The Crystal Mirror of Philosophical Systems

The Library of Tibetan Classics is a special series being developed by the Institute of Tibetan Classics aimed at making key classical Tibetan texts part of the global literary and intellectual heritage. Eventually comprising thirty-two large volumes, the collection will contain over two hundred distinct texts by more than a hundred of the best-known Tibetan authors. These texts have been selected in consultation with the preeminent lineage holders of all the schools and other senior Tibetan scholars to represent the Tibetan literary tradition as a whole. The works included in the series span more than a millennium and cover the vast expanse of classical Tibetan knowledge—from the core teachings of the specific schools to such diverse fields as ethics, philosophy, psychology, Buddhist teachings and meditative practices, civic and social responsibilities, linguistics, medicine, astronomy and astrology, folklore, and historiography.

The Crystal Mirror of Philosophical Systems:
A Tibetan Study of Asian Religious Thought
Thuken Chökyi Nyima (1737–1802)

The *Crystal Mirror of Philosophical Systems (Grub mtha' shel gyi me long),* by Thuken Losang Chökyi Nyima (1737–1802), is probably the widest-ranging account of religious philosophies ever written in premodern Tibet. Thuken was a cosmopolitan Buddhist monk from Amdo, Mongol by heritage, Tibetan in education, and equally comfortable in a central Tibetan monastery or at the imperial court in Beijing. Like most texts on philosophical systems, his *Crystal Mirror* covers the major schools of India, both non-Buddhist and Buddhist, but then goes on to discuss in detail the entire range of Tibetan traditions as well, with separate chapters on the Nyingma, Kadam, Kagyü, Shijé, Sakya, Jonang, Geluk, and Bön. Not resting there, Thuken goes on to describe the major traditions of China—Confucian, Daoist, and Buddhist—as well as those of Mongolia, Khotan, and Shambhala. The *Crystal Mirror* is unusual, too, in its concern not just to describe and analyze doctrines, but to trace the historical development of the various traditions. In evaluating philosophical systems, Thuken favors his own Geluk school, but he generally treats the views of other traditions with sympathy and respect as well—sometimes even defending them against criticisms from his own tradition. All this makes the *Crystal Mirror* an eloquent, erudite, and informative textbook on the religious history and philosophical systems of an array of Asian cultures—and provides evidence that serious and sympathetic study of the history of religions has not been a monopoly of Western scholarship.

HE LIBRARY OF TIBETAN CLASSICS • VOLUME 25
Thupten Jinpa, General Editor

The Crystal Mirror of Philosophical Systems

A Tibetan Study of Asian Religious Thought

Thuken Losang Chökyi Nyima

Translated by Geshé Lhundub Sopa
with E. Ann Chávez and Roger R. Jackson

Special contributions by Michael Sweet and Leonard Zwilling

Edited by Roger R. Jackson

Wisdom Publications • Boston
in association with the Institute of Tibetan Classics

Wisdom Publications
199 Elm Street
Somerville MA 02144 USA
www.wisdompubs.org

Library of Congress Cataloging-in-Publication Data
Blo-bzaṅ-chos-kyi-ñi-ma, Thu'u-bkwan III, 1737–1802.
[Grub mtha' Śel gyi me loṅ. English.]
The crystal mirror of philosophical systems : a Tibetan study of Asian religious thought / Thuken Losang Chökyi Nyima ; translated by Geshé Lhundub Sopa with E. Ann Chávez and Roger R. Jackson ; special contributions by Michael Sweet and Leonard Zwilling ; edited by Roger R. Jackson.
p. cm. — (The Library of Tibetan Classics)
Includes bibliographical references and index.
ISBN 0-86171-464-4 (hardcover : alk. paper)
1. Buddhist sects—China—Tibet—History. 2. Buddhism—China—Tibet—Doctrines—Early works to 1800. 3. Asia—Religion—Early works to 1800. 4. Philosophy, Asian—Early works to 1800. I. Jackson, Roger R. (Roger Reid), 1950– II. Title.
BQ7660.B5513 2009
294.3'9—dc22
2008047842

12 12 11 10 09
5 4 3 2 1

Map on page 24 by XNR Productions. Cover and interior design by Gopa&Ted2. Set in Adobe Garamond Premier Pro 10.5/13.5.

Wisdom Publications' books are printed on acid-free paper and meet the guidelines for permanence and durability of the Production Guidelines for Book Longevity of the Council on Library Resources.

Printed in the United States of America.

This book was produced with environmental mindfulness. We have elected to print this title on 30% PCW recycled paper. As a result, we have saved the following resources: 28 trees, 19 million BTUs of energy, 2,426 lbs. of greenhouse gases, 10,068 gallons of water, and 1,293 lbs. of solid waste. For more information, please visit our website, www.wisdompubs.org. This paper is also FSC certified. For more information, please visit www.fscus.org.

Message from the Dalai Lama

THE LAST TWO MILLENNIA witnessed a tremendous proliferation of cultural and literary development in Tibet, the "Land of Snows." Moreover, due to the inestimable contributions made by Tibet's early spiritual kings, numerous Tibetan translators, and many great Indian *paṇḍitas* over a period of so many centuries, the teachings of the Buddha and the scholastic tradition of ancient India's Nālandā monastic university became firmly rooted in Tibet. As evidenced from the historical writings, this flowering of Buddhist tradition in the country brought about the fulfillment of the deep spiritual aspirations of countless sentient beings. In particular, it contributed to the inner peace and tranquility of the peoples of Tibet, Outer Mongolia—a country historically suffused with Tibetan Buddhism and its culture—the Tuva and Kalmuk regions in present-day Russia, the outer regions of mainland China, and the entire trans-Himalayan areas on the southern side, including Bhutan, Sikkim, Ladakh, Kinnaur, and Spiti. Today this tradition of Buddhism has the potential to make significant contributions to the welfare of the entire human family. I have no doubt that, when combined with the methods and insights of modern science, the Tibetan Buddhist cultural heritage and knowledge will help foster a more enlightened and compassionate human society, a humanity that is at peace with itself, with fellow sentient beings, and with the natural world at large.

It is for this reason I am delighted that the Institute of Tibetan Classics in Montreal, Canada, is compiling a thirty-two-volume series containing the works of many great Tibetan teachers, philosophers, scholars, and practitioners representing all major Tibetan schools and traditions. These important writings will be critically edited and annotated and will then be published in modern book format in a reference collection called *The Library of Tibetan Classics,* with their translations into other major languages to be followed later. While expressing my heartfelt commendation for this noble project, I pray and hope that *The Library of Tibetan Classics* will not only make these important Tibetan treatises accessible to scholars of Tibetan studies, but will create a new opportunity for younger Tibetans to study and take interest in their own rich and profound culture. Through translations into other languages, it is my sincere hope that millions of fellow citizens of the wider human family will also be able to share in the joy of engaging with Tibet's classical literary heritage, textual riches that have been such a great source of joy and inspiration to me personally for so long.

The Dalai Lama
The Buddhist monk Tenzin Gyatso

Special Acknowledgments

THE INSTITUTE OF TIBETAN CLASSICS expresses its deep gratitude to Sandra Esner for generously providing the entire funding for this translation project. As the sponsor of this volume, Sandra wishes to dedicate the publication of this book to her teacher, Geshé Kalsang Mönlam of Drepung Gomang Monastery, from Geshe la's sangha of students. Geshe la's monastery, Gomang, shares a historical connection with the author of this work, Thuken Losang Chökyi Nyima.

We also acknowledge the Hershey Family Foundation for its generous support of the Institute of Tibetan Classics' projects of compiling, editing, translating, and disseminating key classical Tibetan texts through the creation of *The Library of Tibetan Classics*.

Publisher's Acknowledgments

THE PUBLISHER wishes to extend a heartfelt thanks to the following people who, by subscribing to *The Library of Tibetan Classics*, have become benefactors of this entire translation series.

Tenzin Dorjee
Heidi Kaiter
Arnold Possick
Jonathan and Diana Rose
Robert White

Contents

General Editor's Preface

It is with deep satisfaction that I rejoice in the publication of *The Crystal Mirror of Philosophical Systems* in *The Library of Tibetan Classics* series. Completed at the very beginning of the nineteenth century, this acclaimed work by the noted Tibetan scholar Thuken Chökyi Nyima is unique in the annals of Tibetan literature. Beginning with a brief survey of the classical Indian schools, both Buddhist as well as non-Buddhist, the *Crystal Mirror* presents an in-depth treatment of the key schools of Tibetan Buddhism—Nyingma, Kadam, Sakya, Kagyü, Geluk, and Jonang—as well as Bön, covering not only their key philosophical tenets but also providing the reader with an understanding of their historical development. A serious Buddhist practitioner himself, Thuken also endeavors to examine the tenets of the individual Tibetan Buddhist schools in light of their distinctive meditative practices. The final part of the book presents an account of the religions of Tibet's neighbors in the east and north, including China, Khotan, and Mongolia. Thuken's work shows that serious and sympathetic study of comparative religion has not been the sole province of Western scholars.

Two primary objectives have driven the creation and development of *The Library of Tibetan Classics*. The first aim is to help revitalize the appreciation and the study of the Tibetan classical heritage within Tibetan-speaking communities worldwide. The younger generation in particular struggle with the tension between traditional Tibetan culture and the realities of modern consumerism. To this end, efforts have been made to develop a comprehensive yet manageable body of texts, one that features the works of Tibet's best-known authors and covers the gamut of classical Tibetan knowledge. The second objective of *The Library of Tibetan Classics* is to help make these texts part of global literary and intellectual heritage. In this regard, we have tried to make the English translation reader-friendly and, as much as possible, keep the body of the text free of scholarly apparatus, which can intimidate general readers. For specialists who wish to compare the translation with the

Tibetan original, page references of the critical edition of the Tibetan text are provided in brackets.

The texts in this thirty-two-volume series span more than a millennium—from the development of the Tibetan script in the seventh century to the first part of the twentieth century, when Tibetan society and culture first encountered industrial modernity. The volumes are thematically organized and cover many of the categories of classical Tibetan knowledge—from the teachings specific to each Tibetan school to the classical works on philosophy, psychology, and phenomenology. The first category includes teachings of the Kadam, Nyingma, Sakya, Kagyü, Geluk, and Jonang schools, of miscellaneous Buddhist lineages, and of the Bön school. The texts in these volumes have been selected largely by senior lineage holders of the individual schools. Texts in the other categories have been selected primarily in recognition of the historical reality of the individual disciplines. For example, in the field of epistemology, works from the Sakya and Geluk schools have been selected, while the volume on buddha nature features the writings of Butön Rinchen Drup and various Kagyü masters. Where fields are of more common interest, such as the three codes of conduct or the bodhisattva ideal, efforts have been made to present the perspectives of all four major schools. *The Library of Tibetan Classics* can function as a comprehensive library of the Tibetan literary heritage for libraries, educational and cultural institutions, and interested individuals.

On a personal level, to see this beautiful gem of Tibet's classical world made part of the world literary heritage is a source of genuine happiness. To this day I remember the excitement I felt when my own teacher, the late Kyabjé Zemey Rinpoché, lent me his own personal copy of Thuken's *Crystal Mirror*. This was in the summer of 1980, only two years after I had joined Ganden Monastery to pursue the rigorous geshé degree. It was an old woodblock-print xylograph edition, an edition we later consulted for the creation of a critical Tibetan edition used as the basis for this translation. What was most refreshing about Thuken's writing was its fluidity as well as the gentleness of touch with which he analyzed the central tenets of the various schools. Fortunately, a well-edited modern book edition was published in Tibet in 1984, and the work has since been a core volume in my own Tibetan-language library. To now be part of the endeavor of making this important classic accessible to the English-speaking world brings me particular joy.

I offer my deep gratitude first and foremost to His Holiness the Dalai Lama for always being such a shining exemplar and an advocate of Tibet's great classical heritage. I thank one of twentieth century's most eminent Geluk scholars and teachers, Geshé Lhundrup Sopa, for his leadership in undertaking the monumental task of translating Thuken's *Crystal Mirror* into English. To the other members of the translation team, principally Ann Chavez, Roger Jackson, Michael Sweet, and Leonard Zwilling, I owe sincere appreciation for their years of efforts in moving this work toward completion. Especially to Roger Jackson, I express my deep thanks for doing such a superb job of editing the entire volume as well as providing a most illuminating introduction. I owe heartfelt thanks to David Kittelstrom of Wisdom Publications for being, as usual, a most incisive editor; to the Central Institute of Higher Tibetan Studies, Sarnath, for providing full access to its library to my Tibetan colleagues who created the critical edition of the Tibetan text; and to my wife, Sophie Boyer-Langri, for taking on the numerous administrative chores that are part of such a collaborative project. Finally, I express my heartfelt thanks to Sandra Esner, who most generously provided the funding for this translation project, and to the Hershey Family Foundation for its longstanding support of the Institute of Tibetan Classics, without which *The Library of Tibetan Classics* series simply would not have become a reality.

It is my sincere hope that the publication of this volume will benefit many and that it will provide a valuable resource to help people better understand and appreciate the richness of Tibet's classical intellectual and spiritual heritage. May the efforts of all those who have been part of this endeavor help alleviate the sufferings of all beings; may they especially help us humans become wiser so that we may make this world a more caring and a more peaceful place for all.

Thupten Jinpa
Montreal, 2008

Translator's Preface
Geshé Lhundub Sopa

AFTER THE TIBETAN GOVERNMENT was overthrown by Chinese forces, I sought and found political asylum in India in 1959. Three years later His Holiness the Dalai Lama asked me to accompany three young recognized incarnate monks to America to begin their studies there. We went to live at the Lamaist Buddhist Monastery of America in Freewood Acres, New Jersey. One of the key people sponsoring us was Professor Kenneth Morgan of Colgate University. One day he showed me his recently published book on world religions. He felt the section on Tibetan Buddhism, especially the numerous Tibetan schools, such as Nyingma, Kagyü, Sakya, and Geluk, was too scant, since he had not been able to find enough source materials in English. He then urged me to write a book about the religious history, philosophical views, and differences among the schools of Tibetan Buddhism, since no one had explained these in detail before. It was then I thought, "Oh, *Thuken Drumtha*!"[1] At that time (about 1963), I had no means of fulfilling that promise—I barely spoke English!—but I kept Professor Morgan's request in my mind for many years.

I had been expelled from Tibet by the Communists. I had lost my country and my cultural setting, and the Buddhism I had studied for many years was now completely disappearing. The highest Tibetan culture is the great and rich Buddhist culture. In that country was a history of pure and thorough Buddhist study and learning, with great teachings and teachers available over a very long period of time. In the early 1960s, unlike today, virtually no real, essential Tibetan Buddhist teachings existed outside of Tibet. If you mentioned Buddhism, that meant Zen. Tibet had tried to shut off the influence of foreign countries, so almost no foreigners came to central Tibet.[2] Yet, on the borders of Tibet, there existed a very strange mixture of Bön and exotic Buddhist practice that was not authentic or based on education or good sense. I thought how shameful it would be to lose the authentic Tibetan Buddhist teachings. To make available an exposition of the traditional, real teachings of each of the four main Tibetan schools would be of great benefit in the world. When you don't know the different schools, sects, and religions, it can be extremely harmful to yourself and others if they are explained improperly. The exposition must be good, solid, and pure. I strongly resolved that in the future, when I had the language and necessary skills, I would bring this about.

Before I escaped from Tibet, my teacher, the venerable Geshé Lhündrup Thapkhé, had told me about Thuken's wonderful text, the *Crystal Mirror of Philosophical Systems,* containing important information on all the Tibetan schools. This book is unique, because no one in Tibet other than Thuken had written a book covering all the important schools of Tibetan Buddhism. Only in separate books were you able to study the history and sources of the Nyingma, Kagyü, Sakya, and Geluk traditions. A mirror reveals all the beings and things in the world. Similarly, this one book clearly revealed the history and assertions of all these schools, and thus Thuken called it a "mirror." It not only presented the four Tibetan schools, it also presented non-Buddhist religions in India and China, and Buddhism in India, China, and Mongolia. It clearly described how Buddhism came first to India and afterward to Tibet, where, like great rivers, the different philosophical systems flowed into the one ocean of Buddhism. Although Thuken was a great Geluk scholar, he studied all the Tibetan schools—and their history, lineages, and ways of practice—in a very impartial way, which was quite unusual. If certain religious ideas and practices needed criticism, he sharply did so, without regard to school, criticizing even the Gelukpas where necessary. He strove to be completely impartial, and I was very attracted to his style of explanation. He says in the preface to the text:

> Many, under the sway of anger, have deprecated
> The Dharmas and persons of other systems
> Without even knowing how to properly distinguish among
> The various philosophical systems in this land.
>
> Many, under the sway of the four negative tendencies,[3]
> Failing to ascertain any reason
> For the distinctiveness of their own philosophical system,
> And driven only by confusion and desire, still hold their system
> as supreme.
>
> In order to set them in conscientiousness,
> I will briefly discuss here

The sources and standpoints of the philosophical systems
That arose in the Holy Land of India and in Tibet and China.[4]

Everywhere, whether in Buddhism or in any other world religion, people without knowledge see their own religion as superior and, failing to see the value and good of other religions, put them down. Therefore, I thought if I could translate this book, what a wonderful service this would be in the world! Otherwise, Tibetan Buddhism would be seen as the superstitious and foolish beliefs of mountain people with blind faith. That is how the Chinese Communists see it. Now, of course, more has been translated, but at that time so little was available. I felt that the books that very great yogis, teachers, buddhas, and bodhisattvas had written should be made available in the world, and translating the *Crystal Mirror* would bring this about.

In composing the *Crystal Mirror,* Thuken was influenced by his teacher Changkya Rolpai Dorjé, who had himself written on the Indian philosophical systems. Before Changkya, Jamyang Shepa wrote the *Great Treatise on Philosophical Systems,* discussing both the non-Buddhists and the four Indian Buddhist schools in great detail. He was a great scholar. Changkya then wrote a more concise text on the four Indian schools, with clear details, in a sharp and pointed way. Thuken came later, beginning briefly with the non-Buddhists as sources, then the four great Indian schools, but then proceeding to explain how Buddhism came to Tibet, and so forth. He did not divide the Tibetan schools by their correlation to the four Indian schools, but rather by lineage of teachers and place of origin.

The *Crystal Mirror* contains the method and the essence of the things you should adopt or abandon if you seek ultimate happiness for yourself and others. Thuken himself says:

Hey, there! Here is what the wise should do, in thought and action:
Seek a way, a means of liberation from samsara, whose nature is suffering.
Those who never ponder that way, content merely with the appearances of this life,
Appear to be incarnate humans but ought to be counted as cattle.

Further, there are two schools, the non-Buddhist and the Buddhist, who set forth explanations
Of bondage and freedom in this world;

Whichever one you follow, first analyze
The distinction between the deceptive and the nondeceptive.

You allow yourself to weigh incessantly,
In each and every tiny endeavor for this life,
"Although complete, less benefit,
Although incomplete, less harm."

How then could it be right to act so rashly,
Not analyzing what to adopt or abandon,
When being right brings eternal satisfaction
And being wrong brings grave disaster?[5]

Before Thuken, Changkya Rolpai Dorjé wrote that samsara is like an abyss filled throughout with millions of sufferings and hardships. That is the nature of samsara. If samsaric beings are deeply troubled by that, instead of pursuing deceptive pleasures, they need to determine what is the right method of liberation—and what is the wrong method. To investigate this again and again is a very holy thing to do. If we are satisfied with merely filling our stomachs, how are we different from cattle?

Thuken's work also contains a wonderful quality of examination. In order to present the differences among philosophical systems, Thuken uses the traditional style of Tibetan scholastic literature. This has three parts.[6] First, if others' positions are not correct, you refute them with logic and with scriptural references. Next, you present your own position with logical and scriptural support. Finally, you subject your own position to potential criticisms based on different citations and arguments, and then you clear all these doubts away completely with a thorough explanation that resolves all critiques. This is what Thuken does here, and it is the system of the masters. He establishes logically what is to be accepted and refuted in others' positions. He explains what is superior or inferior based on those logical reasons, not on attachment or aversion. For those who want to learn about the different schools, first he establishes the basis—the lineage, sources, and beliefs—and then he lays out the path. Finally, he explains the ultimate goal. In this way, the *Crystal Mirror* demonstrates the proper way to understand and practice, an approach that is not just based on blind faith.

For all these reasons, I felt that it was vital to translate this work. When I came to the University of Wisconsin–Madison in 1967, I began to teach

Tibetan language classes. It seemed that the students were not just interested in the Tibetan language but also wanted to learn about Tibetan religious culture, about Tibetan Buddhism. With funding help from the U.S. Department of Health, Education, and Welfare, I wrote a language book that was designed for this purpose, called *Lectures on Tibetan Religious Culture*. This book showed the highest Tibetan culture of Buddhism in connection with, in part 1, the Tibetan schools and their essence, and in part 2, the stages of the path material. It also built up Tibetan vocabulary.

To prepare a translation of the *Crystal Mirror*, I knew that I would have to learn more about the Tibetan schools. During my university years I received Fulbright fellowships in 1976 and 1987 and was able to go to Tibet, Nepal, and India to do further research on the book. In Tibet, many monasteries had been destroyed by the Chinese Communists, and most of the great scholars and famous lamas had died, although some did get outside to India, Bhutan, and other lands. Texts also were extremely scarce. However, certain things I was able to discuss with my teacher, the great Sera Jé Khensur Rinpoché, Geshé Lhündrup Thapkhé, who had not been able to escape. It was through him and his position as Vice President of the Tibetan Autonomous Region Buddhist Association that I was able to visit Tibet. I spent some time there studying with him. I didn't go to different monastic centers in Tibet because there was nothing available for study and research on Thuken at the time. When I was in Nepal, I scheduled a few meetings with the most famous and highest-ranking leader of the Nyingma tradition, the Ven. Dudjom Rinpoché, and I asked him some questions about the Nyingma section of the text.

In 1978, I was able to teach a seminar related to the *Crystal Mirror*. First, I summarized the contents of the book—the differences among the four Indian Buddhist schools and the Tibetan schools—and then each student in the seminar chose a different chapter of the book to translate. I worked with them to produce basic, rough translations. Further on in my university career and after my retirement, other students helped me to clean up and correct the original translations and to complete the missing chapters. Starting in the mid 1990s, I worked closely with Ann Chávez, who went through the entire text with me, except for the chapters on China. In the late 1990s, Roger Jackson agreed to be general editor for the project. He took the versions Ann had helped me with and worked on smoothing them out. He also generated the notes, bibliographies, and appendixes. The final stages of preparing the translation involved many hours of discussion with Ann and Roger. Now I think it is finally in a form that reflects Thuken's *Crystal Mirror*.

In addition to Roger Jackson and Ann Chávez, I want especially to thank Drs. Michael Sweet and Leonard Zwilling for providing the basic translations and annotations of the chapters on China, and to Dr. Zwilling for providing the same for the section on Mongolia. The two of them also provided valuable critical comments on other aspects of the project at various times. I also would like to thank students from the original seminar who worked on sections of the book: Tony Barber, José Cabezón, Lolly Gewissler, Sharon Hendricks, Roger Jackson, and Jay Weil. Also helpful were the subsequent contributions by Philippe Golden and Lori Cayton.

Thanks also go to those who have commented on drafts of one or more chapters of the translation: Ronald Davidson, Matthew Kapstein, Dan Martin, John Newman, Giacomella Orofino, and Cyrus Stearns. At the Central Institute of Tibetan Higher Studies in Sarnath, India, Wangchuk Dorjé, Sönam Rapten, and Tashi Tsering helped to clarify certain difficult passages, in meetings graciously arranged by Geshé Ngawang Samten. Additional perspective on specific issues was provided by Shahzad Bashir, Tony Duff, Klaus-Dieter Mathes, Guy Newland, Lori Pearson, and Qiguang Zhao. Khachab Rinpoché and Hilary Wehrle, with timely assistance from Roy Li, provided an invaluable service by locating some of Thuken's text references, and Thupten Jinpa and his team of editors in Sarnath identified most of the remainder. Laura Nathan was most helpful in tracking down bibliographic information, and Ann Chávez has carefully prepared the final version of the index.

Gene Smith encouraged this project at the beginning, and has been supportive throughout. Our editor, David Kittelstrom of Wisdom Publications, has been unfailingly patient and effective in bringing this huge work to publication, providing countless helpful suggestions for improving the style and presentation of the volume. I am very pleased that Thupten Jinpa has chosen to include the translation in the *Library of Tibetan Classics* series, and thank him for his enthusiasm and hard work.

Finally, I am grateful for the assistance that I received over the years from the department of South Asian Studies at the University of Wisconsin–Madison, the Fulbright Program, and the U.S. Department of Health, Education, and Welfare; and for the travel grants, sabbatical releases, and collegial support provided to Roger Jackson by Carleton College.

Editor's Introduction[7]

Roger R. Jackson

The Crystal Mirror: An Excellent Explanation[8] *Showing the Sources and Assertions of All Philosophical Systems*[9] was completed in 1802, shortly before the death of its author, the third Thuken[10] *hutuqtu*, or incarnate lama, Losang Chökyi Nyima (1737–1802). Ever since its publication it has, in the words of E. Gene Smith, been considered "one of the most important sources for the study of the comparative philosophical schools of India, Tibet, China, and the Mongol world."[11] In roughly five hundred folio sides, Thuken discusses the development and structure of religious philosophy in India; in the Tibetan traditions of Nyingma, Kadam, Kagyü, Shijé, Sakya, Jonang, several minor traditions, Geluk, and Bön; in Buddhist and non-Buddhist Chinese settings; and in such inner Asian areas as Mongolia, Khotan, and Shambhala. In numerous cases involving Tibetan orders, he also summarizes the strengths and weaknesses of the tradition under consideration. Thuken's scope is not just broad but uniquely so among Tibetan treatises.

Among Tibetan scholars, A. I. Vostrikov observes, the *Crystal Mirror* "enjoys great and fully deserved fame...as the first attempt at expounding not only the history but also the system of views of various philosophical and religious streams of Tibet and neighboring countries."[12] It has been utilized by members of Thuken's Geluk order as a textbook for studying traditions other than their own, but it also seems to have been known, and perhaps even appreciated, by members of other orders, notably the Nyingma.[13] Originally published early in the nineteenth century as part of his collected works by Thuken's home monastery of Gönlung Jampa Ling in Amdo,[14] the *Crystal Mirror* was issued in subsequent editions in Dergé, Ulan Bator (then Urga), and Lhasa, where it forms part of the famous Shöl edition of Thuken's writings.[15] In 1969, through the efforts of E. Gene Smith, the Shöl edition was photocopied and bound in large-book format in Delhi by Ṅawang Gelek Demo, making it accessible for the first time to scholars in universities outside the Indo-Tibetan world.[16] In 1984, the Kan su'u mi rigs dpe skrun khang in Lanzhou, in China's Gansu province, published a different edition of the *Crystal Mirror* in standard book format, thereby increasing its availability still further.[17] In 2007, the Institute of Tibetan Classics published a new, heavily annotated, book-format critical edition, prepared in Sarnath, that should serve as the standard text for the forseeable future.[18]

The *Crystal Mirror* has enjoyed equal or even greater celebrity among non-Tibetan scholars. Its existence was first noted in 1855 by the Russian Tibetanist, V. P. Vasili'ev, and subsequent Russian scholars discussed it as well, including B. Ya. Vladimirotsov and, in his great *Tibetan Historical Literature,* A. I. Vostrikov.[19] The first attempt at translating any of the *Crystal Mirror* was made in the early 1880s by Sarat Chandra Das, who published, in the *Journal of the Asiatic Society of Bengal,* English versions, sometimes partial, sometimes complete, and generally unreliable, of the Nyingma, Bön, China, and Mongolia chapters.[20] In the twentieth century, Western-language translations appeared of the whole or large parts of the chapters on Bön, Jonang, Kadam, India, and China.[21] Chinese and Japanese scholars, such as Li An-che and Tachikawa Musashi employed the *Crystal Mirror* overtly or indirectly for English-language reports on the Nyingma, Kagyü, and Sakya,[22] and they and others have utilized it in scholarship published in their own languages, as well. In 1985, Liu Liqian published a Chinese translation of the entire text.[23]

Why has the *Crystal Mirror* gained such renown? A cynic might point out that as an authoritative text on religious philosophies for the most powerful of the Tibetan orders, the Geluk, the *Crystal Mirror* became a work that members of other Tibetan traditions could ill afford to ignore, and that Geluk lamas could foist on foreign scholars who sought a grand Tibetan summation of a range of Tibetan and other Asian religious systems.[24] There is undoubtedly some truth to this contention, but it overlooks at least two important qualities of the *Crystal Mirror* that do set it apart from much that Tibetans have written about their own and other religious traditions. The first, already suggested in the quote from Vostrikov above, is that the *Crystal Mirror* transcends the usual limits of historical and philosophical literature in Tibet, putting it into a genre of which it is one of the few exemplars, particularly in the age in which it was written. The second is that numerous scholars, Tibetan and non-Tibetan alike, have been impressed, in Matthew Kapstein's words, with Thuken's "relative impartiality...despite the fact that he was no doubt limited with respect to his sources for schools other than the Dge lugs pa."[25] Whether or not this is so, the *Crystal Mirror* does stand as one of the crowning achievements of premodern Tibetan historical and philosophical scholarship. It tells us much about the world in which it was written, and stands as excellent evidence that it is not only Westerners who have attempted to write with "relative impartiality" on the full range of religious and philosophical traditions found in the world known to them.

Thuken's Times, Life, and Works

It is unsurprising that a work as wide ranging as the *Crystal Mirror* should have been composed by someone like Thuken, for he was as cosmopolitan as an eighteenth-century Tibetan could be: Mongol by heritage, Geluk Tibetan by education, hailing from the cultural and religious melting pot of Amdo, and equally at home in a central Tibetan monastery, on the steppes of Mongolia, or at the Qing court in Beijing.[26]

The central Tibetan world during Thuken's lifetime (1737–1802) saw the end of the reign of the Seventh Dalai Lama (1708–57) and most of that of the Eighth (1758–1804), though much of the real power was wielded by lay nobles or monk-regents, and the Panchen Lamas of Tashi Lhünpo served as an important counterweight. Chinese officials or armies occasionally intervened in Tibetan affairs, most notably to repel a Gurkha invasion from Nepal in 1792, but for the most part central Tibet was self-governing. This, however, was not Thuken's world; rather, as a native of Amdo, he passed most of life under the influence of the Manchu imperium of the great Qianlong emperor, whose lengthy reign (1736–95) coincided almost exactly with Thuken's lifetime. The Qianlong was perhaps the last great emperor of China, exercising either direct power or significant influence over a vast area that, to the west, included inner and outer Mongolia, eastern Turkestan, and much of the Tibetan cultural region. In the northwest, as had been the case for centuries, the greatest threat to imperial Chinese power came from various Mongol tribes. Most of these were affiliated with the dominant Geluk order of Tibetan Buddhism, and many became deeply involved in Tibetan politics. It was concerns about the balance of power among Mongol tribes that led the Chinese to intervene militarily in central Tibet in 1720 and establish a loose protectorate over the region.

The Qianlong emperor strongly supported Tibetan Buddhism, especially of the Geluk variety, and frequently hosted Geluk lamas in Beijing, most prominently the Mongolian incarnate Changkya Rölpai Dorjé (1717–86). No doubt the emperor had genuine spiritual interests, but his support for

Tibetan Buddhism was also motivated by his need to use ethnically Mongolian Geluk lamas as intermediaries between the empire and its Mongol subjects, as well as by the Manchus' desire to receive legitimation for their rule over the Chinese from a non-Han religious ideology (though they did cultivate Confucianism, as well). The crucible for these complex interactions among Manchus, Chinese, Mongols,[27] and Tibetans was Amdo, especially the region around Lake Kokonor, where a number of great Geluk monasteries had been established.[28]

It was in this part of Amdo that Losang Chökyi Nyima was born in 1737, in the Phüntsok Lungpa valley of the Porö Langdru region (now in the Chinese province of Gansu). He was identified at an early age as the third incarnation of the Mongolian Thuken line.[29] His two predecessors—Losang Rapten (d. 1679) and Ngawang Chökyi Gyatso (1680–1736) hailed from villages in Amdo in what is now Qinghai province, and centered their activities at Gönlung Jampa Ling, one of the numerous important Geluk monasteries in the Kokonor region. They maintained close connections with Geluk monasteries in central Tibet and with other northeastern incarnation lineages, including the Jamyang Shepa, Changkya, and Sumpa. The second Thuken, Ngawang Chökyi Gyatso, had spent time at the court of the Kangxi emperor (r. 1661–1722) in Beijing and was the main teacher of Changkya Rölpai Dorjé, who would in turn become the root guru of his successor, Losang Chökyi Nyima.

Thuken Losang Chökyi Nyima entered Gönlung Monastery at the age of five and received the second Thuken's novice vows at thirteen from Changkya Rölpai Dorjé, with Sumpa Khenpo Yeshé Paljor (1704–88) also in attendance. He was a star pupil at Gönlung, and in 1755, when he was eighteen, he was sent to Gomang College of Drepung Monastery, near Lhasa, to study with the second Jamyang Shepa incarnate, Könchok Jikmé Wangpo (1728–91), and other accomplished masters, including the Third Panchen Lama, Losang Palden Yeshé (1738–81). At Gomang, as at any major Geluk center, he would have been exposed to the classical monastic curriculum, which focused on study of five basic subjects: Abhidharma (based on Vasubandhu's *Treasury of Higher Knowledge*), valid cognition (based on Dharmakīrti's *Thorough Exposition of Valid Cognition*), Madhyamaka (based on Candrakīrti's *Entering the Middle Way*), the perfection of wisdom (based on Maitreya's *Ornament of Higher Realization*), and vinaya (based on Guṇaprabha's *Vinaya Sutra*). These topics were mastered through immersion in the relevant Indian and Tibetan texts, attendance at discourses by scholar-monks, debate in the monastic courtyard, and, for the most astute, composition of one's own works. Thuken would have been exposed not just to literature on the basic subjects but also to other important texts in the Geluk canon, including such classics as Tsongkhapa's *Great Treatise on the Stages of the Path to Enlightenment,* and various works on the worldly sciences, tantric ritual and meditation, history and biography, and the analysis of philosophical systems. Of the last-mentioned genre, the work that undoubtedly influenced Thuken most was the *Great Treatise on the Establishment of Philosophical Systems,* published in 1747 by his main teacher, Changkya Rölpai Dorjé, which is cited multiple times in the *Crystal Mirror* and serves as a bulwark of Thuken's world view.

When he completed his studies at Gomang in 1759, Thuken was made abbot of the famed Shalu Monastery in Tsang, and in 1761 he returned to Amdo to lead his home monastery, Gönlung. Two years later, at the bidding of the Qianlong emperor, he journeyed to Beijing. He visited Changkya Rölpai Dorjé, who was in residence there, and was received with full honors by the emperor, who even, it is said, "presented him his own robes, which contained one hundred and eight dragons worked in gold, together with a hundred thousand crowns of silver."[30] As he found the Beijing climate unhealthy, Thuken received permission in 1768 to return to Gönlung, traveling there by way of Mongolia, but was called back to Beijing in 1771. He traveled widely for the next twelve years, living variously in the Chinese capital, the nearby border region of Jehol, or at Gönlung, where he occasionally acted as abbot. In the last decades of the century, he remained mostly in Amdo, serving as abbot of Jakhyung Monastery from 1789 to 1793, teaching at Kumbum Monastery, and eventually returning to Gönlung, where he died in 1802. By the time of his death, he was acknowledged as perhaps the greatest Amdo lama of his time, visited, celebrated, and rewarded by monks, potentates, and ordinary people, whether Chinese, Mongolian, or Tibetan.

Although he was far from being the most prolific Geluk scholar of the seventeenth and eighteenth centuries, Thuken amassed an impressive list of publications during his peripatetic life. His collected works amount to 5,746 folios,[31] enough to fill ten large volumes in the book-format edition of his opus published in India.[32] He is credited with well over 250 individual texts, many quite short, but some, especially those on history or philosophy, covering dozens or even hundreds of folios. As is typical of most great Tibetan Buddhist masters, Thuken devoted the majority of his works to tantric ritual. He wrote over fifty texts related to Hayagrīva, around twenty about Vajrayoginī, and lesser numbers on such deities as Tārā, Mañjuśrī, Avalokiteśvara, Vajrabhairava, Kālacakra,[33] and a host of wrathful protectors. He also contributed works on tormas, stupas, and astronomy, and on a such practices as Chö meditation, a method to benefit beings at the time of death, and the fasting ritual of Avalokiteśvara.[34] His nontantric works include biographies of his predecessor, the second Thuken incarnate, and of his main teacher, Changkya Rölpai Dorjé; chronicles of Gönlung and other monasteries; listings of monastic ordinances; surveys of temple images; numerous narrative, propitiatory, and panegyric works in ornate poetic style; and last but not least, the *Crystal Mirror of Philosophical Systems.*

How the Crystal Mirror *Was Composed*

We know just a little of the composition of the *Crystal Mirror,* from Thuken's colophon to the text and the writings of his main disciple, Gungthang Könchok Tenpai Drönmé (1762–1823),[35] who after his master's death would edit Thuken's collected writings and compose many important works of his own. Around 1799, Gungthangpa and a number of Thuken's disciples at Gönlung Monastery requested that he write the work. Thuken mentions that when he was about halfway done, he was urged to complete it by his disciple Ngawang Mipham Dawa. Though in declining health, Thuken pushed through to finish the *Crystal Mirror* because of his disciple's request and the kindness of his lamas. He dates the completion of the text to mid-January 1802, which means that he worked on it for approximately three years, a very fast pace for a work of the *Crystal Mirror*'s length and complexity. Thuken admits that the completed text had not been thoroughly edited, noting, "The corrections I made were rough; since I could not make them in detail, it is possible that some mistakes still remain, and they should be amended."[36] Within the year, Thuken was dead, and the corrections, so far as we know, never were made, so that the *Crystal Mirror* as we have it is probably a first draft.[37]

How was it drafted? In the colophon, Thuken specifies that (like countless Tibetan texts), the *Crystal Mirror* was put into manuscript form not by himself, but by scribes, of whom he names three, all monks at Gönlung Monastery. In the manner of many great Tibetan historical and philosophical works, the *Crystal Mirror* reflects its author's considerable erudition and draws freely on a range of sources already at his disposal, both with and without attribution, footnoting in the Western academic style being unknown to premodern Tibetan scholars. A full investigation of Thuken's sources remains to be undertaken, but it is clear that at least some portions of the text are lifted directly, or in paraphrase, from earlier authors. The portions of the India chapter dealing with Buddhist history, for instance, draw frequently from Butön's *Dharma History* and Changkya Rölpai Dorjé's *Great Treatise on the Establishment of Philosophical Systems*. The chapter on the Nyingma tradition is drawn in part from Gö Lotsāwa's *Blue Annals*. The chapter on Kagyü is partially drawn from treatises on Mahāmudrā by Khedrup Norsang Gyatso and the First Panchen Lama, both Gelukpas. The chapter on Sakya draws in part from a work by the Sakya author Mangthö Ludrup Gyatso,[38] while the Shijé chapter draws largely from the *Blue Annals*. The chapter on Bön draws primarily from a Bön work called the *Ornament of Sunlight in the Breach in the Citadel of Secret Mantra* and from texts critical of Bön by Drigung and Geluk authors.[39] The chapters on China draw in part from the work of his teacher Sumpa Khenpo, and even more so from the account of Chinese religion by the great Mongolian historian, Gönpo Kyap.[40] With or without credit, Thuken did draw on a remarkable range of genres, including Indian sutras, tantras, and treatises; Tibetan histories of China, Mongolia, or Tibet; earlier Tibetan texts on philosophical systems and subjects; polemical treatises; expositions of tantra; biographies; letters; panegyric verses; songs of spiritual experience; and meditation manuals. If the *Crystal Mirror*'s mode of composition was like that of other major Tibetan texts, then we can imagine Thuken consulting the works available to him at Gönlung and drawing on others from memory, stitching them into his own grand narrative, which was dictated to his monk-scribes when time and health permitted.

Beyond the immediate circle of disciples who requested its composition, Thuken's target audience for the *Crystal Mirror* probably consisted mainly of scholar-monks and literate lay officials in the Tibetan cultural sphere, since, as a Tibetan text, it could be understood by precious few Chinese or Mongolians. That it would eventually be translated into Chinese, not to mention English, Thuken could not have foreseen.

Why the Crystal Mirror *Was Composed*

Exactly why Thuken's disciples asked him to write the *Crystal Mirror*, and why he agreed, is not spelled out in detail, but at least three possibilities may be considered:

1. *As a study of religious history*. Certainly, as a lama well educated and well traveled within the Tibetan, Mongol, and Chinese worlds of the eighteenth

century, Thuken had a great deal of experience and wisdom to impart, and his disciples might simply have wanted to have available a single, reliable description of the cultural, historical, and religious cosmos in which they lived.

2. *As an attempt to assess religious systems.* Thuken himself suggests in his poetic preface to the book that he will expound the philosophical systems of India, China, and Tibet so as to help beings toward liberation by dispelling the narrow, deluded partiality felt by so many toward their own tradition, whatever it might be.[41] He returns to this theme in his conclusion but there adds that his exposition, if read carefully by an intelligent reader, will lead inevitably to the recognition that the acme of Buddhist systems is that of "Losang the conqueror," that is the Geluk tradition of Tsongkhapa Losang Drakpa (1357–1419).[42] So, Thuken may have written with the intent to encourage an ecumenical spirit or to promote the Geluk, or both.

3. *As a tool of Chinese imperial policy.* A historically minded outside observer might suggest that as a text concerned not just with Indian and Tibetan traditions, but also those of China and Mongolia, the *Crystal Mirror* may also contain political motives and ramifications. Perhaps Thuken sought not just to justify Geluk dominance in the Tibetan Buddhist world but also to legitimize Chinese hegemony over Tibet.

I now briefly address each of these three suggestions, which, it should be noted, are not mutually exclusive.

1. The suggestion that the *Crystal Mirror* was composed primarily as a source of information about the religious and cultural world in which Thuken and his disciples lived raises the question of just how reliable the text is as a historical source. As we have seen, the text was compiled in some haste near the very end of Thuken's life and was never significantly revised. Thuken does draw on an impressive variety of sources, and this allows him to paint a broad, fairly well-documented portrait of the various traditions with which he is concerned. Nevertheless, the *Crystal Mirror*'s historical reliability is compromised by at least four considerations.

First, whatever the considerable resources at his disposal, Thuken inevitably had better information about some traditions than others, limited perhaps by the libraries at the Amdo Geluk monasteries he frequented. Not surprisingly, his sections on the Kadam and Geluk are the best documented, for these are the traditions in which a Geluk lama would have the most thorough education. At the other extreme are traditions like Shijé, Bön, and Daoism, for which he had to rely almost entirely on hearsay and the writings of others for his accounts. In describing most other systems, he seems to have drawn on the material that happened to be available to him, and put together an account as best he could, but he was still handicapped by not having access to all, or even the best, sources on such schools as the Nyingma, Kagyü, and Sakya, or to the full range of Tibetan historical literature.

Second, even in cases where Thuken provides ample documentation, he does not seem overly concerned to investigate critically the sources that he cites. Admittedly, there are a few instances in which he questions a particular writer's account of an event, or the attribution of a text to a particular author. For the most part, however, rather than attempt to arrive at the most plausible historical account of a given event by weighing all possible sources, he seems intent on laying out a coherent narrative by piecing together whatever textual or legendary material will most help him in the process. This is not unusual in Tibetan historical writing, but Thuken seems in general to display a less critical approach to his sources than a number of his predecessors, like Gö Lotsāwa Shönu Pal, the Fifth Dalai Lama, and Pawo Tsuklak Trengwa. Even if the *Crystal Mirror* does not measure up to the standards of modern critical historiography, or even to the best Tibetan historical writing, it still stands as an ambitious, clearly structured, and generally coherent attempt to take in a vast historical panorama in a fairly concise manner.

Third, it is worth recalling that the approach to history favored by Tibetans in general and certainly by Thuken in the *Crystal Mirror* is, in the words of Kurtis Schaeffer, "overwhelmingly biographical, and thus encourages us to look to individual actors as the prime movers of historical change."[43] Like the "great man" view of history often attributed to Thomas Carlyle in a European context, the Tibetan approach involves the construction of historical narrative through a succession of biographies of eminent individuals. Certainly, such an approach is understandable in Tibet, where lineage is an important religious and political marker, but it does skew historical accounts toward the deeds (especially the religious deeds) of great personages, and away from political, economic, social, or psychological considerations; in short, toward individual history and away from institutional history. This approach has its place on the spectrum of approaches to history, but it does have limitations, particularly in a modern historiographic setting.

Fourth, the *Crystal Mirror* was written at a very particular time in history, when Geluk power, supported by the Qing dynasty, was near its apogee, and many other traditions found themselves in relatively straitened circumstances. The early nineteenth century, after Thuken's death, saw the dawning of the trans-sectarian Rimé movement, which dramatically altered the fortunes of many of the sects on which Thuken commented. The Karma Kagyü, Nyingma, and Sakya, which Thuken viewed as in decline, underwent significant revivals in the nineteenth century that have continued to the present day. Conversely, the nineteenth century was not a particularly vibrant one for Gelukpas, in part no doubt because of the decline of Manchu power. It would be interesting to know how Thuken would have presented the various traditions had he written his history in 1902 rather than 1802.

2. As we have seen, Thuken emphasizes in both the preface and conclusion of the *Crystal Mirror* that he is attempting to provide an impartial and evenhanded account of the various philosophical systems within his purview. On the other hand, we also have seen that he believes that an impartial consideration of the full range of philosophical systems leads inescapably to the conclusion that only the Geluk captures completely the comprehensiveness, profundity, and clarity of the teaching of the Buddha. Is Thuken, then, an ecumenically spirited religious pluralist or an unabashed Geluk triumphalist? Unsurprisingly, there is no simple answer.[44]

If we leave aside his chapters on Indian, Chinese, Mongolian, and other inner Asian traditions (the last two of which are more historical than evaluative) and survey the way Thuken represents the Tibetan traditions that were at the core of his religious world, we find that the overall spectrum of judgments is quite broad. It ranges from the negative extreme of the Jonang, which is roundly condemned and refuted in extraordinary detail, to the positive extreme of the Geluk, which is treated for the most part uncritically and, indeed, explicitly exalted above all other traditions. We may roughly arrange the other Tibetan traditions considered by Thuken between these two poles. Closer to the positive pole, we find the Kadam, which is, of course, seen by Gelukpas as their school's own direct precursor, and the Sakya, which while acknowledged by Thuken to reflect various philosophical strands, including Cittamātra and both Prāsaṅgika and Svātantrika Madhyamaka, is presented descriptively and sympathetically, without any attempt to expose philosophical error. Closer to the negative pole, we find Bön, of which Thuken admittedly knows little, and which he presents primarily through verbatim quotations from works on it by its Buddhist critics, who are especially keen to point out the ways in which "transformed Bön" supposedly consists almost entirely of paraphrased Buddhist texts, ideas, and practices. Somewhere in between, we find the Nyingma, Kagyü, and Shijé, which Thuken regards as rooted in pure views and practices but prone in their latter-day forms to errors that their irreproachable founders would not have countenanced. Typical in this regard is his analysis of earlier and later Shijé: "Because the view that is taught is free of extremes, I think it is coextensive with the Madhyamaka view. Nevertheless, there is no doubt that, in the writings of later generations, there often is an admixture of fish and turnips."[45]

These characterizations are broad and must be qualified by the observation that Thuken's judgments, both positive and negative, are at least partially mitigated in nearly every case. Even the schools most roundly criticized, Jonang and Bön, are acknowledged in passing for, respectively, their transmission of Kālacakra traditions and their appeal to laypeople. Although Thuken does criticize later developments within such "in-between" traditions as Nyingma, Kagyü, and Shijé, he also acknowledges their pure origins and defends their fundamental teachings against attacks, including those by fellow Gelukpas. By the same token, he is careful to note that, having demonstrated the distinctiveness of the Geluk, he does not mean to imply thereby that liberation is impossible through other traditions. If such were the case, he states, it would follow that no philosophy other than Prāsaṅgika Madhyamaka and no method besides highest yoga tantra would lead to liberation, and countless masters who did not employ that view or method would not have been truly enlightened. This is a claim that any number of Gelukpas would have made (and some still do), but Thuken rejects it, saying that, apart from the Jonang, "there does not appear to be even a single system fit for consistent denigration, so those who desire their own welfare should see all of them as pervaded by pure appearance."[46]

Where does this leave Thuken? As is so often the case, it probably depends on where you stand. Jonangpas and Bönpos undoubtedly will feel that Thuken has merely caricatured their traditions and shown virtually no understanding of their subtleties. Nyingmapas and Kagyüpas may well consider Thuken's celebration of their founders while he criticizes latter-day practitioners as damning with faint praise, since few adherents of any tradition in any era will admit that their lineage has been corrupted or misinterpreted. Nyingmapas, Kagyüpas, and Sakyapas are likely to take issue with Thuken's implication that their great founders all were Prāsaṅgika Mādhyamikas. And members of virtually any non-Geluk tradition that was extant in 1800 are likely to find Thuken's account of their decadence during his era misleading and inaccurate.[47] A Geluk triumphalist, on the other hand, may believe that Thuken has conceded far too much spiritual efficacy to other traditions, arguing that such a concession opens the door to a dangerous relativism that threatens to obliterate the great work of Tsongkhapa in presenting Buddhist tradition with unprecedented and inimitable clarity.[48] On balance, if we consider the range of attitudes toward religions not one's own that has been articulated in the West, it probably is safe to characterize Thuken's outlook as falling neither to the extreme of relativistic pluralism, nor to the opposite extreme of triumphalist exclusivism, but under the rubric of inclusivism, which asserts the ultimate supremacy of one's own tradition but admits that salvation may be achieved through other traditions as well.

3. Summarizing Thuken's place in the world and its relation to his inclusivism, Matthew Kapstein writes:

> He was one of a generation of clergymen from Amdo whose spiritual loyalties were unmistakably Gelukpa, but who allied themselves politically with the Qing court. The worldview of these churchmen bore a strange resemblance to that of medieval Latin Christendom, with the Manchus filling the role of Imperial Rome and the Gelukpa hierarchy that of the Catholic Church. These were not the products of a denomination under fire but rather represented the synthesis of a peerless salvific vehicle with a universal temporal order. Not personally threatened by the Central Tibetan feuds, they could afford to regard the situation there only with equanimous compassion. Their intellectual curiosity could be given free rein to explore their own and other traditions impartially.[49]

Quite apart from suggesting a context for Thuken's relative impartiality, this passage raises important questions about the political motivations and implications of his work. As with the question of impartiality, there is a spectrum of possible arguments to be made.

On the one hand, it could be argued that Thuken is fundamentally unconcerned with politics and merely seeks to represent the range of traditions known to him, with an eye cast primarily on questions of philosophical view and religious practice, as they may or may not bear upon spiritual liberation. A modern critical theorist, however, would remind us that there is no nonpolitical writing, especially when it comes to history and religion; only writing that is overt or covert about its political agenda and implications. Furthermore, Thuken gives explicit attention not just to matters of philosophy and religion, but also to the political histories of the various schools, and goes into great detail on Geluk relations with the Mongol and Chinese empires. Thus, the *Crystal Mirror* was not only written from amid Thuken's political and historical situation, but it also displays knowledge of and interest in that situation. In that sense, it has an explicitly political dimension.

Why does Thuken focus on politics as much as he does? It might be maintained that, to the degree that the text is a Geluk tract, its primary political motivation is to demonstrate to a Tibetan-literate audience that the Geluk has enjoyed the patronage of the greatest East Asian empires of both the past and present, and therefore is distinctive not only in religious terms, but in terms of its patronage and worldly power—always for Buddhists a sign of good institutional karma. Thuken's particular emphasis on Geluk relations with the Qing dynasty, however, leads to the question whether he might have sought not only to legitimize Geluk religious and political supremacy in Tibet on the basis of its endorsement by the Chinese emperor, but perhaps even, consciously or unconsciously, to promote Qing imperialism. In this view, the *Crystal Mirror* and other historical works that deal with Sino-Tibetan relations turn out, whatever their authors' purported aims, to serve the interests of those in the Chinese court who would incorporate Tibet into a greater China, since any text that established the spiritual and political supremacy of the Geluk within Tibet and at the same time acknowledged Geluk dependence on the patronage of the empire could be seen by extension as validating imperial claims over Tibet.

It certainly is possible that this has been an unintended consequence of the *Crystal Mirror* and other Tibetan works that dealt with Tibetan-Qing relations. That Thuken self-consciously intended to promote Qing claims over Tibet to his audience, however, is far from evident. Whatever his private views, he never mentions, let alone justifies, those claims in the text. The likelier conclusion, it appears, is that while the *Crystal Mirror* was written within an imperial context, and may be interpreted as an imperial document, its primary political aim was not the promotion of a Chinese agenda but that of the Geluk, and even there, as we have seen, there is room for qualification.

The Genre of the Crystal Mirror

According to its title, the *Crystal Mirror* is a *drumtha (grub mtha')* text, hence part of the genre of Tibetan literature variously translated as "doxography," "religious philosophy," "tenet systems," "philosophical systems," "schools of thought," "philosophical schools," "philosophical positions," and so forth.[50] Even a superficial examination of its contents, however, makes it clear that while the *Crystal Mirror* does present and analyze the views of various schools in a manner suggestive of other drumtha texts, it differs from them in three important respects. First, whereas drumtha texts tend to keep their focus largely on matters of doctrine, each chapter of the *Crystal Mirror* includes not just philosophical and doctrinal material but significant discussions of the historical development of the tradition or traditions to which the chapter is devoted. Second, whereas drumtha texts usually proceed from "lower" to "higher" schools of thought, the *Crystal Mirror,* as Gene Smith notes, "seem[s] to have been arranged more by historical than typological considerations,"[51] moving as it does, like Buddhism itself, from India to Tibet, China, and inner Asia, and generally proceeding within its major sections and individual chapters from earlier to later developments, with the Bön chapter occupying a sort of categorical bardo between Tibetan Buddhist and Chinese traditions. Third, whereas most drumtha texts concern themselves primarily with Indian schools of thought, the *Crystal Mirror* makes a systematic attempt to present and analyze non-Indian traditions, such as those of Tibet, China, and Mongolia. Thus, if the *Crystal Mirror* is a drumtha text, it is a rather unusual one.

Though the question of its actual genre has been little discussed, it is interesting to note the range of views among those who *have* sought to define it as more than mere drumtha. Thus, Vostrikov includes it in his chapter on religious histories *(chos 'byung),* while the website of the Tibetan Buddhist Research Center lists it as both drumtha and logyü *(lo rgyus),* the latter generally being translated as "history," "chronicle," or "narrative." It may simply be a combination of all three, and, indeed, it is in the *combination* of genres that the *Crystal Mirror*'s originality lies. Certainly, Indian traditions had been analyzed both historically and doctrinally by previous Tibetan writers, including two of Thuken's teachers who were masters of traditional drumtha, Changkya Rölpai Dorjé and Könchok Jikmé Wangpo.[52] Another teacher of his, Sumpa Khenpo, wrote the massive *Excellent Wish-Fulfilling Tree,* an institutional history of Buddhism in India, Tibet, China, and Mongolia, which also includes some strong polemics against the non-Geluk Tibetan schools but does not examine doctrinal matters as systematically as a drumtha text generally does.[53] Thus, the genius of the *Crystal Mirror* lies not so much in its creation of a new genre as in the way it brings together intellectual approaches seldom found in Tibet in the same work. In this sense, Vostrikov was quite right to claim that the *Crystal Mirror* has "a special place among the Tibetan historical works of analytical type," and one cannot, in the end, really improve on his plain description of it as a "historico-philosophical work."[54]

As already noted, the very existence of a text like the *Crystal Mirror* demonstrates that the idea of "comparative religion" is not a solely Western invention. Indeed, it might be argued that the Western notion of what is involved in the study of religion ought to be expanded to include comparative works from outside the West.[55] That notwithstanding, it is worth examining briefly how the *Crystal Mirror* might stand as a study of comparative religion, given prevailing Western assumptions about how to compare. Could it serve as a textbook for learning about the religions of India, Tibet, China, and Inner Asia, or is it simply a historical curiosity, an intriguing and erudite, but ultimately quaint, example of premodern approaches to studying religion?

The *Crystal Mirror* clearly is not a text on comparative religion in the modern secular academic style, since it is at least partially concerned with evaluation of the traditions examined, and does on occasion explicitly promote a sectarian agenda. In that sense, whatever the degree of Thuken's impartiality, his text has too much of a normative element to match the contemporary ideal of a "straightforward" text on comparative religion, which seeks, as neutrally as possible, to describe and explain a range of traditions, leaving aside all attempts at evaluation, or perhaps articulating a respect for all traditions equally.[56]

If we look instead to *religious* literature about religions, that is, "theological" works that seek to describe multiple religions from within one particular tradition, we might initially consider the *Crystal Mirror* as an example of heresiography. This genre, of which many instances were produced (and still are) in the Christian and Muslim worlds, often provides considerable information, some of it accurate, about a range of religious traditions, usually within, but sometimes outside, one's own church or community. It does so, however, in the ultimate service of exposing these traditions as heretical. Heresiography is related, but not identical to, apologetics, the branch of theological writing that seeks to defend the tenets of one's faith against the views and critiques of those outside the tradition. While the *Crystal Mirror* may have its triumphalist sections, it does not appear that its *primary* intent is to expose the faults in other traditions and exalt Thuken's, so it does not quite fit the definition of heresiography or apologetics.

What is it, then? Perhaps the closest Western parallel may be found in Christian texts, first written as early as the sixteenth century, and appearing with ever-greater frequency since, that attempt to give accounts of a range of what came to be called "world religions." These texts often claim to be dispassionate in their approach to the various religions, but their descriptions usually are colored by a strong concern for establishing points of comparison with Christianity, and by an assumption, either implicit or explicit, that the world religions, while containing much that is of value, probably fall short of Christianity as fully adequate responses to the human condition.[57] There is actually a significant range within this literature, from works that overtly place other traditions on a par with Christianity but then describe elements common to all traditions that turn out to have their roots in some form of Christianity, to works that analyze the world religions as covert forms of Christianity, practiced by "anonymous Christians" who reflect core Christian values—and may in fact be inspired by God—but express those values through cultural forms that are not obviously Christian.[58] In any case, Thuken's theologically inclusivist account of the traditions of his day, in which relatively impartial description and analysis is conducted with the framework of the assumed distinctiveness of the Geluk, would seem to qualify the *Crystal Mirror* as an Asian example of a sectarian world religions text.

A General Outline of the Text

On the most general level, Thuken divides the *Crystal Mirror* into five sections, on: I. Indian schools, II. Tibetan schools, III. Chinese schools, IV. schools in "other lands" (the central Asian areas of Mongolia, Khotan, and Shambhala), and V. a conclusion. The sections on India and "other lands," as well as the conclusion, consist of a single chapter each. The section on Tibet is subdivided into chapters on: Nyingma, Kadam, Kagyü, Shijé, Sakya, Jonang and minor traditions, Geluk, and Bön. The section on China is divided into chapters on non-Buddhist traditions and Buddhist traditions. Within each individual chapter, Thuken generally proceeds in the following order: (1) the historical origins of the tradition, including major lineages and important persons; (2) the major doctrines and practices of the tradition, with a particular emphasis on philosophical views and meditative practices; (3) a critical analysis of issues raised by the tradition's views and practices; and (4) a poetic summary of Thuken's views of the tradition.[59] Though roughly accurate, this characterization of Thuken's chapters belies the considerable range of approaches that he actually takes in relation to both presenting and analyzing the doctrinal positions of the different traditions.

For example, it appears that only three of the chapters, those on Nyingma, Kagyü, and Jonang, are explicitly organized in the manner just outlined, though this does not mean that the concerns we have emphasized do not find their way into most of Thuken's chapters. Moreover, whatever his rubrics, Thuken does not subject every tradition's doctrines to the same degree of critical scrutiny. His judgments—pro, con, or mixed—are presented quite clearly (though in varying detail) in the cases of the Indian, Nyingma, Kagyü, Shijé, Jonang, and Geluk traditions, but rather less obviously when it comes to Kadam, Sakya, and Bön, as well as Chinese and central Asian schools. Nevertheless, it is fair to say that Thuken generally approaches each tradition by presenting history, doctrines and practices, some analysis, and a poetic conclusion. In the remainder of this introduction, I briefly summarize the contents of each of Thuken's chapters.

Summary of the Chapters

Thuken's preface (not numbered by Thuken; chapter 1 of the translation) is a poetic celebration of the Buddha; various bodhisattvas; Indian masters of sutra and tantra; great Tibetan kings, translators, and masters; and, most especially, Atiśa, Tsongkhapa, the Dalai and Panchen Lamas, and Thuken's own gurus. It also expresses Thuken's wish to compose the text so as to clear away the blind partiality with which so many Tibetans cling to their traditions as the only true one.

The lengthy discussion of Indian schools (Thuken's section I; our chapter 2) is structured along the lines of a traditional Tibetan text on philosophical systems. It is divided into a brief section on non-Buddhist traditions—which includes discussions of the materialist, Jain, and various Hindu schools, as well as an explanation of why we must study these systems—and a much longer section on Buddhist schools. This begins with a discussion of the historical development of the four major philosophical schools—Vaibhāṣika, Sautrāntika, Cittamātra, and Madhyamaka—followed by a summary of the positions of each of the four schools. In summarizing these positions, Thuken spends little time on matters of cosmology, valid cognition, or path theory, focusing primarily on the ways in which each school defines the coarse and subtle selflessness that must be realized by practitioners, and, like any good Buddhist, avoids extreme positions. He also spends considerable time establishing the subtle, but important, differences between Svātantrika and Prāsaṅgika Madhyamaka. In this sense, Thuken's treatment of Indian philosophical systems, especially the Buddhist, touches on some vital ontological issues but is far from a complete account and must be read in conjunction with fuller discussions by scholars of earlier generations, like Jamyang Shepa, Könchok Jikmé Wangpo, and especially his main teacher, Changkya Rölpai Dorjé.[60]

Thuken begins his section on Tibetan traditions with a brief overview of the history of Buddhism in Tibet (his section IIA, our chapter 3). This includes summaries of the "early spread of the Dharma" in Tibet during the imperial period (seventh–ninth centuries) and of the early years of the "later spread of the Dharma," sometimes referred to as the "Tibetan renaissance" (tenth–eleventh centuries).

The first of Thuken's chapters on specific Tibetan traditions (his section IIB1, our chapter 4) covers the "old" tradition, the Nyingma. He summarizes the major differences between "old" *(rnying ma)* and "new" *(gsar ma)* translation traditions, then discusses the early history of Nyingma, beginning with the career of Padmasambhava, and detailing both the nine-vehicle system for organizing Buddhism and the lineages of oral tradition, treasure texts, and pure vision. In his discussion of Nyingma doctrines and practices, he focuses mostly on the philosophical view and meditative practices of the Dzokchen lineage. He then investigates criticisms by new-translation authors that Nyingma is "impure" and concludes that while some more recent practitioners may have lost the tradition, the earlier Nyingmapas and their teachings were pure. He ends the chapter with a summary of political problems faced by the Nyingmapas in the seventeenth and eighteenth centuries and laments their current decadence.

Thuken next turns (his section IIB2, our chapter 5) to the Kadam tradition. He spends most of the earlier part of the chapter extolling the greatness of Atiśa—summarizing his activity in helping restore pure Dharma to central Tibet—and the deeds of his disciples and grand-disciples, including Dromtönpa and the various "Kadam geshés," such as Potowa and Chekawa. He goes on to give a general explanation of the Kadam teaching—their central texts and the lineages of instruction and special instruction—which deals primarily with the establishment of the Prāsaṅgika Madhyamaka philosophical view and the quintessential Kadam practice of mind training *(blo sbyong)*. He does not subject these teachings to critical scrutiny other than to praise them. He concludes by summarizing the great qualities of the Kadam masters.

At over fifty folios, the chapter on the Kagyü tradition (Thuken's section IIB3, our chapter 6) is the longest on any Tibetan school other than the Geluk. Thuken begins by discussing the etymology of the name and the general history of the order, then gives historical accounts of the two major Kagyü lineages as he understood them: the Shangpa and the Dakpo. He describes the development of each of the subschools of the Dakpo: the Karma, Phakdru, Shangtsal, Drigung, Drukpa, Taklung, Barom, Yasang, and Trophu. His section on doctrine focuses on analyzing the philosophical view of the earliest Kagyü masters (concluding that it is Prāsaṅgika Madhyamaka), discussing critically later Kagyü meditations on "seeking the mind," and describing early Kagyü analyses of Mahāmudrā. In the overtly analytical section, Thuken defends Kagyü Mahāmudrā traditions against charges that they distort Indian tradition and entail quietism, investigates the philosophical view involved in the *four yogas* of Mahāmudrā meditation, and considers whether Geluk and Kagyü come down to the same point (he argues that they do).

The considerably briefer discussion of the Shijé tradition (Thuken's section IIB4, our chapter 7) investigates the meaning of the term *shijé (zhi byed),* then describes the major figures in the school's development (especially Phadampa Sangyé and Machik Lapdrön) and the divisions and subdivisions of the major Shijé instruction lineages. Thuken then describes the way in which the Shijé lineage is rooted in the Indian perfection of wisdom literature and helps instill the Madhyamaka view, though he notes that this pure tradition was lost in later generations. He concludes the chapter with a brief discussion of the lineage, view, and practice traditions of the Chö *(gcod)* subschool of Shijé.

Thuken's chapter on Sakya (his section IIB5, our chapter 8) gives a general history of the Sakya order, with special focus on the great masters of the Khön family line, from Khön Könchok Gyalpo through Sakya Pandita and Phakpa. He summarizes the tradition of sutra exposition then turns to the tantric exposition lineages of Ngor, Dzong, and Tsar. After a brief review of current conditions among the Sakyapa (only relatively healthy, he finds), Thuken discusses the history of the "principal Sakya Dharma," the Lamdré ("path and fruit"), and defends it against charges of nihilism. He then presents, in some detail, the viewpoint of the Sakya tradition, including esoteric sutra-vehicle instructions for achieving right view according to lineages rooted in Nāgārjuna and Maitreya, and mantra-vehicle instructions on "identifying the mind," then meditating on how appearances are mind, mind is illusory, and illusions are not inherently existent. As with the Kadam tradition, Thuken has virtually nothing critical to say about the Sakyapas, though he does note the presence of a mixture of Cittamātra and Madhyamaka in certain expositions of their philosophical views and meditative practices.

The chapter on the Jonang school (Thuken's IIB6, our chapter 9) summarizes the history of the tradition, with a special focus on Yumo Mikyö Dorjé and Dölpopa. Thuken explains how the former misconstrued certain meditative experiences and distilled them into the confused philosophical view known as "extrinsic emptiness" *(gzhan stong)*. That view then is refuted in remarkable detail, as Thuken argues, in turn, that Jonang descriptions of ultimate reality are virtually indistinguishable from those of Hindus, and that Jonang interpretations of such Indian Buddhist classics as the *Descent to Laṅka Sutra* and the works of Nāgārjuna are sorely mistaken. Thuken goes on to summarize some Tibetan criticisms of the Jonangpas and gives a brief cautionary biography of Shākya Chokden, a latter-day proponent of extrinsic emptiness who, Thuken claims, repented his views on his deathbed. There follows a brief chapter (Thuken's section IIB7, but folded into our chapter 9) on some minor or syncretic Tibetan philosophical systems, including the Bodong, the Shalu system of Butön Rinchen Drup, and the Lhodrak system of Namkha Gyaltsen.

By far the longest chapter in the *Crystal Mirror* is that on Thuken's own tradition, the Geluk (his section IIB8, our chapters 10–12), which covers nearly one third of the text. The first part of the chapter (our chapter 10) is an extensive (sixty-plus folios) biography of the founder of the Geluk tradition, Tsongkhapa. It includes detailed discussions of his studies of sutra-based and tantric ethics, philosophy, and meditation with a multitude of masters; his inner realizations and visionary encounters with the wisdom bodhisattva Mañjughoṣa; his teaching through oral exposition, debate, and composing texts; and his uniquely exalted status among Tibetan masters.

The second part of the Geluk chapter (our chapter 11) focuses on Tsongkhapa's successors in the order. It enumerates his direct disciples then focuses on the history of the great sutra-based Geluk monastic centers. These include the major monasteries near Lhasa, namely, Ganden, Drepung, and Sera; the seat of the Panchen Lamas, Tashi Lhünpo, in Tsang; centers in the far west; and major sites in Kham and Thuken's home region of Amdo. Thuken then turns to tantra-centered traditions, detailing the life of Tsongkhapa's disciple Sherap Sengé, the development of the Sé and Mé lineages, and the founding of the two great tantric monasteries, Gyütö and Gyümé. He also discusses the

Ensa ear-whispered lineage—a special transmission within the Geluk that includes teachings on guru yoga and Mahāmudrā—and the history of the Dalai and Panchen Lamas.

The third part of the Geluk chapter (our chapter 12) is an argument for the Geluk's status as the greatest of Tibetan traditions. Thuken attempts to show the Geluk's distinctiveness on the basis of its uniquely harmonious synthesis of all the Buddha's teachings; its uniquely lucid and subtle presentation of the Prāsaṅgika Madhyamaka view; its balanced appreciation for the place of meditation on the path and the balance within meditation between tranquility and insight; its scrupulous insistence on maintaining pure vows, whether of a monk, bodhisattva, or tantric yogin; and its sophisticated interpretation of tantric texts and the theories and practices expounded in them. Thuken concludes the chapter by noting that the Geluk not only comprises the entirety of Indian Buddhism but also contains the best of the other Tibetan schools. Of these, he concedes at the very end, all (except the Jonang) contain the basis for achieving enlightenment.

In his short chapter on Bön (his section IID, our chapter 13), Thuken summarizes the history of the three major traditions of Bön: emergent Bön, deviant Bön, and transformed Bön, then discusses the cosmology, metaphysics, rituals, and meditative practices found in the tradition, noting as well some aspects of its monastic organization. He links Bön views and meditations with those of the Nyingma Dzokchen tradition, and makes a point of showing how Bön "transformed," or imitated Buddhist texts and ideas. In his verse conclusion, Thuken observes that despite their apparent contradiction, Buddhism and Bön have to some degree intermingled, and he observes the irony that many Buddhists seek out Bön specialists for help with worldly problems.

Thuken's third major section (covering around fifty folios) discusses Chinese philosophical systems in two separate chapters. That on non-Buddhist traditions (his sections IIIA–B, our chapter 14) focuses primarily on Confucianism ("the Ru system") and Daoism ("the Bön system"), with considerably more attention given to the former. The discussion of Confucianism mentions the great figures and texts in the tradition, devotes some attention to divination practices related to the *Yijing (Classic of Changes),* and expounds in considerable detail Confucian cosmogony, cosmology, metaphysics, soteriology, and ethics. He compares Confucianism to Buddhism, and though he finds Confucian ethics admirable, he faults the tradition, especially in its later, anti-Buddhist phase, for excessive worldliness. The discussion of Daoism, of which Thuken confesses great ignorance, briefly covers the legend of Laozi (a.k.a. Lao tzu or Lao Tse), who he identifies with Shenrap Miwo, the founder of Bön, and whose views he likens to those of certain Hindu schools. The section also surveys Daoist metaphysics, rituals, institutions, and meditative practices and concludes that it is unlikely that Daoist practices lead to enlightenment. In the last section of the chapter, Thuken briefly discusses minor systems, such as a short-lived Brahmanical school and the Islamic tradition of the Uyghurs; he also makes an oblique reference to Christianity.[61]

The second chapter on China (Thuken's section IIIC, our chapter 15) covers Buddhist traditions. It discusses how Buddhism came to China from India and focuses on the exemplary figures, ideas, and practices of what Thuken considers the major Chinese lineages: the vinaya lineage (or Lu school), the secret mantra lineage (Chenyen), the lineage of extensive practice (the Yogācāra tradition of Xuanzang), the lineage of profound view (Tiantai and Huayan), and the lineage of essential meaning (Chan). Interestingly, the Pure Land school receives no mention. Chan is discussed in considerable detail, with a special focus on the life of Bodhidharma; in the end, Thuken likens Chan to the Mahāmudrā traditions of the Kagyü school and suggests that the eighth-century Chan master Heshang Mahāyāna,[62] so notorious in Tibetan lore, did not understand his own tradition. Near the end of the chapter, Thuken briefly discusses the influence of Tibetan traditions in China, touching briefly on Sakya relations with the Yuan dynasty and quite extensively on Geluk relations with various Qing emperors, emphasizing the honors bestowed upon various Geluk masters by their imperial patrons.

The chapter on "philosophical systems in other lands" (Thuken's section IV, our chapter 16) focuses on three parts of central Asia: Mongolia, Khotan, and Shambhala. The section on Mongolia is almost entirely historical, dealing in turn with the thirteenth and fourteenth centuries, when Tibetans (especially such Sakya luminaries as Sakya Pandita and Phakpa) first established preceptor-patron relations with Mongols and the Yuan dynasty and began to influence Mongol culture, and with the later period (sixteenth–eighteenth centuries), in which the Gelukpas spread Buddhism far and wide among the Mongols and received Mongol patronage and military assistance—it was a Mongol prince who invented the title "Dalai Lama," and it was Mongol armies that assured the Fifth Dalai Lama's control of central Tibet. An extremely brief section on Buddhism in Khotan is followed by a somewhat longer discussion of the Dharma's spread to Shambhala. Though the existence of Shambhala is given little credence by modern historians,

Thuken treats it as a real, if vaguely located, place, and discusses the geography, royal line, and Buddhist history of the kingdom (especially as related to the Kālacakra tantra) as well as prophecies regarding Shambhala's role in a future war in defense of the Dharma against Muslim "barbarians."

Thuken's conclusion (his section V, our chapter 17) is largely written in ornate metered verse. With great metaphorical élan, he celebrates the founding of Buddhism in India, its spread to Tibet and other lands, and the importance of understanding the systems of all cultures, both non-Buddhist and Buddhist, so as to overcome narrow partisanship. This will lead, he says, to recognizing the supremacy of Tsongkhapa's tradition and the practice of his unique synthesis of the path. Finally, Thuken dedicates whatever merit there may be in his work and pronounces benediction on the world, practitioners of Buddhism, and the Geluk tradition. The final section is the colophon, explaining briefly how the text came to be written.

Whatever its historical reliability, whatever its degree of impartiality, whatever its political agenda and implications, and whatever its genre in either a Tibetan or a Western setting, Thuken's *Crystal Mirror* stands as an impressive testament to its author's deep curiosity and breadth of interest about the religious world in which he lived. Even if imperfectly, it succeeds in its titular claim to hold up a mirror: to the ideas and practices of a range of Asian religions, to the values of the time and place in which it was written, and to a way of thinking about religion and philosophy that, while not quite modern, is far from out of date.

TIBET
CHINA
Xinjiang (Uyghur)
Xizang
(Tibetan Autonomous Region
LADAKH
Indus
Mt. Kailash
NGARI
TSANG
Tashi
Lhünpo
Jomonang
Shigatsé
Yarlung Tsangpo
Sakya
Shalu
Gya
Mt. Everest
NEPAL
Kathmandu
Delhi
Jamuna
INDIA
Ganges
Bodhgaya
BHU
BANGL
N
0 50 100 150 Miles
76°E
78°E
80°E
82°E
84°E
86°E
88°E
40°N
38°N
36°N
34°N
32°N
30°N
28°N
26°N
24°N

Inner Mongolia
Dunhuang
Gansu
Lake Kokonor
Xining
Gönlung
Kumbum
Lanzhou
Golmud
AMDO
Huang He (Yellow)
Labrang
Qinghai
Choné
Chang Jiang (Yangtze)
Yalung
Mekong
Dzokchen
Dergé
Salween
Chamdo
KHAM
Chengdu
Sichuan
Lithang
Drigung
CHINA
Yunnan
Ü
Brahmaputra
MYANMAR (BURMA)
Cultural Tibet
City
Monastery
92°E
94°E
96°E
98°E
100°E
102°E
104°E
106°E
40°N
38°N
36°N
34°N
32°N
30°N
28°N
26°N
24°N

Technical Note

In preparing our translation, the edition of the *Crystal Mirror* that served as our primary source was the book edition published in Lanzhou by the Kansu'u mi rigs dpe skran khang in 1984, which we refer to as K. We checked problematic readings in the Kansu'u edition against the woodblock print photocopy of the Lhasa Shöl *(zhol)* edition published in 1969 by Ṅawang Gelek Demo as volume II of Thuken's collected works; we refer to this as Z. At the very end of the translation process, the edition prepared in Sarnath and published in Delhi under the aegis of the Institute of Tibetan Classics (which we refer to as S, and for which the default edition is Z) became available. For the most part, our final translation reflects this edition, but we have not been able to check all of its readings against our own, and there are some places (indicated in footnotes), where we may depart from it, preferring readings found in K or suggested by other sources. The bracketed page references included in the text refer to the Sarnath edition. The appendix, which is a detailed outline of Thuken's text, includes page references keyed to each of the three editions we have consulted. Our paragraph divisions often follow those in S or K but in many cases, for ease of reading, we have broken up the sometimes exceedingly long paragraphs in those editions into shorter units. We also have introduced additional text divisions so that the structure of Thuken's work may be as clear as possible; our interpolations are not explicit in the text itself but are clearly set off by brackets in the outline in the appendix.

The conventions for phonetic transcription of Tibetan words are those developed by the Institute of Tibetan Classics and Wisdom Publications. These reflect approximately the pronunciation of words by a modern central Tibetan; Tibetan speakers from Ladakh, Kham, or Amdo (where Thuken was born), not to mention Mongolians, might pronounce the words quite differently. Transliterations of the phoneticized Tibetan terms and names used in the text can be found under the appropriate entry in the index. Sanskrit diacritics are used throughout except for Sanskrit terms that have been naturalized into English, such as samsara, nirvana, sutra, and mandala.

Pronunciation of Tibetan phonetics
ph and *th* are aspirated *p* and *t*, as in *pet* and *tip*.
ö is similar to the *eu* in the French *seul*.
ü is similar to the *ü* in the German *füllen*.
ai is similar to the *e* in *bet*.
é is similar to the *e* in *prey*.

Pronunciation of Sanskrit
Palatal *ś* and retroflex *ṣ* are similar to the English unvoiced *sh*.
c is an unaspirated *ch* similar to the *ch* in *chill*.
The vowel *ṛ* is similar to the American *r* in *pretty*.
ñ is somewhat similar to the nasalized *ny* in *canyon*.
ṅ is similar to the *ng* in *sing* or *anger*.

A note on brackets

In our translation, we have minimized the use of brackets to demarcate implied material, allowing that material to become part of our rendition. That material includes (1) the nouns referred to by pronouns, (2) the word(s) implied by the Tibetan *la sogs pa* ("etc."), (3) the full versions of persons, places, texts, terms, or lists that are given in abbreviated form, and (4) the authors of texts mentioned by Thuken. We beg the indulgence of Tibetologists for this decision, but they will know by looking at the Tibetan what has been added to clarify the original, while readers who do not read Tibetan will, presumably, be able to approach Thuken's text that much more easily for not having to negotiate through countless bracketed expressions. We have utilized standard parentheses for lifespan dates, Western equivalents of Tibetan dates, setting off items in numerical lists, and Tibetan or Sanskrit words that need to be noted in the translation proper, as when Thuken explains etymologies.

A note on dates

In the text itself, we have provided parenthetical dates only for figures who are given significant attention, or whose dates will clarify chronology. We have otherwise supplied the dates for individuals, where these are known or estimated, in the index. In general, greater confidence may be assigned to the dates of later persons than of earlier ones, and Chinese and Tibetan datings are usually more reliable than those for Indians. We have attempted to consult the most recent scholarship on these matters, but our datings should not be taken as the final word. In certain instances, we have cited regnal dates of rulers (prefaced by "r.") rather than birth and death dates, including regnal dates that are speculative at best, as with the earliest emperors of China or the rulers of Shambhala.

A note on notes

In the notes to the translation, we have tried to (1) note our points of departure from the Sarnath edition, (2) explain terms or phrases not spelled out in the text, and (3) provide a sampling of important Western-language sources relevant to the most important traditions, persons, texts, practices, and places mentioned by Thuken. His scope in the *Crystal Mirror* is so wide, however, that we could not possibly provide exhaustive references to the relevant Western-language sources, let alone to the Indic and Tibetan primary sources from which modern scholars have drawn. Fuller references will be found in a number of the works of scholarship noted, and we ask the reader to consult them for further information. In the notes, a single parenthetical italicized term will be Tibetan, unless otherwise identified; where two terms are listed, separated by a comma, the Tibetan is first, the Sanskrit second.

A note on the index

The index to this volume is intended to be a useful reference tool and provides more than just the relevant page numbers for its entries. For historical figures, it also includes their dates when known and sometimes page references to other historical works, such as the *Blue Annals,* where readers can learn more about them. Geographical locales often have brief explanations of their relative location. All Tibetan names and terms in the index are followed by the Wylie transliterated spelling, and readers should therefore consult the index to find the original rendering.

A note on texts

Titles of Indian and Tibetan (as well as Chinese) texts are nearly always rendered in English within the translation and the notes. Texts mentioned but not quoted by Thuken do not appear in the bibliography—their sheer number makes that prohibitive—but they can all be found in the index, along with their Indian and Tibetan titles and, where appropriate, their Tōhoku catalogue number. Works that Thuken quotes, however, do appear in the bibliography as well.

Abbreviations used in the notes

See bibliography for full publication details on the works listed here:

BA: Gö Lotsāwa Shönu Pal. *The Blue Annals*. Translated by George N. Roerich.
Ch: Chinese
GT: Tsong-kha-pa. *The Great Treatise on the Stages of the Path to Enlightenment*. Translated by the Lamrim Chenmo Translation Committee.
K: *Thu'u bkwan grub mtha'*. Lanzhou: Kan su'u mi rigs dpe skrun khang, 1984.
NS: Dudjom Rinpoche. *The Nyingma School of Tibetan Buddhism*. Translated and edited by Gyurme Dorje and Matthew Kapstein.
S: *Grub mtha' shel gyi me long*. Delhi: Institute of Tibetan Classics, 2007.
Skt.: Sanskrit
TBRC: Tibetan Buddhist Resource Center website, tbrc.org.
Tib.: Tibetan
Toh: Tōhoku catalogue number, Dergé edition of the Tibetan Tripiṭaka
TPS: Giuseppe Tucci. *Tibetan Painted Scrolls*.
TR: Ronald M. Davidson, *Tibetan Renaissance: Tantric Buddhism in the Rebirth of Tibetan Culture and the Rise of Sakya*.
TRP: *Taking the Result as the Path: Core Teachings of the Sakya Lamdré Tradition*. Translated by Cyrus R. Stearns.
Z: *Grub mtha' shel gyi me long*. Edited and reproduced by Ṅawang Gelek Demo. Delhi, 1969.

The Crystal Mirror

An Excellent Explanation Showing the Sources and Assertions of All Philosophical Systems

Thuken Losang Chökyi Nyima

1. Preface

[3] *An Expression of Worship and Promise to Compose*

I prostrate to the mighty Muni,[63] the lord of philosophical systems,
Who saw everything in the untold billions of philosophical systems,
Refuted the positions of ill-spoken philosophical systems,
And gave teachings on the principles of pure philosophical systems.

I prostrate respectfully to the Unconquerable and to Mañjughoṣa,[64]
Who possessed the entire secret treasury of the Conqueror's speech
And ordained the banquet of profound and extensive Dharma
With various emanations in countless fields.

May victory come to the two eyes of the world known as Nāgārjuna and Asaṅga, who,
Distinguishing well between definitive and provisional scriptures, illuminated the great chariot-paths of Madhyamaka and Cittamātra
Exactly as prophesied by the Conqueror himself when he said, "There will rise a conjunct sun and moon
Who will open well, respectively, the hundred-petaled lotus and night-lily gardens of the two ways."[65]

I bow respectfully to the ornaments that beautify Jambudvīpa:[66]
Āryadeva, Aśvaghoṣa, Bhāvaviveka, Buddhapālita,
Candrakīrti, Śāntideva, Vasubandhu, Haribhadra,
Sthiramati, Dignāga, Dharmakīrti, Guṇaprabha, and Śākyaprabhā.

I make prostrations as well to the assembly of mighty yogins who,
Drunk on the beer of bliss and emptiness, join with their great secret songs

In the banquet of fortunate supreme adepts
In the palace of the supreme vehicle, highest yoga tantra.

I bow down, remembering the kindness of the translators, pandits, and Dharma kings,
Who, with the strength of the green horse of their arousal of the awakening mind,
Drew the great light of the sun of the holy Dharma to this land,
Which, though surrounded by snow mountains, was covered with the darkness of confusion.[67]

I bow to all the supreme beings who, appearing different yet sharing a single nature,
Spread in this Land of Snows the ways of many different philosophical systems,
Which, though differently elucidated, come down to a single ultimate intention,
Like rivers and streams descending separately but mingling in a single ocean. [4]

I bow from my heart to the great lord Dīpaṃkara, who lovingly and unstintingly bestowed on his Tibetan disciples
The mighty king of teachings on the awakening mind, brought from Suvarṇadvīpa after many hardships.
And I bow as well to the second conqueror and his spiritual sons;[68] he took as his own the complete teaching of the Muni, and through his excellent explanations
And the marvel of a life lived purely, he opened the way of the Gandenpa,[69] the greatest way of all.

I prostrate to the upholders of the Ganden teaching,
Who set atop the victory banner of explanation and practice
The wish-granting jewel of the unstained tradition of the protector[70]
And sent down the inexhaustible rain of all that is virtuous, good,[71] and desirable.

I exalt at my crown Amitābha and Lokeśvara,
The mighty conquerors, father and son,[72]

Who, performing in saffron robes, cause the unremitting increase
Of the highest essence of the teaching of the Muni until samsara ends.

Until enlightenment, may there remain at the center of my heart the incomparably kind three-aspected gurus,[73]
Who, empowered by love for beings as if they were their own children, open the door to the inexhaustible Dharma treasury of the secret mind,
The mentors who freely bestow the essence of the wealth of excellent explanation, and in particular
The actualization of all buddhas, Rölpai Dorjé, and those named Maitripāda and Ratna.[74]

Thus, with words of praise
And with flowers held in the folded hands of faith,
I have worshipped the great lord of the teaching,
The Muni, along with his spiritual sons and their students.

Many, under the sway of anger, have deprecated
The Dharmas and persons of other systems
Without even knowing how to properly distinguish among
The various philosophical systems in this land.

Many, under the sway of the four negative tendencies,
Failing to ascertain any reason
For the special distinctiveness of their own philosophical system,
And driven only by confusion and desire, still hold their system as supreme.

In order to set them in conscientiousness,
I will briefly discuss here
The sources and standpoints of the philosophical systems
That arose in the Holy Land[75] of India and in Tibet and China.

If any there are with honest eyes,
Free of the cataracts of partiality,
They should view the many wondrous forms that appear
In this white crystal mirror of excellent explanation. [5]

A General Explanation of the Project

Now, countless are the ways in which logicians have conceived and established philosophical systems amid the world systems as measureless as space, and likewise the very pure philosophical systems that arose from the awakening mind and deeds of the Muni, the Buddha, the Blessed One[76] are beyond number, so who could discuss the countless ways in which they arose? Here, I will discuss just briefly how different philosophical systems arose in particular lands in Jambudvīpa and the unique standpoints of each system.

This text, then, is fivefold: I. The history of philosophical systems in the Holy Land of India; II. Their history in Tibet, the Land of Snows; III. Their history in the land of Great China; IV. Their history in some other places; and V. The conclusion, which explains the outcome. Part I is twofold: A. The history of the non-Buddhist extremists and B. The history of the Buddhists.[77] Section A is threefold: 1. The story of how the extremists arose; 2. A brief explanation of their standpoints; and 3. The purpose of explaining those.

2. Indian Schools[78]

I. The History of Philosophical Systems in the Holy Land of India[79]
A. The history of the non-Buddhist extremists[80]
1. The story of how the extremists arose

FOR A LONG TIME after this world had come into being, humans here in Jambudvīpa enjoyed uncultivated crops, but then lazy people began hoarding food, so farming became necessary. Then greedy people took what had not been given to them, and because of the discord that resulted, it became necessary to appoint a leader who could pass judgment. The first [6] leader was called King Saṃmāta ("Honored by Many").[81]

Seeing the king punish some evildoers at that time saddened certain beings, who then went to solitary places in the forest and remained there; thus arose the brahmans. Some of these hermits reduced their desires and achieved satisfaction; sitting alone, they isolated mind and body and so attained tranquil abiding. When they then gained supernormal and magical powers, they were called "seers."[82] Of those, many who had attained supernormal powers and trained in logic analyzed their own minds, set forth a path for attaining liberation and higher rebirth, and wrote texts that laid out the logical reasons proving that path. It was through this that the philosophical systems of the extremists spread.

The first to arise was the Sāṃkhya. During the period of measureless lifespans there lived a seer called Kapila ("Yellow-White"), who had long yellow-white hair and possessed the five supernormal powers. Relying on his innate wisdom, he composed many texts. His followers were known as Sāṃkhyas ("Enumerators") or Kāpilīyas. When the human lifespan was twenty thousand years, there lived a seer named Vyāsa ("Spreader").[83] His followers were called Vaiyasins or Nirgranthas ("Naked Ones"). There was also a seer named Lokākṣī ("Eyes of the World") who was quite skilled in logic. He fornicated with his own daughter, denied past and future lives, and composed manifold texts ascribing no benefits to virtue or disadvantages to vice. His followers, the Lokāyatas, were the worst of the extremists. Then came the seer called Handsome One. Mahādeva had made him the protector of his consort, Umā, and Umā lusted after the seer Handsome One. Sitting before him, she displayed many alluring manifestations, but the seer lowered his eyes to his feet. Because he guarded his own austerity, Mahādeva was pleased and permitted him to compose texts. The seer was known as Akṣapāda ("Eyes to Feet"), and his followers were known as Akṣapādins or Naiyāyikas ("Those with Knowledge"). The followers of two later seers, Ulūka ("The Owl One"), who mistook an owl for a god and took pride in attaining knowledge of the six categories, and Kaṇāda ("Grain Eater"), who undertook the austerity of eating the grains [7] thrown out by others,[84] were called Vaiśeṣikas ("Differentiators").

2. *A brief explanation of the standpoints of the extremists*[85]

It is explained in the sutras that there are ninety-six strange views, fourteen indeterminate views, sixty-two debased[86] views, twenty-eight unholy views, twenty debased views, and so forth.[87] There are explanations in Bhāvaviveka's *Blaze of Logic* how there are one hundred and ten categories of views, and in his *Precious Lamp of Madhyamaka* how there are three hundred categories of views.[88] However, as the mighty Lord of Knowledge says, "wrong paths are limitless,"[89] so it is difficult to determine all the debased views of those lacking the intelligence to distinguish the path from the nonpath and say: "This one is and this one isn't." Thus the number of philosophical systems with debased views is not held to be definite. I will just explain in brief the standpoints of some of the more famous ones. I divide the views of the philosophical systems of non-Buddhists into two: proponents of eternalism (Śāśvatavādins) and proponents of nihilism (Uccedavādins). It is said that the proponents of nihilism are the Lokāyatas, while the proponents of eternalism are eight: Sāṃkhyas, Brahmavādins, Vaiṣṇavas, Mīmāṃsakas, Śaivas, Vaiśeṣikas, Naiyāyikas, and Nirgranthas.[90]

a. Lokāyatas

The Lokāyatas are twofold: contemplatives and logicians. Each of those is twofold: proponents of a nihilism in which past and future lives are asserted but cause and effect are not asserted, and proponents of a nihilism that absolutely denies past and future lives and cause and effect.

The way the logicians misstate things: They assert that even with effort no one is able to see the force that causes the sun to rise, the downward flow of water, the roundness of peas, the sharpness of thorns, or the multicolored splendor of the peacock, so these things must arise from their own self-nature; since they say that such things have no causes, they completely deny cause and effect. Furthermore, they illustrate the mind's dependence on the body through three similes: it has the same nature as the body, as in the example of liquor and its capacity to intoxicate; it is an effect of the body, as in the example of a butter lamp and its light; and it is a quality of the body, as in the example of a wall [8] and the mural on it. Therefore, just as an accidental lamp produces light accidentally, likewise, the accidental body produces the mind accidentally;[91] thus, there is no coming into this life from a past life. At the time of death, the body dissolves into the four great elements, and the sense faculties dissolve into space; they are destroyed. Since body and mind are one substance, when the body is destroyed the mind is also destroyed, just as when the wall is destroyed its mural is also destroyed, and there is no transition from this life to a future life. Thus they deny both past and future lives, and so also completely deny liberation. Since there is no habituation to the path over many lives, there is no omniscience, and since there is no cause of suffering and other ills, there is neither a path that brings freedom from that suffering nor any freedom.

The contemplatives[92] say that when you attain the mental absorptions and formless realms, and so forth, you have the perception of yourself as an arhat; but at the time of death, when your concentration degenerates, you foresee rebirth in a lower realm, and because of that, there is no arhatship in the world. Some, having investigated with their clairvoyance and seen someone who had performed charity in this life becoming poor in a future life, say there is no cause and effect and completely deny that which is not seen by their own supernormal powers. Maintaining that perception is the only type of valid cognition—and not asserting generally characterized phenomena, inference, and so forth—this school completely denies past and future lives, cause and effect, liberation, and omniscience. Therefore, among non-Buddhists, they are the worst.

b. Sāṃkhyas

The Sāṃkhyas, or Kāpiliyas, say that effects exist at the time of the cause and then become manifest through conditions. They also are twofold:

the atheistic Sāṃkhyas assert that cause and effect arise only from the principal,[93] while the theistic Sāṃkhyas assert that even though causes and effects have the same nature, they transform into different manifestations through empowerment by the great god, Īśvara.

Sāṃkhyas assert definitively that all objects of knowledge are enumerated into twenty-five: (1) the principal, (2) the great, (3) the I-principle, (4–8) the five sense objects,[94] (9–13) the five elements, (14–24) the eleven sense faculties, and (25) the person, which is self, consciousness, and the knower. Of those, the person [9] is asserted as conscious, while the remaining twenty-four—as aggregate composites—are insentient matter. *Fundamental nature, the general,* and *the principal* are asserted to be synonymous; they refer to an object of knowledge possessing six attributes.[95] *Person, self, consciousness,* and *the knower* are synonyms. *Intellect* and *the great* are counted as a single term, which is asserted as something like the two-sided mirror on which appear reflections both of objects from the outside and of the person from the inside. Sāṃkhyas say that the intellect is necessarily material, while consciousness must be the self.

The way they assert bondage and freedom: Whenever the person generates the desire to enjoy an object, the fundamental nature emanates manifestations such as sound and so forth. Accordingly, from the principal comes the intellect, and from that arise the three I-principles. The *darkness-possessing I-principle* urges forth the other two I-principles. From the *manifesting I-principle* arise the five sense objects, namely, forms, sounds, smells, tastes, and tangibles; and from the *essential-powered I-principle* arise the eleven sense faculties, namely, the five faculties of intellect, the five faculties of the body, and the faculty of mind. In addition, they assert that the fundamental nature, which is like a blind person with legs, and the person, which is like a cripple with eyes, are conflated; and we circle in samsara because we do not understand how manifestations are emanated by the fundamental nature. When, by listening to the instruction directly imparted by a guru, we gain the distinctive ascertainment that "these manifestations are mere emanations of the fundamental nature," at that time we gradually become free from attachment to that object, and through the mental absorptions, we generate the supernormal power of the divine eye. When we regard the principal with that power, the principal is like another's wife, who blushes with shame upon being seen; the manifestations are gathered in, and the fundamental nature abides alone. Then, on the surface of the yogin's intellect, all conventional appearances are turned away, and we abide without using objects and without activity: then, they assert, we have attained liberation.

c. Brahmavādins

The Brahmavādins say that their teacher is Brahmā. They are subdivided into Vaiyākaraṇikas ("Grammarians"), Vedāntins, and Guhyavādins ("Esoterists"). They assert that all the world's environs and inhabitants are created [10] by Brahmā and that the only source of valid cognition is the Vedas. They also state that, since the words of the Vedas are sounds not produced by a person, the Vedas show only true objects. They assert that the method for achieving higher rebirths and the state of Brahmā is the horse sacrifice explained in the Vedic texts.

The Vaiyākaraṇikas state that Brahmā, in the form of the syllable *oṃ,* is the basis for the arising of the world's various environs and inhabitants and is their self-nature. Since it is without birth or death, it is permanent, spatially and temporally partless, truly pervades inner and outer objects, and is of a single nature, abiding absolutely. They state that subjects and objects appear as dual to those who are polluted by ignorance. The standpoint of the Tibetan Jonangpas appears to be close to this. Vaiyākaraṇikas assert that the path effecting the attainment of liberation is, externally, making the fire offering of animal sacrifice, and internally, making the fire offering of dripping the male semen element into the hearth of the woman's vagina; liberation is asserted as the clear emptiness and the bliss that then occur.[96]

The Vedāntins, or Highest Brahmans, assert an entity called the *person.* This is the "person" explained in the Vedas, which are the source of valid cognition; it is single; it is permanent because it is never destroyed; it is pure because it transcends suffering;[97] it pervades all the manifold beings; it is undying because it has no beginning or end; it has the color of the sun; it has transcended the circle of darkness; it has become the great; and it is other than sleep.[98] That person is the self-nature of the gods and also the nature of Maheśvara. From that person alone are produced all the three worlds, happiness and suffering, and bondage and freedom. However, the nature of the person itself is unchanging and inexhaustible. When, based on the mental absorptions, we view the person with the divine eye and see that person as golden colored, then, having equalized virtue and vice, samsara and nirvana, we become free.

The Guhyavādins are mostly like the Vedāntins; based on the Vedas, they assert a self that is conscious, knowing, permanent, partless, and single.[99]

d. Vaiṣṇavas

The Vaiṣṇavas take Viṣṇu as their teacher and say that Viṣṇu has two natures, tranquil and active. Of these, the tranquil nature has: the nature of divine substance, a self-nature that neither exists nor does not exist, and a nature that is immortal; by meditating on that you attain liberation. The active nature they explain as the ten avatars of Viṣṇu—[11] the fish and the others. They maintain that the self is permanent and partless, and explain that there is an end to samsara and that the path to freedom is meditation on the syllable *oṃ,* the vase-breath meditation,[100] and so forth. This system also asserts that samsara has an end; Vedāntins and a multitude of others are explained to be followers of this system.[101]

e. Mīmāṃsakas

The Mīmāṃsakas are followers of Jaiminī, so they are also called Jaiminīyas. They assert that (1) the self is the nature of intellect, is sentient, and is immaterial; (2) that the intrinsic nature of consciousness and the knower is a permanent nature; (3) that self is a discrete substantial existent; and (4) that it is partless. Their viewpoint on the Vedas as a source of valid cognition is like that of the previous schools. They assert that there is attainment of higher rebirths, like the level of Brahmā, solely by sacrificial offerings and other practices. They say that because that liberation is freedom from lower realms, it is a limited liberation; there is no liberation that is the complete pacification of suffering. Also, because of the stains abiding in the intrinsic nature of mind, there can be no omniscience. And, because objects of knowledge are countless, there is no true speech.[102]

Most Mīmāṃsakas assert six sources of valid cognition, while the Cārakīya Jaiminīyas assert eleven sources of valid cognition and also teach a division into forty-eight functional forces, which are not set forth here.

f. Śaivas, Vaiśeṣikas, Naiyāyikas

The trio of the Aiśvaras—or Śaivas—Vaiśeṣikas, and Naiyāyikas take Īśvara as their teacher. Both the Vaiśeṣikas and Naiyāyikas may also include those who have made Brahmā and Viṣṇu their teachers, so members of those two groups may also be designated as Brahmavādins and Vaiṣṇavas.

The Vaiśeṣikas, as previously noted, are followers of a seer who mistook an owl for a god (Ulūka) and a seer who ate grain (Kaṇāda), so they are also called "Owlers" (Ālūkīyas) and "Grain Eaters" (Kaṇādīyas). Also, the Naiyāyikas are followers of the aforementioned seer Akṣapāda, so they are also called Akṣapādins.

They all assert Īśvara to be omniscient and state that all the world's environs and inhabitants proceed from Īśvara's intellect. They say that the path is the blisses arising from the vase-breath meditation, from the bestowal of initiation from the tip of Īśvara's liṅgam, and from the emission of semen[103] during sex with [12] a woman. They assert that liberation is the gnosis of the bliss of intercourse, which arises from the bliss of emitting semen.

The Vaiśeṣikas and Naiyāyikas: the former say that there are many distinctions of the general and the particular to be made via the six categories, so they are known as "Particularizers" (Vaiśeṣikas); the latter, because they are followers of the knowledge system created by the seer Akṣapāda, are known as "Knowledge Possessors" (Naiyāyikas). The Vaiśeṣikas admit three sources of valid cognition: perception, inference, and scripture; the Naiyāyikas admit those three and also admit comparison as a source of valid cognition, making four. Also, both schools assert three types of inference, three aspects of perfect logical reasons that are the basis of those inferences, and three fallacies that subvert a reason. I will not address here their standpoints on the sixteen or eight categories of logic.[104]

The practices for attaining liberation are ablution, receiving initiation, fasting, celibacy when residing in the guru's home, dwelling in the forest, sacrificial offering, charity, and so forth. In time, by cultivating a yoga learned through the guru's instruction, we come to understand that the self is a different entity from the sense faculties, and so forth, and to see the real nature of the self. And, when we fully comprehend the nature of the six categories, then we understand that the self is pervasive in nature but without activity, and we no longer accumulate any wholesome or unwholesome karma. Since no new karma is accumulated, when the old karma is exhausted, the body that has already been taken—the faculties, the intellect, pleasures, pains, attachments, hatreds, and so forth—separates from the self; and since a new body and faculties are not taken, the continuum of rebirths is severed, as with a fire that has exhausted its firewood. When the self abides alone, that is liberation. So say the Naiyāyikas and Vaiśeṣikas.

g. Nirgranthas

The Nirgranthas are followers of the holy Jina and others,[105] so they are known as Jainas. They classify all objects of knowledge into nine categories;

they say that trees and such possess mind; and they assert logical reasons proving that our teacher, the Buddha, is not omniscient. With regard to liberation, they state that based on austerities such as nakedness, silence, exposure to the five fires,[106] and so forth, we exhaust all previously created karma, and by not accumulating any new karma, we go to a place located above the whole world, the so-called *composite world*. This world is shaped like an open upside-down umbrella, white like yogurt or [13] a water lily, and measures 4.5 million leagues[107] across. Because it contains souls, that realm is material; because it is free from samsara, it also is nonmaterial. That abode is called *liberation*. So say the Nirgranthas.

h. Summary

The logical reasons that negate those extremist standpoints are taught extensively in Candrakīrti's *Entering the Middle Way,* the root text and commentary of Bhāvaviveka's *Heart of Madhyamaka* and *Blaze of Logic,* Dharmakīrti's *Thorough Exposition of Valid Cognition* and *Ascertainment of Valid Cognition,* and other texts. Among the extremist philosophical systems, the standpoints of three schools, the Sāṃkhya, Vaiśeṣika, and Naiyāyika, are a little more developed, so many more logical reasons negating them are taught in Dharmakīrti's seven treatises on valid cognition[108] and other texts. Were I to lay out those negations here, I'm afraid it would be too much, so I have not written about them.

3. The purpose of explaining the extremists' views

If you understand these other schools' ways of propounding eternalism and nihilism well, along with the logical reasons negating them that occur frequently in the texts of the great charioteers,[109] you will, induced by the path of reasoning, gain an irreversible faith in the faultless teaching and teacher of our own Geluk system. Thus, as Udbhaṭasiddhasvāmin's *Special Praise of the Holy* says,

> However much I contemplate the aspects
> Of the textual systems of the extremists,
> By that much more, O Protector,
> My mind becomes faithful to you.[110]

Moreover, misconceptions will be stopped—holding that suffering is without cause and that it arises from inappropriate causes, maintaining as the path what is not the path, holding as liberation what is not liberation, and so forth. The seeds of those imprints established in past lives through studying the major texts of debased philosophical systems such as the Lokāyata and others are thereby decreased; and in subsequent lives you will turn away from all wrong views, and the imprints allowing the correct view to arise quickly in your mental continuum will be established. Not only that, since among the various philosophical systems that spread in Tibet, the standpoints of some appear to be similar to those of the extremist systems, it is most necessary that, understanding well the distinctions [14] among them, you arouse such a strong conviction in Buddhist teachings that your own view cannot stray toward some other view, and so forth. Thus, those who desire liberation should not think, "these studies are for countering objections in a debate but are not useful for practice." Instead they should assiduously study and reflect upon the texts of those great charioteers and the excellent explanations of the father, Jé Lama Tsongkhapa, and his spiritual sons. It is crucial that you understand this.

I say:

For anyone here with intelligence,
The principal thing to do in mind and body
Is to find a way to free yourself from samsaric existence;
Otherwise, how are you different from an animal?

Many in this world claim to be teachers,
And though many say they've presented bondage and freedom,
All they've done is show, as the path to peace,
A method that strengthens the root of cyclic existence.

Whose teaching, for those desiring liberation,
Is the supreme and nondeceptive entryway?
Only the Sugata's teaching,
So the Buddha alone is an authority.[111]

If you don't understand even partially the standpoints of other schools,
Then no matter how much you say your own teacher and teaching

Are faultless, your words are like a parrot's:
Mere words, incapable of inducing certainty.

Therefore, understanding well the presentations of non-Buddhist systems—
Perilous footholds on the edge of debased extremist views—
And then rejecting them is the stairway for entry
Into the citadel of liberation. So say the wise.

This has been a brief interlude in verse.

B. The history of the Buddhists[112]

The history of the Buddhists is twofold: 1. The history of proponents of the four philosophical systems; and 2. A brief explanation of the points of view of those philosophical systems.

1. The history of proponents of the four philosophical systems[113]

According to the Mahayana, a thousand buddhas will appear in this eon; according to the Hinayana, there will be [15] five hundred. When the lifespan of the humans of Jambudvīpa degenerated from a measureless lifespan and reached forty thousand years, the Buddha Krakucchanda came. When the lifespan was at thirty thousand years, the Buddha Kanakamuni came; at twenty thousand years, the Buddha Kāśyapa came; and when the lifespan was at a hundred years, and the five impurities were on the rise, our teacher Śākyamuni came to the world and turned the wheel of Dharma in three stages. Following the first pronouncement, the Dharma wheel of the four noble truths, there arose the two śrāvaka schools, propounding Hinayana philosophy; and following the middle and last turning arose Madhyamaka and Cittamātra, the two schools propounding Mahayana philosophy.[114]

a. The history of the śrāvaka philosophical systems[115]

1) Vaibhāṣika

Of the two śrāvaka schools, the Vaibhāṣikas are known as Vaibhāṣikas ("Detailers") because they follow the text called *Ocean of Detailed Explana-*

tion or *Great Detailed Explanation (Mahāvibhāṣā)* and because they argue in detail that the three times are substantially existent. They are divided into four basic schools and eighteen sects.

The four basic schools are: (1) the lineage[116] from the preceptor-arhat Kāśyapa, the Mahāsāṃghika school; (2) the lineage from Rāhula, the Sarvāstivāda; (3) the lineage from Kātyāyana, the Sthavira school; and (4) the lineage from Upāli, the Saṃmatīya school.[117]

The eighteen sects: There are five Mahāsāṃghika sects. Master Vinītadeva (eighth century) says:

> The Pūrvaśaila, Aparaśaila, and Haimavata;
> The Lokottaravāda
> And Prajñaptivāda: these schools
> Are the five Mahāsāṃghika factions.[118]

There are seven Sarvāstivādin sects. Vinītadeva says:

> The Mūlasarvāstivāda and the Kāśyapīya school,
> The Mahīśāsaka school and the Dharmaguptaka school,
> The Bahuśrutīya and Tāmraśāṭīya, along with their disciples,
> And the Vibhajyavāda: these schools
> Are the Sarvāstivāda.[119]

There are three Sthavira sects. Vinītadeva says:

> The Jaitavanīya, the Abhayagirivāsīya,
> And the Mahāvihāravāsīya: these are the Sthavira.[120]

There are three Saṃmatīya[121] sects. Vinītadeva says:

> The Kurukullaka, the Avantaka,
> And the Vātsīputrīya: these are the schools
> Of the Saṃmatīya.[122]

Those eighteen sects also were delineated according to the master of whom there were followers, the country of residence, or the standpoint of the philosophical system. Vinītadeva says:

> By distinctions of region, topic, and master,
> There are eighteen different [16] schools.[123]

That is another, different explanation of the way the schools split into eighteen.[124]

One hundred and sixteen years after the Teacher's nirvana, in the city called Vaiśālī, four elders of the sangha recited the scriptures in four different languages; because of that, the students fell into disagreement and split into the four basic schools. Through divisions in those, there came to be eighteen sects, which quarreled among themselves. In time, they obtained the *Sutra on the Prophetic Dream of King Krikrī*. When they looked into it, they saw its statement that although there would be eighteen sects, the fruit of freedom would not decay, so they came to mutual agreement. This is still another way of explaining the division.

Masters who were well-known proponents of Vaibhāṣika were: Vasumitra, Dharmatrāta, Buddhadeva, Saṅghabhadra,[125] and others.

2) Sautrāntika

The Sautrāntikas ("Sutra Followers") or Dārṣṭāntikas ("Exemplifiers") posit their philosophical system by following the sutras and teaching about all dharmas by means of examples: thus are they known by the wise.[126] Their divisions are two: the followers of scripture, who propound their philosophical system only through accepting literally whatever appears in the sutras; and the followers of reasoning, who follow reasoning as explained in Dharmakīrti's seven treatises. Their renowned masters included Kumārarata, Śrīrirata, Bhadantarata,[127] and others.

b. The history of the Mahayana philosophical systems[128]

After the Teacher's nirvana, the Mahayana teaching was widespread in the regions of the gods and nāgas;[129] it is said to have existed in other worlds as well. Here in Jambudvīpa, many bodhisattvas were abiding on the various bodhisattva stages, and secret mantra yogins were maintaining secret austerities. They themselves practiced, and they explained the practices to a few fortunate people, so the Mahayana teaching was maintained and expanded a little, but overall, because the śrāvaka schools were [17] so widespread, the Mahayana teaching was in decline; in this way a long time passed. By the time the great brahman Saraha[130] came, the Mahayana secret mantra teachings were the main ones propagated. Then, as prophesied by the Conqueror himself, there came the pair of the second Buddha, Nāgārjuna, along with Asaṅga.[131] Based on the words of the Blessed One himself,[132] they divided the scriptures into definitive and provisional. Since, like the sun, they clearly illuminated the complete way of practicing the profound and extensive paths of the Mahayana,[133] they were known as the two great charioteers. From that point on, the teaching of the Mahayana became widespread and extensive.

1) The history of the Madhyamaka philosophical system[134]

a) Nāgārjuna

The protector Nāgārjuna (ca. 150 A.D.)[135] is also the charioteer who opened the way of the Mahayana in general. According to the *Descent to Laṅka Sutra:*

> In the southern region of Vedalī[136]
> Will arise an illustrious and famous monk
> By the name of Nāga
> Who will destroy the positions of existence and nonexistence.
> Having clearly explained my vehicle
> In this world, the unsurpassed vehicle,
> He will achieve the stage of the Joyous[137]
> And will go at death to Sukhāvatī.[138]

In addition, Nāgārjuna was clearly prophesied by the Conqueror in many other texts, such as the *Mañjuśrī Root Tantra,*[139] the *Great Drum Sutra,*[140] and others.

Nāgārjuna was born into a brahman family four hundred years after the Buddha's nirvana, in Vidarbha,[141] in the south. The great brahman Saraha took care of him, ordained him, and prolonged his life—which was not to have exceeded seven days—and then bestowed upon him many instructions on secret mantra. He was fully ordained by Rāhula, the abbot of Nālandā,[142] and was known as Bhikṣu Śrīmata. He was put in charge of provisions for the Nālandā sangha; he provided food for the monks by practicing alchemy. After a śrāvaka partisan named Bhikṣu Ānandakāra wrote a 1,200,000-verse text called the *Ornament of Reasoning,*[143] Nāgārjuna thrice uttered the great Dharma proclamation, annihilating the refutations of the Mahayana made by this master. Arriving in the nāga realm, he taught the Dharma to many nāgas, and he brought back to the human world much nāga mud[144] as well as the *Perfection of Wisdom in a Hundred Thousand Verses* and other sutras that had disappeared from Jambudvīpa; it is for this reason he is known as Nāgārjuna.[145]

Nāgārjuna worked for the benefit of beings in many places, such as Puṇḍaravardhana, Ṣaṭāveṣa,[146] and others. He went to the northern continent of Uttarakuru and other places, performing countless deeds for the benefit of sentient beings through his magical powers, teaching Dharma, and so forth. [18] He erected many stupas and temples. In Bodhgayā he enclosed the Buddha's enlightenment spot with a stone-lattice fence, and he designed and built the stupa of Śrī Dhānyakaṭaka.[147] Doing this and other deeds, he left his legacy and brought limitless benefit to the teaching.

In particular, he established the path of the ultimate definitive meaning, that of the profound Madhyamaka, by means of scripture in the *Compendium of Sutras* and by means of reasoning in the six collections of reasoning, such as the *Fundamental Treatise on the Middle Way*.[148] Moreover, he wrote collections of praises, such as the *Praise of the Dharmadhātu* and others; texts concerned with secret mantra, such as the *Five Stages*[149] and the *Commentary on the Awakening Mind;* and many sutra and tantra commentaries. And, with logical reasoning, he annihilated the proponents of debased views. He revived from the ground up the teaching of the Mahayana, which had disappeared, and with a kindness like that of the Conqueror himself, spread the Conqueror's teaching throughout the land.

Nāgārjuna stayed in the human realm for six hundred years. At the end of this period, the son of King Sātavāhana, named Śaktimāna, begged for Nāgārjuna's head, and Nāgārjuna offered it, but the boy could not cut it off with a sword. Nāgārjuna told the boy that, since he himself had a karmic seed from killing an insect with a blade of kuśa grass, his head could be severed with kuśa grass; thus, the boy severed Nāgārjuna's head. He left carrying the head, but a yakṣī stole it and threw it one league away. Neither Nāgārjuna's head nor his body have decomposed, and it is related that, after coming closer every year, they will reunite, and Nāgārjuna will again work for the benefit of the teaching and of beings.

The *Great Drum Sutra* explains that this master is on the seventh bodhisattva stage;[150] the *Bright Lamp* of Candrakīrti explains that he attained the supreme yogic achievement in this life.[151] Numerous incomparable sages became his disciples, such as Āryadeva, Aśvaghoṣa, Bhāvaviveka,

Buddhapālita, and Candrakīrti.[152] Because he reopened the chariot-path of Madhyamaka by way of the *Fundamental Treatise on the Middle Way (Mūlamadhyamakakārikā)* the followers of Nāgārjuna were called Mādhyamikas and Niḥsvabhāvavādins ("Proponents of Essencelessness").

b) Madhyamaka after Nāgārjuna

Āryadeva (second–third century) was taken by Nāgārjuna's other students to be as authoritative as the master himself. He wrote the *Four Hundred Stanzas,* on the practice of yoga.[153] Although the ultimate meaning of these two, father and son, resides in the Prāsaṅgika system, on the surface their texts do not clearly establish [19] their presentation as uniquely Prāsaṅgika. Rather they dwell more generally on positions common to both Prāsaṅgika and Svātantrika, and so their texts are said to belong to "general Madhyamaka."

Master Buddhapālita (470–540?), in his commentary on Nāgārjuna's *Fundamental Treatise on the Middle Way,* set forth multiple consequential arguments *(prasaṅga)* as the meaning of the logical reasons presented in the *Fundamental Treatise on the Middle Way;* he did not explain those reasons with independent *(svatantra)* syllogisms. In his *Lamp of Wisdom,* however, master Bhāvaviveka (500–570?) noted many faults in Buddhapālita's logic, and giving various reasons why it is necessary to set forth independent syllogisms, he founded the Svātantrika. Later, master Candrakīrti (600–650?) wrote a treatise, *Entering the Middle Way,* and a commentary on the *Fundamental Treatise on the Middle Way,* the *Clear Words.*[154] Showing in various ways that the faults attributed to Buddhapālita did not apply, criticizing the admission of independent syllogisms, and proving that independent syllogisms should not be admitted, he made it clear that the intention of Ārya Nāgārjuna was Prāsaṅgika. There are two positions on the identity of the founder of the Prāsaṅgika: some claim it was Buddhapālita and some claim it was Candrakīrti.[155]

Commentators who explain the intention of Ārya Nāgārjuna as solely either Prāsaṅgika or Svātantrika became known as "one-sided Mādhyamikas." Master Śāntarakṣita (705–62) wrote the *Ornament of Madhyamaka,* master Jñānagarbha (eighth century) wrote *Distinguishing the Two Truths,*[156] and Kamalaśīla (740–95?) wrote the *Light of Madhyamaka.* These three texts are known as the eastern trio of the Svātantrika Madhyamaka. If one divides the Svātantrikas, there are the Yogācāra Svātantrika Mādhyamikas, who maintain a basic presentation in agreement with that of Cittamātra; and the Sautrāntrika Svātantrika Mādhyamikas, who, like the Sautrāntrikas, admit external objects that are composites of the minutest particles; these are the two types of Svātantrika Mādhyamikas. The Yogācāra Svātantrikas also are twofold: Mādhyamikas who reject appearances (false aspectarians) and those who accept appearances (true aspectarians).[157] Masters such as Śāntarakṣita, Kamalaśīla, and Ārya Vimuktisena accept appearances; Haribhadra, Jetāri, and Kambala[158] reject appearances. The false aspectarians also are twofold: tainted and untainted.[159]

The meaning of *Mādhyamikas* or *Niḥsvabhāvavādins:* Mādhyamikas ("Middleists") are so called because they admit a middle that is free from the two extremes; they are called Niḥsvabhāvavādins ("Proponents of Essencelessness") because they propound the idea that dharmas [20] have no truly established essence.

And, as for the meaning of *Prāsaṅgika Mādhyamikas* and *Svātantrika Mādhyamikas:* Svātantrikas are denoted as Svātantrikas ("Independents") because they negate true existence based on correct, three-pronged logical reasons that are established independently; Prāsaṅgikas are denoted as Prāsaṅgikas ("Consequentialists") because they assert that the inferential knowledge in the mind of an opponent that realizes a thesis arises merely through a logical consequence.[160]

2) The history of the Cittamātra philosophical system[161]

a) Asaṅga

As for the history of the Cittamātrin philosophical system: Ārya Asaṅga (fourth/fifth century) founded this system. In the *Mañjuśrī Root Tantra,* the Buddha says of this very master:

> Nine hundred years
> After my final nirvana,
> A monk named Asaṅga,
> Expert in the meanings of treatises,
> Will clearly distinguish in many ways
> The definitive sutras from the provisional.[162]

And:

> In order for the teaching to long remain,
> Asaṅga will summarize the actual meaning of the sutras;
> He will live one hundred and fifty years.[163]

In these and other statements, Asaṅga was clearly prophesied; it is variously asserted that he came nine hundred years after the Teacher had passed or six hundred years after. In any case, after the enemies of abhidharma had thrice emerged in India, the teaching declined.[164] Unable to endure this, a brahman woman named Prakāśaśīlā thought: "I will bear sons, and they will cause the teaching to be spread." From her union with a kṣatriya came Asaṅga; from her union with a brahman came Vasubandhu. After their birth, their mother had an intelligence-sharpening ritual performed for the two, and when they were older, the two boys asked what work their fathers did. Their mother said, "I did not bear you for following your father's profession but for the purpose of spreading the teaching. Therefore, train your minds and spread the teaching." Thus, the younger, Vasubandhu, went to the Kashmiri master Saṅghabhadra. The elder, Asaṅga, thought, "I will spread the teaching after obtaining a vision of Maitreya."

Asaṅga went to a cave on Kukkuṭapāda Mountain.[165] After completing three years of retreat, he had not seen even the slightest sign of Maitreya, so he became depressed. He went outside the cave and saw an old man whittling an iron post down to a needle by rubbing it with a cotton pad. He inquired about this, and the old man replied:

> A person with mental fortitude,
> Can, with practice, do anything, no matter how hard.
> If you do not abandon earnest efforts,
> Then even mountains can be reduced to dust.[166]

Through [21] this statement, certain conditions were fulfilled, and Asaṅga returned to the cave. When he went out after completing three more years, he saw a rock being eroded by drops of water, so it occurred to him to persevere, and he returned to the cave. When he went out after completing three more years, he saw a rock being worn away by the feather of a bird, and, as before, he was inspired and returned to the cave. He completed three more years of retreat and again was depressed that no sign had arisen. When he went out, he saw a she-dog whose rump was infested with worms and whose torso was chewed up by mange, so great compassion arose in him. Thinking to clear away the worms by cutting flesh from his own body, he took a golden razor and cut some flesh from his body. Worrying that the worms would die if they were removed by hand, he thought, "I will shut my eyes and take them off with my tongue." At that moment, he saw it was indeed no dog, but

Holy Lord Maitreya, resplendent. Irritated, Asaṅga said, "No matter how much I practiced, not the slightest sign occurred; Holy Lord, you have little kindness." The Holy Lord said, "I was there from the beginning; you did not see me because of your obstacles. Now, since great compassion has arisen, the obstacles are purified, and you can see me." Asaṅga then beseeched Maitreya, "Please spread the Mahayana." Maitreya said, "Grab hold of my robe!" and off they went to Tuṣita heaven. It is said that Asaṅga stayed there one god-realm[167] moment, or fifty-three human years. There, he received from Maitreya the *Mother Sutra,*[168] the five treatises of Maitreya,[169] and other texts, then returned to the human realm. Asaṅga wrote the five treatises on the stages,[170] the two compendiums,[171] and other texts, and founded the way of the Cittamātrins.

It is explained in the *Exposition of Praises of the Stages* that Master Asaṅga attained the concentration of continuous Dharma.[172] It says in the *Clear Words* of Dharmamitra that even though master Asaṅga reached the third stage—the Luminous—he taught Cittamātra in order to convert Vasubandhu.[173] The lord Asvabhāva explains that Asaṅga abides on the stage of the supreme mundane attainment.[174] Some state that he lived a hundred years, but it is certain he remained for a hundred and fifty.

b) Cittamātra after Asaṅga

Initially a Vaibhāṣika, Vasubandhu (fourth/fifth century), Asaṅga's younger brother, disliked the Mahayana. He made fun of his older brother, saying, for instance:

> Alas, for twelve years in the forest
> Asaṅga tried to gain concentration;
> He didn't gain concentration, but he did write
> An elephant load of works on philosophical systems.[175]

Later, however, after gaining faith in the Mahayana, he received the five treatises of Maitreya and other works from his elder brother. He then wrote the eight [22] dissertations.[176] Thus, the five treatises of Maitreya, the five treatises on the stages, the two compendiums, and the eight dissertations came to be known as the twenty Dharma treatises related to Maitreya.

Vasubandhu had four disciples who were more expert than he: Master Dignāga was more expert in valid cognition; Guṇaprabha was more expert in vinaya; Ārya Vimuktisena was more expert in the perfection of wisdom; and Sthiramati was more expert in abhidharma.[177]

It is said that those who followed in maintaining the way founded by Asaṅga are called Cittamātrins ("Idealists")[178] or Vijñaptivādins ("Representationalists"); they are known thus because they propound that all dharmas are merely the self-nature of mind. There are two divisions: those who assert that the appearance of objects to the sense consciousnesses as gross objects is accurate, and those who assert that appearance as gross objects is inaccurate; these are, respectively, the true-aspectarian and the false-aspectarian Cittamātrins. The true aspectarians are threefold: proponents of an equal number of subjects and objects, split-eggs, and nonpluralists. Because the explanations of scholars regarding the particulars of these three are in disagreement, I will not set them forth here.[179] The false aspectarians are twofold: tainted false aspectarians, who assert that the nature of mind is polluted by the taints of the predispositions of ignorance, and nontainted false aspectarians, who assert that the nature of mind is not polluted. Cittamātrins are also twofold in another way: those following scripture, and those following logical reasoning. Respectively, these are those who follow Asaṅga's five treatises on the stages and those who follow Dharmakīrti's seven treatises on valid cognition.

3) Summary of Mahayana

Accordingly, through the Madhyamaka and Cittamātra ways founded by Nāgārjuna and Asaṅga, the Mahayana teachings grew and spread like rivers in summertime, and with the successive arrival of countless tens of millions of mighty lords who were scholars and adepts, the Buddha's teaching was made to shine like the sun.

2. A brief demonstration of the points of view of the four philosophical systems

Many different standpoints exist regarding the layout of the basis, path, and result of the philosophical systems of Buddhist schools, but I will not elaborate here. For were I to set all those out in detail, this book would be too wordy, and besides, they are already [23] extensively explained in other treatises on philosophical systems. Since the philosophical systems are differentiated by way of view, here I must briefly explain each school's standpoint. This is twofold: a. Each system's standpoint on the object of negation, and b. Each system's position on coarse and subtle selflessness.

a. The standpoint of each of the four philosophical systems regarding the object of negation

There is no difference in any of our schools regarding the admission of dependent arising. Nevertheless, although proponents of philosophical systems from the Svātantrika Madhyamaka on down do not assert, as non-Buddhists do, a self that is established as a different entity from the physical and mental aggregates, they do posit the aggregates themselves as the self. Among the Vaibhāṣikas, some Saṃmatīyas posit the collection of the aggregates as the self. Both the Kashmiri Vaibhāṣikas and the Sautrāntikas posit the continuity of consciousness as an example of the person. The Cittamātrins posit the mind-basis-of-all (Skt. *ālayavijñāna*) as the person. The Svātantrika Mādhyamikas posit the subtle mental consciousness as the person. The Prāsaṅgika Mādhyamikas disclaim all those positions. Also, the way in which everyone from Vaibhāṣikas to Svātantrika Mādhyamikas posits a self that is the basis for action and its result is through asserting that the person or other entity is established conventionally from its own side. Not satisfied merely to impute "I" or "person" on the basis of the aggregates, they inquire: "How is the person established?[180] As the individual aggregates? As their collection? As something other than those?" And, thinking that some suitable example of the person should be found in relation to the aggregates, they posit a conventional self. Apprehending thusly is designated as "apprehending that which is established from its own side," and the object of that as "that which is established from its own side." These schools think: "If, after seeking through that mode of inquiry, you find no person, then that person cannot be established, and the flaw ensues that the person is annihilated."

By the same token, you should also know the particulars of the realists'[181] claims that what is conventionally established is truly established, [24] perfectly established, ultimately established, established in reality, established by its own characteristic, inherently established, essentially established, substantially established, and so forth.[182]

1) *Vaibhāṣika*

The Vaibhāṣikas hold that, in the final analysis, form, consciousness, and other dharmas are necessarily found. They hold also that, in the final analysis, the minutest partless particles and a continuum's briefest partless moments necessarily exist. Thus Vaibhāṣikas maintain that partless particles are the compositional basis of gross physical forms and partless moments are the components of temporal continuity. Since, even upon being broken or destroyed, the partless particle and moment, space, and so forth, are not lost to the mind that apprehends them, they are substantially existent, ultimately true, and ultimately existent; phenomena that are lost to the mind apprehending them by being broken or destroyed are imputed existents, conventional existents, and conventional truths. The Vaibhāṣikas assert that all entities included in the two truths are able to perform a function, and so are substantially established.

2) *Sautrāntika*

The Sautrāntikas assert that dharmas ultimately able to produce a result are specifically characterized, ultimately true, and established by their own characteristics; dharmas ultimately unable to perform a function are generally characterized, not established by their own characteristics, and conventionally true. They also assert that, if both generally and specifically characterized phenomena are not established from their own side, they must be nonexistent. Because they, like the Vaibhāṣikas, admit the minutest partless particles, and so forth, my omniscient guru, Changkya Rölpai Dorjé (1717–86), says in his *Songs on Correct View,* "Matter is a many-colored tiger with stripes."[183]

3) *Cittamātra*

The Cittamātrins assert that dharmas established from their own side, without being merely imputed by thought, are specifically characterized, established by their own characteristics, and truly established; while dharmas established as mere imputations by thought are the reverse. They assert both the dependent nature and the thoroughly established nature as truly established, and the imaginary nature as non–truly established.[184] Therefore, for the Cittamātrins, as for our own Prāsaṅgika-Madhyamaka system, dharmas pertaining to the imaginary nature are asserted as "not established by their own characteristics." However, because they assert that anything not established from its own side must be nonexistent, they do accept the *meaning* of "specifically characterized" according to the Prāsaṅgika Mādhyamikas, even with respect to the imaginary nature. As it says in Tsongkhapa's *Essence of Excellent Explanation*, "Although they do not hold some imaginary bases to exist according to the former sense, as established by their own characteristics, they do hold them according to the latter sense, as established from their own side."[185] [25]

Cittamātrins do not, as the Vaibhāṣikas and Sautrāntikas do, maintain that gross phenomena are composed of partless particles. Rather, they assert that composite dharmas of form and so forth arise from the substance of inner consciousness, and also that noncomposites have the same self-nature as the valid cognitions apprehending them, and so assert that apprehended and apprehender are empty of being substantially different, and that there is no independent external object. Because it is the potential within the preceding consciousness that allows the subsequent consciousness to arise in the aspect of the object, object and subject arise simultaneously as a single substance; that potential is asserted as the objective condition of consciousness. Although the objective condition will induce a consciousness having the aspect of the object, its apprehension by the thought thinking, "It is that object," depends on applying a sign. Thus Cittamātrins assert that dharmas are not established by their own characteristics as the referent objects of the thoughts that apprehend them. Compared to the objectivists,[186] they are very close to the Madhyamaka system. By establishing the nonexistence of the external object in accord with their own assertions, the Cittamātrins will negate the external objects asserted by the two śrāvaka objectivist schools, but a mere negation of the external objects of the two objectivist schools does not establish those objects as only mental. You must understand these differences among the upper and lower philosophical systems in every context.

4) Madhyamaka

a) Svātantrika Madhyamaka

Although the Svātantrika Mādhyamikas claim dharmas as conventionally established in three ways, namely, established by their own characteristics, inherently established, and essentially established, they do not claim, even conventionally, their establishment in five other ways: truly established, perfectly established, ultimately established, established in reality, established by their own entity. Schools from the Svātantrika Madhyamaka on down assert that *coarse* apprehension of a self of persons means apprehending a permanent, partless, independent self, like that asserted by non-Buddhists; *subtle* apprehension of a self of persons, on the other hand, means apprehending the person as a self-sufficient, substantially existent entity. The former apprehension is an imputation that only extremists superimpose. The latter apprehension has two types: (1) the *imputed,* wherein one thinks that a self-sufficient, substantially existent entity is entailed by fallacious logical reasons, such as those that lead the Vātsīputrīyas to apprehend a self by virtue of their philosophical system, and (2) the *innate,* which occurs naturally, without relying on philosophical superimposition. Neither the Vaibhāṣikas nor the Sautrāntikas recognize a selflessness more subtle than that which results from negating the object of this innate apprehension.

Thus the person and aggregates appear as self-sufficient entities with dissimilar characteristics, like a king and his subjects. Apprehending them as being established as they appear is the mode of apprehension that apprehends the person as a self-sufficient, substantially existent [26] entity. Having negated the object of that apprehension—that self-sufficient person that is independent of the aggregates—schools from the Svātantrika Madhyamaka on down, with the exception of the Saṃmatīyas, are alike in claiming that the person is a mere imputation based on the aggregates.

The word *mere* in "mere imputation based on the aggregates": Having negated a self that is a different entity from the aggregates, these schools are in agreement in claiming that the person exists as a mere imputation.

The mode of imputation based on the aggregates: These schools claim variously that the person is imputed on the basis of the mental consciousness, the mind-basis-of-all, or the continuum of consciousness. They also say that the person is imputed on the basis of claiming that the individual aggregates are the self, while some Saṃmatīyas say that all five aggregates are the self. Although schools from the Svātantrikas on down claim that the person is a mere imputation based on the aggregates, they think that if the aggregates are the basis of the imputation of a person, the aggregates necessarily *are* the person; and they believe that the aggregates are imputed as being the person. And, after searching for the object on the basis of which one imputes a person, they believe it is findable; so even though they explain that this means imputed existence, their explanation is clearly incomplete.[187]

b) Svātantrika vis à vis Prāsaṅgika

The Prāsaṅgikas say that the basic object of the innate egoistic view is the self that is imputed on the basis of the aggregates; and not only are the aggregates not the self, they claim, not even a single dharma is findable after searching for the imputed object. Schools from the Svātantrikas on down claim that if such a standpoint were true, admission of dependent arising would be undermined; this is a very important point, but I will not elaborate in detail here.

Both Prāsaṅgikas and Svātantrikas agree that the person established is unable to withstand rational analysis, but they disagree both on the boundary between withstanding and not withstanding rational analysis, and on whether, and to what extent, that analysis constitutes ultimate analysis, and so forth. Unsatisfied with the merely imputed conventional I in such sayings as, "*I* accumulate this karma; *I* experience this result," the Prāsaṅgikas search for the meaning of the imputed conventionality, asking, "Where is it established? In the aggregates individually? In their collection? In something apart from them?" They claim that this constitutes an ultimate analysis and that, after you have searched by that mode of inquiry, if you happen to find the basis of analysis, then it is established as able [27] to withstand rational analysis.

The Svātantrikas claim that that kind of reasoning is a source of conventional valid cognition but is not reasoning analyzing the ultimate, and that even if you find something after searching with that mode of inquiry, it still is not established as able to bear rational analysis. When Svātantrikas search by that mode of inquiry, they find the mental consciousness to be the person, so for them, mental consciousness is posited as the person.

Thus, the Svātantrikas claim that, without dharmas being established "over there" through their appearance to a nondefective mind, when you have analyzed whether or not the object is established from the point of view of its own mode of subsistence, that constitutes an ultimate analysis. If, after searching via that mode of inquiry, you find the basis of analysis, it is established as able to bear rational analysis. The realists do not assert that just that mode of inquiry constitutes an ultimate analysis, or that the object sought is able to withstand rational analysis; they do assert, with respect to searching through logical reasoning, that any dharmas that are found—such as noncomposites, the minutest partless particle, or the shortest partless moment—are established as able to bear rational analysis. Thus, when we analyze a dharma's own way of existing in any system of philosophy, it is very important to know the boundary between a conventional and an ultimate analysis.

The Svātantrikas claim that, without dharmas being established "over there" by virtue of their appearance to a nondefective mind, the apprehension of an object as established from its own side is the subtle apprehension of true existence. That is twofold: the thoroughly imputed, such as apprehension through philosophical systems like those of the Cittamātrins; and the innate, which is independent of philosophical systems. Any referent object of both of these is called truly established, perfectly established, ultimately established, and established in reality; any object established as any of those four does not exist even conventionally. They do claim that any object established by its own characteristics, inherently established, and essentially established is established conventionally; they assert that if objects were not established in that way, you would fall into a nihilistic view. I have explained above the differences among the realists on whether to assert those eight terms as validly established.

The Mādhyamikas claim that when we see that dharmas have no mode of subsistence aside from that posited on the basis of their appearance to the mind, that is the negation of the object of negation. The [28] Prāsaṅgika and Svātantrika systems assert in common that the apprehension of true existence is the cognition that apprehends such an object of negation. The logical analyses are condensed into two: the most important reasoning negating that object of negation is the *sevenfold analysis;*[188] abridging that produces the *analysis free of apprehending the one and the many.*[189] The latter mode of analysis is better known. There are no differences between Prāsaṅgikas and Svātantrikas with respect to negating any existent that is not established through analysis in a mind in meditative equipoise. However, with respect to post-meditation,[190] the Svātantrikas assert that dharmas established by their own characteristics are illusion-like, while the Prāsaṅgikas claim that, after negating such qualities as true existence in meditative equipoise, when we later look for anything remaining, we find only a mere name; this is the unique distinction between Svātantrikas and Mādhyamikas.

Accordingly, the schools from the Svātantrikas on down assert that we are freed from samsara through refuting both the innate apprehension of the person as a self-sufficient, substantially existent entity as well as the object of that apprehension.

The Svātantrikas claim that apprehending both dharmas and persons as objects established by their own mode of subsistence, as opposed to their being established through their appearance to the mind, is the subtle apprehension of a self of dharmas and is the knowledge obstacle. They also claim that we attain omniscience through abandoning the eleven knowledge obstacles—the nine subtle, medium, and coarse obstacles, with the first and last of those nine having two divisions, thus adding two more—through the eleven stages of the path of meditation, from the first bodhisattva stage up to the final continuum.[191]

c) Special features of Prāsaṅgika Madhyamaka

The view of the object of negation and the way of negation, which are special features of the Prāsaṅgikas: Apprehending an existent that is not merely established through a conventional designation is the subtle apprehension of true existence. Apprehending as existent the referent object of that—the person not propounded by way of designation and convention—is apprehension of a self of persons. Apprehending dharmas as existent is the apprehension of a self of dharmas. It is claimed that both innate apprehensions—of a self of persons and dharmas—are the ignorance that is the root of samsara and are the delusion obstacles. It is said that recognizing these kinds of innate apprehensions depends on ascertaining well how persons and dharmas are posited conventionally, how they are imputed by thought. This is a very important point.

The way this system establishes the person: The person is imputed on the basis of the collected aggregates; [29] the phenomenon imputed by that imputation is the person; and the thought that posits the person is the thought that conventionally thinks "I": this must be understood definitely to be the case. That mere "I" that is the object of the mind thinking "I" on the basis of the collected aggregates is called "self" or "person"; that exists conventionally and is called "the self that is the basis of action and result."

The threshold for analyzing the ultimate: Prāsaṅgikas claim that, unsatisfied with merely establishing the I, or self, of our own mental continuum through conventional imputation, we search, asking "How is it established?" This is where the analysis begins. The method of ultimate analysis is observing, for instance, "I sit here. I see. I experience. I remember." We should be satisfied by these conventional sayings; if, however, we are not satisfied, we analyze and discover that "the I is not my own eyes, ears, and so forth, neither individually nor collectively; nor is the I something other than that. *That* is how I am not existent: I don't exist inherently."

Schools from the Svātantrikas on down take the notion of "not inherently existent" to mean entirely nonexistent, and insist that seeing things in that way is nihilistic. For the Prāsaṅgikas, inherent nonexistence does not mean nonexistence. Conventional existence serves the function of existence, and the phrase "dependent arising" removes the two extremes. For while all dharmas are nonexistent inherently, things established by convention are nevertheless admissible.[192] That is the unique feature of this Prāsaṅgika system.

Thus, the two schools, Prāsaṅgika and Svātantrika, have two distinct ways of identifying the object of negation and, because of that, two different demarcations of ultimate analysis. If you do not clearly ascertain this demarcation, you will have difficultly distinguishing the subtle differences between the Prāsaṅgikas and Svātantrikas.

The standpoint on knowledge obstacles: Prāsaṅgikas claim knowledge obstacles are predispositions to delusion that can no longer produce delusions even when conditions are met, as well as the result of those predispositions, namely, the mere illusion of true existence in deceptive dualistic appearances.[193] They claim that one attains the gnosis of complete omniscience through abandoning, on the three pure stages, the three types of knowledge obstacles—subtle, medium, and coarse—or the four types of knowledge obstacles that result when the coarse is made twofold.

Although the assertion in this system—that the apprehension of a self-sufficient substantially existent person [30] is the coarse apprehension of the self of persons—is similar to the standpoint of the Svātantrikas and others, nevertheless that innate apprehension of substantial existence that the Svātantrikas and others assert as subtle apprehension of a self, the Prāsaṅgikas claim as imputed. In the *Essence of Excellent Explanation,* Tsongkhapa states, "That substantially existent self is the object apprehended by non-Buddhists as an existent person, the inner doer imputed as a separate entity from the aggregates."[194] Thus, in this Prāsaṅgika system, the innate apprehension of substantial existence is not apprehension of the self as having characteristics distinct from those of the aggregates. Rather, just as a head merchant is not separate from other merchants yet controls them, so the self, not separate from the aggregates, controls the aggregates by having the same nature as the aggregates. Even though the aggregates are established as dependent on the self, the self is not dependent on the aggregates, as a head merchant is not dependent on merchants; it is taught that this is posited as an innate apprehension of self.[195]

b. Each system's way of establishing coarse and subtle selflessness
1) Vaibhāṣika

The Vaibhāṣikas assert that any established base is necessarily a self of phenomena or *dharmas,* so they admit no distinction between the coarse and subtle selflessness of dharmas. They do posit a coarse selflessness of persons—the person's emptiness of being permanent, partless, and independent—and a subtle selflessness of persons—the person's emptiness of being self-sufficient and substantially existent. They equate *subtle selflessness* and *subtle selflessness of persons.*

Among the eighteen schools of the Vaibhāṣikas, the five schools of the Saṃmatīya[196] admit a self that is self-sufficient and substantially existent, so they do not consider emptiness to be the subtle selflessness of persons. The Prāsaṅgikas aside, proponents of the four lower schools—Svātantrikas, Cittamātrins, Sautrāntikas, and Vaibhāṣikas—take similar positions on the coarse and subtle selflessness of persons. In three systems—Prāsaṅgika, Cittamātra, and Sautrāntika—the subtle selflessness of persons is said to be emptiness. It is well known that Vaibhāṣikas deny the establishment of the three characteristics and assert that emptiness is nonexistence. Nevertheless, it says in the eighth chapter of the *Treasury of Higher Knowledge,* "Signlessness has the aspect of peace;/ Emptiness is emptiness and selflessness,"[197] [31] and we may infer from this that Vaibhāṣikas use the term *emptiness* for two aspects of the truth of suffering: emptiness and selflessness.[198]

2) Sautrāntika

The Sautrāntikas' standpoint on the coarse and subtle selflessness of persons and their nonadmission of a selflessness of dharmas are like that of the Vaibhāṣikas. Of the three characteristics, they assert that dependent phenomena are truly established, and that the other two, imaginary and thoroughly established phenomena, are not truly established. Objection: "If thoroughly established phenomena—emptinesses—are not truly established, then, since the subtle selflessness of persons is both empty and thoroughly established, the thoroughly established would not be suitable as an appearing object of an uninterrupted path.[199] Thus, a direct object of knowledge of an uninterrupted path cannot be posited." Response: There is no fault, because in this Sautrāntika system, the subtle selflessness of persons is asserted as an indirect object of knowledge of an uninterrupted path of the three vehicles, while the construct, which is devoid of a self of persons, is the appearing object and the direct object of knowledge of that uninterrupted path.

According to the Vaibhāṣikas, if you meditate at the conclusion of the fourth mental absorption[200] with a mind based on an object of meditation that is any of the sixteen aspects of the four noble truths—impermanence and so forth—you traverse the last four paths of the pratyekabuddha and bodhisattva;[201] and, by meditating on any of those sixteen objects of meditation—impermanence and so forth—on the basis of any of the nine uncorrupted stages, you necessarily attain the arhatship of a śrāvaka.

In the Sautrāntika system, the last four paths of all three vehicles necessarily arise for the first time solely through taking as your basic object a construct that is devoid of self, or so I think. This should be analyzed further.[202]

The three, Cittamātrins, Svātantrikas, and Prāsaṅgikas, assert that there is no indirect object of knowledge of an uninterrupted path; the Cittamātrins and Prāsaṅgikas claim that the direct object of knowledge of that uninterrupted path must be subtle emptiness, while the Svātantrikas posit it as the coarse and subtle selflessness of dharmas and the subtle selflessness of persons.

3) Cittamātra

The Cittamātra position on the subtle and coarse selflessness of persons agrees with that of the Vaibhāṣika and Sautrāntika, with a slight difference. The Cittamātrins assert that the subtle selflessness of persons is emptiness; and with respect to the selflessness of dharmas, they posit that the subtle selflessness of dharmas is any dharma's (1) emptiness of being established by its own characteristic as the referent object of the thought apprehending it and (2) emptiness of subject-object duality and emptiness of being an external object. They also posit that [32] the coarse selflessness of dharmas is a dharma's emptiness of being an external object that is a collection of the minutest partless particles, while both subtle selflessnesses are posited as emptiness.

4) Svātantrika Madhyamaka

The Yogācāra Svātantrika Madhyamaka standpoint on the coarse and subtle selflessness of persons is also similar to that of the Vaibhāṣikas. With respect to the selflessness of dharmas, they assert that emptiness of subject-object duality, emptiness of being external objects, and emptiness of existing by their own characteristics, as the referent objects of the thoughts apprehending them, are the coarse selflessness of dharmas; while the lack of true existence that is empty of being truly established, as well as ultimate truth, are the subtle selflessness of dharmas. Since they assert that all dharmas are established conventionally by their own characteristics, they assert that all dharmas are established merely through appearing to thought or a mind, without maintaining, as Prāsaṅgikas do, that they are merely imputed by thought or merely established by names and signs.

The Sautrāntika Svātantrikas' position on both the coarse and subtle selflessness of persons and on the subtle selflessness of dharmas is like that of the Yogācāra Svātantrikas, but their position on the coarse selflessness of dharmas is different. They agree with the Cittamātrins in asserting as the coarse selflessness of phenomena the nonexistence of an external object that is a collection of the minutest partless particles. They assert that any established base must be both established by its own characteristics as the referent object of the thought apprehending it and also established as an external object.

5) Prāsaṅgika Madhyamaka

Prāsaṅgikas claim that the coarse selflessness of persons is the person's emptiness of being a self-sufficient, substantial existent, while the subtle selflessness of persons is the absence of an inherently established person. The coarse selflessness of dharmas is the lack of any substantial difference between a gross object composed of partless particles and the valid cognition that apprehends it, while the subtle selflessness of dharmas is the aggregates' or bases of imputation's emptiness of being truly existent. The two subtle selflessnesses are distinguished only by their basis and not by their object of negation. In the subtle selflessness of persons, the object of negation—true existence—is negated with the person as the basis, while in the subtle selflessness of dharmas, true existence is negated with the aggregates, and so forth, as the basis. There is no distinction of subtle and coarse in the subtle selflessnesses of either persons or phenomena; both, it is claimed, are the final, ultimate nature. [33]

3. How proponents of the four philosophical systems avoid the extremes of eternalism and nihilism in each of their own systems

The Vaibhāṣikas say they avoid the extreme of eternalism because the cause ceases when the result arises, and avoid the extreme of nihilism because the result arises right after the cause ceases. The Sautrāntikas assert that they avoid the extreme of nihilism because composites go on without interruption, and avoid the extreme of eternalism because composites are destroyed moment by moment. The Cittamātrins state that they avoid the extreme of eternalism because the imaginary nature is not truly established, and avoid the extreme of nihilism because the dependent nature is truly established. The Mādhyamikas claim they are free of the extreme of nihilism because all dharmas exist conventionally, and of the extreme of eternalism because all dharmas do not ultimately exist. So it is taught.

Accordingly, both the Vaibhāṣikas and Sautrāntikas have to claim that the gnosis realizing impermanence is the ultimate middle path. However, because they definitely must also have abandoned the two extremes based on the definitions of both subtle and coarse selflessness in their respective systems, this statement about gnosis appears to be meant as a loose explanation, or merely as a characterization. If measured by the Prāsaṅgikas, all our Buddhist schools from Svātantrika on down fall to both extremes—eternalism and nihilism—even while boasting that their own systems admit of a middle that is free of the two extremes of eternalism and nihilism and loudly claim to be "middleists."[203]

4. Summary

Although there are degrees of superiority and inferiority among those philosophical systems, it is inappropriate to disparage the Hinayana philosophical systems, saying, "The Mahayana philosophical systems are best," for they also are followers of the Buddha. Not only that, but as the omniscient Second Dalai Lama, Gendün Gyatso,[204] taught, "The view of each of the lower philosophical systems is a stairway to each of the higher."[205] Except for one or two philosophical systems' admission of their own unique positions, the Buddhist view is as taught in the sutras, in the works of the great charioteers Nāgārjuna and Asaṅga, and in the excellent explanations of the great Jé Tsongkhapa—emptiness of a permanent, single, independent self; selflessness that is empty of being a self-sufficient, substantial existent; reality that is empty of a subject-object divide; ultimate essencelessness, even though all dharmas exist by their own characteristics; and the nonexistence of even the merest particle that is established by its own characteristics, even though all dharmas do exist conventionally.[206]

As for the progressive degrees of selflessness that permit the establishment of all actions and agents of cause and effect and samsara and nirvana: the earlier, lower ones are [34] easier to realize than the later, higher ones, and the earlier are the means to enter the later. For some people, being shown the views of the lower philosophical systems allows them to gradually be led to the higher views. If they were shown the higher views at the outset, it would bring more harm than benefit.

The standpoints of the individual non-Buddhist and Buddhist philosophical systems: Since explanations of them occur extensively and in detail in treatises on philosophical systems, I will say nothing more about them here.

Concluding verses

I say:

> Those who are realized know how to distinguish their own teaching from that of others.
> They are able to sound the music of wondrous discourse before the learned,
> And honest people will raise high the banner of their splendid renown.
> Ah! Who would not strive to distinguish the principles of the various philosophical systems!
>
> Nevertheless, many past scholars
> Have already provided
> This very account, extensively and clearly,
> So why do what's already done?
>
> Even if the mass of jewels of newfound eloquence
> Is heaped up in a pile, it's like the riches
> Of wealthy merchants set out in the alleys
> Of an impoverished city. What's the point?
>
> When all the books of excellent explanation by the sages of India and Tibet
> Are perceived as mere things and sit, like ornaments,
> On bookshelves deep within houses, in such times
> Someone like me is little inclined to real effort.

> Therefore, in order to indicate here
> The complete body and limbs of my subject,
> I have revealed just a few supreme limbs
> Of the philosophical systems of the Holy Land and am content with that.

These verses are additional.

From *The Crystal Mirror: An Excellent Explanation Showing the Sources and Assertions of All Philosophical Systems,* this completes the explanation of the history of the philosophical systems of the non-Buddhists and our own Buddhist schools in the Holy Land of India. May all awaken! [35]

3. Introduction to Tibetan Buddhism[207]

II. The History of Philosophical Systems in Tibet, the Land of Snows[208]

> This is but a partial account of the marvelous events whereby, through the kindness of those leading Dharma kings, translators, and pandits,
> The mighty king, the wish-fulfilling gem[209] of the Buddha's teaching, was brought from the precious continent, the Holy Land,
> To the country encircled by snowy mountains and worshipped there atop the victory banner
> Of the people's faith, releasing a rain of good things conducive to benefit and bliss.[210]

The history of philosophical systems in Tibet is fourfold: A. The history of the Buddha's teaching, B. In particular, the history of the different schools, C. As a supplementary topic, the history of the sutras, tantras, and sciences,[211] and D. In addition, the history of the way of Bön.

A. The history of the Buddha's teaching in the Land of Snows[212]

This is twofold: 1. The history of the earlier spread of the teaching and 2. The history of the later spread.

1. The history of the earlier spread of the teaching[213]

For twenty-six generations of kings, from the first king of Tibet, Nyatri Tsenpo (third century B.C.E.?) through Namri Songtsen (seventh century),[214] not even the name "Buddha's teaching" occurred. However, during the time of Lha Thothori Nyenshal (fourth–fifth centuries?), reputed to be an emanation of Samantabhadra, the *Book of the Hundredfold Homage for Amendment of Breaches* descended from the sky[215] to the top of the royal palace. Although its words and meaning were not understood, it was given the name Awesome Secret. Its worship marks the beginning of the holy Dharma in Tibet.

According to a prophecy in a dream of King Lha Thothori, "in five generations one who knows the meaning of this text will arise." So, during the reign of the Dharma king Songtsen Gampo (617–649/50),[216] an emanation of Avalokiteśvara, the minister Thönmi Sambhota was sent to India. After training to the point of expertise in various sciences, he developed two scripts: the basic vertical script with a headstroke [36] was modeled on the Devanāgari alphabet, and the more horizontal script without a headstroke was modeled on the Vivarta alphabet. In this way, he blazed the trail for literacy in Tibet.

King Songtsen Gampo arranged to bring[217] the two main objects of worship to Tibet, an Akṣobhya statue and the Jowo, a statue of Śākyamuni.[218] He erected the great Rasa Trülnang temple and had many Dharma texts translated into Tibetan, including the *Flower Ornament Sutra.*[219] He thereby paved the way for the teaching.

At the time of the Dharma king Trisong Detsen (r. 755/56–97),[220] said to be an emanation of Mañjughoṣa, many teachers were invited to the capital, like the great preceptor Śāntarakṣita, Master Padmasambhava, and others. Seven men—Vairocana and six others—took preliminary ordination. From there, the number of the ordained wearing saffron robes increased. Many great translators spoke both the Tibetan and Sanskrit languages, such as Khönlu Wangpo Sung, Pagor Vairocana, Master Rinchen Chok, Yeshé Wangpo, the trio of Kawa Paltsek, Chokro Lüi Gyaltsen, Shang Yeshé Dé, and others, so many sutras, tantras, and commentaries were translated. The great preceptor Śāntarakṣita took responsibility for explaining the holy Dharma from the vinaya right up to the Madhyamaka and made teaching and study widespread. Master Padmasambhava and others bestowed secret mantra instructions on some qualified students, so some beings became adepts. Later on, a monk named Heshang Mahāyāna came to Tibet from China. He said: "Nonvirtuous thoughts forge the bonds of samsara, of course, but so do virtuous thoughts. Whether gold or iron, our chains still bind us; and since they are the same, we only become free by thinking nothing."[221] When he taught that wrong view, the Tibetans all became his followers. Those maintaining the pure view and conduct taught by the great preceptor bodhisattva Śāntarakṣita and others were few. In order to root out that debased view, the Dharma king invited the mighty sage, Kamalaśīla, who then defeated Heshang in debate.

After refuting Heshang's view through reasoning, Kamalaśīla composed his three *Stages of Meditation* texts, reilluminating the pure view and conduct.[222]

In the reign of Lord Tri Ralpachen (r. 815–38),[223] the pandit Jinamitra and many other scholars were invited [37] to Tibet. They translated many holy Dharma texts into Tibetan, and they definitively established all the texts in the new language. Then Langdarma (r. 838–42)[224] became king, and the Buddha's teaching declined in Tibet to the point where nothing remained.

The view during the early spread of the teaching: King Trisong initially spread the rules by saying, "View and conduct must be according to the system of the great preceptor bodhisattva."[225] Then, after Heshang, he said: "From now on, the view has to be like that of master Nāgārjuna; anyone who acts according to Heshang's system will be punished." So he proclaimed. Thus, some pandits maintained the Cittamātra system during the earlier spread of the teaching, but because the system was mainly that of Śāntarakṣita and Kamalaśīla, the Svātantrika-Madhyamaka view was widespread.

2. *The history of the later spread*[226]

How the later spread occurred: When Langdarma destroyed the teaching, three sages staying at the Palchen Chubo Mountain meditation school escaped and went to lower, or eastern, Tibet. Lachen Gongpa Rapsal (953–1035) took preliminary ordination then full ordination. Ten men—Lumé Tsültrim Sherap and others—came from Ü to take the vows from Lachen Gongpa Rapsal. The ten returned to Ü, where they upheld and propagated the vows. Thus, the embers of the Buddha's teachings were rekindled from lower Tibet, and once again the teaching began to spread. As the teaching was gradually propagated, all of Ü and Tsang were filled with sangha, and the explanatory and practical teachings became widespread. Thus, Lachen Gongpa Rapsal, Lumé, and others were most kind to the denizens of the Land of Snows.

How the teaching was revived from upper, or western, Tibet: During the time of Lha Lama Yeshé Ö, Rinchen Sangpo the Translator[227] (958–1055) was sent to India to study the Dharma. He became a great scholar, translated many Dharma texts of the sutra and tantra classes, and established their teachings through exposition and study. At that time, Razi Kargyal had subdued the nāga Kargyal but was enchanted by him, so [38] mistaken Dharma teachings increased, as did perverted tantric conduct by some, but Rinchen Sangpo put a stop to it. Through his pure teaching, the denizens of the snow mountains were suffused with his kindness. Gö Lotsāwa Shönu Pal states: "That the tantric teachings were for the most part more widespread during the later spread of the Dharma than during the earlier spread is due solely to the kindness of this translator."[228] It seems this is no exaggeration. Later in life, he devoted himself only to practice and went at death to the ḍākinī realm. This great translator's view: He is said to have been a "nonabiding Mādhyamika."[229]

Also, this Lha Lama Yeshé Ö invited from eastern India the sage Dharmapāla, together with the famous trio of his main disciples: Sādhupāla, Guṇapāla, and Prajñāpāla. Shangshung Gyalwai Sherap received the vows from them. He subsequently went to Nepal, where the vinaya master Pretakala requested explanation and praxis related to the vinaya. The lineage from Shangshung's disciples Paljor Sherap, Shangmo Chewa Jangchup Sengé, and others was known as the upper Tibet vinaya lineage. Moreover, during the time of Lord Lhadé, the great Kashmiri scholar Śākyaśrī (d. 1225) was invited to Tibet. He translated many sutras and treatises and made the teaching flourish. The vow lineage transmitted from him was called the vow lineage of the great pandit.

The foundation of the Buddha's teaching is the holy Dharma of the vinaya, and so the earlier and later spread of the teaching are defined through the way in which the vow lineage and vinaya observance were spread. This is just my general summary of how the teaching spread; the topic may be studied in detail in Dharma histories.

Concluding verses

From the headwaters of the aroused awakening mind of many superior beings
To the land of Tibet, the ground that holds the wealth of students' merits,
Descended multiple streams of the pure divine water
Of the Buddha's words and teaching, deep and wide and resonant.

This ocean of the Muni's teaching completely filled Tibet,
Where the jeweled net of three trainings is arrayed,
The thousand-garland waves of scripture and reason roll,
And countless [39] scholar-adepts and nāgas play.

E ma! When I think of the kindness of the successive Dharma kings,
Translators, and pandits who came to enact the unfailing marvels
Of the Holy Land here in this remote country,
I press my palms together at my lotus heart.

B. The histories of the different schools

Thus, through the deeds of the conquerors and their offspring; through the kindness of Dharma kings, translators, and pandits; and by the power of the Tibetan people's merit, the precious teaching of the Buddha became increasingly widespread in the Land of Snows, such that a multitude of philosophical systems arose there.

There are many different designations for the Tibetan philosophical systems. Just as with the eighteen subsects of the Vaibhāṣika, some Tibetan systems are also named for a place or a master, while other philosophical systems are named for a single instruction requested from a single Indian scholar or adept or for a practice instruction related primarily to the nature of reality. Thus, it does not seem to be the case that philosophical systems in Tibet are named only for views, as are some philosophical systems propounded in the Holy Land.

For example, many are named for a place, such as Sakya, Jonang, Shangpa, and Drigung; many are named for a master, such as Karmapa and Bulukpa; and some are named for an instruction, such as Kadam, Dzokchen, Chakchen (Mahāmudrā), and Shijé.

When one briefly discusses these in order, there are two parts: The history of other philosophical systems and the history of the Geluk.[230] [40] The first is sevenfold, discussing the history of the 1. Nyingma, 2. Kadam, 3. Kagyü, 4. Shijé, 5. Sakya, 6. Jonang, and 7. a few minor schools.[231]

4. The Nyingma Tradition[232]

[II. The History of Philosophical Systems in Tibet, the Land of Snows
B. The histories of the different schools]

1. Nyingma[233]

THIS IS TWOFOLD: a. Identifying the general boundaries between the old—Nyingma—and new—Sarma—traditions and b. Explaining the history of the Nyingmapas in particular.

a. Identifying the general boundaries between the old—Nyingma—and new—Sarma—traditions

The establishment of old and new does not occur with respect to the sutras; rather, it is established through the way in which the secret mantra teachings spread. Although there are conflicting ways of explaining it, the best known is this: tantras translated prior to the arrival of Paṇḍita Smṛti (ninth–tenth centuries?) are called *old secret mantra,* while those translated after the coming of the translator Rinchen Sangpo are called *new secret mantra.*[234] If that is true, then the *Mañjuśrī Root Tantra,* translated in Trisong Detsen's time, would have to be accepted as an old tantra. Why then did the great trailblazers of the tantric schools regard it as a new tantra? It seems there are grounds for inquiry. Although the fountainhead of the new secret-mantra translations is identified as the translator Rinchen Sangpo, there were others as well, such as Drokmi, Gö Lotsāwa Khukpa Lhetsé, and Lord Marpa.

At the time when the teaching was on the increase through efforts of Lotön Dorjé Wangchuk (b. tenth century), who came at the beginning of the later spread of the teaching, there were three brothers named Paldé, Ödé, and Kyidé, all sons of Lord Tashi Tsekpa Pal. Tashi Tsekpa Pal was himself the son of Lord Pal Khortsen, who controlled the kingdom in Rulak. These three requested Lotön to give them a preceptor and master capable of developing the teaching,[235] so he dispatched the preceptor Shākya Shönu and Master Yeshé Tsöndrü to Rulak, where they established a monastic community. After the preceptor and the master consulted, they advised both Drokmi and Taklo: "Learn the vinaya because it is the basis of the teaching, [41] the perfection of wisdom because it is the essence, and secret mantra because it is the quintessence." They then sent them to India. Taklo mostly went on pilgrimage and did not study much, but Drokmi practiced as advised and became a great scholar. He helped spread the explanatory and practical teachings of, above all, the mother tantras. The great translator Rinchen Sangpo explained the perfection of wisdom literature and both mother and father tantras, and, in particular, elucidated the yoga tantras. Ārya Gö Khukpa propagated the explanation of the *Guhyasamāja,*[236] mainly the system of Ārya Nāgārjuna. Lord Marpa extensively propagated the initiations, explanations, and special instructions of the father tantra, the *Guhyasamāja,* and those of the mother tantras: the *Mahāmāyā,* the essential mother tantra *Hevajra,*[237] the quintessential mother tantra *Cakrasaṃvara,*[238] and the *Four Seats Tantra* along with its sworn protectors. Therefore, scholars and adepts filled the land of Tibet and became lords of the teachings of secret mantra. It is from these great translators that the secret mantra teachings had their beginning.

b. The history of the Nyingmapas in particular

> I now will relate the history of the famed ancient translation vehicle
> Based on the sweet white-lotus speech of oral instructions from the supreme adepts
> Of the Holy Land, which is undefiled by the beery stench
> Wafting from the blathering mouths of foolish Tibetan tantrists.[239]

The history of the Nyingmapas in particular is fourfold: 1) Their history, 2) The standpoint of their philosophical system, 3) Analyzing a few aspects of that philosophical system, and 4) A discussion of some later events.

1) The history of the Nyingma philosophical system

a) The age of Padmasambhava

First, the Dharma king Songtsen Gampo gave extensive instructions on the generation and completion stages of Greatly Compassionate One and other deities,[240] and there were many practitioners. All of Ü and Kham prayed to

Ārya Avalokiteśvara, and from this time onward, recitation of the six syllables, *oṃ ma ṇi pad me hūṃ,* became [42] widespread. Master Kusara, the brahman Śaṃkara,[241] the Nepalese master Śīlamañju, and others were invited from India, and many portions of the tantras were translated. So it says in the *Testament Drawn from a Pillar.*[242] Five generations later, King Trisong Detsen invited the great pandit Śāntarakṣita to Tibet. The preceptor taught the ten virtues and the dharmas of the eighteen sense fields, and instituted the eight-limbed rule. The powerful local gods did not like this, so the god Nyenchen Thanglha struck Red Mountain[243] with lightning, the god Yarlha Shampo flooded the Pangthang palace in the Yarlung Valley, and the twelve protectresses[244] inflicted many human and animal diseases. The preceptor Śāntarakṣita had stated that, since there were unruly deities and *srin* demons[245] in Tibet that first had to be subdued, Master Padmasambhava[246] should be invited. Accordingly, the king commanded a messenger to do this. Master Padmasambhava knew this through his clairvoyance; heading from India toward Tibet, he met the messenger on the path and was invited to live in Tibet. He imposed oaths on all the malevolent gods and *srin* demons. He displayed the diamond stride in the sky, and after subduing the earth, he erected the threefold Mingyur Lhüngyi Drup temple at Samyé. Through the three-aspected yoga[247] he set Lord Trisong Detsen, twenty-five of his subjects, and many qualified students on the way to spiritual ripeness and freedom. Thus there were many adepts in the land.

It is said that Namkhai Nyingpo rode on sunbeams. Sangyé Yeshé drove a ritual dagger into a rock. Gyalwa Chökyang thrice sounded the miraculous bray.[248] Kharchen Tsogyal raised the corpse of a murder victim. Palgyi Yeshé openly subjugated mother goddesses. Palgyi Sengé converted gods and *srin* demons into servants. Vairocana possessed the eye of gnosis. The lord King Trisong Detsen achieved the immovable world.[249] Yudra Nyingpo possessed the supreme realization. Jñānakumāra displayed magical powers. Dorjé Düjom was unobstructed like the wind. Yeshé Yang went to the ḍākinī realm. The blacksmith Lhapal could hold wild beasts by the neck. Nanam Yeshé flew in the sky like a bird. Palgyi Wangchuk killed whenever he raised his ritual dagger. Denma Tsemang obtained a spell for nonforgetting. Kawa Paltsek read the minds of others. Shübu Palseng reversed the course of rivers. Gyalwai Lodrö turned zombies into gold. Khyeu [43] Chunglo caught birds in the sky. Drenpa Namkha herded wild yaks. Odren Wangchuk swam in water like a fish. Mathok Rinchen ate boulders for food. Palgyi Dorjé passed through mountains and rocks without obstruction. Langdro

Könchok shot thunderbolts like arrows. Gyalwai Jangchup could sit cross-legged in space.[250]

Many other Indian pandits also came, such as the mantra adept Dharmakīrti, Vimalamitra, Buddhaguhya, Śāntigarbha, and others. Dharmakīrti gave initiations into the yoga of the Vajradhātu mandala.[251] Vimalamitra and other masters gave appropriate instructions to a few qualified students. They did not give explanations of the great texts of the definition vehicle,[252] for the time was not right, nor did they greatly diffuse secret mantra, because the oaths are exceedingly strict. Nevertheless, Vairocana, Ma Nyaknup, and others secretly translated the *All-Accomplishing King,*[253] the *Sutra That Gathers Intentions,* and the scriptures and special instructions on the practice of the eight-part *Net of Illusion Tantra.* The great master Padmasambhava hid many profound teachings in mountains, caves, lakes, and other places as treasures for future students, then went away to the southwest, to Cāmaradvīpa.[254] Thus, although a few scattered Nyingma secret-mantra Dharma traditions come from the era of King Songtsen Gampo, most are from the time of King Trisong. These traditions, which come mainly from Master Padmasambhava and those other masters I have just mentioned, are quite numerous.

It would be appropriate at this point to discuss at length the biography of the great master. However, because there are many disagreements about his life, making it difficult to decide on one version, and because I am afraid of writing too much, I have not laid it out here. Some say Master Padmasambhava stayed in Tibet only a few months, and that during that time he only converted gods and *srin* demons and consecrated Samyé Monastery but didn't teach very much. They say that after the master went back to India, an extremist impersonated him, wearing a vulture-feather hat on his head and other parts of a costume known nowadays as the Orgyen Sahorma.[255] The claim that when the impersonator came to Tibet he spread various Nyingma teachings is obviously a biased[256] report. Some [44] also claim that the Nyingma teachings were made up by Guru Chökyi Wangchuk (1212–70) because Chöwang's costume also was what is nowadays called the Orgyen Sahorma; this is just ignorant babbling—Guru Chökyi Wangchuk is a treasure revealer of a later era, so the time frame doesn't make sense.

b) The nine vehicles

In the Nyingma system, the presentation is in terms of nine successive vehicles. The three common vehicles, taught by the emanation body Śākyamuni, are the śrāvaka, the pratyekabuddha, and the bodhisattva vehicles. The three vehicles of outer secret mantra, taught by the enjoyment body Vajrasattva, are the kriyā, upa, and yoga tantras. The three unsurpassable vehicles of inner secret mantra, taught by the dharmakāya Samantabhadra, are the generation-stage mahāyoga, the oral transmission–based anuyoga, and Dzokchen atiyoga. These constitute the nine.

Now, as for the outer tantras and inner tantras: It is explained that the outer kriyā, or action, tantras were taught by Śākyamuni himself, while the upa, or performance, tantras and the yoga tantras were taught by Vairocana. The inner unsurpassable tantras are explained as having been taught by the great Vajradhara in a pure land called Vast Dharma Source.

The unsurpassable vehicle: The primordial protector, the dharmakāya Samantabhadra, spontaneously establishing himself as a perfect enjoyment body, eternally teaches the unsurpassable vehicle effortlessly, spontaneously, free from restriction or partiality, in the four times[257] to bodhisattva students abiding on the pure stages.[258] An enumeration of teachings such as those is impossible, since they are as extensive as space. Still, just a few of these have been elucidated in Jambudvīpa by Garap Dorjé, Śrīsiṃha, Jñānasūtra, Vimalamitra, Padmakara,[259] and other tantric masters who gained the supreme yogic achievement. So it is explained.

c) Lineages

The sequence of lineages is: the meaning lineage of the conquerors, the symbol lineage of the mantra adepts, and the ear-whispered lineage of ordinary persons; these are the basic three.[260] There also is a division into six lineages if one adds the lineage of prophecies of the special oral tradition, the lineage of the karmically projected treasure, and the lineage of the mind-seal prayer.[261] If I were to write about them in detail, it would be too much, so I will not elaborate further.

The Nyingma Dharma is evidently divided into three: (1) the long lineage of oral tradition, (2) the short lineage of treasure, and (3) the profound lineage of pure vision.

(1) The long lineage of oral tradition

As to how the lineages arose in Tibet: It is said [45] that the oral transmission lineage consists of the triad of sutra, magical net, and mind class:

the *Sutra that Gathers Intentions,* the *Net of Illusion,* and the mind-side teachings.[262]

(a) The triad lineage

The cycle on the essential secret of the *Net of Illusion*[263] was explained by Vimalamitra to Ma Rinchen Chok, who translated it into Tibetan. He in turn explained it to Tsukru Rinchen Shönu and Gyiré Chokyong. Those two explained it to Darjé Palgyi Drakpa and Shang Gyalwai Yönten. The lineages descending from Shang had a special-instruction lineage, and Darjé propagated it in many places in the three regions, Ü, Tsang, and Kham; the two lineages derived from him became known as the Ü system and the Kham system.[264]

Further, Nyak Jñānakumāra was the disciple of Vimalamitra, and his disciple was the Sogdian Palgyi Yeshé, whose disciple was master Nup Sangyé Yeshé, so this lineage also arises from them. Nup Sangyé Yeshé had four favorite spiritual sons, So Yeshé Wangchuk and three others;[265] with his holiest spiritual son, Khulungpa Yönten Gyatso, there were five. The father and son, Nup and Yönten, had as their first disciple Nyang Sherapchok, whose disciple was Surpoché Śākya Jungné. His disciples were the "four peaks," with Tsekok making five; and there were the 108 great meditators and others.[266]

The best among the four peaks was Surchung Sherap Drak, or Deshek Gyapopa (1014–74).[267] His disciples were called the four pillars, the eight beams, the sixteen rafters, the thirty-two roof lathes, the two great meditators, the one great braggart, the two simpletons, the two venerables, and the three useless men.[268] One spiritual son of Surchung, who was reputed to be an emanation of Vajrapāṇi, was Jé Drophukpa Chenpo Śākya Sengé (1074–1134). He had twelve disciples: the four fires, the four blacks, and the four teachers.[269] The best of the four blacks, known as Lharjé Chetön Gyanak (1094–1148), became a sage by studying the Tripiṭaka: Madhyamaka, valid cognition, and so forth. He came before Drophukpa to debate Gya Tsönseng and defeated him in debate, so Drophukpa was very pleased and gave Chetön Gyanak all the instructions in their entirety. Chetön also had many good disciples, chiefly the great lama of Wönpo, Yönten Sung, who also had many great disciples. His heart-son was the holy reincarnate Shikpo Dütsi. Of Shikpo's six main disciples, the greatest was Tatön Joyé (1163–1230), who showed great kindness to later generations by writing down all the sayings of his teacher Shikpo.

The tradition passed to Drophukpa's students, the two Tsangpas Chitön and Nyetön, Tsangnak Öbar, [46] Metön Gönpo, and Lama So, from whom Pakshi Shaka Ö and Tanak Düdül received it; and from Tanak Düdül it passed on to Sur Jampa Sengé. Yungtön Dorjé Pal and Jamyang Samdrup Dorjé[270] received it from Sur and further propagated it. It is indisputable that Yungtön Dorjé Pal, whose lifestory is that of a great scholar-adept, was an adept of both new and old tantras. The Drophukpa disciple lineage from Dangpo Sangyé Gongwala spread widely throughout Kham. There were many in Drophukpa's family lineage and disciple lineage with initiations into and explanations of the tantras. From Denbak, Tsangtö Mangar, and Latö, it spread south, north, and in every direction. Another member of Drophukpa's disciple lineage was the man called Kadampa Deshek—his real names were Sherap Sengé and Popa Thayé (1122–92)—who erected a monastery near the banks of the Yangtze River at Pombor on a piece of land shaped like the letter *ka*. There, at the famed monastery of Kathok, the tradition spread even more. That is the context of the main figures in the *Net of Illusion* tradition.

The *Sutra that Gathers Intentions* consists of the root tantra, the *Sutra that Gathers All Awareness,* and the explanatory tantra, the *Sutra that Gathers Intentions*. Dhanarakṣita (eighth/ninth centuries?) expounded it to the Nepali Dharmabodhi and to Vasudhara. Those two expounded it to Chetsen Kyé in Throm[271] and Gilgit and translated it. These three expounded it there to Jetsün Nup Sangyé Yeshé. From Jetsünpa Khulungpa Yönten Gyatso and others, the lineage eventually descended to Lharjé Ukpa Lungpa (1002–62),[272] to whom it was given by Lharjé Shangpa and Togar Namkha Lha. It gradually spread from there. That is the context of the *Sutra that Gathers Intentions*.[273]

Once there was a matchless great sage named Rongsom Lotsāwa Chösang (eleventh century), a reincarnation of master Kṛṣṇācārya. He studied and practiced all three of the sutra-illusion-mind set, and he skillfully instructed others in them; through his activity, they were propagated.

The main practices of the generation stage are known as the eight transmitted precepts.[274] These are known to include five transworldly classes: (1) Manjuśrī [= Yamāntaka], representing buddha's body; (2) lotus [= Hayagrīva], representing speech; (3) purity [= Heruka], representing mind; (4) nectar [= Vajrāmṛta], representing qualities; and (5) dagger [= Vajrakīla], representing deeds. They also include the three worldly classes of practice: sending invitations to the mother goddesses, uttering the destructive wrathful mantra, and praising and making offerings to worldly deities. Of these, the practices of Hayagrīva and Vajrakīla[275] were both bestowed by the great master Padmasambhava himself: Hayagrīva upon the king, and Vajrakīla upon Queen Yeshé Tsogyal and Atsara Salé of Dré. Through [47] them, those practices gradually spread. The Manjuśrī cycle was explained and propagated by master Śāntigarbha, the pure heart by Hūṃkāra, and the nectar by Vimalamitra. The mother goddesses and the other worldly deities: Master Padmasambhava converted the ferocious Tibetan gods and *dré* demons;[276] he initiated them, set them in their pledges, and showed the three types of worldly gods how to practice step by step in order to benefit the world. These practices are similar in arrangement to the worldly mandala practices of performance tantra.[277]

(b) Dzokchen

The heart of the Nyingma Dharma is known as the special instruction on Dzokchen.[278] It is threefold: the mind class, the expanse class, and the special-instruction class. Of the eighteen mother and son texts in the mind class, five originated with Vairocana and thirteen with Vimalamitra.[279] The expanse class also originated from Vimalamitra, while the special-instruction class, known as the *heart drop,*[280] originated from the same Vairocana.

1' The mind class

On what is known as the mind-side division of Dzokchen:[281] It was requested from Vairocana and Yudra Nyingpo by Nyak Jñānakumāra. In him, four great streams of oral tradition were united,[282] and from his ten holy students and others, the lineage came eventually to the Sogdian, Sangyé Yeshé. In addition, Vairocana's student Pang Sangyé Gönpo explained it to Ba Rakṣita. From him, the lineage descended to Yazi Darma Sherap and others. There is also a lineage descending from Vairocana, Queen Dremo, Marpa Sherap Ö, and others. That is the context of the mind-side teachings.

2' The expanse class

The cycle of the expanse class of Dzokchen:[283] Vairocana expounded to Pang Mipham Gönpo[284] the special instructions of the vajra bridge,[285] basing himself on the shorter *Tantra Equal to Space,* whose significance is taught by way of nine expanses, and on the *Secret Gnosis* and other tantras. The tradition came eventually to Dzeng Dharmabodhi (1052–1168),[286] and from him to the quintet of Nyang Dharmasiṃha and four others.[287] Afterward, it was requested by Ngorjé, Dzeng Jhosé,[288] and others and was propagated widely. That is the context of the vajra bridge.

3′ *The special-instruction class*

The special-instruction class, the heart drop of Dzokchen,[289] which is reputed to be very profound, was taught by the early-spread master Vimalamitra to Lord King Trisong Detsen and Nyang Tingzin Sangpo. Nyang erected the temple [48] of Urusha and hid the instructions there as treasure. He expounded the word lineages to Drom Rinchen Bar,[290] who expounded them to Bé Lodrö Wangchuk. Later, the man known as the elder Dangma Lhüngyal revealed the teachings as treasure and taught them to Chetsün Sengé Wangchuk and Kharak Gomchung. Chetsün (twelfth century?) taught the tradition to Nyang Kadampa and hid the teachings in three places[291] as treasures. The treasures were revealed by Chegom Nakpo of lower Rongnar; Shangpa Repa from Langdro[292] Chepa Tak; and Shang Tashi Dorjé, who was born in Lado, in Nuptso Lingu in Yardrok; the latter even met Chetsün himself. The tradition passed to Shang's son Nyibum,[293] and from him to Jober, Trülshik Sengé Gyapa,[294] Melong Dorjé, the tantric master Kumārarāja,[295] and Longchen Rapjampa.[296] Longchen Rapjampa (1308–63) alone rose to the top rank of scholars among upholders of the Nyingma teaching. He wrote on a great many topics, including the sciences, the sutras, and the new and old systems of secret mantra.

What is known as the heart drop of the ḍākinīs[297] was received from Vajradhara by Garap Dorjé; he bestowed it on the tantric master Śrīsiṃha (eighth century). Master Padmasambhava received it from him and bestowed it on Lady Yeshé Tsogyal. She hid it as a treasure, and after Pema Ledrel Tsal (1292–1316) revealed it, the lineage descended to Gyalsé Lekpa Gyaltsen, the omniscient Rangjung Dorjé,[298] Yungtung Dorjé Pal, and others.

(2) *The short lineage of treasure*

The history of the treasure tradition:[299] For the sake of future students, some authoritative beings like Master Padmasambhava and others hid as treasures many instructions that could aid in the accomplishment of supreme and common yogic achievements. They blessed the treasures so they would not be ruined and entrusted them to the treasure protectors. They made prayers so that people with a fortunate karmic connection would encounter the treasures. When it was time for a treasure to be revealed, the way its readiness for revelation was indicated was through a note, put in with the treasure, containing the name and clan of the treasure revealer by whom it would be revealed, along with a signature. At a time when the place, time, and person all coincided, the treasure would be revealed and propagated to many fortunate persons; thus, it is called the *treasure Dharma*.

In general, there were treasure Dharmas even in India, and they also exist in other Tibetan philosophical systems. [49] To argue that all treasure Dharmas are Nyingma Dharmas shows the defect of a narrow education. Although some reputed treasure revealers were impostors who hid what they concocted themselves and then "revealed" it, there were also definitely a great many pure ones, so it is improper to denigrate all treasures categorically. Apart from the authoritative treasure revealers, from Sangyé Lama (990–1070) to Dechen Lingpa (1663–1713), who were prominently prophesied in the *Injunctions* of Padmasambhava, there also were a good many undisputed treasure revealers not directly mentioned in scripture. Chögyal Wangpo Dé (1550–1602) later compiled their names in a single text and wrote the *Supplication to the Hundred Treasure Revealers*. The great sages teach that both the persons and the teachings are completely pure.

Among the treasure revealers were Lord Nyang Nyima Öser (1124–92) and Guru Chökyi Wangchuk (1212–70), who were called the earlier and later treasure revealers, and dubbed the sun and moon of the treasure revealers. The treasure revealer Drapa Ngönshé Bar (b. 1012) established 108 sites, chief among them Drathang. He revealed many treasures, in particular many texts related to healing, such as the four medical tantras[300] and others, so it is evident that he was very great in both kindness and deeds.

(3) The profound lineage of pure vision[301]

Some who had attained the rank of adept gained direct visions of the higher deities, who gave them instructions. This sort of thing occurs within all the philosophical systems, but it seems to have occurred quite often among the Nyingmapas.

2) The standpoint of the Nyingma philosophical system

Consulting the collected writings that expound the standpoint of the Nyingma system in detail is arduous, and so I have not written much. I relate here briefly their presentation of view and meditation.

Their explanation of the way to travel the path, as found in the *Basic Heruka Tantra* and other texts, is similar to new mantra schools' teachings on the six yogas, the five stages, and Lamdré.[302] Also, some of their explanations of, for instance, the *Net of Illusion*'s six stages, three stages, and path of liberation,[303] the special instructions on the path of means of the secret drop and other traditions,[304] the natural meditation of the *Sutra that Gathers Intentions,* the five [50] stages of the eight transmitted precepts, and so forth, are similar to explanations of the new schools. However, later Nyingmapas do not seem to make those the primary focus of their teaching and study.

a) View and meditation in Dzokchen

What they do value greatly are the view and meditation of Dzokchen. Dzogchen is this present stain-free awareness, which is clear, empty, and bare. They give the etymology as follows: It is called "perfection" *(dzok)* because all dharmas appearing in samsara and nirvana are perfected within this empty awareness, and "great" *(chen)* because there is no better means to freedom from samsara.

(1) The three classes

When one analyzes the subdivisions of Dzokchen, there is the mind class, the expanse class, and the special-instruction class. In the mind class, whatever appears is mind, and since mind itself appears as self-originated gnosis, there is nothing other than self-originated gnosis. In terms of how it leads to the end of this path, it is a lot like Mahāmudrā,[305] but the Nyingmapas claim there are great differences in meaning between the two, because Mahāmudrā practitioners put their emphasis on the object, while mind-class practitioners establish the subject, mind itself, as awareness that is empty and primordially pure.

The expanse class: Since there is no destination apart from the expanse of Samantabhadra, which is the dharmadhātu, the Nyingmapas deny that anything arises separately from the dharmadhātu. This teaching places great importance on the clear light, so it is a bit like the new schools' teaching of the five stages; its meaning is very different, however. In the teaching of the five stages, through the technique by which the five winds are bound, you apprehend in its entirety the empty visualized object of meditation, and then, through its subsequent dissolution, you clarify it in the clear light; therefore, there is deliberate activity involved. Practitioners of the vajra bridge, on the other hand, say that the expanse-class practitioner, in effortless meditative equipoise upon the profound technique that is without reference point, possesses a profound method of achieving the diamond rainbow body through the gnosis uniting profundity and clarity. They say that earlier tantric masters who entered this path passed directly into the gnosis body.[306]

The special-instruction class: When the gnosis that is a nondual union free from acceptance and rejection transports you to that state in which all dharmas of samsara and nirvana [51] are seen as empty reality itself, then awareness itself, undivided into samsara and nirvana, directly perceives the dharmadhātu as the object. This ripens into the body of continuous self-awareness[307] and brings about freedom. This liberation on the spot is like moxibustion applied to the proper spot on the body. This emphasis on seemingly transcending the path is like that of the six yogas of the new schools,[308] but there is a great difference in meaning: in the six yogas, the technique of binding the five winds in the central channel effects the appearance of the empty body, leading you gradually along a path of great bliss that involves effort. Here, on the other hand, having severed all analytical thought, you settle directly into the self-luminous ultimate nature; Nyingmapas regard this as especially distinctive. And because this path also releases the gnosis body into the rainbow body, it is distinctive relative to the practices of the expanse class and other Nyingma traditions. Here, it is not merely a question of clarifying the coarse three doors into a brilliant subtle body; through bringing to completion the appearances that are coterminous with the dharmadhātu, all three doors, both subtle and coarse, are clarified into the baseless nature of the body and gnosis. So they say.

(2) Other triads

Alternatively, they use three terms: originally pure nature, spontaneously present intrinsic nature, and all-pervasive compassion.[309] They say that the original essence, empty of basis or arising, is the originally pure nature; the unobstructed radiance of emptiness is the spontaneously present nature; and the energy of that—all pure and impure appearances—is the all-pervasive compassion. They say that the first term refers to the inseparability of awareness and emptiness; the second refers to the inseparability of clarity and emptiness; and the third refers to the inseparability of appearance and emptiness. They say that the difference between mind *(sems)* and awareness *(rig pa)* is that mind is incidental conceptual thought that remembers one thing after another and is controlled by ignorance, while awareness, which is not subject to the polluting control of ignorance, is free of elaborating object and subject, and recognizes that it is itself empty in being empty clarity and nonapprehension. They say that the appearing aspect of mind is samsara while the empty nature of mind is nirvana. And since from the perspective of one's own mind's empty nature there is no cause for distinguishing samsara from nirvana, their outlook is styled "the inseparability of samsara and nirvana."[310]

The logic that identifies awareness for a gradualist is: Determining that all appearances are mind, determining that mind is empty, and determining the nondual union of awareness and emptiness, we realize plainly that all dharmas are [52] awareness and emptiness. The logic that identifies awareness for a simultaneist is: Without meditating gradually, and having awareness merely pointed out by the guru, we realize plainly that whatever appears is awareness and emptiness. The logic that identifies awareness for a transcender is: Even if the union of awareness and emptiness is not plainly manifest in this life, we gain a genuine realization of that in the bardo through the power of our meditation. In brief, they say, we should spontaneously release ourselves into our own stainless, present awareness, which is empty clarity and nonapprehension, without acting to refute or establish any concept or appearance as abiding or moving, good or bad, while maintaining bare empty awareness. This is the essence of the way of meditating on Dzokchen, the unsurpassable essence of the thought of the great master Padmasambhava.

The Nyingmapas' standpoint on the basis, path, and result: They assert that the *basis* is the original ultimate nature, untouched by the mind of samsara and nirvana and untarnished by confusion—the bare ultimate nature, with no experience of confusion, no experience of realization, unfit[311] to exist as anything or to arise as anything. They assert that the *path* is this present awareness, relaxed in meditative equipoise, empty purity free of good thoughts, bad thoughts, and neutral thoughts, abiding as if at the center of luminous space. They assert that the result is what occurs when all the good qualities of the path become manifest, when the dharmadhātu, after clearing ignorance and confusion on its own, becomes manifest.

After collecting the essentials from the explanations in authentic documents of this system, I have written this presentation of view and meditation in Dzokchen for easy understanding.

3) Analyzing a few aspects of the Nyingma philosophical system

You may wonder whether the Nyingma Dharma system is absolutely pure, absolutely impure, or a mixture. In such works as the great translator Rinchen Sangpo's *Distinguishing Dharma from Non-Dharma;* the letters of Lha Lama Yeshé Ö, Shiwa Ö, Tsami Lotsāwa, and Chak Lotsāwa; the *Thorny Plant* of Ngok Lawachen;[312] and Sakya Pandita's *Distinguishing the Three Vows,* no explicit critique of the Nyingma is found. Those texts, however, contain general criticisms of impure Dharma systems in Tibet, and it seems [53] that a few passages are directed at[313] the Nyingmapas. Gö Khukpa Lhetsé and Drigung Palzin set forth many arguments to establish the impurity of Nyingma Dharma, and Shākya Chokden and Karmapa Mikyö Dorjé reiterated them.[314] There is a text critical of the Nyingma purportedly written by Butön Rinchen Drup, but it does not appear in the indexes of his collected works, and stylistically, it does not convey the feel of that sage's language; undoubtedly, some fool wrote it and passed it off as Butön's work. Also, the translator Rongsom Chösang, Künpang Thukjé Tsöndrü, Karmapa Rangjung Dorjé, the adept Urgyenpa, Chomden Raldri, Tharlo Nyima Gyaltsen, the later Drukpa Pema Karpo, Pawo Tsuklak Trengwa, and other famed scholars of other philosophical systems, as well as some on our own Geluk side, like Khöntön Paljor Lhündrup and the Great Fifth Dalai Lama, have explained the Nyingma system as pure Dharma. However, many authoritative scholars, like Butön Rinpoché and the conqueror Tsongkhapa and his spiritual sons, have maintained neutrality. There is a single work said to be written by Gelek Pal Sangpo[315] that proves in numerous verses that the Nyingma is completely pure, but that author is probably some other Gelek Palsang. As is evident to anyone who examines it, the language is not that of the omniscient Khedrup.

You may wonder, then, which of those you should follow. The great biography of Jé Lama Tsongkhapa written by Joden Sönam Lhündrup explains that when someone asked if the Dzokchen view was pure or not, Jé answered, "It is pure, but adulterations fabricated by later ignoramuses have entered into it." When Lama Rinpoché was requested to write a text to eliminate the adulteration, he replied, "I would like to do that, but right now I'm working on the *Commentary on the Guhyasamāja Tantra, Annotations to the Illuminating Lamp,* the *Discussion of the Condensed Meaning,* the *Commentary on Cakrasaṃvara,* and other texts, so I don't have time."[316] Also, I have heard from my omniscient lama, Changkya Rölpai Dorjé, that Tsongkhapa's view is also like that in the biography of Jé Rinpoché composed by Lhula Kachupa.[317] [54]

Therefore, I myself accept the interpretation to the effect that the present-day Dzokchen view is stained by adulteration. I do not, however, dare to say that the view in and of itself is a wrong view. Nevertheless, it appears that a view so elevated was meaningful because it was appropriate to the mental continuums of the sharpest students during that wonderful era when the great master Padmasambhava and others came. I think, however, that in those whose minds are not the least bit distinctive, as in those of present-day ordinary people, a view so elevated might be greatly harmful, and far from beneficial. As Wöntön Rinchen Gangpa has said:

> He who does not practice the Dharma appropriate to his mental continuum
> And pursues the highest vehicle
> Is like a small child mounting a wild horse;
> It is very important to practice what is appropriate to one's mental continuum.[318]

Moreover, even though many impurities are apparent in the Nyingma tantric texts, and in those scriptures that establish view, meditation, and conduct, and the base, path, and result, it is not right to deprecate them for that reason and say they are mistaken Dharma; that would be the same as inappropriately calling tarnished gold brass. As for impurities, when the intelligent analyze in detail, not only the Nyingma, but all Tibetan philosophical systems appear to have them. Thus, if you understand well that this is so, you will gain a definite understanding, induced by faultless reasoning, that our tradition, that of the conqueror Jé Tsongkhapa, is the sole entryway used by those intent on liberation. This is just a brief summary; I will elaborate below.

Thus, the omniscient Butön (1290–1364) states in reply to the translator Rinchen Sangpo, Lha Lama Yeshé Ö, Phodrang Shiwa Ö, Gö Khukpa Lhetsé, and others who regarded the early secret mantra translations of Nyingma as impure:

> My own lamas, the bilingual Nyimai Tsenchen as well as Rikral and others, said that because Sanskrit manuscripts were found at Samyé, and the Sanskrit of *Fragments of the Vajrakīla Root Tantra*[319] appeared in Nepal, those tantras are pure. I think that, as it is said:
>
> The malevolent, whose minds are naturally flawed,
> Are mistaken with respect to the form of what is incorrect,
> Not to mention with respect to things said to be [55] in doubt.
> Thus it is good, not bad, if you remain equanimous.
>
> Saying that good dharmas are not good, and saying that those that are not good are good: this is explained as failing to distinguish[320] cause and effect. Also:
>
> Saying that a dharma does or does not have such and such characteristics
> As distinguished by way of the four causes, when one has neither understood nor seen:
> This is nefarious hairsplitting;
> Disparaging the Dharma is rejected in the Muni's texts.
>
> Just as stated, I will stay neutral.[321]

Thus taught Butön.

4) A discussion of some later events

I have already discussed the many special beings who came earlier and held and propagated the instructions of the oral and treasure transmissions. I might, though, mention some who came later. There were five emanations of Master Padmasambhava, those of his body, speech, mind, qualities, and deeds. The body emanation was Nyang Nyima Öser, the speech emanation was Chöwang, the mind emanation was Ngari Panchen Pema Wangyal, and the emanation of qualities was Wangpo Dé Jangdak Tashi Thopgyal.[322] It is asserted that his deed emanation will arise later, when the time is right. Of those, Ngari Panchen (1487–1543) combined the qualities of both scholar and adept; his writings on Dharma were many. Wangpo Dé Jangdak Tashi

Thopgyal was his incarnation. Ngari Panchen's younger brother was the tantric master Gökyi Demtruchen, or Lekden Düjom Dorjé, the incarnation of Ngödrup Gyaltsen (1337–1409). Gökyi Demtruchen's reincarnation was Jangdak Tashi Thopgyal's son, the tantric master Ngakgi Wangpo. The latter's incarnation was the fourth Dorjé Drak trulku, the tantric master Pema Trinlé (1641–1717).

During his time, Jangdak Tashi Thopgyal (1550–1603) was at odds with the ruler, Shingshakpa Tseten Dorjé. Shingshakpa and Jangpa Namkha Gyaltsen formed an alliance, and Tashi Thopa was exiled. Shingshakpa said with relish:

> You who are called Power *(thop)* are a powerless wanderer:
> I banish you to the region of the city of ghosts.

In reply, Tashi Thopa stated:

> You who are called Field *(shing)* are replete with tenfold guilt
> *(shing chu):*
> I will send you into the mouth of Rāhula.[323]

Having said this, he performed the rituals of Yama and Rāhula, killing Shingshakpa and his retinue. [56] Tashi Thopa had set up a temporary camp for that purpose and named it Evaṃ Chokgar, after the tantric monk named Chokgar who was staying with him. Later, he started Thupten Dorjé Drak, a monastery in Ü that is still standing. Chögyal Terdak Lingpa (1646–1714), the incarnation of Dongak Lingpa of the incarnation lineage of Drapa Ngönshé Bar, founded Orgyen Mindröl Ling Monastery. His younger brother was the great translator Dharmaśrī (d. 1718), who was expert in the sutras, the new and old tantras, and countless worldly sciences, and wrote many treatises.

His highness the Great Fifth Dalai Lama (1617–82)[324] was the body incarnation of Lord Nyang Nyima Öser and met Bhāvaviveka and the Dharma king Indrasena[325] in a pure vision. The teachings transmitted from him were received in their entirety by Sur Chöying Rangdröl and Tratsangpa Lochok Dorjé, who wrote various literary works about them and practiced, expounded, and propagated them. The Great Fifth undertook many practices and activities related to the Nyingma system in Nampar Gyalwa Pen Delek Sheling Monastery and erected a multitude of Nyingma monasteries.

Although the Nyingma teaching was widespread at that time, not long afterward [i.e., in 1718], the Jungar Mongol army pillaged the three monasteries, Dorjé Drak, Mindröl Ling, and Namgyal Ling. Though innocent, the Dordrak trulku, the great translator Dharmaśrī, the great Namgyal scholar Könchok Chödrak, and Terdak Lingpa's son, Pema Gyurmé Gyatso, were all executed. On the pretense of purifying Sera, Drepung,[326] and other monasteries, the Jungars expelled many older monks, and in this and other disgraceful deeds, they claimed they were performing a service for the Gelukpas. Nevertheless, not long afterward, both Dorjé Drak and Mindröl Ling were restored; Namgyal Ling became Geluk.

Later on, the Jedrung trulku, Losang Trinlé (b. 1697), focusing on a treasure text of Terdak Lingpa as well as on the Dharma cycle of the *Secret Gnosis,* wrote many textbooks that mixed the new and old tantras. In that way, alcohol rituals and consort rituals[327] spread everywhere, and all the clergy and lay folk who enjoyed the evils of beer followed him. Some Geluk trulkus and geshés [57] were also involved in that. Many of the monasteries north and south of the Tsangpo River virtually turned into lay centers. Our holy supreme leader, Maitri by name, Phurbu Chok Ngawang Jampa (1682–1762), criticized these practices in accordance with the Dharma, and after he eliminated them, the corrupt practices went into dormancy.

Now Jedrung Trulku himself had certainly attained a high degree of realization, so his actions may have been intentional and advanced some special purpose. Superficially, however, because he mixed new and old systems into one, he does not fit into either line. And those activities were very harmful to pure conduct—the root of the teaching—and likely caused many sentient beings to go to hell.

In Ü and Tsang are two larger monasteries of the Nyingma school, Dorjé Drak and Mindröl Ling, and it seems quite a few smaller monasteries. In Kham are Kathok, Dzokchen, Shechen, and other monasteries. In these monasteries the essential Dharmas of the trio of sutra, magical net, and mind class dissolved long ago into the primordial purity of original space, and the Nyingmapas of the present day merely treat as essential such mimicry as chanting from manuals, giving extravagant ritual feasts, and the threefold practice of suppressing enemies, burning offerings, and casting out tormas, as well as other practices.[328]

Concluding verses

The sea where the six lineages combine as one,
Full of precious treasures of instruction and yogic application,
The place where hundreds of thousands of supreme adepts and
 mighty nāgas play,
Is called the ocean of the unsullied early-translation vehicle.

Striving to travel the stages and paths in succession,
Not looking elsewhere for buddhahood,
Through instructions on transcendence and cutting through, one
 comes to the greatness
Of freeing the corrupted aggregates into a body of light.

Padmasambhava taught it to some with receptive minds,
Who, like peacocks, could eat poison for food;
It is said that they instantly reached the adept stage,
Just like iron transformed to gold by an elixir.

Although the milk of a lioness can be poured
Into a precious vessel, it destroys a clay pot;
The master himself carefully considered this, and entrusting
The holy Dharma to the earth goddess, went off to land of *srin*
 demons.

This account, which discusses such events,
Is as straight as the center line of a mandala[329]
And as pure as [58] the white clouds;
I have published it for those with the eye of intelligence.

From *The Crystal Mirror: An Excellent Explanation Showing the Sources and Assertions of All Philosophical Systems,* this completes the explanations of the history in Tibet of the earlier and later teaching and of the philosophical system of the early translation of secret mantra, that known as the Nyingma.

5. The Kadam Tradition

[II. The History of Philosophical Systems in Tibet, the Land of Snows
B. The histories of the different schools]

2. Kadam[330]

> I now relate the history of the philosophical system known as Kadam,
> Where thousands of learned and perfected nāgas,
> Whose essence is the wish-granting jewel of the supreme thought,
> Played in the great ocean of measureless princely conduct.[331]

THIS BRIEF EXPLANATION of the history of the Kadam philosophical system is threefold: a. The history of the Kadam order, founded through the kindness of the great noble lord Atiśa (982–1054),[332] b. The history of other teachings and teachers based on him, and c. A general explanation of the Kadam teaching.

a. The history of the Kadam order, founded through the kindness of the noble lord
1) Etymology

Earlier lamas discussed the etymology of *Kadam* variously, but when Jé Rinpoché (Tsongkhapa) asked Chenga Rinchen Pal, "What is the meaning of *Kadam*?" Chenga replied, "Without omitting even a single letter *na* from the word *(ka)* of the Conqueror, one takes it as personal instruction *(damngak)*." Jé Rinpoché was very pleased and said, "That's right! That's right!" He went to a monastery and said, "Geshé Rinchen Pal has given me a present of the holy Dharma. What he said is correct." Thus, it is called *Kadam* because the entire content, without exception, of the Buddha's word *(ka)*—the Tripiṭaka—is included in Atiśa's instructions *(dam)* on the stages of the path of the three persons so that one can put them into practice. According to Dromtönpa:

The wonderful [59] word *(ka)* is the Tripiṭaka,
And any being who counts on the precious golden rosary
Of the Kadam, which is beautified by the instruction *(dam)*
On the three persons, will find success.[333]

It is as stated in this and other passages.

2) History

How the extraordinary Kadam order arose: It began with the noble lord, the glorious Atiśa. Dromtönpa Rinpoché blazed the trail for it. The three brothers—Geshé Potowa, Geshé Chengawa, and Geshé Puchungwa—made it widespread. From there, Langri Thangpa and Sharawa, as well as Jayülwa and others, extended it.

a) Atiśa's qualities

Extensive biographies of the noble lord are found elsewhere; this brief account of his greatness is from the *Lamp Illuminating Dharma History of the Kadam:*[334]

He was born as a prince of Sahor[335] in eastern India.
He mastered all the non-Buddhist and Buddhist sciences.
Keeping the three trainings pure, he became an elder, a great vinaya master.
Because he comprehended without confusion the details
Of the four basic Vaibhāṣika schools and the eighteen sects,[336]
He was honored by all, his speech taken as authoritative.
He headed all the great monastic institutions
Of Magadha,[337] such as Vikramaśīla.[338]
He had visions of countless meditational deities,
And there was nothing he did not know about the Dharma of the Tripiṭaka and the tantras.
He fully imbibed the nectar of the awakening mind
That flowed from the precious vase mouth of Serlingpa.
With the roar of positive and refutational reasoning,
He confounded the elephant of base criticism,
And he satisfied the fortunate with the holy Dharma

In accord with their own way of thinking.
He was called "bodhisattva of the fortunate eon."
As prophesied by the Lady Tārā, he was enthroned
By Nāropa as the very lord of the teaching.
That, then, is Śrīmat Dīpaṃkaraśrī.[339]

b) How Atiśa came to Tibet

How the noble lord himself came to Tibet: The teaching has waxed and waned many times in the Land of Snows. The way of teaching established by the threesome of the preceptor Śāntarakṣita, Master Padmasambhava, and the Dharma king Trisong Detsen was corrupted by Heshang.[340] He was defeated by Kamalaśīla, but the pure view and conduct that had become widespread were later destroyed by the evil king Langdarma, and Tibet was a dark land for about seventy years. Then Lachen [60] Gongpa Rapsal revived the embers of the teaching from lower Tibet, that is, Amdo and Kham, and the great translator Rinchen Sangpo resuscitated them from upper Tibet, that is, Ngari, and there was an increase in the number of monasteries in the districts of Ü and Tsang.

However, some who admired the vinaya deprecated mantra, while others who admired mantra deprecated the vinaya, so the teaching became polarized. Most people merely bickered about philosophical systems; needless to say, they didn't know how to put the complete teaching of the Muni into practice. Even partial understanding became rare. Especially during the period after Langdarma destroyed the teaching, some tantric yogins wrote down phrases they had memorized from the tantras, but as they had forgotten the intervening text, they simply inserted into the gaps any corrupt tantric language that came to mind. Likewise, others wrote whatever they wanted in fanciful provincial language and called it "tantra." Some tantric yogins would also say to their wives, "Brew me some good beer today, and I'll write a thick tantric volume." From India came the so-called Red Preceptor, Blue-Cloaked Sage, and others, who spread such perverted versions of Dharma as uniting and freeing: sex with women was called "uniting," and killing sentient beings such as one's enemies was called "freeing." They also spread many types of crude behavior that were designated as "mantra." Because of their influence, those who adhered to pure view and conduct were few, while those who pursued perverted Dharma conduct were many. Even after Lha Lama Yeshé Ö, Phodrang Shiwa Ö, the great translator

Rinchen Sangpo, and others wrote and distributed works critical of perverted Dharma, things did not improve.

At that time, the king of Ngari, Lha Lama Yeshé Ö, found it intolerable that the teaching in Tibet had come to such a state; he thought that the only way to improve things would be to invite a great Indian sage who was an authority on the teaching to rectify the situation.[341] He gave a large quantity of gold to Gya Tsöndrü Sengé and sent him to invite Atiśa, but Gya was unsuccessful. The king decided to seek additional gold then send someone else to invite Atiśa, but when he went in search of gold, he was captured by the king [61] of the Garlok,[342] who would not release him. Yeshé Ö's nephew, Jangchup Ö, obtained a great deal of gold, and though he took it as ransom for his uncle, Yeshé Ö would not hear of turning it over to the Garlok king. Then, Yeshé Ö was killed by the Garlok.

In accordance with his uncle's final wishes, Jangchup Ö sent Naktso Lotsāwa Tsültrim Gyalwa to India with a large quantity of gold to invite the pandit. When Naktso and Gya Tsöndrü Sengé met Atiśa, they reported in detail on the state of the teaching in Tibet and the hardships endured by Yeshé Ö, then requested that he come to Tibet. Earlier, there had been many prophecies to the noble lord about going to Tibet, but that evening he appealed repeatedly to Lady Tārā. Examining the signs, she said that there was a ḍākinī he should ask. Accordingly, he asked the ḍākinī, and she prophesied that if he went to Tibet, it would bring benefit to the teaching, bringing particular benefit through a layman.[343] Thus, he agreed to go to Tibet.

When you know the details of how the teaching waxed and waned and was corrupted, and how for its sake the uncle, Lha Lama Yeshe Ö, his nephew, Jangchup Ö, and the translators underwent great hardships, then you will remember their kindness and recognize how difficult it is to find pure Dharma. As it is vital you do not enter the Dharma rashly but enter it understanding the distinctions that must be made, it would be fitting to write in greater detail. But fearing the weight of my text, I have only elaborated in part here; details may be known from other sources.

c) What Atiśa did in Tibet

How Atiśa acted on behalf of the teaching after arriving in Tibet: As Tsongkhapa's *Great Treatise on the Stages of the Path* says in describing the greatness of the noble lord:

> When he arrived in Ngari in upper Tibet on account of Lha Lama Jangchup Ö's request that he purify the Buddha's teaching, he wrote the *Lamp for the Path to Enlightenment*,[344] a text that collects all the key points of sutra and mantra and condenses them into a sequence of practice; through this and other actions, he propagated the teaching. Also, teaching all the instructions related to sutra and mantra texts to fortunate students for three years in Ngari, nine years in Nyethang, and five years elsewhere in Ü and Tsang, he began anew the teaching traditions that had disappeared, enhanced the traditions that just barely survived, and cleansed away the filthy stain of misconceptions. In short, he freed the precious [62] teaching from its stains.[345]

If we examine this statement closely, we will find that its main points have many implications.

Atiśa remained in Tibet for seventeen years, and having demonstrated final nirvana in Nyethang on the eighteenth day of the ninth month of the male water horse year [i.e., 1054] at age seventy-three, he came before the holy lord Maitreya in Tuṣita heaven, where he was designated as the bodhisattva Stainless Sky.

d) Students

Although the great noble lord had many disciples in both India and Tibet who became scholars and adepts, the one who was given instruction as from one vessel to another, and was blessed as lord of the teaching, was that emanation of Ārya Avalokiteśvara prophesied to Atiśa himself by Tārā, and prophesied in the *Flower Ornament* and the *White Lotus of Compassion* sutras as "the layman who increases Dharma," namely, Drom Rinpoché Gyalwai Jungné, or Dromtönpa (1005–64).[346] If I discussed in detail here the ways in which the precious Dromtönpa blazed the trail of the Kadam, and the three brothers and others further disseminated it, it would be too much; you should study these topics in the Kadam Dharma histories and other texts. Briefly, as stated in the *Lamp Illuminating Dharma History:*

> Then, over the course of up to a decade,
> Geshé Dromtönpa was leader of the group.
> He erected the noble lord's monastic seat, glorious Radreng,

And ripened a circle of utterly pure disciples.
Then, for just over twenty years,
The deeds of the three brothers burst forth.
The Kadam sun rose in northern Ü,
Filling all the Land of Snows with light.
The great seer Potowa
Had disciples whose view and conduct were thoroughly pure:
At one time, there were more than two thousand;
And Chengawa gathered eight or nine hundred.
Puchungwa did not nurture disciples publicly
But ripened countless disciples in a hidden way.
Khampa Lungpa, who taught the *Eight-Session Practice,*
Is said to have gathered eight hundred intent on liberation.
The son nurtured well by the three brothers,
Langthangpa, had around a thousand,
And the great Geshé Sharawa
Gathered together over three thousand whose lives were pure.
Geshé Yagepa had over a thousand,
Jayülwa [63] two thousand seven hundred, and so forth;
Countless spiritual mentors nurtured students by their deeds.
Right at that time, the diffusion of the teaching was great.[347]

In sum, the Ngari kings Lha Lama, uncle and nephew, who were deeply concerned solely with the teaching, and who underwent great hardships without regard to body, life, wealth, or anything else, invited to Tibet the noble lord, the glorious Atiśa. Thus, the darkness of misconduct such as crude behavior claimed to be mantra, and of misconceptions such as holding sutra and mantra to be opposed like hot and cold, naturally disappeared when the sun of Atiśa's teaching rose. All who maintained the pure view and conduct of the later spread of the teaching, those upholding the lineage of Lachen Gongpa Rapsal and others, entered the oral lineage of the noble lord. The whole of Ü and Tsang was completely filled with the teaching and the teachers versed in the oral instructions *(kadam)* of the noble lord, whose life was pure without and pure within, like the bud of a lotus.

All of Ü and Tsang was covered with monasteries upholding the Kadam Dharma system; those still intact today are Radreng in the north as well as the Narthang Jangchup Chenpo retreat center in Tsang. Those were prophesied extensively in the *Book of Kadam*.[348] Radreng, the pure-land headwaters of the Kadam, arose through the gnostic magic of Dromjé Gyalwai Jungné. As to Narthang, after it was established by Geshé Sharawa's student Tumtön Lodrö Drakpa, the lineage of abbots came in an unbroken succession like a rosary of golden mountains. The other main monasteries mostly emptied out over the course of time, and it seems that most are now occupied by nuns. The Kadampas very much shunned women, so when a woman who was the emanation of a ḍākinī came to a monastery and was forcibly expelled, she uttered a curse: "Now you have shunned my kind; in the future, the remaining monasteries will be occupied by women." Therefore, some holy ones say the current situation came about because of that incident. [64]

b. The history of other teachings and teachers based on the great noble lord

Those known as the Kagyü, Sakya, and Geden[349] also all arose based on the deeds of the noble lord. When the forefather of the Kagyü, the great translator Marpa of Lhodrak, went to India for the last time, he met the noble lord and received instructions from him. In particular, the matchless Dakpo Lharjé, or Gampopa, first received the Kadam teaching from Gyayön Dak, a disciple of the great Naljorpa, who was a direct disciple of the noble lord. Then, after hearing Mahāmudrā teachings from Jetsün Milarepa, Gampopa wrote the *Jewel Ornament of Liberation,*[350] an instruction on the stages of the path that combined the two rivers of the Kadam and Mahāmudrā. His disciple Dromgön Phakmo Drupa received the Kadam teaching from Geshé Dölpa and also wrote a treatise on the stages of the teaching.[351] Likewise, Drigung Jikten Gönpo received the Kadam teaching from Geshé Langlungpa, the great Taklung Thangpa received it from Geshé Chekawa, and Karmapa Düsum Khyenpa received it from Geshé Sharawa's disciple Naljorpa Sherap Dorjé, so they performed all the conduct-side practices according to the Kadam system. Thus, the essence of the Kagyü Dharma, which is the instructions on Mahāmudrā and the six Dharmas of Nāropa made into Mahayana Dharma, comes only from the Kadam Dharma lineage of special instructions for generating the awakening mind, which are like yeast as a starter for beer.

Jamyang Sakya Pandita received the Kadam teaching from Geshé Chiwo Lhepa, a disciple of Neusurpa, and in his writings he established all the path practices of the common Mahayana solely according to the Kadam system. Thus, his Sakya followers also practice according to that tradition.

The conqueror, the great Tsongkhapa, is established by authoritative scripture as being in actuality of the same mental continuum as the noble lord. And, even in terms of common appearances, after he received teachings on the stages of the Kadam path from the two great preceptors Namkha Gyaltsen and Chökyap Sangpo, he gradually, over time, cleared away his remaining stains of incomprehension, misconception, or doubt with respect to the noble lord's instructions. He wrote the *Great* and the *Small Treatise on the Stages of the Path* [65] and other treatises whose explanatory excellence was unprecedented. The tradition of Geden[352] Mountain itself is based on the system of the noble lord Kadampa, that is, Atiśa; and though it adds the Madhyamaka view and secret mantra, it is coextensive with the Kadam. In fact, in Dharma histories, the Geden system is given the name New Kadam.

There is a prophecy about that in the *Book of Kadam,* in the prophecy of the future in chapter 26 of the Father Teachings:[353]

> In the end, the embers of the teaching
> Will be rekindled by one named Drakpa,[354]
> Who will accomplish the benefit and happiness of many,
> And his place[355] is a supreme and holy place.[356]

A translator said, "If the name of a limb is a term for the trunk, it is excellent. It is a system where the limbs extend from the body." The verse statement above is prophesying Jé Lama and his monastic seat, Ganden. The apparent meaning of the statement by the translator is that the New Kadam, or Ganden, which is like a limb, will be more widespread than the Kadam, which is like the body.

Moreover, Sülphuwa wrote a long account of the noble lord, and since he received the Kadam teaching from Geshé Tölungpa, all the many vinaya masters in his lineage were solely Kadampas.

Not only that, but the streams of explanation related to the great definition-vehicle texts also arise from the kindness of the noble lord. How did that happen? Here in Tibet, those who mastered completely the Dharmas of Madhyamaka, valid cognition, and the Maitreya literature[357] were the great Ngok Lotsāwa, his disciples, and also their disciples.[358] Ngok Lotsāwa Lekpai Sherap (1018–1115) was not only a direct disciple of the great noble lord, but also was the one heart son who was given the secret Dharma from the *Book of Kadam* at Yerpa Lhari. And, when he erected Sangphu Monastery, he did so in accord with a prophecy given him by the noble lord himself. Loden Sherap (1059–1109), who was both a disciple and nephew of Ngok, wrote the *Stages of the Teaching*[359] after hearing the noble lord's Dharma from his uncle.

Then there were Loden Sherap's disciples: Drolungpa Lodrö Jungné, an expert in all the scriptures; Drechenpo Sherap Bar, an expert in the perfection [66] of wisdom; Gangpa Sheu, an expert in valid cognition; Khyung Rinchen Drakpa, an expert in Madhyamaka; Shang Tsepong, who presided over the actual monastic seat; and others. When Drolungpa was young, he received the Kadam Dharma from the noble lord and Drom. He wrote the *Explication that Binds Together the Inner Meaning of the One Hundred Minor Dharmas,* mainly on the noble lord's shorter texts, and also wrote two *Stages of the Teaching* texts, the *Great* and *Small.* The *Great Treatise on the Stages of the Teaching* is an incomparable commentary on the meaning of Atiśa's *Lamp for the Path to Enlightenment,* so when the conqueror Tsongkhapa saw this book, he received it with various offerings and composed the *Great Treatise on the Stages of the Path* mostly to accord with it. The stream of exposition and study established in many study centers by scholars in the disciple lineage descending from Dro, Dré, Gangpa, Khyung, and Shang eventually went everywhere, like the sky covering the earth, and persists to this day.

In brief, as stated in the *Blue Annals* of Gö Lotsāwa Shönu Pal:

> It is evident from most of the biographies of the virtuous friends and yogins of perfect conduct who came to Tibet in later times that they had encountered the various Kadam geshés. Also, Drom performed deeds whose effects were widespread and long-lasting. Those facts reveal just a portion of the fruits that arose from Dīpaṃkara Śrījñāna turning the Dharma wheel.[360]

As stated, you should understand that all[361] the many pure Dharma systems or philosophical systems of the Land of Snows are the result of the great noble lord turning the wheel of Dharma after coming to Tibet.

c. A general explanation of the Kadam teaching

The general explanation of the Kadam teaching is twofold: 1) The classifications of Dharma and 2) Personal actions and behavior. [67]

1) The classifications of Dharma

Dromtönpa said, "My lama knows how to carry all four corners of the teaching."[362] The great Naljorpa Jangchup Rinchen said, "He understands instructions inwardly: this is said not of one who has mastered just a booklet that fits in the palm of the hand but of one who understands all scriptures as instruction."[363] Lama Gompa Rinchen said, "There is no oral lineage other than that of my lama, who knows how to enlist the vinaya to assist mantra, and mantra to assist vinaya."[364] Thus they have stated.

In general, the special quality of the Kadampas is that they are able to enlist *all* the scriptures of the Conqueror, without rejecting some and accepting others, as the necessary conditions for an individual's enlightenment. Thus, there is no Dharma that is not included in the Kadam. In common parlance, however, it is twofold—*texts* and *instructions.* Sometimes *special instructions* is given as a third.

a) Texts

The texts are of three types: those mainly teaching the view, those mainly teaching conduct, and those teaching the two combined. The first includes *Entering the Two Truths,* the *Instructions on Madhyamaka,* and other texts written by the noble lord. The second includes his *Lamp Summarizing Conduct,* texts on arousing the mind of awakening, rituals for vows, and so forth. The third is *Lamp for the Path to Enlightenment.*

The last is a marvelously excellent explanation that, without discarding even a single letter *na* from the speech of the Conqueror—the Tripiṭaka and the four classes of tantra, together with the commentaries on their meaning—shows how to condense that into a sequence of individual practice. As Jé Lama Tsongkhapa states in his *Great Treatise on the Stages of the Path to Enlightenment:*

> Although the noble lord wrote many texts, the one that is utterly complete, the root, as it were, is the *Lamp for the Path to Enlightenment.* Because it teaches the key points of both sutra and mantra, it completely covers everything expressible. Because it gives primacy to the stages of controlling the mind, it is easy to put into practice.[365] And, because it is adorned by the instructions of the two lamas who were expert in the systems of the two charioteers,[366] it is [68] especially distinctive compared to other systems' texts.[367]

The works known as the six Kadam texts are: Asaṅga's *Bodhisattva Stages,* Maitreya's *Ornament of Mahayana Sutras,* Śāntideva's *Compendium of Train-*

ing and *Way of the Bodhisattva,* Āryaśūra's *Garland of Birth Stories,* and the *Collection of Uplifting Verses.*[368] Of those, the *Compendium of Training* and *Way of the Bodhisattva* unite view and conduct, while the others are texts that mainly teach the conduct of a bodhisattva.

What is known as *One Hundred Minor Dharmas* of the noble lord also is a Kadam text, as are Nāgārjuna's *Fundamental Treatise on the Middle Way, Seventy Stanzas on Emptiness,* and *Precious Garland.*[369]

b) Instructions

The instructions are also threefold: (1) Instructions mainly teaching the view, (2) Instructions mainly teaching conduct, and (3) Instructions teaching the two combined.

(1) Instructions teaching the view

The instructions mainly showing the view: These are the noble lord's special instructions on the guidelines on the four truths in the lineage through Chengawa; the guidelines on dependent arising in the lineage through Puchungwa;[370] and the guidelines on the two truths in the lineage through Naljorpa. The guidelines on the four truths and dependent arising lead to realization of the ordinary selflessness of persons, while the guidelines on the two truths lead to realization of the very subtle selflessness of dharmas.

The disciple of the noble lord with great expertise in the two truths was the great Naljorpa Jangchup Rinchen. He taught it to Drolungpa and Chengawa, and Chenga taught it privately to the duo of Tölungpa and Jayülwa. Tölungpa taught it both ways, privately and publicly, and also wrote many texts. His student Khyungkham also taught it to many disciples, so it became widespread. Sangyé Wön also wrote many textbooks about it, both long and condensed. The *Treatise on Philosophical Systems* composed by Geshé Chekawa and the commentary on it by Lhalung Wangchuk lay out the standpoints of non-Buddhist and Buddhist philosophical systems, and lead one to the nonabiding great Madhyamaka of Nāgārjuna. This is a portion of the Kadampa view.

Thus, through the root text and commentaries of the *Lamp for the Path to Enlightenment,* and the root text and commentaries of the *Instructions on Madhyamaka* and other texts, we learn that the great noble lord upheld the Prāsaṅgika-Madhyamaka view. It also is said that when Dromtönpa offered the noble lord his realization of master Candrakīrti's system, Atiśa was very pleased, and pressing his palms together at his heart, said, "How wonderful! Nowadays in eastern [69] India, this is the only view upheld."[371] In the texts on stages of the path and the sayings of those known as the three brothers—Geshé Potowa, Geshé Chengawa, and Geshé Puchungwa—we find a Madhyamaka view that is strongly in agreement with the system of Candrakīrti. Although Ngok Lotsāwa and his students often quoted Bhāvaviveka and Candrakīrti as textual sources, their way of maintaining the view was more strongly in accord with that of father Śāntarakṣita and his spiritual son Kamalaśīla.[372] The view entailed in some mind training teachings from the lineage of Serlingpa (b. tenth century) appears to be consistent with the false-aspectarian Cittamātra system.[373]

Still, my omniscient lama, Changkya Rölpai Dorjé, stated, "For the most part, the later Kadampas were rarely able to explain and understand the Indian texts without confusing the meaning."[374]

(2) Instructions teaching conduct

The instructions mainly teaching conduct are the teachings on Mahayana mind training,[375] which are a way to traverse the ten stages and the five paths through generating the still-unarisen awakening mind that cherishes others more than oneself and increasing that which has already arisen. The sources of these instructions are, in general, the Mahayana sutras, and in particular such sutra-class texts as the *Flower Ornament* and *Unraveling of Intention* sutras, Nāgārjuna's *Precious Garland, Wish-Granting Jewel Dream,* and *Stanzas Satisfying Sentient Beings,* and Śāntideva's *Compendium of Training* and *Way of the Bodhisattva*. The special instructions condensing the essence of those sutras and treatises are found in such instructional writings as: the mind training texts *The Weapon Wheel* and *Destroying the Peacock's Poison,* written by the noble lord's guru, Dharmarakṣita;[376] the *Vajra Songs on Chanting Meditation* of Lama Jampai Naljor;[377] the *Bodhisattva Stages* and *Crushing Conceptuality* of Serlingpa;[378] and others.

The special instruction on the *Seven-Point Mind Training* was taught by Serlingpa to the noble lord, who gave it to Geshé Dromtönpa as a private Dharma, and Drom taught it as a private Dharma to the three brothers. Although the stages of the path was a public Dharma during the time of the three brothers, it is evident that mind training was given only as a private Dharma. [70] Potowa gave it to Langri Thangpa, Sharawa, and others as a private Dharma.

Langri Thangpa (1054–1123) composed an eight-point outline of meditation topics known as the *Eight Verses on Mind Training,*[379] which he evidently made a public Dharma. Langri Thangpa taught it to Shang Sharawa, Shang Tsünyen, and Shawo Gangpa.[380] The text that mixed the teachings of all those was called the *Multicolored Booklet;* I think it also was known as *Shawo Gangpa's Mind Training.*

Shang Sharawa gave the latter as a private Dharma to Chekawa of Ja; there doesn't seem to be any account of his teaching it to anyone else. Chekawa practiced it on his own for the most part, but, seeing that it would bring great benefit, rather than giving it as a private Dharma to a couple of students, he taught it publicly in Drephu. He organized the text into seven divisions: (1) thinking through the basic Dharma, the preparatory practices, (2) training in the awakening mind, the actual practice, (3) changing adverse conditions into the path to enlightenment, (4) the teaching condensed into practice for a single life, (5) the criteria of mind training, (6) the pledges involved in mind training, and (7) how one studies mind training. He set these out in a root text, which became known as the *Seven-Point Mind Training.*[381] The way of meditating on the awakening mind in which one exchanges oneself with others is taught effectively in Kadam texts on the stages of the path to enlightenment, in Langri Thangpa's *Eight Verses on Mind Training,* and in *Shawo Gangpa's Mind Training,* but the *Seven-Point Mind Training*'s profound visualizations, such as mounting giving and taking[382] on the breath, are not found in those early texts; and since the *Seven-Point Mind Training* also is more extensive than those earlier texts in its sequencing of guidelines, it is especially effective.

Also, there is a text by Narthangpa Sangyé Gompa (1179–1250) called *A Public Explanation of Mind Training*[383] whose explanation is arranged in the order found in the root text of Chekawa. The great Jé Lama Tsongkhapa also recognized the supremacy of the instructions in the *Seven-Point Mind Training* and taught them extensively to his disciples. Jangsem Radrengwa took notes on the teaching and, in particular, Hortön Namkha Palwa (1373–1447) wrote a most profound text called *The Sun Rays of Mind Training.*

The eight-session special instruction of Geshé Dromtönpa: Since Khampa Lungpa (1023–1115) focused on and expounded it, it was known as Khampa Lungpa's *Eight-Session Mind Training.* The eight sessions are the special instructions on: (1) mind training based on food, (2) mind training based on the breath, (3) emanating as many bodies as there are sands in the Ganges, (4) mind training based on [71] flesh and blood, (5) mind training based on tormas, (6) mind training based on the elements, (7) training the mind to emanate the body as a wish-granting jewel, and (8) the time just before death. Khampa Lungpa taught them condensed into eight sessions.[384] Kharak Gomchungwa Wangchuk Lodrö (twelfth century)[385] taught the Dharma called the three cycles of Kharak. That instruction combined two rivers into one: from Gönpawa the instruction on the mind-side[386] transmitted from Aro to Bagom, and the noble lord's mind training instructions, which Kharak had received from Naljorpa and Gönpawa. The instructions were given the name *training in the awakening mind*. Kharak also composed the *Seventy Admonitions,* which set down in verse the special instructions on the stages of the path.

Moreover, the guidelines on the essence of dependent arising transmitted from Geshé Dromtönpa teach a special way of meditating on great compassion; it is an instruction on conduct, as are the rituals for arousing the awakening mind and for vows, and so forth, composed by Shang Sharawa on the basis of the noble lord's texts.

(3) Instructions teaching view and conduct combined

The royal instruction that teaches view and conduct combined is known as the "stages of the path to enlightenment for the three persons"; its text is *Lamp for the Path to Enlightenment.* Since the various texts and special instructions on view and conduct explained earlier are part of the stages of the path, they all are included among the sources for the stages of the path teaching. The stages of the path is a complete instruction on the way to practice, as the noble lord combined in a single work the special instructions of both the extensive-training lineage and the profound-view lineage.[387] Thus, it is called the *instruction that combines view and conduct.*

Those instructions on the stages of the path were taught by the noble lord to Dromtönpa in private. It is said:

> Saying to Drom, "I've found no one to hand this to but you," Atiśa handed Geshé Dromtönpa this special instruction and blessed him to be lord of the teaching; it is because of that that the extent of Dromtönpa's activity was magnified.[388]

Moreover, because Atiśa gave the instruction to Naktso Lotsāwa, there are also stages of the path textbooks in the lineage of Naktso's student,

Laksorwa; and because he gave them to Geshé Sangphuwa, there are the *Great* and *Small Stages of the Teaching,* written by the latter's heart-student, Drolungpa. [72]

Those in the lineage transmitted from father Atiśa and his spiritual son Dromtönpa to Geshé Gönpawa, then Neusurpa and others, and in the lineage transmitted from Dromtön Rinpoché to Geshé Chengawa, then Jayülwa and others, are known as those in the lineage from the upholders of the Kadam special instructions. Those in the lineage from Drom Rinpoché to Geshé Potowa and then Sharawa and others are designated as Kadam textualists. The two are similar in meaning and are only differentiated by whether they expound texts in a very elaborate way.

Although these traditions often disagree on the starting point of the path, it is said they arrive at the same endpoint. Jé Lama used Geshé Potowa's *Blue Udder* as a source when he said, "The main idea in all the collections of special instructions is never to give up the holy virtuous friend,"[389] and he guided his students starting from the way to rely on the virtuous friend.

Evidently, there were many texts on the stages of the path written by Kadampas; the two most famous are the *Blue Udder* and the *Dharma Examples.* The former is a commentary by Lhadri Gangpa on Dölpa Sherap Gyatso's edition of the sayings of Geshé Potowa. Jé Tsongkhapa praised it, saying, "If you are a geshé, then you should read the *Blue Udder,*" and he drew on it often as a source in his stages of the path texts. *Dharma Examples* has three versions. The first, by Geshé Drapa, is the short one. With that as his basis, Geshé Drakarwa added many examples he had heard from Geshé Drapa; his version is the extensive one. Chegom Dzongpa composed a medium-length version that was easier to understand than the previous two; it was called the *Jewel Heap of Dharma Examples.*[390]

c) Special instructions

When special instructions are added to the aforementioned text and instruction lineages, it makes three. Although in general there is no contradiction between the instructions and the special instructions, the special instruction that comprises a third category is known as the *Book of Kadam,* the secret Dharma of the noble lord and his spiritual sons. That special instruction was given by the great noble lord to the trio of Khutön, Ngok Lotsāwa, and Dromtönpa at his retreat place in the upper reaches[391] of Lhari Nyingpo, in Yerpa. What is known as the Father Teachings was requested by the father

[73] Dromtönpa, and what is known as the Son Teachings was requested by the two sons, Ngok Lotsāwa Lekpai Sherap and Khutön Tsöndrü Yungdrung. Although at first Khutön had showed disrespect to Dromtönpa Rinpoché, at this time the great Khu crushed the mountain of his own conceit and bowed his head to the feet of Dromtönpa Rinpoché. This is evident from the *Book of Kadam* in the verses of praise related to Khutön and to his pure visions.[392]

When he was about to pass into nirvana, the noble lord gave these special instructions to Geshé Dromtönpa, saying, "Give the three—the text, the instructions, and the special instructions—to the three brothers, who are, above all, emanation bodies." So, those special instructions were his final advice. Of the three brothers, Puchungwa possessed the instructions completely, Chengawa possessed most of them, and Potowa just a portion of them. Master Namkha Rinchen states:

> Puchungwa Shönu Gyaltsen possessed them completely,
> Chengawa Tsültrim Bar held most of them,
> And Potowa Rinchen Salwa was clear only on portions.
> Nowadays, only I am left.[393]

This is how the special instructions came to Puchungwa: Ngok Lotsāwa Lekpai Sherap handed them over to Ngaripa Sherap Gyaltsen, and he in turn handed them over to Puchungwa Shönu Gyaltsen.

From him, it descended in stages until it came to Drom Kumāramati.[394] Up to this point, it had been a word lineage; Drom broke open the word seal and gave it to a few disciples. After that, the lineage descended in stages, and after the First Dalai Lama, Gendün Drupa, received it from Lochen Thukjé Palwa, it was propagated extensively throughout Ü and Tsang.

The practice of this special instruction is the five recollections. The root text says:

> Remember your lama is the object of refuge.
> See your body in the nature of the deity.
> Make your speech continuously recite the mantra,
> Think of all beings as your parents,
> Analyze the empty nature of your mind: By pulling the oars
> of those five,
> Purify all the roots of virtue.[395]

The essence of the special instruction is the practice of the sixteen drops.[396] The qualities of the practice, it is stated, are such that one will become expert in the practice of anything from the vinaya up to the Vajrayana, even in a single session, and that exacting conduct will arise within the context of an elevated view. The deities are four: Śākyamuni Buddha, Avalokiteśvara, Tārā, and Acala, and the Dharma is the Tripiṭaka: together those are called the sevenfold deities and Dharmas. [74]

You may wonder whether the Kadampas have mantra teachings. The special instruction on the sixteen drops that I have just explained is the union of sutra and mantra. Moreover, the arrangement of the Muni's three pledges—the monastic, bodhisattva, and tantric vows—the cycle of practices of Acala, the fasting ritual based on Ārya Avalokiteśvara,[397] and other practices, were very widespread among the Kadampas. Many Kadam secret-mantra special-instruction traditions have survived to this day: the text known as the *One Hundred Printed at Narthang,* in which Chim Jampaiyang compiled a multitude of scattered special instructions of the noble lord, the instructions on Avalokiteśvara given by the noble lord to Geshé Laksorwa, and also guidelines on the four deities and other practices.

The noble lord wanted to teach Saraha's *Treasury of Dohas* in order to stop the spread of crude Dharma traditions that were claimed as mantra before the noble lord came to Tibet. Dromtönpa stopped him, however, saying, "This is not appropriate for Tibet." The early Kadampas were very strict about secret mantra in general and highest yoga tantra in particular. In actuality, though, the noble lord secretly gave Drom Rinpoché the complete special instructions on the four classes of tantra; and in particular on the ultimate special instructions on the father tantra *Guhyasamāja,* the mother tantra *Cakrasaṃvara,* and highest yoga tantra in general, as well the special instructions on the seven adept texts and the three essential works of Saraha.[398] Thus, the noble Drom was the lord of the complete teaching of sutra and mantra. It is not that the Kadampas do not have secret mantra instructions, therefore, but rather that they do not proclaim them in the marketplace. This may be understood by looking in detail at the biographies of the individual Kadampas.

Not only that, but secret mantra is also central to the practice of the *Lamp for the Path to Enlightenment,* the chief Kadam Dharma teaching. This is so because it would not be a practice of the complete teaching without it, and because it is directly indicated in the *Lamp for the Path to Enlightenment*'s own words.[399] One also may understand it on the basis of the statement in the

Great Treatise on the Stages of the Path to Enlightenment, in the section on the special qualities of the *Lamp for the Path to Enlightenment:* "It was taught as a combination of the essential points of both sutra and mantra, so its subject matter is complete."[400] [75]

2) A general synopsis of the actions and conduct of subsequent holy Kadam beings

The general synopsis of the actions and conduct of those holy Kadam beings who came subsequently: According to the *Lamp Illuminating Dharma History:*

> The Kadampas' personal excellence: The short lineage from Geshé Dromtönpa was a lineage of men who were good and stable. In their equanimity and broad-mindedness, they were not in discord with the values of other philosophical systems or ways of life, yet they did not confuse them. There was little impurity in their relations with sentient beings, and they had the great thought to benefit all. They trained by climbing up from below, yet their view was from on high. In hardship they did not complain, while in happiness their renunciation was even greater. Their mind training was not all obvious, but it covered a great deal of ground. Their lives were very simple, yet they were not distracted even when using fine things. They could be very clearly understood, yet their depth was unfathomable. They were pleasant companions, yet were not conceited when someone admired them. They took praise lightly, yet were very weighty.[401] They used ornate poetry little, relying instead on Dharma language. They had few arguments or idle words yet established their meaning clearly. They used few cutting words or insults, and they were expert at conveying meaning to others' ears. They did not mix up any of the textual systems and yet taught them to be without contradiction. They made the Tripiṭaka a support for the special instructions, and they considered the special instructions to be related to the four aspects of the path of conduct. They did not discuss the flaws in Dharmas or persons, nor did they listen to evil friends. They did not announce the extent of their knowledge and special instructions but were highly familiar with all objects

> of knowledge. They did not take sides with sects and monasteries but were pleased with the faithful. They knew the lama as buddha and saw friends through their great pure vision. Their punctiliousness and strictness were great, their grasping or attachment small. They always reflected when about to act and afterward examined what they had done. Keeping themselves in a low place, they held sway over countless teachings. Abandoning debased worldly acts, they trained completely in the Tripiṭaka. Those great beings are as shown above. Those whose lives were pure like that also are called "the Kadampas of the noble lord," "those possessing the seven deities and Dharmas," and the "word lineage [76] of the great Muni." Emulating action and conduct like theirs, practice from the depths of your heart.[402]

If you consider those statements in detail, each has major implications. A synopsis of the actions and conduct of Potowa and his students is also found in the *Beautiful Lotus Biography,* which is mainly about the actions and conduct of ordinary Kadampas. Thus, although there are some very marvelous stories, I have not laid them out here, for fear of excess. You should learn about them from *Lamp Illuminating Dharma History* and other texts, and cultivate faith in them and make them the basis of your aspiration.

Concluding verses

> In a place far from elaborate thoughts of selfish pursuits,
> Wearing the Benares cloth of shame and modesty,
> They sit upon the deerskin pelt of conscientiousness,
> Legs crossed in the posture of mindfulness and introspection.[403]
>
> At their crown, the three jewels are bound into a topknot;
> On their body the white Brahmā thread of four deities is worn;
> From their mouth the secret words of the Tripiṭaka are recited;
> The vase of their mind is filled with the nectar of the three trainings.
>
> In the hearth of the conventional awakening mind
> Blazes the ritual fire[404] of the ultimate awakening mind;
> Into it, the sticks of the self-cherishing attitude and
> The clarified butter of the egoistic view are offered up for burning.

Hearing the lifestories of the host of Kadam sages,
Who are clean outside and clean inside like the interior
Of a lotus, I relate this, my mind enthralled;
Even my tongue, I think, is fortunate.

Since the Kadam is in harmony with all philosophical systems,
And thoroughly free of bias and contention,
I have held it up as a crown ornament
And spoken only briefly about its history.

From *The Crystal Mirror: An Excellent Explanation Showing the Sources and Assertions of All Philosophical Systems,* this completes the explanation of the history of the Kadam philosophical system.

6. The Kagyü Tradition[405]

[II. The History of Philosophical Systems in Tibet, the Land of Snows
B. The histories of the different schools]

3. Kagyü[406]

> They're drunk on the nectar of the deep definitive meaning,
> Resting forever without arising, entrance, or elaboration [77]
> Within the original clear light, the ultimate, basic nature:
> I now relate the history of the philosophical system known
> as the Kagyü.

THE HISTORY of the Kagyü is threefold: a. The history of the individual Kagyü lineages, b. A presentation of their views, meditative practices, and so forth, and c. A brief analysis of the latter.

a. The history of the individual Kagyü lineages
1) Origins of the name Kagyü

In some later Drukpa Kagyü writings, which only consider that Marpa, Milarepa, and Lingrepa wore white garments, it is written as Kargyü ("white lineage," *dkar brgyud*), but the consensus is that it is Kagyü ("oral lineage," *bka' brgyud*). Since Kagyüpas are upholders of the instruction lineage *(gyü)* of the special oral *(ka)* tradition, they are known as such.

2) History of the Kagyü in general

The Kagyü are twofold: upholders of the lineage of Marpa and upholders of the lineage of Khyungpo. Marpa had the instructions of the special oral tradition that came from Vajradhara through Tilopa (tenth century)[407] and Nāropa (d. 1040/42),[408] so upholders of that Dharma lineage are called Kagyüpas.

How the teachings of the special oral tradition were derived: Tilopa possessed the teachings of the four special oral traditions:

(1) There is the special oral tradition from Vajradhara, King Indrabhūti,[409] the yoginī Lulé Gyurpa,[410] the world-ruler Bhisukalpa, Saraha, Nāgārjuna, and Tilopa, in which the teachings include Guhyasamāja, the *Four Seats Tantra,* and, of the six Dharmas of Nāropa,[411] the instructions on the illusory body and transference of consciousness.

(2) There is the special oral tradition from Vajradhara, Jñānaḍākinī, Kukkuripa,[412] Caryāpa,[413] and Tilopa, in which the teachings include Mahāmāyā and, of the six Dharmas, the instruction on dreams.

(3) There is the special oral tradition from Vajradhara, Vajrapāṇi,[414] Ḍombi Heruka,[415] Bhinasavajra,[416] Kambala,[417] and Tilopa, in which the teachings include countless mother tantras, such as Cakrasaṃvara, and, of the six Dharmas, the instruction on clear light.

(4) There is the special oral tradition from Vajradhara, Vajrapāṇi, Anaṅgavajra,[418] Padmavajra,[419] Dakima Bhagabhadrī, and Tilopa, in which the teachings include Hevajra [78] and, of the six Dharmas, the instruction on inner heat.

Some slight discrepancies in the identification and ordering of the four special oral traditions are apparent in different sources.[420]

In addition, the scholar-adept Khyungpo had the instructions of the special oral tradition that derives from the two wisdom ḍākinīs and others, so the upholders of that lineage are also declared to be Kagyüpas. Thus, the Kagyü is twofold: the Shangpa Kagyü and the Dakpo Kagyü.

3) History of the specific Kagyü lineages

a) Shangpa Kagyü[421]

What is said of its inception: The Shangpa Kagyü is the lineage transmitted from the scholar-adept Khyungpo (d. 1135?).[422] A member of the Khyungpo clan, he practiced Bön during his youth. Displeased with that, he trained in Dzokchen. Unsatisfied even by that, he studied translation in Nepal with Sumati and then went to India, the source of Dharma. For about fifty years, he traveled back and forth among India, Nepal, and Tibet. In India and Nepal, he had a hundred and fifty gurus who were scholars and adepts, and he gained an understanding of countless texts and special instructions of both sutra and mantra. His four ordinary gurus were Mahāvajrāsana, Maitrīpa,[423] Guptayoga, and Rāhula. The extraordinary gurus were the wisdom ḍākinīs Niguma and Sukhasiddhi. Those six were his main gurus.

Niguma (eleventh century?) was the consort of Nāropa. After attaining the rainbow body, she became the leader of an assembly of ḍākinīs and met Khyungpo. She gave him many instructions, for instance on the initiations into the path of the illusory body, the vajra verses related to the six Dharmas, the stages of the path of Mahāmāyā, and so forth. Khyungpo also received from Maitrīpa the Dharma cycle of the gnosis protector Mahākāla.

After Khyungpo returned to Tibet, he took full ordination from Langri Thangpa. When he was staying on Jokpo Mountain in Phenyül, Guru Rāhulaguptavajra brought the Dharma to his doorstep from India, giving him countless instructions, both well known and unknown, on the initiations of the five classes of tantra,[424] the cycles of teaching about the gnosis protector, and so forth. As prophesied by a ḍākinī, Khyungpo went to Yeru, [79] in Shang province, and within three years he founded 108 monasteries, the chief of which was the monastery of Shongshong. Thenceforth, the lineage was called the Shangpa Kagyü. He assembled eighty thousand monks and worked in Shang for the sake of beings for thirty years. There are many amazing stories about him: he simultaneously manifested 108 bodily forms, passed unobstructed through a rocky mountain, dwelled inside a jar for a week, taught the Dharma while sitting in space, and so forth.

Although his disciples were countless, the main ones were:[425] Meutönpa, Yarpo Gyamoché, Ngültön Rinwang, Latö Könchokar, Mokchokpa Rinchen Tsöndrü, and Shangom Chöseng. A disciple of Mokchokpa's was Kyergangpa Chökyi Sengé; his disciple was Nyentön Chökyi Sherap, whose disciple was Sangyé Tönpa. From here on, the lineage is called the lineage of the seven precious lineage members.

Sangyé Tönpa's disciple Ai Sengé administered the monastic seat. The Shangpa split into two schools, Jak and Sam, named after the Jak center, which had been founded by Shangtön, and the Samding center, which had been founded by Khetsün Shönu Drup. Shangtön's disciple was Gyaltsen Bum, from whose disciple, Jakchen Jampa Pal, the great Lama Jé Tsongkhapa received some of the Shang Dharma. The omniscient Khedrup Jé received the cycle of the six-armed gnosis protector from Muchen Namkhai Naljorpa, who was in the disciple lineage of Jakpa. Phagö Künga Sangpo founded Tanak Dorjé Den Monastery. His spiritual son was Drenchok Dönyö Gyaltsen. Drenchok's spiritual son, Jé Künga Gyaltsen—the spiritual father of the

Second Dalai Lama, Gendün Gyatso—as well as the later great adept known as Thangtong Gyalpo were also upholders of the Shang Dharma lineage, so it is clear that the Shang Dharma spread in the Chakzam area as well.[426]

The principal Shang Dharmas are: the initiations of each of the five classes of tantras:[427] Cakrasaṃvara, Hevajra, Mahāmāyā, Guhyasamāja, and Vajrabhairava; the initiation of vow; the illusory body of Maheśvarī:[428] the five ḍākinī oral traditions; the six Dharmas of Niguma;[429] the stages of the path of Mahāmāyā; the miraculous wheel of immortality; the cycle of Sukhasiddhi's transformation practice, and so forth; the amulet-box Mahāmudrā; the Dharma cycle of the gnosis protector;[430] the five deities of Cakrasaṃvara; the secret practice of Vajravārahī; [80] the initiation traditions of Avalokiteśvara, Visphoṭaka, Vajrapāṇi, Acala, and others; and the Kyergang-system practices of Avalokiteśvara, Hayagrīva, and others.[431] These are quite common in all philosophical systems.

The so-called amulet-box Mahāmudrā is the instruction on manifesting clear light through meditating on bliss and emptiness as inseparable, like the joined halves of an amulet box. In its key points, it seems the same as the Mahāmudrā of the Dakpo Kagyü. Since no major works written by the scholar-adept Khyungpo are extant, I do not know in detail how he posited his view. In a sādhana on the inseparability of the lama and the protector Mahākāla, however, such phrases as "realization has arisen when one has cut the cord of thought as though severing a tree trunk at the root," "worldly appearances free themselves," and "there is nothing to be thought," and others, seem similar to the language of Dakpo Mahāmudrā practitioners.

b) Dakpo Kagyü

The Dakpo Kagyü arose from Marpa Lotsāwa Chökyi Lodrö (1012–97).[432] Initially, he studied translation with Drokmi. Later, he went to India three times and to Nepal four times. He met 108 gurus who were scholars and adepts: the great pandit Nāropa, Lord Maitrīpa, the glorious Jñānagarbha, the great adept Śāntibhadra, and others. He trained in detail in the explanations and special instructions, as well as the praxis related to the yogas of the father and mother tantras, such as Guhyasamāja and others. Through his reliance on Maitrīpa, he gained an ultimate realization of Mahāmudrā.[433] When he returned to Tibet, he developed many disciples, the chief of whom were known as the four great pillars: Ngoktön Chöku Dorjé, Tsurtön Wangé, Metön Tsönpo, and Milarepa.

The special oral tradition of the stream of explanation went to three of those, Mé, Ngok, and Tsur, so those who came successively in that disciple lineage spread and propagated widely the explanations of the initiations and tantras of Guhyasamāja, Cakrasaṃvara, Hevajra, the *Four Seats,* Mahāmāyā, and others. The explanation of the initiation and tantra of Guhyasamāja from the lineage of Tsurtön Wangi Dorjé passed down to the omniscient Butön and the great conqueror Tsongkhapa. [81]

The special oral tradition of practice went to Milarepa (1040–1123).[434] He was born in Gungthang, in Ngari. His father died early on, and his uncle and aunt made him miserable. Becoming disconsolate, he studied magic and slew many enemies. Subsequently, he repented of his sinfulness and went to Marpa, who withheld the Dharma for a while in order to purify Mila's sins, making him undergo many hardships, such as building towers and other labors. In the end, Marpa fully bestowed the initiations and instructions Mila sought. Meditating with fierce dedication and hardship, Mila immediately gained the supreme yogic achievement in that very life. His adept-disciples wore simple cotton clothes and came like flocks of birds in flight. The two main ones were the sun-like Dakpo Lharjé and the moon-like Rechungpa.

On the first of his two trips to India, Rechungpa (1083–1181)[435] received from the guru Balacandra the instructions on the wrathful Vajrapāṇi with the lower body of a garuda. Later, Jetsün Milarepa said to him, "Marpa brought five of the nine existing Dharma cycles of the formless ḍākinī; go and bring the remaining four." So Rechungpa went back to India and requested the teachings from Tiphupa, who was a direct disciple of both Nāropa and Maitrīpa. He received many instructions and offered them to his lama Mila back in Tibet. Mila gave them to Ngamzong Tönpa, and the latter wrote various texts. The teachings extending from him are called the Cakrasaṃvara ear-whispered lineage; those extending to others from Rechungpa himself are known as the Rechung ear-whispered lineage.

Mila's sun-like disciple was Dakpo Lharjé (Gampopa, 1079–1153).[436] It is said that in a previous life he was the youth Candraprabha, who asked the Blessed One for the *King of Concentration Sutra.*[437] In this later life, he studied medicine as a youth and became expert in it, so he came to be known as "the physician" *(lharjé).* He took a wife, but his wife died when he was only in his twenties; sad at heart, he took full ordination from the Kadam geshé Shawa Lingpa. He received many Kadam Dharma teachings from Jayülwa, Nyukrumpa, and Chakri Gongkhawa. When he heard of Jé Milarepa, he was captivated; he went to meet him, and Mila happily cared for him. He was given all the instructions in their entirety, and when he meditated, he gained extraordinary [82] realizations. Combining the instructions on the Kadam stages of the path and Mila's Mahāmudrā, he wrote the *Jewel Ornament of Liberation*.[438] Thenceforth, the two rivers of Kadam and Mahāmudrā mingled together. He guided his disciples through the graduated guideline called the yoga of the coemergent Mahāmudrā. The lives of the trio of Marpa, Mila, and Gampopa Dakpo Lharjé are beyond imagining, so I have written of them but briefly; more may be learned about them elsewhere.

The followers of the peerless Dakpo Lharjé are called the Dakpo Kagyü. If one analyzes that by way of its internal divisions, one sees that its individual sections are the Karma Kagyü, and also the Phakdru, Tsalpa, Drigung, Drukpa, Taklung, Barom, Yasang, and Trophu Kagyü.

(1) Karma Kagyü[439]

(a) The Black Hats[440]

The Karma Kagyü is the lineage transmitted from the disciple of the peerless Dakpo Lharjé known as Karmapa Düsum Khyenpa, or Khampa Usé (1110–93). He took preliminary ordination at the age of sixteen from Trewo Chokgi Lama. He received instructions of the noble lord Atiśa's lineage from the noble lord's disciple Yöl Chöwang and others. At the age of nineteen, he went to Ü and received teachings on the Maitreya texts, Madhyamaka, and valid cognition from Tölung Gyamarwa and Chapa Chökyi Sengé,[441] studying them until he became expert. He received teachings on the Kadam stages of the path from Sharawa and Madhyamaka from Patsap Lotsāwa.[442] He received full ordination from Mal Dülzin and studied vinaya with him. At the age of thirty-three, he met Dakpo Lharjé and ceased obscuring the essential meaning with superimpositions. In Loro, he met Rechungpa and received as many teachings as possible about Nāropa's and Maitrīpa's instructions on the six Dharmas and other practices. Moreover, he pondered numerous instructions from many gurus. He practiced in many solitary places and thereby reached a high level of achievement. Later [i.e., in 1185], he founded the monastery of Karma Lhadeng, so he was called "Karmapa." He also founded the monastery of Tsurphu [also in 1185]. He was said to be an emanation of the sixth buddha of the fortunate eon, Siṃha. His disciple was Sangyé [83] Rechen, whose disciples were Bomdrakpa[443] and others. Although some say the Black Hat sect is so called because Düsum Khyenpa wore a black hat, in fact it was only after the Mongol king offered Karma Pakshi[444] a black official hat that the line of reincarnations became known as Black Hat.

Nowadays, the king's ministers are distinguished as to high and low office by the tops of their hats; it is a new custom, from the time of the great emperor of the Qing dynasty.[445] However, in the time of the Mongolian and Chinese empires,[446] rank was distinguished by the shape of the hat. Apparently, because of the tradition of offering a black hat with gold embroidery on the front to honored imperial preceptors, the Yunglo emperor (1360–1424) offered such a hat to Jamchen Chöjé[447] and others. The Karmapas claim that their black hat was made from the hair of a million ḍākinīs, who offered it to Düsum Khyenpa. They make many proclamations of its greatness, but I suspect these reports are exaggerated. By the same token, since the official hat given to Tokden Drakpa Sengé was red, it is obvious why his lineage is called the Red Hat.

Karma Pakshi (1204–83)[448] was a disciple of Bomdrakpa. Some say he was a reincarnation of Düsum Khyenpa, but in no reliable history does he appear as a rebirth of Düsum, although he is reputed to be an emanation of Saraha. Nevertheless, when the Karmapa line was reckoned, he was made the second.

Pakshi is Mongolian for "master," so Karma Pakshi became known thus when he went to Mongolia. His official title was actually Chökyi Lama. Just before Pakshi died, he handed over the monastic seat to the adept Urgyenpa and said, "An upholder of the Black Hat lineage will come from the direction of Nyima Latö.[449] In the meantime, act as regent." He placed on the head of Urgyenpa the black hat with the gold front. Not long after that, he passed into nirvana, and his reincarnation was born in the birthplace of Mila, Latö; this was the trulku Rangjung Dorjé.

Thus, the first of the Karma line was Düsum Khyenpa. The second was Pakshi. From there came the successive trulkus: the third was Rangjung Dorjé (1284–1339);[450] the fourth was Rölpai Dorjé (1340–83);[451] the fifth was Deshin Shekpa (1384–1415);[452] the sixth was Tongwa Dönden (1416–53);[453] the seventh was Chödrak Gyatso (1454–1506);[454] the eighth was Mikyö Dorjé (1507–54);[455] the ninth was [84] Wangchuk Dorjé (1556–1603);[456] the tenth was Chöying Dorjé (1604–74);[457] the eleventh was Yeshé Dorjé (1676–1702);[458] the twelfth was Jangchup Dorjé (1703–32);[459] the thirteenth, now living, is Düdül Drakpa Dorjé (1733–97).[460] That is the sequence.

(b) The Red Hats

Jetsün Tilopa's disciple Dāsānanda died and was reborn in Jālandhara[461] as a brahman disciple of Nāropa named Sarvavid who came to Tibet and met with

Jetsün Milarepa. He died while living a life of austerity in the Nepal-Tibet border area and was reborn as Tsültrim Pal, who became a disciple of Jé Gampopa and Rechungpa. His reincarnation, the fully ordained monk Namkha Ö, was a disciple of Jé Düsum Khyenpa. Namkha Ö's reincarnation, Tashi Drakpa, became a disciple of Karma Pakshi. Tashi Drakpa's reincarnation was Tokden Drakpa Sengé (1283–1349). Drakpa Sengé had many lamas, such as Jé Rangjung Dorjé, and he studied sutra and mantra extensively. He possessed the countless good qualities of scriptural study and inner realization. He also had many disciples, such as Yakdé Panchen. Drakpa Sengé's reincarnation was the second Red Hat trulku, Khachö Wangpo (1350–1405).[462] His reincarnation was the third, Chöpal Yeshé (1406–52). His reincarnation was the fourth Red Hat crown holder, Chökyi Drakpa Yeshé Pal Sangpo (1453–1524).[463] Then came the fifth, Könchok Yenlak (1525–83),[464] the sixth, Garwang Chökyi Wangchuk (1584–1638),[465] the seventh, Palden Yeshé Nyingpo (1639–94),[466] and the eighth, Chökyi Döndrup (1695–1732).[467] After that, there were several purported Red Hat reincarnations, and the rebirth lineages of Gyaltsap, Pawo, and Situ also appeared.

(c) Later history

The members of the Red and Black Hat reincarnation lineages led lives that were mostly those of scholars and adepts, and they also wrote many treatises. The astrological treatise and account of the previous lives of the Buddha and other works written by Rangjung Dorjé spread widely. Mikyö Dorjé was an expert in all the sciences of inner meaning[468] and therefore wrote a great many excellent works. Although on the face of it he wrote refutations of Jé Rinpoché (Tsongkhapa), out of heartfelt respect he urged Sera Jetsünpa to write a reply to Gorampa and Shākya Chokden;[469] and although he himself wrote a textbook on the perfection of wisdom elucidating the meaning of the Maitreya texts as extrinsic emptiness *(shentong),*[470] he stated whatever was proper and necessary for refutation and proof, so when Sera Jetsünpa and his spiritual sons in turn offered written objections, replies, and so forth, he was very pleased. It is also said that he later had a vision of Jé Rinpoché. Be that as it may, [85] he did write a repentant confession and a eulogy of Tsongkhapa.

Mikyö Dorjé's disciple Pawo Tsuklak Trengwa (1504–66) is also rightly reckoned a sage. He wrote many texts, such as the *Great Commentary on the Way of the Bodhisattva,* a treatise on astrology, a Dharma history, and others.[471] Chökyi Nyinjé (1699/1700–1774)[472] of the Situ reincarnation lineage founded the teaching center of Palpung in Dergé, Kham. It seems there was never a latter-day expert in the conventional sciences greater than he. He made new and revised translations, and he wrote a great many texts on the sciences. A biography of him contains this statement:

> Situ first held the Madhyamaka view, but when a Nyingmapa prophesied that he would have a long life if he adopted the Jonang view, he went to the vicinity of the Bodhnāth stupa, renounced the Madhyamaka view, and vowed, "I will uphold the extrinsic emptiness view."[473]

This statement is in a biography whose author's head is so rotten, he cannot smell it himself.

Since each Karmapa had many disciples and grand-disciples, their teaching spread with many Karma-tradition Dharma lineages and monasteries here, there, and everywhere. When the time was right, and they saw that it would be meaningful, Karmapa Mikyö Dorjé, Pawo Tsuklak Trengwa, Drukpa Pema Karpo, and others engaged in extensive activities related to the sciences and other outer pursuits. Since then, most Karmapas and Drukpas have turned their attention to conventional activities, and I think that the assiduous practice of earlier times has deteriorated somewhat.

Norbu Sangpo (d. 1466), who belonged to the line of Rinpung rulers, became the patron of Sempa Shönu Gyalchokpa,[474] and being in a preceptor-patron relationship with the Gedenpas, he erected a great Maitreya statue and performed other works in Jamchen.[475] Some of the Rinpung rulers, however, such as his successor, Künsang Dönyö Dorjé,[476] were very hostile to the Gelukpas and repeatedly assembled armies in Kyishö and made many preparations for an attempt to eliminate the Gedenpas. Later[477] there was a popular uprising against the poet-savant Jikten Wangchuk, and he lost power. Subsequently, Karma Tseten,[478] his son Phüntsok Namgyal,[479] and Phüntsok's son Karma Tenkyong Wangpo[480] ruled in Tsang. When those in a preceptor-patron relationship made trouble for the Gedenpas, it was like the example quoted in Sakya Pandita's *Well-Spoken Advice from Sakya:*

> A torch held downward
> Will scorch the hand of the [86] holder.[481]

[In 1642,] Gushri Tenzin Chögyal (b. 1582)[482] came to Tibet from Kokonor and utterly destroyed the Karmapas' power with his military. If at that time the upholders of the Karmapa teaching had abided in the nature of Mahāmudrā—which, with its impartiality toward philosophical systems, is free from the elaborations of prejudice, anxiety, and so forth—then even though their patrons' power declined, it goes without saying that the great fluctuations of the Karmapa teaching would not have occurred. As a Tibetan sage says, "Mahāmudrā meditators became more and more politically active."[483] Trusting the bad advice of Karma Tenkyong and others, the Karmapas performed all sorts of deluded actions out of inner conviction, and so from then on, the Karmapa teaching went into decline. Much later, [in 1791,] an evil Gurkha army sacked Tashi Lhünpo[484] because of the schemes of the purported Red Hat trulku, Chödrup Gyatso (1741–92), and in retaliation the Chinese emperor obliterated Yangpachen and other Red Hat monasteries.[485]

At the present time, the Karmapa teaching has greatly deteriorated, so the Black Hat trulku just lives in Tsurphu, concentrating on the four trainings of a recluse. That is all that remains.

(2) Phakdru Kagyü

The Phakdru Kagyü[486] is the lineage transmitted from the conqueror Phakmo Drupa (1110–70),[487] who was the main spiritual son of the peerless Dakpo Lharjé and was consecrated as lord of the Kagyü. He was born in southeastern Tibet. When he reached age seven, a state of tranquil abiding arose in him naturally. At the age of nine, he took preliminary ordination at the so-called Jakhyi temple from the preceptor known as Lhingé Yenthup Tsültrim and master Lhingé Öser Gyatso.[488] He was given the name Dorjé Gyalpo. He knew writing and religious drawing without training. While he stayed in Kham, he studied under some sixteen masters. He also gave occasional expositions of the *Way of the Bodhisattva*. At the age of nineteen, he went to Ü. In Tölung, he received the Dharma from Geshé Gyamarwa and Chapa Chökyi Sengé. When he was twenty-five, with Jadül as preceptor, Gyamar as master, and Ar as secret instructor, he took full ordination in Sülphu. He received vinaya teachings [87] from his preceptor and master, the perfection of wisdom from his secret instructor, and the *Way of the Bodhisattva* and other works from Nyangdren, and gained fame as a great sage. Moreover, studying with Mar Chögyal, Palchen Dralo, Sachen

Künga Nyingpo, Jim Lotsāwa, and Jangsem Dawa Gyaltsen, he received many instructions on sutra and mantra. Then he went to Gampo, and by hearing instructions from the peerless Dakpo Lharjé, he gained a supreme realization of Mahāmudrā and reportedly said: "All previous Dharmas have become like skin and husk." After he built his monastic seat on a lovely forest slope in Phakmo Dru, he became known as "Phakmo Drupa Dromgön, the protector of beings"; and when he stayed at the base of the Jewel Heap Boulder, he became known as Tatsawa, "the one at the base." Also, he believed himself to have the same nature as the Blessed One, Śākyamuni. When he developed his disciples, many became adepts. Of the eight hundred monks who were disciples, it is reputed that five hundred became great parasol-bearing scholars.

In particular, there were the great ārya sons. Those called the four utmost sons were: Taklung Thangpa Tashi Pal, utmost in devotion; Lingrepa Pema Dorjé of Naphu, utmost in realization; Parphupa Lodrö Sengé, utmost in wisdom; and Chenbu[489] Gyarepa, utmost in ability. Those called the four sons of the teaching were: Kalden Yeshé Sengé, Tokden Minyak Gomring, Drupthop Nyakri Sewo, and Künden Tsangpa Rechung. Those called the three-and-a-half who realized the single taste were: the Dharma lord Drigung Jikten Gönpo, Bandha Phukpa, the Dharma lord Dum, and the Dharma lord Tum. Those called the four heart sons were: Shengom Karwa, Nyang Shendrongma, Ngok Sengé Khapa, and Tsilungpa. Those called the four literary sons were: Rinpoché Shuktsarpa, Lhapa Gendün Kyap, Drugu Tönpa Lodrö Sengé, and Gyana Thangpo. Those called the four close sons were: Lama Marwa, Yephukpa, Gyergom, and Geshé Sengé Pal. Moreover, there were beings beyond number who became adepts.

After Dromgön Phakmo Drupa, Kyura Rinpoché briefly administered Densa Thil. After him came Chenga Drakpa Jungné, born in the family of Lang Lhasik. Then came, successively: Chenga Thokdukpa, Chunyipa Rinchen Dorjé,[490] Rinpoché Drakpa Yeshé, Nyichöpa Drakpa Rinchen, [88] Tseshi Nyingmapa Drakpa Gyaltsen, and Chunyi Sarmapa Drak Sherap. The latter's elder brother, Jangchup Gyaltsen (1302–64),[491] became the ruler of Ü and Tsang. Tseshi Sarma Drakpa Jangchup's[492] spiritual biography is in a collection of short texts written by the conqueror Tsongkhapa. After Tseshi came many more, such as Dharma lord Sönam Gyaltsen,[493] Chenga Palden Sangpo,[494] and Nyernyi Rinpoché.

In particular, the Dharma lord Sönam Gyaltsen (1345–1407) became a disciple of Jetsün Tsongkhapa the great. He combined in a single text both the old instruction on the six Dharmas of Nāropa and the new instruction on the same six Dharmas as posited by Jé Tsongkhapa; he wrote a guidebook called the *Great Bliss with Thousands of Illuminating Light Rays,* which applied such sources as Saraha's *Treasury of Dohas,* Nāgārjuna's *Five Stages,* and other tantric texts. A great many Kagyü centers and monasteries spread from the monastic seat at Phakdru; some I will explain below.

(3) Shangtsal Kagyü

The Shangtsal Kagyü[495] is the lineage transmitted from Shang Drowai Gönpo Yudrakpa (1123–93).[496] He was born in Kyishö and was named Darma Drak. From age nine to eighteen, he received many teachings on sutra and mantra. At twenty-six, he took full ordination and was given the name Tsöndrü Drakpa. He received many instructions from Galo. He met Dakpo Lharjé's disciple Gampopa Tsültrim Nyingpo and, when he received teachings on Mahāmudrā, won the blessings of the oral lineage *(kagyü).* He plainly saw the nature of mind. He erected the Gungthang temple in Tsal, along with its great image. He had a great purpose in mind, yet he made much trouble, and many ordinary beings amassed evil through this, so Karma Düsum Khyenpa stopped him. From then on he made no trouble. Having manifested seven transformed bodies in seven places, he became known as Seven Names. He did whatever he was told by the raven-headed Dharma protector. He performed [89] countless pure deeds and passed into nirvana at seventy-two.

Although he had many disciples, the chief ones were: Namkha Ö, Kharakpa Dülwa Ö, Lhachukpa Nyida Ö, and Drirawa Shākya Ö. All four of those founded monasteries. Dülwa Ö founded Lutül Monastery in Kharak, and it is said that during his leadership, the assembly numbered some ten thousand monks. The actual monastic seat at Tsal was administered by the peerless Shākya Yeshé, and then by Lopön Jangyé, Lhachukpa Nyida Ö, Sangyé Bum, Sangyé Nyingpo, Sangyé Repa, Serkhang Tengpa, and others. Since those, such as Marpa Ö, who came subsequently at Tsal performed service for the teaching, the lineage is also known as the Tsalpa Kagyü.

As long as Tsal was administered by a succession of great leaders, such as Pönchen Darma Shönu and Sangyé Ngödrup, the teaching survived unimpaired. Later, Tsalpa power declined, and the temples were destroyed by fire. Now only statues, texts, stupas,[497] the chapels of protectors, and other remains are left.

(4) Drigung Kagyü

The Drigung[498] is the lineage transmitted from the guardian Jikten Gönpo.[499] His birthplace was Denma, his family the Kyura. He took birth in the water-sow year (1143). He went to meet Dromgön Phakmo Drupa at an early age. He was given the name Rinchen Pal. When he received instruction, he gained the great gnosis that sees directly the real nature of all dharmas. He fell ill with leprosy, and when he meditated on great compassion, the nāga *tsen* demon[500] and his retinue left his body, and he saw them leave. At that, he recovered from the illness. When he reached age twenty-five, he took full ordination, with Sumtokpa acting as preceptor. At age thirty-seven, he went to Drigung and founded a monastery. It gradually expanded, and a large number of monks gathered there. Once, when Nyö Gyalwa Lhanangpa conducted a religious festival,[501] 55,525 monks attended. It is reported that on one occasion, the ritual counting stick [90] recorded a hundred thousand fully ordained monks. Jikten Gönpo's renown pervaded Jambudvīpa, and it was suggested that he was an emanation of Nāgārjuna. At the age of seventy-five (1217), he pretended to pass away.

Although there were countless disciples,[502] chief among them were the four Chengas; the trio of Nyö Gyalwa Lhanangpa, Gar Dampa Chödingpa, and Chö Mönlam; the twelve Palchens; and others. The heads of the monastic seat were Jé Chenga Rinpoché, Wön Rinpoché, Chung Rinpoché, Nyogyalwa Lhanangpa, Gardampa Chödingpa, Palchen Chöyé, Wön Sherap Jungné, and others.

Sherap Jungné (1187–1241) was of the nephew of the guardian Jikten Gönpo. His service to his lama was unbounded, as was his knowledge. He wrote down the 190 special Dharmas posited by the guardian, which are known as the *single intention*.[503] From him, the teaching went in sequence to many in the monastic succession. In later times, Rinchen Phüntsok and Chökyi Drakpa became great Nyingma tantric masters, and his highness the Great Fifth Dalai Lama praised them extensively. Shapdrung Trulung, however, split from the Kagyü Dharma, and Karma Mikyö Dorjé recounts how misfortune occurred when he made the Nyingma cycle on the iron scorpion his main practice. He also directed sorcery against the Third Dalai Lama, Sönam Gyatso. That omniscient one went into retreat, and for a week he performed the practice of the miraculous wheel of the fierce Yamāntaka, so an illness infected the Drigungpas. It seems that from that time when they cut the precious rope of the lineage of the noble guardian Jikten Gönpo, they became virtually extinct. Now, there are few monks, and the monastic seat, though it is near a main road and has some shrines, also remains in difficulty. That notwithstanding, they are known as Drigungpas by the place name of their monastic seat.

(5) Drukpa Kagyü

The Drukpa is the lineage transmitted from the conqueror Phakmo Drupa's disciples Lingrepa Pema Dorjé and the Dharma lord Tsangpa Gyarepa. The adept Lingrepa (1128–88) was born in upper Nyang. He was given the name Pema Dorjé. He learned to read at the age of nine. At thirteen, he gained mastery of all good qualities. When he [91] reached seventeen, he took his lay vows from Master Ling. At thirty-eight, he met Phakmo Drupa. When he received guidelines and meditated on them, he gained an extraordinary realization in three days. When he offered his realization, the protector of beings was delighted. Lingrepa worked extensively for the sake of beings everywhere.

His main disciple was Jetsün Tsangpa Gyaré (1161–1211). He was born in a section of Khulé, in upper Nyang. He was given the name Yungdrung Pal. When he was twelve, his father left him at his older brother's place, where he put in a great deal of study. When he was thirteen, he cut his hair and was given the name Sherap Pal. Later, he took his preliminary vows from Lama Shang and was given the name Yeshé Dorjé. When he was twenty-two, he met Jetsün Lingrepa, who was staying in Ralung. He presented him a full measure of salt and often sought him out for conversation. Then he went to Ü. He met Lingrepa again in Naphu, and seven days after hearing instructions on the six Dharmas, the yoga of the coemergent, and other practices, he gained the ability to wear a cotton garment.[504] He walled himself in for the winter, and when he meditated, he was able to combine the outer and inner winds[505] and pass unobstructed through walls, and he gained a clear concentration on emptiness vast as space. He revealed the *Six About the Taste of Sameness,*[506] which had been hidden as a treasure by Jetsün Rechungpa. As prophesied by Lama Shang, he founded the monastery of Longdöl. As prophesied by his meditational deity, he founded Ralung. As prophesied by Lingrepa, he founded Druk. When the latter was newly built, fierce claps of thunder *(druk)* resounded over the plain, so the monastery was given the name "Druk." Because of that, upholders of the lineage are dubbed "Drukpas." It is said that Tsangpa Gyaré collected some fifty thousand disciples. He did wondrous things for the sake of beings and was reputed to be an emanation of Nāropa. His disciple lineage spread as far as a vulture flies in eighteen days. It is widely remarked[507] that half of all people were Drukpas, half of all Drukpas were mendicants, and half of all mendicants were adepts.

The chief of Tsangpa Gyarepa's many disciples were the first two great ones, Pariwa and Kyangmo Khapa; the middle two great ones, Gyayakpa and Dremopa; the last two great ones, Lorepa and Götsangpa; the three other cotton-clad ones; the three yogins; the three who had destroyed delusions; and others—there were many. Wönré Darma Sengé[508] presided over the monastic seat. After him, those who came [92] in the family lineage and performed great deeds included Gyalwang Chöjé, his disciple Lhatsepa Ngawang Sangpo, and then the poet-sage Sangyé Dorjé, Bökhepa, and others; this excellent disciple lineage was propagated in many places. In particular, the renowned scholar Pema Karpo (1527–92) wrote many commentaries.[509] His reincarnations were Paksam Wangpo and others. Also, there were the two known as Tsangnyön (1452–1507)[510] and Ünyön, and some amazing adepts, like Druknyön Künlek (1455–1529).[511] Those are known as the middle Druk.

The lives of Lorepa and Götsangpa were quite amazing. Specifically, they did many things that should be taken as examples by those doing serious practice, of which the chief is this: through hardship and dedication, they transformed all evil conditions into the path and brought the practice to completion. This can be seen in detail in their individual biographies. Here, I will mention only the basics.

The conqueror Lorepa (1187–1250)[512] took preliminary ordination at Kyormo Lung from the preceptor Balti; the name he was given was Wangchuk Tsöndrü. He took six great vows, six ancillary vows, and one special vow, so his life is one of thirteen vows.[513] He focused on the Muni's instruction on the fivefold.[514] He had countless disciples who were in the family lineage: the three masters (Jamyang Gönpo and others), the three cotton-clad ones (Tsāri Rechen and others), the three yogins (Ā, Lo, and Shākya), and others. Of these, Jamyang Gönpo (b. 1208)[515] spread widely the Chö instructions called the *heart essence of profound meaning* and the *tenfold door-opener*. Tsāri Repa developed the tradition through his extensive activities, so there were many disciples. Those are known as the lower Druk.

The original name of Götsangpa Gönpo Dorjé (1189–1258)[516] was Döndrup Sengé. He was given the name Gönpo Dorjé when he took preliminary ordination from Tsangpa Gyaré. He has a lifestory that is beyond imagining: twelve mental vows; the thirteen coats of armor;[517] three vows of body, speech, and mind; seven temporary vows; five especially distinctive vows; and others. His four main disciples were: the conqueror Yangönpa, the adept [93] Urgyenpa, Chilkarwa, and Neringpa. Moreover, those disciples had many disciples, including Yangönpa's disciple, Chenga Rinden. His disciple was Surphukpa Rinchen Palsang. Surphukpa's disciple was Barawa Gyaltsen Palsang, who wrote many treatises, including the trilogy on the *Boat of Liberation*[518] and other works. Those many disciples are known as the upper Druk.

The adept Urgyenpa Rinchen Pal (1229/30–1309) went to Bodhgaya, Jālandhara, and Uḍḍiyāna in India. There he was blessed by many ḍākinīs, so his mental continuum was freed through his realizations. Invited by Kublai,[519] the king of Mongolia, he went there, too. Disciples who were upholders of his Dharma lineages were Karma Rangjung Dorjé, Tokden Daseng, and others. Shonglo Dorjé Gyaltsen and Loten also became his disciples. Also in his disciple lineage was Götruk Drakpa Jungné.

Chilkar did not take on any disciples. Neringpa was known as Gangchen Shākya Pal and founded the monastery of Nering. Estimable members of the family lineage succeeded him; Neringpa Chimé Rapgyé, the biographer of Jé Rinpoché,[520] is in the family lineage.

Therefore, the lineage transmitted from Lorepa is called the lower Druk, and the lineage from master Götsang and his disciples is called the upper Druk. They are renowned for being so numerous that "the upper Druk is the stars in the sky and the lower Druk is the greenery of the earth." At the present time, the upper, lower, middle, and other Drukpa are widespread and well off, but it seems that the Dharma lineages are for the most part barely intact.

(6) Taklung Kagyü

The Taklung Kagyü is the lineage transmitted from the great Taklung Thangpa (1142–1210). His family was the Gazi. He was born in Yangshö Bongra Teng. He ordained as a novice with Tönla Gangpa Sherap Dorjé as preceptor.[521] The name given him was Tashi Pal. Although he prepared several times to go to India, his friends and other acquaintances would not let him go. Then, he heard of the fame of Phakmo Drupa, and at age twenty-four, [94] he went to him and became his attendant. Phakdru loved him and gave him the instructions in their entirety. Once, Tashi Pal went to relax in a meadow in Tel,[522] and on that spot he entered meditative equipoise and gained an extraordinary realization. When the protector of beings Phakmo Drupa got there, he pointed his walking stick at Tashi Pal's heart and stated, among other things, "Our noble lord Nāropa said, 'If, in the midst of meditating on all dharmas as empty of inherent existence and without self, you practice various methods through the four immeasurables, then that is the path for attaining the nonabiding nirvana.'"[523] Through being granted a profound and extensive introduction to the nature of mind, Tashi Pal experienced the Mahāmudrā yoga of nonmeditation.[524]

After Phakmo Drupa passed away, Tashi Pal went to Maldro and received Kadam teachings from Chekawa. He took full ordination from Shang Shomrawa.[525] At the age of thirty-nine, he was invited to Taklung by the inhabitants of the three centers, Dar, Bé, and Rong, as well as those in Phödo. As prophesied by the protector of beings, he founded a monastery in that place, so he became known as Taklung Thangpa. He also placed a powerful rock *tsen* demon under a vow.[526] From the time he took preliminary vows, he observed the vinaya rituals scrupulously: he never went to the houses of lay people, never asked for meat or liquor, never served meat or liquor, never brought women inside the compound, and so forth. Just before he left his body, over three thousand monks gathered, and he displayed a multitude of wondrous magical powers. He passed away at sixty-nine.

Wön Rinchen Gönpo was put in charge of the monastic seat. He built a great ritual hall and extended the monastery. After him, Sangyé Yarjön presided over the monastic seat. He had two disciples capable of holding the throne: Wön Tashi Lama and Sangyé Wön. Sangyé Wönpo Drakpa Pal Öser Sangpo went to Kham and founded the monastery of Riwoché. Thenceforth, the teaching was split into the upper-plain Taklung and the lower-plain Taklung. Thirty-eight hundred monks belonged to each. From there, the Taklung monasteries and Dharma lineage were propagated in many areas in Ü, Tsang, Amdo, Kham, and elsewhere. All who succeeded in the abbatial lineage were eminent persons with amazing qualities. In particular, there was a great scholar-adept in later times named Taklung Ngawang Drakpa (1418–96). Because of his great fame, he was honored by the upper classes of Ü and Tsang. His activities, such as reviving the Dharma traditions of Drigung and Taklung [95] when they were on the verge of extinction, were quite extensive.

The man known as Shapdrung Ngawang Namgyal (1571–1626)[527] had deeply studied countless scriptures and was famous for his scholarship, discipline, and goodness. He spread the Dharma in many places, writing the *Wonderful Ocean Dharma History* and other texts. At present, there appear to be quite a few temples and monks from the family line of Gazi and the reincarnation lineage of the trulkus of the upper-field and lower-field Taklung, but as to how the Dharma lineage and other aspects of the tradition are faring, I have no information.

(7) Barom Kagyü

The Barom[528] Kagyü is the lineage transmitted from Barom Darma Wangchuk (1127–1199/1200), who was reputed to be a reincarnation of the tantric yogin[529] Kṛṣṇācārya.[530] He was born in Phenyül. When he was small, a tiny, youthful tantric master came to his residence and spoke favorably of Gampopa. He said that it would be proper for Darma Wangchuk to go to him and accompanied him on the journey. When they arrived at Gampo, the tiny tantric master disappeared without a trace, and Darma Wangchuk knew that he had been an emanation of Gampopa. From then on, he was looked after by Gampopa, and when he practiced the guidelines he had been given, he became supremely realized. He founded the monastery of Barom in the north.[531] He gave the name *mixture and transference* to the bliss-emptiness Mahāmudrā, and the name *sole pursuit of the narrow path of knowledge* to the ultimate-nature Mahāmudrā.[532] He attracted many disciples and gave them guidance. His main spiritual son was Tishri Repa; the monastic seat was held successively by the latter's family lineage. Apparently, the disciple lineage did not become too widespread. I have not found out how it is faring at present.

(8) Yasang Kagyü

The Yasang Kagyü is the lineage transmitted from Kalden Yeshé Sengé (d. 1207), a disciple of the protector of beings, Phakmo Drupa. He was born in Möngar. Once in his youth when he went to herd goats, he merely saw the mountain of Phakmo Drupa's monastery from an opposite mountain and a meditative state dawned on its own. After that, he met [96] the protector of beings; once they were introduced, he was given the name Kalden Yeshé Sengé. His disciple was Yasang Chöjé (1169–1233), whose family was the Nup. He took his preliminary vows from the preceptor known as Chötön; he was given the name Chö Mönlam. Having received vinaya teachings from Shami Mönlam Ö's disciple Lupkar Tsültrim Drak, he mainly focused on the explanation and praxis of the vinaya, so he became known as the vinaya master of Nup. He heard of the fame of Kalden Yeshé Sengé and went to meet him. Merely by seeing Kalden's face, he gained a realization of his lama's mind and his own mind as nondual. When he was thirty-eight, he founded the monastery of Yasang. He met the seer Rāhula[533] directly in a vision and was given special instructions for protection from strokes.[534] He matured and freed countless human and nonhuman students and passed away at sixty-five.

His disciples[535] were known as the four great sons: Nyalmé Pal Riwa Sangyé Jagom, Gorgongpa Sangyé Lhagom, Serdewa Sangyé Legom, and Gönsarpa Sangyé Gyagom. After that, those who followed in the lineage were known as the Yasang Kagyü. Nowadays, only a temple and a statue of Lhamo known as Quick Action remain at the monastic seat.

(9) Trophu Kagyü

The Trophu Kagyü is the lineage transmitted from the brothers Rinpoché Gyaltsa and Künden Repa, who were disciples of Phakmo Drupa.

Rinpoché Gyaltsa (1118–95) was born in lower Shawa, in the family line of Nup Namkhai Nyingpo. From the age of five, he studied writing and calculation. From the time he was young, he was intent on the Dharma. He received Dharma teachings many times from numerous lamas, such as Nur[536] Nyima and others. At the age of nineteen, he went to Ü. He met a direct disciple of Puhrang Lotsāwa named Mar Chökyi Gyalpo, as well as others, and on the advice of Lama Mar, he went to Phakmo Drupa. When he received instructions from him, he gained an extraordinary realization of Mahāmudrā. He requested teachings on Chö from Machik Lapdrön's son, Thönyön Samdrup. He died at seventy-eight. [97]

Künden Repa (1148–1217) was the younger brother of Rinpoché Gyaltsa. He went to take provisions to his brother at Phakmo Dru when the life of Milarepa was being taught there. Thinking, "I should act like that," he nodded his head three times in that Dharma assembly. He asked the protector of beings for instructions, and by meditating he obtained an extraordinary realization. He became a great adept. Once, during a famine, he knocked on the door of the ritual hall of Trophu with his staff, saying, "O yoginīs, I ask for alms for the yogin today," and a great deal of barley came out the doors of the ritual hall. All the people of the region took some, yet after five days the barley was still not exhausted, another sign of his being an adept. Künden Repa died at the age of seventy, in the fire female ox year.

The nephew of the brothers Rinpoché Gyaltsa and Künden Repa was Trophu Lotsāwa (1173–1225). He took birth as the son of Jephen, his father, and Sekma Saljé, his mother. He learned to read at the age of six. When he was eight, he met Gyaltsa. When he was ten, he became a novice, with Gyaltsa and Künden as preceptor and master respectively; he was given the name Jampa Pal. At nineteen, he took full ordination. From Künden and Gyaltsa, he received 136 different systems of instruction and thirteen special oral traditions. When he was twenty-four, he went to Nepal. He met the pandit Buddhaśrī and invited Mitrayogi to Tibet. The latter blessed the land for the foundation of Trophu. On the heels of that, he also invited Buddhaśrī. After that, he went to the trading center of Vaidurya and invited the Kashmiri pandit Śākyaśrī. He erected a great deity image[537] eighty cubits high. Sempa Chenpo became his spiritual son. Trophu Lotsāwa gained the ability to fulfill the aims of beings and perform countless deeds.

Among the disciples of Gyaltsa and Künden were Chegom and Machik Rema; those in the lineage subsequent to them are called the Trophu Kagyü.

Although it seems as if Trophu Lotsāwa Jampa Pal developed a philosophical system unlike that of other Kagyüpas, in the nine-grain instruction, the four-three-twelve heart discourse, the nine-meaning Mahāmudrā, and other practices taught by him, the stated presentations of the view actually appear to be simply the Kagyü Mahāmudrā. Not only that, but the cycles variously taught here and there by the great pandit Śākyaśrī, which are included within the *Hundreds of Basic Special Instructions of Trophu,* [98] as well as the progression of views in the *Treatise on Freedom from Bondage* taught by Dorjé Denpa, that is, Śākaliṅgadeva,[538] as well as other texts, also accord with the Mahāmudrā.

After Trophu Lotsāwa came Lachen Söwang and Sempa Chenpo; the latter's disciple, Yangtsewa Rinchen Sengé; and Yangtsewa's disciple, Butön Rinpoché. A discussion of how Butön upheld a separate system will appear below.[539]

Although the teaching and study of the great texts once spread in Trophu, it then dissolved as a *hūṃ* does, from the *ū* to the *nāda*.[540] At the present time, just a few in the guise of Bhutanese novices sometimes recite the *Ornament of Higher Realization* just once in front of the great Maitreya statue. That is all that remains.

c) Summary

Well, then, what qualities differentiate that multitude of Kagyü schools, which have different individual names even though they are of one nature?[541] It is as explained in the *Wonderful Ocean Dharma History* of Taklung Ngawang Namgyal:

> In short, atop a foundation of Śrāvakayāna renunciation, Mahayana arousing of the awakening mind, and the pure secret vows of secret mantra are the special Dharmas of the precious Kagyü: Marpa and Ngok's explanations of the tantras, Mila's dedication and instructions, Gampopa's cleansing of the nature of mind, the Karmapas' practice for making wind and mind indistinguishable, Shang's supreme and ultimate path,[542] Barompa's hidden path of mixture and transference, Phakdru's secret mantra, Taklungpa's thirty-nine liberations, Drigungpa's three vows with a single key point, Tsangpa Gyarepa's dependent arising and the taste of sameness, and Lo and Gö's devotion to Dharma and disgust for samsara. Although each is "the same, yet distinctive," each fully possesses all the others; it is suitable to establish their distinct qualities based on how teachers, having focused on some particular practice, guided and developed disciples. In their entirety, they are renowned in the three worlds as "the teaching of the precious Kagyü."[543] [99]

b. A partial exposition of the presentation of view and meditation among the Kagyüpa[544]

1) Views

The view of Marpa, the wellspring of the Dakpo Kagyü, is the Prāsaṅgika Madhyamaka view. Marpa's main gurus were Nāropa and the great Maitrīpa, and whenever Marpa explained any view, meditation, conduct, or tantra, he based it on those two; specifically, there is a statement in Marpa's own songs that Maitrīpa is the guru who completely severed his superimposition:

> I went to the east, to the banks of the Ganges River.
> Through the kindness of the great Jé Maitrīpa,
> I realized the foundation, reality itself, as unarisen.

I took hold of the emptiness of mind,
I saw the meaning of the original nature, free from elaboration,
I met the mother, the three bodies, in person.
From then on, I was a man who had severed elaboration.[545]

When he realized through the kindness of Maitrīpa that mind is ultimately unarisen, he took hold of the real nature of mind, the "original nature of mind," which is empty of true existence. When he meditated on that in connection with the profound path of the completion stage, he attained the three bodies in general and, in particular, the encounter of the mother and son clear lights named *dharmakāya;* through that, all elaboration was severed. So it is stated.

Lord Maitrīpa was not just a Mādhyamika; he gave primacy to the system of the glorious Candrakīrti. According to Maitrīpa's vital text, the *Ten Principles:*

Those who wish to know reality
Don't see it with aspects or without aspects;
That Madhyamaka not adorned
By the guru's speech is merely middling.[546]

"With aspects" refers to the view of the Sautrāntikas, and "without aspects" refers to the view of the Vaibhāṣikas, which are both śrāvaka schools. Alternatively, "with aspects" refers to true aspectarians and "without aspect" refers to false aspectarians, which are both Cittamātrins; neither of them realizes the meaning of reality. Not only that, but Maitrīpa also states that a Madhyamaka not adorned by the guru's special instructions is only a middling Madhyamaka.[547] The instructions of the guru are solely the instructions of the glorious Candrakīrtipāda. So it is explained in the commentary by Maitrīpa's direct disciple, the pandit [100] Sahajavajra.[548]

The great pandit Nāropa also upheld only the system of Candrakīrti. In a commentary on the later tantras, he himself states:

In this commentary on the later tantras,
I have relied on Candrakīrti's *Bright Lamp*
To explain the special instructions of Nāgārjuna.[549]

He also states:

> I have relied on the successive special instructions
> Of masters Nāgārjuna and Āryadeva,
> Nāgabodhi and Śākyamitra,
> Candrakīrti, and others.[550]

Because of those and other statements, and because his explanation of the view precisely resembles that of Candrakīrti, Nāropa was a Prāsaṅgika.[551]

It is said that the view in the songs of Jetsün Milarepa also accords for the most part with the Prāsaṅgika:

> To accord with the thought
> Of inferior minds, the omniscient Buddha
> Stated, "Everything exists."
> In terms of ultimate truth, though,
> There is no buddhahood apart from hindrances.
> There are no meditators nor objects of meditation,
> No stages to be traversed, nor signs of the path,
> No resultant bodies nor gnosis,
> And therefore no nirvana:
> These are merely imputed by name and word.
> There is nothing inanimate or animate in the three worlds:
> From the beginning, all are unestablished and unarisen,
> Baseless and noncoemergent;
> There is no karma nor karmic ripening,
> And therefore not even the name *samsara* exists.
> In the ultimate sense, that's how it is.[552]

This shows how all dharmas, from form through omniscience, are ultimately nonexistent. Also:

> Amazing! If there were no sentient beings,
> Whence would the buddhas of the three times arise?
> Since effect is impossible without a cause,
> In terms of conventional truth,
> The Muni has stated: "Samsara
> And nirvana: all exists."[553]

Thus, although they do not truly exist, conventionally samsara and nirvana, action and actor, cause and effect, are all existent. Also:

> Sages with such realization
> Don't see consciousness but see gnosis,
> Don't see sentient beings but see buddhas,
> Don't see phenomena but see reality itself.[554]

The gnosis of an ārya in meditative equipoise sees emptiness through direct perception. While it does not see what appears to a mistaken consciousness, it does see what appears to an unmistaken gnosis. In the seeing in which that gnosis sees reality itself, there is nothing that could be qualified as a sentient being. "Buddha" is reality itself, which is named [101] *dharmakāya*. Thus, it may be said that the view postulated by Milarepa is very much in accord with the Prāsaṅgika Madhyamaka.

Now, Marpa had 108 gurus who were scholar-adepts, and he mastered countless instructions received from them; seeing the mental capacity of some of his disciples, he set out instructions in accord with Cittamātra. Also, in some places in the religious songs of Milarepa, he identifies the four yogas, and it seems that he explains the view in the yogas in terms of Madhyamaka or Cittamātra, as befits the case. Thus, earlier authoritative holy beings like Marpa, Milarepa, and other masters who were expert at guiding disciples saw the intellectual capacity of those requesting instruction and taught quite a bit on view, meditation, and conduct. They were unlike commentators of today, who carelessly expound everything they know, without any limits, so it is not definite that all the views they taught were consistently Madhyamaka.

2) Mahāmudrā

As to the application of the term *mahāmudrā:*[555] In the songs of Mila, phrases such as "the citadel of Mahāmudrā view"[556] and others make only passing reference to the term *mahāmudrā*. The one who made the practice famous was Dakpo Lharjé. In his texts, the view is identified as twofold, a perfection-vehicle system and the mantra-vehicle system,[557] and he gave the name "instructions on Mahāmudrā" to both. Quoting many sutras to the effect that emptiness is taught in the perfection-vehicle system as Mahāmudrā, he composed a treatise proving that emptiness is Mahāmudrā. Before Shang Tsalpa, the term *white simple* was not well known. Shang wrote a treatise focused mainly on the white simple, and from then on, it was well known.[558]

Thus, Marpa, Mila, Gampopa, and their disciples Phakmo Drupa, Drigung Jikten Sumgön of the Kyura, Lingrepa, Düsum Khyenpa, Taklungpa, and others agreed in their presentation of the view. Theirs appears to be a system that placed importance on the appearance side, that is, dependent arising, and did not reject the analytical wisdom that cognizes particulars. Nevertheless, many disciples, scholar and nonscholar alike, inserted confused notations into their collected works, so they do not seem to be reliable. So my omniscient [102] lama has stated.[559]

Well, in a song that Jetsün Mila sang to Gampopa, it says:

> When realizing your own mind to be empty,
> Don't be fettered to the one and the many:
> There's danger of going into a nihilistic emptiness;
> Son, rest in the unelaborated nature.[560]

How do we interpret this quote? It means that when we have definitively established that the mind is empty of inherent existence and are settled one-pointedly on that empty nature, free from the one and the many, we do not analyze. His statement "when realizing your own mind to be empty" shows where to cease analysis.[561]

The Mahāmudrā of those in the early Kagyü is divided into two: sutra and mantra. I will first explain the former. Settling one-pointedly on the nature of mind, you meditate nonconceptually and attain stability. Your clear, aware mind, which is stabilized on the object of meditation thus attained, searches for the mind outside the body, inside the body, and so forth. After that, when you ascertain that mind is a non-true existent, in which you do not find a single nature, you settle one-pointedly on the nature of mind as characterized by non-true existence and meditate on emptiness as an affirming negation.[562] So it is asserted.

The mantra-system Mahāmudrā is posited as the clear-light mind of great bliss that arises from having made the winds enter, abide, and dissolve in the central channel. That is the main subject matter of the famous seven yogic attainment texts[563] and Saraha's three essential works; it is the very quintessence of all the highest yoga tantras. In order to meditate on that, you must first manifest the original mind. For that, you must make the winds enter, abide, and dissolve in the central channel. Thus you establish the nature of the original mind and settle one-pointedly on that; the winds then enter, abide, and dissolve in the central channel. Then, through the ignition of the inner fire at the navel/secret area, the four joys arise, induced by the melting of the drop at the crown. Then the original mind arises in the nature of great bliss. Settled one-pointedly in the bliss-emptiness gnosis—where that original mind and its object, emptiness, are inseparable—you successively traverse the four yogas and attain the supreme. The Mahāmudrā meditation that thus unites bliss and emptiness, method and wisdom, is termed the *white simple*. [103]

Practitioners of Mahāmudrā are twofold: those with sharp and those with dull faculties.[564] Those with dull faculties, who cannot meditate on the path that collects the winds in the central channel, will meditate for the time being on the perfection-system Mahāmudrā. Persons with sharp faculties also are twofold.

(1) If you have trained on the path already in previous lives, or earlier in this life, and from the start settle one-pointedly on the nature of mind, then through that meditation make the winds enter, abide, and dissolve in the central channel so that you experience the original mind directly, you are called a *simultaneist*. It says in *The Epitome:*

> The person who has progressed in training
> Is taught the simultaneist's path.[565]

And, it says in the *Jeweled Stairway* of Phakmo Drupa:

> The simultaneist person is a person who has:
> Collected the collections,
> Trained in the tantric training,
> Tamed the mind to be tamed,
> Gained the experience to be gained, and
> Become supreme.[566]

This also is asserted by Jé Lama, when he says: "It seems that those skilled at making the winds enter the central channel make the winds enter the central channel regardless of the object on which they fix."[567]

(2) If you have *not* already trained on the path in previous lives or earlier in this life, then the common paths, initiations, generation and completion stages, and so forth, must serve as preliminaries. A person such as that is termed a gradualist. In *The Epitome,* it says:

A person with a beginner's karma
Is taught the gradualist's path.[568]

3) Later Kagyüpas: seeking the mind[569]

The later Kagyüpas assert many different ways of meditating on severing the root source of mind. Some say that if you analyze during meditative equipoise how your own mind exists—as external or internal, or as arising, abiding, or ceasing—and see that it does not exist anywhere, that is severing the root source of the mind, that is identifying the mind, that is attaining the meaning of Mahāmudrā. They say that is the meaning of the quote from the *Doha Treasure* of Śavaripa:

The mind and all appearances:
If sought, they are not found, nor is there anywhere a seeker.
Nonexistent, unarisen in the three times, unceasing,
That which does not change into something else
Is the reality whose inherent [104] nature is great bliss.
Therefore, all appearances are the dharmakāya.[570]

Again, others say that when you seek the mind and see that mind does not exist as any part of your body, from your head to the soles of your feet, and does not exist as anything physical, like color, shape, and so forth, then that is seeing the real nature of the mind, and so forth. They think thus because of the statement by Shang Rinpoché:

The ultimate nature of your own mind, which is the seed of all,
Appears as the gnostic dharmakāya,[571] from the start indistinguishable
From the mind of all the conquerors and their sons;
It is not physical, it is naturally clear,
It does not exist as a thing, and it is empty of color and size.[572]

Still others say that, not pursuing a past awareness, not anticipating a future awareness, but settling serenely on the nature of the fresh, uncontrived present awareness, you plainly, directly see the nature of the mind, and at that time the root of the mind is severed and mind is identified. This third view is taught in accord with such statements of Saraha as "put yourself at ease, fresh and uncontrived,"[573] and of great adept Lingrepa:

> If you settle yourself in the uncontrived and fresh, then realization will dawn.
> If you maintain that like a river's flow, then wholeness will dawn.
> Completely abandon all reference points and signs
> And always be in meditative equipoise, O yogin.[574]

Still others say that, whatever objects appear to your mind—forms, sounds, and so forth—and also whatever concepts of good and bad arise—virtue and nonvirtue, and so forth—if you look at their nature plainly, without offering the slightest refutation or proof, they will disappear on their own. After that, you settle in that empty, open blankness, in which there is no identification of anything; seeing like that is the realization of reality itself and identification of the mind. This fourth group explains its view in accord with a passage that occurs in Tilopa's *Ganges Mahāmudrā Instruction:*

> If you want to realize what's beyond thought and inactive,
> Then sever your own mind at the root and rest in naked awareness.
> Let the tainted water of conceptual thought clarify.
> Don't refute or prove appearances; leave them alone.
> When there is no rejection or acceptance, that is Mahāmudrā.[575]

Also, a multitude of others say that any conceptual images that arise should not be released on their own but [105] suppressed. When, on top of that, they are suppressed even more, they are freed on their own, so appearance and freedom coincide. However many conceptual thoughts there are, there are that many dharmakāyas. This group teaches that that is the meaning of the saying by Lama Shang:

> When you have settled yourself like that,
> When a conceptual thought suddenly occurs,
> Do not think it is other than
> The clear-light dharmakāya.
> Therefore, that projected conceptual thought
> Is emptiness projected from emptiness,
> Dharmakāya projected from dharmakāya,
> Union projected from union.[576]

I have transcribed these statements verbatim from Losang Chökyi Gyaltsen's *Lamp Re-Illuminating Mahāmudrā.*

As indicated by the above, most of the later Kagyüpas' written special instructions on seeking mind do not discuss the very subtle original mind; there is only an explanation of what appears when the coarse mind, naturally or impelled, thinks, "I go," "I stay," and so forth—that is, the way of seeking mind through the three: how the mind arises, abides, and ceases. They intended or thought that, to accord with the mental capacity of students in degenerate times, meditators would establish just the actuality of the original ultimate nature of the present mind and get used to it, and then it would be easy to shift over to the very subtle original mind. However, in some writings, there is a deliberate rejection of reasoning establishing an ultimate nature of mind that is other than its conventional nature; such lack of training in the major textual systems is deplorable. Therefore my omniscient lama states:

> If you understand well, then even if you meditate only on the reasoning establishing absence of the one and many, there is no dearth of topics for meditation. Therefore, those boasting that they view the very face of the dharmakāya in their own minds would obviously be better off if they studied just that reasoning and sat up straight.[577]

There is still a great deal to be explained, but fearing prolixity, I have not written about it.

4) Early Kagyü arrangements of Mahāmudrā

Some of the earlier Kagyüpas divided the Mahāmudrā path into four yogas: (1) by meditating one-pointedly on mind, *one-pointedness;* (2) by realizing mind to be unelaborated, *nonelaboration;* (3) by realizing appearances and mind to be of a single taste, the *single taste;* and (4) by the absence of meditation with signs, *nonmeditation.* Those are the four. In relation to the boundaries of the path stages, Jé Götsangpa explains basically that the first is devoted conduct (the paths of accumulation and preparation), the second [106] is the path of seeing (the first bodhisattva stage), the third covers the second through seventh stages (on the path of meditation), and the fourth is the pure stages of that path, the eighth through tenth.[578] Shang Rinpoché states:

> Mahāmudrā severs all at once,
> So the deluded are mistaken in counting stages and paths.
> In order to please the deluded, though,

> The stages and paths of the definition vehicle
> Will be taken into account here.[579]

His way of counting is asserted to be similar to Götsangpa's.

Earlier Kagyüpas, established in their practice of the actual Mahāmudrā, saw the need for a multitude of indispensable techniques conducive to the arising of Mahāmudrā in the mental continuums of beginners, so they produced multiple enumerations of systems of guidance.[580] They guided disciples by instructing them in: Jé Gampopa's yoga of the coemergent; Drigung Jikten Gönpo's fivefold; and the eight great guidelines, the six about the taste of sameness, and mountain Dharma, taught by Tsangpa Gyarepa and others.[581]

a) The yoga of the coemergent

Of those, the meaning of *yoga of the coemergent*[582] is as stated by the protector of beings, Phakmo Drupa:

> The three—mind, conceptual thoughts, and dharmakāya—
> First are coemergent,
> Then, through instruction, are joined into one.[583]

It also is said:

> Mind itself is coemergent with the dharmakāya;
> Conceptual thoughts are the coemergent waves of the dharmakāya;
> Appearances are the coemergent light of the dharmakāya.
> Appearances and mind are inseparably coemergent.[584]

The meaning of the statement is explained as threefold: in light of an emphasis on devotion and disgust, there is (1) the *preliminary,* that is, the four preparations, (2) the *actual,* that is, the two-aspected identification, and (3) the *follow-up,* that is, inner experience in relation to appearing objects. Of these, the preliminary is the same as usual; the two aspects of the actual are tranquil abiding and superior insight.

b) The fivefold

The fivefold[585] is as taught by the world protector, Drigung Jikten Sumgön:

> Mahāmudrā is like a lion:
> If it is not fivefold, it is eyeless.[586]

Because the fivefold is indispensable for the practice of Mahāmudrā, his promulgation of this instruction was a great deed for the Kagyü. It is proclaimed in the world protector's *Root Song:*

> The stallion of awakening mind:
> If you do not decide to race for the benefit of others,
> The crowds of gods and men will not approve,
> So apply your mind to the preliminaries.
>
> Your own [107] body as the royal deity body:
> If you do not hold to this firm, unchanging ground,
> The retinue of servant ḍākinīs will not gather,
> So apply yourself to generating your body as the divine yidam.
>
> The snow mountain of the lama's four bodies:
> If the sun of devotion does not appear,
> The flowing river of blessings will not arise from it,
> So apply your mind to this devotion.
>
> The spacious sky of mind itself:
> If you do not clear away the clouds of conceptual thoughts,
> The planets and stars of the two knowledges will not shine,
> So apply yourself to this nonconceptual mind.
>
> The wish-granting jewel of the two collections:
> If you do not wipe it clean with dedicatory prayer,
> The activities you need and desire will not occur,
> So afterward, apply yourself to this dedication of merits.[587]

The five, then, are: (1) meditation on the awakening mind, (2) meditation on one's own body as the deity, (3) meditation on devotion to the lama, (4) meditation on the nonconceptual view, and (5) stamping with the seal of the dedication prayer.

c) The eight great guidelines

The eight great guidelines are (1) the guidelines on the lama as the three buddha bodies, (2) the guidelines on love and compassion, (3) the guidelines on cause and effect and dependent arising, (4) the guidelines on the fivefold nectar drip,[588] (5) the guidelines on the yoga of the coemergent, (6) the guidelines on the six Dharmas of Nāropa, (7) the guidelines on equalizing the eight worldly dharmas, and (8) the guidelines on meditation to reverse ill fortune through secret conduct.

The guidelines on cause and effect and dependent arising and the fivefold nectar drip are not counted among the six Dharmas of Chenga.[589] In place of those is what are called "the guidelines on cleansing the realms through pure vision." Thus, since there then would be only seven, either love and compassion are counted separately, or we must investigate further. The meditation to reverse ill fortune through secret conduct is mainly just that conduct that enhances the path of the inner heat, and other practices. The others are easy to understand.

d) The six about the taste of sameness

The six about the taste of sameness are (1) using conceptual thoughts as the path, (2) using delusions as the path, (3) using illness as the path, (4) using gods and *dré* demons as the path, (5) using suffering as the path, and (6) using death as the path. The first five of those use Mahāmudrā and the awakening mind as the path; *using death as the path* is an extension of the instruction on the bardo from among the six Dharmas of Nāropa.

e) The mountain Dharma

The mountain Dharma is explained as "the four ornaments of the profound Dharma and that which is adorned by the oral instructions on the three spheres."

The four ornaments are: (1) the mountain Dharma, the source of good qualities, (2) the great ship of the secret initiations, (3) the hidden explanations of the vajra body, and (4) the guidelines on the bardo.

(1) The source of good qualities: it is the context of [108] the yoga of the coemergent and the six Dharmas, which are the actual subject matter of meditation; it involves presentations of the characteristics of any meditation place, and of the three vows that are preliminary to the generation stage and completion stage.[590]

(2) The ship of initiation is a mandala ritual mainly taught in Kṛṣṇācārya's Heruka system; moreover, there is much in it about the objects of meditation required for the yoga of the coemergent and the six Dharmas.

(3) The hidden explanations establish the way things fundamentally exist.

(4) The guidelines on the bardo are a commentary on the teaching Jetsün Milarepa gave to Tseringma on dividing the bardo into six.[591]

The ornament of the oral instructions on the three spheres is threefold: (1) the ornament of the direct guidelines on clearing hindrances, (2) the ornament of the catalogue of the manifold spiritual songs,[592] and (3) the ornament of minor categories.[593] The first clears the hindrances to the earlier mountain Dharma teachings. The main subject matter of the second is the six Dharmas and the yoga of the coemergent. The last consists of miscellaneous sayings.

c. A brief analysis of views, and so forth

1) Is there a perfection-vehicle Mahāmudrā?

A brief analysis of views, and so forth: Quoting many sutras, the peerless Dakpo Rinpoché, Gampopa, wrote treatises to prove that, in the perfection-vehicle system, emptiness is said to be Mahāmudrā. Although some say that those sutra passages do not appear in the Kangyur, those sutras do appear in the Kangyur that was translated into Chinese. Although the words are not exactly the same, phrases with the same meaning appear in some other sutras translated into Tibetan, such as the *Sutra on the Presence of the Present Buddha* and others.[594] So my omniscient lama has stated.[595]

Jamyang Sakya Pandita says in *Distinguishing the Three Vows:*

> Our Mahāmudrā
> Is the gnosis arising from initiation.[596]

Relying on that passage, some say there is no term for Mahāmudrā in the sutra system. I think it is unacceptable to say this, for it has been explained by many pandits, adepts, and scholars that superior, middling, and lesser perfection-vehicle students, abiding with a stable mind in tranquil abiding and superior insight, meditate on the nonduality of method and wisdom, which is Mahāmudrā. Jñānakīrti's *Distinguishing* [109] *Clearly the Entire Sum of the Buddha's Words* says:

> Those with superior faculties who are especially diligent in the perfection vehicle, meditate on tranquil abiding and superior insight, and right from the time they are ordinary individuals, they have a perfect realization arising from Mahāmudrā; because of that, they obtain the signs of irreversibility.[597]

Jñānakīrti also states in the same text:

> These superior students also meditate first on tranquil abiding and superior insight in order to enter the meditation preparatory to the nondual Mahāmudrā.[598]

Not only that; the term Mahāmudrā is used for emptiness. The *King of Concentration Sutra* says, "The intrinsic nature of all dharmas is Mahāmudrā."[599] This point is taught in this and other passages.

If, then, it is objected that all four authenticating seals of the Buddhist view would then be Mahāmudrā, it is not like that: three of them—impermanence, suffering, and peace—seal only some objects, so they will not get the name "great," while the selflessness of all dharmas seals all objects of knowledge, so it has the complete meaning of "great."

2) Does the white simple imply quietism?

Although the objections raised in Jamgön Sapan's *Distinguishing the Three Vows* cover many topics, the main ones appear to be two: (1) the way Shang Tsalpa explains Mahāmudrā as the white simple, and (2) the way the Drigungpas explain the single intention. Echoing the statements of Sapan, many from our own Geluk and other schools have cast aspersions on those positions. It seems that they all raise objections based on having decided that the meaning of Shang Tsalpa's white simple is not thinking anything at all, but if you analyze Shang Tsalpa's statements honestly and in detail, the position of not thinking anything at all clearly is not put forth, and it is evident that the objections in the *Three Vows* are rash statements.[600]

3) Do Kagyü and Geluk have a single meaning?

A disciple of the omniscient Jamyang Shepa, the logician Losang Rinchen (seventeenth/eighteenth century)[601] was at first a Gelukpa. Later, he went to Mindröl Ling to study Sanskrit grammar. He converted to Nyingma, and in a text full of careless statements arising from arrogance, *Harmonizing the Stages of the Path Traditions,* he wrote:

> In his *Proving that the Kagyü and Geluk Have the Same Meaning,* Khedrup Norsang Gyatso insults Sapan's *Distinguishing the Three Vows,* and he states that in seeking the mind, in order to ascertain its non-true existence, the way to meditate is to take emptiness as an affirming negation, and so forth. If he does not [110] state this as a specially required skillful means, then his view accords with the Cittamātra way of meditating on emptiness as an affirming negation; and although that view is the intention of both the dharma lord Nyernyipa[602] and the glorious Dharmakīrti, there still remains in the white simple the flaw that arousing the mind of awakening may or may not be necessary. There is nothing to be heard in it about the common paths, nor is there any mention of the generation stage, and so forth, or the stages of maturing one's mental continuum through the completion stage, or the vows and pledges to be assumed, and so forth. To try to prove that both the white simple called the *Mahāmudrā of abiding mind* and the great synopsis of practice of the entire teaching of the Muni by the conqueror Tsongkhapa have a single meaning is absolutely ridiculous!

In Norsang's *Lamp Illuminating Mahāmudrā,* however, it says:

> When the early Kagyüpas called their Mahāmudrā meditations the white simple, they meant that when the original mind arises in the nature of great bliss, we attain the ultimate result through that single meditation on the ultimate nature.[603]

And:

> Thus, the early Kagyüpas describe Mahāmudrā meditation as the white simple. Regarding that, Sapan asks in *Distinguishing*

> *the Three Vows,* "Is arousing the mind of awakening necessary or unnecessary in your white simple?"[604] His objection is just like the objection of someone who, when told the two collections are singly sufficient for buddhahood, asks, "Is being born from a mother first necessary or unnecessary?"[605]

While Norsang's text says this clearly, Losang Rinchen persists in saying that "there still remains in the white simple the flaw that arousing the mind of awakening may not be necessary." In writing that, he denies what is obvious.

Although Losang Rinchen derides the proof that the Kagyü and Geluk have the same meaning, in Norsang's *Lamp Illuminating Mahāmudrā,* the early Kagyüpas' way of meditating on Mahāmudrā is merely proved to be the way of meditating on the original mind as intended by Saraha; there is no phrase in the beginning, middle, or end of that work that attempts to establish that the Kagyü and Geluk have the same meaning. Later printers, relying on writing that had been added to the cover, wrote the title as *The Lamp Illuminating Mahāmudrā: Proving that the Kagyü and Geluk Have* [111] *the Same Meaning,* and it goes without saying that Losang Rinchen knew it thus. Even if it happened that Norsang did prove that Kagyü and Geluk have the same meaning, when honest people investigate, they learn that there is not the slightest inconsistency between Norsang's method of proof and the assertions of Jé Lama Tsongkhapa. Therefore, Losang Rinchen is ridiculous, for his account is that of someone drunk on partiality, who says whatever comes to mind.

4) Are the four yogas Cittamātrin?

As already noted above, Maitrīpa held the Madhyamaka view, yet Losang Rinchen says, "Apparently, Maitrīpa's view is explained as the practice of the four yogas of the false-aspectarian Cittamātra of Śāntipa." Saying that Maitrīpa held a nonaspectarian Cittamātra view is nonsensical. Therefore, my omniscient lama says, "Some earlier and later logicians say that Maitrīpa was a Cittamātrin because he was a disciple of Śāntipa. The statement that Maitrīpa was a Cittamātrin is the same as a used toilet stone[606] and should simply be thrown away."[607] Losang Rinchen also says:

> Since it is established that the Kagyü view of the four yoga stages—one-pointedness, nonelaboration, the single taste, and

> nonmeditation—is Śāntipa's way of meditating on the view, the Kagyü view is like the Cittamātra view.

Being totally unacquainted with the works of early Kagyüpas and thinking, "as long as there are four yoga stages, it must be Cittamātra," is jumping thoughtlessly to a conclusion. My omniscient lama states:

> Although the term *four yogas* is explained by master Śāntipa as Cittamātra, it is not certain that the four yogas of the Kagyü are part of a Cittamātrin system.[608]

The latter is as explained above.

5) Do the various types of Mahāmudrā have a single meaning?

The First Panchen, the omniscient Losang Chökyi Gyaltsen (1570–1662), states:

> The yoga of the coemergent, the joined amulet box,
> The fivefold, the taste of sameness, the four syllables,[609]
> Shijé, Chö, Dzokchen,
> Guidelines on the Madhyamaka view, and others:
> Many names are applied to each,
> But when the experienced yogin,
> Expert in the definitive meaning of scripture and in reasoning,
> Analyzes them, they all come down to a single meaning.[610]

Wishing to insult him, Losang Rinchen says: "Shijé, Chö, the fivefold, the six about single taste, and other practices are not solely philosophical views; his explanations are lightweight." The Panchen also states:

> Although there are many ways of explaining
> The actual [112] Mahāmudrā,
> It has two divisions, sutra and mantra.
> The latter is the clear-light great bliss
> Arising from skillful means, such as penetrating
> The vital points of the subtle body, and other completion-
> stage practices.

> It is the Mahāmudrā of Saraha,
> Nāgārjunapāda, Nāropa, and Maitrīpa;
> It is the very essence of the highest yoga tantra class,
> Taught in the seven yogic attainment texts and the three essential texts of Saraha.[611]

To this, Losang Rinchen says: "This is difficult to accept, unless it is for the purpose of converting fools." He also says, "The view of Dzokchen accords with the *Sacred Words of Mañjuśrī* by the great master Buddhaśrī Jñānapāda,[612] so there are many reasons for seeing the Panchen's basis of analysis as greatly problematic." Such statements are wanton gossip; they are mere biased chatter.

6) Did Tsongkhapa write the Inquiry into the Pure Noble Intention*?*

The great pandit Jampa Lingpa and others explain that the text known as the *Inquiry into the Pure Noble Intention* is not a work of the great lord Jé Tsongkhapa, for in the middle of it there appear some vulgar phrases, such as "useless as shit." Also, the phrasing is not like the style in other works of Jé. In the colophon, another name is written: "by one called Cared for by Guru Mañjughoṣa";[613] this name is not known to anyone. Also, the *Inquiry* did not find its way into the index to the works of the omniscient Jé compiled by his disciples and grand-disciples, so there seem to be grounds for doubt. However, most in our own Geluk and other schools count it as a text by Jé.[614] The questions were understood as refutations of the great Kagyü meditators, so Drukpa Pema Karpo[615] and others wrote replies, and the Sakyapa Shākya Chokden, in reinforcing his defense of the Kagyüpas, wrote a reply mostly made up of invective.[616] From our own Geluk side, it seems that after Gomchen Ngawangpa wrote on the topic[617] and, in particular, the omniscient First Panchen wrote his *Reply to Questions: Sweet Words of Explanation for Those with Good Minds*,[618] it was assumed that the *Inquiry* was a text by Jé. Thus, it seems difficult to decide one way or the other.

d. Conclusion

Among the Kagyüpas nowadays, it seems that, from minor lamas in a small corner of the monastery on up, no one produces even a single new rational critique. They do write some miscellaneous texts [113] on the three vows and, quoting one or two critical verses by the Kagyüpas and Drigung Palzin, they write many texts refuting the Nyingmapas; to do so is just to tire oneself out, and it's essentially just a waste of paper and ink.

Therefore, to those who desire their own welfare, the omniscient Panchen says:

> The lives of āryas are beyond the purview of ordinary beings, and since the evil incurred by harming the Dharma and holy beings is extremely unbearable, may you cast away the hateful power of partiality, and may you be pervaded by jewel light of pure vision. Thus do I, Chökyi Gyaltsen, pray.[619]

It is fitting to hold in one's heart what he so compassionately advised.

Concluding verses

> The medical elixir whose taste is freedom, mixing into one
> The white simple Mahāmudrā of Maitrīpa,
> The six excellent, deep Dharmas of Nāropa
> And the nectar of the Kadam mind training instructions
> Was given by the physician Gampopa
> To those with gradualist or simultaneist vessels, as appropriate.
>
> Thenceforth, the Kagyü seers who achieved immortality
> Filled every glacier, ravine, and cultivated valley.
>
> Flying about on wings of white cotton,
> They are mistaken for a flock of vultures in the sky,
> And the assembled host of the saffron-clad
> Is like the whole earth covered with ochre dust.
>
> Indra, mightiest of gods, emanates his thousand eyes
> To gaze on that wondrous mass; not only that,
> But oceans of conquerors in untold buddhafields
> Rise to view it from the dharmadhātu, or so I imagine.
>
> For those lacking the fortune to be freed
> By seeing events of the past such as those,

I have related here an account to establish
Something meaningful for those with ears to hear.

From *The Crystal Mirror: An Excellent Explanation Showing the Sources and Assertions of All Philosophical Systems,* this completes the explanation of the history of the Kagyü philosophical system. [114]

7. The Shijé Tradition[620]

[II. The History of Philosophical Systems in Tibet, the Land of Snows
B. The histories of the different schools]

4. Shijé[621]

> I will relate the origins of the philosophical system known as Shijé,
> The ocean of instructions in which the great rains
> Of the pacification of suffering, thrice fallen because of
> The Indian Dampa's concern for Tibet, mingle into one.[622]

THE HISTORY of the Shijé philosophical system is twofold: a. The actual history of the Shijé philosophical system and b. The history of one of its schools, the Chö system.

a. The actual history of the Shijé philosophical system

1) Meaning of the term[623]

According to earlier scholars, the word *Shijé* was applied on the basis of the name of the Dharma teaching called "the holy Dharma that pacifies *(shijé)* suffering." This Dharma is called "the holy Dharma that pacifies suffering" because it instantly pacifies the sufferings of this life—namely, having an inferior body, being sickly, being poor, and being oppressed by nonhumans—which arose through the karma of previous lives, and enables you to endure the practice of yoga. That alone, however does not cover it: the practice of the perfection of wisdom pacifies all the sufferings of becoming and peace,[624] so it also is designated Shijé because the essence of the instruction is the practice of the perfection of wisdom. Were it nothing more than just the alleviation of fleeting negative circumstances, it would not be an extraordinary instruction. It also is claimed that it is designated thusly on the basis of the phrase, "the mantra that completely pacifies all suffering."[625]

2) Major figures

The source from which the instruction arose was Pha Dampa Sangyé (d. 1117).[626] He was born in Kūpadvīpa, in the region of Carasiṃha, in southern India.[627] Because it was his seventh birth,[628] he was unstained by vice and naturally enjoyed virtue. Right from childhood, he trained to the point of mastery in countless sciences, such as grammar. He took preliminary ordination from the abbot of Vikramaśīla, Kṣemadeva, vows for arousing the mind of awakening from Guru Serlingpa,[629] and initiations from many gurus, [115] so that he held all three sets of vows. He received countless instructions from fifty-four male and female adepts: eleven gurus for dialectics and grammar, eleven gurus for moving winds according to the father tantras, eleven gurus for experiencing bliss according to the mother tantras, eleven gurus for the signs of Mahāmudrā, and ten gurus for identifying awareness.[630] In the enumeration of these gurus, there seems to be some inconsistency in the time periods in which those enumerated lived: Indrabhūti, Nāgārjuna, and others came much earlier than Pha Dampa, and some came in a later era. I wonder whether Dampa might not have lived a very long life: my omniscient lama says that it is apparently true, since it seems from some Chinese accounts that Dampa was a disciple of the protector Nāgārjuna.[631] When Dampa meditated in various places over sixty-five years, he had countless visions of the twelve meditational deities, and so forth, and a vision of the thirty-six gurus of the wondrous ḍākinī realm. He gained the common yogic achievements: the eye medicine, speed walking, magic pills, penetration of matter, control of demonesses,[632] the magic sword, and flying.[633] He attained the supreme yogic achievement, the gnosis of the great path of seeing. He practiced tantric conduct in the twenty-four power places[634] and elsewhere. Renowned as an adept, he was called by various names.

He went to Tibet five times; the fifth time, he went from Tibet to China and became famous there. From among the countless disciples he developed in Tibet, the most famous are those of the three lineages—the early, middle, and later Shijé. It is said that the early lineage[635] was taught to the Kashmiri Jñānaguhya and translated into Tibetan by Ongpo Lotsāwa. The middle lineage is said to have been propagated after Pha Dampa gave instructions to the trio of Ma Chökyi Sherap, Sochung Gendün Bar, and Kham Yeshé Gyaltsen. The later lineage: Dampa went to holy Dingri Langkor; of his four supreme disciples there—the holy Charchen, Charchung, Vajrakrodha, and the holy Künga—the main one was the holy Künga, whom Dampa Sangyé had looked after over the course of five lives. In this lifetime, he became the treasury of instruction, so many upholders of the tradition came after him: his disciple Patsap Gompa, then Gyalwa Tené, Rok Sherap Sengé, Shikpo Nyima Sengé, and others. Then Shijé became widespread.

3) Major instructions

I will mention just the names of the instructions of those three lineages.

a) Early Shijé

The first lineage includes the three [116] cycles of the lamp of pacification,[636] the sādhana of Yamāntaka, and others.

b) Middle Shijé: Ma

The middle lineage includes the Ma, So, and Kam systems, along with minor instructions. The Dharma cycle of Ma[637] is twofold: the word lineage and the meaning lineage. Of those, the guidelines on meaning are the sixteen handed-down guidelines, while the word instructions include arousing the mind of awakening, teachings on emptiness, miscellaneous sayings, harsh truths,[638] and extensive conclusions.

c) Middle Shijé: So[639]

The Dharma instructions of the So system are reckoned as twofold: the word lineage and the meaning lineage.

Of these, the word lineage has the great lineage and the small lineage. The great lineage relates to a hundred and three supreme, holy persons: the fifty-four great, the thirty-two middle, and the seventeen lesser. It contains accounts of each adept, the essence of his or her instruction, and each adept's complete system for guiding disciples, so it is said to consist of the fifty-four lineages or the hundred and three lineages; that is why it is called the *great lineage*. The small lineage contains thirty-two classes of Dharma instructions: the five about meaning, the four stages, the long and short sessions on mental absorption, the eight renowns, the trio[640] of the father and two sons, the faulty and the faultless, and others.

The meaning lineage includes the partial and the impartial. The former has: the fifty-four meaning lineages of the fifty-four male and female yoga practitioners, the thirty-two meaning lineages of the thirty-two gurus, and the seventeen meaning lineages of the seventeen holy ones.

The impartial-meaning lineage has the cycle on opening the eye and the cycle of the ḍākinī. The first of those is fivefold, consisting of the four sons and the mother: opening the eye on the hidden text is the mother, and its branches are the four sons—the instruction on time and temporal divisions, the hundred and six identifications, incessant purity, and the secret path of Vajrasattva.

The second impartial-meaning lineage, the cycle of the ḍākinīs, includes the four great headings of the So cycle: (1) for achieving the supreme, the cycle on signs; (2) for gaining ordinary yogic achievements, the cycle on the four syllables; (3) for achieving both, the cycle on *dzagata*[641] and (4) the cycle on the session. (1) The cycle on signs consists of the cycle on the signs of Heruka; the cycle on the signs of the Sugata; the cycle on the signs of Vajraghaṇṭa; and the miscellaneous signs of Pha Dampa. (2) For gaining the ordinary yogic achievements, there is the body sādhana of the white Vārahī, the speech sādhana of the red Vārahī, and the mind sādhana of the black Vārahī. The last consists of the sādhana of Vajravārahī's dharmakāya, the sādhana of her enjoyment body, and the sādhana of her emanation body. [117] (3) The cycle on *dzagata* is the single wheel of inner heat. (4) The cycle on the session is the path of tantric conduct and the system for the development of inner experience.

The essential roots of those, as it were, are the four ear-whispered lineages: (1) Mawai Sengé's meaning lineage, whose Dharma language corresponds with that of tantra; (2) the fourth lineage, a completely unknown meaning lineage whose Dharma language does not correspond with that of tantra; (3) the brief summary of the incomplete chapters; and (4) So's entering straight into awareness.

d) Middle Shijé: Kam

The Kam system is the explanation by Kam Yeshé Gyaltsen of all eight higher realizations according to the instructions of Pha Dampa. He expounded them by quoting from the extensive and medium-length perfection of wisdom sutras and from their poetic distillation.[642] Thus, there were two lineages of disciples, upper and lower. The upper lineage was transmitted from the duo of Khön Wangchuk Dorjé and Gyamé Sherap Lama. At first, both of them were sickly, but Kam used their illnesses to introduce them to the nature of mind. He taught the first chapter of the *Ornament of Higher Realization* as the basic text, the four noble truths as instruction, and miscellaneous texts as praxis.[643] Later, Gyatön Shönu Sengé wrote down the instructions of the Kam system in a text called the *Miraculous Key to Syllogism: The Precious Garland of the Mind Lineage of the Perfection of Wisdom and the Ear-Whispered Lineage of Praxis*. The lower lineage:[644] Kam transmitted it to Dro Chötsön by distinguishing between gradualist persons and simultaneist persons—identifying them in terms of both essential meaning and higher realization—and explaining all the sutras by way of the four steps of dependent arising.[645] The lower lineage was the instruction that focused on meditation.

e) Middle Shijé: Minor and miscellaneous lineages

The minor lineages that occur in the middle Shijé are the three systems of Drapa, Ché, and Jang. Pha Dampa gave Geshé Drapa the instruction on the cycle of the nine lamps of pacification: the *Lamp of the Body Instruction,* the *Lamp of the Speech Vehicle,* the *Lamp of Secret Mind,* the *Lamp of Pure View,* the *Lamp of Precious Meditation,* the *Lamp of Enlightened Conduct,* the *Lamp of Basic Equanimity,* the *Lamp of the Yoga Path,* and the *Lamp of the Ultimate Result.*[646] Dampa gave Ché Candrakīrti the instruction on the combination of sutra and tantra—the perfection-vehicle instruction based on joining the *Verse Summary of the Perfection of Wisdom* with the *Litany of the Names of Mañjuśrī,*[647] and the mantra-vehicle instruction of the fifty-eight male and female adepts.[648] He gave Jang Kadampa the instruction on the unwritten perfection of wisdom; it was said to be no more than a faulty introduction.

The miscellaneous lineages: Dampa gave to Drogom the golden spoon explaining [118] the *Litany of the Names of Mañjuśrī;* to Gugom the instructions on the action seal; to Chugom the instruction on the frank talk from the heart; to Gompa Margom the instruction on the three types of single stroke; to Nyak Lotsāwa the instruction on the solitary hero Heruka; to Chemo Paldrönma the sixteen-section Dharma of the experience of the adepts; to Nyaltö Ngorjé Gompa the yoga of the coemergent; to the elder from Chubar, Jungdrak, the instruction on the perfection of wisdom sutras; to Ngakshé Sherap Gyaltsen the instruction on Kālacakra;[649] to Shangpa Udep the instruction on the four syllables; to Gyatön Kyitsek from Nyemo the instruction on Hevajra; to Shangsak Chungwa the secret practice of Vajravārahī; to

Lama Gönkarwa the instruction on Vajrapāṇi; to Ben Gungyal of Kyishö the ear-whispered lineage of Heruka; and to Machik Lapdrön the instruction on Chö. This concludes the discussion about the middle lineage.[650]

f) Later Shijé[651]

The Dharmas of later lineages are given the name *the cycle of practical guidance on the stainless drop of Mahāmudrā.* This Mahāmudrā is precisely the Mahāmudrā of Maitrīpa, for Pha Dampa Sangyé was a direct disciple of Maitrīpa. "Stainless" is what Dampa's texts are called. "Practical guidance" is the term for that which has a way of practice a little different from other teachings. So its nature is said to be perfection-vehicle instructions in conformity with secret mantra. The *Commentary on the Ten Principles* of Maitrīpa[652] says:

> That system is the perfection vehicle but has a mode of conduct that conforms with secret mantra like that explained in the *Hevajra*. Since it does not rely on deity yoga and does not follow the four seals,[653] it is not secret mantra.

This seems to accord with the statements above. This explanation is given in terms of what is commonly known, but it also is reported that Pha Dampa gave the Kālacakra initiation to Charchen and Ben Gungyal, and that he also bestowed instructions on the action seal on many disciples, so it is not the case that secret mantra is entirely nonexistent in Pha Dampa's pacification of suffering tradition. His own explanations are in conformity with secret mantra, so the vowel-and-consonant blessing and other practices are in conformity with secret mantra. The actual vowel-and-consonant blessing is not secret mantra and should not be mistaken for it, [119] for it is merely similar to the explanation of the dhāraṇī of forty-two syllables in the perfection of wisdom sutras themselves.[654]

This Dharma cycle has two sections: the common Dharma and the uncommon Dharma.

The common Dharma consists of: (1) the sutras and tantras, along with their ritual practices; (2) the special oral tradition, along with the ear-whispered lineage; (3) the stainless, along with the subtle drop; and (4) the cloth filter, along with the manifold explanations.

(1) The first, the sutras and tantras, along with their ritual practices, con-

sists of the general sutra, *The Sutra of the Waterfall's Play;* the special sutra, the *Heart Sutra;* the general tantra, *Illuminating the Collections;* and the special tantra, the *Great Waterfall.*[655] The ritual practices are the great and medium circles of initiation and the three versions of the stages of the path—the great, medium, and small. (2) The special oral tradition, along with the ear-whispered lineage, consists of the four special oral traditions and the four ear-whispered lineages that extend that path.[656] (3) The stainless, along with the subtle drop: the stainless is the six that includes the cycle on the root penetrating the Dharma, and so forth; the subtle drop is the instruction on obstructions causing unhappiness given when Patsap Gompa requested it from Künga. (4) The cloth filter, along with the manifold explanations: The cloth filter is the eight[657] that includes the direct instruction about nectar and so forth, consisting of occasional talks by Patsap that were written down by Tené. The manifold explanations are the explanations written by Tené, Shikpo, Nyemdopa, and others.

The uncommon Dharma class consists of: (1) tantras, along with teachings on emptiness; (2) initiations, along with guidance on the path; (3) the three secret treasuries; and (4) the eight manuals.

[Thuken doesn't elaborate on part 1.]

(3)[658] The three secret treasuries are the guru secret treasury, the meditational deity secret treasury, and the ḍākinī secret treasury.

(2) The second comprises the five path cycles, namely: Virūpa's path cycle of the four doors of the path of means, Saraha's path cycle of the four spheres of the path of means, Serlingpa's eightfold path cycle, Āryadeva's eightfold path cycle, and Nāropa's path cycle on the four unions.

(4) The eight manuals are: the *Manual of the Profound Initiation,* the *Manual of the Root Identification,* the *Manual of the Guidelines of the Ear-Whispered Lineage,* the *Manual of the Vital Points of the Four Doors,* the *Manual of the Various Magical Powers,* the *Manual of the Profound Mantra,* the *Manual of the Ḍākinī Doctrine-Protector,* and the *Manual of the Three-Part Royal Special Instruction.* These make up the uncommon Dharma class, which has the seal of secrecy.

4) *The essence of Shijé*

The essence of the Shijé Dharma: It is the activation of the stages of the path of the perfection of wisdom, [120] a little-known special instruction for putting into practice the entire meaning of the three perfection of wisdom sutras, the extensive, medium-length, and condensed.[659] Generally, Pha Dampa Sangyé mastered six special oral traditions of the lineage of the perfection of wisdom: the lineage from Tuṣita heaven, the lineage from the land of the nāgas, the lineage from Uḍḍiyāna, the lineage from Bengal in eastern India, the lineage from Bhetala in the south, and the lineage from Bhiṣokotacandana in the south. The special instruction for putting into practice the path of the perfection of wisdom, which shows the distillation of the essential meaning of the six special oral traditions, was given by Buddha Dīpaṃkara to Śākyamuni, who gave it to Ānanda. Then, when it had passed through thirty-six lineage holders, up to Bhikṣu Siṃha, a malevolent king cut the line of succession. Then, Ārya Asaṅga, knowing that Maitreya had received the instruction directly from Śākyamuni, performed the practice of Maitreya and had a vision of him; after hearing the perfection of wisdom instruction directly, he gave them to his younger brother, Vasubandhu. The latter gave the instruction to Pha Dampa's maternal uncle, Āryadeva,[660] who gave the instruction to Pha Dampa. So it is explained. Since that instruction condenses the meaning of the Mother sutras[661] for practice according to the special instructions of the treatise called the *Ornament of Higher Realization,* it is a wonderful explanation. How that is so cannot be shown in a few words. If I explained it extensively, it would be far too much, so I have not written about it in detail here.

Although the stream of explanation lasted for a long time, it has now apparently been cut.

5) Sources of the Shijé view

The source of the Shijé view: It reaches back to the wisdom-oriented sutras, while in literature on instructions, Nāgārjuna is taken as authoritative. Also, in Dampa's *Eighty Verses for the People of Dingri,* it says:

> Whirl the spear of awareness into the empty nature.
> O people of Dingri, your view is unobstructed.[662]

Because the view that is taught is free of extremes, I think it is coextensive with the Madhyamaka view. Nevertheless, there is no doubt that, in the writings of later generations, there often is an admixture of fish and turnips. In earlier times, beings beyond number became adepts based on this Shijé philosophical system. The two most famous teaching centers, founded by

Kyemchok Samten Pal (fourteenth century), were Yap Chöding and Gomo [121] Chöding. Following Kyemchokpa, Jangsempa and Guru Könshön presided, respectively, over the two main monasteries. It appears that the Dharma lord Dönrinpa, a mentor of Jé Tsongkhapa, also received instruction from Kyemchokpa. Nowadays, apart from the mere transmission of miscellaneous instructions such as the Sanskrit alphabet, the blessings of the essence of dependent arising, the permission ceremony of Mahādeva Aṃghora,[663] and the medicine bag, and except for the books containing the most important instructions, which just sit there, all the Dharma streams of the Shijé instruction have apparently disappeared.

b. One of the Shijé schools, the Chö system[664]

1) Etymology

The meaning of the term *Chö:* it is applied by way of the function of the instruction. It is designated as it is because the selfish attitude is severed *(chö: gcod)* by love, compassion, and the awakening mind; the root of samsara is severed by the view of emptiness; and the four māras[665] are severed by both in common. It also is known as "conduct" *(chö: spyod)* because the practices of the children of the Conqueror, the bodhisattvas, are conducted on the path of method and wisdom.[666]

2) Lineages[667]

This instruction also arose initially from Pha Dampa Sangyé. When Pha Dampa came to Tibet for the third time and was in Tsang, he gave the Chö instruction to both Kyotön Sönam Lama and Yarlung Mara Serpo. Mara Serpo gave the instruction to his attendant, Nyönpa Serong, who gave it to both Tsetön and Sumtön Rechen. Tsetön gave it to Nyentön, and Sumtön gave it to Kalden Semo, who gave it to Tsangtön, who gave it to Nyentön, and so forth. What extended from them is called the male Chö lineage.[668] Kyotön Sönam Lama gave the instruction to Machik Lapdrön; thenceforth, that lineage was known as the female Chö lineage.[669]

Machik Lapkyi Drönma (1055–1143)[670] was prophesied by the Blessed One in the *Manjuśrī Root Tantra* and other scriptures. A gnosis ḍākinī, she came in the form of a human female and made the Chö instruction pervade all of Tibet. Machik had some sons and daughters; there seem to be conflicting ways of reckoning them in the chronicles. As for Thönyön Samdrup, some explain that he was the son of Machik; [122] others assert that he was her nephew or grand-nephew, but in most of the reliable narratives, he is regarded as her son. In any case, Machik became a great adept and had twenty-one male and female disciples who were adepts, eighteen daughters who were adepts, and so forth. From them, the instructions spread extensively. Although Machik Lapdrön had what are called the four supreme disciples, the stream of the instruction spread most from the lineage of Khugom Chöseng. It has persisted without decline right up to the present day.

Later, there also were some Chö instructions that were revealed as treasures. Gyalthangpa Samten Öser met Machik in a pure vision, and she gave him the Gyalthang system, and she gave Tokden Natsok Rangdröl the profound path ear-whispered lineage, and so forth. A multitude of lineages spread thusly.

In the Dharma cycle of Mañjughoṣa, there is a special instruction on the blessing of the Black Lady of Wrath[671] combined with Chö, which was bestowed on the conqueror, the great Tsongkhapa, by Mañjughoṣa. Transmitted successively from the conqueror Ensapa, that same instruction is nowadays widespread in our own Geluk party.[672]

3) The instruction and the view

The essence of the Chö instruction is practice of the perfection of wisdom that is in conformity with mantra.[673] All scholars and adepts agree that the source of the instruction is the Mother sutras—the extensive, medium-length, and condensed perfection of wisdom sutras—especially the *Verse Summary of the Perfection of Wisdom*. The *Verse Summary of the Perfection of Wisdom* specifically says:

> There are four causes whereby strong and skillful bodhisattvas
> Cannot be moved and are hard for the four māras to control:
> They abide in the empty and do not at all let go of sentient beings;
> They do as they are told and have the blessings of the sugatas.[674]

The four causes stated are: abiding in the empty, not letting go of sentient beings, doing as they are told, and being blessed by the sugatas. The first of those is meditating on the view of emptiness, and the second is meditating on love, compassion, and the awakening mind. These two are the actual practice of pacification Chö. The third cause is relying on a virtuous friend, the root of the path; and the fourth is going for refuge, visualizing the field of assembly, the seven limbs, and offering the mandala. These [123] two are the preliminaries to the practice of pacification Chö. "Hard for the four māras to control" refers to the decisive test,[675] and the instruction about "strong and skillful bodhisattvas" refers to the practice of method by the bodhisattva who has the strength to overcome the sorrows of becoming and peace.[676] Thus it is taught.

You may wonder how this is in conformity with mantra. The *Hevajra* states:

> It is explained that it is good to meditate
> Under a single tree, in a cemetery,
> In the house of a mother deity, at night,
> And also in a solitary hermitage.[677]

And it also says:

> Having given the gift of your body,
> Conduct yourself perfectly on the outside.[678]

And it says:

> Surely, even if some titan
> Or one such as Indra comes before you,
> You should not concern yourself with that,
> And instead roam like a lion.[679]

The Chö instruction is in accord with these statements, because those scriptural passages teach, successively, the place to practice, the way to practice, as well as how, having practiced, you arouse confidence and undergo the ultimate test of Chö.

The view: Since the source of the instruction comprises the trio of the extensive, medium-length, and condensed Mother sutras, as well as their verse summary, it is coextensive with the Prāsaṅgika Madhyamaka. Although this is the case in texts that are definitely Machik Lapdrön's, it seems that in the interim, upholders of the instruction who did not know how to expound her view as it really was mixed in various types of discourse, and because Chö spread impartially to various philosophical systems, explanations of the view and the way to meditate arose according to the dictates of each of the philosophical systems.

Concluding verses

The one who had no conceptual thoughts—of anything whatsoever—
The one who danced emanations—whatever disciplined beings—
The one who performed countless acts—whatever was appropriate—
The one who granted yogic achievements—whatever was desired:

He who was renowned as old father Dampa Sangyé
Taught the countless fathers of the Land of Snows
The essence of the path of the perfections
And the ultimate special instructions of the father and mother tantras.

The distilled intention of every adept,
This supreme medicine, the holy Dharma combining every virtue,
Is called the pacifier of the suffering [124] of every being;
In a single voice, it is praised by every sage.

In conformity with the way of Atiśa,
The supreme instruction for meditating on nonproduction, the meaning of the syllable *a*,[680]
Is this Chö instruction of mother Lapgyi Drönma.
Aho! I think it is the quintessence of Mahayana Dharma.[681]

In the vast forest of manifold philosophical systems,
This account of the history of Shijé
Is music from the throat of the cuckoo,
A great delight to the ear.

From *The Crystal Mirror: An Excellent Explanation Showing the Sources and Assertions of All Philosophical Systems*, this completes the explanation the history of the Shijé philosophical system.

8. The Sakya Tradition[682]

[II. The History of Philosophical Systems in Tibet, the Land of Snows
B. The histories of the different schools]

5. Sakya[683]

> I will relate the history of the philosophical system known as the Sakya,
> In which every portion of the sutra and tantra classes is complete,
> And which possesses the glorious quality of opening the water lily of the Muni's teaching
> With the white light of stainless explanation and practice.

THE HISTORY of the glorious Sakya philosophical system is threefold: a. A general history of the Sakya philosophical system, b. In particular, how the principal Dharmas—Lamdré and other teachings—came about,[684] and c. A presentation of the Sakya view.

a. A general history of the Sakya philosophical system

1) The Khön family line[685]

The widely renowned Sakya arose from Khön Könchok Gyalpo. The family lineage of Khön sprang from the luminous gods.[686] Chiring, Yuring, and Yusé were the three sky-god ancestors, so from there down to Yapang Kyé it is known as the *sky-god lineage*. Yapang Kyé destroyed the *srin* demon Kyareng Trakmé and married the demon's consort, Yadruk Pilima. From that union a son was born, and because he was born from conflict *(khön)* between Yapang Kyé and the *srin* demon, he was known as Khönbar Kyé, "Born amid Conflict." Thenceforth, the successive family lineage was known as the Khön clan. Down to Khön Palpoché (eighth century), those who came in the lineage were exclusively possessed of good temperament from having divine lineage and the glory of powerful merit and were especially distinctive compared to ordinary beings. Palpoché's son, Khönlü Wangpo Sungwa, [125] was the wisest of the seven trial monks[687] who took preliminary vows from the great preceptor Śāntarakṣita; he served Master Padmasambhava and received instructions from him. Thenceforth, until Khönrok Sherap Tsültrim (b. eleventh century), the members of the family lineage only practiced Nyingma secret mantra.[688]

a) Khön Könchok Gyalpo

In Kharok's time, a man named Khön Könchok Gyalpo (1034–1102),[689] an expert in all mantra-vehicle and definition-vehicle subjects, saw many tantric yogins in the middle of the market wearing the masks of the twenty-eight powerful goddesses[690] and performing dances. He reported this to his elder brother, the lama Khönrok Sherap Tsültrim. His elder brother said:

> Now is the time of what is called "corrupt secret mantra." From now on, no one meeting the criteria of an adept will emerge through Tibet's old secret-mantra translation school, the Nyingma, and what we have of them we will hide as treasures. I am old now and you are young. In Mugu Lung lives an expert teacher known as Drokmi Lotsāwa Shākya Yeshé; go there and study the new translations of secret mantra.[691]

When Khönrok Sherap Tsültrim erected three great stupas and inserted into them all the Nyingma images, texts, and sacred substances, the wrath and magical power of the Dharma protectors were apparent, so he removed a few texts on the Dharma cycle of Vajrakīla, the torma rituals of the deities Karmo Nyida Brother and Sister,[692] and other texts and gave them to his younger brother. Then Khön Könchok Gyalpo went to Drokmi and studied the later translations of secret mantra. Moreover, he took on many gurus who were scholar-adepts, such as Gö Lotsāwa Khukpa Lhetsé, the Kashmiri pandit Hangdu Karpo, Ma Lotsāwa Rinchen Chok, Dzinpa Lotsāwa, and others. He examined the land on Pönpo Mountain and, seeing that it was good, [in 1073] founded a monastery on the mountainside in an area where the earth was white. From then on, the tradition was known as Sakya, Gray-White Earth.[693]

b) Sachen Künga Nyingpo

Khön Könchok Gyalpo's son, Sachen Künga Nyingpo (1092–1158),[694] received many Dharma instructions from Bari Lotsāwa Rinchen Drak. When he practiced the meditation of Mañjughoṣa, he had a direct vision in which Mañjughoṣa bestowed upon him the perfection of wisdom instructions on freedom from the four attachments,[695] and so forth. Over the next four years, he received teachings on abhidharma from Drangti Darma Nyingpo, on Madhyamaka and valid cognition from Khyung Rinchen Drakpa and Mé Lhangtsor, on Guhyasamāja and the Dharma cycle of the protective *nyen* demon[696] from Nam Khaupa, on Hevajra from Gyichuwa Dralha Bar, instructions on Heruka and the protector Mahākāla from [126] Gungthangpa Mal Lotsāwa, teachings on Heruka from Puhrang Lotsāwa, and so forth, and in particular, he received instructions on the Lamdré oral-instruction tradition from Shangtön Chöbar. From the great adept Birapa, or Virūpa, who came to Sakya bringing the Dharma to the doorstep,[697] he received in general the instructions on the seventy-two tantras,[698] and in particular the four[699] profound Dharmas not allowed outside the monastery fence and other practices. In short, he was given to satiation the nectar of the profound key points of the short lineage of oral instruction. He first taught the oral instruction to Aseng[700] of Kham, and when he committed it to writing, it became known as the *Text Explanation for Aseng*.[701] Sachen had a lifestory beyond imagining: he had a direct vision of the deity Mañjughoṣa, he cared for students by displaying six different magical emanations at once, and so forth. He was reputed to be an emanation of Avalokiteśvara.

He had disciples: the three who attained the supreme,[702] the seven who attained forbearance,[703] the eighty realizers, the eleven heart sons who upheld the text-explanation tradition, the seven heart sons who commented on the *Vajra Verses*,[704] and others.

Sachen demonstrated nirvana in this realm and acted for the sake of beings after death through four bodily forms in four pure lands: Sukhāvatī, Potala,[705] Uḍḍiyāna, and Suvarṇa in the north, where it is said he still abides.

c) Sons of Sachen

Sachen had four sons: Künga Bar, Sönam Tsemo, Drakpa Gyaltsen, and Palchen Öpo. The first, Künga Bar, went to India and died in Magadha. The second, master Sönam Tsemo (1142–82),[706] studied Madhyamaka and the perfection of wisdom for seven years with Chapa Chökyi Sengé. Before the age of sixteen, he severed superimposition with respect to the tantras and the special instructions. He had direct visions of many higher deities. When living at the monastic seat, he gave instructions on the oral-instruction tradition to many disciples, so there were many who followed his philosophical system. Finally, while preaching the Dharma, he passed on to Sukhāvatī from atop his instruction throne with the manifestation of limitless bodily forms, divine music, and other signs.

Jetsün Drakpa Gyaltsen (1147–1216)[707] took the lay celibacy vow from Jangsem Dawa Gyaltsen (b. eleventh century). His life was like that of an ordained person: not partaking of meat, beer, and so forth. Once, he dreamed that he was given three tantric texts. From then on, he comprehended the real nature of all dharmas. When he was eleven years old, he taught the Saroruha[708] sādhanas of Hevajra; his explanation was very valuable, and everyone [127] was amazed. Up to the age of twelve, he received many Dharma instructions from his father, Sachen. Even after his father passed away, the latter displayed his gnosis body in a vision and taught the elucidation of the meaning of symbols, known as *the very short lineage of Lamdré.*[709] He promised that in a later rebirth, Drakpa Gyaltsen would go to Sukhāvatī, and then, having become the wheel-turning king Countless Qualities in Suvarṇa,[710] he would gain the supreme yogic achievement.

He had many disciples. His holy heart son was Jamyang Sapan himself. Moreover, there were the eight famous men, the four men who requested adornment by the *Vajra Tent,* the four great ordainees, and others.

The fourth son of Sachen, Palchen Öpo (1150–1203), had two sons: the elder was Sakya Panchen Künga Gyaltsen, or Sapan, and the younger was Sangtsa Sönam Gyaltsen.

d) Sakya Pandita

Sapan (1182–1251)[711] spoke the Sanskrit language as soon as he was born. From Jetsün Drakpa Gyaltsen, he received teachings on all the profound key points of sutra and mantra, the distillation of the instructions of the earlier Sakyapas. In dreams, he received teachings on the *Treasury of Higher Knowledge* from the supreme sage Vasubandhu and adamantine songs from the great Kashmiri pandit, Śākyaśrī. He requested the transmission cycle of the five Dharmas of Maitreya and other teachings from Shudön Dorjé Kyap, instructions on valid cognition from Maja Jangtsön and Tsurtön Shönseng, instructions on philosophical systems from Tsekpa Wangchuk Sengé, and various instructions from Chiwo Lhepa Jangchup Ö. At the age of twenty-three, he met the great Kashmiri pandit. With the great pandit and his disciples, Saṅghaśrī, Sugataśrī, and Dānaśīla, he trained completely in the ten sciences: the five major sciences of grammar, valid cognition, medicine, arts and technology, and Buddhism; and the five minor sciences of poetry, lexicography, poetics, metrics, and drama. At the age of twenty-seven, he took full ordination from the great Kashmiri pandit. He wrote the *Treasure of Knowledge* and *Distinguishing the Three Vows,* refuting countless debased propositions and debased views. In Kyirong, he vanquished six debased opponents with his reasoning, the main one being Haridrāyaṇa,[712] a South Indian extremist, and because he introduced them to the teaching, his renown pervaded the land. [In 1247,] he was invited to Mongolia by the Mongol khan, Godan (d. 1251), and he spread the teachings on explanation and practice in that land. At the age of seventy, he withdrew his form body.

It is said that in his next rebirth, he went to the ḍākinī realm, and then, in Mumuni[713] in the east, he became the son [128] of the king Nyima Tophel and traversed most of the stages and paths; after that, he became enlightened in the Abhirati buddhafield and was called Sugata Vimalaśrī. This is just a brief account; more may be learned from the biographical literature.

His disciples included: the three upholders of the lineage of realizations; the two upholders of the lineage of special instructions; the three upholders of the lineage of explanation; the thirteen elder children of the vow; the seven youths; the four great translators; the four hidden yogins; the four learned and righteous heart sons; the upholder of the practice lineage, the conqueror Yangönpa; the hidden great adept Sangtsa Sönam Gyaltsen; and others. All of them lived lives beyond imagining, and through each, the number of disciples and grand-disciples increased manyfold.

e) Phakpa and his successors

The Dharma Lord Sapan's younger brother, Sangtsa Sönam Gyaltsen (1184–1239), had two sons: the protector of beings, the Dharma king Phakpa and his younger brother, the protector of beings Chakna. As soon as Phakpa (1235–80)[714] was born, Sapan said, "He will become someone especially distinctive *(phakpa)* compared to others. Because he was born *(kye)* in the sheep *(luk)* year, name him Phakpa Lukyé." When Phakpa was three years old, he recited the sādhana of Saroruha by heart, and everyone was astonished. It was reported in all quarters that "this one is definitely distinctive," and from then on he was known as Phakpa. He taught the *Birth Stories* at the age of eight and the *Hevajra* at nine, and when he gave a discourse to an assembly of scholars, he severed the scholars' pride, and his fame spread everywhere. When he was ten years old, he took preliminary vows from Sapan before the Jowo in Lhasa. He received many Dharma instructions on the three trainings and other topics from Sherseng, the abbot of Kyormo Lung. At seventeen, he went to Mongolia as Sapan's assistant, and he comprehended most of the good qualities of outer definition-vehicle and inner secret-mantra-vehicle learning possessed by the Dharma lord Sakya Panchen. Sapan was delighted and, giving him the white Dharma conch shell called Sounds-for-a-Furlong and other gifts, enthroned him as lord of the teaching. After Sapan passed away, Phakpa bestowed the Hevajra initiation on the Mongolian king Kublai (1215–94), so he was given the rank of Dishi, or Imperial Preceptor. As offering for the initiation, he was offered thirteen districts in Tibet.

Of the thirteen districts, six were in Tsang: Lho and Jang, Chu and Ja, and Lha and Shang; [129] and six were in Ü: Ya and Phak, Gyal and Tsal, and Dri and Tak. The district of Yardrok made thirteen.[715]

Thenceforth, everyone in Tibet and Kham became Phakpa's subjects, and the Sakyapa gained suzerainty in both political and religious spheres. At the age of twenty-one, Phakpa rode out of Mongolia. At the China-Mongolia border, he took full ordination, with Nyethangpa Drakpa Sengé as preceptor, Joden Sönam Gyaltsen as assistant master, and Yarlungpa Jangchup Gyaltsen as secret teacher. He went to glorious Sakya, where he satisfied everyone, whether superior or inferior, by his endowment of Dharma and material things. Then, with the arrival of a gold-lettered invitation from the emperor, he once again went to Mongolia. As offering for granting initiation to the king, he was granted three provinces—the Dharma province of Ü-Tsang, the populous province of upper Amdo, and the horse province of lower Amdo, namely Kham—and pearls measured by the bushel. Then, he returned to Sakya. At Chumik Ringmo in Tsang he sponsored a Dharma cycle gathering for seventy thousand monks and offered them the gold, tea, silk cloth, and other valuables he had obtained. He attained final peace at the age of forty-six. He had many disciples: two with the special oral transmission of instructions, two with the special oral transmission of the tantras, four with the special oral transmission of the protector Mahākāla, two with mastery of power, six with mastery of greatness, and others. Phakpa's younger brother, the protector of beings Chakna (1239–67),[716] had mastery of magical powers such as reviving the dead and was reputed to be an emanation of Vajrapāṇi.

When the noble lord, the glorious Atiśa, arrived in Tibet, he saw two wild yaks on the slopes of Sakya Mountain and prophesied that good deeds would be performed by two Mahākālas: the two were Gur and Shel.[717] He prostrated toward the whitish earth: there were seven *dhīḥ* syllables and one *hūṃ* syllable, so he prophesied that eight emanations—seven emanations of Mañjughoṣa and one emanation of Vajrapāṇi—would work for the sake of beings.[718] Accordingly, Sachen's son Khöntön Künga Bar, the two Jetsün brothers—Sönam Tsemo and Drakpa Gyaltsen—Chungpal Ö, Sapan, Sangtsa Sönam Gyaltsen, and Phakpa were the Mañjughoṣas; and the lord of secrets, Chakna, was Vajrapāṇi. Sachen himself was Avalokiteśvara. Thus, there were three types of emanations and seven Mañjughoṣas [130] who came in succession. Of these, Sachen, Sönam Tsemo, and Drakpa Gyaltsen were said to be the three lay emanations, while Sapan and Phakpa were said to be the two monastic emanations; those five are known as the five early Sakya manifestations.

Thus, because of the preceptor-patron relationship between Sapan and his nephew Phakpa and the Mongol kings, the Sakyapas controlled all Tibet and Kham. By order of the king, the lama did the work of Dharma and gave worldly commands in conformity with the Dharma, and civil governors did the work of the law; so for just over a century, Tibet was happily ruled by the dual system.

When the Mongol king issued an order that all Tibetans make the Sakya Dharma system their own, Phakpa thought that if that were done, it would result in partisan attitudes and actions. He said that it would be good if the Dharma systems that had come down to each were left in place, so an edict was proclaimed to that effect. Having been handed Tibet when he was just twenty years old, Phakpa ruled until he was forty-six. After him,[719] Dharmapāla[720] ran the monastic seat and the nation for seven years (1281–88), Sharpa Jamyang Shithokpa[721] for eighteen years (1288–1306), Lama Daknyi Chenpo for nineteen years (1306–22),[722] no one for a three-year interval (1322–25), Khetsün Thenpo for nineteen years (1325–43), and Lama Dampa for three years (1343–46). Then, in the third year of the reign of Taen Lodrö Gyaltsen [i.e., 1349], Jangchup Gyaltsen of Situ gained control over most of Ü and Tsang, and Sakya power was destroyed. From then until now, the family lineage has ruled just a fraction of their previous domain.

f) The family lineage

The family lineage controlled the common area around the seat of authority at Sakya up through Sangtsa's son Yeshé Jungné, his son Daknyi Chenpo Sangpo Pal, and the chief of his fifteen sons,[723] the Dishi Künga Lodrö (1299–1327).[724] Künga Lodrö divided the area among the brothers, so the family split into four: the Shithok residence, the Lhakhang residence, the Rinchen Gang residence, and the Düchö residence. Nowadays, the lineages of the first three no longer exist. Later, Jamyang Namkha Tashi of the Düchö residence (b. 1458) erected Tsedong Chödé and Sisum Namgyal, so the monastic seat came to have upper and lower divisions. Still later, [131] during a period of conflict between Desi Sangyé Gyatso (1653–1703/5)[725] and Lhapsang Khan (d. 1717), a member of the Tsedong lineage named Shapdrung Jamyang Künga Yongdu Jawa performed magic against Lhapsang, so that when Lhapsang took control of Tibet, Shapdrung escaped and went to Amdo. From then on, the lower-monastery family lineage was apparently severed. The family lineage in the upper monastic seat has come down without interruption, and the tantric master Wangdü Nyingpo now sits on the throne.

Among those who succeeded in the family lineage, during the earlier time when all Tibet and Kham were completely controlled by Sakya, celibates were called by the honorary titles of *precious highness* and *great lord,* and tantric masters were called *Sakya throne holder.*

Just as it is explained in the sutras that one gains great merit by declaring the Śākya clan supreme among the clans in the world, so do the holy here in Tibet state that the merit is great from speaking of the line of Khön Mañjughoṣa. In the great Sakyapa Sachen Nyingpo's dream, all places—the side of the throne and elsewhere—were covered with countless bodies of Mañjughoṣa beyond imagining, and in particular, in the center of these, there were seven great bodies of Mañjughoṣa, blazing with the thirty-two major and eighty minor marks:[726] this occurred in the dream. Therefore, from among the family lineage, the seven most wonderful emanations of Mañjughoṣa and all the others, too, are explained as manifestations of Mañjughoṣa's compassion. Here, I have respectfully written just briefly about the family line.

2) Philosophical lineages

Although the countless individual upholders of the teaching cannot be enumerated individually, I will mention some of the main ones. With respect to upholders of the teaching of the glorious Sakya, it is known that the main upholders of the teaching on the sutra side are the duo of Yak and Rong, and the main upholders of the teaching on the secret-mantra side are the duo of Ngor and Dzong.

a) Upholders of the sutra teaching

Yaktruk Sangyé Pal (1350–1414)[727] was actually the son of an official from Tsethang, Jangchup Rinchen, but he was called Yaktruk because he was made out to be the son of someone named Yakru, who in aspect was Jangchup Rinchen's attendant. Yaktruk was the disciple of Tsöndrü Pal, who was one of the two leading disciples of Budöl, Nya, and Tsön.

Yaktruk's disciple Rongtön Mawai Sengé (1367–1449)[728] was an emanation of Maitreya, and he so admired the instructions on [132] Shijé and Kamalaśīla's *Stages of Meditation* that he also was reputed to be a reincarnation of Pha Dampa Sangyé and Kamalaśīla. He erected the Nālendra teaching center.[729] He went on the debate circuit for all ten difficult texts.[730] There were sixty-four textual systems he taught to others and forty textual systems on which he wrote explanations. He did nothing but expound texts throughout his entire life, so he had many disciples who were scholars, of whom a multitude became disciples of Jé Tsongkhapa: Sempa Shönu Gyalchok, Markhampa Drakpa Sangpo, Gungru Gyaltsen Sangpo, Narthangpa Sherap Sengé,[731] Drachung Yönten Gyatso, and others. From among the multitude of others, Dakpo Tashi Namgyal[732] ran the main Nālendra monastery, and Jamchen Rapjampa Sangyé Phel founded Kyetsal Monastery in Dreyül. Five monasteries branched off from that: there was the duo of Thupten Wangyal and Yangpachen, plus Nyenyö Jashong, Chökhor Lhünpo, and Kyetsal Ok, so there were six monasteries for dialectics—the mother Kyetsal and five sons. The custom of giving scholars the name *rapjampa*, "the all-encompassing one,"[733] spread during Sangyé Pal's lifetime.

Among his great many disciples was the duo of Panchen Bumtrak Sumpa Jampa Chödrup (1432–1504) and Jamyang Künga Chösang (1433–1503). The former was known as Bumtrak Sumpa, "the three hundred thousand man," because he had memorized the *Perfection of Wisdom in a Hundred Thousand Verses* in a single month.[734] He founded the monastery of Nyenyö Jashong. Jamyang Künga Chösang and his disciple Shungyapa Ngödrup Palbar founded Chökhor Lhünpo. Moreover, there were many scholars in the lineage of disciples: Chakthangpa Jampa Sönam, and then Mangthö Ludrup Gyatso,[735] Khenchen Ngawang Chödrak, and others.

Also, Rongtön's disciple Shākya Chokden (1428–1507)[736] founded Thupten Serdokchen, Sangyé Pal's disciple Gorampa Sönam Sengé (1429–89)[737] founded Thupten Namgyal, and Dedünpa Tenpa Rapsal founded Rawa Mé. The stream of explanation of the definition vehicle was propagated by many disciples and grand-disciples.

It is said in Mangthö Ludrupa's *Almanac of the Teaching* and other texts that the duo of Yak and Shön are the upholders of the teaching of the sutra side [133] of the Sakya.[738] Those two are Yaktruk Sangyé Pal and Rendawa Shönu Lodrö (1349–1412).[739] The latter fully studied the sutras with Nyaön Künga Pal and others. He received Madhyamaka teachings from the great preceptor Jangchup Sengé, and by analyzing with his own intelligence, he understood the subtle key points of the Prāsaṅgika Madhyamaka view and taught them. He himself stated, "At the beginning of my education, when someone said, 'there is a Madhyamaka book,' I thought it not very valuable. Nowadays, I think it something to reckon with, so I have worked on behalf of the teaching."[740] Karma Könshön said, "Nowadays, everyone, wise and the foolish alike, is talking Madhyamaka out of their mouths, Madhyamaka out of their noses.[741] This is due to the kindness of Rendawa. Before that, the Madhyamaka at Thangsak was nothing but a corpse."[742] Rendawa received all the special instructions on the Guhyasamāja and other tantras from Lotsāwa Namsang, Lotsāwa Dragyal, Lotsāwa Kyapchok Palsang, and others, and propagated them extensively. He clarified exactly how the Guhyasamāja accords with the Prāsaṅgika Madhyamaka view, so of the multitude of upholders of the Sakya teaching, he alone is renowned as the kindest.[743] He also was a source of excellent explanations. As was said of him:

> There was a set of ten textual systems that he explained:
> The four great difficult ones[744] of the supreme ornaments
> beautifying Jambudvīpa;[745]
> The trio of the *Fundamental Treatise on the Middle Way,*
> *Entering the Middle Way,* and the *Four Hundred Stanzas;*
> as well as the *Sublime Continuum,*
> The *Treasury of Higher Knowledge,* and the glorious
> *Guhyasamāja.*[746]

Also, it is said that his disciples include the seven virtuous friends who spoke of untold textual systems, the ten who spoke well on the four difficult subjects,[747] and over a hundred disciples who knew the perfection of wisdom and valid cognition. The trio of Jetsün Tsongkhapa and his two spiritual sons, Gyaltsap Jé and Khedrup Jé, are also included among his students.

Before Gyaltsap Jé, those who went on the debate circuit discussing the texts known as the four great difficult ones, the six that were appended to those,[748] and others, were simply called *kashipas,* or experts in the *four* difficult subjects, but after Gyaltsap Jé introduced the custom of explaining the ten books, the custom began of calling debaters *kachupas,* or experts in the *ten* difficult ones.[749]

b) Upholders of the secret-mantra teaching

The upholders of the Sakya secret-mantra teachings were those known as the duo of Ngor and Dzong, or as the two Küngas. They were the duo of Ngorpa[750] Künga Sangpo and Dzongpa Künga Namgyal.

(1) Ngor[751]

There was [134] a division in the lineage of disciples descending from Lama Dampa Sönam Gyaltsen:[752] his disciple was Palden Tsültrim,[753] the latter's disciple was Buddhaśrī,[754] and Buddhaśrī's disciple was Ngorpa Künga Sangpo (1382–1457).[755] [In 1429,] Ngorchen founded Evaṃ Chöden Monastery. He gave innumerable initiations, guidelines, and special instructions; for example, he taught Lamdré eighty-three times and gave the Vajra Garland initiation more than sixty times. Also, he bestowed the full monastic vows over ten thousand times. He kept the vinaya rules purely, so throughout his entire life, he maintained an exclusively vegetarian diet. He was known to have been mentioned in the scriptures of the Conqueror, such as the *Lotus of the True Dharma* and others.[756]

He had many disciples: Jamchen Rapjampa Sangyé Phel, the duo of Gorampa and Shākya Chokden, Bumtrak Sumpa, Künga Chösang, and others. The main one was Muchen Sempa Chenpo Könchok Gyaltsen (1388–1469).[757] Ngorchen gave him a hidden Dharma on the key points of Lamdré that he had not taught to other disciples. Thenceforth, there was a custom of presenting Lamdré as public explanation and private explanation.[758] Later, Könchok Lhündrup,[759] Tartsewa Namkha Palsang, Drupkhangpa Palden Döndrup, and others came successively as upholders of the lineage; it came to be known as the system of Ngor.

(2) Dzong

The Dzongpa tradition[760] is twofold: earlier and later. What is called the earlier Dzongpa or the Musepa includes Lama Dampa Sönam Gyaltsen's disciple Dzongchungwa Ngakchang Sungkyi Palwa (1306–89), and after him Jé Sangpo Gyaltsen, Gyaltsen Könchok, Gewa Sangpo, and others; as well as the disciple lineage of Gyaltsen Könchok's disciple Musepa Dorjé Gyaltsen.[761]

There also were many others: Lama Dampa's disciple Thekchen Chöjé Künga Tashi, the latter's disciple Dzongpa Künga Gyaltsen, Drakthokpa Sönam Sangpo, and others. Drakthokpa's heart son Thutön Künga Namgyal (b. 1442)[762] was said to be an emanation of the tantric masters Śrīsiṃha, Nanam Dorjé Düjom,[763] and others. He was called Thutön because he took birth in the family lineage of Thönmi Sambhota.[764] When he was young, he was called Dranga Gyalpo. He took full ordination from Jé Jampa Lingpa. He founded Gongkar Dorjé Den Monastery [135] in Ü [in 1442], and established ritual practices for multiple mandala rites, the sequence of rituals, dances, and so forth. His deeds were performed with the help of Dharma protectors; he was very famous for his magical powers and abilities. He also wrote many texts. Those in this lineage are called the later Dzongpas or Gongkarwas.

(3) Tsar

Later came Tsarchen Losal Gyatso (1502–66).[765] Intending at first to be a Gelukpa, he entered Tashi Lhünpo Monastery. One day a nun said to him, "Jetsün Doringpa[766] sent me to summon you; I was asked to confer this gift." She handed over a book then disappeared without a trace. His mind shaken by this, Tsarchen went to Doringpa and told him the reason for the visit. Doringpa told him the text had been stolen by Vajrayoginī. When he inserted the book into the empty space in the middle of the pile of manuals from which the ḍākinī booklet[767] had been taken, it fit there perfectly, so Tsarchen gained great conviction. He received from Dakchen Lodrö Gyaltsen and Doringpa Künsang Chökyi Nyima all the instructions that came from Ngor and Dzong, and the ear-whispered-lineage instructions held only in the family lineage and unknown to those in the Ngor, Dzong, and other lineages.[768] He became a great ocean collecting into one the countless rivers of the Sakya teaching. His many disciples included Jamyang

Khyentsé Wangchuk,[769] Mangthö Ludrup Gyatso, Ngakchang Sönam Chöpal, Khenchen Lapsumpa, Bökharwa Maitri Döndrup Gyaltsen, and others. The upholders of the lineage Wangchuk Rabten, Sönam Chokden, Khenchen Ngawang Chödrak,[770] and others propagated the teaching in many places. In later times, too, there were many able upholders of the Tsar-system ear-whispered lineage: Morchen Künga Lhündrup, Nesarpa Künga Lekpai Jungné, and Dakchen Dorjé Chang Ngawang Künga Lodrö and his spiritual sons, and others.

The Third Dalai Lama, Sönam Gyatso, received instructions on Pañjaranātha, Kṣetrapāla, and other deities from Tsarchen; and his highness the Great Fifth Dalai Lama received from Nesarpa Gönpo Sönam Chokden instructions on the thirteen golden Dharmas of the Tsar-system Lamdré,[771] the cycle of instructions on the greater and lesser protectors, and other teachings.[772] Nowadays, [136] the golden Dharmas and the instruction on Kṣetrapāla have spread quite a bit among the Geluk. Thus, the lineage transmitted from Tsarchen is known as the Tsar system, the special instruction of the highly secret disciple-explanation tradition, unheard by the average Sakyapa.

3) Current conditions

In former times, in the lands of Mongolia and China, and in Amdo and Kham and upper and lower Tibet, there were many monasteries where holy upholders of the Sakya teaching, as well as monks, gathered. Nowadays, there are several monasteries, such as Lhündrup Teng in Dergé[773] and others. But apart from rule by the line of Ngor abbots, in other regions there do not seem to be monk practitioners who are upholders of the lineage of the Sakya Dharma.[774]

The glorious Sakya has countless enumerations of the Dharmas of sutra and mantra, and in particular there are extant nearly innumerable initiations, tantric explanations, special instructions, yogic applications, and so forth, in relation to the four classes of secret mantra. Of these, it seems that what is identified as the thirteen golden Dharmas not allowed outside the iron fence of the monastery is separate from these. According to the Tsar system, the thirteen are: the three Khecarī cycles, the three cycles of the great red ones, the three cycles of the lesser red ones,[775] Amāravajradevī, Red Jambala, Siṃhamukhā, and Black Mañjughoṣa; when one adds Siṃhanāda Avalokiteśvara to those, they are called "the fourteen golden Dharmas of Lupa."[776]

Moreover, unbroken lineages beyond imagining have survived to the present time: the initiation of the *Vajra Garland;* the general instructions and side instructions for the *Ocean of Sādhanas,*[777] and others; the Ārya[778] system and the Jñānapāda system of Guhyasamāja interpretation; the Kālacakra; the four special oral traditions of Hevajra; the three Heruka systems—of Lūipa,[779] Kṛṣṇācārya, and Ghaṇṭapa—along with the practice of the Donkey-faced Heruka; the three Yamāntakas, red, black, and Vajrabhairava; and other new tantra traditions. Also remaining are the Dharma cycles of the protectors: the ancestral instruction on the cycles of Yangdak Heruka[780] together with the old tantra Vajrakīla; the protector Pañjaranātha; the four-headed Mahākāla; the lords of the cemetery; the attendant deity of Pañjaranātha, Bektsé; the guardians of Vajrakīla; and others.

b. In particular, the history of the principal Dharmas—Lamdré and others

The history of Lamdré: The essence of the Sakya Dharma is the precious [137] oral instruction on the path together with its result.[781] The actual practice is the succession of practices on the path of the two stages of Hevajra,[782] along with their ancillaries. The stages of the common path are fulfilled in the context of the three appearances, so Lamdré is the complete, inerrant path of the entirety of sutra and mantra.

1) Drokmi and his disciples

The history of Lamdré: The disciple of the glorious protector, Ārya Nāgārjuna, was Śākyamitra (ninth century),[783] whose disciple was Jvalapradhāna,[784] whose disciple was the elder, the glorious Dharmapāla. When the latter devoted himself to tantric conduct, he was given the name Virūpa.[785] His disciple was Ḍombi Heruka, whose disciple was Durjayacandra or Prajñā Indraruci.[786] From the latter, the great lama Drokmi (d. 1064?)[787] received secret-mantra initiations and extensive tantric explanations and special instructions for four years. He also received teachings on Lamdré without its root text. Drokmi went to Tibet and gave many instructions on the tantras, Kuddālapāda's *Special Instruction on the Inconceivable Stage,*[788] and other texts, so many disciples emerged. Gö Lotsāwa Khukpa Lhetsé and Marpa Lotsāwa both were his disciples, but the great lama was so restrictive with the Dharma that a major donation was required for even a minor instruction, so those two, thinking they would meet pandits if they went to India, did not remain long with Drokmi.

When Drokmi was staying in Namkarpo, he received a report that the pandit Gayādhara[789] had come to Tibet. He went to Gungthang to welcome him and greeted him there. He traveled with the pandit and received many Dharma teachings from him, even on the road. Drokmi invited Gayādhara to Mugu Lung and, for five years, received from him there the complete precious oral instruction. Drokmi offered him a donation of five hundred gold *srangs*. The pandit went to India; after returning to Tibet twice, he passed away in Kharak; he had lived for three hundred and fifty years. His other names were Tringyi Shukchen and Lawa Marpo. Apparently, there was a Lawa Marpo in the guru lineage of Devī, who was the pandit Prajñāgupta; and there was another Lawa Marpo who spread *uniting and freeing* and other degenerate practices; they should not be mistaken for Gayādhara.

The complete oral-instruction lineage was given by Drokmi to the trio of Lhatsün Kali,[790] Dromdopa Tönchung,[791] and Setön Künrik.[792] He gave a portion each of the oral instruction to the disciples known as the three males—Gyergom Sewo, Shengom Röpo, and Üpa Drongpoché—and to the four females—Tömo [138] Dorjé Tso, Sangmo Köné, Shapmo Jamchik, and Chemo Namkha—and all seven became adepts. He gave the complete text and explanation lineage to the quintet of Gyijang Ukarwa of Lhetsé, Shapkyi Draktsé Sonakpa, Wangtön Könchok Gyalpo, Khön Könchok Gyalpo of Sakya, and Ngaripa Salwai Nyingpo. This great lama Drokmi had the virtue of being learned in many texts and special instructions, and attained stability in both the generation and completion stages. Through his control of the psychic winds, he sat in full-lotus position in the sky. He wished to become a buddha without giving up his body, through enlisting death onto the path, but his spiritual sons embalmed him, and did other things, which was a small omen that it was not to be. He did, however, gain the yogic achievement of Mahāmudrā in the bardo.[793]

Drokmi gave the complete oral tradition to three disciples, but the instructions did not spread from two of them. According to a prophecy made to Setön Künrik, the spread of the instructions would depend on the brother and sister Shama; the sister-brother pair, Machik Shama and Khönphuwa Chökyi Gyalpo,[794] received the oral tradition from Setön. They practiced and became adepts. It also seems they worked extensively for the benefit of others. More may be learned about them from other, more extensive chronicles.[795]

In general, the lineage of Lamdré spread gradually from the great lama

Drokmi, and it is said that eighteen different oral traditions arose. The main one was the special oral tradition given to the Sakya jetsüns: Khön Könchok Gyalpo received explanatory instructions from Drokmi that were chiefly explanations of the *Vajra Tent* and *Hevajra*. Setön took explanatory instructions on tantra from the great lama Drokmi's direct disciple Ngaripa Salwai Nyingpo, and he also received instructions from Khön Könchok Gyalpo. Setön himself attained high realization and lived to be eighty-eight years old. When he was eighty-seven, Sachen Künga Nyingpo came to meet him and was very pleased. Setön told him, "Come; I will give you instructions." Because of a small hindrance, however, Sachen did not hear them, and the next year, the great Setön passed away. Later, Sachen was tormented by not having received instruction. He asked who had the instructions of Setön and was told that Gönpawa and his younger brother did. The younger had passed away, and when he went to the older one, the omens were somewhat inauspicious, but Shang Gönpawa happily gave him the complete instructions on Lamdré.[796] From then on, [139] the glorious Sakyapas became lords of both the textual and instruction lineages.

2) The nature of Lamdré

Even the Sakyapas have varying ways of explaining Lamdré. Until Ngorpa, the terms "public" and "private" explanation were unknown. Ngorpa Künsang made a distinction between public explanation and private explanation, and from then on it was known that Lamdré was divided thus.

If I elaborate extensively on the nature and workings of the Lamdré instruction, I'm afraid it would be too much, so I will say this:

> "In the sky that is the basis of purification, the thick clouds that are to be purified
> By the purifier—the breeze of the yoga of the two stages—
> Multiply here *en masse,* but self-arising, they are self-freeing,
> And the result of purification—the stainless sky—shows its own face.
>
> "What is present as the basis is pointed out through initiation,[797]
> Cultivated as the path, and, when experienced by means of the view,
> Dawns as the culmination of attainment. The actualized result,
> This inexhaustible treasury unknown to others, is the special wealth of Virūpa.

"When one spreads the water and compost of the four connections
arising from the initiations
On the vast, rich ground of the primordial mandala,
The result is the four bodies. This way of farming,
Which fulfills the wishes of all, is the skillful means of Virūpa.

"Whatever magical apparitions of external demons[798] appear
From the play of the winds and mind in the channel-syllables,[799]
This gold-transforming elixir that changes the iron and copper of confusing appearances
Into gold is the special profundity of Virūpa.

"The primordially unelaborated empty nature
United with the individual channels, syllables, drops, and winds,
Is distinguished according to the initiation[800] as 'apparent yet empty,' 'lucid yet empty,'
'Blissful yet empty,' and 'aware yet empty'; this is the view of Virūpa.

"The path of the entire doctrine is complete in this mode of guidance."
I sing this song that pleases Sarasvatī
And wonder whether Virūpa has passed to me
The great all-conquering banner.[801]

On the basis of the many technical terms of its own language, the Lamdré was criticized in earlier times, as in Ngok's *Thorny Plant*:[802]

The golden Dharmas of Gayādhara arose
From confusion about the transmission of mother-goddess tantras.

There were others, as well, and nowadays, it seems some in our own Geluk party say that study of and reflection on Lamdré do not help us to understand the meaning of the tantras, but this merely shows the fault of their never having received the proper guidance of the four sources of valid cognition and the four ear-whispered lineages.[803] [140]

c. A presentation of the Sakya view

A presentation of the glorious Sakya view: Many, like Jamgön Sapan, Rongtön, and others, gave primacy to the Svātantrika Madhyamaka. Jetsün Rendawa upheld the Prāsaṅgika view. Shākya Chokden at first preferred the Madhyamaka view, in mid-life the Cittamātra view, and at the end the Jonang view. Many others, it seems, took the view of Dzokchen as supreme. The unique Sakya view is the view of Lamdré, which requires nonapprehension of true existence by a clear, empty mind or seeing the inseparability of samsara and nirvana. Accordingly, the presentation of the Sakya view has two divisions, sutra and mantra. The sutra system also is twofold: the special instructions of the followers of Nāgārjuna and the special instructions of the followers of Maitreya.

1) A presentation of the views of the sutra system[804]

a) Special instructions of the followers of Nāgārjuna

Āryadeva states:

> In the beginning, turning away from the nonmeritorious;
> In the middle, turning away from the self;
> And in the end, turning away from all views:
> Whoever knows this is truly wise.[805]

As stated here, in the first of the three stages, by meditating on the disadvantages of samsara, the difficulty of obtaining the leisure and fortune of a perfect human rebirth, karma and its result, love and compassion, and so forth, you turn away from the nonmeritorious. In the middle, you turn away from self. And in the end, in order to turn away all views, you do two things: (1) sever the elaboration apprehending true existence and (2) sever the elaboration apprehending non-true existence.

(1) Severing the elaboration apprehending true existence

First, you identify the apprehension of true existence that apprehends the five aggregates of your continuum as truly established. If your own aggregates are truly established, they should be established from the very beginning, without depending on any causes or conditions. Since the aggregates only exist having arisen from causes and conditions, they are not truly established. Having resolved your thought thus, you fix your mind on that. At first, constraining the mind, you sever the conceptual thought apprehending true existence. In the middle, you relax, relaxing into the view with a relaxed mind, maintaining that through self-liberation from all apprehending. At the end, you alternate constraining and relaxing, or, alternatively, hold to your natural state: without losing mindfulness and introspection [141] of the view, you settle the mind loosely. When you gain confidence in that, Āryadeva says:

> The emptiness of one
> Is the emptiness of all.[806]

In accordance with that and other statements, you freely proceed to an understanding that all dharmas are not truly existent, and all the key points of the Dharma will be understood simultaneously. This is the meaning of "in the middle, turn away from the self." For one with superior faculties who meditates on this first stage of the view, it is possible for the second stage to arise simultaneously. When tranquil abiding has already occurred, then even if the union of tranquil abiding and superior insight does not occur, you may hold the mind of tranquil abiding here on the apprehension of the key point of the view, and the view that is the union of tranquil abiding and superior insight will arise in your mental continuum.

(2) Severing the elaboration apprehending non-true existence

Second, the conceptual thought apprehending true existence, which arises from the conceptual thought apprehending the true existence of the delusions and karma, arises from elaboration or apprehension of a sign, so it must be severed; as Āryadeva states, "in the end, turn away from all views." Thus, after establishing that all dharmas are not truly existent, you also need to sever that part of sign apprehension in which you think that non-true existence exists; through the essential point of dependent arising, you are led to certainty in the view that realizes *all* dharmas are not truly existent. After gaining that certainty, without persisting in that, you also give up clinging to the idea that non-true existence exists. The object, emptiness, is not to be apprehended as having any kind of existence, nonexistence, and so forth,[807] because emptiness is not an object of any kind of mind that apprehends dualistically;

thus should you resolve your thought. Objects are untouched by elaboration; without polluting the mind with impurities, give up all apprehension and signs and elaboration and settle evenly in natural nonapprehension. Thus, in the statement, "if apprehension arises, it is not the right view,"[808] "apprehension" refers to apprehending true existence at the time of the first view stage and apprehending signs at the time of the second.

b) Meditating according to the special instructions of Maitreya

In this system, the basic[809] gnosis being, the natural clear-light mind itself, is the basis of samsara and nirvana. The mind manifesting dual appearance—which does not recognize that, and mistakes apprehended and apprehender as dual—together with its latent disposition, [142] is the innate ignorance that is the root of samsara. Thus, you should sever this root and dissolve it into its original sphere. That is twofold: severing the mistaken appearances of object and of subject.[810]

The first, severing the mistaken appearance of the object, is threefold: (1) seeking the concentration that attains the appearance, that is, heat; (2) seeking the concentration that extends the appearance, that is, peak; and (3) seeking the concentration that realizes that there is no object, that is, acceptance.[811]

(1) Although there abides within your own mind a naturally clear and nonconceptual clear-light mind free of the duality of object and subject, you do not see it. It is obscured by the apprehension of outer objects as truly separate from your own mind, so it is necessary to clear away this obstacle. The way to clear it away is this: Consider, "If these outer objects are just mistaken appearances of my mind, then they do not truly exist apart from my mind." Having concluded this, you strive until the experience of that emerges. Striving thus, you think that these apparent outer objects, apart from being mere mental mistakes, do not truly exist externally. There then will arise a somewhat clear appearance of confidence in that fact. That is called the concentration that attains the appearance, that is, *heat*.

(2) By meditating again, you greatly extend the clear appearance of the former mind; you will gain an experience of confidence that is clearer than the previous confidence; that is called the concentration that extends the appearance, that is, *peak*.

(3) Also, having striven thus, you experience in meditation the clarity and bliss of the clear appearance in your own mind of the manifest fact that the

mistaken appearance of an object to be apprehended is obscuring the clear-light mind in your own mental continuum, and a confidence arises that is greater than before; that is called the concentration cognizing that there is no object, that is, *acceptance*. Although the mistaken mental appearance of an inner subject has not disappeared, the mistaken appearance that appears as an external object has disappeared. Since clinging to external appearing objects as truly existent will not occur at all, that is also called the concentration that attains the appearance of the meaning.

The second, mainly severing the mistaken appearance of the subject: Through renewed effort in meditation, the mistaken mental appearance of an inner subject will also disappear. An experience will occur that is like directly seeing the clear-light of mind as increasingly clear appearance. That is the uninterrupted concentration, that is, the *supreme mundane attainment*.[812] At that time, although innate ignorance has not been fully purified, the clear light arises mostly purified [143] of the manifest mistaken appearance of object and subject extending from that innate ignorance, so the arising of the gnosis of the path of seeing, the first bodhisattva stage, is easily achieved. Through renewed meditation, the latent dispositions to the innate ignorance that is the basis of the projection of the object-subject duality are purified, as are their manifestations. Clear appearance and gnosis arise, like seeing plainly and vividly the natural clear-light mind that is free of the duality of object and subject. The manifest mistaken appearances related to the three stages of appearing, extending, and attaining have manifested and disappeared; the antidotes to those are the clear appearances of appearing, extending, and attaining, that is, the three stages of the path of preparation that occur in succession. After that is the supreme mundane attainment: the great clear light in which the manifest coarse innate ignorance has disappeared. After meditating thus, you see directly with superior insight one part of your own clear-light mind that purifies one part of the innate ignorance and its seed; that is called the *path of seeing*, which is the first bodhisattva stage. Then, at the tenth stage, the clear appearance is greatly extended, purifying each part of the ignorance that obscures your clear-light mind. The eleventh stage is the time of buddhahood: you see without obstruction the natural clear-light mind possessing the two purities.[813] Thus is it explained.

2) A presentation of the views of the mantra system[814]

The view of the mantra system: The view is the realization of the real nature of mind; in order to elicit an experience of that, it is necessary to identify the mind that is the basis of its attributes, so first you must seek the mind. You identify it as the union of clarity and emptiness, and from within that, you point to the innate mind, the original gnosis. You meditate on the meaning of that: without letting the mistaken mind roam, see whatever appearances arise as the play of gnosis, and if mistaken appearances should arise, with mindfulness of the view and with determination, melt them like ice into water, making all mistaken appearances arise simply as gnosis. This is how the view is presented in the highly secret private-explanation system.

a) Identifying the mind

Further, there is the way of seeking the mind: You orient the mind inward, as in the Kagyü way of seeking the mind.[815] [144] You seek by inquiring, "Where is my mind? What kind of shape and color does it have?" When you investigate, you see that the mind is definitely not to be found conventionally, and you identify it as mere clarity, mere cognition, mere motion, cognitive experience, and lucidity. When self-arising experience arises a little from within that identification, that is the realization of the first of the threefold qualities of mind, called *the characteristic of mind: clarity.* When, by seeking in that way, you gain certainty that the mind is the emptiness that is free of the three conditions—arising, cessation, and abiding—that is the realization of the second of the threefold qualities of mind, called *the intrinsic nature of mind: empty.* When you experience it thusly as empty, it is not like empty space in which all and everything is annihilated; rather, it is looking plainly into the very face of that mind, which is mere clarity, mere cognition, fit to appear as anything. Since its intrinsic nature is not apprehended anywhere, you determine that it is emptiness.[816] Although the mind is thus twofold—clarity and emptiness—these are not separable. The intrinsic nature of mind is empty, yet the slightest motion of the empty searcher is clarity, and when there is clarity, it is empty. When from within the empty you determine the union of clarity and emptiness, which arises as self-appearing clarity, that is called *reaching union.* From within the meat of that experience, which is not just intellectual, any appearance that arises, arises as the play of inseparable samsara and nirvana. When such an experience occurs, it is the so-called *uncontrived intrinsic nature of mind,*[817] the complete realization of the quality of the mind as the union of clarity and emptiness. At that stage, it is said that one has gained the *common* identification of mind.

The *uncommon* identification is the identification of the original, innate gnosis. That gnosis is not identified as the mere general mind or the mind of mistaken appearances; it should be identified as an unmistaken basic mind, the union of clarity and emptiness. It is given many different names in the sutras, tantras, and treatises: pure mind, buddha nature, natural clear-light mind, vajra mind, and others; it also is called "the causal mental continuum that is the basis of everything." The mental confusion that innately appears in your mental continuum is the accidental samsara that is to be purified. The intrinsic nature of that, which has accompanied the mind since beginningless time, the previously unidentified innate [145] gnosis, is nirvana. With regard to their intrinsic nature, those two, innate ignorance and innate gnosis, cannot be distinguished; they are inseparable. Accordingly, that is the causal identification of the inseparability of samsara and nirvana. The view when you are meditatively poised on the union of the clarity and emptiness of your mind, which is free of the duality of subject and object with respect to the identification of that innate gnosis, is posited as the view that is the path of the inseparability of samsara and nirvana.

b) Three points related to practice

That view must be stabilized and enhanced by three key points related to practice. The three key points are: (1) proving that appearances are mind, (2) proving that mind is illusory, and (3) proving that illusions are intrinsically nonexistent.

(1) Appearances are mind

First, proving that appearances are mind: It is established by scripture and example that all these externally appearing objects are only mistaken appearances polluted by the ignorance of your own mind; there is no way they are truly established as external. When, through meditation, you determine with certainty that appearing objects are mind, you do not keep your grip on the view of the union of clarity and emptiness, but settle in untroubled clarity. When you thus determine that appearances are mind, the realization that external objects do not truly exist is nearly the same as the view of the true-aspectarian Cittamātra. Stabilized on the natural clarity part, you enhance that realization.

(2) Mind is illusory

Second, proving that mind is illusory: It is established by scripture and example that if external apprehended objects are mistaken appearances polluted by the mistaken mind that apprehends them, then because the object does not exist, the subject, the mind, does not exist, either. Thus, when you meditate, you stabilize the emptiness part and enhance that. Although you may thus realize the object and subject as non-truly existent, if you do not sever the apprehension of true existence in the clear-empty mind that is empty of duality, your realization will be just the same as the view of the false-aspectarian Cittamātra.[818]

(3) Illusions do not inherently exist

The third, the proof that illusions do not inherently exist, is twofold: (a) Proof through dependent arising and (b) Proof through inexpressibility.

(a) Proof through dependent arising

You might think: Even though all apprehended objects and apprehending subjects are not truly existent, perhaps there is a dharma other than object and subject that is truly established. *All* dharmas, however, are not intrinsically established. All compounded phenomena are non-truly established from the standpoint of dependent arising. [146] Uncompounded phenomena are established relative to compounded phenomena. In other words, "uncompounded phenomena" are established as the parts of compounded phenomena that are empty of true existence; there is no additional truly established entity apart from that. Nāgārjuna states:

> Since compounded phenomena do not exist,
> How could uncompounded phenomena exist?[819]

Thus, all dharmas are proven to lack intrinsic nature from the standpoint of dependent arising. By reflecting on the meaning of the above authoritative texts and examples like "a recitation, a butter lamp, a mirror, a seal,"[820] you will sever superimposition by learning and contemplating that all dharmas are empty of true existence. The experience arising in meditation is said to be about the same view as that of the perfection of wisdom and Madhyamaka. The experience of the union of such emptiness of true existence with the clarity of the original innate mind is the view of the inseparability of samsara and nirvana; it is the supreme good path of Madhyamaka, which, through reasoning from dependent arising, is free of the extremes of eternalism and nihilism.

(b) Proof through inexpressibility

Through practicing as explained before, you reduce appearing objects to mind, reduce mental appearances to illusion, and reduce illusion to dependent arising. You will experience with certainty the fact that such apparently contradictory dharmas are not contradictory. Because the nature of these arising dharmas cannot be expressed in such a way as to say, "It is like this," it is simply designated as "inexpressible." Since it is inexpressible by words, in fact there is nothing to think about. Since there is nothing on which to meditate, nor a meditator, there is no object on which to meditate. Since there is nothing to be viewed, nor a viewer, there is nothing to be viewed by wisdom. Since there is nothing to be seen, nor a seer, there is nothing to be seen by viewing. Since there is no one to be liberated, nor a liberator, there is in fact no liberation.

Well, you may ask: If it is unexpressed, the word will not be understood; if it is not thought, the meaning will not be known; if it is not meditated upon, it will not be experienced; if it is not viewed, the ultimate nature will not be seen; and if there is no freedom, there will be no awakening. What, then, should be done? The answer is: In the ultimate sense, no portion of appearance whatsoever—what is to be understood, the understander, and so forth—is dualistic. Nevertheless, you will understand simply through the expression of inexpressibility in conventional discourse. The actual meaning of the ultimate nature is inexpressible, but through gaining certainty by way of profound scriptures of definitive meaning and the guidance of a lama, you will understand mind itself—nondual gnosis—as the actual ultimate nature of the original mind.

Thus, simply by thinking [147] what cannot be thought, you will know: by thinking about that inexpressible object of understanding without concepts of thought or thinker, you will gain certainty regarding the unthinkable realm. Simply by meditating without meditation, you will gain experience: that meditation, free from meditated and meditator, is the supreme way of meditating on reality. Simply by viewing without the viewed, you will see: that very seeing of the meaning of reality as without seen or seer is the best seeing. Simply by realizing that there is nothing to be liberated, you will be liberated: in reality, there is no bondage, and that very realization that there is no bondage is liberation. If you understand thusly, you will become enlightened without enlightenment: primordially, the real nature of mind is not seen anywhere, and that manifest gnosis itself, in which all elaborated signs are stilled, is just what is given the name *buddha;* thus, it is ultimately buddha because it is unseen.

"Well," you may ask, "How can the aims of sentient beings be achieved?" The answer is: Because sentient beings do not ultimately exist as intentional objects, there is no acting for the sake of sentient beings. Conventionally, however, just as all things required and desired come about through the wish-granting jewel, so the aims of sentient beings are effortlessly achieved without thought by force of previous prayers.

With those meanings in mind, Jé Sakya Pandita stated:

> All dharmas are primordially unarisen,
> Arising itself also is unarisen,
> And nonarising itself also appears to arise.
>
> Thus, arising and nonarising,
> Conceptuality and nonconceptuality,
> Appearance and the empty,
> And samsara and nirvana, too,
> Are ultimately not distinct.
>
> Distinctions come about from nondistinction;
> If you can distinguish the distinctions within distinctions,
> You'll realize the real nature of all samsara and nirvana,
> Understand the real nature of all objects of knowledge,
> And know the real nature of all that is good and bad.
>
> When you realize the point that there is no cause of realization,
> Mind itself, which cannot be liberated, will be liberated;
> Objects of knowledge, which are not objects of knowledge,
> will be known;
> The explanation, that there is nothing to be explained, will
> be learned;
> And you'll achieve your desired aim without desire.
>
> Working with all objects of knowledge,
> You'll become the king of all Dharmas.[821]

When the meaning of those verses has been established, then, as Jetsün Rinpoché Drakpa Gyaltsen says:

The second of the three is [148] demonstration through
inexpressibility:
An infant's laughter and a mute's dream,
Tickling a sensitive spot and sexual bliss;
The gnosis of the third initiation and secret union,
Waves of enjoyment and the mandala wheel.[822]

He stated this as the way to identify reality by way of eight examples, in sequence the four common examples and the four uncommon examples. If, through the first four examples, you realize well that all dharmas are just mental, illusory, and without intrinsic nature, the first object of abandonment for tantra, the poison of ignorance, will be extracted. However, the poison that is the deliberate, continuous activity of ordinary conceptual thought, the root of the suffering of samsara, will not be extracted, so it is called *the poisoned view of the time of the cause;* one sets as the view the mere cognition of the object.

Based on the latter uncommon examples of the inexpressible, through the faultless gnosis that arises from initiation and the two stages of highest yoga tantra practice, you will be able to draw out the poison of the deliberate, continuous activity of conceptual thought, so that phase is called *the unpoisoned view of the time of the path*. It is able to indicate the gnosis of the meaning, so it is also called *the gnosis of the indicative example.*[823] It is the view set on concentration-based experience. Thus it is explained. It seems that the view set at the time of the cause is not the Prāsaṅgika Madhyamaka view but just the view common to Madhyamaka and Cittamātra, and that the way that view is elevated is through the view adopted at the time of the path.

That completes my presentation of the glorious Sakya view of the inseparability of samsara and nirvana.[824]

Concluding verses

The lamp of the precious teaching of the Tripiṭaka
And the four classes of tantra is lifted high,
And every direction is filled with Dharma's shining.

The tradition of the glorious Sakya is:
The eye that seeks the liberating path for the fortunate student,

The best medicine to clear up the chronic illness of the delusions,
The wish-granting tree fulfilling all our desires and hopes,
The nectar that grants the deathless stage.

Specifically, it is the wealth of the fortunate, the inner treasury of teaching,
The famous oral instruction that collects
Into a single vessel the mass of precious meanings
Of vast numbers of tantras and the practice of cause, path, and result.

Seeing [149] with his gnosis eye that his very own
Task was to protect this pure way,
The chief of the teaching protectors, Pañjaranātha, came flying,
I think, from the Holy Land, wearing the mask of Sé.[825]

The account describing such events,
Sounding like divine music
And beguiling like a rosary of pearls,
I disburse as an earring for the honest.

From *The Crystal Mirror: An Excellent Explanation Showing the Sources and Assertions of All Philosophical Systems,* this completes the explanation the history of the Sakya philosophical system.

9. The Jonang and Minor Traditions

[II. The History of Philosophical Systems in Tibet, the Land of Snows
B. The histories of the different schools]

6. Jonang[826]

> I will relate the history of the renowned Jonang philosophical system,
> The way opened wide by Dölpopa,[827]
> Who is the white banner known as the Omniscient,
> Unfurled before the learned in every land.[828]

THE HISTORY of the Jonang philosophical system is threefold: a. How it arose, b. The standpoint of the extrinsic-emptiness view of that system, and c. Proving that that view is wrong.

a. How the Jonangpa arose

Künpang Thukjé Tsöndrü (1243–1313) founded a monastery in Jomo Nang. Dölpopa dwelled there and widely propagated this philosophical system, so thenceforth the upholders of the lineage were known as Jonangpas.

1) Yumo Mikyö Dorjé and his successors

The root source of the Jonang philosophical system is Yumo Mikyö Dorjé (eleventh century).[829] At first, he was a yogin; later, he was given the preliminary ordination name Depa Gyalpo. He studied with many lamas, such as Sok Dülzin. He received some Dharma teachings from the Kashmiri scholar Somanātha, and from Somanātha's disciple Drotön Namla Tsek he received detailed teachings on the Kālacakra tantra commentary,[830] along with its special instructions, and Candrakīrti's *Bright Lamp,* along with its special instructions. Then he went to Uyuk, and when he meditated, he gained realization and conceived [150] the extrinsic-emptiness view. He mastered the supernatural powers and performed many magical transformations, into a raven, a magpie, and so forth, so he gained great fame as an adept. He also wrote some textbooks on Kālacakra and other topics. He passed away at age eighty-two.

Although he had many disciples, the main one was his son, Dharmeśvara, who by the age of twenty understood all the instructions on texts mastered by the great adept. He studied with many masters and focused on training in Madhyamaka, valid cognition, Guhyasamāja, and Kālacakra. He was immensely intelligent, supposedly an emanation of Mañjughoṣa. Although he wrote Dharma texts, they have been lost. His great spiritual son was Namkha Öser, whose disciple was Dharmeśvara's son Semo Chewa Namkha Gyaltsen. It is said that up to Demo's disciple Jamsar Sherap Öser, the Kālacakra teaching was restricted, but from Jamsar on, it became open. Jamsar's disciple was the omniscient Chöku Öser, and his disciple was Künpang Thukjé Tsöndrü. The latter wrote textbooks on the six yogas of Kālacakra. His disciple was Jangsem Gyalwa Yeshé. Yönten Gyatso[831] was a disciple of both Künpang and Jangsem.

2) Dölpopa and his successors

Yönten Gyatso's disciple was Dölpopa Sherap Gyaltsen (1292–1361), known as the Omniscient.[832] He received extensive teachings on the Dharmas of sutra and mantra from more than thirty lamas. In particular, having studied the perfection of wisdom, valid cognition, and abhidharma in detail with Kyitön Jamyang Drakpa Gyaltsen,[833] he went on the debate circuit in Ü and Tsang and became a very famous scholar. From Kyitön, he received countless instructions on mantra, as indicated by his receiving seventy initiations and their ancillary teachings. He took his full ordination from Sönam Drakpa, the great preceptor of Chölung Tsokpa.[834] To this point he was an upholder of the Sakya Dharma lineage, but he arrived at Jonang at the age of thirty-one and received many initiations and teachings and, in particular, initiation guidelines on Kālacakra from Khetsün Yönten Gyatso. After that, he belonged to the Jonang Dharma lineage. When he meditated on the six yogas of Kālacakra, a sign occurred that he had completed the stage of breath control. Then, living in the monastic seat, he erected the great stupa.[835] He then gained strong certainty about the extrinsic-emptiness view and wrote texts that focus on that, such as the so-called *Mountain Dharma: The Ocean of Definitive Meaning*[836] [151] and others, so it is said that when he raised the mountain, an ocean broke forth.[837]

He taught many scholars his explanations of the Kālacakra tantra commentary, focusing on the view of extrinsic emptiness. He had visions of many deities and showed signs of gaining yogic achievements, such as displaying three bodily forms simultaneously. He gave many disciples the text explanations and special instructions on sutra and mantra. He undertook many scholarly activities—writing treatises and so forth. Overall, he assembled more than two thousand disciples and more than a thousand serious practitioners. There are many stories about him: Chim Losang Drakpa saw him as Avalokiteśvara, his attendant Namkha Jangchup saw him as Mañjughoṣa, and so forth.

Of his innumerable disciples, two, Lotsāwa Lodrö Pal and Sasang Mati Panchen, became his heart sons,[838] and many sages continued his work, such as Choklé Namgyal, or Chokgyalwa.

Chokgyalwa (1306–86)[839] was educated at Sakya and became a great scholar. At first, Choklé did not accept the extrinsic-emptiness view and went to Jonang to debate. The great Dölpopa gave effective explanations based on scripture and reasoning, so Chokgyalwa overcame his dissatisfaction; he then became Dölpopa's disciple and received many explanations of sutra and mantra, in particular the complete initiation guidelines on Kālacakra. He also received many Dharma teachings from the omniscient Butön. He served as Dharma master of Ngamring[840] and wrote many texts on the perfection of wisdom and valid cognition. His disciple was the great master known as Nyaön Künga Pal.[841] The omniscient Jé Tsongkhapa received teachings on the Kālacakra from Chokgyalwa and the perfection of wisdom from Nyaön, and from then on, he propagated the initiations and explanations of Kālacakra continuously and extensively.

3) Later developments

Because many scholar-adepts thoroughly rejected the view of extrinsic emptiness, it became dormant. Later, however, Jonang Künga Drölchok[842] and, in particular, Drölchok's reincarnation, Tāranātha (1575–1634),[843] revived and illuminated it; they did many things, such as disseminating explanations and composing texts about it. Tāranātha founded Takten [152] Phüntsok Ling: he erected statues and printed many missing texts and the Jonang system's treatises. He also gathered a great many disciples. Because he and the

Rinpung ruler Karma Tenkyong Wangpo[844] had a preceptor-patron relationship, he was greatly renowned in both the religious and political spheres. Not long afterward, however, Rinpung power declined, and after Tāranātha passed away, the Great Fifth Dalai Lama converted Phüntsok Ling Monastery into a Geluk monastery, and named it Ganden Phüntsok Ling. Chölung Jangtsé and other Jonang monasteries were also converted into Geluk monasteries. Most of the prints of the Jonang scriptures were sealed away in hidden places.[845] At the present time, it is reported that there is a monastery founded at Dzamthang in eastern Tibet[846] by Jonang Künkhyen's [i.e., Dölpopa's] disciple and secretary, Kashipa Rinchen Pal, as well as some scattered monasteries that derived from it. Outside those, there is not a single institution in Ü or Tsang where the Jonang philosophical system is upheld, and except for Tāranātha's *Jewel Source of Sādhanas,*[847] the Dharma streams of Jonang have already attained the rainbow body.[848]

4) Origins of the extrinsic-emptiness view

The view of extrinsic emptiness arose from Yumo Mikyö Dorjé. When he meditated on the six yogas of Kālacakra, there arose from within him the aspect of the divine body of empty form.[849] This led to confusion: based on a literal reading of certain sutras of provisional meaning, as well as tantras, he concluded that extrinsic emptiness is the ultimate truth—permanent, fixed, eternal, pervading all things animate and inanimate, existing as an abiding basis, and synonymous with buddha nature. When he practiced the stages of the six yogas, he conceived a mass of contradictions with regard to manifesting the resultant dharmakāya itself, and he termed that the view of extrinsic emptiness. He mixed it with the guidelines on Kālacakra and expounded it covertly. Until it came to Dölpopa Sherap Gyaltsen, that lineage was transmitted one to one in the succession of disciples. Up to that point, aside from just some oral advice, no textbooks focused on that view. The only upholders of that Dharma lineage were yogins who simply had good meditative experiences, so they did not produce extensive or elaborate expositions to prove the view by scripture or reasoning, and because of that, they were not well known. [153]

Dölpopa wrote a treatise teaching the extrinsic-emptiness view, known as *Mountain Dharma: The Ocean of Definitive Meaning,* as well as many miscellaneous works, such as the so-called *Fourth Council.*[850] He set forth many proofs through scripture and reasoning and laid the foundation of the philosophical system called extrinsic emptiness, the ultimate view. His follower Choklé Namgyal wrote both long and short versions of *Destroying Confusion,* and Nyaön Künga Pal wrote the so-called *Clear-Light Ornament of Philosophical Systems* and other texts. Thenceforth, Jonang views and practice became well known.

b. The extrinsic-emptiness view of the Jonangpa

The standpoint of the extrinsic-emptiness view is set forth in the famed *Mountain Dharma: The Ocean of Definitive Meaning* as follows:

> It is asserted that the ultimate truth of the way all dharmas exist is as permanent, fixed, and eternal. In the mind-basis-of-all, it is the gnosis part of the duality of consciousness and gnosis. It is the triple gem of ultimate reality itself. It is the divine assembly of the awareness inseparable from the dharmadhātu that abides pervading all animate and inanimate things. It is buddha nature, the intrinsically existent lineage abiding in all beings, synonymous with the one hundred lineages and other things taught in the tantras. Its mode of abiding is as the continuum of the inseparable basis-cum-result, and its mode of existence is as the three occasions of the dharmakāya.[851] Even though it abides permanently in the basis of all, it is asserted never to appear to consciousness, and it is extensively shown that the way in which the basis exists is the way the result becomes manifested as the dharmakāya itself through successively practicing the six yogas.
>
> These are clearly taught in the *Buddha Nature Sutra, Great Drum Sutra, Sutra Ornamenting the Light of Gnosis, Sutra of the Lion's Roar of Queen Śrīmālā, Sutra Teaching neither Increase nor Decrease, Great Nirvana Sutra, Flower Ornament Sutra, Stack of Jewels Sutra,* and *Holy Golden Light Sutra.* It also has been documented extensively in the root texts and commentaries of the *Sublime Continuum* and other texts that comment on the ultimate meaning of the word of the Buddha, in Nāgārjuna's *Praise of Madhyamaka,*[852] and in other texts.
>
> This ultimate is elucidated [154] by the great charioteers; it is meditated on by yogins who have gained yogic achievements; it is the unmistaken claim of the buddhas of the ten directions and

> the bodhisattvas. On the other hand, things that are part of the conventional—intrinsically empty, nihilistically empty, negationally empty, insignificantly empty, empty from the outset—must be rejected in every way by those desiring liberation.[853]

Thus it is written.

c. Proving that the Jonang view is wrong

1) Jonang views and Hindu views

The proof that that view is wrong: The great, omniscient Dölpopa was reputed to be inconceivably holy, and he was. Although it is possible he had a special basis or intention—like when the Blessed One taught some students on certain occasions that the self of persons exists—the literal standpoint of his view appears to be identical in every way to the assertions of the extremists. How so? The extremists who are proponents of Brahman[854] as sound[855] say: Brahman, which is free of the specifics of directions such as east, west, and so forth, unarisen, indestructible, the intrinsic nature of sound, is, when completely transformed, the assemblage of entities such as form and so forth. So it should be known.

As they explain:

> The Brahman that is without beginning or limits
> Is the real nature of sound and syllable:
> Worldly conventions arise in it;
> It transforms itself into actual entities.[856]

Brahman is the real nature of sound, so it is called "the real nature of sound"; the meaning is that it is the unmistakable nature of sound. The so-called supreme is the self-nature of *oṃ*. *Oṃ* is said to be the intrinsic nature of all sounds and meanings; it also is the Veda. *Oṃ* is the means of realizing the Veda, which abides naturally in the gradations of words and letters; *oṃ* exists as the formal mode of the Vedas.

The proponents of Brahman as sound say that the self-nature of the supreme Brahman holds the quality of the holy result, which is the high state and the definitive good, so it is not seen by the inner agent.[857]

Likewise, the Jonangpas say: The ultimate god, mantra, tantra, mandala, [155] mudra, and so forth, and also the name *buddha nature* demonstrate that the fundamental way these intrinsically empty conventional entities exist is as permanent, fixed, eternal, transcendently holy self, uniquely pure, primordially imbued with strength and all other good qualities, primordially pervading all worldly animate and inanimate things. So they say.

Thus, since extremists who are proponents of Brahman as sound maintain that all entities are transformations of sound and possess its intrinsic nature, and the Jonangpa also appear to assert that a permanent, fixed pervader of all that is animate and inanimate is the way everything exists, there is not the slightest difference between them.

Moreover, the Jonang stance on the way one attains liberation does not appear to be different from that of the Sāṃkhya extremists. The Sāṃkhyas[858] maintain that objects of knowledge are included in twenty-five categories. Of those, twenty-four are material, while the twenty-fifth is a self whose intrinsic nature is the intrinsic nature of knowledge, cognition, and sentience; it is permanent, fixed, pervading everything animate and inanimate, noncomposite, and free from the actions of going and coming. Then, when the person, who is conscious, conceives the desire to enjoy objects, the principal, which is material, emanates the entire transformation complex.[859] The mind, whose intrinsic nature is material, inclines to that, and the person enjoys the object to which the mind inclines.

Thus, while an isolated conscious person has never before been seen in the state of samsara, due to our inclination to identify the person with objects of enjoyment, we circle in samsara and experience suffering. Then we cultivate mental absorption, and when we are thoroughly accustomed to that, then our attraction to objects gets less and less. Viewed with the divine eye, the principal, ashamed, no longer emanates the transformation complex. Further, the transformations first will dissolve into that from which they actually arose, and in the end, the transformations are stilled within the principal. The principal, resting in a state of potentiality, will never again be revealed, so all these transformations seen by worldly beings will fade like a rainbow in the sky. When the self, the conscious person, abides in solitude, and not even the slightest bit of anything else [156] appears, that is the attainment of liberation. So they assert.

Likewise, the Jonangpas assert that although the way all dharmas exist is as permanent from the beginning, because of clinging to objects, we do not see this. Then, by yogic meditation, we see that the objects' real nature is that of a mirage, an imputed snake,[860] and so forth, and when we finally attain buddhahood, a permanent, solitary reality appears, but not even the slightest bit of anything else appears. When all intrinsically empty conventionalities are reduced to nonexistence, and there appears an isolated ultimate, that is the attainment of buddhahood.

Thus, these Sāṃkhya and Jonang standpoints are completely the same and are not the least bit different in terms of right or wrong; this will be apparent to the understanding of any intelligent person who analyzes the matter.

The Jonangpas also say that this present collection of eight consciousnesses[861]—the mind-basis-of-all and the others—have an intrinsic nature that is stained. In saying that, they are just like the Mīmāṃsaka extremists,[862] who maintain that the intrinsic nature of mind is stained. Since the stains have entered the nature of mind, even though you may seek an antidote in order to abandon them, it will be utterly pointless; so even if you assert liberation, you only prove samsara.

The Jonangpas also maintain that these conventionalities are merely mistaken appearances, and they maintain that, when you turn aside the conventional, the ultimate is established permanently. Similarly, various extremist proponents of Vedānta[863] say that this world is only a mistaken appearance, and when you turn that aside, the permanent, all-pervading knower, in which there is no duality of object and subject, abides in natural liberation. The distinctive, separate self possessed by a living being will be dissolved, when liberation is attained, into the nature of the great self. The Vedānta and Jonang assertions are the same, because, mere terminology aside, their meaning is identical—their assertion of liberation as permanent, their way of explaining freedom, and their way of explaining samsara.

Moreover, this view on which the Jonangpas settle appears to commit the mistakes of both eternalism and nihilism. Maintaining that the ultimate intrinsic nature has the intrinsic nature of permanence, one falls to the extreme of eternalism. Saying that superficial truths exist earlier, in the context of samsara, but do not exist in buddhahood, one falls to the extreme [157] of nihilism.

2) Refuting Jonang interpretations of scripture

In support of their assertion that extrinsic emptiness is the ultimate truth, permanent, fixed, eternal, pervading all that is animate and inanimate, the Jonangpas draw on a multitude of scriptures—sutras, tantras, and treatises—such as the *Buddha Nature Sutra,*[864] the Kālacakra tantra, Nāgārjuna's *Praise of the Dharmadhātu,* and others. Taking into account, however, the three fulfillments—of intended meaning, purpose, and conflict with actuality[865]—it is absolutely necessary to interpret those texts as provisional. Take, for instance, the statement that sentient beings have the ten powers, the four fearlessnesses, and other qualities of the Buddha: The meaning is that sentient beings possess the basis for those to arise by cleansing the stains on the naturally pure mind. Although it is stated that buddha nature is permanent and fixed, the intent of the statement is to draw out the meaning of reality for those with extremist views; it is a statement of provisional meaning. Were it definitive, it would not differ from the self view of the extremists.

a) The Descent to Laṅka Sutra

The Buddha himself taught this clearly in the *Descent to Laṅka Sutra:*

> The bodhisattva Mahāmati asked the Blessed One: "The Blessed One has taught buddha nature. The Blessed One has noted that within the body of a sentient being exists the purity that is from the beginning the purity possessing the thirty-two marks. The Blessed One has noted that just as precious and expensive things may be completely wrapped in a stained cloth, similarly, buddha nature is completely wrapped in the cloth of aggregates, sense fields, and sense factors; it is overpowered by attachment, anger, and confusion; it is stained by the stains of thoroughgoing conceptualization; it is permanent, fixed, and eternal. If so, O Blessed One, how is propounding buddha nature different from propounding the self posited by extremists? O Blessed One, extremists also believe in a conception of self propounded as permanent, saying that it is permanent, fixed, without qualities, pervasive, and indestructible."
>
> The Blessed One said: "Mahāmati, my teaching buddha nature is not the same as my propounding the self of the extremists. Mahāmati, the [158] tathāgatas, the arhats, the complete and perfect buddhas, teach buddha nature to be the meaning of such terms as emptiness; the absolute limit; nirvana; the unarisen; the signless; the wishless; and the empty. When they show the door of buddha nature so that the childish may escape the state in which they are afraid of the absence of self, they show the state of the nonconceptual, the domain of the nonappearing.

> "Mahāmati, bodhisattvas who arise in the present and future will not manifestly cling to self. For example, Mahāmati, through his possession of hands, artistry, a hammer, water, string, and pressure, a potter makes various types of containers from a single lump of clay. Likewise, Mahāmati, through wisdom and various types of skillful means, the tathāgatas teach the complete reversal of all conceptual signs to be the absence of self in dharmas, by teaching that as buddha nature or teaching it as selflessness, as is appropriate. Like a potter, they show it by various arrangements of words and letters. Thusly, Mahāmati, the tathāgatas, in order to attract those who cling to the self propounded by the extremists, showed the essential by teaching buddha nature. How can those whose thought has fallen into the conceptual view that the absolutely unreal self is real come to possess the thought that settles in the domain of the three doors of liberation, and completely awaken to unsurpassed, complete, and perfect enlightenment? Mahāmati, it is for the sake of that, that the tathāgatas taught buddha nature. Mahāmati, in order to reverse the views of the extremists, you should recognize that buddha nature lacks a self."[866]

In this passage, Mahāmati is Mañjughoṣa. In order to sever the doubts of students of inferior intelligence, he asked the teacher the question: "If your way of teaching buddha nature is provisional, then what are the intentional basis and the purpose? If it is [159] definitive, then how is it different from the self of the extremists?" The teacher replied to him:

> If the teaching were definitive, what you say would be true, but it is provisional, so buddha nature is not the same as the self propounded by the extremists. The intentional basis is the reality-limit.[867] The purpose is to attract by various methods those extremists who beginninglessly have clung to a self, and who, if immediately taught the way things exist, would be terrified and could not come to the teaching. They will have faith in a teaching taught in the same way as are their own assertions and words about a permanent self, and faith in the Tathāgata, and from then on they will gradually understand reality; thus their teaching will have no faults, and only good qualities will arise.

If that sutra were definitive, then major paradoxes would ensue, such as: (1) the noncomposite would be adorned by the major and minor marks and other physical qualities; (2) the utmost dharmadhātu possessing the two purities would be included in the aggregates and sense fields, which are corrupted; and (3) the Buddha would be overcome by the three poisons.

b) Nāgārjuna's works

Also, the teachings of Nāgārjuna's *Praise of the Dharmadhātu* and other such works to the effect that the conventional intentional basis is this clear, cognitive mind, as well as dependent dharmas that are dependently arisen; that the ultimate intentional basis is suchness and its cognates; and that the stains are the basis for purification: those are merely imputed conventions. Otherwise, those texts would be contradict Nāgārjuna's *Fundamental Treatise on the Middle Way*.

You may say: The *Fundamental Treatise on the Middle Way* and other such works establish just the nonaffirming negation of intrinsic emptiness, but the ultimate, extrinsic emptiness is established by the *Praise of the Dharmadhātu* and other such works, so there is a great difference between them. The reply is: In order to refute others' assertions to the effect that nirvana is either an entity or a nonentity, the *Fundamental Treatise on the Middle Way* says:

> Now, nirvana is not an entity;
> Otherwise, it would follow that it is characterized by aging and death.
> There is no existent entity
> Not characterized by aging and death.
>
> If nirvana were an entity,
> Then nirvana would be composite.
> A noncomposite entity
> Does not exist anywhere.
>
> If nirvana were an entity,
> How could nirvana not be dependent?
> A nondependent entity
> Does not exist anywhere.[868]

That said, if you ask, "Well, what is it?" the reply is as the *Fundamental Treatise on the Middle Way* states:

> Unabandoned and [160] unattained,
> Undestroyed and impermanent,
> Unceasing and nonarising:
> That denotes nirvana.[869]

This contradicts your statement above. If you say that the intention of these verses is to describe intrinsic emptiness, then it undermines your assertion that nirvana is the sole ultimate, with no distinction between intrinsic emptiness and extrinsic emptiness.

Moreover the *Fundamental Treatise on the Middle Way* states:

> Samsara and nirvana
> Are not the least bit different;
> Nirvana and samsara
> Are not the least bit different.
>
> The limit of nirvana
> Is the limit of samsara;
> Even on the subtlest level,
> They are not the least bit different.[870]

How would you analyze this? You must say.

If I were to open all the storehouses of mistaken information about the presentation of the two truths, the standpoints on provisional and definitive in the three turnings of the wheel, and so forth, it would be too much. Extensive explanations can be found elsewhere, and so I will not elaborate here.

3) Critics and defenders of the Jonang view

It is necessary to explain just this much because some who pride themselves on explaining the Dharma nowadays, and in whose hearts the deeds of Māra dwell, say that not only does the Jonang view accord with the Cittamātra but that it also accords with the meaning of the Kālacakra tantra and its commentary, as well as the key points of the mantra system of Mahāmudrā. They appear to proclaim without embarrassment this teaching that is like the talk of an ominous crow, so I have exposed just a little the defects[871] of that wrongful view. However, in the ears of others—those not attached to seeing the good and the flawed, gold and a donkey, as equal—how can such talk even have the effect of a herder's flute song?

In Tibet, the Land of Snows, there are many different standpoints on view. Schools other than the Jonang have found it necessary to identify the sources included among their respective collections of texts and instructions derived from authoritative pandits and adepts. Even if there are some errors in the application of terms, when those who have mastered scripture and reasoning and have spiritual experience analyze with an honest mind, all the views come down to a single crucial point, just as stated in the root text and commentary on Mahāmudrā by the omniscient First Panchen Lama.[872] The Jonang view, however, burst forth on its own and is without lineage sources [161] from Indian pandits and adepts. It elucidates the meaning of many definitive sutras and tantras incorrectly, and it is said in all the sutras and tantras that spiritual fruition is beyond imagining for a sentient being who lays out so debased and lowly, so irredeemable, a view. If that sentient being enters the right path, he will become the protector of countless sentient beings, while if he does not, the vital artery of that being's liberation will be cut, and the cause for the tathāgata body will be destroyed.

a) Critics

Unable to bear that way of seeing, many previous holy beings, as renowned as the sun and moon, wrote many treatises that annihilated that wrong view. The omniscient Butön wrote *The Ornament that Illuminates and Beautifies the Buddha Nature;* his heart son Lotsāwa Rinchen Namgyal wrote *The Ornament of the Ornament that Illuminates and Beautifies the Buddha Nature;* the Tripiṭaka master Tsöndrü Pal wrote *The Lamp Illuminating the Buddha Nature;* Yardrokpa Rinchen Tok[873] wrote many critical treatises, such as *The Vajra of Matchless Might, The Uppermost Gnosis, The Great Vajra Thunderbolt,* and *The Vajra Hammer*. Also, the Sakya sage Nedrukpa Gendün Pal, the Dewachen Tripiṭaka master Rinchen Shönu, Kashipa Rinchen Dorjé, and others also earnestly criticized the Jonang view.

Also, the great, incomparable Rendawa and our very own lama, the omniscient Tsongkhapa, expounded many scriptures and arguments that refuted that wrong view. Further, while staying at Nenying, before touching Jé Tsongkhapa's feet, the latter's elder spiritual son, the omniscient Gyaltsap Jé, wrote a treatise called *Clearing Mental Darkness: Destroying One's Hold on the Extreme View of a Permanent Self Named Buddha.*[874] He later sent the scholar-monks a widely circulated letter that said:

> If refuting the position related to this view is not permitted, people will cling to the thought that it alone is right and other positions are confused. But since ultimate proof is available through scripture and reasoning, and that proof can stand up in debate, let us take as witnesses all the sutras and tantras and their special instructions, the great charioteers of India and Tibet, and the philosophical systems of non-Buddhists and Buddhists, and let's debate whose view accords with these. This letter invites debate at any place and time. [162]

Although there were at that time many adherents of Dölpopa's system who were outstanding debaters—Chokgyal, Nyaön, and others—no one dared to argue against Gyaltsap Jé's position.

b) A defender: Shākya Chokden

Later came Shākya Chokden of Silung (1428–1507), who had sworn to uphold the Sakya teaching and who was renowned as a great pandit. Early in life, in writings such as *Ascertainment of Madhyamaka, Verse Writings on Debate,* and others, with his mind uncontrollably disturbed by the *dön* demons[875] of partiality, he offered many specious refutations of the presentation of view established by Jé Tsongkhapa regarding the ultimate intent of father Nāgārjuna and his spiritual sons.[876] He himself claimed to accept literally the six collections of reasoning of Nāgārjuna and the texts of Candrakīrti, and he expounded the view of neither existence nor nonexistence as the intention of the glorious Candrakīrti. In later life, he wrote *Distinguishing the Two Systems,* in which he claimed that Asaṅga and his brother Vasubandhu were Great Mādhyamikas,[877] that Candrakīrti and others were Madhyamaka proponents of essencelessness, and that that emptiness posited by Candrakīrti and others is a nihilistic emptiness, a nonaffirming negation, so it is not to be practiced meditatively. He repeatedly said this and wrote many execrable things.[878] The end result of a lifetime spent studying textual systems was that, when he was about to pass away, he recognized the baseness of his view, which destroys the cause of the dharmakāya of the Tathāgata. This recognition was a sign of Shakchok's great good fortune, and when he was on the verge of dying, he himself freely accepted the result, which was in accord with the karma incurred by deprecating the right view he had known early in life.[879] In later births, he would experience the meaning of the scriptural passage from Āryadeva's *Four Hundred Stanzas:*

> Someone obstructed by only confusion,
> Who creates obstacles for himself,
> Will not gain goodness,
> Let alone liberation.[880]

Such was his lifestory.

Concluding verses

> In the course of a single philosophical-system moon-cycle,
> The waxing phase draws out the white light of eloquence,
> While the black side gathers the darkness of wrong view;
> The system of the Jomo Nangpa joins them together.
>
> The white dawn of excellent explanation of Kālacakra
> Draws forth the thousand suns that delight the learned,
> While [163] the darkness of irredeemable wrong view
> Obscures the path to liberation: this is the Jonang system.
>
> Sometimes scholars bring down a hail of refutations;
> On occasion they offer flower garlands of praise.
> When someone like me undertakes a decisive analysis,
> It is difficult to express only praise or deprecation: this is
> the Jonang system.
>
> This system, which combines into one
> Both the barbed wire of the view of a permanent, fixed, and
> eternal self
> And the golden thread of tantric initiations and special
> instructions,
> Is known as "obtained from Kailash[881] in the course of Yumo's
> meditative equipoise."

I fashioned this account, which relates such a history,
Like a mirror that naturally clarifies,
And a needle that pulls out
The thorn of faults and defects.

From *The Crystal Mirror: An Excellent Explanation Showing the Sources and Assertions of All Philosophical Systems,* this completes the explanation of the history of the Jonang philosophical system.

7. The history of some minor philosophical systems

There were various different Mahāmudrā lineages, such as the lineages of Kor Nirūpa (1122–62)[882] and others.[883] There also were a variety of other lineages, such as the three cycles of Kharakpa (1186–1271).[884] There was nothing that the lama called Kodrakpa Sönam Gyaltsen (1170–1249)[885] did not know about the Dharma. He was in particular an expert at dispelling hindrances. I have not seen an explanation of what sort of views or practices he upheld, so I do not know. Nonetheless, during his time, there was no Tibetan scholar-adept who did not respect him, so his enlightened deeds must have been vast. Although he had many fine disciples and grand-disciples, it seems that a tradition of which we could say "this is his philosophical system," or "this is his Dharma stream," did not last for long.[886]

There was a great study center at Bodong É from which many scholar-adepts emerged. In particular, there was the man variously called Bodong Choklé Namgyal, Jikmé Drakpa, or other names (1375–1451);[887] his fame spread everywhere for his comprehension of the sutras, tantras, and all the sciences. He directly encountered many meditational deities who were superior divinities, particularly Sarasvatī. Trusting in her, he became [164] a virtuoso in poetry. At the urging of Vajrasattva, he wrote about a hundred volumes, including the *Collected Principles* and others. He debated both Yakdé Panchen[888] and Rongtikpa[889] and defeated them. At Ngamring, he attacked Sakya Pandita's *Treasure of Knowledge,* but Khedrup Jé, still a youth, vanquished him in debate. Although he never met Jé Rinpoché directly, he offered a devout letter of supplication to him. It is reported that he offered up a eulogy of Khedrup Jé, the *Lute of Buzzing Bees,* but that attribution is in error, since that work is by Shangshung Chöwang Drakpa.[890] On one occasion, wishing to establish a philosophical system of his own, he founded some monasteries, such as Palmo Chöding. Although teaching and study went on there, and a Bodong philosophical system arose, apparently it did not grow or flourish much or last very long.

The second Buddha, the venerable Butön (1290–1364),[891] was invited to Shalu Monastery in Tsang.[892] He was sponsored by the Shalu Kushang[893] and others, and for a long time he studied the initiations of the four classes of tantra and the explanations of the tantras along with their special instructions. He built more than seventy mandalas of Kālacakra and of the yoga tantras, mainly the Vajradhātu. The conqueror Tsongkhapa received the cycles of Kālacakra, Heruka, and the yoga tantras from Butön's disciples Gongsumpa Chökyi Palwa, Khyungpo Lhepa, and Dratsepa.[894] After Butön, Dratsepa sat on the throne of Shalu, and Sharchen, Candrapa, and other upholders of the lineage followed. That is known as the Shalu philosophical system or the Bu system.

Namkha Gyaltsen (1326–1401),[895] the great adept of Lhodrak, was inseparable from Vajrapāṇi. Although his paternal ancestors in the Shubu line were Nyingmapas, he combined Kadam teachings he had received with the unique Dharmas on the profound key points that were bestowed on him directly by Vajrapāṇi, and he expounded and propagated them. Although they were not termed the "Lhodrak philosophical system," they seem to be a distinct Dharma system. For fear of fatigue from writing about these, I have not elaborated much. [165]

10. The Geluk Tradition 1: Tsongkhapa

[II. The History of Philosophical Systems in Tibet, the Land of Snows
B. The histories of the different schools]

Introductory verses

I will briefly relate the authoritative account
Of the authoritative teacher, the conqueror Tsongkhapa,
And his authoritative teaching, the tradition of the Geden
philosophical system,
Which was spread by the authoritative upholders of his teaching.

8. The history of the Geluk philosophical system[896]

The Galukpa[897] or Gandenpa is named after its monastic seat. [In 1409,] Jé Rinpoché Tsongkhapa (1357–1419)[898] founded Ganden Nampar Gyalwa Ling Monastery on Drok Mountain, and calling Jé's tradition "the system of the Ganden Dharma lord" *(chöjé gandenpai luk)* is based on his permanent residence there later in life. When people tried to pronounce the abbreviation of that phrase, Galuk, it was not easy to say, so it has consistently been called the Geluk.[899]

The name of Jé's tradition, Ganden Luk, was prophesied in the *Book of Kadam,* in the prophecy of the future in chapter 26 of the Father Teachings:

In the end, the embers of the teaching
Will be rekindled by one named Drakpa,
Who will accomplish the benefit and happiness of many,
And his place is a supreme and holy place.[900]

The "Drakpa" in the second line shows part of Jé's name, Losang Drakpa, and the "supreme and holy place" shows that the name of the Dharma system,

Ganden, is the same as the place name. So state some of the holy ones of our own Geluk tradition.

Some, though, say that because the philosophical system of Jé Rinpoché was held apart *(gerdu)* from others, it was called Gerluk, and later the sound *ger* became corrupted, so it came to be known as Geluk. This claim is sheer fantasy.

Also, just before Lumé Tsültrim Sherap (b. tenth century) went to Ü, the great lama Gongpa Rapsal[901] gave him an extra, broken-in yellow hat and said, "Put this on, and later you will remember me." Because of that, the early great vinaya masters wore yellow hats, and it also was because of that that Jé Lama, as a good omen for the restoration of the vinaya teachings, which were in decline, made yellow the color of the Geluk hat, so as to accord with the early vinaya masters. Therefore, Jé's tradition also is known as "the system that holds the yellow hat." In the *Yellow Beryl,* [166] it says, "Although Jé himself did not wish it, he made yellow the color of the hat in accordance with his inner circle's request that he differentiate his from other philosophical systems."[902] This report is babble by those who project their own dispositions into the lifestory of the great holy ārya.

Thus, if I explain just briefly the history of what is called the Geluk or the system of the holders of the yellow-crown hat, there are four main topics, explaining: a. How the conqueror Tsongkhapa, lord of the teaching, came into the world, b. How his stainless tradition was extended by subsequent upholders of the teaching, c. How that supreme system is distinctive, and as an ancillary, d. How others who try to overturn this system cannot damage it.

a. How the great Jé Tsongkhapa came into the world

Since there are so very many biographies of Jé Lama written by various holy beings, those who want to know his life in detail should look at those. Here, I will relate only some principal points of his biography. My account is twofold: 1) How he himself attained good qualities and 2) How, because of that, he served the teaching.

1) How he himself attained good qualities[903]

This is twofold: a) How he took the moral vows, the foundation of all good qualities, and b) How he actually gained mastery of the good qualities of scripture and realization.

a) How he took the moral vows, the foundation of all good qualities

Our holy guide, the glorious Jetsün Lama Losang Drakpa, whose very name is nearly inexpressible, was in a previous life a greatly heroic bodhisattva,[904] and he made a promise to the Buddha Indraketu to spread in impure lands the good path that delights the conquerors, [167] without regard for his body or life. Again, at the time when our teacher, Śākyamuni Buddha, had come into the world, he was a young brahman boy, and he offered the teacher a white crystal rosary. These two events indicate his arousal of the awakening mind and his offering of prayers. Starting in the distant past, he had repeatedly issued great waves of prayer in sight of many conquerors so that he might uphold the conquerors' holy Dharma. When the force of those prayers fully ripened, he intentionally took birth in the east, in the Tsongkha region,[905] as the son of Lubum Gé, his father, and Shingza Achö, his mother. When he reached the age of three, the Fourth Karmapa, Rölpai Dorjé, conducted the ritual for him to become a full lay follower and offered him the name Künga Nyingpo. At age eight, he accepted from the Dharma lord Rinchen Döndrup the morality of an intermediate renunciant[906] and the vows of a novice monk; the name he was given was Losang Drakpa. From that holy lama, he received many instructions on sutra and mantra. When he reached the age of sixteen, he went to central Tibet.[907] Although it is not clear in his biographies how old he was at the time, at some point thereafter he took full-ordination vows in Yarlung Namgyal, with the abbot of Tsokchenpo Monastery, Tsültrim Rinchenpa, who was from the preceptor lineage of the great scholar Śākyaśrī, serving as preceptor, the Jezing abbot Sherap Gönpo serving as assistant master, the vow-observer Sönam Dorjé serving as secret teacher; and a monk in whom he had confidence filling out the number for a quorum. His mental continuum was utterly suffused with a completely thorough training in superior morality.

b) How he actually gained mastery of the good qualities of scripture and realization

This is twofold: (1) How he gained mastery of the good qualities of scripture through much study, and (2) How he gained mastery of the good qualities of realization through proper practice. [168]

(1) How he gained mastery of the good qualities of scripture through much study[908]

This is twofold: (a) How he severed superimposition through study and (b) How, through reflection, all textual systems arose to him as instruction.

(a) How he severed superimposition through study

Jé Lama's purpose in appearing in this world was solely to activate the teaching. His excellent tradition has not just a portion, but the complete teaching of the Muni, conveying knowledge of how an individual person brings to bear the necessary conditions for awakening, described in all the sutras and treatises, from the *Stanzas on Vinaya* up to the *Guhyasamāja*. His purpose was to clarify like the sun for fortunate students what no previous scholar-adept in the Land of Snows had been able to make clear; as is stated in Dharmakīrti's *Thorough Exposition of Valid Cognition:*

> Since the source of the method is hidden,
> It is difficult to explain.[909]

Thus, one first must ascertain the key points of the complete teaching. For that, Jé saw that it was first necessary to undertake extensive, not partial, study of countless texts of sutra and mantra, so he studied with captains who were expert spiritual friends and raised the white sail of noble intention, the awakening mind, on the great ship of study. Blown by the fierce, strong wind of diligence, he entered the great ocean of scriptures and their commentaries; his diligence in seeking the wish-granting jewel of the meaning of the texts was equal to that of the bodhisattva Sadāprarudita.[910] He did this in two ways: 1' Definition-vehicle study and 2' Mantra-vehicle study.

1' Definition-vehicle study

His study of texts principally composed in the definition vehicle is twofold: a' How he studied the scriptures in general and b' How he studied Madhyamaka and valid cognition in particular.

a' How he studied the scriptures in general

As Jé Lama himself said:

> Therefore, unsatisfied with coarse or polarized understanding
> Of the texts of the invincible Dharma lord Maitreya
> And those renowned as six ornaments and two supremes
> Of Jambudvīpa, I studied all of them in detail.[911]

Jé went to the great monastery of Dewachen: For eighteen days, he listened to Nyethang Tashi Sengé, Densa Yeshé Sengé, Master Yönten Gyatso, and the precious lama Urgyenpa discourse on the root text of Maitreya's *Ornament of Higher Realization* along with its commentary, and he understood them fully. He received teachings on the other four books of Maitreya from Lama [169] Jamrinpa. In particular, when he heard just once a careful explanation of the perfection of wisdom from Nyaön Künga Palwa, he was very satisfied. Moreover, he was not content with vague arguments, as today's students are.

The commentaries on the wisdom side that were asserted by earlier generations of Tibetans to open the chariot-path of the Mahayana: Tsongkhapa studied the *Explication of the Perfection of Wisdom in One Hundred Thousand Verses,* the *Verse Summary of the Perfection of Wisdom,* Nāgārjuna's collection of Madhyamaka reasoning, and Maitreya's *Ornament of Higher Realization.* Also, within these four general areas, with regard to the *Ornament of Higher Realization,* he studied Asaṅga's *Ascertainment of Reality;*[912] Vasubandhu's *Textual Commentary in Twenty Thousand Verses;* Ārya Vimuktisena's twenty-thousand-verse commentary in eight chapters, the *Elucidation of the Twenty-Five Thousand Verses;*[913] Bhadanta Vimuktisena's many-chaptered commentary, the *Thorough Exposition in Twenty Thousand Verses;*[914] Haribhadra's *Commentary Clarifying the Meaning,*[915] *Great Commentary on the Perfection of Wisdom in Eight Thousand Verses,*[916] *Condensed Meaning of the Eighth Chapter,*[917] and *New Commentary on the Verse Summary;* Buddhaśrījñāna's condensed commentary, the *Detailed Explication of the Verse Summary;* Master Śāntipa's *Pure Twenty Thousand,* his commentary on the *Perfection of Wisdom in Eight Thousand Verses,* and his *Supreme Essence;* Vimalamitra's *Extensive Commentary on the Heart Sutra;*[918] the commentaries on the *Diamond-Cutter Sutra* written by masters Vasubandhu and Kamalaśīla,[919] and the explications of the *Ornament of Higher Realization* of Dharmamitra and other followers of Master Haribhadra; the *Explanation of the Ornament of Mahayana Sutras* written by Vasubandhu,[920] and the explanatory commentaries written by Lord Asvabhāva; the Kashmiri scholar Jñānaśrībhadra's *Condensed Meaning of the Ornament of Mahayana Sutras;* the great commentary and subcommentary on the *Ornament of Mahayana Sutras* by Sthiramati; Asaṅga's commentary on the *Sublime Continuum;* and Vasubandhu's *Explications of the Two Distinguishings,*[921] along with Sthiramati's *Subcommentary on Distinguishing the Middle from the Extremes.* Jé comprehended the meaning of every word of those texts, and within two years he had perfectly mastered the Dharmas of Maitreya.

How Jé studied the texts of vinaya and abhidharma: He received from Jetsün Rendawa Shönu Lodrö (1349–1412)[922] precise guidance on Vasubandhu's *Autocommentary on the Treasury of Higher Knowledge.* Rendawa's oral explanation did not depend only on the words written in the text but skillfully arranged the innermost meaning of the whole [170] body of the treatise, so he was able to impart an easy understanding of the entire system. Thus, Jé gained great faith. With everything Rendawa taught, Jé comprehended the meanings of every word after listening just once. He asked good questions about difficult points, so Jetsün Rendawa also was quite impressed, and said to Jé, "To give precise guidelines to you, I really have to be careful!" Jé also received teachings on *Entering the Middle Way* of Candrakīrti from him once. Later, Rendawa gave him a careful explanation of Asaṅga's *Compendium of Abhidharma* and detailed teachings on Dharmakīrti's *Autocommentary on the Thorough Exposition of Valid Cognition,* and he gained a good general understanding of them. He also received teachings on the perfection of wisdom and vinaya from Rendawa. Because it was from Rendawa that he first reached the door of reasoning about Madhyamaka and valid cognition, Jé regarded this unrivaled, matchless teacher as his principal lama.

Jé received teachings on the complete root text of the *Vinaya Sutra,* along with its commentaries and ancillaries, from the abbot of Kyormo Lung, the great expert in vinaya and abhidharma known as Kashipa Losal, and on the side, starting from the beginning, he memorized about seventeen arrow-length folios of the extensive commentary on the root text. The cycle of vinaya and abhidharma texts that he studied and contemplated includes: Guṇaprabha's *Small Commentary on the Vinaya Sutra,* Dharmamitra's *Extensive Commentary on the Vinaya Sutra,* Master Prajñākara's *Exposition of the Vinaya Sutra,* Master Kalyaṇamitra's *Extensive Commentary on the Fundamental Transmission,* Master Vinītadeva's *Commentary on the Division of*

Vinaya,[923] Master Śīlapālita's *Minor Commentary,* Master Viśeṣamitra's *Commentary on the Prātimokṣa Sutra,*[924] Vimalamitra's *Extensive Commentary on the Prātimokṣa Sutra,*[925] the arhat Śakadeva's *Flower Garland of Vinaya,*[926] Master Śākyaprabhā's *Exposition of the Novice Vows in Three Hundred Stanzas,* Master Vinītadeva's *Fifty Stanzas on the Novice Vows,* and so forth.[927]

Jé completely comprehended these vinaya commentaries and subcommentaries, along with their minor limbs, as well as the praxis derived from harmonizing them and the distinction between the permitted and the proscribed. He also established fully the meanings of the earlier and later abhidharmas, based on Vasubandhu's *Treasury of Higher Knowledge* and his *Autocommentary* [171] on it, Yaśomitra's *Clarifying the Meaning of the Treasury of Higher Knowledge,* Pūrṇavardhana's *Tracking the Signs of the Explication of the Treasury of Higher Knowledge,* and the *Commentary on the Compendium of Abhidharma* by Jinaputra.

b' How he studied Madhyamaka and valid cognition in particular

How Jé studied the texts on valid cognition: As he himself said:

> With repeated striving, I studied in particular
> The difficult points of the texts on perfect reasoning,
> Which are the sole door to establishing the nature
> Of entities seen by this-worldly beings.[928]

On the basis of listening first to Lama Jetsünpa Rendawa and later to Lotsāwa Dönsang, Jé examined well and reflected upon Dharmakīrti's seven treatises on valid cognition, along with Dignāga's "sutra," the *Compendium of Valid Cognition.*[929] After harmonizing them, he established their meanings well, and seeing that most Tibetan traditions of explanation did not accord with the Indian commentaries, he studied: Dignāga's *Autocommentary on the Compendium of Valid Cognition* along with its subcommentary;[930] the *Commentary on the Thorough Exposition of Valid Cognition* by Devendrabuddhi and that by Śākyabuddhi; the commentaries on it by the two brahmans;[931] Prajñākaragupta's commentary on it, the *Ornament for the Thorough Exposition of Valid Cognition,* and its two subcommentaries;[932] Dharmakīrti's *Autocommentary on the Ascertainment of Valid Cognition,*[933] and the *Explication* of it written by Dharmottara; and the *Commentary on the Drop of*

Reasoning written by Dharmottara.[934] Establishing well the meanings of the commentaries and subcommentaries on the father Dignāga and his spiritual son Dharmakīrti,[935] along with associated minor texts, he trained his mind so that he thoroughly comprehended the thought of those two mighty lords of logic, and most Tibetan traditions of epistemological explanation were rendered superfluous.

How Jé studied Madhyamaka texts: As he himself said:

> Though I worked exhaustively on the texts of sutra and mantra,
> When I practiced and spoke about their profound meaning,
> I saw that I had not progressed far from the viewpoint
> Of one who had learned nothing and understood nothing.
>
> Thus, above all, I studied well all the key points
> That induce the perfect view through the subtle path
> Of reasoning, which opens the depths of the textual system
> Of Nāgārjuna, and all my doubts were severed.[936]

At that time, the explanatory tradition of Madhyamaka had severely declined in Tibet, so Jé received Lama Rendawa's explanation of Candrakīrti's *Entering the Middle Way,* but he did not hear any explanations of Nāgārjuna's [172] *Fundamental Treatise on the Middle Way* or other texts in the six collections of reasoning. He did hear an oral transmission of Nāgārjuna's six collections of reasoning from the Narthang abbot Künga Gyaltsenpa and from Lama Jamrinpa of Dewachen. In brief, at that time it was difficult for master and disciple both to find a place where one could obtain oral transmissions, not to mention explanations, of the collections of reasoning.

The Madhyamaka texts he studied are: the textual system of Master Nāgārjuna, which includes Nāgārjuna's six collections of reasoning, along with their commentaries, and Nāgārjuna's *Compendium of Sutras;* the texts of Nāgārjuna's followers, for instance Āryadeva's meaning commentary on the *Fundamental Treatise on the Middle Way,* the *Four Hundred Stanzas;* Candrakīrti's commentary on that, the *Bodhisattva's Practice of Yoga: An Extensive Commentary on the Four Hundred Stanzas;* Master Buddhapālita's *Commentary on the Fundamental Treatise on the Middle Way;* Master Bhāvaviveka's meaning commentary on the *Fundamental Treatise on the Middle Way,* the *Heart of Madhyamaka;* his own commentary on that, that is, the *Blaze of Logic;* and his word-by-word commentary on the *Fundamen-*

tal Treatise on the Middle Way, the *Lamp of Wisdom;* the *Explication* of that by Avalokitavrata; Candrakīrti's meaning commentary on the *Fundamental Treatise on the Middle Way, Entering the Middle Way;* Jayānanda's *Explication* of that; Candrakīrti's word-by-word commentary on the *Fundamental Treatise on the Middle Way,* the *Clear Words;* Śāntarakṣita's *Ornament of Madhyamaka,* which explains clearly the words and meaning of the *Fundamental Treatise on the Middle Way,* as well as his *Autocommentary* on that and Kamalaśīla's *Detailed Explication* of it; Jñānagarbha's *Distinguishing the Two Truths,* his *Autocommentary* on it, and Śāntarakṣita's *Detailed Explication* of it. Moreover, he studied Kamalaśīla's *Light of Madhyamaka* and other works.

2' Mantra-vehicle study

How Jé studied the secret mantra vehicle: As he says in his *Song of Realization:*

> To travel to full enlightenment in this life,
> There are two ways: the profound vajra vehicle
> And the perfection vehicle; and mantra, it is said,
> Is very much superior to perfection.
>
> This is known everywhere, like the sun and moon.
> Pretending to accept those words as literal truth,
> Pretending to be a scholar, without asking
> What that profound vehicle actually is:
>
> If a wise person is thus,
> Then how could anyone else be a dullard?
> O, how amazing: carelessly to cast away a path
> So difficult to meet and unsurpassed!
>
> Therefore, I entered that profound treasure of double achievement,
> The supreme vehicle of the conquerors,
> Rarer [173] than a buddha: the Vajrayana.
> And long I studied it with repeated effort.[937]

In Tibet at that time, sutra and mantra were widely held to be contradictory, like hot and cold, so those devoted to the perfection vehicle did not engage in secret mantra, while those devoted to mantra rejected the perfection vehicle. Jé had promised in front of the previous conqueror Indraketu, "I will extend that excellent path that unites the view of emptiness with secret mantra." Accordingly, in order to place the fortunate in that excellent way in which there is knowledge of how to enlist sutra and mantra in mutual support, he thought that first he should study the secret mantra vehicle, not just in part, but very extensively. He said, "I did not need others to urge me toward the mantra side; from the time I was small, I had a fierce desire to understand it, and from the first, I had thought that I should study completely all the texts of the tantric classes."[938] On one occasion, Jetsün Lama Rendawa said to him, "It will take you a long time to do really extensive research into mantra, so for the time being, wouldn't it be better to expound the Tripiṭaka?" Tsongkhapa replied, asking: "Since I have such a fierce desire to understand the mantra side, may I at any rate also research mantra?"

a' Meeting Khyungpo Lhepa

So, Jé himself, having reached the age of thirty-four, in the year of the horse (1390), set his mind on hearing all there was in terms of the initiations, oral transmissions, special instructions, explanatory traditions, and reliable sources of all the higher and lower tantra classes of the Vajrayana. One time, in a dream, Jé found himself seated before a man sitting on a great throne who had an elderly countenance, wore a crown, and was holding a vajra and bell. He said, "I am Lama Khyungpo Lhepa."[939] The lama stood up in a dancing pose and made tantric movements; brandishing the vajra and ringing the bell, he made three clockwise circumambulations of Jé. The syllables *e kā pa tsi kā pa* resounded from his rosary, and he held the vajra and bell on top of Jé's head and said, "You will be called Karmavajra," then went to sit on the throne. That was the dream. When Jé rose from sleep, he [174] experienced great bliss, for it occurred to him that the name given in the dream was similar to his previous secret name, Dönyö Dorjé.[940] He then decided to go to hear about yoga and other topics from Khyungpo Lhepa Rinpoché at his mountain cave at Shalu, and one evening in a dream, Jé found himself seated before a kindly old lama named Precious Khyungpo, who sat on a great throne in the pose of Maitreya.[941] The lama parted the clothing over his heart with both hands, plainly revealing at his heart multiple long mantra-rosary wheels that circled about. Jé could for the most part read those mantras, whose syllables were vivid and distinct.[942]

Having seen those extraordinary sights, Jé went to Shalu and met that very lama, who looked exactly as he had in his dreams, and as a result Jé gained unspeakably great faith and respect. So, as Atiśa's *Lamp for the Path to Enlightenment* says,

> If you desire to practice the secret mantra
> Taught in the action, performance, and other tantras,
> Then in order to receive the master initiation,[943]
> You should please the holy lama
> By every means: respectfully serving,
> Giving precious things, and practicing as instructed.
> When the lama, pleased,
> Fully bestows the master initiation,
> Then all your vices will be purified,
> And you'll be fortunate in gaining yogic achievements.[944]

Jé pleased his lama in thought by seeing him as the actual Vajradhara and in deed by respectfully serving him with body and speech, and offering the daily necessities and jewels, clothes and silks, and so forth. And from time to time he pleased him with the very best pledge substances offered at ritual feasts. Initially, he was drawn to the initiations of the great yoga mandalas: from the action tantras, Sitātapatrā, Trisamayavyūharāja, the Eleven-Faced Avalokiteśvara, Vajravidāraṇa, Amitāyus, and others; and from the performance tantras, the *Tantra of the Manifest Awakening of Vairocana* and others.[945] At that time, he received most of the pure streams of initiation extant in Tibet. Also, within the highest yoga tantra, he received countless traditions: Guhyasamāja-Akṣobhya, the Cakrasaṃvara traditions of Lūipa and Kṛṣṇācārya, and others; the scriptural transmissions possessed by Lama Khyungpo for the most part suffused Jé's mind the way a vase is filled. He stayed for a year. At the end of bestowing such Dharmas, when each [175] initiation was complete, Lama Khyungpo would say sincerely each time, "This was bestowed on me by lama so-and-so, and it is happily given by me." And he also would say, "Since the scriptural transmission has been properly completed, I now have no regrets, because the Dharma has been transferred to its rightful owner." Jetsün Khyungpo Rinpoché distinctly thought: "I have poured into the hands of Jé himself the complete teaching of the Vajrayana, the undeteriorated essence of blessings taken from the oceanic mantra teaching of the omniscient Phakpa Ö and the all-knowing Butön, and the root of the welfare of all the region's beings is now in hand.

b' Studies of the lower tantras

When Jé Rinpoché stayed in Nyangtö Dechen just through one summer and fall, he studied well with the precious Chökyi Palwa and thoroughly mastered the "garland trilogy," consisting of the *Vajra Garland of Mandala Rites,* the *Garland of Perfected Yogas,*[946] and the *Light Blossom* of the pandit Abhayākaragupta, who enjoyed direct visions of Vajrayoginī.[947] Jé did this through receiving the initiations, oral transmissions, precise guidelines, and explanations, together with instructions on dance, line drawing, and chanting, for the forty-two great initiations of the *Vajra Garland of Excellent Explanation,*[948] along with the three mandalas that bring good luck. He also received many oral teachings on such Dharmas as the Great Wheel Vajrapāṇi and others.

In addition, Jé did not just obtain initiations into yoga tantra, but he invited Yogapa Gönsang to stay at Tritsa Khang, between upper and lower Nyang, and studied in detail the ritual practice of Butön Rinpoché with respect to the dance, line drawing, and chanting, the general arrangement of mandala rites, and the application of mudras for the great mandalas of Vajradhātu, Śrī Paramādya, Vajra Peak, and others. Again, he invited the Shalu yoga expert and Tripiṭaka master, Gyaltsen Drakpa, to Penam Phakpa Mountain and refined his ability in yogic chanting, ritual practice, and so forth. He also received the oral transmissions of the many types of tantras and their extensive commentaries: the omniscient Butön's *Great Exposition of the Vajra Source;*[949] the *Compendium of Reality,*[950] *Vajra Peak, Glorious Supreme Primordium,* the *Tantra that Purifies All Lower Rebirths,*[951] and other tantras; and Ānandagarbha's *Light on Reality,* Śākyamitra's *Ornament of Kośala,*[952] Ānandagarbha's *Explication of the Glorious* [176] *Supreme Primordium,*[953] and others.

These are the texts of the three lower tantra classes that Jé studied: Among action tantras, he studied the *Secret Tantra on General Mandala Rites;* the *Tantra of Excellent Yogic Attainments* and Varabodhi's *Condensed Meaning* commentary on that; the *Tantra Based on the Questions of Subahu* and Buddhaguhya's *Condensed Meaning* commentary on that; and the *Higher Contemplation* and Buddhaguhya's commentary on that.[954] Moreover, he studied the *Mañjuśrī Root Tantra;* the great Vajrapāṇi tantra, the *Supreme Awareness;* the *Fierce Vajra Tantra;* the *Vajra Subjugator Root Tantra*[955] and its explanatory tantra, the *Great Meru;*[956] and others. Through those, he established himself on the stages of the path of the action tantras, and he comprehended them.

Although there were many texts of the performance-tantra cycle that had not been translated in Tibet, Jé did study the main text of that class, the *Tantra of the Manifest Awakening of Vairocana.*

Of the principal root tantras of the yoga tantra, he studied the *Compendium of Reality Tantra* together with its supplements; Master Ānandagarbha's extensive commentary on that, the *Light on Reality;* Śākyamitra's extensive commentary on the *Compendium of Reality,* called the *Ornament of Kośala;* Buddhaguhya's *Entrance to the Meaning of the Tantra;*[957] the explanatory tantra, the *Vajra Peak;* the *Glorious Supreme Primordium;* and Master Ānandagarbha's extensive commentary on that in twenty-four thousand verses, the *Explication of the Glorious Supreme Primordium;* the *Tantra of Victory over the Three Worlds* and the scholar Muditakoṣa's *Commentary* on it; the *Tantra that Purifies All Lower Rebirths* and Vajravarman's commentary on it, the *Light Ornament;*[958] and others. In brief, Jé thoroughly studied countless tantras from the three lower classes of tantra along with their commentaries.

c' Studies of highest yoga tantra
1" Masters with whom he studied

How Jé studied the highest yoga tantras: As it says in the *Short Biography:*

> In Shalu, he received most of the initiations and special tantric instructions on all four classes of tantra from Lama Khyungpo Lhepa Shönu Sönam. In particular, he received teachings on and comprehended the yoga systems of the Sakyapas and Butön and, with respect to Guhyasamāja cycles of highest yoga tantra: Marpa's system, Gö Lotsāwa Khukpa Lhetsé's system, the noble lord Atiśa's system, the Ārya system, [177] the Jñānapāda system, Sachen Künga Nyingpo's system, and others, along with their Indian and Tibetan explanatory traditions.[959]

He received the explanatory tradition of the basic Guhyasamāja tantra from Jetsün Rendawa, and it is evident that he also received the Ārya system of Guhyasamāja from Gongsum Dechenpa Chökyi Palwa. Jé says in the *Precious Sprout that Severs*[960] *Extremes:*

> Relying on what I was taught by Jetsün Dampa Kumāramati, or Rendawa; by the venerable Butön's student, the holy noble lord Khyungpo Lhepa; and by Jetsün Dampa Chökyi Palwa—relying on all three, I received in their entirety the Dharma cycles of the Ārya system.[961]

The initiations and other aspects of the Jñānapāda system he received from Butön's heart son, the grammarian and epistemologist Rinchen Namgyal.

How he studied the mother tantras, such as *Cakrasaṃvara, Hevajra,* and others: While staying in lower Amdo, he received from the venerable Dharma lord Döndrup Rinchenpa every type of initiation, explanation, and special instruction related to the five-deity Cakrasaṃvara of the Ghaṇṭapāda system, the Ra system of Vajrabhairava, Hevajra, the Great Wheel Vajrapāṇi, and others. In Shalu, he received from the great preceptor Rinchen Namgyal the initiation of Maitrīpa's thirteen-deity Cakrasaṃvara. In the Dharma fortress in Nyethang, he received from the holy lama Sönam Gyaltsen the body-mandala initiation of the Ghaṇṭapāda-system Cakrasaṃvara and also the permission ceremony for Arapacana Mañjughoṣa. At the mountain cave in Shalu, he received from Khyungpo Lhepa the initiations of the Cakrasaṃvara traditions of Lūipa and Kṛṣṇācārya.

The explanations of the basic *Cakrasaṃvara Tantra:* As Jé says in his commentary on the tantra, *Clarifying the Whole Hidden Meaning:*

> The lama known as Phakpa Ö, who possessed the initiations, guidelines, and explanations of the noble lord Atiśa's system, and the systems of Lochung and the Sakyapa, gave these to the omniscient Butön. Lama Phakpa Ö also said he had received the explanations and oral transmission of Marpa's and Lochung's[962] systems from Yangtsewa Rinchen Sengé, so he also possessed the explanatory traditions of Nāropa, who had transmitted them to the two expert translators, Marpa and Lochung. I listened to the explanation and oral transmission of the venerable Butön's *Great Exposition* of the root tantra from his disciple, the great lama Gongsum Dechenpa Chökyi Palwa.[963]

At Sakya, Jé received from Lama Dorjé Rinchenpa the explanation of the two-chaptered root tantra of Hevajra according to the Sakya system, [178] and at Densa Thil he received from Chenga Drakpa Jangchup the special instructions on Hevajra according to the ritual tradition of the holy lama Sönam Gyaltsenpa: the complete guidelines on the path and its result and the meaning of initiation, arranged into stages of practice.

2" Texts he studied

The tantras and Indian texts related to the cycles of Guhyasamāja, Cakrasaṃvara, and Hevajra that Jé studied:

With respect to the father tantra, the Guhyasamāja, he studied: the first seventeen chapters of the root tantra; the supplementary eighteenth chapter; Candrakīrti's *Bright Lamp* on Guhyasamāja; the pandit Līlavajra's *Explanation of the Preface to the Guhyasamāja;*[964] Śraddhākaravarman's *Unraveling the Seven Ornaments;*[965] Master Praśāntajñāna's *Benefiting the Disciple: A Commentary on Guhyasamāja;*[966] the pandit Vimalagupta's commentary on the first seventeen chapters, the *Ornament of Guhyasamāja;* the pandit Cilupa's *Precious Wish-Fulfilling Tree: A Commentary on Guhyasamāja;*[967] the *Commentary on Guhyasamāja* by Thagana; the pandit Vajrahāsa's commentary on the first seventeen chapters of the *Guhyasamāja;*[968] and Śāntipa's *Handful of Flowers Explaining Guhyasamāja.*[969]

Of explanatory tantras of Guhyasamāja, he studied: the *Vajra Garland, Prophetic Intention, Compendium of Vajra Gnosis, Questions of the Four Goddesses,* and others.[970] In relation to those, he studied the *Commentary on the Prophetic Intention* by Śraddhākaravarman,[971] the *Commentary on the Questions of the Four Goddesses* by Śraddhākaravarman, and the *Explication of the Questions of the Four Goddesses* by Master Ānandagarbha.[972]

Of meaning commentaries on the Guhyasamāja, he studied: Nāgārjuna's *Condensed Sādhanas, Mixture of Sutras,* and *Five Stages;* Āryadeva's *Lamp Summarizing Conduct,* and the explanations of it by Śākyamitra and Nāgabodhi;[973] master Nāgabodhi's *Sequential Presentation;*[974] the seven commentaries on the *Five Stages,* such as Nāgabodhi's and other commentaries;[975] and master Śāntipa's *Precious Garland: A Commentary on the Condensed Sādhanas*. Having harmonized the tantras, their commentaries, the subcommentaries, and the commentaries on the *Five Stages* literature by the pentad of the father Nāgārjuna and his four spiritual sons,[976] along with the special instructions on [179] them, Jé established inerrantly the meaning of the glorious *Guhyasamāja Tantra.*

He studied the two-chaptered root tantra of Hevajra, a yoginī tantra; the unique explanatory tantra, the *Ḍākinī Vajra Tent;* and the common explanatory tantra, the *Saṃpuṭa,* along with its supplement. Of the cycle of Hevajra commentaries, he studied: the *Condensed Explication of the Meaning of Hevajra* by Vajragarbha; Saroruhavajra's *Possessing the Lotus;* Durjayacandra's *Water Lily;*[977] Śāntipa's *Pearl Garland;* the thirteen commentaries, such as *Nāropa's Great Commentary,*[978] and others; the four commentaries on the *Vajra Tent,* such as Indrabodhi's[979] *Orally Transmitted Commentary on Difficult Points in the Vajra Tent;* Master Abhayākaragupta's *Cluster of Instructions;* and others. Relying on the root tantras, the explanatory tantras, and the commentaries, along with their special instructions, Jé established inerrantly the meaning of the *Hevajra Tantra.*

He studied the basic *Cakrasaṃvara Tantra,* a yoginī tantra; and its explanatory tantras, the *Supreme Expression, Vajra Ḍāka, Yoginī*[980] *Conduct, Ḍāka Ocean, Vajra Source,* and so forth. Among commentaries, he studied: Vajrapāṇi's *Commentary in Praise of Cakrasaṃvara,*[981] and the *Detailed Explications* by Jayabhadra of Sri Lanka, Bhavyakīrti, Tiṣyarājacandra,[982] and others; the *Commentary on the Vajra Ḍāka* by Bhavabhadra; Master Vīravajra's *Detailed Explication of Cakrasaṃvara;*[983] *Upholding Reality: Commentary of the Vajra Ḍāka* by the pandit Maṇibhadra; the commentary on the *Ḍāka Ocean* by Padmavajra, the *Conveyance Commenting on the Great Royal Ḍāka Ocean Tantra;* and so forth. Jé trained his mind well in the root tantras and the explanatory tantras along with their commentaries and established the countless meanings of the *Cakrasaṃvara Tantra.*

3" Kālacakra studies

Although Chomden Raldri, Lama Rendawa, and others disagreed, Jé believed that the Kālacakra was a great chariot-path unlike other tantra classes and traditions of explanation. While he was staying in Bau Banyer, at a time when he was considering studying Kālacakra in detail [180] with Gongsum Dechenpa Chökyi Palwa, a voice said to him in a dream: "Chökyi Palwa received teachings on the great Kālacakra commentary, *Stainless Light,* seventeen times from Butön Rinpoché." Then, when he met that lama in Nyangtö Dechen, he offered him a yellow silk as a present. The next day, after offering him a bolt of blue-green silk, he requested teachings on Puṇḍarīka's great Kālacakra commentary along with its auxiliary texts. Chökyi Palwa was delighted, and said:

> Since you arrived just now, at the end of our study of the first chapter of the commentary, at a point where it said, "It is for the purpose of ripening anyone who is great," this is an extremely good omen. The yellow color of the silk from last night is similar to the stage of dissolution of the earth element; it means that you will accomplish the completion stage. The blue-green color of the bolt of silk from this morning is the space element, so you will complete the generation stage. I will give you all the teachings in their entirety.[984]

Delighted, he began teaching the text where he had left off. He completed the *Great Commentary,* then taught it from the beginning up to the phrase where he had left off when Tsongkhapa arrived. Hearing in their entirety the explanation of the tantric commentary, precise guidelines on ritual practice, the experiential guidelines for the six yogas, and so forth, Jé stayed through the fall, winter, and spring. When he asked Chökyi Palwa how many times he had received teachings on the *Great Commentary* from Butön Rinpoché, he was told, "I heard it seventeen times."

After that, at Penam Phakpa Mountain, he received from the precious Chökyi Palwa many ancillary teachings on Kālacakra, such as the *Vajragarbha Commentary,* the *Vajrapāṇi Commentary,*[985] *Nāropa's Great Commentary,*[986] and others besides. And, in Kyormo Lung, he received from the scholar-lama Yeshé Gyaltsen, also known as Tsalpa Tokden Ngonyelma, a detailed explanation of the great commentary, *Stainless Light.* He also studied dialectics, calculation, and various practical arts until he was proficient. At Jonang, he received extensive teachings on the six yogas from Choklé Namgyalwa. He studied the *Condensed Kālacakra Tantra* arranged in 1030 verses, known as the *Garland Holder,* as well as the *Kālacakra Supplementary Tantra,* the *Excerpted Tantra,*[987] and other texts. Of commentaries, he studied the *Commentary in Sixty Thousand Stanzas* by Sucandra; Puṇḍarīka's great commentary, *Stainless Light,* and the commentary on the astronomy in the latter; *Possessing the Lotus,* by Somanātha; Puṇḍarīka's commentary, *Service of the Ultimate;* and Nāropa's [181] *Commentary on a Short Teaching on Initiations.* Jé studied those well and mastered them.

3' Other studies

The list of earlier and later sutra and mantra texts that Jé studied is not an enumeration I made up myself; it accords with what is laid out in the biographies of Jé written by some of his direct disciples. Also, an early Kadampa said, "A practitioner of the path to freedom who does not perform the activities described in an ox-load of volumes, acting as if a mere handbook suffices, will not get anywhere."[988] Thus, I have written this to inform followers who are intent on freedom that they must make those great texts the basis for study and contemplation.

Moreover, from the Dharma lord Dönrinpa, Jé received the various lineages of Ra Lotsāwa, Kyo Lotsāwa, Nyö Gyalwa Lhanangpa, and others, on the initiation, explanation, and special instructions related to the Vajrabhairava trio of Yamāntaka, Red Bhairava, and Black Bhairava. From Lama Umapa, he received many uncommon short lineages that were completely unknown, as well as the cycle of initiations and special instructions of Great Wheel Vajrapāṇi in the lineage from the great adept Śavaripa. From Chenga Drakpa Jangchup, he received in their entirety the essential special instructions of the Kagyü, which come from Marpa and Gampopa: the six Dharmas of Nāropa,[989] the fivefold Mahāmudrā, and the collected works of Phakmo Drupa and Drigung Jikten Gönpo. Also, he received many essential teachings of the Sakya system from the Dharma lord and holy lama Sönam Gyaltsen and others.

In brief, he studied well not only the text collections on the inner sciences but also those on the common sciences: at Tsal, he studied healing practices with Lharjé Könchok Kyap; grammar, poetry, and poetics with Lochen Namsang, Sasang Mati Panchen, and others; and calculation with Tokden Yeshé Gyaltsen. While he was at Tsal, he examined in detail the complete corpus of the Conqueror's word and the treatises that had been translated into Tibetan. In short, there was no science to be mastered that Jé did not study. Deeply learned, he thus crossed to the far shore of the ocean of the good qualities gained [182] through extensively studying the scriptures.

(b) How all the textual systems he studied arose as instruction

If you wish to analyze this topic in detail, you will find extensive discussions in Jé's own *Song of Realization,* but I will explain it briefly here nonetheless. As Jé says in the *Letter of Questions Offered to Lama Umapa:*

In general, there are countless secret-mantra and definition-vehicle instructions nowadays in Tibet. It is not evident that they are *not* transmitted from buddhas and bodhisattvas, so if you find a reason for setting some apart, other than their just having been taught by a particular meditational deity, then you will gravitate solely to whatever directly comes to mind, and you will have no way to cause a pure ascertainment of the unmistaken key points of the path to arise. Thus, intelligent ones who honestly seek an unmistaken path do not clash with or reject texts of the sutra class or the tantra class but rather embrace them. Also, having followed the reasoning of a great charioteer, I distinguished well between the provisional and the definitive. Since it seemed indispensable to establish arguments by reasoning that cannot be interpreted in any other way, I considered it important to study the great texts and the stainless door of reasoning through which one seeks their meaning. And, while I often reached a preliminary level of understanding, I was not content with that, and motivated by the thought directed solely at the Dharma, I made continuous requests to the meditational deity and lama, who are inseparable. By striving in many ways to accumulate merit and purify negativities, I now have experiential knowledge of the complete body, not just a small part, of the general scriptures and of the great treatises that comment on their meaning.

How that came about: Certainty is easily granted to one who crosses to the far shore of the ocean of one's own and others' philosophical systems. I have witnessed with amazement the unmistaken establishment of the stages of the path of the definition and mantra vehicles through the instructions on the stages of the path to enlightenment by the great bodhisattva Dīpaṃkaraśrījñāna, or Atiśa. He understood inerrantly the key points [183] of the three trainings, which are the essence of the three collections of the inner sciences, the Tripiṭaka, and not settling for mere acceptance of doctrinal claims, made them part of his own experience. He was nurtured by many virtuous friends who were scholar-adepts and blessed by countless superior deities. I have been practicing precisely those stages that guide the disciple to enlightenment. Also, that instruction shows how to condense into a single path-sequence countless scriptures, treatises that comment on their

> meaning, and special instructions, so that if one who knows how to explain explains, and one who knows how to listen practices, then, through harmonizing not just a few special instructions, but all the scriptures, understanding will occur. Thus, my enumeration of guidelines is not exhaustive.[990]

Having mostly completed study of the sutra side, Jé went to Rongchö Lung Monastery in Tsang. There, he received various oral transmissions from its abbot, Drakpa Shenyen, and met for the first time the spiritual son of Mañjughoṣa, Lama Umapa Tsöndrü Sengé, whose secret name was Pawo Dorjé.[991] In accord with the advice of Mañjughoṣa, Lama Umapa received from Jé Rinpoché the permission ceremony of Sarasvatī and Candrakīrti's *Autocommentary on Entering the Middle Way.* He said to Jé, "Since my childhood, visions of Mañjughoṣa have come to me constantly; could you please make a detailed investigation of these apparitions?" Jé Rinpoché investigated by interrogating difficult points in various textual systems and determined that they were not just ordinary visions.

Later, when he again met Umapa in Rongchö Lung, he received from him the Dharma cycle of Mañjughoṣa. With Lama Umapa interpreting, he asked Jetsün Mañjughoṣa many Dharma questions, as will be explained below. At that time, Mañjughoṣa urged him to intensive practice so he decided to undertake intensive practice after finishing his study of mantra. Accordingly, when he had finished all his mantra study, both master and disciple went to Gawa Dong Monastery in Kyishö.

After doing a strict retreat, and with Lama Umapa interpreting, Jé asked Jetsün Mañjughoṣa about countless difficult points in the sutras and tantras. Asked how many disciples to take on pilgrimage, Mañjughoṣa stated that Jé should take those known as the eight pure ones.

Up to this point, because Jé Lama had not met [184] Mañjughoṣa directly, he asked his questions with Lama Umapa interpreting; but at this time, because Jé himself had done an intensive retreat, he had a direct vision of Arapacana Mañjughoṣa,[992] sitting at the center of a sphere of rainbow light. Thenceforth, he could see Mañjughoṣa whenever he wished, and he received teachings directly from Jetsün Mañjughoṣa on the profound points of sutra and mantra.

Then, on the advice of Jetsün Mañjughoṣa, Jé decided to go away for intensive practice. Lama Umapa, who was on his way to eastern Tibet, escorted him, and master and disciple arrived in Lhasa. They assembled fine offerings under the eaves of the southern roof of the Jokhang and prayed fervently.

Mañjughoṣa showed himself directly and taught verses that summarized the key points of practice. Jé memorized them and wrote them down, and he offered Umapa initiation into Guhyasamāja-Akṣobhya. In the collected works of Jé, there is a sādhana of White Sarasvatī[993] with the notation: "done at the urging of Jamyang Khaché." In some old manuscripts of earlier times, though, there appears the notation: "Written under the Chinese-style roof of Rasa Trulnang[994] at the urging of Lama Umapa Pawo Dorjé, by the bhikṣu Losang Drakpai Pal, who listened on many occasions to what was taught by Lama Mañjughoṣa." Otherwise, the wording of the poem appears to be the same in the sādhana and the old manuscripts.[995] Umapa went on to eastern Tibet, and when Jé Lama reached the age of thirty-six, nine men—the master and eight disciples—went to Ölkha Chölung for intensive practice. Immediately upon arrival, considering it vital, all of them, master and disciple alike, first worked hard at the confession practice that includes all four opponent powers. Jé himself performed confession of downfalls accompanied by prostrations,[996] to the point where the skin of his fingers and toes cracked, and imprints of his hands, feet, and head appeared in the stone floor. He used a rather large, square stone as the base for his offering mandala, so his forearm skin became raw and broken from wiping it with his forearm.[997] Nowadays, the stone that became so smooth from his prostrations can still be seen.

At that time, Jé trained in a particularly penetrating way in the marvelous bodhisattva conduct that is mentioned in the *Flower Ornament Sutra,* so his mental fortitude greatly improved, and he had no end of [185] pure visions. Then, he went to Menlung in Gyasok, and by diligence in practice, he had many wonderful visions of Indian scholars and adepts, buddhas, bodhisattvas, Vajrabhairava, and others, and his inner realizations increased greatly. At that time, he met Vajrapāṇi's principal spiritual son, the great preceptor from Lhodrak, Namkha Gyaltsen. Since they seemed equally pure, each received many Dharma teachings from the other. In particular, Jé Lama received from the precious great preceptor guidelines on the stages of the path to enlightenment transmitted from the holders of the Kadam instructions, including both lineages of experiential guidelines: that from Gönpawa to Neusurpa and that from Chengawa Tsültrim Bar to Jayülwa.[998] From the great preceptor of Nyal Drakor, Chökyap Sangpo, he received guidelines on the stages of the path transmitted from the Kadam textualists, including both lineages from Potowa—that to Sharawa and that to Dölpa Sherap Gyatso. Remaining at Loro, in Nyal, for about five months, Jé focused on practicing the stages of the path to enlightenment; and when he looked in detail at Drolungpa's *Great Treatise on the Stages of the Teaching,* he gained a special conviction, not a merely intellectual understanding, as to how the entire contents of Maitreya's treatise, the *Ornament of Higher Realization,* can be enlisted as instructions for one person to traverse the stages of the path to awakening. By the same token, countless crucial points in the epistemological treatises, the other books of Maitreya, the Madhyamaka texts, and the four tantra classes of secret mantra also appeared to Jé as instructions. This is well explained in Jé's *Song of Realization;* fearing excess, I will not elaborate here.

These, then, are the unique special qualities of Jé Lama. No previous scholar-adept can be said to have a lifestory in which *every* textual system of the sutras and tantras appears as instruction.

(2) How he gained mastery of the good qualities of realization through meditation

(a) Realizations regarding vinaya

Thus, Jé studied a great deal from the ages of seventeen to thirty-six. When he was thirty-six, at the urging [186] of Jetsün Mañjughoṣa, he took up the renounced life. Through a multitude of practices that accumulate merit—praying to the lama as inseparable from the meditational deity, and so forth—after four years he realized all textual systems as instruction. Then, from ages thirty-eight to fifty-three, he turned his mind to practicing not just a part of the path, but the complete body of sutra and mantra. Thus, unlike those who hope for high realizations but have attained only certain good qualities common to non-Buddhists and Buddhists, he gained authentic inner realizations, just as explained in Dharma texts. As Jé himself stated:

> Whatever others did for me, such as preparing a fine seat, respectfully[999] serving me, and so forth, right there and then, without need of reflection, I thought with overwhelming sadness: "All these are impermanent, untrustworthy, like seductive illusions." Thus, from the very first, I was naturally inclined constantly to transform appearances, rejecting them in the depths of my mind as insubstantial.[1000]

At Sengé Dzong in lower Nyal, he taught many topics related to the vinaya. He practiced vinaya in detail, from minor observances such as the sprinkling of water[1001] up to the major rules, and said: "The pure morality one has taken on is the basis of all good qualities. I have never experienced a prātimokṣa downfall entailing expulsion, suspension, or return; such minor transgressions and infractions as do occur, I confess and vow not to repeat."[1002]

In Ölkha Chölung, Jé examined the *Flower Ornament Sutra* and trained his mind in the awakening mind and bodhisattva conduct. He practiced constantly the meditation that trains the mind in a particularly penetrating way in each of the great waves—both the mental fortitude and the conduct of a child of the Conqueror—that appear in that sutra. Thus, he said:

> Although it is a little difficult at first, later, when you've grown accustomed to those qualities, effortlessly and on your own—hard as it is to fathom the wondrous mental fortitude and conduct of the Conqueror's children—you will never know discouragement, and will engage with others in a natural and joyful manner.[1003]

Once when he was staying at Kyormo Lung, he entered meditative equipoise on the meaning of a sutra being recited in the assembly of monks,[1004] and [187] he did not rise from his concentration even when the assembly of monks was dismissed. And, as he himself said:

> From my early days, whenever I have been involved in detailed analysis of the meaning of scripture, my mind has not been distracted in the slightest, even when others are talking loudly in front of me or doing various things. And since that time in Ölkha Jampa Ling, I also am undistracted when engaging in the practice of virtue.[1005]

(b) Realizations regarding Madhyamaka and tantra

1′ Conversations with Mañjughoṣa

How, in particular, he gained realization of the Madhyamaka view and the bliss and emptiness of the mantra vehicle: In Khedrup Jé's *Cluster of Yogic Achievements: The Secret Biography,* it says that in Tsangrong, when Jé was the questioner and Lama Umapa the interpreter, he asked Jetsün Mañjughoṣa many Dharma questions. In particular, it had been stated by the ārya father Nāgārjuna and his spiritual son Āryadeva that if you do not seek the Madhyamaka view, you will not find the life of the path; that even if you do seek it, it is very difficult to find; and that if you hold it incorrectly, the detours and disadvantages will be greater than those entailed by other mistakes, so Jé sought reality continuously and uninterruptedly, singleminded like the bodhisattva Sadāprarudita. At that time, therefore, he mostly asked the Jetsün questions about the view. On one occasion, he asked, "Is this view of mine Prāsaṅgika Madhyamaka or Svātantrika Madhyamaka?" Mañjughoṣa replied, "It is neither."[1006] At that time Jé was comfortable merely with the unwarranted view that there is nothing to be admitted and nothing to be apprehended.[1007]

After that, when Jé questioned him and probed for contradictions regarding the view, Jetsün Mañjughoṣa stated again and again, "It is incorrect to make the appearance side and the emptiness side completely disparate;[1008] you should give special emphasis to appearances."[1009] Many such statements were made later, too, when Jé was staying at Gawa Dong. In short, Jetsün Mañjughoṣa tried urgently to reject the idea that the supreme Madhyamaka view is the nihilistic view of action and result, which claims that things only exist in the mistaken consciousnesses of others,[1010] unestablished through conventional sources of valid cognition, and that there is no way of establishing one's own system.[1011] [188]

When Jé thus questioned him and probed for contradictions, Jetsün Mañjughoṣa on various occasions taught in a highly distilled manner the seeds of a detailed investigation into the differences between Prāsaṅgika and Svātantrika. The specific differences were the coarse and subtle delimitation of the self and the object of negation of the logical reason, according to how they are apprehended by the two types of self-grasping: innate and imputed; the criteria for realization of the view; the way conventional truth is determined by the Prāsaṅgika system; and so forth. In other cases, he taught in a highly distilled manner the key comparisons and distinctions between the mantra and definition vehicles: the ascertainment of the nature of the five stages of the glorious Guhyasamāja, their ordering, their enumeration, and so forth.[1012] When Jé said he didn't understand, Mañjughoṣa said:

> Write this down so you don't forget it: (1) Praying to and doing intensive retreat on the inseparable lama/meditational deity, (2) striving well in both accumulating merit and purifying delusions, and (3) analyzing the meaning of texts rationally and considering them in detail. Satisfactorily practicing those three in a combined form is not easy, but analyze them well over an extended period, and when the time comes, and the condi-

> tions are right, these seeds that I have just now planted will ripen quickly in a mature understanding.[1013]

Jé had an immense desire to understand the Madhyamaka and Guhyasamāja teachings of the system of the ārya father Nāgārjuna and his spiritual sons, so he asked which lama in Tibet would be the best to study these with. Mañjughoṣa replied:

> There is no one better than Rendawa. However, even he will not be able to arouse in you a complete understanding that severs every extreme. Best would be for me to teach you with Umapa interpreting, but it seems he has to go soon to eastern Tibet. So, from now on, do not teach, but resort to solitude and live a renounced life. As explained before, strive well in practicing the three combined; meditate and perform other practices continuously, and before long, you will get their meaning.[1014]

Also, there is this passage in Lechen Künga Gyaltsen's biographical account of Tsongkhapa's deeds:

> In the autumn of the water male monkey year (1392), when Jé had reached the age of thirty-six, he went together with Lama Umapa to [189] Gawa Dong in the region of Ü. After setting the boundaries of their retreat, they received many cycles of Dharma teachings from Mañjughoṣa. At that time, with Lama Umapa interpreting, Jé put countless questions to Jetsün Mañjughoṣa, on, for example, the Madhyamaka view, the differences between the mantra and definition vehicles, the difficult points of the path of highest yoga mantra, ascertaining the order and enumeration of the five stages of the completion stage of highest yoga tantra, and other issues. Most importantly, Jé, who was relatively content with a "Madhyamaka" view based solely on the perceptions of others, in which there was nothing in one's system to be accepted and nothing to be established, asked the noble lord, "Is this Madhyamaka view of mine a pure view?" Mañjughoṣa replied, "No, because you have ascertained the emptiness side on your own but not the appearance side." When Jé asked what the differences are between Prāsaṅgika and Svātantrika Madhyamaka, Mañjughoṣa

said, "Examine whether overt clinging to mere appearances is or is not stopped." When Jé asked what textual system would be the best to study, Mañjughoṣa said, "Although in general there is no 'good' or 'bad' in the word of the Conqueror, you have a karmic connection to the Madhyamaka, so study that." When Jé asked what kind of tantra would be the best to study, Mañjughoṣa said, "Study the one scripture that has a commentary by master Candrakīrti, the *Guhyasamāja Tantra*." When Jé asked whether it were permissible to hold master Candrakīrti as an authority in every circumstance, Mañjughoṣa said, "How could that great bodhisattva have any confusion?"[1015]

2′ Plans to visit India

Just before Jé met the great preceptor Chakdorwa Namkha Gyaltsen, he thought: "I have studied well such scriptures and treatises, as well as special instructions, as now exist in the Land of Snows, and I have understood them. But now, in order to sever my superimpositions, doubts, and qualms, and in particular to establish certainty about Madhyamaka and mantra, and more specifically about Guhyasamāja and Cakrasaṃvara, I should go to India and meet Nāgabodhi[1016] and others at Odantapuri, Nālandā,[1017] and other monastic universities."[1018] About thirteen of them, master and disciples, examined signs, dreams, and other indicators, and when their aspirations and the omens coincided, they planned with relentless determination to meet and stay with the great adept Mitrayogi[1019] in Śṛṇgeri, then go to Magadha. When the great adept Namkha Gyaltsen found this out, he said, "If you go to India, even though you would become a great pandit who is expert in the five sciences and be made the abbot [190] of Vajrāsana,[1020] it would shorten your life, so it would be difficult to benefit disciples. Thus, if you stay in Tibet and pray to Mañjughoṣa, you will be cared for immediately."

Asked to cancel his plans, Jé promised to do so and resolved not to go. If the great adept had not stopped him then, we who live now in the Land of Snows would have missed the opportunity to taste the essential nectar that is the profound distillate of Jé Lama's mind: the profound key points of the Madhyamaka view and Guhyasamāja, Cakrasaṃvara, and other tantras. Through the kindness of Lama Namkha Gyaltsen, Jé Lama permanently settled in this land. It is because Jé extensively turned the Dharma wheel and left behind so many writings that explain so well the most difficult points of Dharma that, right down to the present, so many of the fortunate have had the opportunity to enjoy here the nectar of the profound and secret Dharmas.[1021] Thus, it is right that we meditate with faith and respect, remembering Namkha Gyaltsen's and Jé Rinpoché's kindness, and in particular, that we ourselves, who have gained a portion of the nectar-like teaching, should make diligent efforts to utilize it, never losing it to the thieves of laziness and distraction.

3′ Definitive realization

Even before he left for the hermitage, Jé constantly examined the key points of the Prāsaṅgika and Svātantrika views but was still unable to gain enough certainty to turn back once and for all his uneasiness about the ultimate points. On this occasion, though, at the Lhashöl hermitage in Odé Gungyal in Lhading, he strove, as instructed by Mañjughoṣa, to develop meditation on the view by way of the combined three requisites.[1022] One night, he dreamed that the holy quintet of the father Nāgārjuna and his four spiritual sons[1023] were engaged[1024] in discussion of the profound meaning, and amid this, one of them, a scholar with a large translucent bluish body, said, "I am Master Buddhapālita" and set an Indian Madhyamaka text on top of Jé's head; this was a sign of blessing.[1025] The next day, when Jé looked into the *Buddhapālita Commentary on the Fundamental Treatise on the Middle Way,* he gained an unprecedented, deeply felt certainty with respect to the ultimate key points of the view of the protector Nāgārjuna and his spiritual sons, the delineation of the object of negation, and so forth. All fixation on apprehended signs thereby dissolved, and the superimposition that imputes the extreme of permanence onto objective reality was obliterated without remainder. By virtue of the faith attained through understanding[1026] the Buddha, Jé wrote what is called the *Praise of the Buddha for His Teaching* [191] *of Dependent Arising: Essence of Excellent Explanation.*[1027]

Where was he looking in the commentary when he severed superimposition? In the words of my omniscient lama:

> When Jé Rinpoché was looking at the *Buddhapālita Commentary on the Fundamental Treatise on the Middle Way,* he saw the commentary on the passage from the eighth chapter of the *Fundamental Treatise on the Middle Way,* "On Agency," that says:

> The agent depends on the action,
> And the action on the agent;
> I see no way of establishing them
> In which they do not arise dependently.[1028]
>
> After that, it was as if he had a new way of realizing emptiness; he cited that scriptural passage many times in his own great commentary on the *Fundamental Treatise on the Middle Way*.[1029]

Thus my lama taught. And, as Khedrup Jé states in his biography of Jé, the *Entryway to Faith:*

> Thus, through reasoning about the meaning of reality, he severed every last superimposition and applied himself to the concentration of single-pointed meditative equipoise on emptiness. Through his extraordinary meditative development, nurtured well by perfect mindfulness and introspection, as Jé himself said:
>
> > Now I am well developed, so even after meditation, all these various appearances arise as empty, like illusory appearances, while ordinary appearances not sealed by emptiness rarely arise on their own.
>
> Thus he taught. So, since this lifestory that delights the wise is hard to fathom, and is celebrated with a series of praises even by the conquerors and their children, it goes without saying that we should praise it, too.[1030]

Therefore, through the kindness of Jetsün Mañjughoṣa, Jé Lama attained the profound Prāsaṅgika Madhyamaka view, which had never been revealed in Tibet just as it is by any previous sage. Because of that, it is proven that our Geden view is distinctive relative to the views of the famed Kagyü, Sakya, Jonang, and Dzokchen. "Well, then," someone might ask, "didn't even Lama Rendawa understand the view just as it is?" In the words of my omniscient lama, "Although on most elements of the presentation of the view, the claims of Rendawa and Jé Lama are identical, still, when it comes to clearing away the affirmative extreme by appearances and the negative extreme by emptiness, and when it comes to the way emptiness appears in cause and effect, Jé

Lama's presentation is unique."[1031] Thus, I think this was the point of Jetsün Mañjughoṣa's saying earlier, "even [192] Rendawa will not be able to produce in you a complete understanding that severs every extreme."[1032]

(c) Realizations regarding highest yoga tantra

How Jé attained realization of the two stages of highest yoga tantra: It says in Khedrup's *Secret Biography:*[1033]

> When Jé was forty-eight and forty-nine, while staying at Jampa Ling temple in Sangngak Monastery in Ölkha, he wrote the *Exposition of the Presentation of Stages of Guhyasamāja* and the *Great Treatise on the Stages of Mantra.* At that time, he stated:
>
> > I understood thoroughly and well the rough meaning of, in general, the five stages and, in particular, how to achieve the illusory body of the third stage, as taught in the basic and explanatory tantras of glorious Guhyasamāja, and the uncommon meaning taught in the texts of the quintet of the ārya father Nāgārjuna and his spiritual sons. After that, more than ten years passed when I could not speak of it; after that, I spoke of it just a little.[1034]
>
> In Okar Drak, while doing intensive retreat on Cakrasaṃvara and practicing the guidelines on the six Dharmas of Niguma, he gained many wonderful experiential realizations of what had been explained. At Sengé Dzong in Nyal, he practiced the experiential guidelines on the sixfold yoga of Kālacakra and gained a special realization of the sixfold yoga. He had a vision of the solitary Kālacakra, who told him, "For the Kālacakra tradition, your coming will be like the arrival of Sucandra."[1035]
>
> At Samten Ling in Ölkha, he had a vision in which the principal deity of the Guhyasamāja mandala, Mañjuśrīvajra, was discussing the Dharma with Mañjughoṣa and Maitreya. The principal mandala deity gave Jé a vase filled with water, and the omniscient Butön Rinchen Drupa, sitting in the style of Maitreya on a precious throne, entrusted him with the root tantra of Guhyasamāja, saying, "Master this," and Jé saw signs of being

> blessed by mantra and mudra. And he attained a special ascertainment of the instruction by Marpa of Lhodrak on the ninefold cycle on mixing and transference.[1036]
>
> While living in strict retreat at Ganden, he saw the thread-like light of the letters *evaṃ* streaming from the beginning of the central channel at the tip of his nose, down through the path of the central channel, to the lower openings. At that, he gained the gnosis, possessed of the four joys and the four empties, that unites a special uncommon melting bliss with the realization of emptiness. From then on, he continuously developed the special gnosis of bliss and emptiness so he could remain in equipoise on the gnosis of bliss and emptiness taught in the tantras. And, [193] as described in the texts of the great adepts, he attained meditative equipoise in a concentration unlike that to which some want to attach the name "gnosis of bliss and emptiness," but that is merely akin to the concentration common to both non-Buddhists and Buddhists. Also, whatever appeared in post-meditation appeared as the sport of bliss and emptiness in the circle of the deity. His time passed like that.[1037]

Khedrup's text also says:

> On one occasion, Jetsün Mañjughoṣa prophesied, "From now on, if you direct your efforts mainly at practicing the yogas of the generation and completion stages, then, through highest yoga mantra, you will gain a special realization; not only that, each of your seven fortunate disciples will also gain a special realization of the path." About that, Jé said, "Visions that are experienced when our inner elements are unbalanced are not[1038] very reliable, so I should ask Tokdenpa Jampal Gyatso about it." When asked, Tokdenpa said:
>
> > There is no need to ask again. Mentally renounce this life, and after showing the complete paths of sutra and mantra to suitable disciples, set them to meditating. Jé, you yourself said that Mañjughoṣa stated: "If you apply yourself mainly to practice while on retreat, then since the inner causes for the path to arise quickly in your mind—the special gnosis

> of bliss and emptiness, and so forth—have already arisen in your mind, then the outer conditions—such as special helpers like human messenger goddesses—will come soon. Since you also are blessed by the supreme deity Mañjughoṣa, you have completed the requisites, and you will quickly gain the path."[1039]

If, on that occasion, Jé had resorted to an action seal,[1040] it would have been the cause for his manifesting the stage of union[1041] in that very life. So that his followers would honor their celibacy—the root of the teaching—he did not resort to an action seal. Help on the path was provided by an innate seal,[1042] as suggested by the words of Jetsün Mañjughoṣa; and, as Tokden Jampal Gyatso states:

> A beautiful woman continually came before Jé, wearing attractive clothes and a Tang-style flat red hat. Her not coming in the aspect of a goddess seems to have resulted from his fault of showing [194] the secrets of mantra to unsuitable recipients. After Jé wrote the *Wish-Fulfilling Commentary on Lūipa's Cakrasaṃvara System,* she came in the aspect of Vajrayoginī and other female buddhas and gave him special help. Apparently, when erecting the three-dimensional Cakrasaṃvara mandala in the Lhasa cathedral, Jé saw goddesses singing the words and tune of the concentration blessing song[1043] and other offering songs.[1044]

Alternatively, it is said that the goddess Sarasvatī was his action seal.[1045] Jé himself said:

> With unfettered power to achieve that path,
> May the heroes and ḍākinīs of the twenty-four power places
> Of Jambudvīpa, along with their retinues,
> Always assist us unstintingly.[1046]

And Jé also said:

> Through communing quickly with the helpful messenger,
> May there be the auspicious blazing of the banquet of bliss.[1047]

This will be apparent to the understanding through these various quotes. With that goddess's crucial help, Jé attained the supreme yogic achievement in the bardo. As stated by Khedrup Jé:

> At death you manifested the clear-light dharmakāya,
> Your body turned into a sphere of light,
> And in the bardo, you attained the complete enjoyment body;
> I pray to the one who gained the supreme yogic achievement.[1048]

(d) Pure visions

If the pure visions he saw in just one session of concentration meditation are beyond imagining, who could describe all of them? You may learn about them roughly from the *Secret Biography* and other texts. And, as for Mañjughoṣa acting as the virtuous friend, it is stated in Khedrup Jé's *Entryway to Faith:*

> In particular, he had direct visions, again and again, of the one father of all the conquerors, Jetsün Mañjughoṣa.[1049] Because Mañjughoṣa acted as his virtuous friend, he did not become confused about the meaning of any text. If he had difficulty in realizing what a text meant, however, he first analyzed it in detail through reasoning, and most of the time, the meaning came to him. When such analyses were incapable of inducing the mental certainty in which extreme views are severed, Jé would offer a mandala and pray intently to the lama and Jetsün Mañjughoṣa, who do not differ. Immediately thereafter, he could effortlessly and thoroughly consider those points and gain an irrefutable grasp of them. Moreover, although the biographical details [195] of Jé's visions and other experiences of the body and speech of Jetsün Mañjughoṣa cannot openly be described to everyone, my account of the way he analyzed the meaning of the scriptures, of whether the analysis was complete or incomplete, of the key points of his practice, of the way his disciples were guided, of the kind of retinue he had, of the places he stayed, and so forth, is nevertheless not influenced by my own fabrications.[1050]

That is how it was.

2) How he served the teaching

How Tsongkhapa acted on behalf of the teaching is twofold: a) How he laid the foundations of the teaching, and b) How he propagated and extended the teaching through the three activities of scholars.

a) How he laid the foundations of the teaching

Earlier, when Jé was staying in Drabo Monastery in Lhodrak, having already accomplished the restoration of the Dzingchi temple, he thought that observing the pure vinaya training rules would be an especially good omen, one of extensive benefit to the teaching, so he prepared three Dharma robes, a begging bowl, a staff, and so forth, and a song of praise he had written, the *Crown of Brahmā,*[1051] and sent them to be offered to the statue of Maitreya the protector at Dzingchi. After that, at Sengé Dzong in lower Nyal, he taught many topics related to the vinaya. He practiced vinaya in detail, from minor observances such as the sprinkling of water on up to the major rules, and said: "The pure morality one takes on is the basis of all good qualities. I have never experienced a prātimokṣa downfall entailing expulsion, suspension, or return; such minor transgressions and infractions as do occur, I confess and vow not to repeat."[1052] He practiced thus, and his retinue also joined him in practicing that way.

Later on in particular, Jé Lama, Lama Rendawa, and the great translator Kyapchok Palsang met together at Namtsé Ding.[1053] Just over six hundred monks, headed by many Tripiṭaka masters, took the vow for the summer retreat; all three Dharma lords intended [196] to undergo purification for the sake of the precious teaching. Also, their minds resonated with the saying, "As long as the Conqueror's inmost treasure, the vinaya, exists in full, the teaching of the Buddha will exist; without it, there is no teaching." So, with their minds intent solely on the teaching, they each gave an extensive explanation of the *Vinaya Sutra*. At that time, they established well the way of pure observance according to the explanations of (1) all the rules taught in the *Great Group,*[1054] from the subtlest up to the most important, which even present-day people can practice; and (2) the rites found in the *Great Division,*[1055] which repair by name and kind all the downfalls that transgress the rules. At the time, most of the monks who received teachings on the vinaya also examined their own minds. They put into practice, just as they are explained, the specifications as to how many objects of confession are required for all the subtle and coarse downfalls;[1056] and when, prior to a confession-punishment, one has to forego a forbidden substance,[1057] and so forth, and they thereby corrected those downfalls. From then on, most of the regular attendants examined their own minds daily and corrected their downfalls without delay. Since they even took great effort in practices such as blessing the requisites, setting up the kitchen, guarding rules regarding temporary shelter, and so forth, what need is there to mention those not so hard to accomplish? Thus, Jé completely restored the root of the Buddha's teaching, the prātimokṣa foundation; his service to the teaching was extraordinary.

Therefore, in the biography by Khedrup Jé, the *Entryway to Faith,* it says:

> Nowadays, when those involved in study and reflection actually apply themselves to study and reflection and honor the basis of the training, only a certain few Tripiṭaka masters, though meditating intensely, engage in shameful wanton behavior—drinking beer, eating at the wrong times, and so forth. Formerly, most of those at the great monasteries who had taken preliminary ordination found it difficult even to recognize the requisites of a recluse—the seat cover, begging bowl, and so forth.[1058] And as for the arrangement of vertical and horizontal squares on the upper robe and lower robe, and so forth, it was unheard of. Nowadays, everywhere from Kashmir to China, practitioners [197] are in accord with the training in virtue, where one applies oneself to everything from the subtle basis of the training on up, like maintaining the pure marks and attire of recluses, giving up beer and afternoon meals, and guarding the rules about the giving and taking of food, water offerings, the maximum number of nights sleeping under one roof, and so forth. If this situation is not due solely to the kindness of our glorious lama, Jetsün Rinpoché, by whom else, then, do you think it has occurred?"[1059]

Also, the great sage Gö Lotsāwa Shönu Pal says:

> Times being what they were, quite a few fully ordained monks were lax. Thus, the holy Jetsün Losang Drakpai Pal first trained well in the vinaya at Kyormo Lung with the great scholar Kashipa Losalwa. Later, he performed the essential practices in a solitary place and never strayed from vinaya conduct. Still later, when

> caring for his retinue, he trained his entire inner circle and, just as explained in the vinaya, made them keep the necessary requisites: the three Dharma robes, the mat, the begging bowl, and so forth. Based on the special instructions of the uniquely divine noble lord Atiśa, he trained in the systems of the three types of persons, and having mentally renounced all of samsara, he arranged all the vows for the purpose of authentic individual liberation.[1060] Through others' emulation of his actions, the teaching of the vinaya appeared like the rising sun everywhere in the realm of Tibet.[1061]

This expression of praise is exactly right.

Moreover, thinking that if those sworn to the Mahayana did not observe the pure morality of the bodhisattva, they would become Mahayanists in name only, and that if those engaged in secret mantra did not properly guard the vows and pledges, they would only open the door to the lower realms, Jé gave many Tripiṭaka masters extensive explanations at Gawa Dong Monastery on the morality chapter of Asaṅga's *Bodhisattva Stages,* Aśvaghoṣa's[1062] *Fifty Stanzas on the Guru,* and Lakṣmīṅkara's *Fourteen Root Downfalls;* and he composed explanatory texts on the morality chapter, the *Fifty Stanzas on the Guru,*[1063] the *Fourteen Root Downfalls,* and so forth. Because of that, the practice of striving to guard the two higher vows and repairing them if they degenerate has persisted right up to today, and it should be recognized that this, too, stems from the kindness of Jé Lama. [198]

b) How he propagated and extended the teaching through the three activities of scholars

This is threefold: (1) How he served the teaching by way of explanations, 2) How he served the teaching by way of debate, and (3) How he served the teaching by disseminating his writings, which are a garland of excellent explanation.

(1) How he served the teaching by way of explanations

When staying at Tashi Dong in Möngar, Jé taught the various biographies of Indian and Tibetan scholar-adepts. He stated that the kashipa Sherseng had taught eleven volumes in one Dharma course; he said that that seemed to be the most taught at one time in the later period in Tibet. Then, when his whole inner circle—Geshé Shatön and others—asked Jé himself to teach that many at one time, he said that it seemed he could teach that many if he made the effort. When they urgently requested him again, he promised to do so.

That month, he isolated himself from the tenth to the new-moon day,[1064] reading and analyzing manuscripts. On the day of the new moon, he bound all the manuscripts with a belt. He had hoped to start the Dharma course on the first of that month, but he had to await the arrival of many Tripiṭaka masters who were coming from particular monasteries like Sangphu and others, so for about three days he taught some miscellaneous oral traditions of Marpa, Milarepa, and others. On a single day, the fifth day, he simultaneously began teaching fifteen texts, from their opening "In the language of India."[1065] Each day, teaching without break from early morning until midnight, he gave explanations in fifteen sessions. When he had finished teaching the two shortest volumes of the original fifteen, he started two other short ones in their place.

He explained seventeen treatises: Dharmakīrti's *Thorough Exposition of Valid Cognition;* the perfection of wisdom, that is, Maitreya's *Ornament of Higher Realization;* the pair of abhidharmas, the higher, which is Asaṅga's *Compendium of Abhidharma,* and the lower, Vasubandhu's *Treasury of Higher Knowledge;* Guṇaprabha's *Vinaya Sutra;* the other four of the five books of Maitreya; five of Nāgārjuna's six collections of Madhyamaka reasoning; Candrakīrti's *Entering the Middle Way;* Āryadeva's *Four Hundred Stanzas;* and Śāntideva's *Way of the Bodhisattva.* For some of the most difficult texts, he established, with refutations and proofs, many modes of commentarial explanation that went beyond those set out in the great Tibetan commentaries. For most other texts, he gave detailed explanations on every hard or easy passage on the basis of their own commentaries. He finished this task in three months.

On that same occasion, whenever he was free from Dharma teaching, he uninterruptedly performed the yogas of the two stages of his meditational deity, Vajrabhairava, including [199] self-initiation, and so forth. At that time, too, everyone agreed that it could not have happened thus unless it were certain either that he was directly blessed by a superior deity or that he was a great bodhisattva who had attained the power of nonforgetting. Reports are in agreement on this.

This is a most unusual ordinary biography; there is no such story about any previous sage.

At Radreng,[1066] after harmonizing well such great texts as Maitreya's *Ornament of Mahayana Sutras* and Asaṅga's *Distinguishing the Middle from the*

Extremes,[1067] *Compendium of Abhidharma, Stages of the Śrāvakas,* and others, he gave a thorough explanation of tranquil abiding, and when he allowed his students to meditate, a special experience of tranquil abiding, concordant with scripture, arose in the minds of some. He taught the quintessence of the Kadam special instructions, which is the teaching on how to meditate on the conventional awakening mind of equalizing and exchanging self and other, condensed into a clear order for practice, and adorned it with Mañjughoṣa's special instructions on ultimate awakening mind. The *Rays of the Sun of Mind Training* and other texts were developed based on the notes taken by Hortön Namkha Pal during the teachings.

At Lhepu Gönsar,[1068] he taught to many Tripiṭaka masters all the principal subjects of Dharmakīrti's *Thorough Exposition of Valid Cognition* as they apply to practice.[1069] When he taught his interpretation of the text according to the stages of the path, the scholars were utterly captivated by the nectar of this unprecedented excellent explanation. Before then, it was said that studying valid cognition was necessary only for broadly understanding external phenomena but had no relevance to internal practice. Thenceforth, though, the *Thorough Exposition of Valid Cognition* became a supreme treatise for showing practice.[1070] Gyaltsap Jé Rinpoché took notes on what Jé taught at that time. Jé wished to teach the perfection of wisdom, so he suggested to his retinue that they each offer butter lamps. Gyaltsap Jé put a wick into a huge copper pot filled with clarified butter. Seeing it lit, Jé thought it was a particularly good omen, so he collected all the other butter lamps into that huge pot. Then Jé Rinpoché taught the application of yogic practice to the meaning of the perfection of wisdom according to the special instructions taught to him by Jetsün Mañjughoṣa. Gyaltsap Jé [200] also took notes on that and then wrote the *Ornament of Essential Expositions,* which is a great treasure that eloquently explains what no previous sage could evince.

When it comes to secret mantra, Jé's spiritual heir Khedrup Jé wrote a great commentary to accord with Jé's extensive teaching at Ganden on the great Kālacakra commentary, *Stainless Light*. Also, after harmonizing all the tantras and Indian texts of the Yamāntaka cycle, Khedrup Jé wrote the *Great Generation Stage of Vajrabhairava* according to what Jé had taught, and Dülzin[1071] wrote a textbook according to Jé's teachings on the three families of the action tantras and on the performance tantras. Moreover, many disciples took notes on Jé's teaching on the generation and completion stages of Cakrasaṃvara and Guhyasamāja.

In brief, even when Jé was very young and living in lower Amdo, he gave explanations of Maitreya's *Ornament of Mahayana Sutras*. Having arrived in central Tibet, he began in Nenying with an explanation of Asaṅga's *Compendium of Abhidharma*. At the temple at Keru in Ön, he taught many topics, such as the perfection of wisdom, valid cognition, Madhyamaka, and so forth[1072] to the governor of Tsakho[1073] and others. At Dewachen and Jayül in upper Ü, he repeatedly taught the perfection of wisdom, valid cognition, Madhyamaka, and Asaṅga's *Compendium of Abhidharma*. At Kyormo Lung, Dewachen, Tölung Tsomé, and the five lineage temples on Ngangkar Sinpo Mountain, he repeatedly taught the Tripiṭaka. At the rock cave at Kyormo Lung, he repeatedly taught Kālacakra, the perfection of wisdom, Madhyamaka, and other topics. At Rapdrong in upper Nyal, he repeatedly taught the profound and extensive Dharma to many Tripiṭaka masters, and he repeatedly taught the Dharma at Lungra Chenmor Drak, Garphuk in Ölga, Ei Teura, and Nyangpo Dangdo. At the Potala,[1074] he repeatedly taught such topics as Kamalaśīla's *Light of Madhyamaka,* the vinaya, the stages of the path, and so forth, to many hundreds of disciples, principally many scholars headed by the abbots of the great monasteries: the trio of Sangphu, Dewachen, and Gungthang, and the trio of Ganden, Kyormo Lung, and Sül Chölung. At this time, the upholder of the Sakya teaching, Rongtön Shākya Gyaltsen, bowed at Jé's feet and received teachings on the stages of the path, although in the biographies of Rongtön written by Shākya Chokden and others, this fact, like a buried treasure, is not revealed.

At Gawa Dong, Jé gave extensive explanations of the morality chapter of Asaṅga's *Bodhisattva Stages,* Aśvaghośa's *Fifty Stanzas on the Guru,* and Lakṣmīṅkara's [201] *Fourteen Root Downfalls.*[1075] At Radreng, he taught many topics at different times: the earlier and later versions of the stages of the path, and so forth. At Drigung, he frequently taught the Dharma to the Tripiṭaka masters there, headed by Gushri[1076] Döndrup Gyalpo and Drigung Lotsāwa. At Ön Dechen Teng, he taught many guidelines for the stages of the path and about difficult points of Madhyamaka and valid cognition. At Ölkha Jampa Ling, he taught the generation and completion stages and, at Jangchup Lung, the stages of the path of mantra. While in retreat at Sera Chöding,[1077] he taught the five stages of Guhyasamāja and some of the completion-stage practices of the mother tantras. At Sera, before about six hundred monks, he taught Nāgārjuna's *Fundamental Treatise on the Middle Way,* his own *Distinguishing Provisional and Definitive,*[1078] Āryadeva's *Four Hundred Stanzas,* his own *Stages of the Path of Secret Mantra,* his *Exposition of the Basic Downfalls,* Aśvaghoṣa's *Fifty Stanzas on the Guru,* and other texts; and he also gave extensive guidelines on the stages of the path. Then, at Drumbu Lung in Kyimé before at least a thousand monks, he repeatedly taught the stages of the path, the completion stage of the mother tantra Cakrasaṃvara, and other topics. Again, at Sera Chöding, before about six hundred Tripiṭaka masters, he repeatedly taught on Nāgārjuna's *Fundamental Treatise on the Middle Way,* the morality chapter of Asaṅga's *Bodhisattva Stages,* Vitapāda's *All-Good Sādhana Collection,* the stages of the path, and other topics. At Sangri Chin, before Chenga Sönam Sangpo and others, he repeatedly taught the sutra and mantra approaches to the stages of the path, and so forth. At Samten Ling in Ölkha, he taught various topics.

Then he went to the great throne site at Ganden Mountain and gave countless teachings on the difficult points of: the stages of the path, Candrakīrti's *Bright Lamp,* Nāgārjuna's *Five Stages,* Asaṅga's *Compendium of Abhidharma,* Asaṅga's five treatises on the stages, valid cognition, and other topics. Again, at Tashi Dokha in Ön, before hundreds of Tripiṭaka masters, he extensively taught Madhyamaka, valid cognition, the stages of the path, and so forth. After that, he returned to Ganden; for many years there, he taught innumerable profound Dharmas, principally the explanatory traditions of the four classes of tantra, and so forth. He gave countless teachings, these above all: teachings on Candrakīrti's Guhyasamāja commentary, *Bright Lamp,* including the annotations; extensive guidelines on Nāgārjuna's *Five Stages;* extensive guidelines on the six yogas of Kālacakra; extensive teachings on Puṇḍarīka's great Kālacakra commentary, *Stainless Light;* many teachings about Cakrasaṃvara; explanations of Madhyamaka and valid cognition; guidelines for the stages of the path; and other topics. Then, at glorious Drepung, before about two thousand scholars, he made the Muni's teaching as bright as sunlight, turning the vast wheel of such Dharmas as: guidelines for the stages of the path, guidelines for the six Dharmas of Nāropa, Candrakīrti's *Entering the Middle Way,* [202] the Guhyasamāja tantra, and so forth. In this regard, it says in the *Blue Annals,* "The great being Künsangwa stated: 'Because he was lord of the teaching, even one explanation by Jé Lama on topics explained hundreds of times by others became a victory banner that never disappeared.'"[1079] This quotation is exactly right.

(2) How he served the teaching by way of debate

When Jé was nineteen years old, he went on the debate circuit[1080] related to the perfection of wisdom, traveling to Sangphu, Dewachen, Sakya in Tsangrong,

Dar Sangden, Garong Chödé in Ngamring, Chödra Chenpo É, Nenying, and other places. Later, he went on the debate circuit related to the other four greatly difficult subjects,[1081] traveling to Sakya, Sangphu, Tsethang, and other places. On those occasions, before many hundreds of experts on scripture and reasoning, he established the meaning of the major textual systems through refutation and investigation; his reasoning, supported by the evidence, destroyed the arrogance of countless opponents. The assembly of impartial scholars was moved to deeply felt[1082] faith by his splendid discipline, and spontaneously bowed in respect. At that time, reports of his sagacity filled Jambudvīpa, so whenever a debate circle was assembled in front of Jé Lama, no one would step forward to debate him. Although some at first came wanting to debate him, when they met him and heard his excellent explanations of the teaching, they were utterly captivated and became his disciples.

For example, when the three lamas came together at Namtseng Deng to turn the wheel of Dharma, Karma Könchok Shönu said:

> Lotsāwa Kyapchok Palsang and I can debate, with Rendawa and Tsongkhapa as witnesses. Alternatively, Rendawa and I can debate; that would also be fine. But, at this point, I should not debate Lama Losang Drakpa. He has the excellent awakening mind from previous lives, so he has no prejudice, even against those who propound debased philosophical systems.

It is known that he was scolding Kyapchok and Rendawa for being biased. It says in the *Short Biography* by Tokden Jampal Gyatso:

> He was renowned for having the three qualities [203] of sagacity, purity, and goodness, so his fame pervaded this Land of Snows, and it seems that he was also held in respect by all who, like Karma Könshön, are high minded.[1083]

Still, if they are not refuted through scripture and reasoning, incorrect statements, even if they occur in texts by this or that famous sage of India or Tibet, lead to detours on the perfect path and should not be politely ignored. When it comes to making refutations with hundreds of scriptural and rational arguments, it is obvious that what is clear and extensive in the precious writings of Jé does not exist in the teachings of even the most elevated of other scholars of the Land of Snows, such as Sakya Pandita, Ngok Lotsāwa, Butön, and others. Likewise, when it comes to Jé's own point of view, even when opponents trained in logic disputed and analyzed it hundreds of times, they could not move him even an inch from his thesis. Thus, Khedrup Jé says:

> Even examined a hundred times by countless opponents
> With training in logic, your words, O protector,
> Cannot be altered by even an inch;
> To you who possess a mind that is pure, I pray.[1084]

Later, such scholars as Rongtön Mawai Sengé, Ngorpa Künsang, Gorampa Sönam Sengé, Shākya Chokdenpa, Taktsang Lotsāwa, and others secretly wrote a great deal of literature opposing the writings of Jé, using whatever native intelligence they had, but Khedrup Jé and, later, the omniscient Sera Jetsünpa, Khedrup Lekchöpa, and other direct disciples and grand-disciples of Jé reduced them to ashes with a scriptural and logical deluge of diamond fire. Their own analytical limbs became bound by the tattered ropes of the negations and affirmations they propagated; as this is an appearing object perceived by those with the eye of wisdom, I have not bothered to prove here what is already proven.[1085]

(3) How he served the teaching by disseminating his writings, which are a garland of excellent explanation
(a) How he wrote great texts on sutra-vehicle traditions

At the upper monastery of Radreng, Jé prayed for many days and nights before the statue of the noble lord Atiśa known as the "great image whose head inclines left,"[1086] and he had a vision for a month of the lineage gurus, from Śākyamuni down to the great preceptor Namkha Gyaltsen, and in particular of the noble lord Atiśa, Dromtönpa, Potowa, [204] and Sharawa. They gave him many instructions and follow-up teachings, and at the end, Potowa, Dromtönpa, and Sharawa dissolved into the lord. Atiśa placed his hand on Jé's head and said, "You must perform expansive service for the teaching, and I will also help you achieve enlightenment and act for the sake of sentient beings." Then he disappeared. At that time, Jé wrote the *Prayer to the Lineage of the Stages of the Path, Which Opens the Door to the Supreme Path.* Since special signs like that arose and the omens were well configured, he wrote the *Great Treatise on the Stages of the Path of the Three Persons.*[1087] Then, leaving out many of the refutations and proofs and scriptural quotations, he wrote the *Small Treatise on the Stages of the Path, Which Clearly Shows the Essential Meaning of the Great Treatise.*[1088] The stages of the path literature is distinctive because of five special qualities: (1) distinctive subject matter, that is, the three principal aspects of the path, the teaching given to Jé himself by Jetsün Mañjughoṣa, which is adorned by the noble lord Atiśa's special instructions regarding the three types of person, (2) distinctive mode of exposition, that is, cutting off detours from the path and presenting the nature of the path without error, the order of the path without confusion, and the enumerations of the path without excess or deficiency, (3) distinctive requesters, that is, the great preceptor Sülphuwa, the great translator Kyapchok Palsang, Drigung Chöjé, and others, (4) distinctive place, that is, Radreng, the conqueror Dromtönpa's hermitage, and (5) distinctive retinue, that is, great beings such as the two spiritual heirs, Gyaltsap and Khedrup Jé, and others.

Although there are many Kadam stages of the path texts, Jé's stages of the path texts are distinctive compared even to those. As Khedrup Jé states:

> The stages of the path teaching tradition of the great noble lord, the glorious Atiśa; the many levels of written instructions composed by the great geshés of the textual and special-instruction lineages; the many earlier and later examples of sayings from the great bodhisattvas Potowa, Chengawa, and Chekawa; and the *Great* and *Small Treatises on the Stages of the Teaching* by the great geshé Drolungpa, who followed the teachings of the great geshé Khampa Lungpa, and so forth: all these are stages of the path traditions that delight the conquerors, follow the great scriptures, are adorned with the oral teachings or speech of the lineage of the holy gurus, and are marvelous entryways [205] to pleasing the wise. Even so, these books of excellent discourse written by the omniscient Jé—the teachings of the *Great* and *Small Treatises on the Stages of the Path to Enlightenment*—are unsurpassable, uniquely marvelous texts, such as have never before been revealed in the Land of Snows by anyone. They incorporate every single scripture, as well as the commentaries on their meaning, and the enumeration and ordering of the full body of the path—which are the necessary conditions for an individual's

> awakening—as well as the general body of the path—the way to integrate successive meditation topics into your own experience by turning them over in your mind—and all the individual limbs of the path. Making a detailed investigation with unbiased intelligence as to how this is so, you should develop conviction of this. [1089]

At that time, many virtuously inclined primeval great gods, such as Nyenchen Thanglha,[1090] Shoklha Gyukpo, and others, provided the cooperative conditions: they came directly before Jé in nomad costumes and, after offering him yogurt, cheese, and so forth, petitioned him: "Include us in your prayer." Thus, Jé wrote:

> In all their lives, may every human and nonhuman who has provided
> Cooperative conditions for arranging this text on the good path
> And has cleared away contradictory conditions
> Never be separated from the pure path praised by the conquerors.[1091]

When Jetsün Mañjughoṣa said to Jé, "Isn't my teaching on the three principal aspects of the path sufficient?" Jé replied, "I made that the principal subject; I wrote more extensively by adorning it with the special instructions of Atiśa." There is that and other wonderful stories as well.

At Gungthang in Tsal, he wrote a commentary on the perfection of wisdom, the *Golden Rosary of Excellent Explanation,* and the scholars were captivated. Even Taktsang Lotsāwa, on seeing this excellent explanation, had his mountain of pride cast down, and attained the faith of a Dharma follower with regard to Jé Lama and praised him sincerely:

> I see the extent of the lotus garden of the perfection of wisdom sutras
> and the *Ornament of Higher Realization*
> Opened by your sun-like intellect, though you are still a youth,
> And the night lily of my conceit closes up;
> I pray to you, O treasury of knowledge deep and vast.[1092]

At Sera Chöding, when he was planning to write a commentary on Nāgārjuna's *Fundamental Treatise on the Middle Way,* he encountered difficulties [206] on some of the subtle points of reasoning. He prayed intently to Jetsün Mañjughoṣa and saw, filling space, a list of the twenty emptinesses of the perfection of wisdom sutras[1093] in letters the color of refined gold. He thereby resolved every single point of doubt and wrote the *Ocean of Reasoning Explaining the Fundamental Treatise on the Middle Way*.[1094] In that same place, he wrote the *Essence of Excellent Explanation: A Treatise Distinguishing Provisional and Definitive in the Scriptures*.[1095] The difficult points in that text were such that no previous Tibetan sage realized those points just as they are: not such deeply learned men as Ngok Lotsāwa, Sakya Pandita, Butön, and others; not those known as the eight great lions, such as Chapa Chökyi Sengé and the others who had struggled along the path of reasoning; not the omniscient Dölpopa and others not lacking in qualities of higher realization. Jé, on the other hand, through the kindness of the noble lord Mañjughoṣa, saw them clearly, and as stated in the *Essence of Excellent Explanation*:

> Even those deeply learned in the scriptures,
> Those who struggled along the path of reasoning,
> And the many who did not lack in accumulation of qualities of higher realization:
> Strive though they did, they did not gain such realization.
> Through the kindness of Lama Mañjughoṣa, though, I have seen well,
> And I will explain with thoughts of utmost love.[1096]

(b) How he wrote great texts on mantra-vehicle traditions

When Jé was staying in upper Gyasok, he had visions of the actual physical forms of many scholars, such as Ārya Nāgārjuna, Āryadeva, Buddhapālita, Nāgabodhi, Candrakīrti, Asaṅga and Vasubandhu, Dignāga, Dharmakīrti, Guṇaprabha and Śākyaprabhā, Devendrabuddhi, Prajñākaragupta, Kamalaśīla, Abhayākaragupta, and others; and many great adepts, such as King Indrabhūti, the great brahman Saraha, Master Lūipa, Ghaṇṭapa, Kṛṣṇācārya, and others. Thinking the visionary experiences were probably unreliable, Jé asked Jetsün Mañjughoṣa, who replied, "These visionary experiences did not come randomly, so you should make strong prayers. This is an omen that extensive benefits will accrue to you and others from relying on the texts of these beings." Later, when Jé was staying in the Lhashöl hermitage at Jampa Ling Monastery [207] in Odé Gungyal, the Jetsün told him, "You should write an explanation of Master Nāgabodhi's *Sequential Presentation*;[1097] great benefit will accrue."[1098] Thus exhorted, Jé immediately wrote the *Exposition of the Presentation of Stages*. Jé stated:

> I understood thoroughly and well the rough meaning of, in general, the five stages and, in particular, how to achieve the illusory body of the third stage, as taught in the basic and explanatory tantras of glorious Guhyasamāja, and the uncommon meaning taught in the texts of the quintet of the ārya father Nāgārjuna and his spiritual sons. After that, more than ten years passed when I could not speak of it; after that, I spoke of it just a little.[1099]

At that place, at the urging of Lotsāwa Kyapchok Pal Sangpo, and at the particular urging of the glorious Phakmo Drupa regent, Chenga Sönam Sangpo, Jé also wrote the *Great Treatise on the Stages of the Path of Vajradhara,*[1100] a great treatise that elucidates the entirety of the paths of the four classes of tantra. In the words of Jé himself, "Apart from being told at Gyasok Phu that great benefit would be accomplished through relying on the texts of those earlier great adepts and Abhayākaragupta, I did not have any other particular reasons for writing. When I wrote the text, the time passed very quickly, and I did not pray or perform other practices for a long time."[1101]

While living in strict isolation at Samten Ling in Ölkha, Jé prayed intently to the lama who was inseparable from the meditational deity many times and arrived at the decision to write the *Lamp Illuminating the Five Stages,*[1102] on the completion stage of glorious Guhyasamāja. While setting down notes for the book, he had a wonderful dream in which someone said, "moon above tiger." You can learn the meaning of those words in detail from Khedrup Jé's *Secret Biography,* but essentially it indicates that the special instructions on the Ārya system of Guhyasamāja and on Cakrasaṃvara will be elucidated by Jé himself.[1103] In the *Lamp Illuminating the Five Stages,* Jé says, "Because I prayed for a long time, I obtained the special sign giving me permission to write the text."[1104] Also, in the *Direct Explanation of the Five Stages,* he says, "I obtained the firm sign I desired."[1105] The meaning of both is the same. Having realized this meaning in that very place, Jé wrote that great treasure of excellent explanation of Guhyasamāja called the *Lamp Illuminating the Five Stages,* [208] as well as the *Direct Explanation of the Five Stages* and expositions of the two explanatory tantras, the *Questions of the Four Goddesses* and the *Compendium of Vajra Gnosis.*

At the great monastic seat of Ganden, he made detailed corrections to the translation of Candrakīrti's Guhyasamāja commentary, *Bright Lamp,* and wrote the *Precious Sprout that Severs Extremes,* which, through annotations that explain in detail the meanings of the words of the *Bright Lamp,* covers both the individual chapters and the general points of difficulty; he also wrote the *Condensed Meaning of the Bright Lamp,* which examined the individual topics of the *Bright Lamp.* He also wrote many textbooks on the Cakrasaṃvara cycle, such as the *Rite Based on Lūipa's Higher Realization;* the commentary on that, *Wish-Fulfilling;* the commentary on the root tantra, *Clarifying the Whole Hidden Meaning;* the extensive and condensed discussions of the great completion stage;[1106] and, also on the completion stage, the *Eye-Opener for Viewing the Hidden Meaning;* and so forth.

As just described, the writings of the great Jé are not just what he felt like writing; rather, he saw definite signs that his writing would be of benefit to the teaching and to beings, as when he had a vision of the great adepts in bodily form, and other experiences. Urged to write this or that by Jetsün Mañjughoṣa, he did just that. Since the essential meaning, ordering, and other elements, even of such shorter texts as the *Crown of Brahmā: Praise of Maitreya,*[1107] *Precious Illuminating Lamp,*[1108] the *Sukhāvatī Prayer,*[1109] and other works, were formulated according to Mañjughoṣa's word, it goes without saying in regard to the great treatises.

In these great texts, by basing himself on the works of Ārya Nāgārjuna and his spiritual sons, which reveal the key points of the two stages hidden in the root tantras of the highest yoga tantras, Jé clarified the marvelous teaching that is revealed when the basic and explanatory tantras are properly connected. This had been beyond the ken of any previous scholar-adept. In the *Annotations Clarifying the Meaning of the Five Stages,* he states:

> In the great nectar ocean of glorious Guhyasamāja,
> Through Nāgārjuna's special instruction, which clarifies the meaning hidden there,
> I have churned again and again with the supreme churning rod of the explanatory tantra,
> Which is tied by the excellent churning rope of intelligence that, in relation to the king of tantras,
> Distinguishes between practice that arises as instruction and the subtle path of reasoning;
> I have found the vase, never before seen in this land,
> Filled with the nectar of the meaning of the tantra's words,

> Clarifying the essential meanings of the words [209] from
> every angle.[1110]

Also, in the *Cluster of Yogic Achievements*, a text on the completion stage of Cakrasaṃvara, he states:

> Regarding the completion stage of the great adepts,
> The points most difficult to realize
> Through the basic and explanatory tantric texts
> Were not till now well elucidated in this land.
> But I, with great diligence
> And through long striving, have understood them.
> Listen now, as I explain them here.[1111]

Thus, Khedrup Jé stated:

> Seeing just as they are the profound key points
> Of the two stages of the ultimate path, which had not till now
> Been experienced by others in this land, you made attainment
> Of that goal your essential practice; to you I pray.[1112]

What he said was exactly right and not just poetic hyperbole.

Suppose someone were to ask, "Well, then, what are the profound points of the two stages that were never previously revealed?" Well, with respect to the generation stage, many teachings on the full meaning of the sādhanas elucidated by the great adepts, on such topics as the meditative objects intended for the tantras—from meditation with gnosis to the dissolution of the mandala[1113]—had not been revealed by any previous Tibetan lama. With respect to the completion stage in particular, Jé provided many singular explanations of the individual stages of the path, beginning from the isolated body and going up to how one arises in divine form in the union of no more learning.[1114] Above all, he clarified precisely the intent of the ārya father Nāgārjuna and his spiritual sons as to the marvelous way you achieve the illusory body based on the wind-mind that has traversed the four empties. If such things are not clear even in the writings of Marpa, Gö Khukpa, the early Sakyapas, the omniscient Butön, and others, what need be said about other lesser sages?

3) Faith in Tsongkhapa

When the intelligent are long acquainted with the writings of Jé and his spiritual sons and see their exceptional qualities, they arouse the faith that follows from seeing things as they truly are.[1115] As stated in the biography of Jamyang Chöjé:[1116]

> At the Potala, Chöjé said: "It says in the *Wishing Tree of Higher Realization,* by the great Jetsün Drakpa Gyaltsen:
>
> When I remember the kindness of the assembled gurus
> Who teach these things, I shed tears of faith.
> Always, I bow to the stainless lotus feet
> Of those most supreme gurus.[1117]
>
> "We ourselves [210] cannot measure the minds of the great Jetsün and Jé Rinpoché. The Dharma texts they wrote, the *Wishing Tree of Higher Realization* and the *Lamp Illuminating the Five Stages,* are so vastly and immeasurably distinguished that tears flow when we recall the kindness of the assembly of gurus who have taught these things. The *Lamp Illuminating the Five Stages* should evoke tears because it has the rare quality of being well explained. It is the one pure door for entering the teaching, yet no one enters—and my own ability only goes so far."
>
> He said this, his voice shaking, weeping, and all the officials and servants wept, too.

Even Taktsang Lotsāwa praised him, saying:

> To you who are the great treasure of unprecedented excellent explanation
> Regarding all of sutra and mantra, especially the Vajrayana,
> All the tantra classes, especially highest yoga,
> And everything within the two stages, especially the illusory body; to you I bow.[1118]

This, it seems, reflects the judgment of one with impartial intelligence. Through long, detailed acquaintance with the writings of Jé, one will understand them, but how can someone like me express them exactly? Those who claim to uphold the Geluk teaching should at the very least be able just to identify Jé's uniquely excellent explanations. Nowadays, however, it seems that most of those who are in the position of being great upholders of the teaching are satisfied exclusively with the color of their hats.

4) Final years

In the year of the female earth ox (1409), Jé commemorated in Lhasa the miraculous deeds of the Buddha.[1119] After that, as prophesied by the conqueror,[1120] he founded Ganden Nampar Gyalwa Ling on the great Drok Mountain, and he turned the Dharma wheel there for a long time.[1121]

At the age of sixty-three, in the year of the female earth pig (1419), he manifested final nirvana at Ganden Nampar Gyalwa Ling. According to authoritative scripture, he took birth before Maitreya in Tuṣita heaven and was called Mañjuśrīgarbha, the Conqueror's son; and, in the future, he will attain manifest, perfect buddhahood and will be called Tathāgatha Siṅghasvara.[1122]

5) Why Tsongkhapa is extraordinary

These expressions of the qualities of greatness of Jé Lama have been compiled from just some of the most important material I have seen in written biographies and heard through authoritative statements. [211] At this degenerate time, I wrote this mainly to show how Jé, like the sun, illumined the pure teaching in the land of Tibet. There are some significant biographical details that did not emerge here, but faith may be developed through learning them from other sources.

In terms of detailed expressions, Vajrapāṇi said to the great adept from Lhodrak, Namkha Gyaltsen, "Even I, Vajrapāṇi, cannot comprehend the extent of the good qualities of Matibhadra."[1123] If even the holder of the treasury of the secret teachings of all the conquerors, Vajrapāṇi, says he cannot fathom the extent of Jé's qualities, than what is there to say of others? As to the main biography of Jé, Tokden Jampal Gyatso asked Jetsün Mañjughoṣa for the lifestory of Jé Rinpoché. Mañjughoṣa replied, "The lifestory of Jé cannot be encompassed by thought. The main point of his lifestory is how he comprehended all dharmas in their profundity through clearly discerning the nature of dharmas, and how he comprehended the triad of basis, path, and result through reasoning based on the way things are; this is it."[1124] And, as Mañjughoṣa also said, "He established authoritatively how the approaches of the mantra and definition vehicles are effective methods for one individual's awakening; this is the principal meaning of the extraordinary lifestory of this great being."[1125]

In short, as my own omniscient lama wrote in his *Great Treatise on the Establishment of Philosophical Systems:*

> Although the common and the uncommon lifestories of the great lord Jé cannot be encompassed by thought, still, in all of them, the main point is how he himself, without even the subtlest bit of confusion, and without mixing them up, ascertained by means of stainless scripture and reasoning the intended meanings of the countless scriptures of sutra and mantra of the conquerors, exactly as they had been opened by the great charioteers; and how, when he gave teachings to others, his kindness in completely explaining the precious teaching of the Muni made the teaching pervade the whole world—it's just that. This should be known by the wise.
>
> Thus, on the sutra side from the fine points of the practice of the vinaya on up to the great philosophical systems, and on the mantra side from the fine points of mandala rites and praxis [212] on up to the great tantric commentaries, any and all of these Jetsün Tsongkhapa traced back to the intention of the great scholars and adepts, who opened the way for each system, never covering his teachings with the flaws of "easy Dharma" or personal invention. What's more, his teachings can be traced back to the word of the Conqueror. Also, one is granted certainty about every subtle point that is analyzed through scripture and reasoning; in that way, and in the way that all teachings are presented as noncontradictory and mutually supportive, the teachings are arranged as necessary conditions for the awakening of one individual. No previous scholar-adept in the Land of Snows had such a lifestory, in which both parts of the teaching, the explanatory and the practical, were upheld and propagated. Not only that, but even someone like Ārya Nāgārjuna of the Holy Land of India is in no way superior to Jé; this is proven by the fact that Jé's mode of reasoning is also stainless.

> Therefore, what chance is there that Jé's lifestory is like the lifestories that rely on the mere prophecy of others who say, "This being was prophesied by so and so and such and such"? Although one learns from them that he obtained many visions of meditational deities, and many concentrations and supernormal powers, and so forth, the principal aspect of his lifestory is what was just explained.
>
> Jé Lama himself said:
>
> > In the beginning, I frequently sought extensive study.
> > In the middle, all the textual systems arose as instruction.
> > At the end, I practiced all through the day and night.
> > All of that I have dedicated to extending the teaching.[1126]
>
> At the very start, Jé Rinpoché's approach was to seek far and wide to study in detail the words of the Conqueror and the countless textual systems of the great charioteers who had commented on the meaning of those words, and not just in a vague or biased manner. And based on that, through appropriately condensing countless sutras and treatises, from the *Stanzas on Vinaya* up to the glorious *Guhyasamāja,* into the main and ancillary aspects of a path that awakens one individual, all textual systems arose for Jé as instruction. And accordingly, based on his practice of spontaneously engaging all the time with the perfectly complete body of the path that arose for him, he ascertained the key points of the path through experiences whose doorway was stainless reasoning. So, the result of the perfect reasoning by which he nailed down an unmistaken understanding was, [213] in general, that his actions enlisted all teachings without contradiction, and in particular, there were Jé's own texts on sutra and mantra. No matter how much you examine Jé's words, you will not find in them even an iota to blame, whether for irrelevance, repetition, contradiction, or going outside the authoritative scriptures of the Muni, for they are established through direct perception.[1127]

Whatever I have stated accorded with this; this teaching is a particularly distinctive synopsis of Jé's lifestory.

For these reasons, that sun of speech, Khedrup Jé, said:

To you who have the power of limitless prayer and, with skillful methods,
Effortlessly and spontaneously leads the assembly of countless students
Onto the path that delights the conquerors,
To you, the refuge of all the worlds, I pray.

At a time when the clergy only generalized about explanation, practice,
And reasoning, and the "teaching of the Muni" was only nominal,
You shone the sun on every holy Dharma of the Conqueror—
The scriptures and realizations of the three trainings—so to you I pray.[1128]

I scatter with faithful hands the flowers of praises of the abiding meaning.

11. The Geluk Tradition 2: Tsongkhapa's Successors

[*II. The History of Philosophical Systems in Tibet, the Land of Snows*
B. The histories of the different schools
8. The history of the Geluk philosophical system]

b. How the stainless tradition of Jé Lama was expanded by subsequent upholders of the teaching

THE DISCUSSION of how Jé Lama's stainless tradition was expanded by subsequent upholders of the teaching is threefold: 1) How his system was expanded by Jé's direct disciples, 2) How subsequent disciples served that system, and 3) A general synopsis of the biographies of those upholders of the teaching.

1) How his system was expanded by Jé's direct disciples

This is twofold: a) An enumeration of direct disciples and b) How they extended the teaching. [214]

a) An enumeration of direct disciples

The disciples of the omniscient Jé Tsongkhapa also abided in the morality of the three vows and seriously practiced the yogas of the three types of persons and the two stages of highest yoga tantra. The sages who continuously sounded the great drum of the Tripiṭaka and the four classes of tantra were like a constellation of stars in the expanse of space, or a grove of trees rooted in the earth, or springtime trees adorned with flowers. I will discuss some of the most important of those inconceivably great disciples who came after Jé.

The four lamas from whom Jé received his Dharma connection[1129] were:

Umapa Tsöndrü Sengé, the great preceptor Namkha Gyaltsen, Jetsün Rendawa, and the great preceptor from Dragor, Chökyap Sangpo.

The four spiritual sons from before Jé went to live a renounced life were: the guide from Tsakho, Ngawang Drakpa;[1130] Drakpa Lodrö from upper Amdo; Dongtön Jñānaśrī; and Geshé Shatön.

The eightfold retinue of later times was: the four from Ü, that is, Jampal Chösang, who was known as Lama Jamkarwa; the venerable Sangkyongwa; the venerable Rinchen Gyaltsen; and the venerable Jangsengwa; and the four from lower Amdo, in other words, Tokden Jampal Gyatso; Geshé Sherap Drak; Geshé Jampal Tashi; and Geshé Palkyongwa; these are the eight. Those eight had qualities of scriptural and experiential realization beyond imagining and all were nurtured by the meditational deities.[1131]

The two known as "the two principal spiritual sons" were the omniscient Gyaltsap Darma Rinchen and the great bodhisattva, Drigung vinaya master Drakpa Gyaltsen.[1132]

The especially holy threefold retinue prophesied by Vajrapāṇi was said to be the two principal spiritual sons and Lama Jamkarwa.

On account of his very great kindness with respect to Jé's teaching, the sole inner heart son was the omniscient Khedrup.

The four great sons whose deeds were vast as space were: Jamyang Chöjé Tashi [215] Palden, the unequaled Dharma lord Gungru Gyaltsen Sangpo, Jetsün Sherap Sengé, and the omniscient Gendün Drupa.[1133]

The ten lamps of the teaching from Ü and Tsang were: the Sangphu Dharma lord Könchok Tsültrim, Nyalgö Rinchen Samdrup, Khyenrap Wangchuk Drakpa Sangpo, Gyalwang Khaché of Sangphu, Nyalchen Sherap Gyaltsen, Hortön Namkha Pal, the Dharma lord Lodrö Chökyong, Baso Chökyi Gyaltsen, the Dharma lord Palden Sengé, and Narthangpa Rapchok.

The six bodhisattvas who spontaneously worked for the sake of others were: the Radreng bodhisattva Shākya Sönam, the bodhisattva Künga Sangpo, the Demo Thangpa bodhisattva Lodrö Gyaltsen, the bodhisattva Tsültrim Palsang, the bodhisattva Shönu Gyalchok, and the bodhisattva Gyaltsen Draksang.

The two imperial preceptors who were honored by rulers were the Jamchen Dharma lord Shākya Yeshé[1134] and Jangdarma. The two nephews who studied the teachings extensively were Machik Önpo Namkha Pal and the guide from Yargyap, Sönam Nampar Gyalwa.

The two, the greater and lesser, who upheld the good qualities of the training were Tashi Gyatso of Shalu and the Shalu Dharma lord Lekpa Gyaltsen.

The two sages with extraordinary intelligence were Musepa Lodrö Rinchen Sengé and Shangshungpa Chöwang Drakpa.

The six great flags who protected the teaching in every direction were: Tö Shersang, Mé Shersang, Gugé Ngawang Drakpa, Lhopa Gyaltsen Sengé, Lama Palden Sherap, and Lama Yönten Palwa.

The two translators who spoke two languages were Gö Lotsāwa Shönu Pal—or Yisang Tsewa—and Taklung Lotsāwa.[1135]

The six Dharma lord rulers were: the precious Palden Sangpo, the precious Sönam Sangpo, [216] the precious Jangchup Dorjé, the precious Sönam Gyaltsen or Nyernyipa, the Drigung trulku Döndrup Gyalpo, and the Taklung trulku Tashi Pal Ö.

The eight upholders of the teaching who knew many scriptures were: Dromtön Sherjung Lodrö, Gyalwa Rinchen Samdrup, Drakpa Rinchen of Jamling, Sönam Rinchen of Ngari, Jamyang Rinchen Gyaltsen, Gugé Sangyé Gyaltsen, Jamyang Rinchen Drakpa, and Gyalsé Dejungwa.

The four sages of Amdo and Rong were Do Öser, Do Leksang, Do Sönam Sherap, and Rongpo Chenak.

The two descendants of the one who reached the ḍākinī realm were the Treshing trulku Jangchup Palwa and Rinchen Palwa.

The two amazing beings were Kyemchok Mönlam Thayé and Rimi Bapa Sönam Rinchen.

The eight presences[1136] were: Chenga Künga Lodrö, Chenga Shönu Ö, Chenga Lodrö Gyaltsen, Chenga Palsangwa, Chenga Namkha Gyaltsen, Chenga Sönam Lhündrup, Chenga Rinchen Gyaltsen, and Chenga Rinchen Palwa.

The four great lamas who beautified the top of the throne were: the Gungthang Dharma lord Dzepa Pal, Nyenpo Shākya Gyaltsen, Takphu Gushri Palden Döndrup, and Teurapa Chöjé Pal.

The four abbots who ruled the assembly were: the great Kyormo Lung abbot Chögyal Palsang, the great Phakmo Dru abbot Gyalsangwa, the great abbot Künga Dorjé, and the Chenyé abbot Jangchup Palwa.

The five greats of Tramo Monastery were: the great Drakpa Sangpo, the great Dakpo Öser Sengé, the great Lodrö Phel, the great Künga Gyaltsen, and the great Tashi Gyaltsen. [217]

The two Dharma directors of initiation were the Densa Thil Dharma director, Jamyang Khaché Punyé Śrī; and the Drigung Dharma director, Tashi Rinchen.

The four masters who raised the victory banner of teaching and study were: Master Tsöndrü Drakpa, Master Lekdenpa, Master Taklep Jangchup Gyaltsen, and Master Jangchup Palwa.

The four experts in the ten difficult texts who propounded reasoning were: Kachupa Darma Sangpo, Baser Kachupa, Tsotsa Kachupa Yönten Gyaltsen, and Lhula Kachupa Lekpa Pal.

The ten experts in the four difficult subjects who apprehended both words and meaning were: Tilchung Kashipa Dönyö, Drakgön Kashipa Rinchen Pal, Gyalwa Kashipa Rinchen Chögyal, Gyeré Kashipa Sangyé Wangchuk, Takphu Kashipa Sangyé Sangpo, Yakdé Kashipa Sönam Sangpo, Drö Kashipa, Tsurphu Kashipa, Kashipa Chöseng, and Kashipa Drakpa Gyaltsen.

The four nobles[1137] who upheld discipline were Joden Dawa Lodrö, Joden Sönam Lhündrup, Joden Lekrinpa, and Kongpo Joden.

The six venerables whose morality was pure were: the venerable Chösangpa, the venerable Gyaldingpa Döndrup Pal, the venerable Gyamawa Gendün Gyalpo, the venerable Öser Tashi, the venerable Shönu Sangyé, and the venerable Künga Bum.

The five realizers[1138] who had renounced this life were: Kuchor Tokden Sangyé Palsang, Tokden Namkha Shoré, the Götruk Dharma lord Drakpa Jungné, Tokden Ralshikpa, and Bulewa Namkha Gyaltsen.

In addition, there were Lhasik Drakpa Gyatso, Gyatön Losang Drakpa, Drung Shönu [218] Palwa, Khenpo Samgyalwa, Lama Serthupa, the Yarding trulku Shilo Pönpo, Drung Namkhawa, Lama Gönpo Jangchup, Lama Sörin, Drung Chöphakpa, Lama Shaka Rinpa, Lama Dawa Sangpo, Lama Chö Gyaltsen, and Gyara Sangyé Yeshé.

Of those, except for the four masters of teaching and study, I wrote the names according to Panchen Sönam Drakpa's *Beautiful Ornament of Thought*.[1139] Also, not appearing in that text are: Dülzin Lodrö Bepa, Phakö Yönten Gyatso, the great Narthang preceptor Sönam Chokdrup, the great Sülphu preceptor Könchok Palsang, Gyalwa Drakpa Tashi, Lama Künsang Rinchen, Lama Söwang, Jamyang Dorin, the Gyama trulku Künga Lodrö, the Dharma lord Gyaltsen Draksang, Jatang Rinchen Sangpo, and Tsangpa Losangpa. Still, after examining various biographies and Dharma histories in detail, I felt that those not included should be inserted here. If one takes into account the mere possession of a Dharma connection, then it is also appropriate that Rongtön Shākya Gyaltsen and Ngorpa Chöjé Künga Sangpo be counted. In Sangsing Neringpa, or Chimé Rapgyé's, biography of Jé, the *Golden Shrine,* the way of listing direct disciples is unlike that above; I have not written of it for fear of including too much.

In brief, there does not seem to have been a Dharma master from the trio of Sangphu, Dewachen, and Gungthang monasteries; the trio of Gawa Dong, Kyormo Lung, and Sül Chölung; the trio of Loro, Jayül, and Rinchen Gang; the trio of Gyal, Langthang, and Drö; the trio of Radreng, Cheka, and Kyilbu; the trio of Drigung, Taklung, and Tsalpa; the trio of Ei Teura, Nyal Drakor, and Takten Phüntsok Ling; nor a Dharma master from such Yorside monasteries as Thangpoché and others who did not bow down before Jé Rinpoché.

All those mentioned above were included by virtue of their greatness in scripture and realization, their family lineage, or their high status. There also were those who extensively received the Dharma connection of an inferior or middling being and those who attained a mere Dharma connection;[1140] there were so many of these each year that they cannot be enumerated.

If one makes a list based on benefactors, there were Neudong Gongma Chenpo, Shika Neuzongpa, Shika Drakarwa, Gyama Tripön, Yarlung Jowo, Ölga Dzongpön, Dzingchi Drakpa [219] Rinpoché, Gompa Chögyal, Tölung Wön Yönten Gyatso, Rinpungpa Namkha Gyaltsen, and others. All the nobles of Ü and Tsang raised Jé's feet to their heads. They made offerings of wealth and homage. And even the great emperor Yunglo, who wielded worldly sovereignty, invited Jé to his kingdom, offering many of his own possessions and expressing praise for him with golden scriptures.[1141]

Although in this Land of Snows many have opened the way for their own philosophical systems and made them self-sufficient, the coming to the Land of Snows of Jetsün Tsongkhapa the great is comparable to how our original teacher, the fully enlightened Buddha, came into this world sphere. It is explained in the *Scholars' Banquet Dharma History* that when Jé was very small, the Fourth Karmapa, Rölpai Dorjé, gave him the layman's vows and told him, "If you go to Ü and Tsang, you will perform deeds for the Muni's teaching that equal those of the Muni himself."[1142] And when Jé went to Tsāri,[1143] at the bottom of Mola Pass, Jetsün Maitreya told Jé himself, "Noble son, know that your coming will be like the coming of the Buddha into the world"; and so it came to pass.[1144]

And, as the great and glorious Yisang Tsewa stated, "At present, it is as if this great land is being shielded by the white umbrella of Jetsün Tsongkhapa."[1145] This expression of praise is exactly right.

b) How his disciple sons expanded the teaching

By virtue of achieving the power of prayers that uphold the holy Dharma, all Jé's direct disciples had their own respective qualities of greatness and ways of serving the teaching, which are beyond imagining, so how can one like me express all of that? This will mainly be an explanation of how just a few of the disciples expanded Jé's tradition. Tokden Jampal Gyatso, Gyaltsap Jé, Dülzinpa, [220] Khedrup Jé, Jamyang Chöjé, Jamchen Chöjé, Jé Sherap Sengé, and the great scholar Gendün Drup are the ones who, through both teaching and practice, made Jé's tradition of sutra and mantra widespread in Ü and Tsang. The duo of Sherap Sengé and Gungru Gyaltsen Sangpo were the main disseminators of the teaching in the outlying areas.

(1) Abbots of Ganden

(a) Gyaltsap Jé and Khedrup Jé

Of those, the duo of the omniscient Gyaltsap and the lion of speech Khedrup sat successively on the Dharma throne of Jé Lama at Ganden and firmly established the Geden teaching. Just before Jé attained nirvana, he gave Gyaltsap Rinpoché (1364–1432)[1146] his robe and scholar's hat, making it understood that this meant that Gyaltsap Jé was to preside over the monastic seat. Accordingly, all the disciple sons, such as Dülzinpa, the venerable Rinchen Gyaltsen, and others, prayed to Gyaltsap Jé with a single voice and consecrated him on the fearless lion's throne. Khedrup Jé expressed his praise of Gyaltsap Jé in the *Glorious Good Qualities,* and the great scholar Gendün Drup praised him poetically in the *Marvelous Wheel of Utter Goodness.*

Like the great lord Jé Tsongkhapa, Gyaltsap Jé purely pursued the teaching and study of the vinaya, the practice of the three bases, and so forth. Taking those as a basis, and with his own inner experience and stainless scripture and reasoning, for thirteen years he gave explanations of, on the sutra side, the higher and lower abhidharmas, valid cognition, the perfection of wisdom, Madhyamaka, and so forth; and, on the mantra side, secret mantra in general and, in particular, the explanations of the tantras of Guhyasamāja, Cakrasaṃvara, Kālacakra, Hevajra, and Vajrabhairava, the guidelines on the two stages, and so forth. In short, he transmitted the countless excellent explanations of Jé Lama, which were not within the purview of earlier Tibetans. Most of Jé's direct disciples and countless other fortunate and intelligent beings were utterly captivated, and they respected and honored Gyaltsap Jé without distinguishing him from Jé Rinpoché. Thus the son followed his spiritual father and firmly established Jé's tradition of teaching and practice.

After Gyaltsap Jé, the omniscient Khedrup (1385–1438)[1147] presided over the monastic seat and, like him, maintained the tradition without degeneration.

In particular, he taught even the most subtle of Jé's teachings without mixing [221] them with other teachings. Not only did he destroy by reason countless thinkers who wrote critiques of the works of Jé, but he refuted the Dharma lord Gungruwa and others who, through listening to statements made by the great lord himself but failing to analyze the view fully, explained Jé's version of emptiness as an affirming negation. Moreover, he also refuted all those whose way of explaining how to maintain certainty about the view did not go along with Jé's claims. Therefore, because Khedrup Jé freed Jé Lama's unique tradition of sutra and mantra from stains, his kindness toward this teaching is matchless and unrivaled.

He thought that the essence of the Buddha's teaching was found only in the teaching of Jé Lama and that the main thing for him to do was to establish it firmly in Ü. It seems that because he assumed that responsibility, he did not even accept invitations from Ngari and Kham urgently requesting he visit between Dharma sessions. There was, for instance, the letter sent to Geshé Shersang:

> The great burden of the complete teaching,
> Which is the matchless teaching tradition of the holy father Jé,
> Is so heavy it weighs on my heart,
> Yet I do not feel at all exhausted.
>
> Previously, even when it came
> To establishing the lamp of stainless teaching
> In dark hinterlands far from the sun
> Of the Muni's teaching, I did not become discouraged.
>
> Nevertheless, the Land of Snows is the base of the teaching,
> The place where many superior beings established it,
> The source of all present-day holy Dharma,
> Renowned as the pure land of Ü and Tsang.
>
> If you examine well, however, the teaching is only a facade;
> It, too, is like a lamp whose oil has been depleted.
> All the cherished treasures of the Muni are being tossed away like grass,
> And debased minds and distorted textual systems are increasing by the day.

The messenger demons[1148] of behaving however one likes,
Those appearing as spiritual teachers honored by the multitude,
And the many massed troops who strive mightily to throw down
The victory banner of the teaching, those three cover every corner
of this land.

It has come to that, and those with the eye of intelligence,
Those undiscouraged in distinguishing Dharma from non-Dharma,
Those great spiritual teachers who bear the burden of the teaching
are very [222] rare,
And so their followers are also extremely rare.

Finding this situation almost unbearable,
I zealously take on responsibility for the teaching.
I've been strongly moved by intelligence to uphold right here
The perfect tradition of holy father Jé.

When the wish-granting tree of the teaching is being cut right here
At its root with the ax of non-Dharma and faulty explanation,
I see that for a branch to grow elsewhere just once
And just a little would have little value.

Right now, right here, the massed army of non-Dharma is the
enemy,
And I am holding the weapon of the well-explained teaching.
Therefore, if I abandon the struggle right here,
Who, pray tell, will maintain the Muni's cherished treasures?

Therefore, though your lofty intent is virtuous,
I cannot consent to your proposal,
However much you may wish it.[1149]

Such was the reply that Khedrup wrote.

He feared that the continuum of Jé Lama's unique explanatory tradition would be cut, so although he could be punished by the ḍākas and ḍākinīs for widely propagating teachings on the difficult points in secret mantra, which are like the heart blood of the ḍākinīs, he nevertheless, without regard for body or life, and deeply concerned solely for the teaching, elucidated these by way of teaching and writing. In *Biography of Khedrup Jé*, Jamyang Chöjé says:

> If you explain mantra, it seems, you incur the suffering of having your heart blood taken by the ḍākinīs: when Khön Könchok Gyalpo taught the Hevajra to seventeen people, Drokmi Shākya Yeshé sent a man to ask, "Is your life indestructible?" thereby rebuking him. Renouncing this life, Khedrup Rinpoché taught the exposition of mantra.[1150]

This roaring lion lived on the snow mountain of the tradition of father Jé. When he roared his roar of scripture and reasoning on the secret heights, all the foxes who propounded misconceptions were terrified and intimidated, while the herd of deer who upheld the teaching thrived under his protection. Khedrup Jé governed the monastic seat for eight years.

More may be learned about both Gyaltsap Jé and the omniscient Khedrup from other detailed biographies. [223]

(b) Other Ganden abbots

After Khedrup Jé, the mighty wonder worker from Shalu, Lekpa Gyaltsen, occupied the golden throne, and then Jé Lodrö Chökyong. The latter was an expert in the four classes of tantra in general and the Kālacakra in particular, so he wrote a supplement to Khedrup Jé's *Great Commentary on the Kālacakra*. Next was Khedrup Jé's younger brother Baso Chökyi Gyaltsen. Through studying with Tokden Jampal Gyatso, he became an expert in the teachings of Jé's ear-whispered lineage. He wrote *Guidelines on the View*, a text on the generation and completion stages of Kālacakra,[1151] and other texts. Next was Jé Lodrö Tenpa. He founded Dakpo monastic college and thereby began to make Jé's tradition of teaching and practice widespread in that area. He wrote many excellent expositions, including the *Great Commentary on the Ornament of Mahayana Sutras*, the *Commentary on the Other Four Dharmas of Maitreya*, the *Arrangement of the Path According to the Thorough Exposition of Valid Cognition*, and other texts. Next to sit on the golden throne was Jé Mönlam Palwa. Those up through him are known as the sevenfold Mañjughoṣa lineage from Tsang. Although Mönlam Palwa never met Jé Tsongkhapa in person, he did meet him directly in a dream and received the Dharma from him, so he is included in the enumeration of direct disciples. He was believed to be the rebirth of Atiśa's disciple Khutön Tsöndrü Yungdrung. He wrote the *Great Commentary on the Thorough Exposition of Valid Cognition,* whose use has been widespread up to the present day.

There was a line of succession of abbots at the monastic seat at Jangtsé, such as Gyaltsap Rinpoché's follower, Hortön Namkha Palwa, and at the monastic seat at Shartsé, such as Sharpa Rinchen Gyaltsen, Wön Dadrak, and others.

Jangtsé monastic college and Nyakrong monastic college: When Khedrup Rinpoché occupied the Ganden throne, he selected four masters from the study centers and gave them courses of study; afterward, the study centers were combined into two. In Jangtsé, there were Nyenpo Chökyi Wangchuk, Nyaltön Paljor Lhündrup, and others, and in Nyakrong, there were the all-encompassing Dharma lord Tsema Wangyal, the Dharma lord Gyalwangpa, and others. They kept the lineage of lamas unbroken and developed the tradition of Jé Lama without any degeneration.

(2) Drepung abbots

The great lord Jé said to Jamyang Chöjé Tashi Palden (1379–1440), "You should found a fine monastery; from the mother monastery, joy will become greatly widespread among the offspring." And, as Jé himself gave Jamyang Chöjé the Dharma conch that had been taken as a treasure from Gokpa Mountain,[1152] Neupön [224] Rinsang became the benefactor, and [in 1416] the great monastery of Drepung was founded. Jé Rinpoché told Jamyang Chöjé, "Explain a hundred volumes from memory," so the latter memorized all the words and meanings of the 108 volumes of mantra and definition-vehicle texts[1153] and explained them. He gave courses of study continuously on the stainless explanatory system of the tradition of Jé Lama regarding Madhyamaka, valid cognition, the perfection of wisdom, and so forth, so that the disciples produced by the teachings, such as Musepa Lodrö Rinchen, were as numerous as constellations in the sky. Each of seven selected Dharma-expounding masters individually gave courses of study, and because of that there came to be seven monastic colleges: Gomang, Losal Ling, Deyangpa, Shakor, Thösam Ling or Gyalwa, Dülwa, and the tantric college. Later, they merged into four: Gomang, Losal Ling, Deyangpa, and the tantric college.

After Jamyang Chöjé came Palden Sengé. The great adept Śavaripa appeared before him in a vision and gave him direct instruction, and so forth, on the glorious protector, Mahākāla. Next came Rinchen Jangchup, Jé Ön Losang Nyima, Rongtön Losang Drakpa, Nyenpo Shākya Gyaltsen, Jé Mönlam Palwa, and Jamyang Lekpa Chöjor. The latter had a vision of Mañjughoṣa, who said to him, "What joy when there is someone of your intelligence!" so the name he was given was Jamyang [= Mañjughoṣa] Gawai Lodrö, "Whose Intelligence Inspires Joy." He was an unrivaled scholar-adept beyond compare. He gave explanations of the great texts for many years and had many disciples, including the omniscient Second Dalai Lama, Gendün Gyatso, and others. Jamyang wrote many excellent expositions, such as his textual commentaries on the *Ornament of Mahayana Sutras, Ornament of Higher Realization, Fundamental Treatise on the Middle Way, Entering the Middle Way,* the epistemological tradition,[1154] and so forth. He wrote the *Meteor Wheel* in response to Gorampa and annihilated his debased claims.

After Jamyang Gawai Lodrö, Yönten Gyatso came to the abbot's throne, and after him the omniscient Gendün Gyatso and Panchen Sönam Drakpa (1478–1554).[1155] The latter performed many great deeds: he occupied the golden throne of Ganden and was the preceptor of the Third Dalai Lama, Sönam Gyatso. Also, his writings on Dharma include textbooks on vinaya, abhidharma, Madhyamaka, the perfection of wisdom, and the *Thorough Exposition of Valid Cognition;* nowadays, these are the main course texts for study at Losal Ling. Moreover, he wrote many expositions of mantra, for instance on the generation and completion stages of Guhyasamāja; the Dharma history called the *Beautiful Ornament of Thought;* and *An Almanac* [225] *of the Teaching.*

After that came the Third Dalai Lama, Sönam Gyatso; the Fourth Dalai Lama, Yönten Gyatso; the omniscient First Panchen, Losang Chökyi Gyaltsen;[1156] and the mighty conqueror, the Great Fifth Dalai Lama; thenceforth, each successive Dalai Lama occupied the abbot's throne of Drepung.

Were I to write on the line of lamas of each individual monastic college, it would become excessive, so I will discuss just some of the main ones. At Losal Ling, as already mentioned, there was the pair of Jamyang Lekpa Chöjor and Panchen Sönam Drakpa; at Deyang, there was Drachung Yönten Gyaltsen; at Shakor there was Narthangpa Rapchok; at Thösam Ling there was Nyenpo Shākya Gyaltsen; those were the especially illustrious ones. At Gomang, there were Rinchen Jangchup, Jampa Lhündrup, Shukhangpa Gelek Lhündrup, Gungru Sangyé Tashi, and in particular, Gungru Chökyi Jungné, whose textbooks and courses of study were better than others.

In later times, there was Jamyang Shepai Dorjé (1648–1721). This great scholar-adept, who was the equal of the Indian ornaments who beautified Jambudvīpa, wrote textbooks on all of sutra and mantra and, in particular, on the exegesis of the five root texts.[1157] These became treasures of unprecedented excellent explanation, so that nowadays the textbooks of Jamyang Shepa are the only Dharma texts upheld at Gomang. Indeed, not just those at Gomang, but countless philosophers in both central Tibet and the outlying areas made them the foundation of their study and reflection, and because of that, it seems, most of the other textbooks were put away.

(3) Sera abbots

Jamchen Chöjé Shākya Yeshepa (1354–1435) went to China and became the guru of both the emperor Yunglo and his son, Sönté Gyalpo;[1158] and he began to spread the tradition of Jé Lama in the land of China. He returned to Tibet and [in 1419], as ordered by the great lord Jé, founded Sera Thekchen Ling.[1159] When he again went to China, he selected Kachupa Dargyé Sangpo for the abbot's throne. After that, Gungru Gyaltsen Sangpo (1383–1450), known as the incomparable Dharma lord, sat on the throne.

Some of the latter's explanations of the view and other topics did not accord with the teachings of Jé Rinpoché, so Khedrup Jé said, "Gyensangwa, [226] when you teach by saying 'moreover,' you serve up explanations that do not accord with Jé's; I rebuke you." Gyensangwa was upset, and sadly said:

> Losang Drakpa has gone to abide in Tuṣita,
> Jamchen Chöjé is celebrated in the emperor's palace,
> And Gungru Gyaltsen Sangpo is abandoned on the snow
> mountain.[1160]

The *Biography of Tsültrim Rinchen of Shalu*[1161] states:

> When Tsülrinpa went to hear the Dharma from Jamyang Chöjé Tashi Palden, the omens were unfavorable, so he went to Sera to hear the Dharma from the incomparable Dharma lord, Gyaltsen Sangpo. His way of explaining the view did not agree with the way Jé's direct disciples explained it, and when asked the reason for this, Gyensangwa said, "They did not know what to say to others; Jé Lama told me that the proper way to meditate on emptiness is as an affirming negation."

In Gungruwa's guidelines on view, the way it is explained is like that, so perhaps Jé taught Gungruwa before having completed his analysis of the view.

Gungruwa wrote a multitude of treatises that were appreciated by other scholars, such as commentaries on the *Ornament of Mahayana Sutras* and *Ornament of Higher Realization,* and the three *Doses of Madhyamaka Emptiness* texts—extensive, middling, and abbreviated. He also had many disciples because of his teachings, such as Khedrup Palden Sengé, Rinchen Jangchup, and others. After Gyensangwa, Shalu Rapjampa occupied the abbot's throne, and after him Lodrö Rinchen Sengé,[1162] known as the all-knowing one. The latter wrote extraordinary textbooks on Madhyamaka and other topics, though a few of his explanations did not accord with Jé's thought; later, Sera Jetsünpa and others wrote refutations of them. Nowadays, even those who proudly depict themselves as geshés merely skim the textbooks of Gyensangwa and the all-knowing one, looking for what is unsuitable. But when the intelligent examine them, the texts appear as treasures of excellent explanation pleasing to the wise.

After Lodrö Rinchen Sengé, Netenpa, Lhepu Chöjé, and Nyaltön Paljor Lhündrup sat on the monastic seat. The last was a great scholar: when he debated the great Sakya scholar Shākya Chokden, he rendered Shakchok speechless. He also defeated Tsenyak in debate, so his fame as a scholar became widespread. He wrote a commentary on the difficult points in Tsongkhapa's *Essence of Excellent Explanation: A Treatise Distinguishing* [227] *Provisional and Definitive.* After him, the erudite Palden Lodrö; Jamyang Dönyö Palden; the Second Dalai Lama, Gendün Gyatso; and Jetsünpa Chökyi Gyaltsen (1469–1544) sat on the throne. The last was an unrivaled lord of knowledge beyond compare. He wrote many textbooks on Madhyamaka and other topics that were treasures of excellent explanation. He responded to refutations of Jé's teachings by both Gorampa and Shākya Chokden and wrote a treatise that corrected mistakes in the perfection of wisdom textbook by the Eighth Karmapa Mikyö Dorjé, which he offered to the Karmapa; the latter was very pleased and wrote an expression of praise to Jetsünpa. He gave courses of study for many years on the stainless tradition of Jé, and he had many disciples as a result of those teachings. After Jetsünpa, the abbot's throne was occupied by Panchen Sönam Drakpa; Chödrak Sangpo; the Third Dalai Lama, Sönam Gyatso; Tongkhor Yönten Gyatso; the Fourth Dalai Lama, Yönten Gyatso; the First Panchen, Losang Chögyen; and the mighty conqueror, the Great Fifth Dalai Lama.

From then on, successive Dalai Lamas were made the master throne holders. Although at first there were five monastic colleges, they later merged into two, Sera Jé and Sera Mé.

The first, Sera Jé: When Musepa Lodrö Rinchen Sengé, a disciple of Jamyang Chöjé, was staying in Drepung, he was disturbed that some monks were involved in dubious practices, so he went to Sera and was followed by about a hundred disciples who were themselves sages; those who came with him settled there permanently, and it became known as Sera Jepa monastic college.

Sera Mé: Through courses of study given by Jangchup Öser, known as the all-knowing Jangchup Bumpa, there was a steady increase in disciples. Later on, a tantric college was established, too.

Those who were in the line of abbots or were scholar-adepts at Sera Jé and Sera Mé are countless, so I will not write about all of them here.

Thus, both Sera and Drepung were established on the basis of the monastic seat at Ganden Mountain, and from them—like sons, grandsons, and great-grandsons—grew many centers of teaching and practice, and the tradition of Jé Lama pervaded the whole of Tibet, both central and outlying areas. Although there are prophecies of such developments in the *Precious Book*[1163] and other texts, from fear of excess I did not write about them.

(4) Tashi Lhünpo abbots

The omniscient Gendün Drupa Pal Sangpo (1391–1474)[1164] made Jé's teaching widespread [228] in the Tsang region. Drepung was founded eight years after Ganden [in 1416], Sera was founded eleven years after Ganden [in 1419], and twenty-nine years after that [in 1447],[1165] Jé Gendün Drupa founded the monastery of Tashi Lhünpo as prophesied by the lama/meditational deity. Although he was earnestly requested to ascend the Ganden throne after Shalupa Lekpa Gyaltsen, he did not, saying, "In war, it is necessary to establish a foothold in enemy territory; it is my hope that this place will come to be just like Ganden." Apparently, he said that because at that time there were many in the vicinity of Tashi Lhünpo Monastery who had mistaken views about Jé's tradition, such as Ngorpa Künga Sangpo, Gorampa, and Shākya Chokden.[1166] Later, because of the steady increase of the brilliance of Tashi Lhünpo, Sakya monasteries such as Ngor, Tanak Thupten, and Serdokchen became as dim as fireflies in sunlight.

For thirty-eight years, Jé Gendün Drupa gave courses of study primarily at the monastic seat at Tashi Lhünpo and went forth to teach the Dharma in many areas south, north, west, and east of the Tsangpo River. He thought only of the teaching: he gave courses of study on the great texts and wrote many treatises, such as the *Commentary on Vinaya,* the *Hundred Thousand Stories,* the *Short Commentary on the Thorough Exposition of Valid Cognition,* the *Ornament of Reasoning,* and others. He had innumerable disciples who were scholar-adepts: in the early period, his disciples included Künkhyap Mönlam Palwa, the duo of Dülkar and Dülnak, Jatang Sempa Chenpo, Panchen Sangpo Tashi, Shangtön Drimé Shenyen, Gyüpa Jinpa Palwa, and others; in the middle period, they included Panchen Lungrik Gyatso, Jé Drakpa Samdrup, Topden Öser, Chöjor Palsang, and others; in the later period, they included Nenyingpa Künga Delek, Jé Ön Losang Nyima, Panchen Yeshé Tsemo, and others.

After Gendün Drupa, the monastic seat at Tashi Lhünpo was occupied by Panchen Sangpo Tashi, Panchen Lungrik Gyatso, and Panchen Yeshé Tsemo. At this time, the Second Dalai Lama, Gendün Gyatso, was staying at Tashi Lhünpo. Panchen Yeshé Tsemo appeared to be jealous of him, so he did not remain at Tashi Lhünpo but went to Drepung. Then, Gendün Gyatso established Chökhor Gyal Monastery,[1167] and at a time when his activities were very successful there, he went at the urging of Panchen Yeshé Tsemo and presided over the monastic seat of Tashi Lhünpo. After him came Ngari Lhatsün [229] Tenpai Nyima, Panchen Shantipa Lodrö Gyaltsen, Panchen Dönyö Gyatso, and Shangtön Lodrö Leksang, who wrote textbooks that gave excellent expositions. Subsequent abbots were Nenying Chöjé Chökyi Gyaltsen, Shangtön Chöpal Gyatso, Chukshungpa Sönam Gyaltsen, Shangtön Samdrup Palsang, Nyangtön Damchö Yarphel, Nyangtön Lhawang Lodrö, and the omniscient Panchen Losang Chökyi Gyaltsen, from whom the lineage of Panchen Lamas originates.

Three monastic colleges formed at Tashi Lhünpo. It would be too much for me to write about all of the lineage lamas in them, so I will not elaborate much. At Shartsé, the first main instructor was Shangtön Drimé Shenyen, and the sixth was Lodrö Gyatso. At Kyilkhang, the eighth main instructor was Panchen Shantipa Lodrö Gyaltsen, and the tenth Tenpa Darsang. At Thösam Ling, the first main instructor was the all-knowing Chöjor Palsang, and the fourth was Trukjampa Tashi. All these wrote textbooks that gave excellent explanations of Madhyamaka, the perfection of wisdom, and the other main subjects. Even though the First Dalai Lama, Gendün Drupa, set his mind on establishing a tantric college, he did not succeed. The omniscient Panchen Losang Chökyi Gyaltsen did establish a tantric college, though, and some authoritative masters, such as the great mantra practitioner Dorjé Dzinpa Könchok Gyaltsen, came from there.

Accordingly, based on these four great monasteries of Ü-Tsang, new Geluk monasteries and practice centers increased manyfold, and a multitude of monasteries of the other philosophical systems were converted to Geluk centers. Through the efforts of the upholders of the tradition of Jé Lama, the Geluk came to pervade the Land of Snows, both in the central and outlying areas. For details, the Dharma histories should be consulted.

(5) Geluk centers in the far west and east

The spread of Jé's teaching in the regions of upper Tibet, that is, Ngari, and lower Tibet, that is, Amdo and Kham, was initially due to the kindness of the two Shersangs.

(a) In the far west

Jé's direct disciple, Tö Sherap Sangpo, founded the monastery of Takmo in the Śītā River basin in the Mangyül region of Ngari,[1168] and Wönpo Sherapa of that center founded the monastery of Triksé, and both prospered [230] greatly. The Dharma system of Jé also was established at the monastery in Zangskar. Moreover, Gugé Ngawang Drakpa became the lama of the three brothers—Gugé Dakpo Tashi Ödé, Tri Namgyal Ö, and Shākya Ö—and he established and extended Jé's superlative system in many older monasteries, such as the temple of Toding Ser—the monastic seat of the great translator Rinchen Sangpo—the monastery of Tsaram, and Lötang. Khedrup Jé's disciple Sangphuwa Lhawang Lodrö revived the temple of Pethup, which had been built by Ödé, the younger brother of Lha Lama Jangchup Ö;[1169] and he founded both the Barkya monastery and the Liging monastery. Thenceforth, new monasteries were built in many areas, and most of the old ones came to uphold the Geluk philosophical system, so that the Geluk came to cover the entire Ngari area.

(b) In Kham

The first to spread Jé's teaching in Amdo and Kham was Mé Sherap Sangpo. When the Dharma lord Dargyé Sangpo was staying at the monastic seat of Jamchen Chöjé, that is, Sera Thekchen Ling, the bodhisattva from Mé, Sherap Sangpo, was a visiting teacher, and by offering explanations that accorded with the tradition of the father Jé and his spiritual sons, he attracted an ocean of scholars. At that time, he wondered, "If I go in the direction of my own birthplace, Kham, and—retaining this attire of pure vinaya morality—modify the Dharma lineage and the view and conduct there, will the benefits to the teaching of Jé Rinpoché and to sentient beings be very extensive?" When this occurred to him, the all-knowing Jangchup Bumpa knew it through his clairvoyance, and he invited the bodhisattva to visit. He gave him good, devoted service and, bestowing on him a woolen blanket and a hat, said without further ado, "You should leave quickly for Kham and do whatever benefits the teaching in the Kham region." Sherap Sangpo thought, "He told me, without any discussion, 'Leave quickly for Kham.' Would it then be proper to remain here? In any case, I'll ask Gyaltsap Rinpoché, for he might tell me to stay here for now." He then went to Ganden, and when he asked Gyaltsap Rinpoché where he should reside, the latter reportedly said, "Don't even think about delaying; it is much better you go to Kham. At a place there in the vicinity of the famed [231] Riwo, students will come and great deeds will be performed." Gyaltsap gave him a prophecy and parting gifts.

Later, Sherap Sangpo founded Chamdo Monastery. He built a school of dialectics, attracting about three thousand monks. The aims of beings were served extensively in middle Kham and lower Amdo, so the clairvoyance of the all-knowing Jangchup Bumpa was confirmed.

Then Gyalwa Phakpa Lha (1439–87)[1170] was born as the son of the direct disciple of Jé Rinpoché, Kuchor Tokdenpa or the yogin Öpak Dorjé, and successive emanations followed. The incarnation lineages of Phakpa Lha's disciples Shiwa Sangpo, Chakra Trulku, and Gyara Trulku, and the revered Tatsak Jé emanations of Baso Chökyi Gyaltsen, followed, as did the incarnation lineage of Jé's direct disciple, Gushri Palden Döndrup; the Takphu trulkus; the reincarnations of Ngok Lotsāwa Loden Sherap and Ngok Lotsāwa Lekpai Sherap—that is, the greater and lesser households of the Drakyap trulku; and others. In short, many great reincarnates held the rosary of incarnate lines. Moreover, there were many beings—scholars and adepts—who built monasteries in different areas and propagated the teachings on explanation and practice; those known as the six from Gang, the nine from Rong, the ten from Shö,[1171] and the three from Ru[1172] spread the Geluk teaching in all parts of Kham.

(c) In Amdo

In the region of Domé, that is, Amdo, the Dharma lord Döndrup Rinchen (1309–85) founded a monastery at Jakhyung Drak. In the birthplace of the conqueror Tsongkhapa, where the Kumbum stupa stands, there were some monks who were mingling with townspeople. So when the Third Dalai Lama, Sönam Gyatso, arrived there, the vinaya Dharma lord Öser Gyatso built Tsangön Monastery at his suggestion. After the passing of some generations of lamas, courses of dialectical study and a tantric college were started there, and later a medical college was built.

The mighty Fourth Dalai Lama, Yönten Gyatso, sent Gyalwai Sepo Dönyö Chökyi Gyatso to start a monastery in Domé (in 1604). Gyalsé Rinpoché founded Gönlung Jampa Ling,[1173] and started courses of study, so that it became the first school of dialectics [232] in the area. Later, Jé Jamyang Shepa started a tantric college. From this monastery emerged many great beings who benefited the teaching. In particular, the successive sages Changkya Ngawang Losang Chöden, Jé Thukenpa Ngawang Chökyi Gyatso,[1174] and the omniscient Rölpai Dorjé served as objects of veneration for the Mañjughoṣa of the East, the great emperor of China, and worked to sustain the teachings of Ganden Mountain. The tenth abbot of Gönlung, Lama Tsenpowa Döndrup Gyatso, founded a great monastery in Serkhok, Ganden Damchö Ling. It was developed by the former abbot of Gomang, Hor Ngawang Trinlé Lhündrup, and became prosperous. Its four monastic colleges were presided over by the successive incarnations of Mindröl Nomin Han:[1175] a pair of dialectics colleges—upper and lower—a tantric college, and a medical college.

Losang Tenpai Gyaltsen, who was known as Rongbo Chöjé Rinpoché (seventeenth century), had a cousin named Kalden Gyatso who was known as Kachu Rinpoché (1607–77). The latter gave himself over entirely to essential practices comparable to those described in the biography of Jetsün Milarepa and gained the elevated status of adept. He founded the hermitage of Tashi Khyil at the practice site of his lama and instituted the course of study at the great monastery of Rongbo. Later, he founded colleges for Kālacakra and tantra that still flourish today. Kalden Gyatso had many disciples, so eighteen practice centers, and others besides, were founded. At present, these have expanded into many more centers.

Yershong Ngakrampa Jamyang Lodrö (1651–1753) was a main disciple of the great tantric yogin Könchok Yarphel, Changkya Dorjé Chang, and Jé Jamyang Shepa. He was proficient in the meanings of the scriptures in general and the tantras in particular, and he built the monastic college at Yershong. He gave many initiations, guidelines, and instructions, both at the monastic seat and in areas above and below it. From him came a multitude of excellent disciple lineages, such as that of Tongkhorwa Sönam Gyatso, and reincarnation lineages as well.

The crown ornament of the millions of scholar-adepts, Jé Jamyang Shepai Dorjé, founded the great monastery of Tashi Khyil[1176] in the southern part of Domé. The great scholar Ngawang Tashi developed the center well, and wrote many textbooks. Jamyang Shepa Lama himself returned as a protector [233] of the teaching and of beings as the Dharma king Mañjughoṣa, Könchok Jikmé Wangpo (1728–91). He presided over Tashi Khyil for a long time in a dual role,[1177] until there were four subdivisions: Thösam Ling, the tantric college, the Kālacakra college, and the medical college. Nowadays, of all the study centers of Domé, Tashi Khyil is manifestly the best, like the crown of a victory banner. It also has a great many branch monasteries that are study centers and retreat centers.

The Dharma lord Rinchen Lhünpo (1475–1527?), who was born into the lineage of rulers of Choné, founded Choné Monastery. Later, the one known as Drakpa Shedrup, the author of many Dharma texts, started the courses of study and the tantric college there. Print blocks of the Kangyur and Tengyur are housed at Choné, and there are also many branch monasteries.

Thus, in the same way as limbs and their extensions grow from the body, study and retreat centers spread from those great monasteries to many places, so that every place in Domé, south and north, was filled with them. Although in earlier times there were in the Amdo region some who upheld the Sakya and Kagyü Dharma lineages, it has now become solely the province of upholders of the Geden tradition.

(6) The transmission of secret mantra

Having briefly explained how Jé's tradition of teaching and practice spread in both the central and outlying areas, I will now explain briefly how, in particular, Jé Lama's secret-mantra teaching spread.

(a) Sherap Sengé

From among Jé's disciples, who came forth like the sky covering the earth, those who practiced secret mantra and those who gave explanations to others were countless, but those who had the special oral tradition of Guhyasamāja became the source of the teachings of secret mantra. One lama, the scholar-adept Sherap Sengé (1383–1445), experienced the profound view, mastered the stable concentrations of the generation and completion stages, was blessed by his meditational deity, and accomplished deeds with the help of the Dharma protectors. He was strengthened by his prayer that he enhance the work of Jé. He held every one of Jé's special instructions on Guhyasamāja and Cakrasaṃvara, and it is said that he also possessed many unwritten special instructions and oral directions that were not given to other disciples.

How the teachings of secret mantra were propagated after being entrusted to Jamchen Chöjé by Jé Lama: After Jé Rinpoché suggested to Jamchen Chöjé that he start a tantric college, Jé went above Sera and, before many, many [234] great scholars who were his disciples, gave one Dharma session each, right from the beginning, on the root tantras of both Guhyasamāja and Cakrasaṃvara. Then he held up in his hand a book that included four Guhyasamāja commentaries and asked, "Who is able to master this?" Even though he said this three times, no one was able to reply. Then, Jé Sherap Sengé stood up amid that ocean of scholars and replied, "I'll do it!" Having ritually recited this three times, he accepted the book.

Although it is written in the *Dharma History* of the Drukpa scholar Pema Karpo that Khedrup Jé derided him, there is no evidence for this in any other Dharma history or biography. Pema Karpo's *Dharma History* also says, "When the duo of Rongtön Shākya Gyaltsen and Gyaltsap Darma Rinchen debated at Sangphu, the victory drum was beaten by Rongtön";[1178] and "Although the Gedenpas say that Gyaltsap and Khedrup were the heirs of Jé Rinpoché, it appears from our investigations that Gendün Drup was the real heir."[1179] Those and other statements appearing in certain writings are sheer fantasy because they are hearsay with no source; this is just an aside.

Then, the great lord Jé prophesied to Sherap Sengé:

> You need not be afraid; I will entrust you to Dharmarāja.[1180] You will go to Tsang, and on top of a mountain shaped like a downward-facing bell, there will be a yogin practicing Yamāntaka; he will make your teaching flourish. Atop a mountain shaped like a

> supine demoness will be a demoness; she also will make your teaching flourish. Then you yourself will know what is to come.[1181]

Then the two of them, the father Sherap Sengé and his spiritual son Gendün Drup, went to Tsang. The vinaya master Lodrö Bepa received many Dharma teachings on sutra and mantra from both father and son. Many disciples who were scholar-adepts gathered to receive teachings on secret mantra from Sherseng and on the definition vehicle from Gendün Drup. The vinaya master acted as an assistant teacher, and the courses of study were very successful. Khedrup Norsang Gyatso said:

> In the days of my youth, in Rikhu, I saw the Dharma lord Sherap Sengé, the omniscient Dharma lord Gendün Drup, and the Dharma lord and vinaya master Lodrö Bepa staying together with their great spiritual sons; it was like when the Teacher, the Buddha, lived on earth with his retinue.[1182] [235]

Thus, once while staying in Tsang enhancing the course of study, Sherap Sengé suddenly remembered the promise to propagate the tantras that he had made previously to Jé, so in order to give a course of study on Guhyasamāja, he went to Lhünpo Tsé. The lama of that monastery, Phakö Yönten Gyatso, along with his retinue, requested and received Dharma teachings. Phakö Yönten Gyatso wrote a tantric commentary called *Ascertainment of the Illuminating Lamp* and maintained well the Geluk way of explaining the tantras; he was also the Yamāntaka yogin prophesied by Jé. At that monastery, Sherap Sengé instituted the mandala practice ritual according to Jé Rinpoché's system as well as courses of study on the tantras. Thinking it a good omen, Jé Rinpoché had left there a Dharmarāja mask, along with a stick and noose, taken from his treasury. Apparently, they can be found there even now.

Then Sherap Sengé went to Sengé Tsé. He took the female master of that place as his benefactress and instituted the mandala ritual and tantric course of study at the monastery as it had been before. This female master was the demoness prophesied by Jé Tsongkhapa.

(b) Sé and Mé

During his stay at Sengé Tsé, in accordance with the remaining part of the earlier prophecy, namely, the statement that "then you yourself will know what is to come," Sherap Sengé decided on his own to go and advise Dülnakpa to establish the Sé tantra tradition. One day, when Jé Gendün Drup was sitting at the head of the right-hand tea-drinking row before Sherap Sengé, with Dülkarwa and others behind, and Dülnakpa Palden Sangpo (1402–73) was sitting at the head of the left-hand row, Jé Sherseng asked Dülnakpa, "Which is your year?" "The horse," he replied. "That is good," said Sherseng. "There is an exemplary proverb that says, 'At the place where the yak dies, the horses will frolic,' so you should go to the region of Yakshi[1183] and give courses on the tantras." Having said this, Sherseng gave Dülnakpa Jé's pandit hat and robe. Dülnakpa said, "This is more suitable for Jé Gendün Drupa. Please give me Jé Tsongkhapa's *Four-Part Commentary on Guhyasamāja*[1184] along with the book carrier[1185] and begging bowl." He took them and went to the upper part of the Sé region, which is also called the region of Yakshi. He founded a tantric college at Ganden castle in Sé, which became the tantric college of upper Tsang.[1186]

Although twenty-one monastic successors came between Dülnakpa and Gyüchen Könchok Yarphel, the members of the lineage with uninterrupted Dharma transmissions were: Dülnakpa, Jamyang [236] Gendün Phel, Dorjé Chang Tashi Phakpa, Panchen Samdrup Gyatso, Gyüchen Tsöndrü Phakpa, Khedrup Dorjé Sangpo, Gyüchen Sangyé Gyatso, and Gyüchen Könchok Gyatso; these great tantric yogins who preceded Gyüchen Könchok Yarphel appear to be the only ones who gained high realizations of the generation and completion stages. The principal tantric expositions that they gave were on Jé's *Four-Part Commentary* and his larger and smaller commentaries on Guhyasamāja[1187] and also Dülnakpa's *Arrangement of the Vajra Path*. They expounded these and also gave expositions on what were known as the eight great guidelines: (1) the direct instructions on the five stages of Guhyasamāja, (2–3) the two guidelines on Cakrasaṃvara, by Lūipa[1188] and Ghaṇṭapa, (4) the stages of the four yogas of Vajrabhairava,[1189] (5) the six yogas of Kālacakra, (6) the fourfold blessing of the Great Wheel Vajrapāṇi, (7) the six Dharmas of Nāropa, and (8) the opening of the golden door to the guidelines on transference of consciousness. Of those, the Great Wheel Vajrapāṇi and the guidelines on transference were omitted at some point. The six other great guidelines were expounded, so the two sets later came to be known as the six great guidelines of the Sé tantra system and the eight great guidelines of the Mé tantra system.

The branch guidelines: There are those known as the three instructions, that is, the guidelines on the sixty-three,[1190] the guidelines on the miraculous wheel,[1191] and the guidelines on the *Ocean of Yogic Achievement Related to Fire Offerings*.[1192] There are the guidelines on great torma of the protector. There are guidelines on the four great reversals, related to Sitātapatrā and others.[1193] Moreover, there are in this lineage many special instructions on the principal mantras on the generation and completion stages of the trio of Guhyasamāja, Cakrasaṃvara, and Vajrabhairava, as well as a multitude of very profound sutra and mantra teachings, such as guidelines on the stages of the path to enlightenment.

Although Gyüchen Könchok Yarphel (b. 1602) had some earlier disciples of his own who studied the Sé tantra tradition, none emerged to uphold the Dharma lineage. Later in Gyüchen's life, Megen Lama Ngawang Lodrö and Shalu Khenchen Jamyang Tenzin venerated him, but they did not hear the great key points of the initiations and explanations of Guhyasamāja and other tantras. When Gyüchen was eighty years old, the all-knowing Jamyang Shepai Dorjé and, when he was eighty-one, Changkya Dorjé Chang Ngawang Losang Chöden and Thangsakpa Ngödrup Gyatso came from Ü to venerate him, and he gave them the initiation of Guhyasamāja, an explanation of the tantra, and a vase filled to the brim with the teachings of the Sé tantra tradition, which are primarily [237] the guidelines on the two stages. Not long afterward, Gyüchen himself went to final peace; I think he had waited until he could pass on his Dharma to the rightful owners and remained in the world accordingly.

Having also received the complete teachings on sutra and mantra that came from the Mé tantra tradition and the Ensa lineage, those three holy beings combined all three streams together into a single river of teachings. Both Jé Ngawang Chöden and Jamyang Shepai Dorjé also wrote many textbooks, and Thangsakpa also wrote about the generation and completion stages of Vajrabhairava and other topics. After that, the great adept Jamyang Dewai Dorjé, Gurmönpa Dönyö Khedrup, Jé Phurbu Chokpa Chenpo, Trichen Ngawang Chokden, the Seventh Dalai Lama Kalsang Gyatso, the omniscient Changkya Rölpai Dorjé, and others made the tantras widespread in every corner of Tibet, from the central to the outlying areas.

(c) Gyümé and Gyütö[1194]

Having founded the Sé tantra tradition, the scholar-adept Sherap Sengé returned to Ü and started the Gyümé tradition, giving courses of study on the king of tantras, Guhyasamāja. Through disseminating expositions of Guhyasamāja, the eight great guidelines, and other topics, he made Jé Lama's secret mantra teachings widespread. After Sherap Sengé, Gyüpa Jinpa Palwa occupied the throne and gave courses and wrote tantric commentaries. After him came many generations of lamas who were certified upholders of the lineage. They wrote many guidebooks and other texts; of those, the *Guhyasamāja Generation and Completion Stage* of Dakpo Namkha Drak was especially popular.

Nenyingpa Künga Döndrup (1419–86), who had met Jé Sherap Sengé only breifly, arrived at Gyümé and received special instructions on the tantras and their commentaries from Gyüpa Jinpa Palwa. After Jinpa Palwa, Draksangpa occupied the throne; the two of them, Jinpa Palwa and Draksangpa, passed away in the earlier and later parts of the same year. Although Künga Döndrup was qualified to be the tantric course master, Treu Tashi Gyaltsenpa was selected by the lead chanter Dönyö and others as teacher; appearing somewhat displeased, Künga Döndrup took religious items—a painting of a protector and a skull cup—and went to the upper part of Ü.

At the outset, master and disciples together made six; then, when there came to be thirty-two, it was a good omen, since that is equal to the number of deities in the Guhyasamāja mandala. Even though the lineage successors of Tashi Gyaltsenpa invited Künga Döndrup back to Gyümé to be [238] the master, he did not come. With the tantric explanation tradition established in upper Ü, the assembly of monks grew larger each year. The great tantric yogin himself developed the center for thirteen years, so it became the Gyütö monastic college of Ü. Of the line of lamas who came subsequently, there were some who performed extensive deeds: Panchen Sönam Drakpa, Gomdé Namkha Gyaltsen, Jé Könchok Chöphel, and others.

It was Jé Sherseng who laid the foundation of the great school of dialectics at Tashi Lhünpo. He started courses of study of the tantras in Tsang and Ü that, right up to the present day, have not degenerated. This being so, the Dharma lord Yisang Tsewa praised him, saying, "Of the disciples of Jé Tsongkhapa, there is none whose deeds were greater than Sherap Sengé of Narthang."[1195] This is exactly right.

Sherseng wrote such texts as the *Commentary on the Thorough Exposition of Valid Cognition, Guidelines on the View,* and *Explication of the Guhyasamāja Root Tantra.* Also, his direct disciples include many renowned scholar-adepts, such as the omniscient Gendün Drup, Phaköpa, Gyüpa Jinpa Pal, Jé Mönlam Palwa, the duo of Dülkar and Dülnak, and others.

Moreover, Jé Panchen Sangpo Tashi explained many tantras and their commentaries, the elder Döndrup Pal established the explanatory tradition of Candrakīrti's *Bright Lamp* in Lhodrak, and the Dharma lord Dagyenpa gave courses of study on the tantras at Nyiding and Dzingchi. Later, monastic colleges started by the followers of the traditions of Gyütö and Gyümé multiplied in Amdo and Kham, and the exposition and study of Guhyasamāja according to Jé Lama's explanatory tradition spread in all directions.

(7) The Ensa ear-whispered lineage

As to how the Ensa oral lineage came about:[1196] At Geden Mountain monastery there were prophecies regarding requests made by Tokden Jampal Gyatso (1356–1428) and five or six fortunate disciples to the holy lord Mañjughoṣa and to Jé Lama himself. Although the omniscient Khedrup grasped some of the rough sense of what was known as the emanated book of extraordinary instructions of the ear-whispered lineage that had been taught by the holy lord Mañjughoṣa and Jé Lama himself, the full and complete teachings, along with the emanated [239] book, were not given to anyone but Lama Tokden Jampal Gyatso.[1197] Later, the great pandit Baso Chökyi Gyaltsen (1402–73)[1198] received the teachings that had belonged to Khedrup Jé and, in particular, received the full and complete teachings that had belonged to Tokden Jampal Gyatso himself. The great pandit Baso Chökyi Gyaltsen said:

> I only taught this to three qualified persons, and those three, if they should encounter a couple of qualified disciples who have renounced the activities of this life, should explain the instruction to them; they should not even mention this topic to anyone else.[1199]

He made this very strict commitment, which was witnessed by the meditational deity, ḍākas and ḍākinīs, and Dharma protectors.

Those three disciples were those known as the three Dorjé brothers.[1200] The three were: the great adept Chökyi Dorjé,[1201] Palden Dorjé of Tölung, and Rinchen Dorjé of Kham. The latter apparently had his name written as "Dorjé Pal." In the history by the Great Fifth Dalai Lama called the *Vajra Life-Tree of Long-Life Initiations*, it is stated that the great adept Chökyi Dorjé lived in the lotus cave on Jomo Lha Mountain, in the area of upper Nyang; Palden Dorjé of Tölung lived in Drip in a divine mansion of massive rocks that looked like piled-up vajras; and Khampa Yeshé Rinchen Dorjé lived in a solitary place in upper Jokpo in Phenyül; they had immortal vajra bodies not visible to ordinary beings.[1202] There are also explanations to the effect that Palden Dorjé lived in Gephel, a hermitage above Drepung. In the Fifth Dalai Lama's biography of the Third Dalai Lama, Sönam Gyatso, it says:

> In the private room called Sunlight, the Dalai Lama received initiation into the Cakrasaṃvara of Lūipa's tradition from the great adept called Palden Dorjé, who had attained the rainbow body, and the great adept offered a long-life initiation to the Dalai Lama that he himself had received directly from Master Padmasambhava.[1203]

Of the great adept Chökyi Dorjé, it is said:

> The one who came from the divine path of the pure clear light,
> Who possesses the immortal vajra rainbow body,
> Who guides beings by displaying himself as they wish:
> To the feet of Chökyi Dorjé I make supplication.[1204]

Since, according to that statement, he obtained the immortal vajra body, it is reputed that he is still living.

That great adept gave the conqueror Ensapa Losang Döndrup (1505–66)[1205] the ear-whispered lineage along with the emanated [240] book. Although on the surface many years elapsed between the great adept Chökyi Dorjé and the conqueror Ensapa, Chökyi Dorjé stayed in the rainbow body and was met by the conqueror Losang Döndrup in pure visions; because of that, some prattlers deny the secret qualities of those great āryas.

Jé Ensapa Losang Döndrup gave the ear-whispered lineage to the scholar-adept Sangyé Yeshé (1525–91), and he in turn gave it to the omniscient First Panchen, Losang Chökyi Gyaltsen (1570–1662).[1206] The first two holy ones and, especially, the omniscient Panchen set down in writing some of the teachings of the ear-whispered lineage. Thus, Jé Lama's multitude of essential instructions on sutra and mantra, which were the principal contents of the ear-whispered lineage and the emanated book, and which came down through the lineage to father Ensapa and his spiritual son mainly from Tokdenpa and also from Khedrup Jé, were known as the Ensa ear-whispered lineage.

2) How subsequent disciples served Jé's teaching

How subsequent disciples served Jé's teaching: Of the myriad supreme beings who upheld the Geden tradition in later times, the two who, like the sun and the moon, are without rival or compare are the mighty conquerors, the father and son—the Panchen and Dalai Lamas.[1207]

a) The Panchen Lamas

Of those, Panchen Losang Chökyi Gyaltsen was believed to be of a single mental continuum with Master Padmasambhava, the noble lord Atiśa, and the matchless Gampopa. His prior incarnations included: the śrāvaka Subhuti, who was the supreme interlocutor before the mighty Muni—the Buddha—and the clan chief Mañjuśrīkīrti, who compiled the *Kālacakra Root Tantra* in Shambhala.[1208] In the Holy Land of India, it included Master Abhayākaragupta, who composed the Garland Trilogy and spread the teachings of secret mantra. In Tibet, it included: the great translator Gö Lotsāwa Khukpa Lhetsé of Tanak, who illuminated the excellent path of Guhyasamāja; Jamyang Sakya Pandita Künga Gyaltsen; Yungtön Dorjé Pal, the scholar-adept [241] of Nyingma secret mantra; Khedrup Rinpoché, the sole heart son of the great lord Jé; the great scholar-adept Sönam Chokkyi Langpo; and the conqueror Ensapa Losang Döndrup, who gained the supreme achievement in this very life.

In his life as Panchen Chökyi Gyaltsen, he was lord of the full and complete teaching of the Muni and was expert, in particular, in the explanatory and practical teachings of Jé Lama. In general, Panchen Chökyi Gyaltsen's ordinary and exalted lifestories are beyond imagining; in particular, his deeds on behalf of upholding and enhancing the tradition of Jé Lama were as vast as space. His next rebirth was as the Second[1209] Panchen, Losang Yeshé (1663–1737), then as the Third Panchen, the great Vajradhara, the mighty Losang Palden Yeshé (1738–81). His supreme precious emanation body, the Fourth Panchen Lama Losang Tenpai Nyima (1781–1854),[1210] presently serves as the glorious holy protector of the teaching and of beings.

b) The Dalai Lamas[1211]

The omniscient mighty Dalai Lamas:[1212] Although according to the genealogy of his highness the Great Fifth, there are a great many in the rebirth line, the most renowned are: in the Holy Land of India, Prince Ratnadāsa; and in Tibet, Ārya Avalokiteśvara, who showed the aspect of a nobleman as the Dharma king Songtsen Gampo; the grandfather of the Kadam, Dromtön Gyalwai Jungné; the lord of the ocean of tantric texts, Sachen Künga Nyingpo; and the supreme spiritual son of Jé Lama, the First Dalai Lama, the omniscient Gendün Drupa.[1213] The latter wrote:

> From now until I attain the essence of enlightenment,
> I pray I will always be diligent,
> Jé, in upholding your teaching.[1214]

In accordance with the prayer that had been made, each successive reincarnation extended Jé Lama's tradition: the Second Dalai Lama, Gendün Gyatso (1475–1542),[1215] became the head of all scholar-adepts, performing greatly extensive deeds for the teaching; the Third Dalai Lama, Sönam Gyatso (1543–88),[1216] made the light of Dharma pervade the area of darkness in the wild borderlands;[1217] the Fourth Dalai Lama, Yönten Gyatso (1589–1617), annihilated those who sought to overturn Jé's teaching;[1218] and the mighty conqueror, the Great Fifth Dalai Lama (1617–82),[1219] made the white umbrella of the unification of religious and secular deeds cover the earth.

The next incarnation, the Sixth Dalai Lama, Tsangyang Gyatso (1683–1706),[1220] did not complete his activities due to the small merit of his students.[1221] The next, the omniscient [242] Seventh Dalai Lama, Losang Kalsang Gyatso (1708–57),[1222] identified with the lifestory of the First Dalai Lama, Gendün Drup: he became the great glorious protector of all the teachings and upholders of the teaching of Geden Mountain, and he also wrote many texts explaining well the difficult points of the teachings. Now, the omniscient Eighth Dalai Lama, Losang Jampal Gyatso (1758–1804),[1223] lives and assumes responsibility as guardian and protector of all beings, including the gods.

c) Summary of the deeds of Tsongkhapa's followers

From Jé Lama's arrival in the world right up to the present, upholders of the teaching who combined the three qualities of learning, discipline, and goodness rival in number the dust motes in the whole world, so I cannot discuss how each and every one served the teaching; here is just a general synopsis.

Some of those supreme and holy beings assured that the continuum of explanation was preserved through exposition and teaching to collected assemblies of the wise in the great monastic centers, according to Jé Lama's clarifications of the textual systems of the six ornaments and two supremes who beautified Jambudvīpa.

Some served the teaching through disseminating expositions according to the eightfold special instruction: the textual guidelines and direct instructions—along with the oral advice—on the stages of the path to enlightenment, which collect the key points of the entire teaching for practice in a single session.[1224]

Some assured that Jé's tantric teaching was preserved and increased through expounding the stainless explanatory tradition of the great tantric systems—of which the main two are the king of tantras, the glorious Guhyasamāja, as well as Cakrasaṃvara—and through imparting the streams of initiations, guidelines, special instructions, and so forth.

Some freed the teaching of stains through refuting by scripture and reasoning those from other schools who created systems opposed to that of the texts of Jé, and by refuting those from even our own Geluk school whose debased statements did not capture Jé's intent.

Some, for the sake of students of future generations, exerted themselves in the methods for assuring the preservation of the teaching until the end of time through appropriate writings that explained well how those of lesser intelligence could easily realize the meaning of Jé Lama's excellent explanations.

Some assured the preservation and increase of the teachings of Jé Lama's practice lineage through pure practice of the excellent paths of the sutra and mantra [243] traditions of Jé Lama that were unsullied by the stains of the eight worldly dharmas, and through upholding them in their own minds and disseminating them to others.

Some, too, thinking that the teaching depended on the various classes of sangha, extended the teaching through protecting existing study and practice centers and establishing new ones.

Some influenced the great kings of various countries and made them devoted to the Dharma, and for those beings in the wild borderlands with no prior faith in the Dharma, they skillfully spread the teaching by making it directly meaningful.

Also, some yogins freed the precious teaching of hindrances by employing the special conduct explained in the tantras to annihilate those who did not allow themselves to be subdued peacefully but who malevolently sought to overturn the tradition of Jé Lama.

There were also some holy great beings who by themselves accomplished all the liberating activities just explained.

If I discussed in detail how they did all that, I fear it would be far too much, so I have not elaborated. Those who wish to know the details may learn them from Dharma histories and the biographies of each holy being; it is right to make them objects of faith, rejoicing, and aspiration.

3) Giving just a general synopsis of the ordinary biographies of those holy Geden scholar-adepts

If I give just a general synopsis of the ordinary biographies of those holy Geden scholar-adepts, it is as stated by my omniscient lama:

> One who studies and reflects impartially,
> For whom all textual systems arise as instruction,
> One who propounds the rational path that deserves to be heard:
> That one is called a *scholar*.
>
> One who stabs through the delusions,
> Who is able to tame their own and others' minds,
> One confident that view and meditation are free from error:
> That one is called an *adept*.
>
> The adept not overwhelmed by scholarship,
> And the scholar not overwhelmed by practice:
> One who accomplishes benefit for the teaching
> Is also called [244] a *holy being*.[1225]

Since the foundation of all good qualities is morality, their first main praxis was guarding the purity of their vows. Then, they severed superimposition through study and reflection on the key points, not merely of partial or minor textual systems, but the entirety of the sutra and mantra vehicles. When meditating on the meaning of what they had studied, they did not discriminate the Muni's word in terms of rejection or acceptance. They took as their essential practice the practice of the totality of the teaching, which serves as a necessary condition for the enlightenment of a single individual, bearing without contradiction all the key points of sutra and mantra, from the most basic teachings of the *Vinaya Sutra* up to the highest Guhyasamāja practice. In the wake of meditation, they did not have pride in lofty realizations when they had just some minor experiences of the channels, drops, and so forth; rather, they investigated whether or not their practice was an antidote to the delusions.

Nor, rather than traversing the stages of the path from the bottom up, did they drool over such states as transcendence and cutting through;[1226] for even if one is overflowing with inner realizations, this does not contradict conformity with disciplined outer conduct. Nor, rather than being embarrassed about even the subtlest action and its result, did they generate the lax attitude that says of each subtle flaw, "What harm can it do?" Nor, rather than focus on the explanations of meditation deities in authoritative tantric texts or an undiminished lineage blessed with the complete methods for achieving the supreme through sādhanas and special instructions, did they trust the mere say-so of those who lack special qualities but promise great blessings and quick results. Nor, rather than relying on a gnosis-being Dharma protector who has the power to effect the appropriate conditions for clearing away obstacles on the path to enlightenment, did they entrust themselves to a principal guardian who is the type of worldling with just a little transient power.

By virtue of their solemn sense of full responsibility solely for the teaching and for beings, they spent their time exclusively in pursuits that benefited themselves, others, and the teaching. Such is the synopsis of the biographies of the previous holy Gedenpas. [245]

12. The Geluk Tradition 3: The Distinctiveness of Geluk

[II. The History of the Philosophical Systems in Tibet, Land of Snows
B. The histories of the different schools
8. The history of the Geluk philosophical system]

c. The way that excellent system is distinctive
1) The general distinctiveness of Geluk

WHETHER YOU DESIGNATE it a teaching, a Dharma system, or a philosophical system, the quality that determines it as authoritative is as stated in the *Beautiful Adornment of the Mount Meru of the Sage's Teaching: A Clear Explanation of the Establishment of Philosophical Systems,*[1227] written by my omniscient lama Changkya Rölpai Dorjé:

> Whatever definitely possesses
> The intended meaning of the Tripiṭaka,
> Abiding in it well and without contradiction:
> That is the teaching of the great Muni.
>
> In the practice of the three trainings,
> Whatever is oriented toward
> Abiding well in faultlessness:
> That is the Mahayana teaching.
>
> The view that is free from extremes,
> Analytical meditation equal with stabilizing meditation,
> Conduct unopposed to the teaching and practice of sutra and mantra:
> That is the faultless teaching.[1228]

In general, for a teaching to be a teaching of the Buddha, its view, meditation, and conduct must not contradict the Tripiṭaka—the scriptural Dharma—and it must conform with internal practice of the three trainings—the realized Dharma. In addition, for a teaching to be a Mahayana teaching, some portion of it must possess the path of the inseparable union of wisdom and method—meditation on emptiness motivated by compassion.[1229] In short, a teaching is faultless if the view, meditation, and conduct are faultless, that is, concordant with achieving liberation. If a teaching were deemed faultless merely because it cannot be contradicted by scripture or reasoning, then, impossibly, only the Prāsaṅgika would be faultless, and other philosophical systems would contain no faultless teachings, and their teachers, too, would be faulty.

Well then, if you ask how these qualities are fulfilled in the Geden tradition, this is the reply. First, it possesses the three *piṭakas* and the three trainings. The Sanskrit word *piṭaka* is rendered in Tibetan with the syllables for "groups" and "container" *(sde snod).* [246] *Piṭaka* is a north Indian term for a "great liter," which comprises ten liters of grain, and a container that accommodated a lot of grain was accordingly described as a *piṭaka. Piṭaka* also refers to all the words and meanings of the scriptures, or the objects of knowledge that are to be established, from the basis—the aggregates, sense fields, and sense factors—on up to the result, the body and gnosis of the Buddha. Thus, because the Tripiṭaka collects all groups or kinds, it is called a "group container." When *piṭaka* is defined like that, there are three *piṭakas*—the Sūtrapiṭaka, the Vinayapiṭaka, and the Abhidharmapiṭaka—or two *piṭakas,* of the Mahayana and Hinayana. There is no scriptural Dharma not included in those. Since all the principal topics of the Tripiṭaka are included in the three trainings, there also is no Dharma to be understood that is not included in those three.

The great majority of Tibetan philosophical system adherents have, when referring to those who have studied many scriptural collections, made "logician" and "teacher" pejorative terms. Have abandoned study, they meditate in the hope of being freed merely by meditating on the channels, winds, and drops, or by being introduced to seeing the bare nature of mind, which are minor practices. Even those who are proud of their studies are content with incomplete or minor textual systems. The *Ornament of Mahayana Sutras* says, "Here, it is on the basis of study that proper thinking will arise,"[1230] and so forth. Your mental continuum should be trained gradually through study, reflection, and meditation on the scriptures of the Tripiṭaka. Those texts that do not conform with that presentation of practice leading to liberation and omniscience through the three trainings are deficient. They lack the qualities definitive of a teaching that are explained in authoritative textual systems.

In the Geden tradition, you study and reflect upon the Sūtrapiṭaka, and you practice all three trainings with respect to both the higher and lower vehicles. You study and reflect upon the Vinayapiṭaka and practice the two trainings—in morality and concentration. You study and reflect upon the Abhidharmapiṭaka, and having generated the wisdom that unerringly knows the characteristics of all dharmas, you practice the training in wisdom and directly attain it. In particular, Gedenpas focus on the Mahāyānapiṭaka, studying, reflecting, and meditating upon the teaching through the vast conduct related to the awakening mind, the bodhisattva stages, and the perfections, as well as countless forms of subtle reasoning about selflessness. Thus, this supreme system possesses the totality of the characteristics [247] that establish the Buddhist teaching in general and the Mahayana teaching in particular.

If you believe that secret mantra is deficient in the qualities thus established, here is the reply. Secret mantra in general is said by the *Tantra Based on the Questions of Subahu* and by great Indian pandits to be included in the Sūtrapiṭaka. And, within the subdivisions of secret mantra, there are examples of all three *piṭakas*. On the occasion when the hundred holy deities[1231] were taught, the explanation of the color, shape, appearance, and other aspects of form; the classification of footless, many-footed, four-footed, and other beings; and the teaching chiefly on the empty part of the unique gnosis of bliss and emptiness: all fit into the Abhidharmapiṭaka. On the occasion when the generation and completion stages were taught, the teachings on how to achieve uncommon concentration by way of divine pride and clear appearance of oneself as the deity, fit into the Sūtrapiṭaka. And the general and specific teachings on mantra vows and pledges fit into the Vinayapiṭaka. Thus, it is unnecessary to distinguish secret mantra as separate from the Tripiṭaka.

No other philosophical system in the Land of Snows is equal to the Geden, which lacks even the slightest fault with respect to view, meditation, or conduct, so the Geluk is distinctive relative to all other philosophical systems in those three ways.

2) How its view is distinctive

a) Mistaken views

Some Tibetans of earlier generations maintained that the meaning of emptiness is nothingness, and held as supreme the debased nihilistic view that asserts that virtue and vice, cause and effect, and so forth, are entirely nonexistent. This is unacceptable. The lowliest of the extremists, the Lokāyatas, were twofold: the logicians and the contemplatives.[1232] Of those, some contemplatives accepted karma and cause and effect for a span of a hundred lives, and so forth, but they did not accept liberation. The logicians asserted that cause and effect and liberation were equally nonexistent. No philosopher in any other philosophical system, non-Buddhist or Buddhist, accepts a path to liberation after alleging that cause and effect are entirely nonexistent. Some philosophers, too, say that emptiness is truly existent;[1233] and some say that extrinsic emptiness—the enlightened mind's emptiness of any conventional dharmas extrinsic to it—is the final, ultimate nature.[1234] Those, too, are unacceptable. The *Fundamental Treatise on the Middle Way* says:

> Those for whom emptiness is a view,
> It is said, are incorrigible.[1235]

Thus, Nāgārjuna taught that one cannot recover from an eternalist ultimate view; [248] and Nāgārjuna was said by the Conqueror himself, in the *Descent to Laṅka Sutra* and elsewhere, to be a reliable authority on the exposition of the definitive meaning.[1236]

Some say that, if you apprehend something as merely existent, it entails apprehending a sign, so it cannot be that all dharmas are existent, nor can it be that they are nonexistent. Therefore, they say, when meditating, you should settle on thinking nothing, about either existent self or nonexistent self, emptiness or nonemptiness, and so forth. Thinking nothing is meditation on reality, and that very nonseeing is proper seeing. Saying this, those people are stuck in the view and meditation of the system of Heshang.[1237] That, too, is unacceptable. Concepts such as existent and nonexistent, permanent and impermanent, and one and many, have been proven through the scriptural analysis and reasoning of the great Indian pandits to be contradictory in terms of mutual exclusion through direct opposition.[1238] And since that very thought, "I will think nothing," is thinking something, and that very nonseeing is both seeing and not seeing, this view seems only a mass of contradictions.

In addition, those who pretend to be contemplatives say that it is only necessary to meditate on the meaning of the ultimate nature—elaborate virtuous practices are nothing more than distractions and rational analysis is unnecessary. They say that without any conceptual thought or analysis—with the mind not pursuing the past and not anticipating the future—you settle without fabrication or contrivance on the fresh awareness of the present, rejecting all conceptual fabrication with regard to the clear, empty, and ungrasping reality, relaxing comfortably into thinking nothing; when you do this, you come face to face with dharmakāya itself. That, too, is unacceptable. If, while absorbed in thinking nothing, a buddha gnosis for which nothing is unknown should arise in your mind, then a result would emerge from an incompatible cause; anything could arise from anything. This is treated extensively in the omniscient Jé Tsongkhapa's *Essence of Excellent Explanation,* his stages of the path texts, and his explanations of the *Fundamental Treatise on the Middle Way* and *Entering the Middle Way;*[1239] and in the *Dose of Emptiness that Opens the Eyes of the Fortunate*[1240] and the *Guidelines on View that Clear Away the Darkness of Wrong Views* written by Jé's spiritual heir Khedrup Jé.

b) Correct view[1241]

Thus, when those of earlier generations undertook analysis through reasoning that examines the ultimate, it was inferior, [249] because they did not know how to establish the combination of (1) thoroughly refuting the object of refutation and (2) knowing how to determine, non-nihilistically, what is left over after refutation: cause and effect, deed and doer, and so forth. When you follow the texts of the tradition of the glorious protector, Ārya Nāgārjuna, who was prophesied by the Conqueror himself as a commentator on the definitive meaning, you do not find, among all the dharmas of samsara and nirvana, even an atom that is ultimately existent from the side of its own basis of imputation. They are, however, established authoritatively as mere conventional labels through name and conceptual thought applied to their bases of imputation. Dharmas are established as this or that dharma conventionally by reason of their emptiness of inherent nature, and when you know how to posit deed and doer, and so forth, acceptably, then even if inherent existence is refuted conventionally, it is permissible in our own Geluk system to accept that all deeds and doers involved in karma and its result, and so forth, are authoritatively established, regardless of how others see things. Not only that, inducing certainty about dependently arisen dharmas gives you greater certainty about lack of inherent existence, so you know that emptiness and dependent arising are mutually supportive. This profound information was obtained only by the great lord Jé, through the kindness of Jetsün Mañjughoṣa. Apart from Jé, who taught it clearly, no previous Tibetan sage established this precisely and then taught it.

Thus, the omniscient Gyaltsap said:

> Until I met Jetsün Tsongkhapa,
> I did not even partially realize
> The path that severs the root of existence—
> The Madhyamaka, dependent arising free of extremes.[1242]

If even that great lord of reasoning, who nearly rivals the six ornaments of Jambudvīpa, said that before meeting the great lord Jé face to face, he did not even partially realize this Madhyamaka view free of extremes, then it goes without saying that it does not enter the purview of others who—pretending to be scholars—have not tasted the nectar of the great lord Jé's excellent explanations. Needless to say, earlier Tibetans did not know Jé's wonderful Madhyamaka system either. Also, with respect to the Vijñāptimātra system,[1243] no one at all had been able to explain precisely how the nature and imputed particulars of form and so forth are imputed, or how to establish the selflessness of dharmas through denial that they exist [250] by way of their own characteristics. In explaining the Cittamātra philosophical system, Khedrup Jé states:

> No one anywhere
> Could teach the scriptures; he opened the precious treasury
> Of the intended meaning of the profoundest points
> And thus aroused delight.[1244]

You may well ask, "Well, then, must it be said that even such previous holy beings as the father Marpa and his spiritual son Milarepa, the father Sachen Künga Nyingpo and his spiritual sons, the father Dromtön and his spiritual sons, and Butön, Ngok Lotsāwa, Rendawa, and others, did not realize the profound meaning?" The reply is: Although there is no certainty regarding their followers, it cannot be said that those eminent beings did not realize the Madhyamaka view. Nonetheless, when it came to writing great texts that established the profound Madhyamaka system through flawless scripture and reasoning, elucidating without confusion the intention of father Nāgārjuna and his spiritual sons, nothing like what the omniscient Jé wrote had previously appeared. You can see this when you examine the texts of those others. In Jé's own words, in the *Essence of Excellent Explanation:*

> Many who were very learned in scripture and reasoning,
> Who had taken great pains on the path of reasoning,
> Who were not deficient in their accumulation of the qualities of
> higher realization:
> Strive though they might, they did not gain realization,
> While I have seen that abiding reality quite well,
> Through the kindness of the protector-lama Mañjughoṣa.[1245]

In expounding the meaning of this passage, some apparently explain that the one who is very learned in scripture and reasoning is Butön, those who had taken many pains on the path of reasoning were Sakya Pandita and Chapa Chökyi Sengé of Tsang, and those who were not deficient in their qualities of higher realization were Marpa, Milarepa, Gampopa, and others.

Thus, with respect to the Gedenpas, Jé himself prayed:

> Thoroughly rejecting all wrong and debased views that,
> Out of fear of the profound meaning of the ultimate nature,
> Hold as supreme a mind-made or partial emptiness,
> May I realize that all dharmas are primordially empty.[1246]

Accordingly, the explanation and practice of the excellent profound Madhyamaka view, which is the ultimate intended meaning of the Conqueror, describing an emptiness that is not just mind-made or partial, but established by refuting the object of refutation—inherent existence, with respect to all dharmas, from form to complete omniscience—is like the common property of every Gelukpa. Although [251] some in other philosophical systems have refuted the extreme of mere existence, it is not common to all in those systems, so the Geluk is distinctive in terms of view.

3) How it is distinctive in terms of meditation

a) Refuting some mistaken views

The tradition of Ganden Mountain is also distinctive in terms of meditation. (1) Some renowned in Tibet as contemplatives say that all conceptual thought is to be abandoned, so it is necessary to stop thinking. (2) Some, too, say that all conceptual thought is movement of the dharmakāya, so realizational experience will increase to the same degree that conceptual thought increases. (3) Some, by saying "conceptual thoughts are the great ignorance that plunges you into the ocean of samsara,"[1247] say that conceptual thoughts are ignorance. (4) Some say that conceptual thoughts are the dharmakāya. (5) Some say when the mind abides clearly and vividly without elaboration, that is buddha or nirvana, and when the mind elaborates even a little, that is sentient beings or samsara. (6) Some say that when you are established in darkness with the body perfectly still, the eyes staring upward, and nothing present in the mind, then all the strange experiential appearances that arise, such as smoke and so forth, are the dharmakāya and the nature body, so that even ordinary beings can see the dharmakāya directly. (7) Some say that seeing those appearances is not seeing the totality of the dharmakāya but, rather, seeing just a part of the dharmakāya. (8) Some say that although those appearances are not the dharmakāya, they are path signs previewing your imminent vision of the dharmakāya. (9) Some say because those ephemera are mistaken appearances of a confused mind, they have no essence whatsoever. (10) Some say they are produced phenomena, while (11) others say they are unproduced. And so on: many mistaken statements are made about the nature of meditation.[1248]

Those claims are quite unacceptable. (1) The first claim is unacceptable because if all conceptual thought is to be abandoned, then even inferential reasoning that realizes emptiness must be abandoned, so emptiness could never be perceived directly, and yogic perception could never be attained. (2) The second is unacceptable because it would entail that our own realization is even higher than that of a complete buddha. (3) The third is unacceptable because conceptual thought is general and ignorance is [252] particular. (4) The fourth is unacceptable because it is unsuitable for both the thing to be purified and the purified part to be the same, and because it would entail that all sentient beings are freed without effort. (5) The fifth is unacceptable because it is impossible that a buddha's abandonments and realizations deteriorate. (6) The sixth is unacceptable because it is explained in all sutras and treatises that the three and four bodies are achieved through collecting merit and gnosis over three great countless eons and are the ultimate attainment. (7) The seventh is unacceptable because even though a subtle partless particle is asserted by the Vaibhāṣikas, no Buddhist school asserts an isolated part unrelated to a whole. (8) The eighth is unacceptable because the mere experience of the dissolution of elements has been mistaken for virtuous qualities of the higher stages and paths. The rest (9–11) are only accounts of fruitless exertion.

Not only that, when it comes to meditation, some, thinking that all meditation must only be placement meditation and, holding the practice of analysis to be faulty even when one meditates on the view and so forth, block the door that leads to the ascertainment of the ultimate nature. And, when first practicing tranquil abiding, they do focus on the stabilization part, but they give up nonconceptual placement through raising and tightening the level of the mind.[1249] This is because, confused by the mere wording of such passages as Saraha's to the effect that

> The mind itself, so strictly bound,
> Is freed when released, no doubt,[1250]

they say "the best relaxation is the best meditation," and lowering the heightened awareness[1251] and releasing the well-guarded mind, they reinforce subtle sinking; confusing that with good meditation, they waste their lives in that state.

b) Definitions of abiding and insight

With regard to the essential definitions of tranquil abiding and superior insight, the criteria for achieving each, the way to posit the union of tranquil abiding and superior insight, and so forth, not only are the very terms unknown to these others, but most of them do not recognize subtle sinking. They conflate sinking and torpor, and they also conflate distraction and excitation.[1252] In short, they cannot even distinguish the difference between sinking and real meditation, so there are many who have not even come close to the pure way of achieving concentration taught by the Conqueror.

When Lama Umapa Pawo Dorjé first thought to hear special instructions on meditation, there was a famous pair of teachers in Tibet at that time, Barawa Gyaltsen Palsang and Jakchen Jampa Pal; he received the instructions from Barawa Gyaltsen Palsang. Later, when he asked the holy lord Mañjughoṣa, "Does the superior insight posited by Barawa fit the definition of superior insight?" Mañjughoṣa said, [253] "Not at all!" This story occurs in the biography of Jé by Khedrup Jé.[1253] So, if the superior insight of even those leonine realized beings does not fit the definition, what need be said about others?

The great lord Jé refuted in general the idea that meditation is only placement meditation and, in accordance with what is taught in the mighty sage Kamalaśīla's *Stages of Meditation* and other texts, taught how, when analytical meditation is required, you apply analytical meditation; how, when placement meditation is required, you apply placement meditation; and how, when you must alternate analytical and placement meditation, you do that. He relied upon the extensive elucidations of the prerequisites for both tranquil abiding and superior insight found in the five books of Maitreya, Asaṅga's five treatises on the stages, Kamalaśīla's *Light of Madhyamaka* and *Stages of Meditation,* and other texts that expound the meaning of the instructions in the sutras on how to achieve faultless concentration.

He also taught: the differences among meditative objects; the distinction between analytical meditation and placement meditation; the criteria for achieving the similitude of tranquil abiding and superior insight once you have meditated in possession of the nine methods for stabilizing the mind and the eight factors for abandoning obstacles; the criteria for initial fulfillment of the definitions of tranquil abiding and superior insight; the ordering of the two; the criteria for fulfilling the definition of the concentration that unites tranquil abiding and superior insight; the way experiences arise at the beginning, middle, and end of those; the special signs that occur in the body and mind; the identification of sinking and confusion and the differences between them; the identification of distraction and excitement and the differences between them; which antidotes clear them away and how; the identification of mindfulness and introspection and the differences between them; the moment and the way to rely on each of those; the way a beginner first practicing concentration, not content just with the abiding side, requires the keenness of clarity; and so forth. In short, Jé correctly established the exact meaning of the texts of the great charioteers, so all aspects of his teaching are free from confusion.

Precisely because of that, at the end of the tranquil-abiding section of the *Great Treatise on the Stages of the Path,* he said:

> The stages of achieving concentration are taught well
> In the sutras and treatises commenting on their intended meaning,
> But because they are so hard to fathom, those with little discernment
> Do not understand them as they are; the fault is in their own minds.
>
> When they spread this ignorance to others, thinking that in those
> excellent

Texts there is no teaching for nurturing nonconceptuality,
They do not search in the texts where the teaching is,
And [254] search mightily where it is not, thinking to find it there.

Searching like that, they will not be able even to distinguish
The concentration of non-Buddhists from that of Buddhists;
Needless to say, they will not properly distinguish
The differences between the concentrations
Of the superior vehicle and the lesser vehicle, or
The vajra vehicle and the perfection vehicle.

Seeing this, I have explained, in words easy to understand,
How to nourish concentration as it is taught in the major texts.

Friends! You who have studied the great texts for years:
Do not cast away your own precious jewel
And take up the trinkets of others;
Know that you yourself possess a precious jewel.

Seeing that there are no divided meanings
In the instructions of the texts you have studied,[1254]
It is right to ponder the meaning of what the mighty Muni
taught:
"Those who have studied much will find bliss in the forest."[1255]

Thus, those who study many texts and

Contemplatives pinning their hopes on exertion alone
Do not gain the understanding that well discerns
Either the way of initial practice or the criteria of achievement
For the path to tranquil abiding placed in nonconceptuality.

To know how to develop concentration,
They should rely on an expert;
If not, they'd do less harm
If they let the Conqueror's teaching rest[1256] a while.[1257]

These words of advice and instruction were compassionately offered to those satisfied by mere foolish talk about meditation.

Thus, this tradition of Geden Mountain is also proven distinctive in terms of its good qualities of higher concentration.

4) How it is distinctive in terms of conduct

The Geluk also is especially distinctive in terms of conduct. Earlier Tibetans mostly said that what is taught in the vinaya about drinking intoxicants, avoiding afternoon food, and so forth, was influenced by those devoted to the lower, lesser vehicle, while for those who know the higher vehicle and the nature of their own mind, these practices are binding nets and so are unnecessary. Those who carelessly rejected the thoroughly pure conduct of the ordained were not only thoughtless, but some, purposely rejecting even such marks of a monk as the upper and lower robes and so forth, destroyed the pure vinaya training rules [255] of the holy Dharma, so that the teaching of the Conqueror became a mere reflection. In fact, most of them did not even know how to cut and measure the upper and lower robes. As it says in the biography by Khedrup Jé called *Entryway to Faith,* the great lord Jé, finding such a situation unbearable because the foundation of the Buddha's teaching is the training in higher morality, put into practice even the subtle vinaya rules—avoiding liquor and afternoon food—and among other things, preserved the rituals of giving and receiving before eating, sprinkling water before the evening drink, and not sleeping more than three nights in the house of someone not fully ordained.

Even when engaging in secret mantra, it was as taught in a tantra:

> Maintaining a śrāvaka's conduct on the outside
> And experiencing the joy of Guhyasamāja on the inside.[1258]

In conformity with that statement, Jé maintained completely pure conduct, practicing the yoga of the two stages, and so forth, while properly observing the entire code of conduct specified in the vinaya. On top of that, he protected, as he would his own eyes, the rules prescribed in the bodhisattva and tantric vinayas—his life was that pure.[1259] Even the scholar Taktsang Lotsāwa wrote to Jé Rinpoché:

> Some focus on vinaya and abandon tantra;
> Others, inclined to mantra, reject the vinaya.
> I bow down to you who know how to practice,
> Well and without contradiction, the Conqueror's entire teaching.[1260]

And:

> Some emphasize the definition vehicle and use secret mantra
> to make a living;
> Others are arrogant about mantra and just give lip service to
> the definition vehicle.
> I bow down to you who see there is no way to progress to full
> enlightenment
> Without all of sutra and mantra being complete.[1261]

Taktsang had initially issued refutations of eighteen "cartloads of contradictions" in the teaching of Jé Rinpoché,[1262] but later, seeing good qualities such as those stated above, he wrote in praise of him. Thus, the omniscient Fifth Dalai Lama, Ngawang Losang Gyatso, prayed:

> His marvelous life was lived observing the rules of purity;
> His great mental strength was a giant wave of bodhisattva conduct;
> His yogic conduct was the two stages of supreme bliss-emptiness;
> May I meet with the teaching of Losang the conqueror.[1263]

5) How it is distinctive in terms of secret mantra
a) In terms of view

The Geden system is also distinctive in terms of secret mantra. Other Mahayanists [256] on the definition vehicle, and āryas practicing the three lower tantras, are able to abandon the coarse knowledge obstacles based on the gnosis that directly realizes emptiness and on a limitless accumulation of merit. Since they are unable to abandon the subtle knowledge obstacles, however, it will take them a long time to reach buddhahood. In contrast, the highest yoga tantra vehicle is able to abandon every knowledge obstacle in a single, short life in this degenerate age. This difference in speed is due to the subject—innately blissful awareness—that realizes the object, emptiness. Since the student for whose sake highest yoga mantra is taught needs to have sharper faculties than even the sharpest perfection-vehicle student, that emptiness—which for such a disciple is a union of bliss and emptiness—must be solely the subtlest emptiness, as established by the Prāsaṅgika Madhyamaka.

For a student who is not so advanced and merely aspires to the path of mantra, there is a common bliss-emptiness, which is like the emptiness established by Svātantrika and the emptiness established by Cittamātra—

that is, empty of subject and object being substantially different. But the unexceptional student has no gnosis of bliss and emptiness that is applied to the emptiness of a substantially existent, self-sufficient person.

Because of that key point, Jé Lama stated in his *Essence of Excellent Explanation:*

> This pair of chariot-paths for establishing reality, that is, Cittamātra and Madhyamaka, is widely used in the perfection vehicle, and even scholars and adepts who comment on secret-mantra texts teach no third position on the meaning of reality that does not conform with those two. Thus, you need to know the key points establishing reality in all the texts of sutra and mantra. If you seek reality without relying on the twofold way of the great charioteers, you are like a blind person running through a treacherous area without a guide.[1264]

Thus, the emptinesses concocted by Tibetans—there is nothing whatsoever, things neither exist nor don't exist, open wakefulness is the view of emptiness, truly existent entities are extrinsically empty, and so forth—are not even close to the Vaibhāṣika, Sautrāntika, or Vijñaptimātra views, let alone the Madhyamaka view. If these are not even equal to the profound nonduality of the profound and the clear found in the lower-tantra classes, how could they ever be equal to the emptiness of [257] the union of bliss and emptiness found in highest yoga tantra? Since they are not equal, their proponents may claim to propound a system of meditation of the path of the generation and completion stages, but it is just a lifeless facsimile: it lacks the meditative path that establishes the imprints for the dharmakāya, and it separates method and wisdom. So not only will it be incapable of bringing about the stage of union, but it will also be incapable of weakening the root of samsara in the slightest.

Thus, the secret-mantra path of the Gedenpa is also distinctive in terms of view.

b) In terms of the two stages

Most others, not knowing the requirement that the fourth initiation[1265] introduce the inseparable union of the two truths,[1266] introduce only emptiness, and the emptiness merely involves doing the meditation of Heshang, which is thinking nothing whatsoever. Some, a little better than those, say they are introducing bliss and emptiness, but their standpoint on emptiness is like that just explained, so it is bliss and emptiness in name only.

With regard to the requirement that the generation stage come first so that the mind is ripened for the completion stage, some say that the generation stage was taught by the Conqueror to students of lesser intellect just for the attainment of common yogic achievements, and that those who desire the supreme yogic achievement must meditate on the completion stage from the outset; they say that the generation stage is not a cause of buddhahood.

Also, with regard to the completion stage, some say it is meditation only on the definitive meaning, and some say it is meditation on the union of deity yoga and the definitive meaning, and that meditation on the definitive meaning means placement of the mind without thinking anything. In short, thus, they do not assert as the cause of buddhahood anything other than Heshang's meditation.

Some also say that the completion stage is meditating like this on the meaning of the fourth initiation: when the inner fire is kindled at the navel cakra through fixing your meditation on the short *a* syllable, and by the power of that meditation, the white bodhicitta at the crown cakra melts and bliss arises, then when you look intently at the nature of that bliss and an empty, clear appearance dawns, you place the mind nonconceptually on the nature of that bliss—that is the completion-stage meditation of the inseparable bliss and emptiness.

Also, the *Hevajra Tantra* says about the time of the fourth initiation:

> This gnosis is very subtle
> And is, like the center of adamantine space,
> Dirt-free, complete, tranquil;
> You yourself are also the father of that.[1267] [258]

Reflecting on the meaning of this verse, some look up into space with their eyes after reciting those words, and when that space has expanded farther and farther, they think finally that the extent of space is the extent of mind—that, they say, is the nature of the fourth initiation. On the basis of that scriptural passage, they take empty, clear space to be the meaning of the ultimate nature, not understanding how to relate metaphor and meaning: just as space is the negation of obstruction, so in bliss-emptiness, emptiness is the negation of the projection of true existence. The meditative equipoise on empty, clear space becomes the source-concentration of infinite space of the first formless absorption, but it is nowhere near the profound completion stage taught in the tantras.[1268]

Some say that when the innate gnosis becomes manifest simply through your becoming accustomed to the mind's abiding in bliss, clarity, and nonconceptuality, then you awaken in this life. There is no awakening, however, without the achievement of a complete enjoyment body possessing the seven integrated factors and adorned with the major and minor marks. Achieving that in this life is impossible without a cause, and the cause must be of a similar type. In that regard, this impure body cannot be transformed into the enjoyment body, so you have to discard it. Knowing the antidote through which you discard it and, having discarded it, the way to achieve the enjoyment body—you have to have the fortune to practice those paths. If, however, you could awaken just by settling the mind in bliss, clarity, and nonconceptuality, without any basis for achieving a conqueror's body adorned by the major and minor marks, then you would awaken in the body of an ordinary person. You would be a buddha who is solely dharmakāya, without any of the major or minor marks, the enjoyment body, the emanation body, or other aspects of the form body.

Definitely attaining buddhahood in this very life is said to depend on whether you know how to achieve the illusory body. The identification of the illusory body does not come across clearly in the teachings of the system of Gö Lotsāwa Khukpa Lhetsé. Those adhering to the system of Marpa take *illusory* as appearances not inherently existing, and *body* as the divine body, and identify the *illusory body* as the divine body's not inherently existing as it appears. Jé Lama, on the other hand, clarified through extensive explanation how when the yogin who has established the basis for achieving the illusory body abides in isolated mind, with vajra recitation[1269] as the inner condition and [259] union with the consort as the outer condition, the isolated mind enters the stages of death exactly as wind and mind do during the stages of dissolution of earth, water, and the other elements, and transforms into the three empties;[1270] when you rise from the clear light of the final isolated mind of the reverse order, the immediately subsequent instance of the primordial wind that is the vehicle of that clear-light mind rises as the illusory body.[1271] Since even the duo of Marpa and Gö, who were top experts on Guhyasamāja, did not think of this, then needless to say, others claiming to be tantric yogins did not either. The essential subject matter of highest yoga tantra is twofold: innate gnosis and the illusory body; since Jé Lama alone really clarified those two according to the special instructions of the tantras and great adepts, and there is no clearer explanation than his, it is proven in this way that the Geden teaching tradition is also distinctive in terms of secret mantra.

Moreover, whatever the context—from the enumeration of tantric texts, to initiations, pledges, ritual service, the stages of activity of the mandala, and so forth—the Geden is distinctive in each, but I cannot take up every topic; you should learn about them through long acquaintance with the texts of father Jé and his spiritual sons.

c) In terms of interpreting the tantras

The cause for other Tibetans saying only mistaken things: The concealed key points of the two stages in the root tantras must be distinguished according to the intention of the great adepts who elucidated the meaning of the root texts through analyzing the explanatory tantras. Some Tibetans, not understanding that, treated the tantras and the texts of the great adepts as merely academic in value. Transmitting orally some essential points that they did not wish to publish, or putting them on tiny paper scrolls, they understood them as separate special hidden instructions, and when they integrated those instructions with the tantras and pure Indian texts, even if the points were contradictory, they fixated on the thought, "This is special instruction, so it is superior." For holding this, they should be criticized.

Also, when you do just a little explanation and practice based on a tiny bit of special instruction and do not study or reflect upon the entirety of the Dharma, nor practice the entirety of the path, you will be satisfied with some subtle sign, such as bodily heat, where the requisites are incomplete, and develop vivid pride, arrogantly believing you have obtained definite knowledge. For example, [260] the basic *Guhyasamāja Tantra* says:

> Kill living beings.
> Take what is not given.
> Speak lying words.
> Take another's wife.[1272]

For practitioners who have not reached the level where conduct is based on nonelaboration, that passage appears to endorse many sorts of wrongful conduct; they do not see how the explanatory tantras teach the meaning of "kill" to be dissolution into the central channel of the "life," or winds, abiding in the right and left channels; of "take" to be practice involving one's own innate wind and mind, even if it is "not given" by other buddhas;[1273] of "lies" to be the utterance and explanation of words that show dharmas to be illusion-like; and of "taking another's wife" to be meditation on emptiness.[1274] It is taught in many tantras that this misunderstanding yields inexhaustible negative results. Thus, Jé taught in the *Great Treatise on the Stages of Mantra:*

> Seeing the tantras and the great texts that comment on their meaning as merely academic in value and as a means for making a living through Dharma, you fixate on the thought, "An especially profound, unexplained separate instruction is concealed within them"; doing so, you show no interest in the ultimate Dharma nor develop great respect for the great mantra texts. This prevents the great texts from appearing as instruction and is a major condition for their rapid disappearance; spurn such an approach like poison. Rather, relying on the special instructions of the holy lama, strive in the method whereby the great texts arise as instruction. As stated in Nāgārjuna's *Five Stages:*
>
> > In the glorious *Guhyasamāja Tantra,*
> > These realities are concealed;
> > Following the explanatory tantras,
> > Try to realize them as taught by the guru.[1275]

Thus, in any situation related to the generation and completion stages and other aspects of tantra, even if you are dealing with straightforward texts of instruction coming from an uninterrupted lineage, do not reject any of the great texts out of partiality, and instead harmonize the root tantras, the explanatory tantras, and tantras with similar approaches, and combine those in a noncontradictory way with the authoritative texts of the great adepts that comment on those tantras. Establishing unmistakenly each topic—the nature of the paths, their number and order, the system through which realization arises based on practice, the way to prevent detours and clear away obstacles, the method for enhancing practice, and the system for achieving the result—and enlisting all textual systems as instruction: this should be understood as the special, unique Dharma [261] of this Geden philosophical system.

6) Further discussion

Moreover, of the many teachings that other philosophical systems have taken as the essence of their Dharma, this system lacks none of them: it includes all vinaya-vow lineages, explanations, and practices from those earlier traditions known as the vinaya of upper Tibet and the vinaya of lower Tibet;[1276] the Kadam-lineage stages of the path teachings from the noble lord Atiśa; the renowned teachings on mind training; and the explanatory tradition, transmitted from father Ngok Lotsāwa and his spiritual sons, on the great texts of abhidharma, the perfection of wisdom, Madhyamaka, valid cognition, and so forth. It also includes limitless profound teachings explaining the initiations and tantras related to the great mandalas of the four classes of tantra, guidelines for the generation and completion stages, and so forth, as exemplified in brief by: the Guhyasamāja lineage from Marpa, Gö Lotsāwa Khukpa Lhetsé, and others; the Kālacakra teachings transmitted from Ra Lotsāwa, Dro Lotsāwa, and Shong Lotsāwa; the Cakrasaṃvara and Hevajra teachings transmitted from father Sachen Künga Nyingpo and his spiritual sons; the Great Wheel Vajrapāṇi teachings transmitted from Lama Mar; the teachings on the Red, Black, and Vajrabhairava forms of Yamāntaka transmitted from Ra Lotsāwa, Kyo, and Shang;[1277] the essence of the Kagyü Dharma, the Mahāmudrā of bliss and emptiness; the six Dharmas of Nāropa and Niguma; and also the practices known as Chö, transformation,[1278] the taste of sameness, and so forth. The Gedenpas possess all of those, as many as there are, lacking none, taking them as profound special instructions. Those teachings that had, in the interval, been covered with the faults of not being understood or being wrongly understood, father Jé and his spiritual sons purified, as gold is purified by burning, cutting, and rubbing, so Geden alone is distinctive in what it offers.

The Geluk possesses, flawlessly and perfectly for anyone whenever they wish, instructions for practicing the four activities—peaceful, increasing, empowering, and wrathful—that occur in stainless tantras, were transmitted from those holy beings who were adepts, and are not polluted by Bön, extremism, or other debased traditions. Thus, there is no situation where it is necessary to rely on another system for lack of the requisites for the four activities. [262]

Moreover, the conventional sciences of grammar, logic, art, medicine, poetry, mathematics, and so forth also are widespread among the Gedenpa. Thus, this matchless precious teaching of Ganden Mountain should be known as the great Dharma ocean that incorporates every river of the profound and extensive sutra and mantra that issue from the snowy mountain of the mighty Muni.

Now, when I explain why the Geluk philosophical system is distinctive, someone may mistakenly think, "If what you say is true, then other Tibetan philosophical systems cannot lead you to liberation and omniscience." Our response is that many problems ensue from such a misconception: explaining the Prāsaṅgika view as superior would mean the Svātantrika and lower schools had no liberating paths; explaining highest yoga tantra as the summit of all the vehicles would mean the lower tantras had no method for achieving enlightenment; and so forth. Thus, of the various philosophical systems that arose in Tibet, the Jonang view involves the worst wrong view, being utterly irredeemable, and it is hard to admire faulty formulations like those of Taktsang Lotsāwa and Shākya Chokden. Apart from these, however, there does not appear to be even a single system fit for consistent denigration, so those who desire their own welfare[1279] should see all of them as pervaded by pure appearance. That, I think, is the root of one's own benefit.[1280]

d. How others trying to refute Jé Tsongkhapa's system could not find any faults

It does not seem necessary to discuss the fourth outline topic mentioned above. If I were to write about it here, this section would be too bloated. I will write about it separately in the future if the occasion arises.

Concluding verses

All dharmas—the mass of names that dissolve into the ultimate sphere,
Everything, written with the brush of analysis, that is to be known in the three times—
All objects are comprehended instantly, without confusion, in his *excellent mind (losang)*. This melody of his *renown (drakpa)*
Is raised by all the conquerors, a song of praise to the omniscient Tsongkhapa.

Even though the merits of countless beings can barely carve even a drop of a syllable

From [263] the deep expanse of space pervaded completely by the amassed clouds of Jé's wisdom and love,
The great nectar rain of the profound and extensive holy Dharma is yielded without effort and swirls into a single ocean;
The Geden tradition is famed in this world as an ocean of precious qualities.

This ocean, because its nature is pure morality,
Is free from pollution by the corpses of faults and downfalls;
Pure concentration is undisturbed in its profoundest depths,
So the stars of experiential realization shine, and everything easily appears.
The swelling series of wisdom waves
Sprays the droplets of the Madhyamaka of profound meaning.

This teaching with nectar-like qualities
Grants the glory of deathlessness to all the fortunate;
But since the profound definitive meaning is obscure,
And it is hard to measure the extent of scripture and reasoning so vast,
This teaching frightens the mass of ignorant fools
Whose potential for the Mahayana family is not ripe.
For the unfortunate who rest at the bottom
Of the well of partiality, there is no progress.

The sweet renown of the upright is pervasive,
Like the sound of millions of dragons thundering forth.
In the treasury of the precious profound meaning,
The merit they possess blazes like the crown jewel of a nāga;
And for the fortunate, whose discernment is as lofty as a nāga's crest,
Those millions are like mighty nāga kings cavorting in their supreme abode.

E ma! If even the Conqueror's children would exhaust
Their intellects in trying to express as they are
All the wonders of this teaching, then what's the value
When one such as I expresses just a portion of it?

Nevertheless, saying: "In all my successive lives,
May I not be separated from this excellent system,"
Drawn on by attachment to my own goals,
I wrote this as a banquet for the ears of the wise.

From *The Crystal Mirror: An Excellent Explanation Showing the Sources and Assertions of All Philosophical Systems,* this completes the explanation of the history of the Geden philosophical system. [264]

C. The supplementary topic of the history of sutra, mantra, and the sciences[1281]

When it comes to the supplementary topic of the history of how sutra, mantra, and the sciences—that is, vinaya, Madhyamaka, valid cognition, and study of the *Thorough Exposition of Valid Cognition* on the sutra side,[1282] the initiations, explanations, and special instructions of the four classes of tantras on the mantra side, and the conventional sciences—first originated and then spread in India and Tibet, were I to extensively discuss the ultimate implications of the presentation of the express meaning of each, it would be an excellent explanation pleasing to the wise, but fearing prolixity, I must content myself with merely listing them.

13. The Bön Tradition[1283]

[*II. The History of the Philosophical Systems in Tibet, Land of Snows*]

D. The history of the way of Bön[1284]

I will relate the origins of the philosophical system known as Bön,
The pre-dawn messenger,
The Shen system, which opened the way
For the rising sun of the holy Dharma in the dark land of Tibet.

1. History of the Bön philosophical system

I WILL EXPLAIN the history of Bön briefly as an aside. A Bön text says, "During this eon, it is said, as the lifespan decreases from limitless to ten years, eighteen teachers will appear, from Tsomchok Künsang to Thangma Medrön. Among them, appearing at a time when the lifespan is one hundred, will be Shenrap, the teacher of present-day Bön. The one called Shenrap Miwoché[1285] appeared in Ölmo Lungring in the land of Shangshung.[1286] Some say that he was an emanation of the Buddha, while others say that our teacher appeared at the same time as the Buddha."[1287] This passage occurs in the *White Beryl:*

Intending to subdue Bön in the land of Shangshung,
The Buddha manifested as Shenrap Miwo:
He practiced the twelve deeds of Bön;
He taught the nine-vehicle stages;
He opened the divine door for the living;
He blocked the tomb door for the dead;[1288]
He laid out the swastika path for beings.[1289]

In any case, it is known that Shenrap, possessing supernormal powers, miraculous abilities, and other powers, went to many places in Tibet where he bound to oaths and subdued many worldly gods and *nyen* demons: the place called Önda Serkhang Tsé, which is now [265] Ngari Monastery; Rinchen Pung Mountain; Bön Mountain, which is to the east of the Kongyül Buchu temple; and others. He explained the *swastika Dharma heap,* which refers to the four doors, with the treasury as fifth,[1290] and so forth. He had many followers: his heir, Mutso Demdruk; the Tazik sage Mutsa Trahé Sé; Trithok Bartsam;[1291] Gu Hili Parma;[1292] the Indian sage Lhadak Ngakdro; the Chinese sage Lektang Mangpa; the Throm sage Serngok Chejam; the Tibetan sage Demgyin Tsamé Gé; the Minyak[1293] sage Chetsa Gargu; the Sumpa sage Mupung Sangtang; the Shangshung sage Shir[1294] Buchen; and others. They propagated the Bön Dharma in every direction and made it widespread.

2. History of individual Bön traditions

The Bön that spread in Tibet is threefold: a. emergent Bön, b. deviant Bön, and c. transformed Bön.[1295]

a. Emergent Bön

During the time of Tridé Tsenpo, who was sixth in the royal line stemming from Nyatri Tsenpo,[1296] a thirteen-year-old boy from a family of priests[1297] in what was called Amshö Ön,[1298] in Ü, was abducted by *dré* demons and carried all over central Tibet and Kham for thirteen years. When he was twenty-six, he was put back among humans; since he had superhuman powers, he had knowledge of various things, and would state: "In thus and such a place, there is thus and such a god or *dré* demon, who does thus and such benefit or harm; make prayers and offerings to it, and when you have performed the rite of effigy offering, it will help."[1299] The royal chronicles do not give any explanation other than to say that the government was administered by Bönpos through twenty-six generations of kings, from Nyatri Tsenpo to Trithok Jetsen, but it is evident that the initial spread of Bön in Tibet began from the sixth ruler, Tridé Tsenpo. However, in the Bön of that time, which was just threefold—with subjugation of *dré* demons and *sri* demons[1300] below, offerings to ancestral gods above, and home-hearth exorcisms[1301] in between, [266]—there was no terminology such as "the view of the Bön system," and so forth, so some Dharma histories and royal chronicles explain that the spread of Bön dates from Drigum Tsenpo. The tradition prior to Drigum Tsenpo is also known as *blackwater causal Bön.*

b. Deviant Bön

Deviant Bön: The Tibetan Bönpos[1302] did not know how to perform the knife funeral[1303] for King Drigum Tsenpo.[1304] They summoned three Bönpos to the knife funeral from three places, Kashmir, Gilgit, and Shangshung. One, by worshipping Gegö Garuda[1305] and the fire god, showed himself able to fly through the sky on his drum, draw out blood, cut iron with a bird's feather, and so forth. Another practiced divination through thread-reading,[1306] oracular speech, scapulamancy, and so forth, and thereby determined what was good and bad. The other knew the particulars of funerals, such as handling the dead, controlling the knife, and so forth. Until those three arrived, there was no saying that "This is the Bön view." From then on, a Bön view took hold.[1307] It is said that the philosophical system of the extremist theists[1308] became mixed with deviant Bön.

c. Transformed Bön

Transformed Bön is threefold.

The first transformation: It is said that in India a blue-robed pandit buried some distorted Dharmas as treasure then revealed them himself and mixed then with Bön.[1309]

Second, the middle transformation: It is said that during the time of Trisong Detsen, it was decreed that Bönpos had to be inducted into the Dharma. A Bönpo named Gyalwai Jangchup was made to listen to the Dharma by Rinchen Chok. He did not accept it, and angered by the king's chastisement, he cast his lot with Bön and transformed some Buddhist scriptures into Bön scriptures. When the king heard of this, he ordered the beheading of those who transformed the scriptures of the Tathāgata. Many were beheaded, so the frightened Bönpos hid their transformed texts, along with others, as treasures, and when the texts were later taken out of hiding, they claimed these were Bön treasures. [267]

Third, the final transformation: After the Buddhist teaching was suppressed by Langdarma, at a Bön holy place in Ü called Daryül Drolak, a man from Nyangtö in Tsang named Shengur Luga[1310] transformed many Buddhist scriptures into Bön texts. He called the *Perfection of Wisdom in a Hundred Thousand Verses* the *Big Piece,* the *Perfection of Wisdom in Twenty-Five Thousand Verses* the *Little Piece,* the *Establishment in Perpetuity*[1311] the *Bön Sutra,* and the *Five Classes of Dhāraṇīs* the *Black and White Hundred Thousand*

Nāga Verses.[1312] He did so by altering various Dharma terms and topics. He hid the texts as treasures under a rock at Tsonga Dreuchung. Later, he himself took them out, pretending he had discovered them.[1313] After that, Khyungpo Bönshik[1314] and others transformed many texts along similar lines.

Those three transformed Böns—early, later, and middle—were called *whitewater Bön* and given the name *resultant Bön.*

3. The Bönpo Dharma system

The Bön Dharma has a rough equivalent to the Kangyur.[1315]

Texts showing the view are:[1316] the *Golden Rosary of the Precious Completion,* the root text and commentary of the *Razor-Wind,* the *Clear-Light Wheel of Instruction,* and others.

Texts on meditation are: the *Cycle of Nine Drops Self-Transforming the Aggregates,* the *Drop of Gold,* the *Inner Experience of Body and Mind,* the *White Primordial Throne Scripture of Mind,* and others.

Texts about conduct are: *A Hundred Thousand*[1317] *Verses for Establishing the Eight Elements, A Hundred Thousand Verses on the Systematized Meaning of Primordial Shen, A Hundred Thousand Verses on the Ten-Stage Path of the Swastika, A Hundred Thousand Verses on the Pure Vinaya Morality, A Hundred Thousand Verses on Completing the Great Collection of Extensive Virtue,* as well as the *Black Hundred Thousand Verses on Sickness,* the *Variegated Hundred Thousand Verses on Lifespan,* the *White Hundred Thousand Verses on Medicine,* the *Black Hundred Thousand Verses on Apotropaic Ritual,* and others.[1318]

Texts about deeds are:[1319] *360 Apotropaic Methods, 84,000 Methods of Diagnosis,* the *Four Chanting Meditations, Eight Lamentations, 360 Funeral Methods,*[1320] *Eighty-One Methods of Subjugation,* and others.

These are called the Bön of the blackwater tantras of existence.

Texts about the generation stage, completion stage, and result are: the *General Heap of Bön Treasure,* the collection of the nine wrathful father tantras, the *Rising of the Nine Suns of Mother Tantras,* the *Expanse of the Great Sutra of Wrathful Tantras,* and others. These are called the Bön of whitewater mantra.

In relation to guardian deities there are: practices related to the great and small Rasp of Life,[1321] the web of the Red and Black Razors,[1322] and the slow-spreading blood of the Mother Demoness,[1323] and others; practice cycles related to messenger demons, royal demons,[1324] *tsen* demons, *mu* demons,[1325] nāgas, planetary deities, Īśvara, [268] and so forth; the cycle on the nine wheels of animals; the cycle on harmful rites;[1326] the cycle on the cry of the running wolf corpse,[1327] and so forth.

These texts contain scattered references to impermanence; karma and its result; love, compassion, and the awakening mind; the six perfections; and so forth; and also presentations of the five paths, the ten stages, the three bodies, and so forth. There also are equivalents to Buddhist discussions of initiation, the generation stage, the completion stage, pledges and vows, consecration, burnt offerings, practices and offerings related to mandalas, death rites, and so forth, and also many minor activities.[1328] Their mode of explanation may conform with the Dharma or disagree, as the case may be. They use such terms as: *primordial shen* for the Buddha, *Bön body* for the dharmakāya, Satri Esang[1329] for the great wisdom mother, Samantabhadra for the enjoyment body, *purifier*[1330] *of becoming* for the emanation body, *son of a shen* for arhat, *swastika being* for bodhisattva, *divine guide* for lama, *amenyi*[1331] for emptiness, and for the ten stages, *the stage of stainless crystal, the stage of the cloud mass of a tantric master emitting light rays, the stage of the transformed seal,* and so forth.[1332] So it seems that in many cases, their symbols and terms were imitations.

4. The Bön standpoint on view, meditation, and other aspects of the path

a. View

In general, Bön is known to be twofold: outsider Bön and insider Bön. Some Bön texts say, among other things:

> Primordially, there was empty nonexistence;
> Then, primordial existents barely came to be;
> Then just a whitish hoarfrost came to be;
> And then just dripping dew drops came to be.[1333]

Drigung Jikten Gönpo states:

> Ultimately, there appears to be a system in which the world and its inhabitants arose from an egg, and a system in which they were made by fate, Īśvara, and so forth; they were deviant, extremist views.[1334]

Nowadays, many phrases like those above also appear in texts on healing rituals that are common everywhere.[1335]

Chenga Lodrö Gyaltsen taught:

> It says in the Bön text called the *Precious Collection Tantra:*[1336]
>
> > Conventionally, entities exist because of clinging.[1337] They do not exist ultimately, when attachment has been abandoned. Both perspectives are just partial perspectives of the mind, and when mind is without attachment and without movement, that is called the *gnosis of emptiness*. When that gnosis is nonconceptual, all-pervasive, clear, and vivid,[1338] it is itself [269] the object of meditation. When you conduct yourself thus in uniting both view and meditation, you will definitely attain the fruit of liberation in this birth.
>
> Their way of explaining this and other statements is similar to the explanations and meanings found in Buddhist scriptures and treatises.[1339]

Apparently, too, the all-knowing Sherap Ö[1340] and Taktsang Lotsāwa[1341] also taught that the nine vehicles of Bön are similar to those of the Dzokchen of Nyingma.

I saw the following in a Bön text:

> The basic, naturally pure ultimate nature: In the past, prior to either buddhas or sentient beings, there existed the clear-light, empty Bön body, whose essence is naturally pure, unclothed by predispositions or obstacles; it is nothing at all, yet it is luminous. Primordially abiding in the nature of buddha, it is not accomplished through causal activities, and is independent of productive conditions; it is effortless, spontaneous, and self-existent. It does not improve with realization, nor worsen with nonrealization, and because it exists in buddha and sentient beings, there is no better or worse in either of them. All-pervasive, thoroughly diffused, it is the basic ultimate nature. From it, all things in samsara and nirvana spontaneously occur, and all dharmas abide in its nature. Its creativity operates ceaselessly. When it is realized, it

appears as gnosis; when it is not realized, it appears as karma and the delusions. When, its meaning ascertained, it becomes manifest, it is the realization of the ultimate nature of the abiding basis. When you realize it, it appears on its own in your mind. After it arises, you attain the manifest result, the three bodies. The essence of that ultimate nature, unobstructed, shines plainly and vividly, knowledge appearing as gnosis: plain, uncovered by conceptual thought, analysis, movement, or effort. At that time, the blankness of nonrecollection, the movement without fixed reference, plain nonconceptuality, wakeful nonapprehension: that is called the *self-arisen gnosis of awareness,* and plainly viewing *that* is called the view.

b. Meditation

In the center of the divine palace of the precious essential mind, abiding on the eight petals of the veins, are the five elemental essences. In the center of that are the five gnoses, like a ball of rolled-up colored threads. In the center of that is a sphere of light, which is the Bön body. That has an empty nature, so it does not go to the extreme of permanence, and it is cognitive and clear, so it does not go to the extreme of annihilation. There is nothing to be taken as a meditative object in any way. The Bön body's creativity, sound, and clear light unimpededly appear as the three doors, the six types of sensory equipment, and the six types of object. When, with view and viewer [270] nondual, the nature of that is plainly viewed, and you place your mind on that limpid appearance without movement or separation from it, that is called meditation.

When you divide it, it is threefold: sessional meditation, natural meditation, and expanse meditation.

(1) Sessional meditation: Having identified the Bön body and determined the number of recitations and the number of sessions, you meditate. At first, you abide on the object a little; in the middle, you abide and do not abide in equal measure; at the end, you enter entirely into concentration. Thus, if you settle on the object, it stays; if you release it, it goes; if you hold it, it is held; if it arrives when needed, you have fulfilled the criteria of sessional meditation.

> (2) Natural meditation: Once you have the experience of the self-liberation of appearances, there is no collection or separation in your concentration, so when you abide on the object meditationless and unmoving, you have fulfilled the criteria of natural meditation.
>
> (3) Expanse meditation: When you meditate on that awareness in that way, the goal is manifest: you transcend meditated and meditator, apprehend things as if they were of the nature of space, and transcend conceptual thought and intellect. At that time, all the delusions appear as gnosis, and all appearances are realized as the pure sphere of Bön. After samsara and nirvana, good and bad, and rejection and acceptance have become inseparably of a single taste, the Bön body remains in its own state, so you have reached the terminus of expanse meditation.[1342]

These views and meditations are in conformity with the system articulated by the later Dzokchen practitioners, so it seems that the two, Bön and Dzokchen, are intimately related.

5. *The organization of Bön*

It is said that Bön texts are organized in terms of nine vehicles.[1343] The nine are: The four causal vehicles, those of (1) the shen of prediction, (2) the shen of appearance, (3) the shen of magic, and (4) the shen of existence; the four resultant vehicles, those of (5) the layperson, (7) the white *a*,[1344] (6) the seer, and (8) the primordial shen; with one more, (9) the especially great vehicle, that makes nine.[1345]

It is said that (1) the shen of prediction has 360 types of divination rituals and 84,000 types of medical diagnoses, (2) the shen of appearance has four chanting meditations,[1346] eight lamentations, and forty-two types of pledge, (3) the shen of magic has texts on magical powers for purifying view,[1347] (4) the shen of existence has 360 death rites,[1348] four doors of subjugation, and eighty-one methods for subduing demons, (5) the layperson has the sutra-class texts on the arising and maturation of the world and its inhabitants, and so forth, (6) the seer[1349] has four classes of hundred thousands,[1350] (7) the white *a* has many tantric scriptures, (8) the primordial shen has four classes of scriptures on mind, and (9) the especially great vehicle has five classes of special instruction.[1351]

The four causal Bön vehicles (1–4) abandon the four parts of conceptual thought related to apprehended and apprehender.[1352] The layperson and seer vehicles (5–6) purify the delusion obstacles, while the white *a* and primordial-shen vehicles (7–8) purify the knowledge obstacles. The especially great vehicle (9) eradicates the innate impurity. Also, [271] by training for many eons in the four vehicles of causal Bön, you attain the four stages of devoted conduct.[1353] Traversing the path of the layperson and the seer for three countless eons, you attain liberation. By means of the white *a* and primordial shen, you attain liberation in a single lifetime. By means of the especially great, you attain the Bön body in a single life.[1354] Thus is it explained.

I have not found texts that explained the spread or standpoint of Bön in detail, so I have written on Bön's history in Tibet in the early, late, and middle periods as stated in the *Single Intention of Drigung*.[1355] I have written on the Bön standpoint on view, meditation, the vehicles, and so forth, according to its treatment in what is called the *Ornament of Sunlight in the Breach in the Citadel of Secret Mantra*,[1356] a summary of the 84,000 portals of Bön composed when countless tantric masters and scholars from Taksik,[1357] India, China, Tibet, and other lands had gathered in the secret Bön cave of Yülmang Khar.

6. Bön monasteries

Monasteries that existed in Tibet, such as Shendar Ding, Yungdrung Lhading in Gyalmo Rong, and others were destroyed later by the Chinese imperial army, and the Geluk monastery called Ganden[1358] was newly established at Lhading. Even though a mild edict forbidding the Bön system was proclaimed, it seems that nowadays quite a few Bön centers still exist in Gyalmo Rong, Tsakho, and other places.[1359]

Concluding verses[1360]

Dharma and Bön are considered contradictory, but
Dharma has Bön mixed in, and Bön has Dharma mixed in,
So one such as I, lacking the dustless eye of Dharma,
Is wary of trying to make distinctions between Dharma and Bön.

You denigrate Bön, but when you reach a crisis,
You ask a Bönpo with his divining cords what to do and not to do;

You enjoy Bön-style chanting and collect ritual materials,
And everyone hopes to be helped by Bön devices.

When you think about it, in this lifetime
What leisure is there to do elaborate things like these?
Now, when you have some leisure, attained just once,
Who would not constantly cultivate contemplation?

If you do only a few deeds, then act on the holy Dharma;
If you utter only a few utterances, then utter the talk of Dharma;
If you think only a few thoughts, then ponder karma and its results;
If you go to only a few destinations, then go to solitary places.

This account is neither Dharmic nor worldly;
It is neither useful nor [272] useless;
It is neither extensive nor condensed;
What I have related is neither clear nor unclear.

From *The Crystal Mirror: An Excellent Explanation Showing the Sources and Assertions of All Philosophical Systems,* this completes the explanation the history of the Bön philosophical system. [273]

14. Chinese Traditions 1: Non-Buddhist[1361]

III. The History of Sciences and Philosophical Systems in the Land of Great China

I shall relate how, in due order, from out of the broad path
Of the cosmic wind of the Conqueror's deeds,
The sun, moon, and stars of Dharma, Bön, and Veda appeared[1362]
In the sky-like vastness of the great land of Mahācīna.[1363]

The third basic outline topic is the history of the philosophical systems in China. This great country, China, is called Shenzhou in the native language and is known far and wide as "the sacred continent." There are also those who identify Shenzhou[1364] with the continent of Videha.[1365] The Indians call it Mahācīna. *Mahā* means "great" and *cīna* is a corruption of the Chinese Qin. Among the Chinese kings, there was, during the Qin dynasty, a mighty and powerful king named Shihuang (255–210 B.C.E.) who conquered many countries on the frontiers and in the central regions. On account of this the people of the frontier applied the name of his kingdom to the larger country, calling it "the realm of Qin." Apparently, the pronunciation of Qin gradually became corrupted, so that it came to be pronounced as "Cīna." The Tibetans call it Gyanak, because the Chinese people mostly wear black-colored *(nag)* clothes, and they call the Holy Land Gyagar, because the people of the Middle Country mostly wear white *(dkar)* cotton cloth. However, when writing it, Tibetans do not write *rgya dkar* but *rgya gar,* because in the vernacular it is customary to read *dkar po* as *gar po*. Some scholars offer other etymologies, but these are just figments of their own imagination.

How various traditions arose among the philosophical systems in this great country: A reliable Chinese history[1366] explains it thus:

> Although a number of miscellaneous minor traditions appeared in this land, they were of short duration; there are, however, three great traditions that clarify the ultimate nature of things: Ru,[1367]

> Dao, and Jing.[1368] Of those, the first is like a star, the second is like the moon, and the third is like the sun.

Here, accordingly, I shall explain A. The histories of the first two traditions, B. The histories of some miscellaneous traditions, and C. [274] The history of the Buddhist tradition.

A. The histories of the first two traditions

1. The history of the tradition known as the "star-like Ru"

The history of the tradition known as the "star-like Ru": Although *ru* is a term for letters and means "the way of letters," the master Anu[1369] says:

> I shall explain the joining of letters
> Because it is the basis of all Buddhist instruction,
> The ground for reciters of the Veda,
> And the basis of all names, words, and expressions.[1370]

In conformity with this statement, this tradition is not merely a system for reading and writing letters but also includes many other subjects—various sciences, the principles of worldly conduct, and so forth.[1371] Thus, if one translates the sense of *ru,* it means "a book of instruction" or "means for conveying knowledge."[1372]

a. The history of Ru

The first of all the kings of China, Fu Xi,[1373] was capable of founding on his own the sciences and the principle of distinguishing between what should be adopted and what should be rejected. He bestowed these upon his wise minister, Cang Jie, who was the first to invent Chinese letters, which he established in terms of six types: pictograph, simple ideograph, compound ideograph, phonetic compound, mutual explanatories, and phonetic loans.[1374] He also introduced the practice of writing with a lacquer stylus on a bamboo slate. The letters of that time were round in shape and called *zhuanzi* (seal characters). Later on, Li Si, the minister of the King Qin Shihuang, set to work with the idea of facilitating writing, and invented the letters known as *lizi* (clerical style). General Meng Tianyong made a brush from the tail of a hare and ink from pine soot, and wrote on silk cloth. Again, in later times, the eunuch Cai Lun (first–second century C.E.) invented paper. Then, the "regular style" of writing called *zheng kai* and the "running script"[1375] called *caozi* (cursive characters) gradually appeared. Because of their convenience, [275] they gradually spread and writing became an exceedingly easy matter, but for the most part, the *caozi* conflicted with the six original types. Because of the spread of many treatises that were specious, meaningless, and mistaken, the contributions of Li Si and Meng Tian, while immediately useful, were in the end recognized as highly inadequate. This is the account found in impartial sources of later times.[1376]

The origin of the treatises: The first king, Fu Xi, composed a text on the *bagua* (eight trigrams) called *Lianshan;* it was the first of the great texts to appear, and it became the principal treatise on the subject. He also composed a work entitled *Neijing* on the inner principle for clearly knowing the ways things are in reality.[1377] Then there appeared what are known today as the *wujing,* or "five classics": the *Yijing (Classic of Changes),* the *Shijing (Classic of Odes),* the *Shujing (Classic of Records),* the *Lijing (Classic of Rites)*, and the *Chun Qiu (Spring and Autumn Annals)*. The *Yijing* was written by the aforementioned Fu Xi; the authors of the remaining four have not been determined. These five texts are the basis for the Ru tradition. However, the five texts themselves are not called[1378] *Ru* but are referred to as *Jing* (classics). The actual Ru consists of those five texts along with their annotations and supplementary literature.

The founding teacher is known as Kongfuzi (Confucius) or Kongzi (551–479 B.C.E.). The Tibetans do not pronounce his name as it is in Chinese but call him Kongtse.[1379] He was born in the country of Shandong, one of the thirteen great provinces of China, toward the end of the dynasty known as Zhou Wang during the time of Zhou Jing Wang, not many years after Buddha's appearance in the world. Accounts and biographies of him are well known throughout China, and he was regarded as an especially eminent person. The systematic treatises composed by him are the authoritative basis for contemporary Chinese law and for the code of conduct for the three types of persons: the powerful, the weak, and the middling. From his time down to the present, despite many changes of government, it is the system of Kongzi alone that has been regarded as preeminent. Even the royal custom of honoring Kongzi's portrait and his title of National Preceptor has continued down to the present. From earlier times down to the present, the lineal descendent of Kongzi has been granted the hereditary title of *gong* (duke), and it is said that the *gong* of the present day is the [276] seventy-third lineal descendent of Kongzi. The

Tibetans call Kongzi "miraculous king" and believe him to have been a king possessed of magical powers. In some Chinese divinatory rituals, the principles of meditating on Kongzi's higher realization, and so forth, are presented. Some other texts call him "Kongzi the craftsman," as he was understood to be skilled in craftsmanship. All of this seems to me just groping in the dark.[1380]

Now, Confucius was the illuminator of the Ru tradition, but he wrote only a few of its basic verse texts; his disciples and grand-disciples commented extensively upon them in what are known as the *sishu,* or "four textbooks." All Chinese scholars first study these later writings and make them the basis of their education. The four textbooks are the *Daxue (Great Learning),* the *Zhongyong (Doctrine of the Mean),* the *Lunyu (Analects),* and the *Mengzi (Book of Mencius).* The first of them, the *Daxue,* is a small text by Kongzi that was added to by Zengzi, who put a series of questions to Kongzi. The *Zhongyong* was written by Zi Si. The *Lunyu* was edited by Zi Lu, Zi Chang, and Zi Xia. The *Mengzi* takes its title from the name of its author. These authors were either pupils of Kongzi or pupils of the pupils. Beginning with the establishment of the Zhou dynasty, the number of treatises greatly increased. We also know that both earlier and later on, hundreds of teachers who explained the sciences and composed many miscellaneous instructional texts that were added to those earlier texts as appendixes and amplifications.

The tradition of legal writings regulating governmental administration: During Han rule, there was a learned master named Xiao He, who expanded upon the teaching of Kongzi, and so illuminated the Ru way. Later, a scholar named Zhu Xi (1130–1200),[1381] who had studied many religious systems, composed numerous treatises that many have regarded as authoritative down to the present day.

Also, both in earlier and later times, there appeared a great many books called *gangjian* (annals), which are authoritative historical works resembling what [277] are called in Tibet *depther.*

b. Confucian divination

Of the many sciences that emerged from this way called Ru, the first to appear concerned divination.[1382] This is because divination is the principal subject matter of the *Yijing,* the first of the aforementioned *wujing.* Because *yi* has the sense of "exchange" and "change," when Chinese divination was translated into Tibetan during the Tang dynasty, it was called *Spor thang (Thang Changes).*[1383]

1) The earlier and later heavenly systems

Its history: As already explained above, the first kings to appear in the land of China were the three Huang and then the five Di.[1384] At the time of the first Huang monarch, King Fu Xi, there emerged from the great Huang He (Yellow River) in the province now called Henan, a dragon-horse, with a mid-section like a horse and a head and tail like a dragon. On its back were the *bagua* or eight designs (trigrams), which, in Tibetan, owing to mispronunciation, are called *parkha.* Seeing them, Fu Xi created the *bagua* emblems. He expanded the eight *bagua* to sixty-four [hexagrams] by combining the eight trigrams with each other and explained them in a text he composed called *Lianshan,* which emphasizes *gen,* the image for which is a mountain.[1385] The designs on the back of the dragon-horse were called *Hetu* (river chart) because *tu* means "design" or "pattern," and *he* is the name of the river, that is, the place from which the dragon-horse emerged. The system of the *bagua* explained by Fu Xi is called the Early Heavenly System. Subsequently, Shen Nong composed a work on the *Spor thang* called *Guizang yi,* which emphasizes the trigram *kun,* the image for which is earth. It is also said that an eagle brought this book from the mountain called Xianyuan, and while there is a text that says, "It was written based on a book in the eagle language," its account is not credible.

The third Huang king, Yi Xuan Shi (Yellow Emperor), having meticulously observed the planets and stars, and methodically divided the five elements into male and female, then arranged time into years, months, and days and subsumed them under the ten roots and the twelve branches[1386] of rat, ox, and the other animals. As a means to teach this practically, he constructed a useful device in the form of a globe called a *huntianyi* (armillary sphere). He also designed charts in order to make the revolutions of the planets and stars easy to understand. The *zimingzhong* (chiming clocks), *biao* (watches), and so forth of the present day are similar kinds of things. Moreover, he was the first to build chariots, boats, and [278] forts, and to construct musical instruments, such as the twelve *lülü* (pitch pipes), weapons of various kinds, and so forth. Even the various types of common bodily adornments apparently originated with him.[1387]

The later heavenly system:

> In the wood-dragon year, the first heavenly year of the fourth of the five Di kings, Yao Tao Tang Shi[1388] (third millennium B.C.E.?),

> a southern commoner named Yue Shang Shi found a wonderful tortoise, which he presented to the king. Looking at it, the king saw that on the tortoise's back was an extensive diagram of the divisions of time. Fully comprehending it, he greatly clarified the subject of divination. From the wood-dragon year down to the fire-dragon year of the twelfth sexegenary cycle when King Qianlong (1711–99) ascended the throne (1737), 4092 years have elapsed.[1389]

Again, according to other authorities:

> Although there are stories that a commoner presented a wonderful tortoise to King Yao, there is nothing to the effect that he did anything like utilizing the marks on its shell. Later on, King Yu of Xia wrote a work on divination based on the *bagua* designs found on the back of an extraordinary miraculous tortoise, the *shengui,* which came from the Luo River in the area of Henan. He called his work *Luotu (Luo Chart), tu* meaning "pattern," and *luo,* the aforementioned place of origin.

In any case, the difference between the earlier and later heavenly systems evidently refers to the time prior to the division of heaven and earth in the case of the former and the time after their division in the case of the latter. Thus, it is believed that the very nature of the *bagua* is eternally and inherently unchangeable.

The histories merely state that elemental divination was created based on the designs found on the back of a tortoise. The story of the tortoise being the creator of all things is unknown to Chinese literature or authoritative traditions, so Tibetan writers on Chinese divination who say, basing themselves on those accounts, that the "great golden tortoise" is the eternal, self-originated creator are arrogantly propagating a fiction. Having pointed that out, there are also many false accounts of the origin of the *bagua*, the twelve-year cycles, and so forth, but I shall write no more, as it is inopportune to do so. [279]

2) Further developments

Wen Wang (1148–1051 B.C.E.?), the father of the first king of the Zhou dynasty, was an especially eminent person. Accepting the early heavenly system as conceived by Fu Xi, he expanded the eight *bagua* of the later heavenly system into sixty-four (hexagrams) by combining the eight trigrams with each other, and he composed an explanatory text on the *Spor thang* called the *Zhou yi,* which emphasizes the hexagram *qian,* the image of which is heaven.[1390] These three texts—the earlier *Lianshan* and *Guizang yi* along with this one—are widely renowned as "the three texts on the *Spor thang.*"

After the rule of the Zhou clan came to an end, a violent and ignorant king of the Qin dynasty conceived the idea that divination was a threat to the kingdom because by means of it one could know things that were secret, and he instituted a system of forcibly collecting all the texts, which he then had burned. The first two treatises disappeared, and only the text of Wen Wang remained, so all later works follow it.[1391]

Wen Wang's son, Zhou Gong, composed a text that clearly elucidated his father's thought. Although it is known that later on even Kongfuzi elucidated the thought of his predecessors very clearly, there appears to be some doubt as to whether the actual text composed by Kongzi on the *Spor thang* is extant. It is said that during the period of the Zhou dynasty, several men of discernment wrote quite a number of miscellaneous texts based on the text of Zhou Gong, and that some disciples of Kongzi compiled them into what is called the *Shijing (Classic of Yarrow Stalk Divination);* I think that is why the *Shijing* is attributed to him. Chinese scholars of later times call Fu Xi, Wen Wang, Zhou Gong, and Kongzi the *four great men.* Those whom the Tibetans call the *four receivers* are probably those four. However, owing to orthographic errors or mispronunciation, they write Gong Zi for Kongzi, Ji Gong for Zhou Gong, Ji Nong for Shen Nong, and Wang Tai for Wen Wang.

Although the history of divinatory science in the land of China has just now been explained, the Tibetans of old nevertheless propagated various threads of false information, for example, "Divination originally was taught in China at Five Peaks (Wutai Shan) by Mañjughoṣa," or "It emerged from the crown of the head of the goddess Vijayā," or "It was taught [280] by Master Padmasambhava." What's more, the divination texts of reputed Chinese origin that spread in Tibet are unknown in China, not even their titles, so that one has to consider whether they might actually have been written by Tibetans.[1392] In general, one cannot prove that those four great men were emanations of Mañjughoṣa—not even the merest fragments of such stories are known in China, nor do we read that those four men were prophesied by the Buddha. But I think it can be accepted on the basis of the circumstantial evidence and unanimity of opinion.

c. Other Confucian sciences

The history of medicine: The second of the three original Huang kings, Yan Di Shen Nong Shi, wrote the first treatise on medicine. The diagnosis of illness based on the pulse and the method of understanding the fluctuations of the five elements are distinctive features of his work not found in India or any other country. I think that even the four tantras of Tibetan medicine have their ultimate origin in China, because in them, the five elements are not reckoned as they are in the Indian system, that is, earth, water, fire, wind, and space, but as wood, fire, earth, metal, and water, and the arteries are called *tshön, kan,* and *chak,* which are obvious mispronunciations of the Chinese *cun, guan,* and *chi.*[1393]

A minister of King Shun named Yu invented the five-stringed *qin* (guitar) and the twenty-five-stringed *se* (zither), which are musical instruments. He composed a treatise on song called *Shao,* and I think the contemporary dance-opera called *changzhi* is based upon it.[1394]

Many texts on poetics appeared over time, and it seems there are many more poetical figures of speech than are known in Tibet.

Moreover, historical literature and writings on technology, geomancy, physiognomancy, prognostics, and other topics have existed from earliest times. Later on, the number of such compositions greatly increased, but although they were popular, they appear not to have been included among the great texts. [281]

d. The standpoint of the Confucian system

1) Soteriology

A brief explanation of the standpoint of the system known as Ru: Among the actual root texts of this school there is no explanation at all of the principles of samsara or nirvana, bondage and freedom, the designation of the six classes of beings, past and future lives, karma and its result, and so forth. Consequently, of the multitude who studied Ru, except for one or two who have a predisposition toward Dharma from a previous life, the vast majority are contented with just the things of this life. When someone explains the principles of cause and effect and so forth, others say, "If there were such principles, they necessarily would have been explained in the texts of the early kings, Kongzi, and others, but such is not the case." Extraordinary persons like King Fu Xi Shi, Kongfuzi, and others thought that the people of their time were not vessels to whom the principles of samsara and nirvana and the like could be taught, and so in the *wujing* and *sishu* they chiefly explained the principles of human conduct and other methods beneficial for the time, but they never wrote a single word to prove that there were no past and future lives, karma and result, and so forth, as did the extremist Lokāyatas. In response to a disciple who asked Kongzi, "What happens after death," he did not say, "There is no future life," but replied, "That belongs to what is hidden; I explain the principles of what is presently manifest." Again, when Kongzi was explaining the characteristics of the great man, his disciple Yan Hui asked, "Is the man possessing such characteristics so-and-so of such-and-such a place?" mentioning the names of some. To each, Kongzi said, "No." "Are you such a one?" his disciple asked. "How could I be?" he said. "Well, if there is some such individual at present, who is it?" he asked. In reply, Kongzi said, "Such a one will appear in the West," implying that only the Buddha is such a model individual.[1395]

Even the principles of the stages and path are to be found among what seem to be the hidden meanings of the texts written by Fu Xi and Kongfuzi. According to some of the direct disciples of our glorious lama, the omniscient Rölpai Dorjé, he said, "It is permissible to explain the meaning of the *Yijing* in accordance with the highest secret mantra." According to one history, at the time of the Jin dynasty, two experts in exegesis, the *heshang*[1396] Faxian[1397] [282] and Daoming, elucidated the meaning of both Ru and Daoshi texts in conformity with Buddhism. Again, in a later history of religion in China, it is written that, "The texts of the Ru teacher Kongzi outwardly teach governance and inwardly the stages of ascending the noble path, so they do not contradict the teaching of the Buddha." As it is difficult for those who have not studied Buddhism to understand such a point, it obviously cannot enter the minds of those who have studied only Ru.

The principal subject matter of the five great texts are the *wuchang* (five virtues) and so forth, that is, *ren, yi, li, zhi,* and *xin*. In Chinese, *wuchang* means the system of five "traditions" or "constants." *Ren* is gentleness of character; *yi* is kindness or affection; *li* is proper ritual behavior; *zhi* is wisdom; and *xin* is reliability. The four textbooks known as the *sishu* also elucidate them extensively. What noble worldly persons have said, that "One must hold those five as dear as life," has become proverbial.

2) Cosmogony, cosmology, and eschatology

According to the *Yijing,* the origin of heaven, earth, and humanity apparently are as follows: "The time before the formation of heaven and earth is called *huntun* (chaos). It was mixed and tangled, cloudy and indistinct." "It" seems to refer to something that cannot be identified, analyzed, or designated. In most apotropaic rituals, it is said that "At first, there was nothing whatsoever"; the *Yijing* is evidently the source for that. Then came the *taiji,* or the "ultimate superiority," meaning "inherent nature," and "inherent character," "reality itself," or "the ultimate nature." Just as all entities have their individual efficacious capacity, in the same way *huntun,* too, is believed to have a special capacity for producing the heaven and so forth. By its own nature it shook and quaked, and from that there arose the *liangyi,* the "two aspects" or the "two inherent natures." Those two are the male aspect and the female aspect. They also refer to a capacity like that of a father and mother as the planter and receiver of a seed. [283]

Then those two met, joined like a male and a female, and shook and settled, owing to which there emerged the *sixiang* or "four transformations": great male and little male, great female and little female. Once again, from the union of the male and female aspects arose what are known as the *bagua,* or *spar kha*, and the *jiugong,* or the nine palaces. After that, the capacities of both became clear and shone, lit up, and shook, and that which stayed up above, the sharper parts, was called *tian,* or heaven: that time was called "the time of the separation of heaven." The parts that were muddy and unclear, heavy, firm, and dull, remained permanently below, and were called *di,* or earth: that time was called "the time of the closing of the earth." After heaven and earth had come into existence, the vital power of heaven descended, and the vital power of earth ascended, and as a result of their contact, humanity came into being: that time is called "the time of the coming into existence of humanity." The trio of heaven, earth, and humanity are also called the *three excellences,* the *three powers,* and the *three finalities*. In apotropaic rituals, it is said: "The vigorous father, say, is the pinnacle in heaven. The vigorous mother, say, is the maternity on the earth. From the coming together of the two in sexual intercourse..." and so forth.[1398] This also appears in the chants. *Heaven* has the sense of "capacity" or "system of conduct"; *earth* is believed to have the capacity to generate things. However, the pale blue sky and the ground are also termed heaven and earth, and the sky is thought by most people to be dark blue and round, the earth yellow and square.

Although in this system the heavens are counted as nine in number, there is no distinction between higher or lower. This scheme occurs in Tibet, where the nine were thought to be equivalent to the seven underground levels, so that by adding the word "level," a chant says: "Of the nine heavenly levels, above"; but this seems to be a fabrication.

The period of time from the initial coming into being of heaven, earth, and humanity until their final destruction is called *yi yuan,* that is, "one root" or "one beginning." The length of one *yuan* is 129,600 human years, which evidently is the same as the kalpa accepted in our own system. It is believed that with the destruction of heaven and earth, the *huntun* and the *taiji* once again will convulse, and so forth, and so cycle [284] endlessly.

A human being is held to be a material object that is a coagulation of the vital power and liquid essence of other material objects. Since the Chinese have no notion of the four kinds of birth, they cannot say to which birthplace humanity belonged when it first came into being. Nor is there any explanation in the early texts of this system to the effect that when heaven and earth were divided into two, heaven had human features.[1399] Not only that, there was no notion of what occurs after death or of the six classes of beings. In a text written by a later scholar named Zhu Xi, who had studied many religious systems, there is a statement that:

> After a person dies, their life-soul or vitality—the *sanhun,* or "three souls," obtained from the father—soars upward into the sky and becomes *shen* (spirit), whereas the *liupo*—the six souls or vitalities obtained from the mother—sink into the earth, where they become a demon called a *gui* (ghost).[1400]

It would appear that the notion of six souls in the Tibetan rituals for calling the wandering soul and for the violent destruction of enemies has its origin in some similar conception. Later on, the Chinese say that all worldly happiness and suffering are effected by *tian,* or heaven, and that pigs, sheep, and other animals have been created by heaven as food for humans, so they are like vegetables, and there is no fault in killing them. There are many gods that have human features, such as Yu Huang (the "jade emperor")[1401] and others, and an array of many *guishen,* or gods and demons. They bury the corpse of the deceased under the ground and worship it, making food offerings to it in the belief that the deceased will be capable of enjoying them. It seems that these are a mix of various barbarian, Daoshi, and other systems, and that some even blend in Buddhism.

e. Confucianism vis à vis Buddhism

In the root text of Kongzi's textbook, the *Daxue,* it says:

> The Way of Great Learning depends on clarifying illustrious good qualities; doing good to people depends on achieving the highest good. After that is understood, it is proper that it be upheld; after it has been upheld, it is proper that it be stabilized; after it has been stabilized, it is proper that one become happy; after one has become happy, it is proper to offer instruction; after instruction has been offered, it is proper to understand it. Whatever there is has an origin and an end, and activities have [285] their beginning and end. When one understands what comes before and what comes after, one is close to the Way.[1402]

It is easy to understand that what is explicitly shown by those words is the principle of human conduct, but I think it teaches something like this as its hidden meaning: To clarify what is and is not the path is what is meant by "illustrious good qualities." *Ru,* or the Way of the Great Learning, illuminates it. "Doing good to people" means leading sentient beings to the good path. Knowing that leading others there depends on achieving the highest good, you should initially achieve the good yourself and assist others afterward. Further, those who are happy should be stabilized in their happiness, and those who are not happy should be made happy. When you have made them happy and they have become suitable vessels, instruct them in what they should accept and what they should avoid, and it then will be proper to make them understand the principles of samsara and nirvana, and so forth. Thusly, whatever exists has an initial origin and a subsequent end, so when you fully understand those two, you are close to the Way. I think the passage has that meaning; the idea of initially ripening your own mind and after that ripening the minds of others is similar to what is found in the subject matter of the Mahayana Dharma system. Although the text does not use the term *buddha,* the phrase "achieve the highest good" suggests to my mind that perhaps Kongzi accepted what we call "the stage of a buddha."

Chinese scholars who have studied those texts and mastered them are given the title *xiansheng* (teacher). Although translated literally it means "firstborn," the sense it has is of "great man." In addition, when they have completed their education in the five texts, they receive the title of *xiucai* (scholar) or *zhuangyuan* (premier) depending on the degree of their learning. Studying the textual system thusly, they themselves become scholars. In addition, when they have mastered the literature of the legal system, they will know how to instruct others in right and wrong. When scholars have acquired those two qualities, they are worthy to be officials who govern the common people through the legal system and administer the imperial government. In conformity with their degree of merit, they are appointed to the ranks of officials with their varying official duties. To make an analogy with [286] Tibet, the five texts are like the five root texts (of the traditional curriculum), Ru is like the entirety of the Buddhist canon, and receiving the titles *xiansheng, xiucai,* and *zhuangyuan* through the study of those texts is similar to the way Tibetans are given the titles of *geshé, kachu,* and *rapjampa.*[1403] Appointment to the rank of an official who instructs the people in what is right and wrong is similar to the appointment of a qualified educator as a master in charge of courses at a larger or smaller monastery. Nowadays, because of the time we live in, such standards are rare, and this seems to be the case both in China and Tibet.

There are also those who have a good understanding of the great Chinese textual systems and have no interest in official rank and the like, nor the desire for the householder's activities of business or farming, and they go to isolated ravines and reflect on the meaning of the textual systems they have studied. If a disciple should appear, they teach him, and they live out their lives with few goals or activities. They resemble those Dharma practitioners who, when they have brought their study and reflection to completion, renounce worldly life and practice in solitude; yet in both countries, such persons appear to be very few.

Kongzi evidently respected the Buddha, but at that time the doctrine of the Buddha had not yet come to China, so neither good nor bad opinions of Buddhism are expressed in the textbooks composed by him. Zhufuzi, who also had knowledge of Buddhism, praises the Dharma in his works and writes not a word in condemnation.[1404] A later minister by the name of Zhouzi[1405] expressed prejudiced opinions. He said:

> Because all the happiness and prosperity of the commoners comes from the power of the king's merit, the one having the greatest kindness toward all the people is the king; and because your parents have produced your body, those who are the kindest to you are your parents. Therefore, you must repay their kindness. Intelligent commoners should administer the laws, the courageous should wage war, and the ordinary people should pay their taxes. So long as your parents are alive, you should honor and serve them, and after they have died, you should make offerings to their bones and their name. [287] Acting in this way is the excellent system of the nobles of former times. Later, a certain Śākyamuni, ignoring the kindness of his king and parents, left home and taught a Dharma system in which one provides food and clothing for oneself alone. The foolish king Han Ming of the Yongping era (r. 58–76 C.E.) spread that Way in the land of China, and the family lines of many people died out, and the excellent Way of earlier times declined.[1406]

Now Buddhism is not concerned just with the kings and parents of the present life, but aims to free all sentient beings in numbers as vast as the sky from suffering and establish them in happiness, and it aims to free them not merely from transitory sufferings, but from all the general and specific suffering belonging to samsara, and to place them in inexhaustible, utmost bliss. And so we answer this ignorant person: To compare the extent of gratitude in our system with that of theirs is to compare the magnitude of the sky with the eye of a needle.

Although there are other scattered written accounts denigrating Buddhadharma along the lines of the foregoing, not a single logical reason is offered in support; there is only nonsense uttered under the influence of clinging to wrong views. From the introduction of the teaching into China down to the present, with the exception of one or two emperors, most have been devoted solely to the teaching, and as a consequence, such vulgar talk is like an echo. Although some common Chinese of the present day repeat those criticisms, there is an apt proverb:

> If an old dog barks,
> The others run for no reason.[1407]

2. The history of the moon-like Dharma system, the tradition of Bön called Daoshi

a. Origins

The history of the moon-like Dharma system, the tradition of Bön called *Daoshi* (Priests of the Dao): The founding teacher of this system was called Laojun (Lord Lao). There seems to be both a divine and a human Laojun. The former, the divine Laojun, is called Taishang Laojun, which, in Tibetan translation, is Most Excellent [288] Chief Lord. It is said that he appeared when, according to the Chinese system, heaven and earth first came into being. According to some, he is identified with the god Brahmā, which I think is acceptable, as it seems to agree with the explanation in the abhidharma and elsewhere that in the beginning, when the world came into being, the immeasurable palaces of Mahābrahmā and Brahmā emerged sequentially, and that his name, Most Excellent Chief Lord, fits with the standpoint of those who say that Brahmā is the creator of the world. It is said that from then on Laojun revealed eighty-one human emanations, among which our teacher the Buddha is counted.[1408] This seems to conform with the view of proponents of the principle of the ten avatars of Viṣṇu. The human Laojun is apparently identified as one of the emanations. The time of his appearance is roughly the same as that of Kongzi. Having spent eighty-two years in his mother's womb, he had white hair when he was born, so he was called Laozi, "Old Man." Later, it seems, his followers gave him the pleasant name of Laojun.

I have seen an account to the effect that he obtained seventy-two chapters of heavenly Dharma from a cave, studied them, and spread the system of Daoshi. My omniscient lama said: "Laojun was the same as Shenrap, the teacher of Bön"; I think perhaps *xian,* in *shengxian,*[1409] or "great man" in Chinese, was called *shen (gshen)* through mispronunciation.

There also appeared Yuanshi Tianzun, who was similar to Laojun. Although I have not seen his history, I think after researching him he may be identified as one of the eight-one emanations.[1410] Thus, the source of the Way of Daoshi is Taishang Laozhun, who is identical to the god Brahmā, and in the human realm his emanations Laozi, Yuanshi Tianzun, and others, who spread it extensively.

b. Teachings

The characteristics of the Daoshi Dharma: It is said that they accept what is formless, shapeless, colorless, and unsurpassable as the great self-originated path. Because I have not seen the great Daoshi texts, I do not know the details concerning their standpoints on samsara and nirvana, bondage and liberation, and so forth. According to some small books [289] of selections I have seen, it seems there are many gods with human features, and powerful spirits—the lords of the five great rugged mountains of China,[1411] the lords of the four great rivers, and the lords of the wind, rain, lightning, and so forth—in relation to whom various rituals are prescribed. When worshipping them, there are mantras for purifying the body, mouth, and tongue. There are instructions for rites of bathing and purity, and there are a multitude of explanations included in the special instructions on concentration, such as the means for suppressing the breath, praising *shen,* that is, the vital power of the gods,[1412] and remaining with the mind undisturbed. There are histories of the famous *badong shengxian,*[1413] or "eight great men," and others who attained the worldly supernormal powers, and of the mighty Zhang Dashi,[1414] who intimidated many wicked spirits and commanded all the local and guardian deities in the area of the present-day great palace in Beijing. It is known that when his clan descendents approach the palace, the great spirits of that place welcome them. Moreover, there are many about whom stories are told regarding their attainment of supernormal powers, magical powers, and so forth. To judge by that, there are evidently instructions for accomplishing a simple one-pointed concentration of the desire-realm mind, but I think it unlikely that they have a correct method for realizing the path of liberation. There are a great many instructions dealing with the performance of activities related to sacred objects, the analysis of lightning, good-luck ceremonies, and spells and mantras composed by the gods, seers, and others. There are two kinds of practitioners: householders and those who have forsaken family life. The latter take something like vows, which they apparently guard well.

Although I heard it said that the southern Chinese were diligent in their studies and that there were many scholars, I had no useful discussions with them. The north is a great nation, with an excess of diversions, and those who have studied deeply are rare, so that when I questioned those who claimed to be scholars, few could elucidate flawlessly and perfectly the individual traditions[1415] without confusing the three systems. Since I, who had not studied

Chinese literature, could not read many of the texts myself, [290] I had to listen to what others read, so that I have just a partial view of the origins and standpoints of Ru and Daoshi, and I dare not write more than just this.

B. The history of some miscellaneous traditions

The history of some miscellaneous traditions: During the time of the great Han,[1416] there came from the island of Singhala a non-Buddhist pandit called the Great Brahman. When he related to the Chinese king Yao Xiang (fourth century) the reasons why it was necessary for him to promulgate his philosophical system, a *heshang* named Daoyong fluently recited the Vedas in Sanskrit as well as many other Vedic texts known to non-Buddhists. As the *heshang* was versed in three times more texts than he, the pandit was cowed and prostrated to the *heshang*. Then the king, realizing the pandit's religious system was useless, sent him back to his own country. It is for that reason that down to the present day, the debased views of the extremists have not appeared in China.

During a period of disorder in the time of the Tang, many troops from Tukhara[1417] were brought in who settled permanently in China. Gradually increasing in numbers, they came to be called Huizi (sons of Hui) or Huige (Uyghur).[1418] Also, after Genghis Khan (ca. 1162–1227) had conquered the western regions,[1419] a commoner from the ocean island of Xiyang[1420] who was an expert in a Dharma system called Tianzhu, or the "Lord of Heaven," followed him on his return home and came to the land of China, where his Dharma gradually increased and has existed down to the present day.[1421]

The descendents of the Tokharians practiced their own tradition and dwelled among the Chinese, but it seems that not only did the Chinese not adopt their religion, they did not even intermarry with them. They say: "all worldly happiness and suffering, and good and bad, is ordained by heaven." It seems that *Tian* means god and heaven, and has other senses as well, but the Huizi and others like them do not make any distinctions beyond the general senses of the word *Tian*. It seems they do not take refuge in or offer worship to worldly gods. They say that Tian collects the consciousness of a dead person and Tian ordains where it is [291] to be born again. As to how consciousness takes birth, they state various things: they say that it takes birth when, after this world has been destroyed, a new world comes into existence, consciousness having in the interim subsisted mixed in with the sky; they say that souls take birth immediately; or they say that their continuity as a human being is cut. The consciousness of an animal killed by an adherent of their philosophical system is sent to Tian, who takes care of it; but the consciousness of an animal killed by another who is not of their religion is thrown into limbo, where it wanders; thus, to eat the flesh of an animal killed by others is a great sin. Unfortunate adherents of this tradition whose continuity as a human being has been cut are born as pigs: if you eat pork, your continuity as a human being is cut. If you do not keep yourself clean, Tian is displeased, so they say that purificatory practices such as bathing and so forth are very important. Apart from these things, they know nothing of the principles of samsara and nirvana, bondage and freedom, view and conduct, and so forth. Thus, these people have no system of reasoning like that in the philosophical systems of true extremists, so they resemble those who are categorized as barbarians. Although nowadays the Huizi are greatly increasing in all countries, nevertheless, it will not be long before they are subdued by the kalkin Raudracakrin, who will clear away their wrong views as the sun clears away the darkness and set them on the right path. How that happens will be explained below.[1422]

Concluding verses

Those confused even about what to do and not to do in this realm of appearance
Were unfit vessels for the ever-desirable Dharma,
So the Conqueror selected, as the first Chinese teachers,
Sages who illumined an authoritative code of worldly conduct.

Those who understood the difference between appropriate and deceptive methods
Composed quite a number of purificatory texts,
So the stains of confusion were washed away, and the minds of disciples
Made fit to be vessels for the nectar of holy Dharma.

Although some were purified in that way, those clay pots
So unfortunate that they could not in their present life contain
The lion's milk of the holy Dharma, reached their goal by gaining
A visual and auditory connection with the Conqueror's doctrine.

Not long after the kalkin Raudracakrin has come to Shambhala,
Even the barbarians, with their ironclad debased views,
Will certainly be changed into the precious jewel of converts
Through the excellent alchemy of his deeds.

This account of the origins of the Veda
And Bön in the land [292] of China
Is related in the manner of one who has seen things only hazily,
Not of one who has attained exact certainty.

From *The Crystal Mirror: An Excellent Explanation Showing the Sources and Assertions of All Philosophical Systems,* this completes the explanation the history of the Vedic and Bön philosophical systems in the land of Mahācīna.

15. Chinese Traditions 2: Buddhist[1423]

C. The history of the Dharma system of the insiders, the Buddhists

> I will now relate how the ambrosial rain of the holy Dharma,
> which bestows an abundance
> Of benefits and happiness, descended on the land of China
> From the self-created cloud mass of the Conqueror's deeds,
> Gently saturating all the fields of converts.

THE ACCOUNT of how the sun-like Dharma system known as *Jing*, the precious teaching of the Buddha, came to the land of China, is twofold: 1. How it came from India, and 2. How it came from Tibet.[1424]

1. How Buddhism came from India

a. Historical developments

1) Before Buddhism

It seems that even before the dissemination of the actual teaching in the land of China, there were some teachings that resembled it in part. The teacher Mozi (ca. fifth–fourth centuries B.C.E.) taught that you should devote yourself solely to the welfare of others without regard for your own body or life, and that the nature of the mind is primordially pure but polluted by adventitious stains and altered by karma.[1425] The teacher Liehzi[1426] taught that everything is dependently originated. At that time, there were no relations with India, so that not even the word *buddha* was known in this country, yet Liehzi, cognizing through his clairvoyance, wrote in one of his texts: "In the west there will appear one who performs great deeds naturally and possesses extraordinary perspicacity, a noble being beyond the realm of expressibility; his name will be Buddha."[1427] This is the first time the sweet name of Buddha was uttered in this country. There is also the story of the teacher Zhuangzi (369–298 B.C.E.?), who dreamed he was a butterfly and, after awakening, reflected upon it and realized that everything that appears is [293] without any existence at all.[1428] The teacher Ye Su (Jesus), or Protector of the World, is known to have had a miraculous birth. He composed a treatise that taught a ten-limbed vow of not taking human life, and so forth, that the experience of happiness arises as a result of virtuous actions, that one falls into hell through the ripening of evil acts and suffers agonies there forever, and that deliberately committed misdeeds are not purified by confession.[1429] All of this is explained in the *History of Buddhism in China*. While it seems these were excellent ways that arose due to Buddha's deeds, their spread was neither extensive nor long lasting.[1430]

On the eighth day of the fourth month of the wood-male-tiger year, in the twenty-sixth year of the reign of Zhao Wang, the fifth king of the Zhou dynasty,[1431] a great effulgence of golden light appeared in the southwest border region and pervaded all the land. The king saw it and questioned the oracles, who said it was a sign that a great lord had been born in that direction, and they prophesied that when a thousand years had passed his philosophical system would appear in China. That phenomenon was recorded in the annals. From that wood-tiger year to the fire-hare year of the thirteenth sexegenery cycle (1747),[1432] 2773 years passed, and to the iron-monkey year of the thirteenth sexegenery cycle (1800),[1433] 2826 years have passed. Again, some also say that this occurred in the twenty-fourth year of King Zhao, a water-bird year; according to some Tibetan texts, it was in the twenty-fourth year of King Mu,[1434] which is obviously a scribal error. According to the writings of the *heshang*s:

> Our teacher was born at that time. Then, when he was twenty-nine years old, on the eighth day of the second month, he entered the homeless life. When he was thirty, on the eighth day of the second month, he became a buddha, and for the next forty-nine years he turned the wheel of Dharma. When he was seventy-nine, on the fifteenth day of the second month in the water-monkey year, he entered nirvana.[1435]

Although such a chronology is acceptable, I suspect that the source might be the "Lion's Roar" chapter of the *Great Nirvana Sutra,* where this question-and-answer may be found:

> The birth of the Blessed One, the entrance into homelessness, the attainment of complete buddhahood, and the turning of the

> wheel of the Dharma all took place on the eighth day in the first half of a lunar month; why is only the appearance of his uncorrupted nirvana associated [294] with the fifteenth day?[1436]

2) The coming of Buddhism

The nirvana of the Teacher occurred in the fifty-third year of King Mu[1437] (949 B.C.E.). Counting 1013 years from then, the teaching came to China in the eighth year of the Yong Ping era (29–75 C.E.) of King Ming Di of the great Han dynasty.

During the night of an auspicious day in the third year of that king's reign, the king dreamed that a great being more than three fathoms in height, of a golden complexion, adorned with the marks of a great being, and radiating sunlight, came down from the sky and approached the golden-throne room in the palace.[1438] When the king questioned his ministers the next day, minister Fu Yi suggested: "I have heard it said that in the time of a Zhou king there was in India a sage called Buddha, whose body was well proportioned and more than three fathoms tall, whose skin was of a golden complexion and radiant, and who could move through the sky. Perhaps there is a connection between this and his majesty's dream." Then the king looked into the old records and found the prophecy from the time of King Zhao of the Zhou dynasty; calculating the date, he saw that it tallied with the 1010 years that had passed. The king was very happy and sent an envoy, Wang Zun, to India in search of Buddhism.[1439]

At that time, the arhat Mātaṅga, who was of the clan of Kāśyapa, and the pandit Bharaṇa, who, owing to a mispronunciation of the Sanskrit, was called Falan in China, saw that the time had come to spread the teaching to China. They loaded a white horse with a portrait scroll of the Teacher and some Mahayana and Hinayana sutras, along with a quantity of relics, and set out from India. They met the envoy in that part of China called Loyokhyi[1440] and, together with Wang Zun, arrived at the royal palace, where the king welcomed them and paid them homage. When they presented the supports of the teaching to the king for him to see, he was very pleased with the portrait of the Teacher, which appeared identical to the figure he had seen in his former dream. The arhat instilled faith in the king by performing some miracles, and the king erected a temple called Baima Si (White Horse Monastery) and installed the two Indians as recipients of offerings.

The indigenous Bönpos,[1441] after offering many reasons, said to the king,

"This tradition conflicts with our own [295] and is unfit to be spread in this country." The king replied, "Well, then, cast the scriptures of both into a fire; the ones that remain unburned will be worthy of reverence." His command was carried out, and the scriptures of the Daoshi were burned up, but the Buddhist scriptures were untouched by the flames, so the two chiefs of the Daoshi, Fei Shucai and Chu Shanxin, jumped into the fire. The two pandits then ascended into the sky and displayed extraordinary miracles, so that the king, along with his ministers and the common people, gained faith in the Dharma. The king spoke verses of praise:

> A fox is not found among lions;
> A lamp does not shine like the sun and moon;
> A pond is not as wide as an ocean;
> A hill does not have the splendor of a lofty mountain.
>
> The auspicious cloud of Dharma covers the world;
> Its pure rain will quicken the seeds of beings.
> Deeds without precedent are now plainly seen
> And will serve to convert many beings in every direction.[1442]

The king had seven temples built in the palace of Henan Fu, the main one being Baima Si, and three temples for nuns. The king took lay practitioner's vows, and more than a thousand men, led by several great ministers, became monks.

Again, the king asked: "Are there any holy great beings permanently dwelling in our kingdom who are working for the benefit of beings?" The arhat then described how Ārya Mañjughoṣa dwelt on Five Peaks (Wutai shan). Then the arhat and the pandit went off to Five Peaks, the field of Mañjughoṣa, and with their divine eye beheld the marvels of that miraculous place. On their return, they told the king; "During the time of the Buddha Kāśyapa, King Aśoka[1443] (304?–232 B.C.E.), with the assistance of the spirits, built 84,000 stupas in a single night containing relics of the Buddha in their inner chambers; we have identified one of them on Five Peaks." Then the king erected a great stupa containing that very stupa in its inner chamber, which is known nowadays as Dabao Ta (Great Precious Temple), and he founded the monastery of Xiantong Si (Illuminating the Universe Temple). At Five Peaks and elsewhere, he erected many stupas containing relics in their inner chambers; one of these is contained in the inner chamber of the stupa known nowadays as the White Stupa of Beijing. Six hundred and twenty men became monks and two hundred and thirty women became nuns. The [296] arhat translated the *Sutra in Forty-two Sections,* which is a collection of important passages from the Hinayana sutras, and the first sutra to be translated into Chinese; it still exists today.[1444] The pandit is known to have translated five sutras, including the *Sutra of the Ten Stages,* but due to the ebb and flow of the teaching, they no longer exist.

Moreover, the teaching was initially established at Jiangnan in the south by a group of six pandits, including Master Āryakāla,[1445] the elder Cilukākṣa, the layman Suvinaya, and three others; along with a group of four, consisting of the pandit Dharmakāla,[1446] two other upholders of the Mahayana and Hinayana vinaya, and another pandit; as well as the scholar Gaṇottarasena,[1447] the layman Zhi Qian,[1448] and others. They were the very best translator-scholars during the time of the great Han dynasty.

3) Later developments

After that, throughout the reigns of the thirteen kings of the Han dynasty, the fourteen kings of the Jin dynasty, the many kings of the former Qin, Huige (Uyghur), and Sui dynasties, the twenty Tang kings and the eighteen Song kings, a great many scholars and adepts arrived in succession from India. There were innumerable learned *heshangs* some of whom went to India and others who, even though they did not go, still possessed unimaginably good qualities of scriptural realization. They translated the word of the Buddha and many treatises into Chinese, and while a great many of them are the subject of wonderful stories of how they served the teaching, I will not write about them out of fear of prolixity; but they may be known from the *History of Buddhism in China* and elsewhere. From the time of the Mongol kings on, many Tibetan holy men went to China, too, so that the teaching of the Conqueror increased immensely, as will be discussed below.

The enumeration of the translations of the Buddha's words and their commentaries: In the time of the Sui king Wen Di (r. 581–605), the translations that had been made up till then were catalogued. After that, twice during the time of the Tang and twice during the time of the Song, the new translations that had appeared in the interim were added and catalogued. Finally, in the time of the Mongol King Sé Chen (Kublai Khan, 1215–94), the Tibetan and Chinese Kangyurs were compared, and those [297] texts lacking in the Chinese were translated from Tibetan. At the end of the compilation were appended twenty-one volumes of Indian treatises and 153 volumes of large texts written by learned *heshangs*, making 740 volumes in total—for which a new catalogue was made—among which are many sutras, tantras, and treatises that have never been translated into Tibetan.

b. Buddhist teaching lineages in China

Among the Buddhist teachings that spread in the land of China, five lineages are recognized: 1) the vinaya lineage, 2) the secret-mantra lineage, 3) the extensive-practice lineage, 4) the profound-view lineage, and 5) the essential-meaning lineage.

1) The vinaya lineage

Although the continuity of vows that had been transmitted from the arhat Mātaṅga lasted for a while, the continuity was later broken, apparently, and a tantric master named Kumāraśrī,[1449] an expert in countless subjects and possessor of clairvoyance and magical powers, came to the land of China. At the time of his arrival [in 401], the sandalwood statue of Lord Buddha also was brought. King Hong Shi[1450] paid Kumāraśrī honor, and the latter, along with eight hundred learned disciples headed by Seng Zhao (384–414),[1451] translated many sutras and treatises, and the Mahayana doctrine was spread widely through their explanations. In particular, many were allowed to take the vows of a monk and the vows of a bodhisattva. The *heshangs* then introduced the custom of taking the bodhisattva vows after receiving those of the layperson. Also, the three vinaya masters, Buddhajñāna,[1452] Vimalacakṣu, and Dharmāruci, who had come to China with Kumāra, translated many vinaya cycles, such as the four texts, and taught precise guidelines for the training of monks. Moreover, the elder Saṅghavarma (fifth century) also came and spread the tradition of the vows and the particulars of training in the vinaya, so that the continuity of prātimokṣa vows and bodhisattva vows transmitted from Kumāraśrī and Saṅghavarma has lasted down to the present day.

While there is an account of ten nuns coming to China from India, including the Sinhalese nun Devasarā (fifth century) and others, we do not know whether there was a transmission of nun's vows descending [298] from them. It is said that from the four basic transgressions down to the seven Dharmas for resolving disputes, the Chinese vinaya is not different from that of

Tibet; the difference is in the matter of various religious practices, which may conform to the customs of the country or be taken from other sects. The Chinese Buddhists do not eat meat and they do not ride on animals; they carry a begging bowl of the smallest capacity, and the pieces making up the monk's robe overlap like birds' feathers. As there is only a single class of monk in this country, one need not worry about making a mistake in identification, so there is no tradition of sectarian markings for distinguishing one from another. In Chinese tradition, yellow is the auspicious color of the king and red of the ministers, and the king of that time explicitly forbade either color to clerics. By virtue of the fact that according to Chinese tradition it is shameful for bare flesh to be exposed, the *heshang*s spread the custom of wearing dark-colored robes with sleeves. Later on, Tibetan lamas came who wore the clerical robe according to Tibetan tradition, but they were given explicit permission to do so, as it was the time of the Mongol kings. The separately developed customs, whereby the *heshang*s wear dark-colored cloth and the Tibetan monks wear red or yellow robes, persist to the present day.

2) The secret-mantra lineage

The elder Śrīmitra (fourth century) was the first mantra master to come from India, but apart from the translation of a few dhāraṇīs, such as the *Great Peacock,* he did not propagate mantra teachings. While quite a number of contemporary experts in secret-mantra knowledge came with him from India, apart from translating a few mantra texts, they did not give the initiations, instructions, and so forth, to even a single person. Even the tantric master Kumāraśrī did not generally give them to anyone but one or two suitable persons. Those who propagated it a bit more widely were Vajrabodhi (671–741), a scholar from Malaya in southern India, and his disciple Amoghavajra (705–74). These two arrived together during the time of Tang Ming Wang (Minghuang)[1453] and initiated a few of the fortunate, headed by the *heshang*s Chan Shi Yeshé Thayé (Zhiguang Chanshi) and Sherap Thayé (Huigang). Vajrabodhi and Amoghavajra explained the tantric texts, gave special instructions, and performed various religious rituals for the benefit of others. Amoghavajra initiated the king into the great mandala of Vajradhātu, so [299] the king offered him the title Tripiṭaka Master, Treasury of Gnosis. On the appearance of an inauspicious star, Amoghavajra performed the worship and fire ritual of Vajradhātuvāgīśvara, and the inauspicious star disappeared. When he repulsed a foreign army by setting Vaiśrāvaṇa on it, the king offered him a high rank and three thousand householders as his subjects. He translated seventy-seven volumes of the principal texts of secret mantra. After initiating his disciple Huilang, or Yeshé Ö, as his successor and as a tantric preceptor, he entered nirvana. Although some disciples and grand-disciples of Vajrabodhi and Amoghavajra attained mantric accomplishments, the continuity of the teaching declined not long afterward. Although some pandit-adepts, such as the great abbot Dānarakṣita, Dharmabhadra, and others arrived from the Holy Land during the time of the Song[1454] and repaired the way, its continuity did not last long because they put too many restrictions on imparting the Buddha word. Among latter-day *heshangs,* apart from the widespread recitation of a few dhāraṇīs or mantras, such as the long dhāraṇī of Amoghapāśa and some others, there does not seem to be any practice of the teachings of secret mantra.

3) Xuanzang and the lineage of extensive practice

The lineage of extensive practice: The person known as Thangpa[1455] Lama (the "Tang Lama," i.e., Xuanzang, 602–64)[1456] was a descendent of the great Han minister Zhong Gong. He became a monk while still quite young. His inborn wisdom and self-confidence were matchless. At the age of eleven, he could fluently recite the *Teachings of Vimalakīrti Sutra* and the *Lotus of the True Dharma Sutra*. Initially, he mastered the cycle of abhidharma texts and then read extensively in the sutras and commentaries that had been translated into Chinese. As it had been his heart's desire to travel to India, he learned the vernacular, and at the age of twenty-nine, he skillfully petitioned the king, who granted him a travel permit. Then, making his way by stages through many countries, he arrived in India.

He went everywhere in India, from the border lands to the central region, and to many different countries, such as Kashmir and others, visiting many holy sites. He heard many Dharma teachings of both the higher and lower vehicles from many scholars, including Jitāri, that is, Dralé Namgyal. He chiefly attended the great abbot, the 106-year-old Vinītabhadra,[1457] [300] who upheld the Cittamātra philosophical system and dwelled at glorious Nālandā. According to some, his name was Vinītadeva, and there are those, too, who say that he was, or was not, master Vinītasena, a disciple of Uttarasena. Moreover, Tang Sanzang Fashi ("Tang Tripiṭaka master," i.e., Xuanzang) also met Jetāri, the guru of Atiśa, but there are many gurus between Jetāri and Vinītasena, and the chronological inconsistency warrants further investigation.

In any case, over the course of one year and three months he heard the cycle of the five treatises of Maitreya from Vinītabhadra. Once again, over nine months he heard detailed teachings on valid cognition and abhidharma. Then, over a three-year period, he heard many other Dharma teachings. He defeated an extremist opponent in debate and wrote a treatise annihilating wrong views from the Mahayana perspective in 6,600 verses that captivated the minds of all the scholars. Moreover, when the scholar Haraprabhā[1458] composed a treatise in refutation of Cittamātra, master Xuanzang composed a treatise in three thousand verses called *Proof of Harmony,* which he presented to the scholar Vinītabhadra, who was very pleased. As a result of those activities, his renown as a scholar was quite extensive, and the people of the Holy Land called him Mahāyānadeva, or God of the Mahayana, and in a reversal of the usual custom, several Indian scholars received Dharma teachings from him. He was greatly revered by many rulers, such as King Śīlāditya,[1459] King Kumāra,[1460] the South Indian king Dhātubhadra, and others. Although many *heshang*s who were masters came to India both before and after him, it is certain that he was the only one to attain the rank of master in India and become the recipient of royal offerings.

After an absence of seventeen years, including three years spent in travel, Xuanzang returned to China. King Zhen Guan (Emperor Taizong, r. 627–50) honored him elaborately, and he presented to the king over six hundred volumes of Indian manuscripts written on palm leaves, many relics and images, and goods of various kinds. The king installed him in the monastery of Hongfu Si (Monastery of Extensive Happiness), where together with twelve scholar-*heshangs,* he translated 657 volumes of Indian works, both the word of the Buddha and its commentaries, the most important of which were the *Perfection of Wisdom in a Hundred Thousand Verses* and the five treatises of Maitreya. He also revised many of the old translations.

Then he revived Cien Si, or Jampa [301] Ling (Loving Kindness Monastery). At that time, there were 3,716 monasteries in China. By recruiting monks from those monasteries and ordaining new monks, Xuanzang built a monastery with a population of 18,630 monks, and the master took up residence there. After the death of King Zhen Guan, his son, King Gao Zong (r. 650–84), gave to every fifty monks at the Siming Si Monastery (Western Light Monastery) a novice and three betweeners[1461] to support them and presented the monastery to the master. The master then served as abbot of all three monasteries, Hongfu Si, Cien Si, and Siming Si.

He instituted the way of the three stages of the path and the five methods of meditation. He wrote many treatises, including a commentary on the *Perfection of Wisdom in a Hundred Thousand Verses* according to the Cittamātra system; an eight-chapter summary of the extensive practice; commentaries on several sutras, such as the *Descent to Laṅka* and *Unraveling of Intention;* a commentary on bodhisattva vows, a commentary on abhidharma, a summary of valid cognition, and so forth. He widely spread the doctrine in general and the Mahayana in particular, most especially the Cittamātra system.

Just to the south of Cien Si, he constructed a very large stupa in the Indian style and offered for deposit Indian manuscripts and relics. Moreover, he set up many supports, such as a million images made from various materials; he ransomed the lives of ten thousand animals destined for slaughter, distributed alms to ten thousand people, offered a hundred million lamps, and so forth. Having worked for the welfare of beings for nearly forty years, he entered nirvana at the age of sixty-five.

The lineage of extensive practice, then, is as follows: the Teacher, the Blessed One; the conqueror Ajita; Master Asaṅga; his younger brother, Vasubandhu; Dharmarakṣita; Master Ānanda; Master Vinītabhadra; and after him, Tang Sanzang, or Tang Tripiṭaka Master (Xuanzang). It was through that master that the lineage spread in China. The masters Zhiyan, Xianshou (Fazang), and others in the lineage of the profound view heard teachings from Kuiji Fashi,[1462] a disciple of Tang San (Xuanzang), and from then on, the lineages of view and practice were united.

4) The lineage of profound view[1463]

The lineage is as follows: The Teacher, the Blessed One; Jetsün Mañjughoṣa; the glorious protector, Ārya Nāgārjuna; Master Nīlanetri (Having Blue Eyes), that is, Candrakīrti, who was so called [302] because he had a blue mole resembling an eye on each of his cheeks; the noble Bhāvaviveka the Later, or Bhāvaviveka the Lesser; the noble Prajñāraśmi; and the Chinese master Yeshé Pal.[1464] He may have received the direct transmission that originated with Nāgārjuna himself. Next came the master Yeshé Lodrö (Huisi), from whom the *zhizhe dashi,* that is, the great master Yeshé Den (Zhiyi, 531–97), heard it.

a) Zhiyi and the Tiantai

Zhiyi was like a great chariot from whom the lineage of the view spread in China. He was very highly educated, and his practice was excellent. His clairvoyance was unimpeded, and through the power of his awakening mind, he required no assistance in taming those to be tamed. He became religious instructor to two kings of the southern Chen dynasty[1465] and to the great king Wen Di of the Sui dynasty. His deeds were incomparably great. He constructed a great monastery on Mount Tiantai called Guoqing Si (National Purity Monastery) and a great monastery on Yuchuan Mountain as well. With those two monasteries as the principal centers, he founded thirty-six monastic schools for teaching and study, printed fifteen copies of the complete Kangyur and Tengyur, and erected 800,000 images of buddhas and bodhisattvas made from gold, silver, brass, sandalwood, and other materials.

He had more than 14,000 disciples who took vows, thirty-two of whom definitely carried on the lineage, and countless persons with whom he had a Dharma connection. He organized the vows by dividing the precious scriptures into five periods: the *Sutra of the Ornamented Tree* period, the Deer Park period, and the *Great Extensive Sutra, Perfection of Wisdom,* and *Great Nirvana Sutra* periods.[1466] He instituted a Way called the eight entrances: *dunmen,* or the sudden entrance; *jianmen,* or the gradual entrance; *mimi,* the secret or special entrance; the indefinite entrance; the entrance to the *piṭakas;* the entrance to awareness; the entrance to discrimination; and the entrance to perfection.

Encouraged by King Wen Di, he wrote nearly forty volumes of treatises, including the *Stages of Entry into the Dharmadhātu* and others. The notes written by his disciples on the public explanations he gave in classes on the *Flower Ornament Sutra,* the cycle of perfection of wisdom sutras, the *Lotus of the True Dharma Sutra,* and the *Fundamental Treatise on the Middle Way* fill fifty volumes.

Having turned the wheel of Dharma, above all the system of the protector Nāgārjuna, for thirty years, at the beginning of his sixtieth year (597), in the seventeenth year of the reign of Kai Huang (Emperor Wen Di), on [303] the twenty-fourth of midwinter,[1467] he entered nirvana while in meditation. He had bound to a vow the great war god of China, Guan Yunchang, that is, the King of Long Clouds, also known as Guan Laoye (Old Gentleman), and appointed him a guardian of the teaching.

Of the thirty-two lineage holders, the greatest were: the venerable Zhangan,[1468] the venerable Wei of Fahua,[1469] Venerable One of Dongyang Tiangong Si (Eastern Sun Heavenly Palace Monastery),[1470] the venerable Xuanlang of Zuoqi,[1471] and Venerable One of Jingqi (711–782).[1472] It seems that after that, the lineage, known as the Tiantai Zong, became gradually more widespread in that part of present-day southern China known as Jiangnan.

b) Chengguan and the Huayan

In northern China, toward Zhongyuan, there was another sect. Its lineage was transmitted from the father Zhizhe (Great Master Zhiyi) and his spiritual sons through the fivefold spiritual succession of Dashi Di Xin Fashun,[1473] Dashi Zhiyan of Yunhua,[1474] the Xianshou (Sage Leader) Dashi Fazang,[1475] the Guoshi (National Preceptor) Chengguan of Qingliang,[1476] and Dashi Zongmi of Guifeng.[1477] It spread extensively through the teaching and study of the *Flower Ornament Sutra,* so that those five were known as the "five masters of the *Sutra of the Ornamented Tree.*"

The Guoshi Guan of Qingliang, whose actual name was Chengguan or, in Tibetan, Drimé Sik (Stainless Sight) resided permanently at Five Peaks, so he was known as the Guoshi of Qingliang. He flourished during the time of Tang Ming Wang (the emperor Xuanzong) (713–55). There was nothing he did not know in the fields of the ten sciences, governmental administration, and so forth. He possessed the awakening mind. Although he had never gone to India, he was the equal of Indian scholars in the Sanskrit language, so he required no assistance in the work of translation. He was endowed with many of the major and minor marks of a buddha: he was nine cubits, four inches tall; his hands hung below his knees; he had forty teeth; his eyes never blinked; and so forth. The mere sight of him captivated the minds of everyone, high and low. In the land of China, he was the Great Pandit, without rival or compare. In the hymn of praise to Five Peaks composed by my omniscient lama, it says:

> The great being of eastern China,
> Who is none other than the protector Ajita,
> Is the one known by the name of the Guoshi of Qingliang.[1478]

He also was reported to be an emanation of Jetsün Mañjughoṣa. He translated the remainder of the *Flower Ornament Sutra* and illuminated the

Tripiṭaka through his three-volume commentary on the stages of the *Flower Ornament Sutra,*[1479] his one-volume work on the vows,[1480] the one-volume work entitled the *Mirror Showing the Profound Meaning of the View in the* [304] *Dharmadhātu,*[1481] the one-volume work entitled the *Treatise on the Mirror-Lamp,*[1482] the *Five Entryways into the Stages of the Path,*[1483] and so forth. All in all, he wrote more than three hundred volumes of systematic treatises, which gather the scattered and reveal the hidden. It is reputed that there never appeared in China a greater expert on the *Flower Ornament Sutra* than he. He gave detailed explanations of the *Sutra of the Ornamented Tree* to the king and his court on two occasions, and he explained the sutras to them many times. He was esteemed as a lama by seven generations of kings. He lived to the age of 102. His mode of instruction on the extensive stages of the path was in terms of five path stages: (1) middling and ordinary persons, (2) preliminaries to the Mahayana, (3) the two actual bases, (4) the sudden approach, and (5) the gradual approach. This sequence is called the Xianshou (Worthy Leader) system. Although it seems that the aim of this system and the aforementioned Tiantai system are one and the same, when it comes to the stages for guiding students, the mode of guidance of the former involves the eight entrances, while that of this system involves the five stages, and they maintain their separate lineages based on just that.

Thus, when some Tibetan Dharma histories distinguish the *dunmen* and *jianmen* as distinct philosophical systems, this is an error, because it seems that both *dunmen* and *jianmen*—that is, sudden entrance and gradual entrance—differ only in their methods for guiding disciples. It is said that the twenty-first successor to the fifth *Sutra of the Ornamented Tree* master, You Anpu Taifashi (Blessed Ārya Dharma Master Anpu) went on a pilgrimage to Five Peaks, where he encountered the holy lord Maitreya, who was actually dwelling there in a miraculous temple. Over the course of a month, he perfectly received Maitreya's detailed explanation of the five treatises. Although the southern and northern disciple lineages of those masters were unbroken, the stream of the proper explanation of the Madhyamaka view as presented by father Zhizhe (Zhiyi) and his spiritual sons apparently did not last long.

5) The lineage of essential meaning, Chan[1484]

The lineage of essential meaning: The lineage is as follows: the Teacher, the Blessed One; the ārya Mahākāśyapa; the ārya Ānanda; the arhat Śānavastrī;[1485]

and the arhat Upagupta. From Upagupta, it went to the ārya Dhītika[1486] and Madhyāhrika.[1487] From Dhītika,[1488] it was transmitted to the arhat Kṛṣṇa, [305] and it went from him to Sudarśana and Vibhāga. From Vibhāga, it went to Buddhānanta; Buddhamitra; Bhikṣu Pārśva; Sunaśada;[1489] Aśvabhaka,[1490] that is, "He Who Has a Horse's Voice," who is not the same as the master Aśvaghoṣa; Amṛta; Nāgārjuna; Āryadeva; Rāhula, who is the same as Rāhulabhadra; Saṅghananti; the bhikṣu-arhat Ghalaśa; Kumārata; Śayata; Vasubandhu; Manota; Hakalikaśa; Bhikṣu Siṃha; Bhaśyasiddha; Viśvamitra; and Prajñādhara. From Prajñādhara, it was transmitted to Bodhidharmottara (sixth century?), that is, "He Whose Highest Dharma Is Enlightenment,"[1491] who was the twenty-eighth successor to Kāśyapa.[1492] During that time, the special instruction on the essential meaning was handed over without interruption from one master to another.

This master Bodhidharmottara handed over the teaching to Viśvamitra the Later, then went to China himself. Initially, he had an audience with the king of the Jiangnan region, Liang Wu Di (Emperor Wu of Liang). When he was questioned on the Dharma by the king, his ministers, and some scholars, he did not teach according to the text but taught only in enigmatic speech and allegory; they were displeased and took him to be an advocate of nihilistic views. The master, realizing that it would be purposeless to stay, left there and went north, to the land of Huige.[1493] While he was en route, when he had to cross the great river Jiang,[1494] he made his way to the other side by riding on a single reed, without sinking into the water. A general who was traveling by boat saw this, developed faith, and recounted the story. The king of the Jiangnan region, his ministers, and others heard it, and repented. There were also among the Huige many learned Indian and Chinese masters, like master Bodhiruci and others, so that it was a period of extensive teaching and study. Because master Bodhidharmottara could not find in that country anyone fortunate enough to be able to carry on his legacy, he waited for a while, as if in hiding.

As it happened, a *heshang* named Huike (484–590?) from the country of Jiangnan heard the lifestory of the master and, impelled by faith, sought him out and met him. He and three Huige disciples were the four to whom Bodhidharmottara taught the special instruction on the essential meaning. The other three had a general understanding of the meaning, but Huike alone encountered the meaning directly, so the master handed over to him the teachings of the essential instruction, and prophesied:

> Before, when I was crossing the river, there were five leaves on the reed that supported my feet; this omen signifies that the transmission of the word lineage will increase greatly from your fifth successor. From him, it will divide [306] into five independent schools.

Then the master appeared to enter nirvana. Afterward, some who had come from India said they had met the master on the road returning to India carrying a sandal. When his disciples, their doubts having been raised, opened the casket containing his remains and looked inside, there was nothing there but a single sandal.[1495]

Through a corruption of the Sanskrit *dharmo,* most people later on called him Damo Zushi (Damo the First Patriarch). He is depicted in art as crossing the river atop a single reed, bearing a staff on his shoulder to which a single sandal is attached; this seems to be based on the story recounted above. Some say: "This master is the Indian Pha Dampa; it is widely known that he went to China, and in some teachings of the Shijepa it says that 'When he assumed the form of the vajra body of Pha Dampa Sangyé, he bore on his shoulder a ceremonial cloth similar to the costume in which Dharmo is depicted.' It seems there also is a story of Pha Dampa going to India bearing a sandal on his shoulder." However, because I have not seen that story recounted in my sources, it is difficult to credit.

In accordance with the prophecy of Master Bodhidharmottara, from Huike to Liuzu Chanshi (Huineng, 638–713) the word instruction was transmitted to five masters; Liuzu Chanshi gave it to many disciples, so it split into five lineages: the Linji lineage, the Caodong lineage, the Yunmen lineage, the Guiyang lineage, and the Fayan lineage. Of those, the Linji and Caodong[1496] lineages have lasted down to the present; the other three have disappeared.

The lineage of the essential meaning is called Zongmen (Gate of Realization). Its approach seems equivalent to the Tibetan Kagyü, the Mahāmudrā-symbol lineage.

While it seems that the Heshang Mahāyāna who came to Tibet (eighth century) was a follower of the Zongmen, what he taught does not seem to be the same as the standpoint of the general Zongmen view. The followers of Zongmen teach that, when influenced by neither renunciation nor the awakening mind, virtuous and nonvirtuous actions yield, respectively, happiness and suffering, but neither virtuous nor nonvirtuous actions can become causes of liberation or omniscience. This is like white clouds [307] and black clouds, which appear distinct but obscure the sky in equal measure. Failing to make that distinction, Heshang Mahāyāna said that good thoughts and bad thoughts alike produce bondage. Although the instructions on how to meditate on the Zongmen view say that you should "do nothing and think nothing," this is for the person who has directly realized the ultimate nature. Heshang Mahāyāna, on the other hand, said that from the very beginning, you are freed by thinking nothing at all. Thus, it is inappropriate to regard the views of all *heshangs* as wrong simply because a flawed system was taught by one.

6) Summary of India-based traditions

Thus, the teaching of the Buddha came down in five lineages or stages; since the time of Gung Yöl of the Tang dynasty,[1497] however, it has been reduced to three schools: the Lumen, or vinaya lineage, the Jiaomen, or explanation lineage, and Zongmen, or realization lineage. This classification into three schools continues to be current.[1498]

2. How Buddhism came from Tibet

a. In general

Until the Mongol (Yuan) dynasty, no Tibetan holy person had ever gone to China. At the time of the great Mongol dynasty, Sakya Pandita Künga Gyaltsen, along with his disciple and successor, the world-protecting Dharma king Phakpa, went to China, as did the three Karmapas, Karma Pakshi, Rangjung Dorjé, and Rölpai Dorjé, and the Nyingmapa Yungtön Dorjé Pal. Although King Yonglé (1403–25) of the Da (Great) Ming dynasty invited the conqueror Tsongkhapa, he did not go; Jamchen Chöjé Shākya Yeshé went as his representative. The Dharma lord Tashi Palden,[1499] who was a direct disciple of both Jé Tsongkhapa and the Karmapa, as well as Karmapa Deshin Shekpa and others, went and worked extensively for the teaching in China.

b. In particular, how the matchless Ganden Mountain tradition spread

Although Jamchen Chöjé went to China in the time of King Yonglé and introduced the teaching there, it became very widespread only in the time of the Great Qing. When the emperor Shizu Huangdi[1500] (r. 1644–62) was residing at Mukden,[1501] the omniscient Panchen Losang Chökyi Gyaltsen urged the Great Fifth Dalai Lama: "If you establish a relationship [308] with the present king of Mukden and obtain his patronage, he may help our teaching later on." The Dalai Lama agreed, and the two conquerors, father and spiritual son, sent an envoy to present a letter along with gifts. The great emperor was quite delighted and sent to each a direct reply along with generous gifts; that was the beginning of the preceptor-patron relationship.[1502] Not long afterward, when the bandit chief Li Zicheng[1503] seized the realm of King Chongzhen,[1504] the troops of Emperor Shizu the Great decisively defeated the bandit chief, and he took the empire for himself. At that time, when the emperor was staying at Mukden,[1505] there was a lama-adept who had been dispatched by Panchen Rinpoché to perform religious rituals. He predicted the day, the minute, the hour, and so forth when the empire would be conquered, and the adept himself went with the king to Beijing. After the emperor ascended the golden throne, he constructed a stupa on the top of a mountain called Jing Shan in the center of the capital[1506] in order to strengthen his rule. In front of the stupa, he erected statues of Lhamo and her two attendants, with the faces (of a lion and crocodile), and three religious flagpoles. Nowadays, because their significance is no longer understood, those three flag staffs have been converted into three tall flagpoles in the Chinese style, called *qigan*. Moreover, behind the outer walls, he constructed the Yellow Temple[1507] and its statuary, which guard the kingdom, as it were. Occasionally, a good-luck ceremony was performed on top of the palace involving the blowing of horn trumpets and circumambulation; this custom has continued down to the present day. For that reason, the emperor bestowed upon him[1508] the rank of Consecrated Seal Lama,[1509] which the chief figures in the lineage continue to hold.

Furthermore, the forty-nine banners of the Inner Mongols recognized Neichi Thoyon Hutuqtu (1557–1653) as guru. At his urging, most of the Mongols, principally the Khorchin, submitted to the emperor, as did all the Khalka, on the basis of the activities of the holy lord Losang Tenpai Gyaltsen (1635–1723), who was the rebirth of Jamyang Chöjé.[1510] Because of the valuable service rendered to the empire by those Geluk lamas, the great emperor became an extraordinary patron of our teaching, and he and the Dalai and Panchen Lamas sent envoys back and forth, so that in time the relationship became even [309] deeper. When the mighty conqueror, the Great Fifth, was invited to the capital, the emperor presented him with a letters patent proclaiming him "Mighty Conqueror of the Field of Supreme Virtue in the Western Quarter, The Master of All the Buddha's Teachings on Earth, the Omniscient Dalai Lama Vajradhara," along with a crystal seal.[1511] The Emperor King Dekyi (Kangxi, 1661–1722) invited the omniscient Changkya Ngawang Losang Chöden and presented him with a golden letter praising him as Da Guoshi, or Great National Preceptor, together with a golden seal. The preceptor and patron erected several temples in the imperial city and restored the great temple at Seven Lakes (Dolonor), establishing a monastery there.

During the lifetime of that same emperor's son, Yongzheng the Great (r. 1722–35), my alleged previous birth, the great being Thuken Ngawang Chökyi Gyatso (1680–1736) was enthroned as Seal Lama[1512] for having well taught the precepts of the two systems[1513] to the yellow-clad lamas of the imperial city, and was presented with a golden letter proclaiming him Jingxiu Chanshi, or Master of Contemplation Possessed of the Pure Teaching, and a seal. The supreme Changkya emanation body, the omniscient holy lord Rölpai Dorjé (1717–86), was invited to China when he was just eight years old, and homage beyond imagining was paid to him; not long afterward, he was given the seal of Da Guoshi. The omniscient Second Panchen, Losang Yeshé, was given letters patent and a seal, and a fiefdom in the region of Tsang. The Seventh Dalai Lama, the omniscient Kalsang Gyatso, was given letters patent and a crystal seal, as in the time of the Fifth Dalai Lama. To a multitude of holy men worthy of honor, such as the noble Jamyang Shepai Dorjé, he gave the title of Nomin Han (King of the Dharma)[1514] and a seal, and he distributed gifts impartially to the upholders of the Geluk Dharma, regardless of whether they resided in the border or central lands.

His son, the emperor, the great sovereign Qianlong (1735–96), proclaimed Changkya the omniscient as the Crown of the Human Race, heard many Dharma teachings from him on sutra and mantra, and put them into practice. He established innumerable temples and instances of the three supports. In the imperial city, he renovated the temple of Ganden Jinchak Ling[1515] and instituted colleges for sutra, mantra, and worldly subjects there; and in the place known as Jehol, he established many different temples and colleges. Many great, holy men from Tibet and Amdo were invited and granted [310] the title of Samati Pakshi (Concentration Master). I, too, who am to be regarded as a pebble is to gold, was given very generous rewards and the seal of Chanshi (Master of Contemplation). The omniscient Third

Panchen, Palden Yeshé, was invited, and the emperor paid him incomparable honor, presented him with letters patent, and heard Dharma teachings from him. When the Gorkhas of Nepal attacked the teaching and the government in Tibet, troops sent by the emperor defeated them decisively.[1516] A proclamation was issued that the Ganden tradition should be the foremost everywhere under the sun.

Thus, through his gnostic insight, the Panchen, who is the omniscient aspect of Amitābha, discerned that it would be particularly necessary in the future, and so auspiciously inaugurated a relation of preceptor and patron between the Bogdo of the Jurchid[1517] and the Gedenpas. Based on that, the precious teaching of Jé Tsongkhapa, the second conqueror, which is without even the slightest stain of confusion about any of the three—view, meditation, and conduct—with regard to either sutra or mantra, and is the source of benefit and happiness of all people, has flourished like a wishing tree in the land of China, its splendor blazing like the orb of the sun.

Concluding verses

Many very powerful great beings, who prayed
To uphold the holy Dharma, brought to the land of China
From the Dharma treasury of the Holy Land
As many precious texts as their own intellectual ability could carry.

And many merchants of the Dharma—scholars and adepts—
Rich with the wealth of learning and realization,
Bearing the instructions on sutra and mantra, the wealth desired by all,
Forged sincerely on, and arrived in this country.

As the treasure of the holy Dharma flourished in that way
In the world of converts in the eastern lands,
The hand of hope for all beings
Was adorned with the glory of the ever-desirable jewel.

From out of the dharmadhātu, so clear, so clear,
The beautiful moonlight of the Buddha's deeds, so deep, so deep,
Spontaneously shines everywhere unimpeded
Upon the pools of fortunate converts, whoever they may be.

With the brush of intelligence dipped
In the colors of the topics of many histories,
I have drawn a sketch of this marvelous account
As a curiosity for the connoisseur.

From *The Crystal Mirror: An Excellent Explanation Showing the Sources and Assertions of All Philosophical Systems*, this completes the explanation the history of the Dharma system of the insiders—the Buddhists—in the land of China. [311]

16. Central Asian Traditions

IV. The History of Philosophical Systems in Some Other Lands[1518]

> I will relate how the Muni's teaching, the source of benefit and happiness,
> Came to Great Hor,[1519] Khotan, and Shambhala
> Through the Conqueror's deeds and, like beautiful music,
> was performed in harmony with the disciples' karmic lot.

In many countries great and small, such as Kashmir, Nepal, Persia, Campaka,[1520] Kiṣkindha,[1521] Sermik,[1522] Rugma,[1523] Ramma,[1524] Tāmradvīpa, Siṅgaladvīpa, Priyaṅkudvīpa, Yamunadvīpa,[1525] Suvarṇadvīpa,[1526] Candradvīpa,[1527] Mecca, Kaśya,[1528] Kyi Jang,[1529] Shangshung, Gilgit, Achai,[1530] Sumpa,[1531] Sahor,[1532] Xixia,[1533] Jang,[1534] Xinjiang, Tukhara, Uḍḍiyāna, Draviḍa,[1535] Longpo,[1536] Cola, Kaliṅga, and others, the Dharma spread and declined in various ways due to the degree to which those countries encountered the three vehicles of the Buddhadharma in its entirety, and the differences among the peoples of those lands as ordinary or extraordinary fields for conversion. To discuss all of that, as well as all of the many varieties of wrong views held in those countries, is beyond my capacity. Therefore, I will briefly relate here how the Dharma spread in A. Mongolia, B. Khotan, and C. Shambhala.

A. How the teaching spread in Mongolia
1. The thirteenth and fourteenth centuries: Sakyapas, Karmapas, and the Yuan
a. Genghis Khan's era[1537]

There are no historical accounts of Indian scholars, adepts, or others coming to this land and opening the way for the teaching; the Dharma was introduced from Tibet. The first teaching to arrive was the Dharma system of the

Sakyapas. Genghis Khan, (1162–1227), who turned the wheel of power, came to Tibet and brought under his control all three myriarchies of Ngari,[1538] the four horns of Ü and Tsang,[1539] and Lho, Kham, and [312] Gang. He sent emissaries to Tsang and through an exchange of gifts and so forth with Sachen Künga Nyingpo, established a preceptor-patron relationship with him. Subsequently, Genghis invited him to Mongolia and also requested that he bring with him some examples of the three supports. As a result, all of the Mongols came to have faith in the teaching, which was the beginning of the worship of the Buddha. Some even took lay and other vows. This marks the establishment of the teaching among the Mongols.[1540]

This event took place in the fire-hare year of the fourth sexegenary cycle (1207). According to those who maintain that the Buddha's nirvana occurred in an iron-dragon year, 2,087 years had passed, and for those who accept that it occurred in a fire-hare year, 2,041 years. From that year (1207) to the iron-dragon year of the thirteenth sexegenary cycle (1760), 553 years have elapsed.[1541]

b. Godan and Kublai's era

When Genghis' grandsons, the brothers Guyug (mid-thirteenth century) and Godan (d. 1251), ruled the kingdom from Lanzhou,[1542] Godan, who had heard of the fame of Sakya Panchen, sent an emissary to Tibet with an invitation for him to visit Mongolia, which he accepted. Sapan did so because it accorded with a prophecy that his predecessor, the venerable Drakpa Gyaltsen, had made to him, that when a man from a borderland wearing a hat like a hawk and shoes like pigs' snouts would come to invite him there, it would be beneficial to both the teaching and living beings were he to go. Together with his nephews Phakpa and Chakna, he went and met with King Godan in the fire-sheep year of the fourth sexegenary cycle (1247).[1543] The king, who was stricken with an illness caused by earth demons, was completely cured by Sapan by means of the Lion's Roar ritual.[1544] Sapan bestowed the Hevajra initiation on the king and his retinue and performed miracles of various kinds, so that they became devotees.

Up to that time the Mongols had no written language. Sapan, wishing to design an alphabet for them, happened to see a woman holding a wooden hide-rubbing tool that resembled the edge of a saw, and based on its shape he modeled the Mongolian letters: *a e i, na ne ni, pa pe pi, ha he hi,*[1545] *gha ghe ghi, ma me mi, la le li, ra re ri, sa se si,*[1546] *ta te ti, tha the thi, tsa tse tsi, tsha tshe tshi, ya ye yi, wa we wi.* Dividing the letters into male, female, and neuter, and tight, loose, and slack, he introduced literacy in Mongolian.[1547] Both Sapan and the king died in the iron-pig year (1251). As everyone knows, the physical remains of Sapan lie within the stupa of Trüldé (Miraculous Monastery), outside the palace at Lanzhou.[1548] [313]

Later on, during the reign of King Mongké (1209–59), Karma Pakshi and others arrived. Mongké's younger brother, Kublai Sechen Khan (1215–94), greatly expanded Mongol power by bringing under his control all of China, Tibet, Mongolia, and about half of India, as far as the border of Kashmir. Sapan's nephew, Phakpa Lodrö Gyaltsen, was invited from Tibet, and he met with the king in the water-ox year (1254). The king questioned him about the Dharma and so became his devotee. However, prior to that he had been a devotee of Karma Pakshi and in a private conversation had said, "Phakpa's knowledge of scripture is the greater, but it appears that when it comes to realization, the bearded[1549] lama is far superior." The queen, named Dzema Sangmo (Beautiful and Good), was a devotee of Lama Phakpa and secretly reported the king's remark to him, imploring him to compete with Pakshi in a contest of miracles so that the king might come to have full faith in him. This Phakpa accepted. According to some accounts, in the presence of the king and others, Pakshi rose cross-legged into the sky and abruptly[1550] passed right through a mountain and displayed other feats as well. Phakpa demonstrated such miracles as severing his own five limbs, scattering them about, turning them into the conquerors belonging to the five families, reuniting them with his own body, and so forth.[1551] According to the *Blue Annals:* "Kublai met Pakshi and promulgated a gracious decree:[1552] 'You may practice your Dharma in the land of Tibet or wherever you like, and may I be the recipient of your good wishes.'"[1553] This story is found nowhere else. According to some holy men the so-called Stupa of Karma Li Shi located within the palace of Lanzhou is actually the stupa of Karma Pakshi, which, through a garbled pronunciation, came to be known as the Stupa of Karma Li Shi. While there is no doubt that Karma Pakshi died in Lanzhou, there are, nevertheless, in the *Blue Annals* and elsewhere, accounts of his having returned to Tibet.[1554]

The king did not ask Phakpa for initiation for some time. First, he had the queen request the Hevajra initiation. When he asked her what kind of vows were required and she described them to him, the king said: "While I can keep my other promises, it is impossible for me, a great king, not to transgress the orders of a guru." The queen replied that it would be acceptable if the king were to be supreme in worldly matters and the guru supreme in matters of Dharma. The king found this agreeable, and together with a retinue of twenty-four who were able to keep the vows, he received the Hevajra initiation. As the initiation tribute he offered [314] two great golden mandalas, one patterned with flawless pearls the size of sheep droppings piled up in heaps, and the other patterned with Mt. Meru, the continents, and so forth also made of gold, as well as gifts of horses, mules, camels, gold, silver, and silk beyond imagining. The king also offered him a title that in Chinese is Sanjie Daguoshi (Great National Preceptor of the Three Realms), or Dharma King of the Three Realms. The king gave him the territory around the city of Lixin[1555] together with its inhabitants, and later, in stages, all three provinces of Tibet[1556] to be his subjects.[1557] When the king said that he was going to decree that all Tibetan monks should follow the Sakya Dharma system, Phakpa Rinpoché replied that it would be best if everyone adhered to their own long-flourishing Dharma systems, and the king established a policy of impartiality as a result.

Phakpa Rinpoché went back to Tibet in the wood-ox year (1266) but returned to the land of Hor in the earth-snake year of the fifth sexegenary cycle (1269). In the iron-horse year (1271), he designed Mongolian seal letters that were square in shape and so established the practice of teaching, study, meditation, and realization; thus did he greatly promote the welfare of the teaching and living beings.[1558] The king, having obtained from India many examples of the three supports, such as buddha relics and so forth, had temples built, established monasteries, and so spread the teaching.

c. Later developments

The Dharma, however, could not be translated into Mongolian using the seal letters, so when the Mongols recited the Dharma, they did so in the Uyghur language. In the time of King Öljeitü (1265–1307), the Sakya teacher Chökyi Öser[1559] came to Mongolia and added many letters with tails to the letters previously invented by Sapan and so made it possible to translate the Dharma. Later, in the time of King Heshan Külüg (1281–1311), the word of the Buddha, such as the five dhāraṇī texts, and other texts and their commentaries were translated into Mongolian. In the time of Buyantu Khan (1285–1320), Jamyang, a pupil of Narthang Rikral (fourteenth century), came to the land of Hor. While at Narthang he had put on a mask and frightened Rikral so that his lama had become displeased with him;[1560] however, he later regained his lama's favor by sending him from Mongolia much of the equipment necessary for producing a Kangyur, and in particular by offering him a box of the best Chinese ink. It was owing to the dispatch of the equipment by Jamyang that a Kangyur was produced, and he requested that it be kept in the Mañjughoṣa temple at Narthang. With that as a model, [315] copies of the Kangyur proliferated.

It is said that some time later, the Third Karmapa, Rangjung Dorjé, came and initiated a king of Hor who, I think, may have been Jayatu (1304–32). Togon Temur (1320–70) invited the Fourth Karmapa, Rölpai Dorjé, who arrived in Mongolia at the age of nineteen, in the earth-male-dog year (1359). During the time of the fourteen kings from Genghis to Erdeni Chogtu (1326–32),[1561] many Sakya and Karmapa lamas went to Mongolia, and more than a few were honored by the king with the title Dishi (Imperial Preceptor).

2. The sixteenth and seventeenth centuries and beyond: Mongol-Geluk relations
a. Altan Khan and others

How the relationship of preceptor and patron with the Gedenpa came about: During the time of Altan Khan (1557–82) of the Tümed, the Third Dalai Lama, Sönam Gyatso, came to Mongolia, abolished the practice of the ritual sacrifice of living creatures in the worship of the Ongghot,[1562] and introduced the Yellow Hat tradition. The Third Dalai Lama having died in Mongolia, his incarnation, the Fourth Dalai Lama Yönten Gyatso, was born in Mongolia [in 1589], which was beneficial to the wide diffusion of the teaching, especially in Mongolia. All the Mongols became patrons of the Gedenpa. Subsequently, Shirgetu (fl. early seventeenth century) translated the three mothers into Mongolian.[1563] In the time of the Chahar Ligden (d. 1634) many translators, under the direction of Künga Öser, translated the entire Kangyur into Mongolian.[1564] Ligden, the last minor king of Hor, destroyed his very own kingdom in a civil war, and the Hor dynasty came to an end. During the time of the emperor Kangxi (1661–1722), the Mongolian-letter Kangyur was corrected and printed. By order of the Mañjughoṣa[1565] Emperor Qianlong (1711–99), the entire Tengyur was translated into Mongolian and printed. During that time, Changkya Rölpai Dorjé wrote the *Dictionary: A Sourcebook for the Wise,*[1566] which was indispensable for translating the Dharma into Mongolian and was, for later translators, the eye for viewing the meaning of scriptural terminology.

When Sönam Gyatso was traveling to the land of Sog for the second time, King Taiji Abadai (1554–88) met him in Khalkha territory [in 1587]. The king built the temple of Erdeni Juu.[1567] The First Jetsün Dampa Losang Tenpai Gyaltsen, the rebirth of Tāranātha, was born as the son of Abadai's grandson Dorjé Tushetu Khan (1594–1655). Jetsün Dampa became the crown jewel of all seven sections of the Khalkha. Even the great Mañjughoṣa Emperor greatly esteemed him and praised him. [In 1654,] Jetsün [316] Dampa established the monastery of Riwo Gegyé Ling. From that time on the rebirths have proceeded in succession. In addition, both Jaya Pandita Losang Trinlé, who had been a pupil of both Panchen Losang Chögyen and the Fifth Dalai Lama, and Erdeni Pandita Losang Tenzin founded monasteries and promoted the teaching widely. Ever since then, the land of the Khalkha has been filled with holy men and monasteries, and instruction in both teaching and practice has flourished.

Döndrup Gyatso (b. seventeenth century), the head teacher of Gomang, who was famous for being a bodhisattva on the path of preparation, came to the land of the Torgod and introduced the teaching; however as the Torgod came under the control of Russia the teaching did not make much progress. Later, when the Torgod emerged from Russian control and were put under the control of the Mañjughoṣa Emperor, the emperor divided the territory up among the various chiefs who settled there, and the Torgod zealously applied themselves to the veneration and support of the precious teaching.[1568]

When, from among the four sections that make up the Oirat or Ölöt, the Khoshot were in power, Galdan Boshugtu Khan (1644–97) of the Choros clan[1569] grew in strength and wealth, overthrew the Khoshot Ocirtu Sechen[1570] Khan, and brought the entire realm of the Oirat under his control. He established many colleges for instruction in the sutras and tantras. After him, Erdeni Jorigtu Hong Taiji Tsewang Rabten (1643–1727)[1571] came to have strong faith in the Conqueror's teaching in general, and in the doctrine of Geden in particular. From Tashi Lhünpo he invited in turn the great tantric master Gelek Rapgyé and Paljor Gyatso. Later, he invited many scholars from Drepung, such as Washül Tenpa Rapgyé and others. He encouraged the taking of one-day vows by householders and had the novices and monks adhere to the two texts by Tsongkhapa on *Training According to the Namtsé Ding Tradition;*[1572] in this way the purity of the rules of discipline was established. Although he founded no colleges for the study of dialectics, he did focus upon promoting the teaching and study of *The Great* and *Small Stages of the Path*. In his respect for the teaching, he was the equal of the Tibetan king Tri Ralpachen, as shown by such deeds as giving every novice and monk a gift of three households to support him, six camels, forty cows and horses, and two hundred sheep. After him, his son Ganden Tsering Wangpo (r. 1727–45) invited [317] many who possessed the eye of Dharma: from Tashi Lhünpo the head teacher of Thösam Ling college, the renowned and accomplished great scholar the Third Panchen Palden Yeshé; from Drepung the venerable vinaya master and head teacher of Gomang college, Losang Phüntsok, and the high official Gendün Drakpa; from Sera, the head teacher of Jé college; and others. Ganden Tsering instituted the teaching and study of dialectics, built many temples, and furnished many material supports of the Buddha's body, speech, and mind.[1573] Through rich rewards and praise for each newly graduated class of geshés, the pure way of the teaching flourished for quite some time. However, the kingdom was later on destroyed by civil war, so that today it is barren like fields in autumn.[1574]

b. Gushri Khan and the Fifth Dalai Lama[1575]

From among the four sections that make up the Oirat, the third son of the Khoshot chief Ha-nai Noyan, Gushri Khan (1582–1654), known as Tenzin Chökyi Gyalpo (Righteous King Upholder of the Teaching)[1576] was born in the water-male-horse year. His given name was Thorol Baihur. According to a prophecy by the treasure revealer Drimé Lhünpo, he was an emanation of Vajrapāṇi; he was a stage-abiding bodhisattva[1577] who appeared in the form of a righteous king. When he was thirteen years old, he led his troops and fell upon an army of ten thousand Gokar,[1578] crushing the entire opposing force. From that battle he acquired a reputation for military prowess. At that time the Dharma had not yet spread into his country. As everyone knows, when someone remarked to him that the holy Dharma had spread in other Mongol lands owing to the kindness of the pair—the preceptor, the Dalai Lama Sönam Gyatso and the patron, the Golden King [Altan Khan]—immediately upon hearing that single word *Dharma* he gained great faith, and he prostrated so many times in the direction of those lands that his forehead swelled up. When he was twenty-five his mother died, and as part of her funeral rites he lavishly gave alms to the poor.

Meanwhile, owing to a disagreement, there had been a battle between the Khalkha and the Oirat. Moved by compassion, he went without hesitation among the Khalkha and brought about a reconciliation between the two parties. For that, Lama Tongkhor Chöjé[1579] and the Khalkha king and ministers were overjoyed and gave him the title of Da Guoshi (Great National Preceptor). He then returned to his own country. [318]

During one of his journeys to Mongolia, the Third Dalai Lama, Sönam Gyatso, was asked by a man from the Oirat to lay his hands on a copy of the *Holy Golden Light Sutra*. When the Dalai Lama asked him its Mongolian title and the man replied, *Altan Gerel (Golden Light)*, the Dalai Lama prophesied that in twenty years time the Dharma would spread to his country. In accordance with that prophecy, with Gushri Khan as patron, many scriptures such as the *Holy Golden Light Sutra* were translated, and the way of the teaching was established.

Due to the turmoil provoked by the king of the Chahar among the six great divisions of the western Mongols, some of the chiefs fled to the Khalkha, but because of internal dissension among the Khalkha chiefs themselves, the Khalkha Chogtu was driven out of his own country and went to Kokonor, where he brought all of Amdo under his control. For a while his power was great, and he inflicted as much damage as he could on the teaching in general and on the teaching of Mount Geden in particular. The news of these events reached the king. With the teaching of Jé Rinpoché as his sole concern, he left his country with a large army and, in the first month of the fire-ox year (1637), arrived in Kokonor, where in battle he utterly destroyed Chogtu's forty thousand troops and so brought every part of eastern Tibet under his control. He then went to Ü to meet with the conqueror father and son. He had an audience with the Great Fifth Dalai Lama and Panchen Losang Chökyi Gyaltsen and took them as his crown-of-the-head ornaments. Although it was nighttime on the twenty-seventh day of the lunar month[1580] when he went to Ganden for his audience, the assembly hall was so bright that even small stones were visible; thus the omens concurred that all religious and secular government would be white and smooth. He then returned to Kokonor in the winter of the fire ox-year (1637).

In middle Kham, King Dönyö of Beri was extremely hostile to the teaching of the Buddha and honored the Bön tradition exclusively. Learning of this, in the fifth Hor month of the earth-hare year (1639) Gushri Khan with a huge army fell upon Beri and made most of them his subjects. The King of Beri fled elsewhere but was captured on the twenty-fifth day of the eleventh month of the iron-dragon year (1640) and imprisoned. All the lamas and chiefs of the Sakyapas, Gelukpas, Karmapas, Drukpas, Taklungpas, and others who had been incarcerated were released and sent back to their original places. The people of every land, up to those of the king of Sa Dam in Jang, paid their taxes and earnestly rendered him homage.

At that time the ruler of Ü-Tsang was the [319] regent Tsangpa (1606–42),[1581] who patronized the Karmapas primarily and plotted actively against the Gelukpas. Gushri Khan, with a mighty army, invaded Ü-Tsang and destroyed the forces of Tsangpa. He captured the ruler Tsangpa and his ministers, imprisoned them at Neu Shikha in Ü, brought all of Ü-Tsang under his control, and became king of the three provinces of Tibet. The white umbrella of his law extended to the pinnacle of the cosmos. He eliminated all wicked persons challenging the Gelukpas. In addition, many lesser kings from the border regions, such as the Indian king Raghu Singh,[1582] the king of Kathmandu in Nepal, the king of Ngari, and others offered him gifts according to the custom of their countries. Gushri Khan offered the subjects of Ü-Tsang to the omniscient Dalai Lama. The majesty of the heaven-appointed political administration of the Ganden Palace[1583] reached to the sky. It is understood that the reputation that Ganden enjoys to this day as Heavenly Ganden is due to the kindness of this king.

This king had ten sons, from among whom Dayan Khan (d. 1668) and, in turn, his grandson Lhapsang Khan (r. 1703–17) became kings of Tibet. Gushri Khan's youngest son, A Khu Tashi Batur (1632–1714), became king of Kokonor [in 1660]. Thus, the line of Gushri Khan split among separate independent princes who were powerful and rich and able to stand on their own without relying on others. However, they all later came under the control of the Mañjughoṣa Emperor as a result of the war initiated by Tenzin Wang [in 1723].[1584] The emperor restored them to their respective fiefdoms and presented them with gifts, and in accordance with the custom of their ancestors, the princes enthusiastically worked for the Dharma, honoring and supporting the teaching of Ganden and its upholders by building monasteries in their territories and so forth.

Thus did the teaching spread through the various lands of the Sog. Over the course of time it became customary for Mongolian monks to go to Ü and Tsang for their education, so that many of them, having received a standard Tibetan education, were able to uphold and further the Dharma in various ways through teaching and practice. In addition, holy great men came time and time again—from Ü-Tsang, Eastern Tibet, and elsewhere [320]—so that at present the entire land of Hor is filled with temples and monasteries. Schools of dialectics have spread, and as a result the precious teaching has spread and flourished. Apart from some places such as Solon and Barga,[1585] even the names of the debased views of the infidels and barbarians are unknown in the vast land of Sog. At present, even upholders of the earlier Dharma lineages of the Sakya and Karmapa are not to be found; the Yellow Hat tradition alone fills the land.

B. How the teaching spread in Khotan[1586]

As prophesied by the Blessed One in such sutras as the *Liyül Prophecy*[1587] and *Langru Prophecy,*[1588] in Khotan, 117 years after the passing of the Buddha, Vaiśrāvaṇa gave to the king of China a boy named Kustana,[1589] who had been born to Vaiśrāvaṇa and a queen of the Dharma king Aśoka.[1590] Kustana, who had gone on an expedition with ten thousand troops, and Dharmarāja Aśoka's minister Yaśa and his retinue of seven thousand, who had been exiled by king Aśoka, converged in Khotan and took over the land. In the time of Vijayasaṃbhava of the Yaśa lineage, who was an emanation of Maitreya, Mañjughoṣa emanated as the bhikṣu Vairocana and created and taught the Khotanese alphabet. King Vijayasaṃbhava built the temple of Tsārma. Many people wanted to establish temples and stupas, so they built temples and stupas for as many relics of the Buddha as there were. At the urging of the king, the bhikṣu Vairocana invited sixteen elders, and they were worshipped and honored. Then, at the time of the seventh in the Khotanese royal line, Vijayavīrya,[1591] four arhats came from India. The Kāśyapa stupa, which had been prophesied by the Teacher, and the Gaotoshan temple were erected on top of Ox-Head Mountain. A prince took preliminary ordination and obtained arhatship.[1592] From then on, the teaching of the Buddha spread widely in that land; there were multiple Dharma kings, who established many temples and stupas. [321]

C. How the teaching spread in the land of Shambhala[1593]

1. Overview

How the teaching spread in Shambhala: The Kālacakra teaching arose there during the Buddha's lifetime, has existed there until the present day, and will also be widespread there in the future. Shambhala is said to be known thus because it was controlled by the so-called Shambhaka clan of the Śākyas. It also is said that *Shambhala* means "Held by Śambhū"; Śambhū is a name for Īśvara, and the land he controls is Shambhala.

As to the layout of the land: Its shape is circular; it has the shape of an eight-petaled lotus inside an encircling border of snow mountains. The interstices of the petal shapes are cut by rivers, and at the center sits a great pistil-like snow mountain. Each petal contains 120 million cities, so there are 960 million cities all together. Each set of ten million cities has ten million districts, and each set of ten million cities is ruled by a governor. In the center of that land is an area like the four continents divided by snow mountains, and in the center of that is Kalāpa city. To the south of that, in the Malaya garden, is the great three-dimensional Kālacakra mandala constructed by the Dharma king Sucandra; to the east is Upamānsara Lake; to the west is Puṇḍarīka Lake; and to the north is the great palace that was the residence of Dharma kings and kalkins.

The first king to rule there is said to have been Sūryaprabhā. Then came seven Dharma kings and twenty-five kalkins.[1594] According to the *Kālacakra Root Tantra:*

> Sucandra (d. 877 B.C.E.), Sureśvara, and Tejin,
> Somadatta and Sureśvara,[1595]
> Viśvamūrti and Sureśāna.[1596]

Those are the seven Dharma kings. And:

> The kalkin Mañjughoṣa Yaśas, the first of the clan
> (r. 277–177 B.C.E.),
> Thence the kalkin Puṇḍarīka,
> The kalkin Bhadra, who was third,
> Likewise, the fourth, Vijaya,
> Sumitrabhadra, Ratnapāṇi,
> The seventh, Viṣṇugupta,
> Sūryakīrti and Subhadra,
> Samudravijaya, Aja,
> And the [322] kalkin Sūrya, the twelfth,
> Viśvarūpa[1597] and Śaṣiprabha,
> Ananta and then Mahīpala,
> Śrīpala, Siṃha,[1598] Vikrama,
> Mahābala, and Aniruddha,
> Narasiṃha, Maheśvara,
> The kalkin Ananatavijaya,

And again the kalkin Yaśas[1599]—
As Ananatavijaya's son, the great wheel holder,
The kalkin Rudra (r. 2327–2427)—all these will come.[1600]

Those are the twenty-five kalkins.

2. History of the Buddha's teaching

The Blessed One awakened to complete enlightenment in the water-horse year called "the various" (878 B.C.E.).[1601] A year later, on the full moon of Caitra in the water-sheep year called "the sun," he taught the perfection of wisdom sutras on Vulture Peak[1602] and simultaneously at Śrī Dhānyakaṭaka assumed the form of the main deity of the mandala, Kālacakra, who projected, in the lower section of the stupa, the mandala of the twelve-part ultimate truth, Dharmadhātu Vageśvara, and in the upper section, the glorious sixteen-part astrological mandala.

With the Dharma king Sucandra at their head, the ninety-six emanated[1603] Dharma kings of northern Kalāpa,[1604] as well as innumerable pure courtiers, were initiated into the great Vajradhātu mandala and were taught the *Kālacakra Root Tantra*. The Dharma king Sucandra wrote out the root tantra in book form; having taken it to Shambhala, he erected a three-dimensional Kālacakra mandala and wrote a twelve-thousand-verse[1605] commentary on the tantra. Six hundred years later, the first kalkin, Mañjughoṣa Yaśas,[1606] came and taught the root tantra for a hundred years. And, especially for the purpose of maturing the seer Sūryaratha[1607] and others, he taught the *Condensed Kālacakra Tantra*. Because he brought the castes into a single caste, he took the name kalkin, or "caste leader." After that, the kalkin Puṇḍarīka[1608] ascended the throne; he taught the root tantra and condensed tantra for a hundred years and wrote the great commentary called *Stainless Light*. Eventually, the great pandit Cilupa, Kālacakrapāda the Elder, and others spread the Kālacakra from Shambhala to the Holy Land of India. Twenty-five translators who came over time spread the teaching of the Kālacakra in the land of Tibet—the glorious Bhadrabodhi, Dro Lotsāwa Sherap Drak, and others.

At the present time, the nineteenth kalkin, Vikrama, reigns in Shambhala, and this [323] iron-monkey[1609] year (1801), called "the fierce," is the seventy-fifth year since that kalkin assumed the throne.

3. The future

The fire-sky-ocean era[1610] began in the wood-monkey year called "freeing the sun" (624 C.E.), during the reign of the tenth kalkin, Samudravijaya. In the land of Mecca dwelt the barbarian teachers and their retinues:[1611] Adam, Enoch,[1612] Abraham, Moses, Jesus, the White-Clad One,[1613] Muhammad, and the Mahdi. The seventh of those, called Ngarden or Drangtsi Lodrö, that is, Muhammad,[1614] composed the astrological texts used by the extremists and spread the barbarian teaching. At that time, the extremists also adopted the barbarian teaching, so they destroyed many Buddhist temples. As for a rough calculation of the duration of the barbarian era: it is explained that it will last for 1800 years after the Hijra.

About 537 years after this present iron-monkey year, in the fire-sheep year of the twenty-second cycle, called "the ape" (2327 C.E.), the twenty-fifth kalkin, Raudracakrin, will occupy the Shambhala throne and teach the Dharma. After about fifty years, half the abhidharma texts of the sutra-vehicle portion of Buddha's teaching will have disappeared. Toward the end of the Kali Yuga,[1615] the last of the four ages described in the mantra texts, starting in the fire-monkey year called "ugly face" (2378 C.E.), a barbarian king who is the emanation of a titan[1616] will appear with his massed vassals and army at a place called Delhi in the western part of the Holy Land; he will subjugate the lands south of the Śītā River: Madhyadeśa together with the region of Tibet.[1617] Having taken control of about half of Jambudvīpa, he will commence to wage war on Shambhala.

At that time, according to the *Kālacakra Root Tantra:*

> The kalkin Rudra will arise
> And put an end to the barbarian religion
> Through the concentration called *the supreme steed of the lord of speech*.[1618]

As stated there, the twenty-fifth kalkin, Raudracakrin, who is an emanation of Mañjughoṣa, will annihilate those barbarians. The way that will happen is that that kalkin will come to Jambudvīpa from Shambhala to subdue the barbarians with 90 million horses with the strength of the wind, 400,000 elephants, 500,000 chariots, and an army of soldiers extending as far as the eye can see, and will fight a battle with the barbarians [324] on the banks of the Indian river called the Śītā.[1619] At that time, Raudracakrin will pierce the barbarian king Muhammad[1620] with his spear, and the kalkin's two generals, Hanuman and Rudra, will in turn pierce the barbarian generals, Mahācandratanaya[1621] and Indranātha, with their spears and defeat them. On this occasion, all the gods will take the side of the kalkin, and the titans will take the side of the barbarians. Thus, having utterly destroyed the host of barbarians in combat, the kalkin will have control over the whole expanse of the earth. The Mahayana Dharma will spread extensively, and because of that, people's lifespans will increase to 1800 years, and they will enjoy the splendor of an unprecedented perfect age.[1622]

This is just a brief account; further details may be learned from Khedrup Jé's *Great Commentary on Kālacakra* and other sources.

4. Distinguishing barbarians from extremists

Barbarians and the extremists are not the same: there were extremists in Shambhala before the barbarians entered, and it is explained that their standpoint agreed with that of the Indian extremists, and that there were also some who were a bit different from the Indian extremists. I have not elaborated here on the way they expound their standpoint or the reasoning refuting those debased views, which are taught in the Kālacakra; those wanting more information should look into the tantric commentaries.

The system of the barbarians, unlike that of most extremists, is not based on logic, meditative equipoise, and so forth. Like worldly human conduct, it apparently is a system founded on confusion, clinging, and ego-fixation; it seems that it mainly propounds harming others as Dharma. It seems that nowadays, in China and other lands, there also are types of barbarians called Houzi and Thaendru.[1623] There are many others like them, and I have heard it said by holy people that the barbarian clans gradually will expand in different directions, and that in the future, when all the great barbarian armies assemble in the Delhi region, they will join forces and will gain control of about half of Jambudvīpa.

5. Secret prophecies

The secret teaching of the omniscient Third Panchen, Palden Yeshé, states:

> At the present [325] time, not just the Kālacakra, but all the teachings of sutra and mantra are flourishing in Shambhala; even the

> well-expounded texts of Jé Tsongkhapa, the second conqueror, were magically brought to Shambhala by ḍākas and ḍākinīs and are widespread there.[1624]

I also have heard prophecies, seen in pure visions by authoritative persons, to the effect that when the kalkin Raudracakrin has annihilated the barbarians and the teaching of the Buddha is flourishing, the body and head and other limbs of the past glorious protector, Ārya Nāgārjuna—which had been separated and came to rest in different places—will gradually draw closer together. At that time, the parts will reintegrate, and Nāgārjuna will live again. Also at that time, the wish-fulfilling jewel, the remains of Jé Lama, will be taken to India by a master, and Jé Lama will live again. Those two once more will perform greatly extensive deeds on behalf of the teaching.[1625]

The kalkin Raudracakrin will be an emanation of the First Panchen, the original Buddha, Losang Chögyen:

> I pray to the wheel-turning king Raudracakrin, who in the future
> Will destroy the forces of the dark, demonic barbarians;
> He is the ornament *(gyen)* beautifying the aim of the noble-minded
> Dharma *(losang chö)*
> Of Tsongkhapa, who is an emanation of Mañjuśrīvajra.[1626]

General Hanuman will be an emanation of the Seventh Dalai Lama, Sumatikalpabhadrasamudra, or Losang Kalsang Gyatso. A prayer in his *Secret Biography* says:

> In the future, in order to destroy the barbarian forces,
> Let virtue and goodness be bestowed on the whole of Jambudvīpa
> Through the appearance of the one with splendid, inexhaustible
> Vajra weapons: the ruler of the twelve lords.[1627]

And, as already discussed in my *Biographical Ornament Beautifying the Geden Doctrine,* as shown in the secret prophecy of Panchen Śrīmajjñāna, that is, Palden Yeshé, General Rudra will be an emanation of my own guide, Jñānaśasanasyadīpiśrībhadra, that is, Changkya Rölpai Dorjé.[1628]

Concluding verses

Although the lotus's friend [i.e., the moon] is high in the sphere of the sky,
Its radiant light falls on all the earth; likewise,
Although the friend of the sun [i.e., the Buddha] came to the center of Jambudvīpa,[1629]
His holy Dharma spread widely, throughout the world.

In [326] Khotan, moistened by the prophetic rain
That came from the cloud of the Mighty Muni's mouth,
The golden grain-cluster of the holy Dharma bowed down
Atop of the ripening sprout of the merits of embodied beings.

The Mongol lands have been ruled by many lion men,
Endowed with mighty shoulders of potent faith
That can carry the Dharma throne of the Buddha's teaching;
Nowadays these lands contain as well the glory and wealth of the Land of Snows.

The great rain of the kalkin Rudra's army
Will wash away all stains of debased views, as rain cleanses the earth;
Sweet as well is this summer thunder of prophecy
That reveals the smile of a new perfected age.

The great sunlight of the Conqueror's teaching
Opens the lotus of auspiciousness;
I have spoken briefly of its marvelous rise
In Mongolia, Khotan, and Shambhala.

From *The Crystal Mirror: An Excellent Explanation Showing the Sources and Assertions of All Philosophical Systems,* this completes the explanation of the history of philosophical systems in some other lands. [327]

17. Conclusion

V. Conclusion

THE FIFTH TOPIC of the basic outline, concluding by an explanation of the final outcome, I will discuss in metered verse.[1630]

In the beginning, in the golden ground of his mental continuum,
the Buddha planted the stable root of the virtuous arousal of the awakening mind;
In the middle, through the power of that, he drank for many eons
the streaming water of the two virtuous collections;
At the end, by growing and developing it in such a way, he completed
the creation of the tree of virtuous enlightenment.
And so, through constant virtue, the cool shade of deeds that take away the torments of existence, the power of the Muni, protects beings completely. (19)

The Kailash of his gnostic understanding
Is struck by the solar heat of great kindness,
So the streaming rivers of the 84,000 Dharmas
Pour down into the fields of converts. (9)

The swirling waters of the purifying Tripiṭaka,
Containing the essence of the jewels of the three trainings,
When moving in waves of explanation and practice
Are called "the great ocean of the Muni's teaching." (7)

In that very ocean of scripture and reasoning, the blazing,
brilliant light of the jewels of excellent explanation, raised high by the nāga kings,
Illuminates the ultimate nature of what is to be adopted and abandoned, destroying all the submerged darkness of debased views;

The assembled nāga potentates, upholders of the teaching who are expert at bringing down the rain of longed-for goodness, hold as their own
The precious treasure of good qualities that, in every world, protects all the fortunate minor nāgas.[1631] (17/15/17/17)

The lotus pond of pure morality has become
The playground of a flock of swans, who sound a song
Of the deep, extensive Dharma, diligent in the vows
That pacify conduct and subdue the senses. (9)

The source of precious things, the oceanic teaching of the Muni,
Fills the center, borderlands, and everywhere;
It surges up and overflows, descending to the land
Outside the rim of snowy peaks.[1632] (7)

Drawn down to the valleys
Of differing inclinations, that water
Swirls into the many philosophical-system ponds
Beautified by the lotuses of explanation and practice. (7)

Although it came in a single purifying
Stream from Kailash, the Mighty Muni,
It became unfit to drink, polluted by the brine
Of certain persons' [328] fantasies.[1633] (7)

At that time, Mañjughoṣa, performing as a human,
Cleansed away the stains of sullied impurity
With the *ketaka* stone[1634] of Losang the conqueror's[1635] discernment,
Turning the way of Dharma into the nature of nectar. (9)

Hey, there! Here is what the wise should do, in thought and action:
Seek a way, a means of liberation from samsara, whose nature is suffering.
Those who never ponder that way, content merely with the appearances of this life,
Appear to be incarnate humans but ought to be counted as cattle. (15)

Further, there are two schools, the non-Buddhist and the Buddhist,
who set forth explanations
Of bondage and freedom in this world;
Whichever one you follow, first analyze
The distinction between the deceptive and the nondeceptive. (9)

You allow yourself to weigh incessantly,
In each and every tiny endeavor of this life,
"Although complete, less benefit,
Although incomplete, less harm." (7)

How then could it be right to act so rashly,
Not analyzing what to adopt or abandon,
When being right means eternal satisfaction
And being wrong brings grave disaster? (7)

So, when you know the standpoint
Of the non-Buddhist extremists,
And see how that system is destroyed
By valid knowledge, you can reject it like poison. (7)

And when you establish reliably,
Through reasoning based on the way things are,
The ways in which we enter or leave samsara,
As taught by our Teacher, (7)

You will gain certainty that this teaching alone
Is the supreme entryway for those desiring liberation
And that this very teacher is an undeceiving
Authoritative being. Another teaching or teacher (7)

You will not seek, even for the sake of your life.
You will not abandon the Three Jewels;
Held in your heart as eternal objects of refuge
They are the basis for fulfilling[1636] every goal. (7)

Likewise, in this land of Tibet as well,
The various philosophical systems of the Dharma schools

Are like the designs on Chinese silk—
With elements both different and alike. (7)

To understand distinctly the mode
Of presentation of view, meditation, and conduct
In those philosophical systems, you need to distinguish,
Using scripture and logic, what is true from what is fake. (7)

Some are under the sway of partiality,
Some act only from obstinate ignorance,
Others meditate on everything as pure appearance:
Mostly, the Dharma goes unanalyzed. (7)

The system of the wise is not like that.
Giving up taking sides, they search out
With an honest mind the distinctions between
Errant and inerrant, superior and inferior. (7)

When you take the Conqueror's scriptures as witness
And analyze with reasoning based on [329] the way things are,
Then faith derived from understanding reasons will arise
Toward the system of Losang the conqueror. (7)

Otherwise, praising their own side
And denigrating the other side out of partiality alone,
Those who proudly claim to evaluate the teaching
Simply disgust the wise. (9)

Among as many scriptures of the Conqueror as there are,
There is not even a single thing
That is unavailing at the time of practice
For those who are intent on liberation. (7)

Although the Buddha taught various provisional and definitive
scriptures,
They all come down to a single ultimate meaning;
Although he taught different vehicles,
They all incline toward the ultimate one, the Mahayana. (7)

Therefore, from the *Stanzas on Vinaya*
Up to the *Guhyasamāja,* everything extant
In the scriptural tradition is a necessary condition
For one person to become a buddha. (7)

Thus, the fortunate desiring liberation,
Unsatisfied with rough or partial understanding,
Pursue studies that go to the essential points
In untold textual systems. (7)

Because the point of study is to accomplish goals,
Do not take a solely external view;
Focus on a method that establishes
How to practice by way of meditation.[1637] (7)

If you do not obtain your own allotted share
Of the banquet of secret mantra, the Vajrayana,
Which is rarer even than a buddha's arising,
That's an opportunity for this teaching missed. (9)

By learning and practicing
Just a small deity sādhana,
You will not cover the distance to enlightenment;
So it's vital that the tantras' meaning appear as instruction. (7)

After obtaining initiation and abiding in the pledges,
The way to advance to the stage of Vajradhara
Is the path-traversing system of the two tantric stages
And the stages of yogic achievement ensuing from those. (7)

Well understanding the stages taught in the tantras,
The yogin who practices those exactly right
Is called a secret-mantra yogin
By sages who see the mantra way. (7)

The fortunate one who has brought into experience
The Dharma to be practiced in that way
Will not waste a human life distracted
By the spectacle of this realm of appearances. (7)

Living in satisfaction with few desires
In a solitary place praised by the Conqueror,
Practicing the union of sutra and mantra:
That's how life and practice are equalized. (7)

Thus, precise study, reflection, and meditation
On the key points of the complete teaching of the Conqueror:
This is the intention of Losang the conqueror;
It's the excellent path traveled [330] by the conquerors of the three
times. (9)

Weary of a way such as this,
You may hope for immediate freedom
Merely through identifying the mind;
But that's just making your own head spin. (7)

This conclusion of my discussion
Of the necessity for understanding philosophical systems
And the history of philosophical systems
Should be taken to heart by those desiring attainment.[1638] (7)

In terms of concluding through an explanation of the final outcome, that's it!

Afterword

Furthermore, I say:

Everywhere in this world, when lovely lines of bright
White light-waves descend from the milk-ocean moon orb,
The seas, replete with water, are made fortunate by the addition
Of twinkling starlight and the mass of laughing moonflowers. (11)

Likewise, too, this undefiled account,
Which discusses the teaching, upholders
Of the teaching, and the history of philosophical systems,
Brings good fortune to oneself and others. (7)

Many, however, are the styles of debased view that pave the way
To samsara's edge,[1639] and many, too, the stairways
Of philosophical systems that lead to the doorway
Of the 84,000 Dharmas in the fine house of the Muni's teaching. (9)

If discussing those styles of debased view
Completely fatigues the intelligence
Of even the highest sages,
For someone like me to speak is ridiculous! (7)

Thus, though a child who would swim to the sea's far shore will
not get far,
The dark clouds drink the ocean's essence and spit it out
as rain.
Just so, though the real nature of our own and others' complex
philosophical systems are not within the compass of my mind,
Who would reprove me for putting into writing what I have
partially seen and heard? (15)

Therefore, in order to arouse amazement
In the hearts of those with the clear eye
Of wisdom, and to multiply my own merits,
I took pains to strive in this way. (7)

Were I to write in detail, this would become a massive tome,
with far too many words;
If it were a massive tome, people seeking the proper view would
get discouraged just seeing it;
If they got discouraged, the book would lie neglected on a dusty
shelf in a dark recess of the house;
Rather than write a treatise that will lie neglected, it's better this
old man should lie neglected. (15)

Therefore, though not prolific in foliage of words,
This account—which bundles together twigs of sandalwood
That sprout many [331] flowers of essential meaning—
Springs up just inside the mental fence of the less intelligent. (9)

May the merits of my striving here become
A mighty, royal wish-fulfilling jewel that piles up
Clouds of Samantabhadra's offerings in the conquerors' fields
And fulfills the hopes of beings in all the worlds. (9)

May the victory banner of the teaching,
Beautified by the crown jewel of the three trainings
And trimmed with the ribbons of the Tripiṭaka,
Be raised in every direction and never list. (7)

In particular, may this stainless tradition
Of sutra and mantra of Losang the second conqueror,
The supreme essence of the Muni's teaching,
Be triumphant until the end of existence. (7)

May the upholders of the teaching have long lives and their wholesome deeds extend in the ten directions;
May the various classes of sangha exert themselves in explanation and practice, with minds harmonious and morals always pure;
May every ruler have faith in the teaching and guard their dominions according to Dharma, without contention;
May beings enter the path of the ten virtues and proceed to the city of liberation. (15)

May I, too, in all my lives, gain leisure and fortune,
And be cared for by perfect virtuous friends;
Through study, reflection, and meditation, and through teaching, debate, and composition,
May I uphold the teaching of Losang the conqueror and augment it. (9)

With the incomparable courage to bear alone
The burden of the great waves of deeds of the conquerors and their children;
May I, like Mañjughoṣa, be the ally and friend
Of beings infinite as space, as long as existence continues. (9)

I confess to the supreme refuges the entirety
Of the mass of contradictions, errors, and mistakes due to childish faults
In this account describing the history of the philosophical systems;
By your merciful compassion, please purify my flaws. (9)

All those who provide sponsorship for the writing,
Printing, and so forth of this account, and who read and reflect upon it:
Through all their lives may they not be separate
From the pure path praised by the conquerors. (9)

The compassion of the Three Jewels, just like the rays of the sun, extends equally to all;
The deeds of the Dharma protectors, like the ocean tide, are never untimely;
By the force of dependent arising, as by the wish-granting tree, all desirable things are yielded up:
By the power of these truths, may what I have hoped for come to pass. (15) [332]

Colophon

This *Crystal Mirror: An Excellent Explanation Showing the Sources and Assertions of All Philosophical Systems:* Könchok Tenpai Drönmé—the holy scholar-adept who controls all desirable things through his independent[1640] discernment of all the untold textual systems, and who is the reincarnation of Gungthangpa Gendün Phüntsok, who in turn was the spiritual heir of the crown ornament of all the scholar-adepts, the omniscient lama Jamyang Shepa—offered a silver mandala and divine silk cloth, ardently exhorting me, "Write such a book." Likewise, Lharampa Yeshé Döndrup, the throne holder of Thumé Peisi Monastery and reciter of a hundred texts,[1641] exhorted me repeatedly by letter. Moreover, I also undertook this because of the requests of a multitude of intelligent monks from the great monastery of Gönlung Jampa Ling, such as the logician Ouhan Kachu Yönten Palsang, Trensin Kachu Tenzin Gyatso, and others.

When the writing was about half finished, the unrivaled and matchless

Rongpo Bipa trulku, Ngawang Mipham Dawa, saw it and, presenting a long silk scarf, exhorted me, "Please bring the book all the way to its conclusion." Because of that, and through the kindness of my holy tutors, numbering more than thirty, on the dust of whose feet I place my head—including the holder of the vajra of definitive meaning, the omniscient Changkya Rinpoché, Rölpai Dorjé; the lord of the complete teaching of the Muni, if I may say his name, my precious preceptor, the holy Phurbu Chok Ngawang Jampa; the great wheel turner of the holy Dharma, Mañjughoṣa Könchok Jikmé Wangpo; the pervasive lord, the great Takphupa, Hasavajra Shap; the lord of the ocean of the three trainings and all the sciences, Paṇḍita Jñānaśrībhuti Sumpa Khenpo Yeshé Paljor; and others—I, who am called Losang Chökyi Nyima, a lazy man in the form of a monk whose confidence in his own intelligence is not too low to give an account that pleases the wise, completed the text at the source of the teachings of explanation and practice, the great monastery of Gönlung Jampa Ling, when I had reached my sixty-fifth year, on a day good for nectar practice: the eighth day, that is, the second "conqueror" day, of the waxing moon of the twelfth month of the female iron-bird year, [333] the Durmati year.[1642] The transcription was made by the scribes: the bhikṣu from Ordusu Hangzin, Losang Darma; the bhikṣu from Othok, Ngawang Phüntsok; and the bhikṣu from Chundrar, Yeshé Palden.

Through this, may the stainless tradition of the conqueror who is the essence of Mañjughoṣa, Tsongkhapa, be widespread in all directions, times, and circumstances, and may it remain for a long time to come.

When I got near the end of writing this treatise on philosophical systems, I was ill for a long time; nevertheless, with determination, I brought it to completion. The corrections I made were rough; since I could not make them in detail, it is possible that some mistakes still remain, and they should be amended. May goodness increase![1643]

Appendix: Detailed Outline of Thuken's Text

NOTE: Text divisions indicated by Thuken's text are unbracketed except for occasional explanatory interpolations; those added by the translators for the sake of clarity are entirely bracketed. The page numbers after each section title refer to the appropriate page and line numbers in, respectively, the ITC's Sarnath edition (S), the book-format edition published in Kansu/Gansu (K), and Ṅawang Gelek Demo's photocopied book version of the Shöl edition (Z).

1. Preface

An Expression of Worship and Promise to Compose (S 3:1, K 1:1, Z 6:4)
A General Explanation of the Project (S 5:1, K 4:1, Z 11:2)

2. Indian Schools

I. The History of Philosophical Systems in the Holy Land of India (S 5:14, K 4:14, Z 11:6)
   A. The history of the non-Buddhist extremists (S 5:15, K 5:3, Z 12:1)
      1. The story of how the extremists arose (S 5:16, K 5:3, Z 12:1)
      2. A brief explanation of the standpoints of the extremists (S 7:2, K 7:7, Z 13:5)
         [a. Lokāyatas] (S 7:14, K 8:3, Z 14:3)
         [b. Sāṃkhyas] (S 8:17, K 9:15, Z 15:6)
         [c. Brahmavādins] (S 9:21, K 11:11, Z 17:5)
         [d. Vaiṣṇavas] (S 10:20, K 12:20, Z 19:2)
         [e. Mīmāṃsakas] (S 11:5, K 13:9, Z 19:5)
         [f. Śaivas, Vaiśeṣikas, Naiyāyikas] (S 11:14, K 14:2, Z 20:3)
         [g. Nirgranthas] (S 12:17, K 15:17, Z 22:1)
         [h. Summary] (S 13:4, K 16:8, Z 22:4)

3. The purpose of explaining the extremists' [views] (S 13:9, K 16:14, Z 22:6)

B. The history of the Buddhists (S 14:16, K 18:13, Z 24:5)

1. The history of proponents of the four philosophical systems (S 14:17, K 18:17, Z 24:8)

[a. The history of the śrāvaka philosophical systems] (S 15:7, K 19:9, Z 25:3)

[1) Vaibhāṣika] (S 15:7, K 19:9, Z 25:3)

[2) Sautrāntika] (S 16:11, K 21:7, Z 26:6)

b. The history of the Mahayana philosophical systems (S 16:17, K 21:14, Z 27:3)

[1) The history of the Madhyamaka philosophical system] (S 17:7, K 22:9, Z 28:2)

[a) Nāgārjuna] (S 17:7, K 22:9, Z 28:2)

[b) Madhyamaka after Nāgārjuna] (S 18:20, K 24:14, Z 30:4)

[2) The history of the Cittamātra philosophical system] (S 20:5, K 26:15, Z 32:4)

[a) Asaṅga] (S 20:5, K 26:15, Z 32:4)

[b) Cittamātra after Asaṅga] (S 21:18, K 28:20, Z 34:6)

[3) Summary of Mahayana] (S 22:15, K 30:4, Z 36:2)

2. A brief demonstration of the points of view of the four philosophical systems (S 22:19, K 30:10, Z 36:4)

a. The standpoint of each of the four philosophical systems regarding the object of negation (S 23:5, K 31:1, Z 36:8)

[1) Vaibhāṣika] (S 24:3, K 32:8, Z 38:1)

[2) Sautrāntika] (S 24:10, K 32:16, Z 38:4)

[3) Cittamātra] (S 24:16, K 33:4, Z 38:6)

[4) Madhyamaka] (S 25:12, K 34:8, Z 40:2)

[a) Svātantrika Madhyamaka] (S 25:12, K 34:8, Z 40:2)

[b) Svātantrika vis à vis Prāsaṅgika] (S 26:13, K 35:18, Z 41:6)

[c) Special features of Prāsaṅgika Madhyamaka] (S 28:14, K 38:19, Z 44:6)

b. [Each system's] way of establishing coarse and subtle selflessness (S 30:9, K 41:11, Z 47:5)

[1) Vaibhāṣika] (S 30:9, K 41:11, Z 47:5)

[2) Sautrāntika] (S 31:1, K 42:9, Z 48:4)

[3) Cittamātra] (S 31:19, K 43:12, Z 49:5)

[4) Svātantrika Madhyamaka] (S 32:3, K 43:20, Z 50:1)

[5) Prāsaṅgika Madhyamaka] (S 32:14, K 44:15, Z 50:6)

3. How proponents of the four philosophical systems avoid the extremes of eternalism and nihilism in each of their own systems (S 33:1, K 45:6, Z 51:3)

[4. Summary] (S 33:14, K 46:3, Z 52:3)

[Concluding verses] (S 34:7, K 47:3, Z 53:3)

3. Introduction to Tibetan Buddhism

II. The History of Philosophical Systems in Tibet, the Land of Snows (S 35:1, K 48:1, Z 55:1)

- A. The history of the Buddha's teaching in the Land of Snows (S 35:10, K 48:11, Z 56:4)
  - 1. The history of the earlier spread of the teaching (S 35:11, K 49:3, Z 56:4)
  - 2. The history of the later spread (S 37:10, K 51:18, Z 60:2)
  - [Concluding verses] (S 38:18, K 53:17, Z 62:2)
- B. The histories of the different schools (S 39:4, K 54:6, Z 62:5)

4. The Nyingma Tradition

- 1. Nyingma (S 40:5, K 55:10, Z 63:5)
  - a. Identifying the general boundaries between the old—Nyingma—and new—Sarma—traditions (S 40:6, K 55:14, Z 63:6)
  - b. The history of the Nyingmapas in particular (S 41:14, K 57:13, Z 65:5)
    - 1) The history of the Nyingma philosophical system (S 41:17, K 57:17, Z 65:6)
      - [a) The age of Padmasambhava] (S 41:17, K 57:17, Z 65:6)
      - [b) The nine vehicles] (S 44:4, K 61:6, Z 69:3)
      - [c) Lineages] (S 44:18, K 62:5, Z 70:3)
        - [(1) The long lineage of oral tradition] (S 44:22, K 62:14, Z 70:6)
          - [(a) The triad lineage] (S 45:2, K 62:14, Z 70:6)
          - [(b) Dzokchen] (S 47:6, K 65:19, Z 74:2)
            - [1' The mind class] (S 47:11, K 66:4, Z 74:3)
            - [2' The expanse class] (S 47:16, K 66:11, Z 74:5)
            - [3' The special-instruction class] (S 47:20, K 66:17, Z 75:1)
        - [(2) The short lineage of treasure] (S 48:15, K 67:19, Z 76:2)

[(3) The profound lineage of pure vision] (S 49:13, K 69:5, Z 77:4)
2) The standpoint of the Nyingma philosophical system (S 49:16, K 69:9, Z 77:5)
[a) View and meditation in Dzokchen] (S 50:3, K 69:20, Z 78:2)
[(1) The three classes] (S 50:8, K 70:6, Z 78:4)
[(2) Other triads] (S 51:11, K 71:19, Z 80:2)
3) Analyzing a few [aspects of] the Nyingma philosophical system (S 52:16, K 73:14, Z 82:1)
4) A discussion of some later events (S 55:6, K 77:5, Z 85:5)
[Concluding verses] (S 57:13, K 80:9, Z 89:1)

5. *The Kadam Tradition*

2. Kadam (S 58:5, K 81:5, Z 91:1)
a. The history of the Kadam order, [founded] through the kindness of the noble lord (S 58:12, K 81:14, Z 92:3)
[1) Etymology] (S 58:12, K 81:14, Z 92:3)
[2) History] (S 59:4, K 82:11, Z 94:1)
[a) Atiśa's qualities] (S 59:7, K 82:15, Z 94:2)
[b) How Atiśa came to Tibet] (S 59:19, K 83:11, Z 95:1)
[c) What Atiśa did in Tibet] (S 61:15, K 86:3, Z 97:6)
[d) Students] (S 62:6, K 86:20, Z 98:6)
b. The history of other teachings and teachers based on the great noble lord (S 64:1, K 89:12, Z 101:4)
c. A general explanation of the Kadam teaching (S 66:17, K 93:11, Z 105:3)
1) The classifications of Dharma (S 67:1, K 93:14, Z 105:4)
[a) Texts] (S 67:11, K 94:7, Z 106:2)
[b) Instructions] (S 68:7, K 95:9, Z 107:2)
[(1) Instructions teaching the view] (S 68:8, K 95:10, Z 107:2)
[(2) Instructions teaching conduct] (S 69:9, K 96:20, Z 108:6)
[(3) Instructions teaching view and conduct combined] (S 71:11, K 100:2, Z 111:6)
[c) Special instructions] (S 72:19, K 101:20, Z 113:6)
2) A general synopsis of the actions and conduct of subsequent holy Kadam beings (S 75:1, K 105:5, Z 117:1)
[Concluding verses] (S 76:8, K 106:20, Z 118:6)

6. The Kagyü Tradition

3. Kagyü (S 76:20, K 107:16, Z 121:1)
   a. The history of the individual Kagyü [lineages] (S 77:4, K 108:3, Z 122:3)
      1) Origins of the name Kagyü (S 77:4, K 108:3, Z 122:3)
      2) History of the Kagyü in general (S 77:9, K 108:10, Z 122:4)
      3) History of the specific Kagyü [lineages] (S 78:6, K 109:14, Z 124:4)
         a) Shangpa Kagyü (S 78:6, K 109:14, Z 124:4)
         b) Dakpo Kagyü (S 80:9, K 112:15, Z 127:4)
            (1) Karma Kagyü (S 82:9, K 115:12, Z 130:3)
               [(a) The Black Hats] (S 82:9, K 115:12, Z 130:3)
               [(b) The Red Hats] (S 84:3, K 118:1, Z 132:6)
               [(c) Later history] (S 84:15, K 118:17, Z 133:5)
            (2) Phakdru Kagyü (S 86:12, K 121:13, Z 136:4)
            (3) Shangtsal Kagyü (S 88:12, K 124:8, Z 139:3)
            (4) Drigung Kagyü (S 89:12, K 125:15, Z 140:5)
            (5) Drukpa Kagyü (S 90:18, K 127:11, Z 142:4)
            (6) Taklung Kagyü (S 93:17, K 131:15, Z 146:6)
            (7) Barom Kagyü (S 95:6, K 133:18, Z 149:2)
            (8) Yasang Kagyü (S 95:17, K 134:12, Z 149:6)
            (9) Trophu Kagyü (S 96:13, K 135:14, Z 151:1)
         [c) Summary] (S 98:10, K 138:7, Z 153:5)
   b. A partial exposition of the presentation of view and meditation among the Kagyüpa (S 99:1, K 139:3, Z 154:4)
      [1) Views] (S 99:1, K 139:3, Z 154:4)
      [2) Mahāmudrā] (S 101:10, K 142:15, Z 158:1)
      [3) Later Kagyüpas: seeking the mind] (S 103:17, K 146:4, Z 161:4)
      [4) Early Kagyü arrangements of Mahāmudrā] (S 105:19, K 149:3, Z 164:5)
         [a) The yoga of the coemergent] (S 106:10, K 150:1, Z 165:5)
         [b) The fivefold] (S 106:18, K 150:11, Z 166:2)
         [c) The eight great guidelines] (S 107:9, K 151:9, Z 167:1)
         [d) The six about the taste of sameness] (S 107:16, K 151:19, Z 167:4)
         [e) The mountain Dharma] (S 107:20, K 152:4, Z 167:5)
   c. A brief analysis [of views, and so forth] (S 108:10, K 153:1, Z 168:4)
      [1) Is there a perfection-vehicle Mahāmudrā?] (S 108:10, K 153:1, Z 168:4)

[2) Does the white simple imply quietism?] (S 109:11, K 154:11, Z 170:1)
[3) Do Kagyü and Geluk have a single meaning?] (S 109:18, K 154:20, Z 170:4)
[4) Are the four yogas Cittamātrin?] (S 111:5, K 157:1, Z 172:5)
[5) Do the various types of Mahāmudrā have a single meaning?] (S 111:17, K 157:16, Z 173:4)
[6) Did Tsongkhapa write the *Inquiry into the Pure Noble Intention*?] (S 112:8, K 158:14, Z 174:4)
[d. Conclusion] (S 112:20, K 159:10, Z 175:3)
[Concluding verses] (S 113:9, K 160:3, Z 176:1)

7. The Shijé Tradition

4. Shijé (S 114:1, K 161:1, Z 177:1)
   a. The actual history of the Shijé philosophical system (S 114:6, K 161:7, Z 178:2)
      [1) Meaning of the term] (S 114:6, K 161:7, Z 178:2)
      [2) Major figures] (S 114:15, K 162:4, Z 179:3)
      [3) Major instructions] (S 115:22, K 163:18, Z 181:4)
         [a) Early Shijé] (S 115:22, K 163:18, Z 181:5)
         [b) Middle Shijé: Ma] (S 116:1, K 163:20, Z 181:5)
         [c) Middle Shijé: So] (S 116:5, K 164:4, Z 182:1)
         [d) Middle Shijé: Kam] (S 117:5, K 165:13, Z 183:3)
         [e) Middle Shijé: Minor and miscellaneous lineages] (S 117:15, K 166:6, Z 184:1)
         [f) Later Shijé] (S 118:10, K 167:8, Z 185:2)
      [4) The essence of Shijé] (S 119:22, K 169:15, Z 187:4)
      [5) Sources of the Shijé view] (S 120:16, K 170:16, Z 188:4)
   b. One of the Shijé [schools], the Chö system (S 121:7, K 171:12, Z 189:3)
      [1) Etymology] (S 121:7, K 171:12, Z 189:3)
      [2) Lineages] (S 121:12, K 171:18, Z 189:5)
      [3) The instruction and the view] (S 122:12, K 173:7, Z 191:2)
   [Concluding verses] (S 123:17, K 175:2, Z 193:1)

8. The Sakya Tradition

5. Sakya (S 124:7, K 175:17, Z 195:1)
   a. A general history of the Sakya philosophical system (S 124:12, K 176:6, Z 196:3)

[1) The Khön family line] (S 124:12, K 176:6, Z 196:3)
[a) Khön Könchok Gyalpo] (S 125:4, K 177:3, Z 198:1)
[b) Sachen Künga Nyingpo] (S 125:18, K 178:1, Z 198:6)
[c) Sons of Sachen] (S 126:12, K 179:3, Z 200:2)
[d) Sakya Pandita] (S 127:9, K 180:9, Z 201:3)
[e) Phakpa and his successors] (S 128:9, K 181:19, Z 202:6)
[f) The family lineage] (S 130:17, K 185:8, Z 206:3)
[2) Philosophical lineages] (S 131:16, K 186:16, Z 207:5)
[a) Upholders of the sutra teaching] (S 131:18, K 186:19, Z 207:6)
[b) Upholders of the secret-mantra teaching] (S 133:21, K 190:1, Z 211:1)
[(1) Ngor] (S 133:22, K 190:3, Z 211:2)
[(2) Dzong] (S 134:14, K 191:1, Z 212:1)
[(3) Tsar] (S 135:4, K 191:16, Z 212:6)
[3) Current conditions] (S 136:4, K 193:5, Z 214:3)

b. In particular, the history of the principal Dharmas—Lamdré and others (S 136:20, K 194:7, Z 215:4)
[1) Drokmi and his disciples] (S 137:4, K 194:14, Z 215:5)
[2) The nature of Lamdré] (S 139:2, K 197:12, Z 218:4)

c. A presentation of the Sakya view (S 140:1, K 199:1, Z 220:1)
1) A presentation of the views of the sutra system (S 140:9, K 199:12, Z 220:4)
[a) Special instructions of the followers of Nāgārjuna] (S 140:9, K 199:12, Z 220:4)
[(1) Severing the elaboration apprehending true [existence]] (S 140:15, K 200:1, Z 220:6)
[(2) Severing the elaboration apprehending non-true [existence]] (S 141:8, K 200:18, Z 221:5)
[b) Meditating according to the special instructions of Maitreya] (S 141:19, K 201:13, Z 222:4)
2) A presentation of the views of the mantra system (S 143:13, K 204:3, Z 225:2)
[a) Identifying the mind] (S 143:20, K 204:13, Z 225:5)
[b) Three points related to practice] (S 145:4, K 206:8, Z 227:3)
[(1) Appearances are mind] (S 145:7, K 206:11, Z 227:4)
[(2) Mind is illusory] (S 145:13, K 206:19, Z 228:1)
[(3) Illusions do not inherently exist] (S 145:19, K 207:5, Z 228:3)
[(a) Proof through dependent arising] (S 145:20, K 207:8, Z 228:3)

[(b) Proof through inexpressibility] (S 146:10, K 208:4, Z 229:2)

[Concluding verses] (S 148:16, K 211:12, Z 232:5)

9. The Jonang and Minor Traditions

6. Jonang (S 149:7, K 212:7, Z 235:1)
    a. How the Jonangpa arose (S 149:12, K 212:14, Z 236:2)
        [1) Yumo Mikyö Dorjé and his successors] (S 149:16, K 213:1, Z 236:4)
        [2) Dölpopa and his successors] (S 150:12, K 214:2, Z 238:3)
        [3) Later developments] (S 151:19, K 215:20, Z 240:4)
        [4) Origins of the extrinsic-emptiness view] (S 152:11, K 216:18, Z 241:3)
    b. The extrinsic-emptiness view of the Jonangpa (S 153:6, K 218:1, Z 242:4)
    c. Proving that the Jonang view is wrong (S 154:5, K 218:1, Z 242:4)
        [1) Jonang views and Hindu views] (S 154:5, K 218:1, Z 242:4)
        [2) Refuting Jonang interpretations of scripture] (S 157:2, K 223:15, Z 247:5)
            [a) The *Descent to Laṅka Sutra*] (S 157:10, K 224:6, Z 248:3)
            [b) Nāgārjuna's works] (S 159:12, K 227:9, Z 251:4)
        [3) Critics and defenders of the Jonang view] (S 160:10, K 228:18, Z 252:6)
            [a) Critics] (S 161:5, K 229:20, Z 254:1)
            [b) A defender: Shākya Chokden] (S 162:3, K 231:8, Z 255:3)
    [Concluding verses] (S 162:19, K232:9, Z 256:3)
7. The history of some minor philosophical systems (S 163:10, K 233:4, Z 257:2)

10. The Geluk Tradition [1: Tsongkhapa]

[Introductory verses] (S 165:2, K 235:10, Z 262:1)

8. The history of the Geluk philosophical system (S 165:4, K 235:13, Z 262:2)
    a. How the great Jé Tsongkhapa came into the world (S 166:9, K 237:12, Z 265:3)
        1) How he himself attained good qualities (S 166:14, K 237:17, Z 266:1)
            a) How he took the moral vows, the foundation of all good qualities (S 166:17, K 238:1, Z 266:1)

- b) How he actually gained mastery of the good qualities of scripture and realization (S 167:18, K 239:6, Z 267:5)
  - (1) How he gained mastery of the good qualities of scripture [through] much study (S 167:20, K 239:9, Z 267:5)
    - (a) How he severed superimposition through study (S 168:1, K 239:11, Z 267:6)
      - 1' Definition-vehicle study (S 168:14, K 240:7, Z 268:5)
        - a' How he studied the scriptures in general (S 168:17, K 240:11, Z 268:6)
        - b' How he studied Madhyamaka and valid cognition in particular (S 171:4, K 244:3, Z 272:4)
      - 2' Mantra[-vehicle] study (S 172:16, K 246:9, Z 274:5)
        - [a' Meeting Khyungpo Lhepa] (S 173:15, K 247:17, Z 276:2)
        - [b' Studies of the lower tantras] (S 175:8, K 250:6, Z 278:5)
        - [c' Studies of highest yoga tantra] (S 176:19, K 252:9, Z 280:5)
          - [1" Masters with whom he studied] (S 176:19, K 252:9, Z 280:6)
          - [2" Texts he studied] (S 178:4, K 254:8, Z 282:5)
          - [3" Kālacakra studies] (S 179:20, K 256:19, Z 285:2)
      - [3' Other studies] (S 181:3, K 258:14, Z 287:1)
    - (b) How all the textual systems [he studied] arose as instruction (S 182:2, K 260:2, Z 288:3)
  - (2) How he gained mastery of the good qualities of realization through meditation (S 185:19, K 265:10, Z 293:6)
    - [(a) Realizations regarding vinaya] (S 185:19, K 265:10, Z 293:6)
    - [(b) Realizations regarding Madhyamaka and tantra] (S 187:5, K 267:8, Z 295:6)
      - [1' Conversations with Mañjughoṣa] (S 187:5, K 267:8, Z 295:6)
      - [2' Plans to visit India] (S 189:14, K 270:18, Z 299:4)
      - [3' Definitive realization] (S 190:10, K 272:4, Z 300:6)
    - [(c) Realizations regarding highest yoga tantra] (S 192:2, K 274:11, Z 303:2)
    - [(d) Pure visions] (S 194:13, K 278:4, Z 306:5)
- 2) How he served the teaching (S 195:5, K 279:3, Z 307:5)
  - a) How he laid the foundations of the teaching (S 195:8, K 279:7, Z 307:6)

b) How he propagated and extended [the teaching] through the three activities of scholars (S 198:1, K 283:3, Z 311:5)
(1) How he served the teaching by way of explanations (S 198:2, K 283:5, Z 311:5)
(2) How he served the teaching by way of debate (S 202:5, K 289:5, Z 317:5)
(3) How he served the teaching by disseminating his writings, which are a garland of excellent explanation (S 203:18, K 291:11, Z 320:1)
[(a) How he wrote great texts on sutra-vehicle traditions] (S 203:18, K 291:11, Z 320:1)
(b) How he wrote great texts on mantra[-vehicle traditions] (S 206:14, K 295:12, Z 324:2)
[3) Faith in Tsongkhapa] (S 209:17, K 299:20, Z 328:6)
[4) Final years] (S 210:15, K 301:9, Z 330:2)
[5) Why Tsongkhapa is extraordinary] (S 210:21, K 301:18, Z 330:5)

11. The Geluk Tradition [2: Tsongkhapa's Successors]

b. How the stainless tradition of Jé Lama was expanded by [subsequent] upholders of the teaching (S 213:12, K 305:14, Z 334:4)
1) How [his system] was expanded by Jé's direct disciples (S 213:18, K 306:2, Z 334:5)
a) An enumeration of direct disciples (S 214:1, K 306:5, Z 334:6)
b) How his disciple sons expanded the teaching (S 219:17, K 314:11, Z 342:4)
[(1) Abbots of Ganden] (S 220:5, K 315:2, Z 343:2)
[(a) Gyaltsap Jé and Khedrup Jé] (S 220:5, K 315:2, Z 343:2)
[(b) Other Ganden abbots] (S 223:1, K 319:4, Z 347:3)
[(2) Drepung abbots] (S 223:20, K 320:10, Z 348:4)
[(3) Sera abbots] (S 225:17, K 323:3, Z 351:3)
[(4) Tashi Lhünpo abbots] (S 227:22, K 326:9, Z 354:5)
[(5) Geluk centers in the far west and east] (S 229:18, K 329:1, Z 357:3)
[(a) In the far west] (S 229:20, K 329:3, Z 357:4)
[(b) In Kham] (S 230:9, K 329: 17, Z 358:2)
[(c) In Amdo] (S 231:14, K 331:13, Z 360:1)
[(6) The transmission of secret mantra] (S 233:12, K 334:9, Z 362:6)

[(a) Sherap Sengé] (S 233:13, K 334:11, Z 363:6)
[(b) Sé and Mé] (S 235:11, K 337:5, Z 365:5)
[(c) Gyümé and Gyütö] (S 237:9, K 340:2, Z 368:4)
[(7) The Ensa ear-whispered lineage] (S 238:17, K 341:20, Z 370:3)
2) How subsequent [disciples] served Jé's teaching (S 240:11, K 344:6, Z 372:5)
[a) The Panchen Lamas] (S 240:15, K 344:12, Z 372:6)
[b) The Dalai Lamas] (S 241:10, K 345:13, Z 374:1)
[c) Summary of the deeds of Tsongkhapa's followers] (S 242:5, K 346:17, Z 375:2)
3) Giving just a general synopsis of the ordinary biographies of those holy Geden scholar-adepts (S 243:14, K 349:1, Z 377:3)

12. The Geluk Tradition [3: The Distinctiveness of Geluk]

c. The way that excellent system is distinctive (S 245:1, K 351:1, Z 379:2)
[1) The general distinctiveness of Geluk] (S 245:1, K 351:1, Z 379:2)
[2) How its view is distinctive] (S 247:13, K 354:17, Z 383:1)
[a) Mistaken views] (S 247:13, K 354:17, Z 383:1)
[b) Correct view] (S 248:22, K 356:18, Z 385:1)
[3) How it is distinctive in terms of meditation] (S 251:3, K 359:19, Z 388:2)
[a) Refuting some mistaken views] (S 251:3, K 359:19, Z 388:2)
[b) Definitions of abiding and insight] (S 252:15, K 362:3, Z 390:3)
[4) How it is distinctive in terms of conduct] (S 254:16, K 365:4, Z 393:4)
[5) How it is distinctive in terms of secret mantra] (S 255:21, K 366:18, Z 395:2)
[a) In terms of view] (S 255:21, K 366:18, Z 395:2)
[b) In terms of the two stages] (S 257:6, K 368:16, Z 397:1)
[c) In terms of interpreting the tantras] (S 259:13, K 372:4, Z 400:3)
[6) Further discussion] (S 261:2, K 374:7, Z 402:4)
[d. How others trying to refute Jé Tsongkhapa's system could not find any faults] (S 262:15, K 376:12, Z 404:5)
[Concluding verses] (S 262:18, K 376:15, Z 404:6)

C. The supplementary topic of the history of sutra, mantra, and the sciences (S 264:1, K 378:6, Z 406:3)

13. The Bön Tradition

D. The history of the way of Bön (S 264:7, K 378:14, Z 407:1)
1. History of the Bön philosophical system (S 264:10, K 379:1, Z 408:2)
2. History of individual Bön [traditions] (S 265:9, K 380:8, Z 410:2)
    a. Emergent Bön (S 265:11, K 380:11, Z 410:3)
    b. Deviant Bön (S 266:3, K 381:9, Z 411:2)
    c. Transformed Bön (S 266:12, K 382:1, Z 411:6)
3. The Bön Dharma system (S 267:8, K 383:3, Z 412:6)
4. The Bön standpoint on view, meditation, and other [aspects of the path] (S 268:12, K 385:1, Z 414:3)
    [a. View] (S 268:12, K 385:1, Z 414:3)
    [b. Meditation] (S 269:18, K 386:20, Z 416:3)

[5. The organization of Bön] (S 270:13, K 388:3, Z 417:4)
[6. Bön monasteries] (S 271:9, K 389:8, Z 418:5)
[Concluding verses] (S 271:14, K 389:14, Z 419:1)

14. Chinese Traditions [1: Non-Buddhist]

III. The History of Sciences and Philosophical Systems in the Land of Great China (S 273:1, K 391:1, Z 421:1)
[A. The histories of the first two traditions] (S 274:3, K 392:15, Z 424:3)
1. The history of the tradition known as the "star-like Ru" (S 274:4, K 392:15, Z 424:3)
    [a. The history of Ru] (S 274:12, K 393:7, Z 424:6)
    [b. Confucian divination] (S 277:2, K 396:15, Z 428:3)
        [1) The earlier and later heavenly systems] (S 277:6, K 397:1, Z 428:5)
        [2) Further developments] (S 279:1, K 399:13, Z 431:3)
    [c. Other Confucian sciences] (S 280:6, K 401:10, Z 433:2)
    [d. The standpoint of the Confucian system] (S 281:1, K 402:9, Z 434:1)
        [1) Soteriology] (S 281:1, K 402:9, Z 434:1)
        [2) Cosmogony, cosmology, and eschatology] (S 282:13, K 404:13, Z 436:3)
    [e. Confucianism vis à vis Buddhism] (S 284:18, K 407:18, Z 439:6)

2. The history of the moon-like Dharma system, the tradition of Bön called Daoshi (S 287:18, K 412:5, Z 444:3)
    - [a. Origins] (S 287:18, K 412:5, Z 444:3)
    - [b. Teachings] (S 288:20, K 413:19, Z 445:6)

B. The history of some miscellaneous traditions (S 290:3, K 415:15, Z 447:6)

[Concluding Verses] (S 291:14, K 417:19, Z 450:1)

15. Chinese Traditions [2: Buddhist]

C. The history of the Dharma system of the insiders, the Buddhists (S 292:4, K 418:5, Z 451:1)

1. How [Buddhism] came from India (S 292:9, K 419:5, Z 452:3)
    - [a. Historical developments] (S 292:9, K 419:5, Z 452:3)
        - [1) Before Buddhism] (S 292:9, K 419:5, Z 452:3)
        - [2) The coming of Buddhism] (S 294:2, K 421:11, Z 455:6)
        - [3) Later developments] (S 296:10, K 424:20, Z 459:5)
    - [b. Buddhist teaching lineages in China] (S 297:5, K 426:2, Z 460:6)
        - 1) The vinaya lineage (S 297:8, K 426:5, Z 461:1)
        - 2) The secret-mantra lineage (S 298:12, K 427:19, Z 462:6)
        - 3) [Xuanzang and] the lineage of extensive practice (S 299:12, K 429:7, Z 464:3)
        - 4) The lineage of profound view (S 301:20, K 432:14, Z 468:2)
            - [a) Zhiyi and the Tiantai] (S 302:4, K 433:1, Z 468:4)
            - [b) Chengguan and the Huayan] (S 303:6, K 434:14, Z 470:3)
        - 5) The lineage of essential meaning, [Chan] (S 304:19, K 436:20, Z 472:6)
        - [6) Summary of India-based traditions] (S 307:7, K 440:12, Z 476:6)
2. How [Buddhism] came from Tibet (S 307:11, K 440:17, Z 477:2)
    - [a. In general] (S 307:11, K 440:17, Z 477:2)
    - [b. In particular, how the matchless Ganden Mountain tradition spread] (S 307:18, K 441:9, Z 477:5)

[Concluding verses] (S 310:12, K 445:7, Z 481:6)

16. Central Asian Traditions

IV. The History of Philosophical Systems in Some Other Lands (S 311:1, K 447:1, Z 483:1)

A. How the teaching spread in Mongolia (S 311:16, K 448:6, Z 485:4)
    - [1. The thirteenth and fourteenth centuries: Sakyapas, Karmapas, and the Yuan] (S 311:16, K 448:6, Z 485:4)

[a. Genghis Khan's era] (S 311:16, K 448:6, Z 485:4)
[b. Godan and Kublai's era] (S 312:8, K 449:4, Z 486:5)
[c. Later developments] (S 314:14, K 452:10, Z 490:3)
[2. The sixteenth and seventeenth centuries and beyond: Mongol-Geluk relations] (S 315:6, K 453:9, Z 491:3)
[a. Altan Khan and others] (S 315:6, K 453:9, Z 491:3)
[b. Gushri Khan and the Fifth Dalai Lama] (S 317:8, K 456, Z 494:5)
B. How the teaching spread in Khotan (S 320:6, K 460:15, Z 499:3)
C. How the teaching spread in the land of Shambhala (S 321:1, K 461:16, Z 500:3)
[1. Overview] (S 321:1, K 461:16, Z 500:3)
[2. History of the Buddha's teaching] (S 322:5, K 463:13, Z 502:1)
[3. The future] (S 323:2, K 464:18, Z 503:3)
[4. Distinguishing barbarians from extremists] (S 324:10, K 466:18, Z 505:4)
[5. Secret prophecies] (S 324:22, K 467:13, Z 506:3)
[Concluding verses] (S 325, K 468:19, Z 507:6)

17. Conclusion

V. Conclusion (S 327:1, K 470:1, Z 508:4)
[Afterword] (S 330:6, K 476:10, Z 513:4)
[Colophon] (S 332:1, K 479:17, Z 516:3)

Notes

1 In Tibetan transcription: *Thu'u bkwan grub mtha'.* This is the name by which most Tibetans know the text; literally, it means "Thuken's Text on Philosophical Systems."
2 That is, the areas of Ü and Tsang.
3 *'Gro ba bzhi:* According to the vinaya, these are the four tendencies that impede receiving secret teachings: desire, fear, anger, and confusion. Alternatively, it may refer to the sorts of beings *('gro ba)* who are controlled by these tendencies.
4 See below, p. 35.
5 See below, p. 388–89.
6 The three are, in Tibetan: *dgag, gzhag,* and *spong.*
7 Some passages in this introduction are excerpted or paraphrased from R. Jackson, "Triumphalism and Ecumenism in Thu'u bkwan's *Crystal Mirror,*" and are reprinted with the kind permission of the *Journal of the International Association of Tibetan Studies.*
8 The term *legs bshad (subhāṣita)* is very difficult to convey adequately in English. In the most general sense, it refers to anything that is well spoken. It may refer to a genre of literature that the French would describe as *bon mots,* i.e., well-spoken advice or aphorisms. More broadly, it refers to an explanation or exposition that is of high quality. We have mostly opted in this volume to render it as "excellent explanation."
9 The full Tibetan title of the text is: *Grub mtha' thams cad kyi khung dang 'dod tshul ston pa legs bshad shel gyi me long.* It most is commonly referred to by Tibetans as *Thu'u bkwan grub mtha' (Thuken's Text on Philosophical Systems)* or the *Grub mtha' shel gyi me long (Crystal Mirror of Philosophical Systems).*
10 According to Wang (p. 185), the incarnation lineage is named after the village in which the first Thuken incarnate was born. "Thu'u bkwan" (or sometimes Thu'u kwan) is a Tibetan transcription of the Chinese word *tuguan,* referring to an "indigenous official" or "local ruler" who, in various non-Han areas, would govern on behalf of the emperor. Though the Tibetan transcription approximates the Chinese original if pronounced as written, most central Tibetans would pronounce the name Thuken (or, *"Too-ken"*), and so we have used that phonetic spelling throughout.
11 E. G. Smith, pp. 147–48.
12 Vostrikov, p. 155.
13 Kapstein, *The Tibetan Assimilation of Buddhism* (hereafter *Tibetan Assimilation*), p. 256n62. The reason for this is said to be that Nyingmapas in Amdo appreciated

their protection from persecution by the Thuken and other Mongol incarnates. It is interesting that the deity on whose practice Thuken wrote by far the greatest number of works is a form of Hayagrīva popular among Nyingmapas.

14 See E. G. Smith, pp. 154–58. The monastery is located to the east of the city of Xining, in Qinghai province; it is referred to by the Chinese as Youning Temple.

15 Vostrikov, pp. 155–56; E. G. Smith, p. 147.

16 See Z. For further information on editions of Thuken's writings, see Chandra, *Materials for a History of Tibetan Literature,* vol. I, p. 52; and E. G. Smith, p. 308n473.

17 See K.

18 See S.

19 Vostrikov, p. 156.

20 See Das, "Contribution on the Religion, History, etc., of Tibet."

21 On Bön, see Hoffman, *Quellen zur Geschichte der tibetischen Bon-Religion;* on Jonang, see Ruegg, "The Jo naṅ pas"; on Kadam, see A. Chattopadhyaya; on India, see Mittal. Guilaine Mala has translated the China chapters as part of her thesis for Oxford University, completed in 2006, and unavailable to us. In addition, D. S. Ruegg utilized the *Crystal Mirror* to a significant degree in the annotations to his 1966 *Life of Bu ston rin po che.*

22 See Li, "Rñiṅmapa, the Early Form of Lamaism," "The Bkaḥ-brgyud Sect of Lamaism," and "The Sakya Sect of Lamaism"; Tachikawa.

23 See Liu.

24 Needless to say, the compass of Thuken's work does not extend to all of Asia, as he omits entirely any discussion of the traditions of Japan, Korea, or Southeast Asia, which would have registered faintly, if at all, on the radar of an eighteenth-century Tibetan or Mongolian.

25 Kapstein, *Tibetan Assimilation,* p. 255n60.

26 There is very little biographical information on Thuken available in English. Earlier sources include Das, "Contribution on the Religion, History, etc., of Tibet," vol. L, part 1, no. 3 (1881), pp. 187–88; and Chandra, *Materials for a History of Tibetan Literature,* vol. I, pp. 51–54. More recently, see E. G. Smith, pp. 147–70; and Wang, pp. 186–89. Thuken's collected works include (in vols. 9–10 of Z) a massive biography of him written by his disciple Gungthang Könchok Tenpai Drönmé (1762–1823). This work is deserving of further study; here, we have drawn most of our information from Wang and from the foreword to K. See also the listing for Thuken (P170) on the Tibetan Buddhist Resource Center [TBRC] website: http://www.tbrc.org/cgi-bin/tbrcdatx?resource=P170. This page has links to pages for Thuken's works, teachers, students, and monasteries.

27 The Mongol people of this region are generally identified as Monguors. The Monguor language is related to other Mongolian dialects but is unusual in its adoption of many Tibetan loan-words. See, e.g., Rona-Tas; Schram.

28 On the history of this era from the Tibetan point of view, see, e.g., Shakabpa, pp. 125–52; Snellgrove and Richardson, pp. 204–32. For Chinese developments at this time, see, e.g., Mote, pp. 841–948; Fairbank and Goldman, pp. 143–65. For the Manchus, see Crossley. On Sino-Mongolian relations, see, e.g., Perdue. On Mongolia, see Grousset, pp. 513–42. On Qing relations with Tibetan Buddhists, see Berger; Chan.

29 Most scholars identify Thuken as a Mongolian, or "Tibetanized Mongol" (e.g., E. G. Smith, p. 133). It is worth noting, however, that his biographer, Gunthang Könchok Tenpai Drönmé, traces his ancestry to the Dra *(bra),* a Tibetan clan that migrated from Ü to Amdo in ancient times (*White Lotus Expressing Realization of the Marvelous Triple Secret of Jetsün Losang Chökyi Nyima;* in *Collected Works of Thu'u bkwan,* vol *ta,* 7b–8a). Given what we know about the ethnicity of the important Amdo reincarnation lines of the Qing period, it must be supposed that Thuken's Tibetan bloodlines had at the very least been mixed with Mongol strains.

30 Das, "Contribution on the Religion, History, etc., of Tibet," vol. L, part 1, no. 3 (1881), p. 188. I have been unable to identify the source of this claim, which is not cited by Das, but the sort of assertion involved is not unusual in hagiographic literature related to great lamas.

31 Wang, p. 187.

32 Z. The most easily available listing of Thuken's works is on the TBRC website, but see also Chandra, *Materials for a History of Tibetan Literature,* vol. I, pp. 215–28. Summaries of a number of Thuken's nontantric works may be found in E. G. Smith, pp. 147–70, and a most interesting discussion of a polemical work not found in his collected works is in Kapstein, *Tibetan Assimilation,* pp. 121–37.

33 For a translation of a Kālacakra sādhana by Thuken, see Berzin, "Abbreviated Single-Deity Kalachakra Sadhana."

34 His text on the latter is still widely used among Gelukpas. It has been translated in R. Jackson, "A Tibetan Fasting Ritual."

35 Also known as Gungthangpa Könchok Gendün Phüntsok, or just as Gungthangpa.

36 See below, p. 396.

37 It is possible that Thuken's disciple Gungthangpa, who edited his collected works, might have introduced some changes of his own composition; this is a topic deserving of further study. I thank Leonard Zwilling for drawing my attention to this possibility, and for providing some of the information in this paragraph on the basis of his readings in Gungthangpa's works.

38 See Tachikawa.

39 Dan Martin has researched this matter thoroughly; see his *Unearthing Bon Treasures,* chap. 12; see also Bjerken.

40 See, respectively, Sumpa Khenpo; Gönpo Kyap. On the latter, see Mala, "A Mahayanist Rewriting of the History of China," pp. 145–54.

41 See below, p. 35.

42 See below, p. 388–89.

43 Schaeffer, "Future Directions for Modern Tibetan Studies," p. 18.

44 For perspectives on the question, see, e.g., Kapstein, *Tibetan Assimilation,* pp. 121–37, R. Jackson, "Triumphalism and Ecumenism."

45 See below, p. 164.

46 See below, p. 318. In this, Thuken is identifying with what might be called the ecumenical wing of the Geluk, pioneered most strikingly by the First Panchen Lama, Losang Chökyi Gyaltsen, who in his verses on the Geluk Mahāmudrā system, famously remarked (in a passage cited twice by Thuken) that all the great meditative traditions come down to the same point. See Dalai Lama and Berzin, pp. 98, 123, 271; R. Jackson, "The dGe ldan bka' brgyud Tradition of Mahāmudrā."

47 A striking instance of this is to be found in Dudjom Rinpoche's history of the Nyingma, where he suggests that Thuken's analysis of the decayed state of the Nyingma in his own time could not possibly have been written by a scholar as great as Thuken and must be a later interpolation. See Dudjom Rinpoche, pp. 735–36.

48 An example of such a view in Thuken's era is found in some of the writings of his own teacher, Sumpa Khenpo, whom Thuken went so far as to criticize in defense of Nyingma claims about the authenticity of their treasure traditions. See Kapstein, *Tibetan Assimilation,* pp. 121–37.

49 Kapstein, *Tibetan Assimilation,* p. 130.

50 On this genre in general, see Hopkins, "The Tibetan Genre of Doxography."

51 E. G. Smith, p. 148.

52 On the latter, see Sopa and Hopkins.

53 Vostrikov, p. 151; Martin, *Tibetan Histories,* p. 287.

54 Vostrikov, p. 154. In unpublished remarks from a panel at the University of Wisconsin–Madison in 2003, John Dunne described Thuken's contribution along somewhat similar lines, as the introduction of institutional history into the *grub mtha'* genre.

55 An especially interesting argument to this effect, based in Chinese texts on multiple religions, is found in Campany. Interestingly, Thuken's approach to describing religions, along largely doctrinal lines, tends to fit better with early modern Western approaches to the topic (criticized by Campany), which were similarly doxographical. On these issues, see also Sweet, "Jesus the World Protector."

56 It is worth noting that the notion of neutrality or impartiality in the Western ideal of comparing religions has been subjected to severe critical scrutiny, especially by those who argue that the entire enterprise masks an implicit liberal Protestant agenda; see, e.g., Fitzgerald.

57 For a brief survey of texts of this type, see J. Z. Smith, pp. 275–80.

58 An exemplar of the former outlook is John Hick, of the latter Raimundo Pannikar, though the concept of "anonymous Christians" is usually traced to Karl Rahner. For one of the most balanced examples of this genre, see Kung et al.

59 The first three elements of this structure were first suggested by E. G. Smith, p. 148.

60 For translations of the works of the first two (with commentary), see, for Jamyang Shepa, Hopkins' *Maps of the Profound* and Cozort and Preston; for Könchok Jikmé Wangpo, see Sopa and Hopkins. A translation of Changkya's text will appear as volume 24 in the *Library of Tibetan Classics* series, tentatively under the title *A Beautiful Adornment of Mount Meru: Presentation of Classical Indian Philosophies.* It must be remarked that the general approach of Tibetan writers on philosophical systems is usually quite ahistorical, with ideal positions constructed with only limited regard to the evolution of particular viewpoints, whether by individuals or by schools. On this, see, e.g., Cabezón, "Canonization of Philosophy."

61 On the treatment of Christianity by Tibetan historians of the eighteenth century, see Sweet, "Jesus as World Protector."

62 *Hvā shang ma hā yā na* (a transcription of the Chinese *heshang mohoyen*) is pronounced *Hashang Mahayana* by Tibetans. We have maintained the spelling *Heshang* for the sake of consistency.

63 Muni here refers to the historical Buddha. The Sanskrit term *muni* carries a range of connotations, denoting an ascetic, a visionary, and/or someone who has taken a vow of silence. The Tibetan equivalent, *thub pa* or *thub dbang (munendra),* additionally implies someone with great spiritual ability or power.

64 The Unconquerable *(mi pham)* is an epithet most often associated with Maitreya, and despite the absence of the copulative *dang* here, it is probably both Maitreya *and* Mañjughoṣa who are being referred to. The likelihood of this is increased by the subsequent reference to profound *and* extensive Dharma, which are connected to Mañjughoṣa and Maitreya, respectively. Likewise, Nāgārjuna and Asaṅga, mentioned in the next verse, are connected to the same two qualities of Dharma and are seen as opening the way to the promulgation of the traditions of Mañjughoṣa and Maitreya, respectively.

65 The reference, perhaps to a sutra, is unknown. The hundred-petaled lotus *('dab brgya ba)* refers to a flower opened by the sun, or metaphorically, the Madhyamaka school. The night-lily *(ku mu ta)* refers to a flower opened by the moon, or metaphorically, the Cittamātra school.

66 In the sacred geography that has Mount Meru at its center, Jambudvīpa ("Rose Apple Island") is the southern continent and the region most easily identifiable with the known human world.

67 In Indian mythology, the sun and moon are drawn by seven heavenly horses around Mount Meru. In this metaphor, the green horse is like the bodhicitta dedication of the great translators, pandits, and Dharma kings, drawing the Dharma sun around the mountains of Tibet, which had been darkened by ignorance.

68 Tsongkhapa Losang Drakpa (1357–1419) and his disciples Gyaltsap Jé Darma Rinchen (1364–1432) and Khedrup Jé Gelek Pal Sangpo (1385–1438).

69 An alternative name for the Gelukpas.

70 Tsongkhapa.

71 *Dge legs* ("virtuous and good") is yet another name for the Geluk.

72 The Panchen and Dalai Lamas, respectively.

73 This probably refers to Thuken's three major teachers, Changkya Rölpai Dorjé (1717–86), Phurbuchok Ngawang Jampa (1682–1762), and Könchok Jikmé Wangpo (1728–91).

74 Maitripāda is Phurbuchok Ngawang *Jampa* and Ratna is *Könchok* Jikmé Wangpo.

75 Despite the Western connotations of the term *Holy Land,* we believe that it reflects accurately the Tibetan perception of India as the source of Buddhadharma, and hence is a proper translation of the Tibetan *'phags pa'i yul* or Sanskrit *āryavarta*—literally, "land of the noble or exalted."

76 The precise dates of the Buddha have long been disputed and will probably never be known with certainty. Tibetan traditions based on the chronology used in the Kālacakra tantra corpus place his final nirvana in 881 B.C.E. Chinese tradition generally has opted for 949 B.C.E. On the basis of a "long chronology" of masters, Theravāda tradition has favored 544 B.C.E., on the basis of which the world's Buddhists celebrated the 2,500th anniversary of the final nirvana in 1956. Until late in the twentieth century, most modern scholars, basing themselves on a corrected Theravādin "long chronology," accepted a nirvana date of 483 (or

486 or 480) B.C.E. More recently, a number of scholars have used the Chinese "short chronology" to argue for a date as late as 383 B.C.E. For our purposes, it is sufficient to suggest that the Buddha and his major disciples lived sometime during the fifth century B.C.E.

77 The terms "outsider" *(phyi rol pa)* and "insider" *(nang pa)* connote non-Buddhist and Buddhist, respectively, and we generally have translated them accordingly.

78 For an alternative translation of this chapter, see Mittal and Jamspal. Lori Cayton contributed to an earlier version of the present translation of the chapter.

79 For either translations or accounts of Tibetan presentations of Buddhist and non-Buddhist schools of Indian philosophy, see, e.g., Mimaki; Sopa and Hopkins, pp. 139–322; Guenther, *Buddhist Philosophy in Theory and Practice;* Tsultrim Gyamtso Rimpoche; Hopkins, *Maps of the Profound* and *Meditation on Emptiness,* pp. 305–428; Cozort and Preston. For traditional Tibetan historical accounts of Indian Buddhism (those of Butön Rinchen Drup and Tāranātha), see Obermiller, *Jewellery of Scripture* and *History of Buddhism in India and Tibet;* Chimpa and Chattopadhyaya.

80 The Tibetan *mu stegs pa* is sometimes glossed as meaning "one who holds up the edge." For most educated readers, it evokes the *mu bzhi,* the "four extremes" through which any phenomenon may be analyzed: is, is not, both is and is not, and neither is nor is not. The Sanskrit *tīrthika* is "one who makes a ford"; it may refer to Hindus and others who make journeys to pilgrimage places at sacred riverbanks (Skt. *tīrtha*), a practice often criticized by Buddhists, or more abstractly, it may to refer to those who have forded philosophically beyond what is reasonable. For general accounts of non-Buddhist schools of Indian philosophy, see, e.g., Dasgupta, Radhakrishnan, Sharma. For anthologies, see, e.g., Radhakrishnan and Moore, Koller and Koller. For more critical analysis, see, e.g., Potter, *Presuppositions of India's Philosophies;* Smart; Matilal. See also Potter's exhaustive *Bibliography of Indian Philosophies.*

81 The Sanskrit (most often *mahāsaṃmata*) actually conveys the sense of "The [Great] Elected One."

82 The Sanskrit *ṛṣi (drang srong)* refers to a visionary; it is the term most widely used in Hindu traditions for the great sages who conveyed the Vedas to humanity. The Tibetan *drang srong* denotes one who is upright or straightforward.

83 All available Tibetan editions have *rgyas pa,* meaning "one who spreads"; this is, however, unattested as an epithet of Mahāvīra, whereas a small orthographic shift would give us *rgyal ba,* Sanskrit *jina* ("victor"), a well-known title for any *tīrthaṅkāra* and the source of the tradition's most common name, Jaina. The fact that Thuken himself later (p. 43) uses *rgyal ba* to refer to the tradition's most recent representative makes it likely that the *rgyas pa* here is a misprint for *rgyal ba.*

84 Although Thuken identifies Ulūka and Kaṇāda as separate sages, they most often are alternative names for the same person.

85 For Lokāyata, see D. Chattopadhyaya. For Sāṃkhya, see Larson. For Vaiyākaraṇikas, see Coward and Raja; for Vedānta, see Deutsch; Potter, *Advaita Vedānta up to Śaṃkara and His Disciples;* Rambachan. For Mīmāṃsā, see Verpoorten. For Nyāya-Vaiśeṣika, see Halbfass; Potter, *Indian Metaphysics and Epistemology.* For Jainism, see Jaini.

86 The semantic range of *ngan* is difficult to capture in a single English word. It connotes inferior or lowly but often implies evil as well. We have generally opted for "debased" when views are described as *ngan* because it implies both inferiority and moral deficiency.

87 The most famous of these lists is probably that of the sixty-two debased views enumerated in the *Brahmajāla Sutta* of the Pāli *Dīgha Nikāya;* see Bodhi. For references to the sutra sources for these lists, see S, nn. 9–15, pp. 335–36.

88 *Blaze of Logic,* chap. 9; Toh 3856 Tengyur, dbu ma, *dza,* 278a4; *Precious Lamp of Madhyamaka;* Toh 3854 Tengyur, dbu ma, *dza,* 263b2.

89 Dharmakīrti, *Ascertainment of Valid Cognition,* chap. 3; Toh 4211 Tengyur, tshad ma, *ce,* 229b5.

90 The order followed by Thuken is exactly that found in the texts of his great predecessors, Jamyang Shepa *(Great Exposition of Philosophical Systems;* see Hopkins, *Maps of the Profound)* and Changkya Rölpai Dorjé *(Great Treatise on the Establishment of Philosophical Systems).*

91 The emphasis on the "accidental" *(blo bur ba)* here reflects the Lokāyata's rejection of causation, alluded to above.

92 Where before Thuken used the term *bsam gtan pa,* literally, "one who practices absorption," here he uses the term *snyoms 'jug pa,* literally, "one who practices meditative equipoise." The two are roughly synonymous, involving as they do the concentration of the mind in advanced meditative practice.

93 The principal, *pradhāna,* is synonymous with *prakṛti,* the fundamental nature or "procreatrix" that is one of the two fundamental realities for Sāṃkhya.

94 The five sense objects (forms, sounds, smells, tastes, tangibles) are, more literally, the five "just thats" *(de tsam, taṅmātra).*

95 This probably refers to its being divisible into objects of eye, ear, nose, tongue, body (i.e., touch), and mind.

96 Note the foreshadowing here of notions of liberation to be found in Buddhist highest yoga tantra, where a gnosis of inseparable bliss-emptiness is likened to, or even said to be equivalent to, enlightenment.

97 *Tshangs pa* means "pure," or "complete," but also is the term for Brahmā. The clause may also be read as asserting that the person is *brahmanirvāṇa,* a common Vedāntin term for the liberated state.

98 That is, although as an experience it may resemble deep sleep, it is beyond that, a state of consciousness sometimes called *the fourth* (Skt. *turīya, caturtha*), so as to distinguish it from waking, dreaming, and deep sleep.

99 Mittal (p. 29) identifies the Guhyavādins as an Upaniṣadic school.

100 This meditation is also incorporated into Buddhist highest yoga tantra completion-stage practices.

101 The fact that Vedāntins could also be Vaiṣṇavas indicates that the systems identified by Thuken include both philosophical schools and devotional traditions.

102 There can be no utterly authoritative human speech because the infinity of objects of knowledge and the inevitability of mental stains will forever leave truth claims limited.

103 *Khams (dhātu)* literally means "element" but here connotes semen.

104 According to Mittal (p. 31n), the sixteen categories are: sources of valid cognition (Skt. *pramāṇa*), objects of valid cognition *(prameya),* doubt *(saṃśaya),* purpose *(prayojana),* example *(dṛṣṭānta),* established conclusion *(siddhānta),* premises *(anavaya),* argument *(tarka),* ascertainment *(nirṇaya),* debate *(vāda),* disputation *(jalpa),* destructive criticism *(vitaṇḍā),* fallacies of the reason *(hetvābhāsa),* quibbling *(chala),* refutation *(jāti),* and point of defeat *(nigrahasthāna).* The eight categories probably represent a condensation of this list, not, as Mittal speculates, some version of the Nyāya category list.

105 The "holy Jina" is presumably Mahāvīra (sixth/fifth century B.C.E.), the most recent of the twenty-four Jain *jinas* or *tīrthaṅkaras.*

106 Mittal (p. 32n) identifies these as the fires of the four directions, with the sun overhead.

107 In Indian calculation, a league *(dpag tshad, yojana)* is approximately four and half miles, as opposed to the three miles of Western systems.

108 The *Thorough Exposition of Valid Cognition* (see, e.g., Mookerjee and Nagasaki; R. Jackson, *Is Enlightenment Possible?;* Franco; Tillemans), *Ascertainment of Valid Cognition* (see Steinkellner), *Drop of Reasoning* (see Stcherbatsky, *Buddhist Logic,* vol. 2), *Proof of Other Minds, Analysis of Relations, Principles of Debate,* and *Drop of Reasons.*

109 The great charioteers *(shing rta chen po)* are usually reckoned as Nāgārjuna (ca. 150 C.E.), who is the "trailblazer" *(shing rta'i srol 'byed pa)* for the attainment of profound perfect wisdom, and Asaṅga (ca. fourth century C.E.), who is the trailblazer for the development of vast skillful means.

110 Udbhaṭasiddhasvāmin; Toh 1109 Tengyur, bstod tshogs, *ka,* 4b3.

111 *Tshad ma'i skyes bu (pramāṇapuruṣa)* is literally a "person of (or who is) valid cognition," also known as a *tshad mar gyur pa (pramāṇabhūta),* i.e., "one who has become valid cognition." The term was coined by Dignāga and analyzed most extensively in the second *(tshad ma'i sgrub pa, pramāṇasiddhi)* chapter of Dharmakīrti's *Thorough Exposition of Valid Cognition.* On this topic, see, e.g., R. Jackson, *Is Enlightenment Possible?;* Franco.

112 Literally, the Insiders *(nang pa).* For general histories of Indian Buddhism, see Lamotte, *History of Indian Buddhism;* Hirakawa; Warder; Williams and Tribe.

113 For general accounts of the schools and texts of Indian Buddhist philosophy see, e.g., Warder; Nakamura; Kalupahana; Lamotte, *History of Indian Buddhism;* R. Jackson, "Buddhism in India"; Potter, *Buddhist Philosophy from 100 to 350* A.D., and *Buddhist Philosophy from 350 to 600* A.D.; Williams and Tribe. See also the Tibetan accounts by Üpa Losal (see Mimaki); Butön (Obermiller, *History of Buddhism in India and Tibet* and *Jewellery of Scripture*); the Second Dalai Lama (Mullin, *Selected Works of the Dalai Lama II,* pp. 153–82); Jamyang Shepa (Hopkins, *Maps of the Profound*); Könchok Jikmé Wangpo (Sopa and Hopkins); and Mipham Gyatso (Guenther, *Buddhist Philosophy in Theory and Practice*).

114 The reference here is to the three turnings of the Dharma wheel, as laid out in chapter 7 of the *Unraveling of Intention Sutra* (see Lamotte, *L'Explication des Mystères;* Powers, *Wisdom of Buddha*), which are the Buddha's teaching of: dharma realism through Hinayana sutras at Sarnath; emptiness through the perfection of wisdom sutras on the Vulture Peak at Rājagṛha; and mind-only and/or buddha nature through various sutras at Mount Malaya and/or Vaiśālī.

115 For scholarly accounts of Hinayana schools, see Hirakawa; Lamotte, *History of*

Indian Buddhism; Bareau; Dutt; Jayatilleke; Hoffman; Stcherbatsky, *Central Conception of Buddhism;* Potter et al.; as well as the Tibetan accounts in Sopa and Hopkins; Hopkins, *Maps of the Profound;* Guenther, *Buddhist Philosophy in Theory and Practice;* Cozort and Preston. For translations of important Hinayana philosophical texts, see, e.g., Rhys Davids; Aung and Rhys Davids; La Vallée Poussin; as well as the synopses in Potter, *Buddhist Philosophy from 100 to 350* A.D.

116 As a noun, the Tibetan *brgyud* may in most cases be translated with equal accuracy as "lineage" or "transmission." We have opted for "lineage," reserving "transmit(ted)" for its verbal occurrences.

117 Each of the four lineage founders is a famous disciple of the Buddha, and so can tentatively be assigned, like the Buddha himself, to the fifth century B.C.E.

118 *A Summary of the Teachings of the Various Sects by Way of a Progressive Reading of Various Critiques;* Toh 4140 Tengyur, 'dul ba, *su,* 154b3.

119 *A Summary of the Teachings of the Various Sects by Way of a Progressive Reading of Various Critiques;* Toh 4140, 'dul ba, *su,* 154b4.

120 *A Summary of the Teachings of the Various Sects by Way of a Progressive Reading of Various Critiques;* Toh 4140 Tengyur, 'dul ba, *su,* 154b4. These are the "sects" related to the three major monasteries of Anuradhapura, the ancient capital of Sri Lanka, namely, Abhayagiri, Mahāvihāra, and Jetavana. Of these, the Mahāvihāra is most closely associated with orthodox Sthaviravāda (in Pali, Theravāda).

121 The school is also known as the Saṃmitīya.

122 *A Summary of the Teachings of the Various Sects by Way of a Progressive Reading of Various Critiques;* Toh 4140 Tengyur, 'dul ba, *su,* 154b5. Later (p. 64), Thuken refers to *five* Saṃmatīya sects.

123 *A Summary of the Teachings of the Various Sects by Way of a Progressive Reading of Various Critiques;* Toh 4140 Tengyur, 'dul ba, *su,* 154b5.

124 For more details on Tibetan scholastic views of these divisions, see Hopkins, *Maps of the Profound,* pp. 211–15.

125 These four are featured prominently in the *Great Detailed Exposition* and criticized by Vasubandhu in the *Autocommentary on the Treasury of Higher Knowledge.* They probably lived before or during the first century, the usual date assigned to the *Great Detailed Exposition.*

126 The Tibetan term *mkhas pa,* which translates the Sanskrit adjective *kuśala* or the noun *kauśala,* means above all someone who is expert or skillful, especially but not exclusively in intellectual or spiritual matters. Depending on the context, we translate it as either "expert," "scholar," "sage," or "the wise."

127 These three were probably Sautrāntikas following scripture. Kumārarata also is known as Kumāralāta or Kumāralabhda, Śrīrirata as Śrīlāta or Śrīlabhda, and Bhadantarata as Bhadantalabhda; see Mittal, pp. 37, 125–26.

128 For scholarly accounts of Mahayana schools, see, e.g., Warder; Williams, *Mahāyāna Buddhism;* Williams and Tribe; as well as the Tibetan accounts in Sopa and Hopkins; Hopkins, *Maps of the Profound;* Guenther, *Buddhist Philosophy in Theory and Practice;* Cozort and Preston.

129 On these aquatic spirits, which have both Indic and Tibetan prototypes, see, e.g., Nebesky-Wojkowitz, p. 290.

130 For information on and works by Saraha, see, e.g., Robinson, pp. 41–43; Dowman, *Masters of Mahāmudrā,* pp. 66–72; Templeman, *Seven Instruction Lineages,* pp. 2–3; Kvaerne, *Anthology of Buddhist Tantric Songs;* Cleary, *Ecstasy*

of Enlightenment; Shahidullah; Snellgrove, "Saraha's Treasury of Songs," Guenther, *Royal Song of Saraha* and *Ecstatic Spontaneity;* R. Jackson, *Tantric Treasures;* Thrangu, *Song for a King;* Schaeffer, *Dreaming the Great Brahmin.*

131 The chronology cited here by Thuken would find little support among contemporary historians, who place the development of Buddhist tantra well after the time of Nāgārjuna. Thuken's chronology presupposes that Saraha was the teacher of Nāgārjuna, and that Nāgārjuna appeared just a few centuries after the nirvana of the Buddha. It rests on the further assumption (common to nearly all Tibetan exegetes) that there was only one Nāgārjuna, who authored both Madhyamaka texts and tantric treatises. Contemporary historians generally accept two Nāgārjunas, the second-century philosopher who perhaps had as his teacher a figure named Rāhula or Rāhulabhadra (the latter is credited with authorship of the *Praise of the Perfection of Wisdom*), and a late-first-millennium tantric exegete who perhaps had as his teacher Saraha, the composer of tantric songs. Adding to the confusion, Saraha sometimes is identified with Rāhula(bhadra), though as will become evident below, Thuken considers them separate, both active as early as a few centuries after the passing of the Buddha.

132 Most notably, in chapter 7 of the *Unraveling of Intention Sutra.*

133 The former relates to the collection of gnosis, which eventuates in a buddha's dharmakāya, while the latter relates to the collection of merit, which eventuates in a buddha's form bodies.

134 See, especially, Ruegg, *Literature of the Madhyamaka School.*

135 For historical information on Nāgārjuna, see, e.g., Streng; Lindtner; Walser. For translations of texts by Nāgārjuna, see, e.g., Lindtner; Garfield; Komito; Hopkins, *Buddhist Advice for Living and Liberation.* For fuller bibliographic information, see Hopkins, *Maps of the Profound,* pp. 1073–74.

136 Vedalī was in what is now Andhra Pradesh, the area generally associated with Nāgārjuna. The Tibetan *be ṭa* (or *be ta*) also comes to be associated with Vidarbha, further to the west, in what is now northeastern Maharashtra (see Das, *Tibetan-English Dictionary,* p. 875). This may explain why, below, Thuken explicitly states that Nāgārjuna was born in Vidarbha.

137 This is the first of the ten levels (Skt. *bhūmi*) through which advanced bodhisattvas pass en route to buddhahood. Among the five paths to liberation, it is equivalent to the third, the path of seeing. It marks the first time that meditative tranquil abiding and superior insight are brought together so as to realize directly the true nature of entities, as either without self or as empty; it is the basis for the eradication—as opposed to the suppression—of the delusions that, in coarse, subtle, or residual form, prevent one from attaining liberation or omniscience.

138 *Laṅkāvatārasūtra;* Toh 107 Kangyur, mdo sde, *ca,* 165b4. Cf. Suzuki, *Laṅkāvatāra Sūtra,* pp. 239–40. Sukhāvatī is the western pure land of Buddha Amitābha.

139 Toh 543 Kangyur, rgyud 'bum, *na,* chap. 36, 200b1.

140 Toh 222 Kangyur, mdo sde, *dza,* 124b2.

141 See above, note 136.

142 Here and elsewhere, Thuken has *nā lendra,* an alternative name for the great monastic university northeast of Bodhgayā in present-day Bihar. Nālandā's development probably postdates Nāgārjuna if we regard him as having lived in the second century. On Rāhulabhadra, see Ruegg, *Literature of the Madhyamaka School,* pp.

54–55. For a brief discussion of the problem of Rāhula(bhadra)/Saraha vis à vis Nāgārjuna, see above, note 131.

143 This text is unknown to modern scholarship.

144 *Nāga mud (klu'i 'dam)* refers to soil from the nāga realm, possession of which empowers its owner to return to that realm once he or she has left it.

145 Tib. *klu sgrub.* Literally, the one who accomplished *(sgrub, arjuna)* great things in or through the nāga *(klu)* realm.

146 Mittal (p. 39) suggests that this is Śrāvastī, a city in the Gangetic plain that already was important during the Buddha's time.

147 This is generally identified with the stupa at Amarāvatī, in present-day Andhra Pradesh.

148 The *Fundamental Treatise on the Middle Way* (see Garfield), *Sixty Stanzas on Reasoning* (see Loizzo), *Seventy Stanzas on Emptiness* (see Komito), *Finely Woven Scripture, Refutation of Objections* (see, e.g., Streng, pp. 222–27), and *Precious Garland* (see Hopkins, *Buddhist Advice for Living and Liberation*). See also Ruegg, *Literature of the Madhyamaka School,* and the bibliographic information in Hopkins, *Maps of the Profound,* pp. 1073–74.

149 On the five stages, see, e.g., Cozort; K. Gyatso, *Tantric Grounds and Paths;* for a translation of a portion of Nāgārjuna's text, Thurman, *Essential Tibetan Buddhism,* pp. 249–60.

150 Toh 222 Kangyur, mdo sde, *dza,* 100b6.

151 Toh 1785 Tengyur, rgyud 'grel, *ha,* 200b1.

152 Direct discipleship by the last three would require extraordinarily long lifespans for them, for Nāgārjuna, or for all of them, and Tibetan tradition does indeed assign most of them Methuselah-like longevity, largely as a way of showing that Madhyamaka masters who earlier propounded emptiness later wrote treatises on tantra.

153 Sometimes, this gloss is incorporated into the title of the text, so that the title becomes *Yogācāra-catuḥśataka.* On this text, see Lang.

154 On the former, see, e.g., Huntington; on the latter, see, e.g., Sprung.

155 On this question, see Dreyfus and McClintock, especially the introduction and chapters 1–2.

156 On the *Ornament of Madhyamaka,* see Blumenthal; on *Distinguishing the Two Truths,* see Eckel.

157 According to Könchok Jikmé Wangpo, "True Aspectarians assert that [e.g.,] an appearance of blue as blue to an eye consciousness apprehending blue exists as it appears, whereas False Aspectarians maintain that an appearance of blue as blue does not exist as it appears to an eye consciousness apprehending blue" (Sopa and Hopkins, p. 250).

158 In Tibetan, Labapa *(lwa ba pa),* the "blanket-clad one"; he is better known as one of the eighty-four mahāsiddhas than as a philosopher, but he is credited with several texts on Perfection Vehicle topics. See Mittal, pp. 42, 168–69; Robinson, pp. 117–20, 300; Dowman, *Masters of Mahāmudrā,* pp. 179–85; Templeman, *Seven Instruction Lineages,* pp. 33–36.

159 According to Könchok Jikmé Wangpo, "Tainted False Aspectarians are so called because they assert that the nature of the mind is polluted by the latencies of ignorance and...Non-Tainted False Aspectarians are so called because they assert that the entity of the mind is not in the least polluted by the latencies of ignorance" (Sopa and Hopkins, pp. 258–59).

160 In other words, such realizations arise not from making use of independent syllogisms, as Svātantrikas claim; rather they arise organically whenever we pursue the logical consequences of any position. On the distinction between the two schools in general, see Dreyfus and McClintock.

161 See translations of important Cittamātra/Yogācāra texts by, e.g., Powers; Suzuki, *Laṅkāvatāra Sūtra;* Anacker; for an exhaustive analysis of Tibetan perspectives on Cittamātra, see Hopkins, *Absorption in No External World.*

162 Toh 543 Kangyur, rgyud 'bum, *na*, chap. 36, 309b1.

163 Toh 543 Kangyur, rgyud 'bum, *na,* chap. 36, 309a2.

164 The three suppressions of abhidharma, according to Butön, followed three separate occasions on which statements or actions by Buddhists were taken as insults by non-Buddhists, and the community was oppressed as a result. See Obermiller, *History of Buddhism*, pp. 136–37.

165 In Magadha; it has strong associations with the Buddha's disciple Mahākāśyapa.

166 This quote is found in Butön Rinchen Drup, *Dharma History,* p. 153; cf. Obermiller, *History of Buddhism,* p. 137.

167 Although all editions have *lha'i gro,* we read it as *lha'i 'gro.*

168 That is, the *Perfection of Wisdom in a Hundred Thousand Verses.*

169 The *Ornament of Higher Realization* (see Conze, *Abhisamayālaṃkāra*), *Ornament of Mahayana Sutras* (see Thurman et al.), *Sublime Continuum* (see Obermiller, "Sublime Science"; Thrangu, *Uttara Tantra*), *Distinguishing the Middle from the Extremes* (see Stcherbatsky, *Madhyānta-vibhaṅga*, Dharmacakra Translation Committee), and *Distinguishing Dharmas from the Dharma Realm* (see Thrangu, *Distinguishing Dharma and Dharmata*). See also the bibliographic references in Hopkins, *Maps of the Profound,* pp. 1071–72.

170 For fuller bibliographic information on these texts—Asaṅga's *Stages of Yogic Practice, Compendium of Bases, Compendium of Ascertainments, Compendium of Enumerations,* and *Compendium of Explanations*—see Hopkins, *Maps of the Profound,* pp. 1060–61.

171 Asaṅga's *Compendium of Mahayana Sutras* (see Lamotte, *La Somme du Grand Véhicule d'Asaṅga*) and *Compendium of Abhidharma* (see Rahula).

172 Toh 4043 Tengyur, sems tsam, *'i,* 69a1.

173 Toh 3796 Tengyur, mdo 'grel, *nya*, 9a1. The implication is that, by reaching this stage, he would have seen past Cittamātra and mastered Madhyamaka, but he taught the former to his Hinayanist brother out of compassion.

174 *Explication of the Ornament of Higher Realization;* Toh 4029 Tengyur, sems tsam, *bi,* 60b2. This is the fourth, and highest, of the four stages of the path of preparation—the second of the five paths; it directly precedes attainment of the path of seeing, wherein tranquil abiding and higher insight are fused, the nature of reality is directly realized, and delusions begin to be uprooted.

175 This quote is found in Butön Rinchen Drup, *Dharma History,* p. 155; cf. Obermiller, *History of Buddhism,* p. 143.

176 Vasubandhu's *Twenty Stanzas, Thirty Stanzas, Dissertation on the Five Aggregates, Rational System of Exposition, Dissertation on the Proof of Deeds, Explanation of the Ornament of Mahayana Sutras, Explication of Distinguishing the Middle from the Extremes*, and as the last either the *Treasury of Higher Knowledge* (see Hopkins,

Maps of the Profound, p. 1078) or *Commentary on Distinguishing Dharmas from the Dharma Realm* (see NS, vol. II, p. 7n95). Anacker translates 1, 2, 3, 5, 7.

177 These represent four of the five major subjects studied by candidates for the Geluk degree of geshé *(dge bshes)*. The fifth, whose mastery we should not expect from any Cittamatrin, is Madhyamaka.

178 The translation of *sems tsam/cittamātra* ("mind only") by "idealist" is controversial, but to the degree that a central tenet of Cittamātra is that external appearances exist as "mind only," the view is similar to that of idealism in Western philosophy.

179 *Proponents of an equal number of subjects and objects*, e.g., Śākyabuddhi, assert "that the aspects of the various apprehended objects and concordant types of consciousnesses arise simultaneously"; *split-eggs (sgo nga chad tshal ba)*, e.g., Śaṃkarānanda, assert "that the two, apprehended objects and apprehending subjects that are the nature of consciousnesses, are different substantial entities in terms of the time of their establishment"; and *nonpluralists*, e.g., Dharmakīrti, hold that "the aspects of consciousness to which the various [appearances] of the blue and yellow of a mottle, etc., appear are in the entity of one consciousness" (Cozort and Preston, p. 193). The split-eggs sometimes are said to be so named because they are "half like Sautrāntika, half like Cittamātra. They say that an object produces a subject, but that both are of the nature of mind" (Cozort and Preston, p. 193n1). These characterizations of the three positions are quite general; as Thuken notes, there is considerable disagreement among Tibetan scholars as to the precise definitions of each.

180 The term *grub pa* (Skt. *siddha*) can also mean "exists," but because Thuken uses another word, *yod,* for "exists," we translate *grub* as "is established," with the understanding that it is nearly synonymous with "exists."

181 From a Prāsaṅgika Mādhyamika standpoint, *realist (dngos smra ba, *vastuvādin)* refers to the proponent of any Buddhist school from Cittamātra down; Svātantrika Mādhyamikas are not considered realists.

182 Although these terms are distinguishable in subtle ways, they are treated by Thuken (and many Tibetan scholars) as roughly synonymous. All of them refer to ways in which one might express the idea that some (or any) entity is or possesses self. See Hopkins, *Maps of the Profound,* p. 823; Cozort and Preston, p. 239.

183 *Collected Works,* vol. *nga,* 2b3. This passage is quite difficult, and the translation conjectural. The implication may be that, on the Vaibhāṣika and Sautrāntika view, solid matter does not have the reality that it seems to, because it is actually atomic in nature. For an alternative translation of this passage, see Jinpa and Elsner, p. 111, where it is rendered: "Atomic matter—is she a beaming tiger?" The "she" is the "mother," the nature of reality, which is the poem's subject.

184 These are the three "natures" *(rang bzhin, svabhāva)* or "characteristics" *(mtshan nyid, lakṣaṇa)* into which, according to Cittamātrins, all existents may be divided: the *dependent (gzhan dbang, paratantra),* the *thoroughly established* or *absolute (yongs grub, parinispanna),* and the *imaginary (kun btags, parikalpita).*

185 *Essence of Excellent Explanation: Distinguishing Between Provisional and Definitive;* in *Collected Works,* vol. *pha,* 5a5. According to Cittamātra, there are two types of imaginary entities: (1) nonexistent (or impossible) imaginaries, such as the horns of a rabbit or a barren woman's son; and (2) existent imaginaries, which include all permanent phenomena except for emptinesses, e.g., space. The latter are claimed

by Cittamātrins not to be established by their own characteristics but nevertheless to exist from their own side. Because for Prāsaṅgika Madhyamaka anything that exists from its own side *must* be established through its own characteristics, the Cittamātrins fall into realism when they assert that some imaginary entities do exist from their own side.

186 Objectivists *(don smra ba)* assert the ultimate existence of objects of knowledge; the term is used to refer to the two Hinayana philosophical schools, Vaibhāṣika and Sautrāntika. Objectivists are a subset of the larger category of "realists," which, as we have seen, from the Prāsaṅgika standpoint, also includes Cittamātra.

187 The explanation by Svātantrikas and others is incomplete, or inadequate, because it supposes that a basis of imputation for the concept of a person, namely, the aggregates, *will* be found after analysis, and that these turn out to be "the person." From the Prāsaṅgika perspective, though, anything that is findable after analysis cannot be "merely" imputed; hence, the lower schools' claim to have located the basis of imputation for the person, which in some sense, then, *is* the person, belies their failure to understand what "mere" imputation really means, and their failure to understand the meaning of "mere" imputation means that they do not really know what the imputed object is, either.

188 In Madhyamaka, the investigation whether an entity exists: as separate from its components, as identical to its components, possessing its components, inherently dependent upon its components, as the basis upon which the components depend, as the collection of components, or the shape of its components. The *locus classicus* is Candrakīrti's *Entering the Middle Way* 6:150–64; see Huntington, pp. 175–77.

189 This is a mode of analysis in which you determine that the self you seek must be one or many. Neither possibility stands up to analysis, however, and since they are exhaustive and mutually contradictory options, the self cannot be found.

190 Literally, "subsequent attainment" *(rjes thob, pṛṣṭhalabhda),* this is a non-buddha's experience subsequent to a meditation session in which emptiness has been directly perceived.

191 The nine levels of knowledge obstacles are derived by identifying gross, medium, and subtle levels of obstacles on each of three general levels: gross, medium, and subtle. As noted in the text, the count of eleven is arrived at by dividing the gross-gross and subtle-subtle into two. The eleven levels are related to the ten stages of the bodhisattva: the last moment of the first bodhisattva stage is the first moment of the path of meditation, which then is followed by the other nine stages. The tenth stage is divided in two, with the stage itself and the last moment before buddhahood (the *final continuum*) being counted separately. For their part, the Prāsaṅgikas maintain that no knowledge obstacles are eliminated until the eighth bodhisattva stage.

192 That is, the fact that dharmas are dependent assures their ultimate emptiness, while the fact that they do arise assures that they do exist conventionally.

193 By the time knowledge obstacles begin to be eliminated, the seeds for delusion have been entirely destroyed; but there remain certain traces of those delusions, and a subtle predisposition still to see reality incorrectly, though not to grasp at that incorrect vision.

194 *Collected Works,* vol. *pha,* 71b2.

195 The point here is that for non-Prāsaṅgika schools, the innate apprehension of a self involves apprehension of a self that is separate from but in control of the aggregates, as a shepherd is in charge of a flock. The Prāsaṅgikas regard such a mode of apprehension as imputed, or intellectually derived, rather than innate. For them, the innate apprehension of a self involves apprehension of a self that is identified with yet appears to be separable from and in control of the aggregates, when in fact the "self" is dependent on the aggregates—just as a head merchant appears to be separable from and in charge of other merchants but is not really thus separable. See Hopkins, *Meditation in Emptiness,* pp. 303–4.

196 Above, following Vinītadeva, Thuken listed only three Saṃmatīya sects.

197 Vasubandhu, *Abhidharmakośa* 8:24ab; Toh 4089 Tengyur, mngon pa, *ku,* 24b3. Cf. La Vallée Poussin, vol. 4, p. 1257.

198 The implication is that although the Vaibhāṣikas may claim that emptiness is simply nonexistence, they do utilize the term in certain contexts, as in discussions of the three doors to liberation—the signless, the empty, and the wishless—or the sixteen aspects of the four noble truths, of which emptiness (related to the truth of suffering) is the fourth.

199 The path of seeing is divided into sixteen moments: eight pairs consisting of an uninterrupted path and a path of liberation. Here, an uninterrupted path is roughly synonymous with direct perception. See Sopa and Hopkins, p. 207.

200 The Buddha traditionally attains final nirvana via the fourth mental absorption.

201 In both śrāvaka and Mahayana five-path schemes, these are: preparation, seeing, meditation, and no more learning, though the definitions of what is accomplished on each path will of course differ from school to school.

202 Because Sautrāntikas deny that a mere absence can be an object of cognition, the actual object that is intended when you realize selflessness is some constructed object that has selflessness as an aspect.

203 *Dbu ma pa* refers either to those who claim to find the "middle" or to those who adhere to the Madhyamaka (middle way).

204 Following standard practice, Thuken refers to *rgyal ba dge 'dun rgya mtsho.* To reflect modern appellations, we translate this as "the Second Dalai Lama, Gendün Gyatso." We follow this pattern, including the interpolation of the ordinal number, throughout in translating references to Dalai Lamas, Panchen Lamas, Karmapas, and other important trulku lineages.

205 *A Ship to Sail the Ocean of Philosophical Systems,* p. 51. For the context of the passage quoted by Thuken, see Mullin, *Selected Works of Dalai Lama II,* p. 156.

206 The contradiction between the last two statements is only apparent: dharmas exist *(yod)* by their own characteristics in that they have conventional definitions but are not established *(grub)* by their own characteristics as possessing any ultimacy.

207 A. W. Barber and N. Jay R. Weil contributed to an earlier version of the present translation of the chapter. For an alternative, rough translation of this chapter, see Das, "Contribution on the Religion, History, etc., of Tibet," vol. LI, part 1, no. 1 (1882), pp. 1–6.

208 For general accounts of Tibetan Buddhism, see, e.g., Dalai Lama, *World of Tibetan Buddhism;* Samuel; Ray, *Indestructible Truth* and *Secrets of the Vajra World;* Powers, *Introduction to Tibetan Buddhism;* Snellgrove and Richardson; Lopez, *Religions*

of Tibet in Practice, pp. 3–36; Stein, *Tibetan Civilization,* pp. 164–91; Tucci, *Religions of Tibet,* chaps. 1–5; Kapstein, *The Tibetans,* chap. 7.

209 Literally, "the source of all we need and want" *(dgos 'dod kun 'byung).*

210 *Phan bde* may connote either temporary benefit *(phan)* or final bliss *(bde).*

211 The "sciences" *(rig gnas),* as classified by Sakya Pandita and accepted by most subsequent Tibetan scholars, are divided into five minor sciences (grammar, poetic theory, prosody, drama, and lexicography) and five major sciences (linguistics, logic, medicine, arts and technology, and "inner meaning," or Buddhism). See D. Jackson, *Entrance-Gate for the Wise,* vol. 1, p. 11n17; Cabezón and Jackson, pp. 17–18. When the section related to this heading actually appears in the text (at the very end of chapter 12 in this volume), Thuken notes that it would be too much to examine the subject in depth and is satisfied to merely list its contents.

212 For overviews by modern scholars, see, e.g., TPS, vol. 1, pp. 81–92; Shakabpa; Snellgrove and Richardson; Richardson, *Tibet and Its History;* Snellgrove, *Indo-Tibetan Buddhism,* vol. II; Samuel; Powers, *Introduction to Tibetan Buddhism;* Kapstein, *The Tibetans,* chaps. 3–5, 7, and *Tibetan Assimilation of Buddhism.* For Tibetan presentations, see, e.g., BA; Ahmad, *A History of Tibet by Ṅag-dBaṅ Blo-bZaṅ rGya-mTsho;* Obermiller, *History of Buddhism,* pp. 181–224. For anthologies, see Lopez, *Religions of Tibet in Practice;* Thurman, *Essential Tibetan Buddhism;* Batchelor.

213 See, e.g., BA, pp. 1–62, 102–203; NS; S. Gyaltsen; Tucci, *Religions of Tibet*, chap. 1; Snellgrove and Richardson, part 1.

214 Namri Songtsen is generally agreed to have been Songtsen Gampo's father, so he probably lived from the late sixth to the early seventh century. Dates for Tibetan kings prior to this time are conjectural at best.

215 The text was probably brought from India. However, according to the then-prevalent Bön mythology, sacred things "come from the sky." Other texts "descending" at this time include the *Jewel Chest Array Sutra,* which is dedicated to Avalokiteśvara. On the latter, see, e.g., Studholme.

216 See, e.g., Ahmad, *A History of Tibet by Ṅag-dBaṅ Blo-bZaṅ rGya-mTsho,* pp. 17–49; Obermiller, *History of Buddhism,* pp. 183–85.

217 Literally, "invite" *(spyan drangs).*

218 This is the statue that dominates the Jokhang, the main temple in Lhasa.

219 For a translation, see Cleary.

220 See, e.g., Ahmad, *A History of Tibet by Ṅag-dBaṅ Blo-bZaṅ rGya-mTsho,* pp. 50–68; Obermiller, *History of Buddhism,* pp. 186–96.

221 *Yid la mi byed pa (amanasikāra)* literally means "putting nothing into the mind." It is a common term in the Indian literature at the root of Mahāmudrā traditions, including the so-called Twenty-Five Works on Unthinking, attributed to Maitripa (or Advayavajra, eleventh century), on which see, e.g., Broido, "Sa-skya paṇḍita, the White Panacea and the Hva-shang Doctrine," pp. 55–57; for a Sanskrit edition of most of the texts, see Shastri.

222 On the debate between Kamalaśīla and Heshang, see, e.g., Obermiller, *History of Buddhism,* pp. 191–96; Demiévelle; Tucci, *Minor Buddhist Texts;* Ruegg, *Buddha-nature, Mind and the Problem of Gradualism.* For translations of one or another of the *Stages of Meditation (Bhāvanākrama)* texts, see, e.g., Beyer, *Buddhist Experience,* pp. 79–89; Dalai Lama, *Stages of Meditation.*

223 See, e.g., Ahmad, *A History of Tibet by Ṅag-dBaṅ Blo-bZaṅ rGya-mTsho,* pp. 69–74; Obermiller, *History of Buddhism,* pp. 196–97.

224 See, e.g., Ahmad, *A History of Tibet by Ṅag-dBaṅ Blo-bZaṅ rGya-mTsho,* pp. 75–82; Obermiller, *History of Buddhism,* pp. 197–200.

225 That is, Śāntarakṣita's Yogācāra Svātantrika Madhyamaka view.

226 See, e.g., BA, pp. 63–101, 204–398; Tucci, *Religions of Tibet,* chap. 2, and TPS, vol. 1, pp 3–80; Snellgrove and Richardson, part 2; TR.

227 *Lo tsā ba* ("Translator") is a title reserved for the very greatest of translators, and occasionally for great scholars who may not be translators.

228 *Blue Annals,* 62:5; cf. BA, p. 68.

229 That is, a Mādhyamika who abides in none of the possible extreme positions (is, is not, both, neither). Since Madhyamaka is in general defined by adhering to a middle beyond extremes, the phrase may simply indicate that Rinchen Sangpo was a Mādhyamika of undetermined affiliation.

230 Like K and Z, we have ignored these two subdivisions in representing Thuken's account of the Tibetan schools. Thus the first page of the discussion of each tradition refers only to the heading encompassing *all* Tibetan Buddhist schools: (1) Nyingma, (2) Kadam, (3) Kagyü, (4) Shijé, (5) Sakya, (6) Jonang, (7) minor schools, (8) Geluk.

231 For alternative organizational schemes, see, e.g., BA; Kapstein, *"gDams ngag";* Ringu; Kongtrül, *Esoteric Instructions.*

232 A. W. Barber and N. Jay R. Weil contributed to an earlier version of the present translation of this chapter. Sönam Rapten, of the Central Institute of Tibetan Higher Studies, Sarnath, and Matthew Kapstein provided invaluable help with difficult passages. For an alternative, rough translation of the first portion of this chapter, see Das, "Contribution on the Religion, History, etc. of Tibet," vol. LI, part 1, no. 1 (1882), pp. 6–14.

233 On Nyingma in general, see, e.g., BA, chap. III; TPS, vol. 1, pp. 87–88, 108–16; Batchelor, part 4; Powers, *Introduction to Tibetan Buddhism,* chap. 12; Ray, *Indestructible Truth,* chap. 5; Karmay, *The Great Perfection;* Tucci, *Religions of Tibet,* pp. 76–87; Lopez, *Religions of Tibet in Practice,* chaps. 2, 13, 15, 18, 19, 22, 30, 35; and, most especially, NS.

234 For a later, synoptic view of the tantric systems of both the old and new translation schools, see Kongtrül.

235 See BA, p. 205.

236 On the Guhyasamāja, see, e.g., Matsunaga; Wayman, *Yoga of the Guhyasamājatantra;* Yangchen; Boord and Tsonawa, chap. 9; Davidson, *Indian Esoteric Buddhism, passim.*

237 On the Hevajra, see, e.g., Farrow and Memon; Snellgrove, *Hevajra Tantra;* Davidson, "Preliminary Studies on Hevajra's *Abhisamaya*" and *Indian Esoteric Buddhism,* pp. 263–69 *et passim.*

238 On the Cakrasamvara, see, e.g., Tsuda; Gray; Beyer, *Buddhist Experience,* pp. 140–53; Huntington and Bangdel; K. Gyatso, *Clear Light of Bliss.*

239 In all Tibetan editions, these verses appear before the section heading, but we have moved them to better indicate their function of introducing the section.

240 According to tradition, these teachings had been brought to Tibet by Thönmi Sambhota and taught to the king. Greatly Compassionate One is Avalokiteśvara.

241 Presumably not the famous Advaita Vedānta philosopher, who generally is said to have lived in the late eighth or early ninth century.

242 In *Ma ṇi bka' 'bum,* p. 279ff. On the *Ma ṇi bka' 'bum,* see Kapstein, *Tibetan Assimilation of Buddhism,* pp. 144–55. Thupten Jinpa notes in his introduction to *The Book of Kadam* (p. 20): "One of the most interesting aspects of the nineteenth chapter [of the Father Teachings] is its close connection with another important Tibetan work of some antiquity that appeared to be a key text in the propagation of the tradition of identifying Tibetan imperial figures with Avalokiteśvara. This is the famous *Kakholma Testament* (literally, *Testament Extracted from a Pillar*), purportedly authored by the seventh-century Tibetan emperor Songtsen Gampo and later rediscovered as a revealed treasure text. According to a tradition dating back to the twelfth century, Atiśa is credited with having retrieved this text in Lhasa toward the end of the 1040s. In fact, in the present redaction of the testament, the text opens with an interesting discussion of Atiśa's visit to the Lhasa cathedral and some miraculous visions he experienced relating to the image of the self-originated Avalokiteśvara icon there. In the text's colophon, Atiśa is quoted as saying that he saw the manuscript of the testament written on a blue silk cloth with gold letters and that there were three versions of the text. He also explicitly states that the text was discovered as a treasure in the cathedral of Lhasa."

243 The site of the Potala.

244 These are indigenous earth goddesses; according to NS, vol. II, p. 170, their names vary from list to list.

245 Attempts to translate the types of various Tibetan indigenous "demons" into English often end up being misleading, so we generally have opted to refer to them by their phoneticized Tibetan name followed by "demon." The *srin* demon (or demonesses) is often said to be the Tibetan equivalent of the Indic *rakṣasa* or *rakṣasī,* but the class was in place before the introduction of Buddhism. On this class of deity, see Nebesky-Wojkowitz, p. 280 *et passim.*

246 See, e.g., Zangpo, *Guru Rinpoché;* TPS, vol. 2, pp. 373–86; NS and BA, *passim;* Thurman, *Essential Tibetan Buddhism,* pp. 97–98, 261–64.

247 This probably refers to the three inner tantric yogas of the Nyingma: mahāyoga, anuyoga, and atiyoga, which will be discussed below.

248 This is the sound of Hayagrīva, a wrathful emanation of Avalokiteśvara.

249 Z has *ting 'dzin,* or "concentration," which is equally if not more plausible. The immovable concentration implies supreme achievement.

250 Orgyen Lingpa, *Five-Part Edict,* p. 131. For a variant account, see NS, vol. I, pp. 535–36.

251 This is one of the two great mandalas of the yoga tantra buddha Vairocana, the other being the Garbhadhātu. It was important during the imperial period in Tibet and is of great importance in the Shingon tradition of Japan.

252 The definition vehicle, or *vehicle of characteristics (mtshan nyid theg pa),* is another name for the perfection vehicle or the sutra vehicle, which is contrasted with the vehicle of tantra. It is referred to as the *definition vehicle* because its texts establish the basic categories, terms, and meanings that must be understood prior to undertaking tantric practice.

253 For a translation, see Norbu and Clemente.

254 This is traditionally said to be the abode of demons (Skt. *rākṣasas*), whom Padmasambhava subdued. See, e.g., NS, p. 520.

255 Orgyen, also known as Urgyan (Uḍḍiyāna in Sanskrit), is traditionally said to be the home of Padmasambhava; it is generally identified with what is now the Swat Valley in Pakistan. Sahor *(za hor),* from a Persian word for "city," has been identified both with the Kangra district of what is now Himachal Pradesh (see Das, *Tibetan-English Dictionary*, p. 1089) and with Sābhār, which is near present-day Dhaka, Bangladesh (see BA, p. 241). Although there may be more than one place with that name, it is the one in Bengal that is said to be the birthplace of both Śāntarakṣita and Atiśa.

256 Literally, "[based on] desire and anger" *(chags sdang).*

257 Past, present, future, and indefinite time; see, e.g., NS, vol. II, p. 125.

258 The eighth, ninth, and tenth bodhisattva stages, on which one has transcended ordinary samsaric suffering.

259 This is either an alternate name for, or a manifestation of, Padmasambhava.

260 See NS, vol. I, pp. 452–57.

261 The final three—also known as, respectively, the lineage empowered by enlightened aspiration, the lineage of prophetically declared spiritual succession, and the lineage of the ḍākinīs' seal of entrustment—are all related to treasure transmissions. See, NS, vol. I, p. 745.

262 These are related to the mahāyoga, anuyoga, and atiyoga vehicles, respectively (NS, vol. I, p. 396). Thuken reverses the *Net of Illusion* and *Sutra that Gathers Intentions,* but we have placed them in the order we have so as to show their connections to each member of the triad.

263 See, NS, vol. I, p. 533.

264 This entire paragraph, and the beginning of the next, are drawn nearly verbatim from Gö Lotsāwa, *Blue Annals,* chap. 3, 3b–4a; cf. BA, p. 108.

265 The other three were Lönchen Phakpa, Lekpai Drönmé, and Dengyi Yönten Chok; see NS, vol. I, p. 613.

266 See NS, vol. I, p. 622.

267 See NS, vol. I, pp. 635–45, and Dilgo Khyentse. The other three of the "four peaks" were Menyak Khyungdrak, Shang Göchung, and Zangom Sherap Gyalpo (NS, vol. I, p. 622).

268 For a detailed listing, see NS, vol. I, p. 642; see also BA, pp. 118–21.

269 For a complete listing, see NS. vol. I, pp. 648–49; see also BA, p. 125.

270 He is also known as Tanak Drölmema.

271 Throm *(khrom),* a name that may bear distant echoes of "Rome," is difficult to locate, but is most often associated with portions of the eastern Byzantine empire. For a discussion, see Garrett, p. 368.

272 He is also known as Zurpoché Śākya Jungné.

273 See NS, vol. I, pp. 537, 607–16, 717ff.

274 See NS, vol. I, pp. 534–35, 475–81.

275 On Vajrakīla, see, e.g., Boord.

276 See Nebesky-Wojkowitz, *passim.*

277 See Hopkins, *Yoga of Tibet,* pp. 82–101.

278 There are far too many works on Dzokchen to list here but see, e.g., Karmay, *The Great Perfection;* Germano, "Architecture and Absence"; van Schaik; Tulku Thondup, *Buddha Mind;* Dowman, *Flight of the Garuda;* J. Gyatso, *Apparitions of the Self;* and the many references in NS.

279 For a complete list, see NS, vol. II, p. 221.

280 The Tibetan term *snying thig* has received a range of translations; NS renders it as "innermost spirituality," Tulku Thondup as "heart essence," and David Germano as "seminal heart" ("The Elements, Insanity, and Lettered Subjectivity," p. 315).

281 See NS, vol. I, pp. 325–26.

282 According to NS, vol. I, p. 601, these are the streams of conventional textual exegesis, instruction of the ear-whispered lineage, blessing and empowerment, and practical techniques.

283 See NS, vol. I, pp. 326–29, 540–53.

284 He also is known as Pangen Sangyé Gönpo.

285 A practice that leads to the attainment of the rainbow body in a single life. See below, p. 86, as well as BA, pp. 175–91; NS, vol. II, p. 45n591.

286 Following NS, we read *'dzeng* for *'dze.*

287 The four or five others, are, according to NS, vol. I, p. 552: Serlungpa, Du Dorjé Gyaltsen, Zik Yeshé Wangpo, Yaktön Dawa Özer, and Kyetsé Yeshé Wangchuk.

288 Following NS, we read *'dzeng* for *'dze.*

289 See BA, pp. 191–203; NS, vol. I, pp. 554–74.

290 He also is known as Dro Rinchenbar.

291 According to NS, vol. I, p. 558, these are: Langdro Chepa Tak, Uyuk, and the upper valley of Jal.

292 Following K and NS, we read *lang* for *mas.*

293 Following K, we read *'bum* for *'bu.*

294 Following K and NS, we read *rgyab pa* for *rgyal ba.*

295 We read *ku mā ra rā dza* for *ku mā rā dza.*

296 See BA, pp. 200–202; NS, vol. I, pp. 574–96; E. G. Smith, pp. 33–35. For translations of Longchenpa's work, see, e.g., Tulku Thondup, *Buddha Mind;* Barron; Berzin et al.; Thurman, *Essential Tibetan Buddhism,* pp. 116–28, 172–75. See also the forthcoming volume 3 of *The Library of Tibetan Classics,* a translation of Longchenpa's *Great Chariot (Shing rta chen po).*

297 See NS, vol. I, pp. 554–55.

298 The Third Karmapa of the Karma Kagyüpas. See NS, vol. I, pp. 572–74.

299 See, e.g., NS, vol. I, pp. 743–881; Tulku Thondup, *Hidden Teachings of Tibet;* Doctor; TR, chap. 6; J. Gyatso, "Drawn from the Tibetan Treasury."

300 These are the *Root Tantra (rtsa ba'i rgyud), Explanatory Tantra (bshad rgyud), Tantra of Special Instruction (man ngag gi rgyud),* and the *Follow-up Tantra (phyi ma'i rgyud).* See NS, vol. II, p. 229.

301 See NS, vol. I, p. 747.

302 The six yogas are the completion-stage phases described by the Kālacakra tantric tradition: withdrawal, mental absorption, breath control, retention, recollection, and concentration; see, e.g., Khedrup Norsang Gyatso, part 5. The five stages are the completion-stage phases described by the Guhyasamāja tantric tradition: isolated speech, isolated mind, illusory body, clear light, and union; see, e.g., Cozort; K. Gyatso, *Tantric Grounds and Paths.* Lamdré is the "path and result" tradition dominant in the Sakya tradition; on this see below, chapter 8.

303 On the various enumerations of processes involved in the *Net of Illusion* tradition, see NS, vol. I, pp. 275–83.

304 The path of means generally entails complex yogic practices focused on the channels, winds, and drops of the subtle body. The secret drop *(gsang thig)* is probably syn-

onymous with the heart-drop tradition *(snying thig)* within the special-instruction class, described above.

305 Mahāmudrā, the "great seal," is a dominant meditative style in the Kagyü tradition; see chapter 6 below.

306 The gnosis body *(ye shes sku, jñānakāya)* is the "cognitive" aspect of a buddha's dharmakāya.

307 The *rang rig lu gu rgyud kyi sku* is equivalent to the dharmakāya.

308 Again, a reference to the six yogas of the Kālacakra tantra, which is accepted by all the new-translation traditions.

309 In Tibetan, these are, respectively, *ngo bo ka dag, rang bzhin lhun grub,* and *thugs rje kun khyab.*

310 This term also has importance in the Sakya school; see chapter 8.

311 Although all editions have *ma btub,* the dropping of the negative *ma* would bring the passage closer to conformity with standard Nyingma views on the capacity of the ultimate to manifest.

312 On this Ngok, whose dates are unknown, see Martin, *Unearthing Bon Treasures,* p. 108n4.

313 Literally, "hit the head and hit the foot of" *(dbu phog zhabs phog).*

314 Many of these passages critical of the Nyingma are found in Soksokpa Lodrö Gyaltsen's *Dragon's Roar of Definitive Meaning,* a defense of the Nyingma against its critics that may well have been available to Thuken. See S, pp. 341–42nn46, 48–49.

315 The full name of Khedrup Jé, one of Tsongkhapa's two greatest disciples.

316 Joden Sönam Lhündrup's *Biography of Tsongkhapa* was unavailable for consultation; it is listed as TBRC W18630.

317 We have been unable to identify this text.

318 In TBRC, the only work listed for Wöntön Rinchen Gangpa is the *Great Treatise on the Stages of the Path,* W17171. The quotation is found in Chenga Lodrö Gyaltsen's *Seven-Point Mind Training;* in *Collected Works,* vol. *nga,* 5b6.

319 The Tibetan version of the latter is found in vol. *ta* of the Nyingma Gyübum (see, e.g., *Taipei Tibetan Tripitaka,* vol. 64) but not in the Kangyur; for a study, see Boord.

320 Literally, "equalizing" or "leveling out" *(mnyam par).*

321 Butön Rinchen Drup, *Dharma History,* p. 266.

322 Following K and NS, we read *rgyal* for *rgyas.*

323 We have been unable to locate a textual source prior to Thuken for this well-known dialogue.

324 See NS, vol. I, pp. 682–84, 821–24.

325 That is, the king of the Heaven of the Thirty-Three, Indra.

326 Sera and Drepung, core monastic institutions of the Geluk lineage, lie just outside Lhasa.

327 Literally, "nectar offerings and wisdom-lady offerings" *(bdud rtsi'i mchod pa dang rig ma mchod pa).*

328 See the translation at NS, vol. I, pp. 735–36, and Dudjom Rinpoche's following comment: "Such uncritical prattle is exceedingly false. Since a great scholar like Thuken, who bears up to examination, would never present a corrupt account, we think that this statement was undoubtedly an interpolation made later on by some foolish fanatic."

329 Literally, the "Brahmā line" *(tshangs pa'i thig).*

330 Lolly Gewissler contributed to an earlier version of the present translation of the chapter. We also benefited from comments by Leonard Zwilling and Michael Sweet. The first two-thirds of this chapter have been translated by A. Chattopadhyaya, pp. 377–96. On Kadam in general, see, e.g., TPS, vol. 1, pp. 88–89; BA, chap. V; Ray, *Indestructible Truth,* chap. 6; Snellgrove, *Indo-Tibetan Buddhism,* vol. II, pp. 479–94; Batchelor, part 2; Wangyal; Decleer; TR, chaps. 3–4, 7–8; and, most especially, Jinpa, *Mind Training* and *The Book of Kadam.*

331 Nāgas can be symbolic of bodhisattvas; the "supreme thought" is the awakening mind *(bodhicitta);* "prince" is a common epithet for bodhisattvas, who are sons or daughters of the Buddha.

332 Atiśa, or Dīpaṃkara Śrījñāna, is usually referred to in this chapter as the lord *(jo bo),* the noble lord *(jo bo rje),* or the great noble lord *(jo bo rje chen po).* On Atiśa, see A. Chattopadhyaya; BA, pp. 241–63; Ahmad, *A History of Tibet by Ṅag-dBaṅ Blo-bZaṅ rGya-mTsho,* pp. 83–88; K. Gyaltsen, *The Great Kagyu Masters,* pp. 145–86; TR, chaps. 3–4; Lopez, *Buddhism in Practice,* chaps. 24, 42, and *Religions of Tibet in Practice,* chap. 8; Jinpa, *Mind Training,* chaps. 1–5, 17, 25, 27.

333 Cited in Jamgön Anyé Shap, *Collected Works,* vol. *cha,* 53b3. The title of the text cited is *Lha chos bdun ldan chung ba,* or *Short Work on the Sevenfold Divinity and Teaching.*

334 See Martin, *Tibetan Histories,* p. 81.

335 See above, note 255.

336 See above, pp. 46–48.

337 The north Indian "heartland" of Buddhism, with its capital at Rājagṛha, covered much of present-day Bihar (including Bodhgaya) and West Bengal.

338 In the eastern part of present-day Bihar.

339 Lechen Künga Gyaltsen, *Lamp Illuminating the Dharma History of the Kadam,* 623a4–624b4. Cf. GT vol. 1, pp. 36–37.

340 See above, p. 72.

341 See BA, pp. 244–45.

342 The Qarluqs, a Turkic Muslim group inhabiting what is now the border region between Xinjiang and Russia.

343 A reference to Dromtönpa.

344 For translations, see, e.g., Sherburne; Rinchen and Sonam, *Atisha's Lamp for the Path;* Davidson, "Atiśa's Lamp on the Path."

345 *Collected Works,* vol. *pa,* 6b4. Cf. GT vol. 1, p. 41.

346 *White Lotus of Compassion Sutra,* chap. 6; Toh 111 Kangyur, mdo sde, *cha,* 84a2.

347 Lechen Künga Gyaltsen, *Lamp Illuminating the Dharma History of the Kadam,* 625a2–626b2.

348 See Jinpa, *The Book of Kadam,* especially his introduction, which discusses the origin of the text and its role in establishing Dromtönpa's reputation. For the prophecy about the founding of Radreng, see pp. 297–303.

349 That is, the Geluk.

350 See translations by Guenther, K. Gyaltsen; see also below, p. 122.

351 Following K, we read *bstan rim gyi bstan bcos* for *bstan bcos.*

352 That is, Ganden.

353 The *Book of Kadam* is divided into the Father Teachings *(pha chos)* and the Son Teachings *(bu chos)*. The Father Teachings consist primarily of a series of dialogues between Atiśa and Dromtönpa in a twenty-six-chapter text called *The Jewel Garland of Dialogues*. Chapters 24–26 actually appear in volume 2 of the *Book of Kadam* following the Son Teachings and may be a later addition. See Jinpa, *The Book of Kadam*, pp. 20–21.

354 Tsongkhapa's name is Losang Drakpa (Blo bzang grags pa).

355 Namely, Ganden Monastery.

356 *Book of Kadam*, p. 754. Cf. p. 215 below, in the Geluk chapter, where the verse is quoted again.

357 That is, the five treatises of Maitreya and their commentarial corpus.

358 On Ngok and his lineage, see BA, chap. VI.

359 On this and other texts on stages of the teaching, see D. Jackson, "The *bsTan rim*."

360 Gö Lotsāwa Shönu Pal, *Blue Annals*, p. 289, lines 6–7; cf. BA, p. 327. Dīpaṃkara Śrījñāna is another name for Atiśa.

361 Thuken does not list the Nyingma, which follows scriptures translated during the earlier spread of the teaching, but latter-day Nyingmapas used gradual schemes derived from Atiśa as surely as members of the new translation schools did.

362 Literally, "is one who knows how to carry all the teachings with the four-cornered path" *(bstan pa thams cad gru bzhi lam gyis 'khyer shes pa)*. The image of the four corners connotes completeness. Thuken has probably drawn this quote from Tsongkhapa's *Great Treatise on the Stages of the Path to Enlightenment;* in *Collected Works*, vol. *pa*, 11a5. Cf. GT vol. 1, p. 49; 382n61.

363 This quote also is drawn from Tsongkhapa's *Great Treatise on the Stages of the Path to Enlightenment;* in *Collected Works*, vol. *pa*, 12a5. Cf. GT vol. 1, p. 51.

364 Lechen Künga Gyaltsen, *Lamp Illuminating the Dharma History of the Kadam*, 3a4.

365 Literally, "easy to take in hand" *(lag tu blang bde ba)*.

366 These are Serlingpa, an expert in the thought of Asaṅga, and Vidyākokila the Younger (a.k.a. Avadhūtipa, tenth century), an expert in the thought of Nāgārjuna.

367 Tsongkhapa, *Collected Works*, vol. *pa*, 8b1. cf. GT vol. 1, p. 45.

368 For translations of the *Ornament*, see Thurman et al.; of the *Compendium*, see Bendall and Rouse; of the *Way of the Bodhisattva*, see, among many others, Crosby and Skilton, Padmakara Translation Group; for the *Garland*, see Aryasura; for the *Collection of Uplifting Verses*, see Rockhill; and Sparham, *Tibetan Dhammapada*.

369 For translations of the *Fundamental Treatise*, see, e.g., Garfield; of the *Seventy Stanzas*, see, e.g., Komito; of the *Precious Garland*, see e.g., Hopkins, *Buddhist Advice for Living and Liberation*.

370 See Jinpa, *Mind Training*, pp. 423–29.

371 Cited in Changkya Rölpai Dorjé, *Great Treatise on the Establishment of Philosophical Systems;* in *Collected Works*, vol. *cha*, 450:1.

372 That is, the Yogācāra Svātantrika Madhyamaka position.

373 See above, p. 55.

374 Changkya Rölpai Dorjé, *Great Treatise on the Establishment of Philosophical Systems;* in *Collected Works*, vol. *cha*, 450:4.

375 The most complete set of translations of texts on this topic is Jinpa, *Mind Training*.
376 See Sopa; Jinpa, *Mind Training*, pp. 133–70.
377 See Jinpa, *Mind Training*, pp. 171–75.
378 For both, see Jinpa, *Mind Training*, pp. 177–96.
379 See, e.g., Jinpa, *Mind Training*, pp. 275–76.
380 See BA, p. 271; Jinpa, *Mind Training*, pp. 105–6, 484–86.
381 See, e.g., Jinpa, *Mind Training*, pp. 83–86.
382 This is tonglen *(gtong len)*, a visualization practice in which you take on the sufferings of others and send to them all your happiness and attainments.
383 See Jinpa, *Mind Training*, pp. 313–418.
384 See Jinpa, *Mind Training*, pp. 225–37.
385 See BA, p. 332; Jinpa, *Mind Training*, pp. 639–40n848.
386 Related to the Dzokchen tradition of the Nyingma school; see above, p. 84.
387 These are the lineages related to the development of, respectively, compassionate methods and wisdom, with the former traced to Asaṅga, the latter to Nāgārjuna.
388 We have been unable to locate the source of this quotation.
389 Tsongkhapa, *Great Treatise on the Stages of the Path to Enlightenment;* in *Collected Works,* vol. *pa,* 6b4–7a1; cf. GT vol. 1, p. 70. The passage quoted by Tsongkhapa is found in Geshé Potowa, *Blue Udder;* in *Gangs can rigs brgya'i sgo 'byed lde mig,* vol. 10, 47a3. A translation of this text will appear in volume 10 of this series.
390 For a partial translation of this text, see Bentor.
391 Literally, the "neck" *(mgul)*. It refers to a narrow, partly sheltered area below the summit of a mountain.
392 These are found in the twenty-first chapter of the Son Teachings in the *Book of Kadam*. Chapters 1, 2, 20, and 22 of the Son Teachings are translated in Jinpa, *The Book of Kadam*.
393 *Book of Kadam,* vol. 1, p. 302.
394 This Drom is obviously different from Dromtönpa. For the intervening line of succession, see Jinpa, *The Book of Kadam,* p. 20.
395 *Book of Kadam,* vol. 1, p. 634.
396 This is a cycle of initiations and practices related to a tantric form of Avalokiteśvara, Jinasāgara *(rgyal ba rgya mtsho)*. For Gelukpas, it is the most important tantric lineage handed down from Atiśa. See Miller, chap. 2. For a detailed explanation of the practice of the sixteen drops, see Khenchen Nyima Gyaltsen's *Elucidation of the Heart-Drop Practice* in Jinpa, *The Book of Kadam,* pp. 395–452.
397 See R. Jackson, "A Tibetan Fasting Ritual."
398 The latter are the *People Dohā Treasury* (see Shahidullah; Snellgrove, "Saraha's Treasury of Songs"; Guenther, *Ecstatic Spontaneity;* R. Jackson, *Tantric Treasures;* Schaeffer, *Dreaming the Great Brahmin*), the *Queen Dohā Treasury* (see Guenther, *Ecstatic Spontaneity*), and *King Dohā Treasury* (see Guenther, *The Royal Song of Saraha* and Thrangu Rinpoche, *A Song for the King*).
399 *Bodhipathapradīpa,* vv. 61–67. Toh 3947 Tengyur, dbu ma, *khi,* 286b3.
400 Tsongkhapa, *Collected Works,* vol. *pa,* 8b1; cf. GT vol. 1, p. 45.
401 Following K, we read *lcid* for *lced.*
402 Lechen Künga Gyaltsen, *Lamp Illuminating the Dharma History of the Kadam,* 621a5–623a4.

403 These are two crucial procedures in tranquil abiding meditation, which allow one to maintain concentration on one's chosen object.

404 Literally, the southeast *(byin za),* which is the traditional directional location of Agni, the Vedic fire god.

405 Wangchuk Dorjé, of the Central Institute of Tibetan Higher Studies, Sarnath, provided invaluable help with several difficult passages in this chapter, as did Tony Duff.

406 On Kagyü in general, see, e.g., TPS, vol. 1, pp. 89–91; BA, chaps. VIII, XI; Ray, *Indestructible Truth,* chap. 7; Snellgrove, *Indo-Tibetan Buddhism,* vol. II, pp. 492–506; Powers, *Introduction to Tibetan Buddhism,* chap. 13; Batchelor, part 3; Lopez, *Religions of Tibet in Practice,* chaps 5, 7, 9, 11, 16, 27.

407 Also known as Telopa, Tailopa, Tillipa, or Tillopāda; Thuken uses all these variants, but we have standardized them to the best-known version, Tilopa. See, e.g., Robinson, pp. 98–99; Dowman, *Masters of Mahāmudrā,* pp. 151–55; Thrangu, *The Life of Tilopa and the Ganges Mahamudra;* Templeman, *Seven Instruction Lineages,* pp. 45–49; Guenther, *Life and Teaching of Nāropa;* Chang, *Six Yogas of Naropa and Teachings on Mahamudra;* Bercholz and Kohn, pp. 266–72; Thaye; Nālandā Translation Committee, "Life of Tilopa" and *Rain of Wisdom,* pp. 126–29; K. Gyaltsen, *The Great Kagyu Masters,* pp. 33–54; R. Jackson, *Tantric Treasures;* TR, pp. 46–49; Brünnholzl, *Straight from the Heart,* pp. 93–118.

408 See e.g., TR, pp. 44–49, 144–48; Guenther, *Life and Teaching of Nāropa;* Kunga and Cutillo, *Drinking the Mountain Stream,* pp. 26–29; K. Gyaltsen, *Great Kagyu Masters,* pp. 55–89; Templeman, *Seven Instruction Lineages,* pp. 46–49; Thaye; Thrangu, *Songs of Naropa;* TR, pp. 44–49, 142–48 *et passim.*

409 See, e.g., Robinson, pp. 150–52; Dowman, *Masters of Mahāmudrā,* pp. 229–34; Templeman, *Seven Instruction Lineages,* pp. 24–25.

410 Literally, "the yoginī transformed from a nāga."

411 Of the six (inner heat, illusory body, dream, clear light, transference of consciousness, and the bardo), the last is not included in the four special oral traditions. On these, see, e.g., Chang, *Six Yogas of Naropa and Teachings on Mahamudra;* Evans-Wentz, *Tibetan Yoga and Secret Doctrines,* pp. 155–252; Mullin, *Readings on the Six Yogas of Naropa* and *Tsongkhapa's Six Yogas of Naropa.*

412 See Robinson, pp. 128–30; Dowman, *Masters of Mahāmudrā,* pp. 199–203.

413 An alternative name for Kāṇha/Kṛṣṇācārya.

414 The tantric deity rather than the student of Maitrīpa who transmitted certain Mahāmudrā traditions; see BA, p. 843ff.

415 See TR, pp. 55–56, 196–99; Templeman, *Seven Instruction Lineages,* pp. 19–22.

416 Following K, we read *bhi na [sa] badzra* for *bhi nas badzra.* She was a female disciple of Ḍombi Heruka.

417 See above, note 158.

418 See Robinson, pp. 247–49; Dowman, *Masters of Mahāmudrā,* pp. 368–71.

419 Best known as the author of the *Secret Yogic Achievement,* later classified as one of the Seven Yogic Achievement Texts.

420 See, e.g., Nālandā Translation Committee, *Life of Marpa,* pp. xxxii–xxxiii, note; and the comparative chart on the Samye.org website: http://www.samye.org/other4.htm.

421 See, e.g., Kapstein, "The Shangs-pa Bka' brgyud" and "The Journey to the Golden Mountain"; Riggs; Zangpo, *Timeless Rapture.*

422 See, e.g., BA, p. 732ff. Matthew Kapstein ("Chronological Conundrums in the Life of 'Khyung po rnal 'byor") has suggested a lifespan of 1040–1140.

423 See, e.g., Tatz, "The Life of the Siddha-Philosopher Maitrīgupta"; Templeman, *Seven Instruction Lineages,* pp. 11–13; BA, pp. 227–28 *et passim;* Brünnholzl, *Straight from the Heart,* pp. 125–90; Mathes, "Blending the Sūtras with the Tantras."

424 These probably refer to the five tantric cycles described below (p. 120), those of Cakrasaṃvara, Hevajra, Mahāmāyā, Guhyasamāja, and Vajrabhairava.

425 See BA, p. 733.

426 That is, the "iron bridge" area in Tsang, not far from Lhasa. Thangtong Gyalpo is credited with building a number of iron bridges in Tibet. See Lopez, *Tibetan Buddhism in Practice,* chap. 16; J. Gyatso, "Genre, Authorship, and Transmission in Visionary Buddhism"; Stearns, *King of the Empty Plain.*

427 Although the same word *(sde)* is used as for the different categories of tantras, here it refers to the five highest yoga tantra practice cycles mentioned.

428 She is the consort of the Hindu god Śiva, or Maheśvara.

429 These have the same names as the six Dharmas of Nāropa (inner heat, illusory body, dream, clear light, transference, and bardo), but the details of the teachings vary somewhat; see, e.g., Mullin, *Selected Works of the Dalai Lama II,* pp. 92–151.

430 That is, sādhana, puja, meditation, activities, etc.

431 For an alternative enumeration of Shangpa practices, see Ringu, p. 180.

432 See, e.g., TR, pp. 141–48 *et passim;* Nālandā Translation Committee, *Life of Marpa* and *Rain of Wisdom,* pp. 129–64; Thaye; Lhalungpa, *Life of Milarepa* and *Mahāmudrā, passim;* K. Gyaltsen, *Great Kagyu Masters,* pp. 97–122. Davidson (TR, pp. 142–43) disputes these dates for Marpa, which are taken from the *Blue Annals,* and notes that earlier sources point to Marpa's birth date as either 1009 or 1021.

433 The phrase that we generally translate as "gained a realization" (or variants thereof) is in Tibetan *rtogs pa thugs la 'krungs* (or variants thereof), which literally means "realization arose in his or her mind."

434 See, e.g., BA, p. 448 *et passim;* Quintman; Lhalungpa, *Life of Milarepa* and *Mahāmudrā, passim;* Chang, *Hundred Thousand Songs of Milarepa;* K. Gyaltsen, *Great Kagyu Masters,* pp. 123–44; Kunga and Cutillo, *Drinking the Mountain Stream* and *Wonderful Journey;* Beyer, pp. 75–76, 174–84; Nālandā Translation Committee, *Rain of Wisdom,* pp. 165–215; Thrangu *Teachings from the 100,000 Songs;* Martin, "The Early Education of Milarepa."

435 See, e.g., BA, pp. 436–40; Lhalungpa, *Life of Milarepa;* Chang, *Hundred Thousand Songs of Milarepa,* pp. 110–25, 190–210, 248–76; Nālandā Translation Committee, *Rain of Wisdom,* pp. 216–17; Brünnholzl, *Straight from the Heart,* pp. 219–30.

436 See, e.g., BA, pp. 451–62; Guenther, *Jewel Ornament of Liberation;* K. Gyaltsen, *Jewel Ornament of Liberation,* and *Great Kagyu Masters,* pp. 187–204; Karthar; Chang, *Hundred Thousand Songs of Milarepa,* pp. 211–45; Stewart; Nālandā Translation Committee, *Rain of Wisdom,* pp. 217–42, 275–82; Lhalungpa, *Mahāmudrā, passim;* D. Jackson, *Enlightenment by a Single Means,* chaps. 1–2; Kragh; Trungram. Dakpo is in southwestern Kham.

437 On this text, which is important in tracing Mahāmudrā lineages, see, e.g., Régamy; Cüppers; Thrangu, *King of Samadhi.*

438 See translations by Guenther; K. Gyaltsen.

439 See, e.g., Richardson, "The Karma-pa School."

440 See Douglas and White.

441 See, e.g., Tauscher.

442 Patsap Nyima Drak was crucial in the introduction of Prāsaṅgika Madhyamaka into Tibet; see Lang, "Spa-tshabs Nyi-ma-grags."

443 TBRC lists him as Pomdrakpa *(spom brag pa),* but the BA (p. 485), Thuken's probable source, has *sbom brag pa.*

444 The "Mongol king" is the Yunglo emperor of the Yuan dynasty (1360–1424); Karma Pakshi was Düsum Khyenpa's successor, the second Karmapa.

445 Probably the first great Qing emperor, Kangxi (1661–1722).

446 That is, the Yuan and Ming.

447 The founder of Sera Monastery; see below, p. 278.

448 See BA, pp. 485–88; Richardson. "The Karma-pa School," pp. 142–45; Kapstein, *Tibetan Assimilation,* pp. 97–106.

449 BA, p. 487, has *stod lungs phar tshan.*

450 See BA, pp. 488–93; Chang, *Six Yogas of Naropa and Teachings on Mahamudra,* pp. 31–36; Richardson, "The Karma-pa School," pp. 145–46; Nydahl; Schaeffer, *Enlightened Heart of Buddhahood;* Thrangu, *Transcending Ego.*

451 See BA, pp. 493–506; Richardson, "The Karma-pa School," pp. 146–47.

452 See BA, pp. 512–17; Richardson, "The Karma-pa School," pp. 147–49.

453 See BA, pp. 512–17; Richardson, "The Karma-pa School," pp. 149.

454 See BA, p. 517; Richardson, "The Karma-pa School," pp. 149–50.

455 See, e.g., Richardson, "The Karma-pa School," pp. 151–54; Nālandā Translation Committee, *Rain of Wisdom,* pp. 16–26, 310–13; Williams, "A Note on Some Aspects of Mi-bskyod rDo-rje's Critique."

456 See Richardson, "The Karma-pa School," pp. 154–55; Wang-ch'ug Dor-je; Nālandā Translation Committee, *Rain of Wisdom,* pp. 27–33, 313; Thrangu, *The Ninth Karmapa's Ocean of Definitive Meaning.*

457 See Richardson, "The Karma-pa School," p. 155; Nālandā Translation Committee, *Rain of Wisdom,* pp. 34–44, 313–14; Dewar.

458 See Richardson, "The Karma-pa School," p. 160.

459 See Richardson, "The Karma-pa School," p. 160; Nālandā Translation Committee, *Rain of Wisdom,* pp. 62–63.

460 See Richardson, "The Karma-pa School," p. 160; Nālandā Translation Committee, *Rain of Wisdom,* pp. 64–66, 318–19. By the time Thuken completed the *Crystal Mirror,* the thirteenth Karmapa had died, but Thuken may have been unaware of the fact.

461 In the Punjab.

462 See BA, pp. 540–45; Nālandā Translation Committee, *Rain of Wisdom,* pp. 45–48, 314–16.

463 See Brünnholzl, *Straight from the Heart,* pp. 321–330.

464 See Nālandā Translation Committee, *Rain of Wisdom,* pp. 49–53.

465 See Nālandā Translation Committee, *Rain of Wisdom,* pp. 54–57, 316; Brünnholzl, *Straight from the Heart,* pp. 343–82.

466 See Nālandā Translation Committee, *Rain of Wisdom,* pp. 58–59.

467 See Nālandā Translation Committee, *Rain of Wisdom,* pp. 60–61, 317.

468 That is, the range of Buddhist ideas and practices.

469 On this dispute, see Williams, "A Note on Some Aspects of Mi-bskyod rDo-rje's Critique"; Cabezón and Dargyey; Jorden.

470 On this concept *(gzhanstong),* which is central to the view of the Jonang school, see below, chap. 9.

471 The Dharma history mentioned is the *Scholar's Banquet,* an important, but so far untranslated, text; see also Brunnhölzl, *Center of the Sunlit Sky,* part 2.

472 Better known as Chökyi Jungné. See E. G. Smith, pp. 87–96; Eighth Situpa; Thrangu, *The Eighth Situpa;* Nālandā Translation Committee, *Rain of Wisdom,* pp. 67–71, 319–21.

473 The source of this quotation is uncertain. Material about Situ's views may be found in Situ Panchen Chökyi Jungné, *Spotless Crystal Mirror;* in *Collected Works,* vol. *a,* 267a1.

474 A great Kadam/Sakya master of the mind training tradition; see TBRC, P1943.

475 See Ahmad, *A History of Tibet by Ṅag-dBaṅ Blo-bZaṅ rGya-mTsho,* pp. 161–62; Shakabpa, pp. 86–90.

476 See Ahmad, *A History of Tibet by Ṅag-dBaṅ Blo-bZaṅ rGya-mTsho,* p. 163.

477 Perhaps in 1517; see Shakabpa, p. 90.

478 Also known as Karma Tensung Wangpo.

479 1597–1621. See Shakabpa, p. 98ff.; TBRC (P1367) lists his death date as 1632.

480 See TBRC, P1366; Shakabpa, p. 102ff.

481 Sakya Pandita, *Well-Spoken Advice,* v. 91; in *Collected Works,* in *Sa skya pa'i bka' 'bum,* vol. *na,* 119a3. Verse 91 in Davenport's translation (p. 83) appears to be of a different, if distantly related, Tibetan original.

482 Better known as Gushri Khan; see, e.g., Ahmad, *A History of Tibet by Ṅag-dBaṅ Blo-bZaṅ rGya-mTsho,* pp. 191–97; Shakabpa, pp. 120–24; Snellgrove and Richardson, pp. 193–99; and below, pp. 317–20.

483 We have been unable to trace the source of this well-known saying.

484 The great Geluk monastery in Shigatsé in Tsang; see below, pp. 280–82

485 On these events, which led to a long suppression of the Red Hat lineage, see Shakabpa, pp. 152–72; Richardson, "The Karma-pa School," pp. 161–64.

486 See Ahmad, *A History of Tibet by ag-dBaṅ Blo-bZaṅ rGya-mTsho,* chaps. 15–19; TPS, vol. 1, pp. 17–39; Shakabpa, pp. 73–79.

487 See, e.g., BA, pp. 552–63; K. Gyaltsen, *Great Kagyu Masters,* pp. 205–19; Lhalungpa, *Mahāmudrā, passim*; TR, pp. 332–35.

488 Following K and TBRC, we read *rgya mtsho* for *rgyal mtshan.*

489 Following K, we read *mchan bu* for *mtshan bu.*

490 See Ahmad, *A History of Tibet by Ṅag-dBaṅ Blo-bZaṅ rGya-mTsho,* p. 127; BA, pp. 580–81.

491 See Ahmad, *A History of Tibet by Ṅag-dBaṅ Blo-bZaṅ rGya-mTsho,* chap. 16; Shakabpa, pp. 73–83; Snellgrove and Richardson, pp. 182–85.

492 See Ahmad, *A History of Tibet by Ṅag-dBaṅ Blo-bZaṅ rGya-mTsho,* pp. 144–45; BA, pp. 585–86.

493 Also known as Drakpa Gyaltsen; see Ahmad, *A History of Tibet by Ṅag-dBaṅ Blo-bZaṅ rGya-mTsho,* pp. 146–50; BA, pp. 589–94.

494 See Ahmad, *A History of Tibet by Ṅag-dBaṅ Blo-bZaṅ rGya-mTsho,* p. 127; BA, pp. 587–88.

495 Also known as the Tsalpa. See Ahmad, *A History of Tibet by Ṅag-dBaṅ Blo-bZaṅ rGya-mTsho,* pp. 107–10; Sørensen and Hazod.

496 See BA, pp. 711–15; TR, pp. 328–32; Martin, "A Twelfth-Century Tibetan Classic of Mahāmudrā" and "Meditation Is Action Taken"; D. Jackson, *Enlightenment by a Single Means,* pp. 42–66; Lhalungpa, *Mahāmudrā, passim;* Broido, "Sa-skya Paṇḍita, the White Panacea and the Hva-shang Doctrine."

497 Literally, "receptacles of body, speech, and mind" *(sku gsung thugs kyi rten).*

498 See Ahmad, *A History of Tibet by Ṅag-dBaṅ Blo-bZaṅ rGya-mTsho,* pp. 110–13.

499 See, e.g., BA, pp. 596–601; K. Gyaltsen, *Prayer Flags;* Lhalungpa, *Mahāmudrā, passim;* K. Gyaltsen, *Great Kagyu Masters,* pp. 220–55.

500 See Nebesky-Wojkowitz, *passim.*

501 Literally, "showing dharma" *(chos ston),* an occasion on which food and money are given to monks.

502 See BA, p. 601.

503 In the *Textbook on the Single Intention,* from which Thuken draws liberally in his chapter on Bön; see Martin, *Unearthing Bon Treasures,* chap. 13.

504 Tib. *ras thub pa.* This may refer to the development of inner heat, one of the six Dharmas of Nāropa, whereby one can wear cotton even in winter.

505 This refers to the process of drawing outer winds into the central channel of the subtle body, generating "inner heat" through *tumo* practice, then warming the outer air through the internally generated heat.

506 The root text for this tradition is attributed to Rechungpa's Indian teacher, Tiphupa (eleventh/twelfth centuries)

507 Literally, "reported as on the wind" *(lung ltar grags).*

508 See BA, p. 671. He is said to be a nephew of Tsangpa Gyaré, and as a result the lineage descending from him is called the "family (or nephew) lineage" *(dbon brgyud).*

509 See, e.g., TPS, vol. 1, pp. 125–28; Evans-Wentz, *Tibetan Yoga and Secret Doctrines,* pp. 101–54; Beyer, pp. 76–78, 124–30, 140–53; E. G. Smith, pp. 81–86; Broido, "Padma dKar-po on Integration as Ground, Path and Goal," "Padma dKar-po on Tantra as Ground, Path and Goal," "Padma dKar-po on the Two *Satyas,*" and "Sa-skya Paṇḍita, the White Panacea and the Hva-shang Doctrine."

510 Best known as the author of the lifestories of Marpa (Nālandā Translation Committee, *Life of Marpa*) and Milarepa (e.g., Lhalungpa, *Life of Milarepa*). See also E. G. Smith, pp. 59–80.

511 See Stein, *Vie et chants;* Dowman, *Divine Madman.*

512 See BA, pp. 672–76; Nālandā Translation Committee, "The Yogin Lorepa's Retreat" and *Rain of Wisdom,* pp. 246–55.

513 BA, p. 674, lists seven.

514 The same fivefold as is highlighted in the Drigung Kagyü tradition; see below, pp. 147–48.

515 See BA, pp. 676–79; Nālandā Translation Committee, *Rain of Wisdom,* pp. 268–71.

516 See BA, pp. 680–86; Nālandā Translation Committee, *Rain of Wisdom,* pp. 268–71.

517 This translation of *go cha dang bcu gsum* is conjectural, and the reference obscure.

518 See Martin, *Tibetan Histories,* p. 76.

519 *Ju pi;* also known as Qubilai Qan, or Khan.
520 For information on Nering's biography of Tsongkhapa, see TBRC, W23937.
521 All editions have *mkhan po na,* though *mkhan po ni* probably is preferable.
522 Or *thil;* this undoubtedly refers to the area around Phakmo Drupa's monastery, Densa Thil.
523 In Mahayana Buddhism, nonabiding nirvana *(mi gnas pa'i mya ngan las 'das pa, apratiṣṭanirvāṇa)* is the nirvana attained by a buddha, who abides neither in the tumult of samsara nor the quietistic peace of final nirvana. It signifies that in Mahayana, enlightened beings remain active in the world, though they are not "of it."
524 This is the highest of the four yogas of Mahāmudrā: one-pointedness, nonelaboration, single taste, and nonmeditation.
525 Following Z and BA, we read *shom ra ba* for *sha ra ba.*
526 That is, he made him a Dharma protector.
527 See Martin, *Tibetan Histories,* p. 101.
528 Or: Baprom *('bab rom).*
529 Literally, "one who practices disciplines" *(rtul bzhugs spyod pa),* i.e., who has assumed demanding vows or practices the path of tantric conduct.
530 Presumably the Kṛṣṇācārya/Kāṇha revered as one of the great tantric adepts *(grub thob, mahāsiddhas)* of Buddhist India. See, e.g., Robinson, pp. 81–85; Dowman, *Masters of Mahāmudrā,* pp. 123–31; Templeman, *Tāranātha's Life of Kṛṣṇācārya/Kāṅha;* Kvaerne, *Anthology of Buddhist Tantric Songs;* Beyer, *Buddhist Experience,* pp. 258–61; R. Jackson, *Tantric Treasures;* Farrow and Menon.
531 That is, northern Latö, in southwestern Tsang.
532 These are the subjective and objective Mahāmudrā, respectively.
533 It is unclear which Rāhula this is; perhaps the Rāhula who sometimes is conflated with Saraha, perhaps the arhat who was the Buddha's son.
534 *Gza';* this refers both to strokes (or paralysis) and to the planetary deities believed to cause them.
535 See BA, p. 657.
536 Following K, BA, and TBRC, we read *gnur* for *gcung.*
537 The *lha mo che* was a statue of Maitreya.
538 In the Tōhoku catalogue, the author is listed as Niṣkalaṅka (b. twelfth century?).
539 At the end of chap. 9.
540 This reflects a typical dissolution process in tantric visualizations, whereby the Sanskrit or Tibetan letter *hūṃ* (often symbolic of the mind) dissolves from the bottom up, starting with the *u,* then the *hā,* the top line, the crescent, and finally the drop indicating nasalization, which includes the *nāda.* For its symbolic connotations, see, e.g., Evans-Wentz, *Tibetan Yoga and Secret Doctrines,* pp. 335–42.
541 The phrase *ngo bo gcig la ldog pa tha dad* is often used in logical analysis to explain entities that are ontologically the same but are conceptualized differently. Examples given include such pairs as persons and the five aggregates, or things and being impermanent.
542 This is also the shortened title of his great Mahāmudrā text, *Shang's Special Instruction on the Ultimate Profound Path of Mahāmudrā.*
543 Taklung Ngawang Namgyal, *Wonderful Ocean Dharma History,* 690b2–13.
544 For other works exploring this subject, see, e.g., the various works of Broido; Ruegg,

"A Kar ma bKa' brgyud Work"; Williams, "A Note on Some Aspects of Mi-bskyod rDo-rje's Critique"; and, especially, Brunnhölzl, *Center of the Sunlit Sky.*

545 Tsangnyön Heruka, *Biography of Marpa;* in *Biographies of the Kagyüpa,* vol. 1, p. 401. Cf. Nālandā Translation Committee, *Life of Marpa,* pp. 144–45; BA, p. 402.

546 *Tattvadaśaka;* Toh. 2236 Tengyur, rgyud 'grel, *wi,* 113a1.

547 In line with Thuken's interpretation of the first two lines, "middling Madhyamaka" would be Svātantrika Madhyamaka. Although *madhyamaka* means "middle," there is no pun in the Tibetan, for which Madhyamaka is *dbu ma* and "middling" *'bring po.*

548 *Explication of the Ten Principles;* Toh 2254 Tengyur, rgyud 'grel, *wi,* 164a3.

549 *Explication of the Lamp on All Secrets;* Toh 1787 Tengyur, rgyud 'grel, *ha,* 234a5.

550 *Explication of the Lamp on All Secrets;* Toh 1787 Tengyur, rgyud 'grel, *ha,* 234a6.

551 Thuken's claim rests on a conflation of the Madhyamaka philosopher Candrakīrti with the tantric commentator Candrakīrti, an identification modern scholars would be unlikely to accept.

552 Tsangnyön Heruka, *Hundred Thousand Songs of Milarepa,* p. 483; see also Chang, *Hundred Thousand Songs,* p. 325. We acknowledge the assistance of Tony Duff in construing parts of this and the following two poetic passages.

553 Tsangnyön Heruka, *Hundred Thousand Songs of Milarepa,* p. 483; cf. Chang, *Hundred Thousand Songs,* p. 325.

554 Tsangnyön Heruka, *Hundred Thousand Songs of Milarepa,* p. 483; cf. Chang, *Hundred Thousand Songs,* p. 325.

555 As with Dzokchen, there are far more works in print than can be listed here. See e.g., however, BA, chap. XI *et passim;* R. Jackson, "Mahāmudrā"; D. Jackson, *Enlightenment by a Single Means;* Lhalungpa, *Mahāmudrā;* Martin, "A Twelfth-Century Tibetan Classic of Mahāmudrā"; Wang-chug Dor-je; Evans-Wentz, *Tibetan Yoga and Secret Doctrines,* pp. 101–54; Eighth Situpa; Kragh; and the various works of Broido.

556 Tsangnyön Heruka, *Hundred Thousand Songs of Milarepa,* p. 523.

557 See, e.g., Gampopa, *Collected Works,* vol. *ga,* 2a2.

558 On Gampopa's and Shang Tsalpa's approaches to Mahāmudrā, see, especially, D. Jackson, *Enlightenment by a Single Means.* The term *white simple (dkar po gcig thub)* may also be translated as "white panacea" or "self-sufficient white remedy." It refers to a single medicine—a simple—that is efficacious in curing disease.

559 Changkya Rölpai Dorjé, *Great Treatise on the Establishment of Philosophical Systems;* in *Collected Works,* vol. *cha,* 21a1.

560 Tsangnyön Heruka, *Hundred Thousand Songs of Milarepa,* p. 657; cf. Chang, *Hundred Thousand Songs,* p. 494.

561 Literally, "to hold the line" *(mtshams 'dzin).*

562 An affirming negation *(ma yin dgags)* is one in which the negation of one sort of entity implies the existence of another. Here, the negation of the true existence of mind implies its luminosity and blissfulness.

563 Late Indian Buddhist texts on advanced tantric practice: Padmavajra's *Secret Yogic Achievement,* Anaṅgavajra's *Yogic Achievement Ascertaining Wisdom and Means* (see Snellgrove, "The Attainment of the Realization of Wisdom and Means"), Indrabhūti's *Yogic Achievement of Gnosis,* Lakṣmīṅkarā's *Yogic Achievement of Nonduality* (see Mishra), Dārikapa's *Special Instruction on the Reality*

of the Greatest Secret, Yoginī Cintā's *Yogic Achievement of Reality Following the Clarification of Entities,* and Ḍombi Heruka's *Yogic Achievement of the Innate* (see Shendge). For an edition that includes all but number 5, and adds Kuddālapāda's *Special Instruction on the Inconceivable Stage* and Padmavajra's *Accomplishing Ascertainment of the Wisdom and Method that Opens Up the Nondual,* see Samdhong and Dvivedi.

564 The following discussion seems to be drawn from Khedrup Norsang Gyatso's *Lamp Illuminating Mahāmudrā,* p. 7.

565 Nāropa, *The Epitome;* Toh 2331 Tengyur, rgyud 'grel, *zhi,* 271a4; see also Lhalungpa, *Mahāmudrā,* p. 123.

566 *Collected Works,* vol. *ga,* 84b2.

567 Tsongkhapa, *Lamp Illuminating the Five Stages;* in *Collected Works,* vol. *ja,* 194b4.

568 Nāropa, *The Epitome*; Toh 2331 Tengyur, rgyud 'grel, *zhi,* 271a4; cf. Lhalungpa, *Mahāmudrā,* p. 123.

569 As Thuken acknowledges below (p. 144), most of this section is taken verbatim from Losang Chökyi Gyaltsen's (the First Panchen Lama's) *Lamp Re-Illumining Mahāmudrā;* cf. Dalai Lama and Berzin, pp. 300–303.

570 Śavaripa, *Doha Treasure Mahāmudrā Instruction;* Toh 2273 Tengyur, rgyud 'grel *zhi,* 122b1; cf. Thaye, p. 81; Lhalungpa, *Mahāmudrā,* p. 193. The text is misattributed to Saraha in the Tengyur.

571 The dharmakāya is sometimes divided into a natural dharmakāya *(ngo bo nyid sku, svabhāvikakāya),* which is the enlightened mind's emptiness, and a gnostic dharmakāya *(ye shes chos sku, jñānadharmakāya),* which is the enlightened mind's omniscience, compassion, and power. Alternatively, the gnostic dharmakāya simply is another term for the single, indivisible dharmakāya.

572 Shang Yudrakpa Tsöndrü Drakpa, *Shang's Special Instruction on the Ultimate Profound Path of Mahāmudrā;* in *Collected Works,* vol. *nga,* 41a4; see also Martin, "A Twelfth-Century Tibetan Classic of Mahāmudrā," p. 257.

573 We have been unable to find this statement in the works of Saraha.

574 *Collected Works,* vol. 1, 26a6.

575 Toh 2303 Tengyur, rgyud, *shi,* 243a3; cf. Bercholz and Kohn, p. 268; Chang, *Six Yogas,* p. 29; Thrangu, *Life of Tilopa,* p. 39.

576 Shang Yudrakpa Tsöndrü Drakpa, *Shang's Special Instruction on the Ultimate Profound Path of Mahāmudrā;* in *Collected Works,* vol. *nga,* 51a; cf. Martin, "A Twelfth-Century Tibetan Classic," pp. 267, 268. Thuken treats the first four lines as if they immediately precede the last four; in Shang's text, however, they are separated by numerous verses.

577 Changkya Rölpai Dorjé, *Great Treatise on the Establishment of Philosophical Systems;* in *Collected Works,* vol. *cha,* 115b1.

578 For a discussion of these issues, see Lhalungpa, *Mahāmudrā,* p. 404.

579 Shang Yudrakpa Tsöndrü Drakpa, *Shang's Special Instruction on the Ultimate Profound Path of Mahāmudrā;* in *Collected Works,* vol. *nga,* 14b3; cf. Martin, "A Twelfth-Century Tibetan Classic," p. 287 and p. 311n114; for Tsangpa Gyarepa's discussion of the topic, see Lhalungpa, *Mahāmudrā,* pp. 403–4.

580 Much of the material in the following subsections is drawn from Losang Chökyi

Gyaltsen's (the First Panchen Lama's) *Lamp Re-Illumining Mahāmudrā;* see Dalai Lama and Berzin, pp. 262–67.

581 These five practices are described in the sections that follow. According to the Dalai Lama and Berzin (p. 233), Tsangpa Gyarepa taught all three practices listed; Li ("Bkaḥ-brgyud Sect," p. 58) credits him only with the first two.

582 The Dalai Lama and Berzin (p. 263) translate the term *lhan cig skyes sbyor* as "simultaneously arising as merged."

583 *Joining the Coemergent;* in *Collected Works,* vol. *nga,* 3a1; cf. Lhalungpa, *Mahāmudrā,* p. 224. *Joining* and *yoga* are synonymous.

584 Phakmo Drupa Dorjé Gyalpo, *Verses on the Four Yogas;* in *Collected Works,* vol. *nga,* 67a4; cf. Lhalungpa (*Mahāmudrā,* p. 223), where both Gampopa and Gomchungwa are quoted to similar effect.

585 See K. Gyaltsen, *Garland of Mahamudra Practices* and *Prayer Flags,* pp. 72–86.

586 We have been unable to locate this quotation.

587 *Collected Works,* vol. *tha,* p. 96; cf. K. Gyaltsen, *Prayer Flags,* pp. 55–56; Dalai Lama and Berzin, pp. 267–69.

588 This reference is not entirely clear; it may relate to the five nectars sometimes utilized in highest yoga tantra practice (urine, feces, blood, semen, and marrow), or it may denote processes in which drops of "nectar" drip down through the subtle body in advanced highest yoga tantra practices, e.g., on the basis of inner-heat meditation.

589 The reference here is unclear, and Thuken's discussion leads one to believe that there were eight, rather than six, Dharmas identified by Chenga.

590 That is, the prātimokṣa, bodhisattva, and tantric vows.

591 See Chang, *Hundred Thousand Songs,* vol. I, pp. 347–49. There are several listings of six bardos, which only partially overlap (see, e.g., *RangjungYesheWiki,* http://rywiki.tsadra.org/index.php/bar_do_drug). It is not completely clear what Mila's sixfold bardo consists of, but his discussion seems generally consonant with a list that includes the bardos of (1) this life, beginning from birth, (2) the stages of dying, (3) the ultimate expanse experienced at the moment of death, (4) the process of "becoming" one's next rebirth over up to forty-nine days after death, (5) dreaming, and (6) meditative absorption.

592 These may refer specifically to the teachings given in Milarepa's *Hundred Thousand Songs,* but may also refer more generally to collections of songs of spiritual realization.

593 Tib. *sil bu'i sde tshan phran tshegs gyi rgyan.* We have been unable to determine what the referent is.

594 *Pratyutpannasamādhisūtra.* On this text, see, e.g., Harrison.

595 Thuken probably heard this directly from Changkya (S 352n268).

596 Sakya Pandita, *Distinguishing the Three Vows* 3:164; in *Complete Works,* in *Sa skya pa'i bka' 'bum,* vol. *na,* 25b4; cf. Rhoton p. 117.

597 *Tattvāvatārākhyasakalasugatavacastātparyavyākhyāprakarana;* Toh 3709 Tengyur, rgyud 'grel, *tsu,* chap. 3, 40a3.

598 *Tattvavatārākhyasakalasugatavacastātparyavyākhyāprakaraṇa;* Toh 3709 Tengyur, rgyud 'grel, *tsu,* chap. 3, 40a5.

599 *Samādhirājasūtra;* Toh 127 Kangyur, mdo sde *da,* chap. 17, 59a6. In fact, this passage—often quoted in Tibetan writings on Mahāmudrā—does *not* mention

Mahāmudrā *(phyag rgya che);* rather, it is best translated as "Whatever is the intrinsic seal of all dharmas..." (Tib. *chos rnams kun gyi rang bzhin phyag rgya gang,* Skt. *yā sarvadharmānaṃ svabhāvamudrā* [Vaidya, p. 112]).

600 On this issue, see, e.g., D. Jackson, *Enlightenment by a Single Means;* Lhalungpa, *Mahāmudrā,* pp. 105–9; Ruegg, *Buddha-nature;* Broido, "Sa-skya Paṇḍita, the White Panacea and the Hva-shang Doctrine"; for Sapan's text, see Rhoton, p. 154; for Shang's text, see Martin, "A Twelfth-Century Tibetan Classic," pp. 290–92.

601 Some works by Losang Rinchen are listed in the recently published catalogue of the holdings of Drepung Monastery in Tibet, but to our knowledge, they have not been studied or made available outside the monastery.

602 We have been unable to identify this person, though it may refer to Nyernyipa Rinpoché Chökyi Gyalpo (1340–1407), the eleventh abbot of Drigung.

603 Khedrup Norsang Gyatso, *Lamp Illuminating Mahāmudrā,* pp. 7–8.

604 Sakya Pandita, in *Collected Works,* in *Sa skya pa'i bka' 'bum,* vol. *na,* 26a2.

605 Khedrup Norsang Gyatso. *Lamp Illuminating Mahāmudrā,* p. 10.

606 The *'phongs phyis pa'i rdo* is a Tibetan equivalent of toilet paper.

607 Changkya Rölpai Dorjé, *Great Treatise on the Establishment of Philosophical Systems;* in *Collected Works,* vol. *cha,* 19b4.

608 Changkya Rölpai Dorjé, *Great Treatise on the Establishment of Philosophical Systems;* in *Collected Works,* vol. *cha,* 20b1.

609 These are the syllables that make up the Sanskrit term *amanasi* ("unthinking"), each of which is given a specific equivalency to a stage in Mahāmudrā meditation. See, e.g., Dalai Lama and Berzin, p. 270.

610 Losang Chökyi Gyaltsen, *Root Text on Mahāmudrā: The Main Path of the Conquerors;* in *Collected Works,* vol. *nga,* 2a5; cf. Dalai Lama and Berzin, pp. 98, 261–71.

611 Losang Chökyi Gyaltsen, *Root Text on Mahāmudrā: The Main Path of the Conquerors;* in *Collected Works,* vol. *nga,* 2a2; cf. Dalai Lama and Berzin, pp. 98, 216ff.

612 Presumably the founder of the Jñānapāda tradition of Guhyasamāja interpretation.

613 Tsongkhapa [sic], *Inquiry into the Pure Noble Intention;* in *Collected Works,* vol. *ka,* 85a4.

614 Indeed, as evidenced by the previous note, it did make its way into the standard edition of Tsongkhapa's collected works, where it is item 68 in the Miscellania *(gsung thor bu)* found in volume *kha.*

615 In his *Storehouse of Mahāmudrā;* in *Collected Works,* vol. *zha.*

616 In his *Reply to the Inquiry into the Pure Noble Intention;* in *Collected Works,* vol. *'a.*

617 In his *Garland of Yogic Attainments* and *Reply to Questions about the View and Meditation of the Inquiry into the Pure Noble Intention,* both in *Collected Works,* vol. *kha.*

618 Losang Chökyi Gyaltsen, *Reply to Questions: Sweet Words of Explanation for Those with Good Minds;* in *Collected Works,* vol. *nga.*

619 Losang Chökyi Gyaltsen, *Root Text on Mahāmudrā: The Main Path of the Conquerors;* in *Collected Works,* vol. *nga,* 30b2.

620 An earlier version of this chapter was prepared by N. Jay R. Weil. We are par-

ticularly appreciative to Giacomella Orofino for her assistance with some of the difficult passages found here.

621 On Shijé in general, see, BA, chap. XII, on which Thuken has relied heavily; see also TPS, vol. 1, p. 92; TR, *passim.*

622 This probably refers to the three main lineages of Shijé: early, middle, and later.

623 Most of this section is drawn from the *Blue Annals,* chap. XII; see BA, p. 867.

624 *Srid zhi* refers to the torments of samsaric becoming and the temptation to rest in the false peace of a Hinayana nirvana.

625 *Heart Sutra;* Toh 21 Kangyur, sher phyin, *ka,* 145b4; cf. Conze, *Buddhist Wisdom Books,* p. 101.

626 See BA, pp. 902–26 *et passim;* Aziz; Molk; Martin, "Padampa Sangye"; TR, pp. 150–51, 245–49, *et passim;* Evans-Wentz, *Tibetan Book of the Great Liberation,* pp. 241–52; Chang, *Hundred Thousand Songs of Milarepa,* pp. 606–13; Kunga and Cutillo, *Drinking the Mountain Stream,* pp. 84–89; Brünnholzl, *Straight from the Heart,* pp. 203–16. In some cases where Thuken refers to him as Dampa, or Dampa Sangyé, we have added a Pha for clarity, as it is under the name Pha Dampa Sangyé that he is best known.

627 Most likely in what is now Andhra Pradesh.

628 This refers to the seventh rebirth after attainment of the path of seeing, after which rebirth is no longer necessary.

629 Presumably, the same teacher from whom Atiśa learned the mind training practices, though this would make Pha Dampa very long-lived indeed.

630 See BA, p. 869; it is in the last category that the female gurus are found.

631 Traditional Tibetan histories credit Nāgārjuna with a six-hundred-year lifespan, but even with this extraordinary longevity, he would have died several hundred years before the time of Pha Dampa—hence Thuken's suggestions that Pha Dampa must have had a very long life as well.

632 Literally, "harmful demoness" *(gnod sbyin mo);* see Nebesky-Wojkowitz, p. 188.

633 The usual list of these (see, e.g., NS, vol. II, p. 157) has eight, with invisibility added, and control of harmful demonesses replaced by suppression of diseases.

634 These are various sites in India that are sacred to the traditions of Hevajra, Cakrasaṃvara, and Vajrayoginī. They have internal equivalents in syllables and deities visualized in body-mandala practices in these tantric systems. The Buddhist sites partially overlap with sacred sites known in Śakta traditions of Hinduism. See, e.g., Snellgrove, *Hevajra Tantra,* vol. I, p. 70; Davidson, *Indian Esoteric Buddhism,* pp. 206–11.

635 See BA, pp. 871–72.

636 Rather than *sgron ma* (lamp) here, BA (p. 871) has *sgrol ma,* the usual name for the bodhisattva Tārā. Either way, the reference is not entirely clear.

637 See BA, pp. 872–76.

638 *Khar phog snar phog* literally means "hit the nose, hit the mouth." The idea is that one casts about wildly, not worrying about what one will hit.

639 This section appears to be taken nearly verbatim from the *Blue Annals;* cf. BA, pp. 886–88. We have been unable to find details of the various teachings and traditions listed.

640 Following K and BA, we read *gsum ma* for *gsum mam.*

641 *Dza ga ta* refers to a ritual liquor-offering.

642 The extensive perfection of wisdom sūtra is the *Perfection of Wisdom in a Hundred Thousand Verses;* the medium-length is the *Perfection of Wisdom in Twenty-five Thousand Verses* (see Conze, *Large Sutra on Perfect Wisdom*); the poetic distillation is the *Verse Summary of the Perfection of Wisdom* (see Conze, *Perfection of Wisdom in Eight Thousand Lines*).

643 To this point, the paragraph is taken verbatim from the *Blue Annals;* cf. BA, p. 899.

644 See BA, pp. 900–901.

645 The reference is not entirely clear, but these may be connected to the fourfold analysis of dependent origination in terms of projecting causes, projected effects, manifesting causes, and manifested effects.

646 This sentence is taken verbatim from the *Blue Annals;* see BA, pp. 905–6. The correct Tibetan title of the *Lamp of the Ultimate Result* is, according to the Tōhoku catalogue, *Mthar thug 'bras bu'i sgron ma,* not *Dngos grub 'bras bu'i sgron ma,* as cited by Thuken.

647 On this text, see, e.g., Davidson, "The *Litany of Names.*"

648 Most of this sentence is taken verbatim from the *Blue Annals;* see BA, p. 910.

649 Of the many publications on Kālacakra, see, especially, Wallace, *Kālacakratantra* and *Inner Kālacakratantra;* Newman, *Outer Wheel of Time* and "Vajrayoga in the Kālacakra Tantra"; Gnoli and Orofino; Mullin, *Practice of Kalachakra;* Sopa, Jackson, and Newman.

650 This paragraph is taken verbatim from the *Blue Annals;* cf. BA, p. 911.

651 This entire section is taken verbatim from the *Blue Annals;* cf. BA, pp. 976–79.

652 The only commentary on Maitrīpa's *Ten Principles* in the Tripiṭaka is Sahajavajra's *Tattvadaśakaṭīkā* (Toh 2254 Tengyur, rgyud *wi*), but the passage that follows does not occur there.

653 These are four procedures particularly important in the highest yoga tantras. Though there are various enumerations and orderings of them (see, e.g., Lhalungpa, *Mahāmudrā,* pp. 99–101), one common list is: action seal *(karmamudrā),* dharma seal *(dharmamudrā),* pledge seal *(samayamudrā),* and great seal *(mahāmudrā).*

654 Symbolism related to the forty-two vowels and consonants (Skt. *ālikāli*) of Sanskrit has both tantric and nontantric contexts. The former, as noted by Giacomella Orofino (private communication) may be found both in the *Secret Matrix Tantra* (see NS, vol. I, p. 292, and vol. II, p. 275) and in meditations related to the bardo between death and rebirth, where the forty-two peaceful deities that appear have these syllables as their seed syllables. Thuken, however, is intent on showing that there is a nontantric source for vowel-and-consonant symbolism in the perfection of wisdom sutras—references to which we have not been able to locate.

655 See BA, p. 978. With the exception of the *Heart Sutra,* these texts are apocryphal and may have been composed by Pha Dampa Sangyé or, as noted by a Nyingma scholar, revealed by him as treasures; see TR, p. 247.

656 The former are probably not the same as those transmitted to Tilopa (see above, pp. 117–18); their precise contents, like those of the four ear-whispered lineages, are unknown to us.

657 BA, p. 978, says eighteen.

658 The discussion here proceeds in ascending order based on the number of items in

the category rather than in the sequence Thuken initially listed them. We have been unable to find details of any of the treasuries, cycles, or texts listed below.

659 The extensive is in 100,000 verses; the middle-length in 25,000 verses (see Conze, *Large Sutra on Perfect Wisdom*), and the condensed in 8,000 verses (see Conze, *Perfection of Wisdom in Eight Thousand Lines*).

660 As with Nāgārjuna and Candrakīrti, we only can assume that the Āryadeva mentioned in this context is the later, tantric author, and not the second/third-century Madhyamaka philosopher. He is credited with a *Special Instruction on the Perfection of Wisdom;* for a translation, see Edou, pp. 15–23.

661 Another term for the perfection of wisdom sutras.

662 Pha Dampa Sangyé, *Hundred Basic [Verses] for the People of Dingri;* in *Bka' rnying gi skyes chen du ma'i phyag rdzogs kyi gdams ngag gnad bsdus nyer kho rin po che'i gter mdzod,* vol. *sha,* 3b6; cf. Evans-Wentz, *Tibetan Book of the Great Liberation,* p. 247. Although Thuken refers to an eighty-verse text, the passage is in fact found in Pha Dampa's hundred-verse text. Thuken may have seen the quotation in Losang Chökyi Gyaltsen's *Root Text on Mahāmudrā,* where it is inserted without specific textual attribution.

663 A form of Mahākāla.

664 See, especially, BA, chap. XIII; J. Gyatso, "Development of the *Gcod* Tradition"; Edou; Orofino, *Contributo* and "Great Wisdom Mother"; Harding; TR, pp. 290–93.

665 Māras in general are obstacles on the path and sometimes take the form of demons. The four māras are: the aggregates, delusions, death, and the divine youth, a euphemism for the desires that prevent us from overcoming the first three māras. This last is sometimes taken as Kāma, the god of lust. On this class of deity in a Tibetan context, see, e.g., Nebesky-Wojkowitz, pp. 274–78.

666 For alternative discussions of the etymology of the term, see BA, pp. 980–82; Edou, pp. 39–40.

667 See Edou, pp. 79–94.

668 See BA, pp. 996–99; Gö's version of the lineage is rather different.

669 See BA, pp. 983–96.

670 See BA, pp. 983–84; Edou; Orofino; Harding; TR, pp. 290–93.

671 An especially wrathful manifestation of Vajrayoginī.

672 In the late 1940s, Dongpön Rinpoché made the practice of Chö so popular at Drepung Losal Ling that the hillside outside Drepung was dotted with small tents occupied by monks engaged in the practice. To counter this trend and bring monks back into the scholastic fold, a polemic against Chö was written by Geshé Dönden.

673 On this issue, see, especially, Orofino, "Great Wisdom Mother."

674 *Verse Summary of the Perfection of Wisdom,* v. 27:3; Toh 13 Kangyur, sher phyin, *ka,* 15b5. Cf. Conze, *Perfection of Wisdom in Eight Thousand Lines,* p. 59; BA, p. 981; Edou, p. 40; J. Gyatso, "Development of the *Gcod* Tradition," p. 324.

675 The decisive test or definitive sign *(chod tshad)* marks the point where one has severed the self-cherishing and egotistic view, and requires difficult, all-night meditations in a cemetery. Edou (p. 75) states: "Experiencing directly the truth of suchness of phenomena and the very nature of non-self, he or she realizes the dharmakāya, while also establishing others, such as the lord of the soil and local

gods and demons, on the path of liberation. This is called the definitive sign *(chod tshad)* in the realization of Chod."

676 The bodhisattva does not abide in the extreme of samsara, which is severed by realization of emptiness, nor in the extreme of peaceful nirvana, which is severed by love, compassion, and the enlightened thought.

677 *Hevajra Tantra* I:6:5; Toh 417 Kangyur, rgyud 'bum, *nga,* 7a1; translated from Sanskrit at: Farrow and Menon, p. 63. Also cf. the translation of this and the following two passages at BA, p. 980; given their juxtaposition, the *Blue Annals* likely was Thuken's source for the quotations.

678 *Hevajra Tantra* I:6:19; Toh 417 Kangyur, rgyud 'bum, *nga,* 7b1; cf. Farrow and Menon, p. 67.

679 *Hevajra Tantra* I:6:25; Toh 417 Kangyur, rgyud 'bum, *nga,* 7b4; cf. Farrow and Menon, p. 69.

680 This is the primordial sound of the Sanskrit language, and so is in that sense the mother of all sounds; analogously, it is equivalent to emptiness, which is the primordial nature of entities, itself seen as the "mother" goddess, Prajñāpāramitā. It is also virtually the entire content of a sutra entitled the *Perfection of Wisdom in One Syllable.*

681 Each of the first four stanzas is an "alphabetical" poem, tied together by the repetition of an initial letter or word. In the first, all four lines begin with *gang la* ("who"); in the second, all four begin with *pha* ("father," or the first syllable of the word for "perfection"); in the third, all four begin with *ma lus* (every); in the fourth, all four begin with *a* (as in *A*tiśa, the meaning of the syllable *a, a ma* ["mother"], and the exclamation *a*ho). It is almost impossible to convey this in English.

682 Sharon Decker Hendricks and Philippe Golden, at different points, contributed to earlier versions of the present translation of the chapter. Tashi Tsering, Ronald Davidson, and Cyrus Stearns provided invaluable help with difficult passages.

683 On Sakya in general, see, e.g., TPS, vol. 1, pp. 7–17, 91; BA, chap. IV; Ahmad, *A History of Tibet by Ṅag-dBaṅ Blo-bZaṅ rGya-mTsho,* chap. 13; TR; Chogay; Ray, *Indestructible Truth,* chap. 6; E. G. Smith, chaps. 8–9; Batchelor, part 6; Powers, *Introduction to Tibetan Buddhism,* chap. 14; Deshung; Stearns, *Luminous Lives* and TRP; Ngorchen.

684 Following K, we read *byung* for *byon,* though the meanings are very similar.

685 On the Khön in general, see, e.g., TR, pp. 267–74; E. G. Smith, chap. 8.

686 These are the gods who abide on the third level of the second meditative absorption.

687 Literally, the "seven men who were tested" *(sad mi mi bdun).* There are several different listings of these seven; see, e.g., NS vol. II, p. 155.

688 On these developments, see, e.g., E. G. Smith, pp. 102–6.

689 See, e.g., BA, pp. 210–11; E. G. Smith, pp. 106–9; Stearns, *Luminous Lives,* pp. 109–11, and TRP, pp. 184–87; TR, pp. 271–74.

690 These goddesses *(dbang phyug ma, īśvarī)* are important in certain Nyingma practices; they are connected to twenty-eight lunar mansions, or, alternatively, to the sevenfold emanations of each of four female gatekeepers for the forty-two peaceful deities in the *Net of Illusion* tradition.

691 Jamgön Anyé Shap Ngawang Künga Sönam, *Wonderful Treasure-House of Sakya Genealogy,* p. 18.

692 See Chandra, *Tibetan-Sanskrit Dictionary,* vol. I, p. 74; E. G. Smith, p. 299n326.

693 The implication is that the earth was not pure white *(dkar po)* but grayish white *(skya po).*

694 See, e.g., BA, *passim;* Chogay, pp. 7–15; TR, pp. 293–316; Stearns, *Luminous Lives,* pp. 133–57, "Sachen Kunga Nyingpo's Quest," and TRP, pp. 23–126, 213–26.

695 Or "clingings" *(zhen pa).* The four are: this life, samsaric existence, one's own aims, and the self. See six texts on "parting from the four clingings" at the end of the *Blo sbyong rgya tsa* translated by Jinpa, *Mind Training,* pp. 517–66. See also Thurman, *Essential Tibetan Buddhism,* p. 112; Batchelor, pp. 209–47; Powers, *Introduction to Tibetan Buddhism,* pp. 381–84; TR, pp. 295–96.

696 See Nebesky-Wojkowitz, p. 288.

697 This episode, almost certainly visionary in nature, forms an important basis for the Khön family's claim to priority among the Sakyapas. It is probably an invention of the thirteenth century; it is not mentioned by either Drakpa Gyaltsen or Sönam Tsemo (Ronald Davidson, personal communication, August 4, 2003). See also TR, pp. 303–4.

698 These are all highest yoga tantras.

699 Following Z, we read *bzhi* (four) for *bcu bzhi* (fourteen).

700 Following K and TBRC, we read *a seng* for *a sing.*

701 See Stearns, *Luminous Lives,* pp. 18–19.

702 These are a Sri Lankan śrāvaka named Sendapa, Gompa Kyibar, and Jangchup Sempa Tak (Stearns, *Luminous Lives,* pp. 149–51).

703 Perhaps a reference to the third phase of the path of preparation, the second of the five stages of the path; for a list of the seven disciples, see Stearns, *Luminous Lives,* p. 151.

704 This is the root text (not, in fact, in verse) for the Lamdré tradition *(Lam 'bras rtsa ba)* attributed to the great adept Virūpa but not found in Sanskrit; for discussion of this seminal but mysterious text, see TRP, pp. 13–22; TR, pp. 183–94, 303–21, 353–60, and 477–88.

705 Traditionally said to be the abode of Avalokiteśvara, whence the name for the palace in Lhasa occupied by the Dalai Lamas, who are said to be emanations of Avalokiteśvara.

706 See BA, *passim;* Chogay, pp. 15–16; TR, pp. 337–70; TRP, pp. 232–33.

707 See BA, *passim;* Chogay, pp. 16–17; Stearns, *Luminous Lives,* p. 157, and TRP, pp. 233–38; TR, pp. 337–70 *et passim.*

708 The great adept also known as Saroruhavajra or Sakara; he probably lived in the ninth century. See Robinson, pp. 229–30; Dowman, *Masters of Mahāmudrā,* pp. 342–46; TR, *passim.* For a discussion of the disputed identification of Saroruhavajra with Padmavajra, see TR, pp. 199–200.

709 The *brda don gsal* is a teaching on internal mandalas; see TR, p. 351.

710 On Drakpa's visions, see TR, pp. 350–52.

711 See, e.g., BA, *passim;* Chogay, pp. 17–20; Stearns, *Luminous Lives,* pp. 159–69; D. Jackson, *Enlightenment by a Single Means* and *Entrance-Gate for the Wise;* Rhoton; van der Kuijp, *Contributions to the Development of Tibetan Buddhist Epistemology;* Ruegg, *Buddha-nature, Mind and the Problem of Gradualism;* Davenport; Wangyal and Cutillo.

712 This is a speculative Sanskritization of *'phrog byed.*

713 Citing a Kālacakra text, Das (*Tibetan-English Dictionary,* p. 967) places this in Bengal, but we have been unable to find further information on its location or significance.

714 See, e.g., BA, pp. 211–12, 234–37 *et passim;* Chogay, pp. 20–21; Shakabpa, pp. 64–70.

715 For a slightly different list, see Ricard.

716 See BA, p. 212 *et passim;* Chogay, p. 21.

717 See Chogay, pp. 49–50.

718 According to Chogay (p. 1), Atiśa also saw a *hrīḥ* syllable, symbolic of Avalokiteśvara.

719 See BA, pp. 212–14, 217–18.

720 See Chogay, p. 21.

721 TBRC gives his dates as 1288–1339, but this does not correspond well for the dates suggested for his abbacy.

722 It may be that Daknyi Chenpo is being credited with the three-year interregnum that followed his abbacy; only thus do the dates match.

723 BA, p. 213, says twelve.

724 See Chogay, p. 21.

725 See, e.g., TPS, vol. 1, pp. 136–37.

726 For an enumeration of the latter, see Thurman, *Holy Teaching of Vimalakirti,* pp. 156–57.

727 See BA, p. 1017; Davidson, "Ṅgor-pa Tradition," p. 82.

728 Also known as Rongtön Shākya Gyaltsen; see, e.g., BA, *passim;* Cabezón, "Rong ston Shākya rgyal mtshan on Madhyamaka"; Martin, *Tibetan Histories*, p. 74; Hookham, *passim;* Chogay, pp. 30–31; Cabezón, "Two Views of the Svātantrika-Prāsaṅgika Distinction."

729 In Ü, to the northeast of Lhasa.

730 The ten usually are listed as: Dharmakīrti's *Thorough Exposition of Valid Cognition* (see, e.g., Mookerjee and Nagasaki; R. Jackson, *Is Enlightenment Possible?;* Franco; Tillemans), Maitreya's *Ornament of Higher Realization* (see Conze, *Abhisamayālaṃkāra*), Guṇaprabha's *Vinaya Sutra,* Asaṅga's *Compendium of Abhidharma* (see Lamotte, *La somme du Grand Véhicule d'Asaṅga*), Nāgārjuna's *Fundamental Treatise on the Middle Way* (see, e.g., Garfield), Candrakīrti's *Entering the Middle Way* (see Huntington), Āryadeva's *Four Hundred Stanzas* (see Lang), Maitreya's *Sublime Continuum* (see Obermiller, "Sublime Science"; Thrangu, *Uttara Tantra*), Vasubandhu's *Treasury of Higher Knowledge* (see La Vallée Poussin), and the *Guhyasamāja Tantra.* Cf. below, p. 178.

731 He founded the Gyümé tantra college of the Geluk tradition.

732 Not to be confused with the Kagyü scholar of the same name.

733 A title of scholastic achievement roughly equivalent to the Geluk *geshé.*

734 The text contains a hundred thousand verses; the tripling of the number in Bumtrak Sumpa's epithet is simply an exaggeration for effect.

735 For a discussion, see, e.g., TRP, pp. 260–61; for a text by Mangthö, see ibid., pp. 573–83.

736 See, e.g., Komarovski; Dreyfus, *Recognizing Reality;* Jorden. See also below, pp. 208–9.

737 See, e.g., Dreyfus, *Recognizing Reality;* Jorden; Cabezón and Dargyay; Thakchoe.

738 Mangthö Ludrup Gyatso, *Almanac of the Teaching,* p. 193. On this text, see Martin, *Tibetan Histories,* p. 94.

739 See BA, pp. 339–40 *et passim;* Thurman, *The Central Philosophy of Tibet, passim.*
740 Cited in Mangthö Ludrup Gyatso, *Almanac of the Teaching,* p. 195.
741 *kha dbu ma sna dbu ma* literally means "Madhyamaka from the mouth, Madhyamaka from the nose."
742 We have been unable to locate the source of this statement.
743 Mangthö Ludrup Gyatso, *Almanac of the Teaching,* p. 195.
744 Following K, we read *dka'* (difficult) for *bka'* (Buddha's word), though each is a plausible reading.
745 The list of "supreme ornaments" can be quite extensive, as for instance above, p. 33. The *four great difficult ones (dka' chen bzhi)* are usually taken to be the subject matters and/or basic texts of (1) Madhyamaka (Candrakīrti's *Entering the Middle Way*) or, alternatively, valid cognition (Dharmakīrti's *Thorough Exposition of Valid Cognition*), (2) the perfection of wisdom (Asaṅga's *Ornament of Higher Realization*), (3) vinaya *(Vinaya Sutra),* and (4) abhidharma (Vasubhandu's *Treasury of Higher Knowledge*). Here, however, given that two of these texts are listed among the six specified in the next lines, the *four great difficult ones* probably are a different set; given their importance at the time in Tibet, the likeliest candidates are the *Thorough Exposition of Valid Cognition, Ornament of Higher Realization, Vinaya Sutra,* and Asaṅga's *Compendium of Higher Knowledge* (on which see Rahula).
746 This verse, which is probably drawn from Mangthö Ludrup Gyatso, is found in Yongzin Yeshé Gyaltsen, *Biographies of the Masters of the Stages of the Path Lineage,* p. 901.
747 In Tibetan monastic education, the subject matters of Madhyamaka (or valid cognition), the perfection of wisdom, vinaya, and abhidharma, as well as the basic texts for each course of study: Candrakīrti's *Entering the Middle Way* (see Huntington) or Dharmakīrti's *Thorough Exposition of Valid Cognition* (see Mookerjee and Nagasaki; R. Jackson, *Is Enlightenment Possible?;* Franco; Tillemans), Maitreya's *Ornament of Higher Realization* (see Conze, *Abhisamayālaṃkāra*), *Vinaya Sutra,* and *Treasury of Higher Knowledge* (see La Vallée Poussin).
748 See above, note 730.
749 On the Sakya system of education, see, e.g., D. Jackson, *Entrance-Gate for the Wise;* Dreyfus, *Sound of Two Hands Clapping.*
750 Or Ngorchen.
751 See, e.g., Davidson, "Ngor-pa Tradition" and "Preliminary Studies on Hevajra's *Abhisamaya.*"
752 See BA, *passim;* Ngorchen, p. xv; Stearns, *Luminous Lives,* pp. 36–39 *et passim.*
753 See Stearns, *Luminous Lives,* pp. 183–84.
754 See Davidson, "Ngor-pa Tradition," p. 84.
755 See, e.g. BA, *passim;* TPS, vol. 1, pp. 124–25; Davidson, "Ngor-pa Tradition"; Deshung; TRP, pp. 245–46.
756 See Chogay, p. 28, for alternative titles.
757 See Davidson, "Ngor-pa Tradition," p. 89; TRP, pp. 246–47.
758 *Tshogs bshad* and *slob bshad.* Technically, *tshogs bshad* is an "explanation for the assembly," and *slob bshad* an "explanation for disciples." See, e.g., Davidson, "Preliminary Studies on Hevajra's *Abhisamaya,*" p. 124ff.; Powers, *Introduction to Tibetan Buddhism,* p. 399.

759 Davidson, "Ngor-pa Tradition," pp. 90–91; Ngorchen.

760 See, e.g., Stearns, *Luminous Lives, passim.* It is named for Dzong Monastery in Tsang.

761 See Martin, *Tibetan Histories,* p. 72; TRP, pp. 663–64, 693.

762 See Chogay, pp. 32–33.

763 Both are important figures in Nyingma lineages, from time of Padmasambhava.

764 *Thu bo* is an heir, so perhaps his being called Thutön *(thu ston)* refers to his being a teacher who is an heir of Thönmi.

765 See Chogay, pp. 34–36; Stearns, *Luminous Lives,* 41–43 *et passim,* and TRP, pp. 257–59; TR, p. 176. His monastic seat was at Dar Drongmochen in Tsang, though Nālendra in Ü became an important center for the tradition in later times.

766 That is, Doringpa Künsang Chökyi Nyima. See Chogay, p. 34; Stearns, *Luminous Lives,* pp. 40–41 *et passim* and TRP, pp. 255–56.

767 *Mkha' spyod ma'i be'u 'bum* refers to a collection of texts on Vajrayoginī practice.

768 The grammar of the passage indicates that Tsarchen recived teachings from both Dakchen and Doringpa, but in fact Dakchen died seven years before Tsarchen was born. Either Thuken was unaware of this fact, or he is implying that Tsarchen received Dakchen's teachings through Doringpa, who was Dakchen's disciple.

769 See Stearns, *Luminous Lives, passim,* and TRP, pp. 259–60; Martin, *Tibetan Histories,* p. 156. For translations of four seminal works on Lamdré by Jamyang Khyentsé, see TRP, pp. 319–538.

770 See Martin, *Tibetan Histories,* p. 103; TRP, pp. 265–66.

771 See below, this page; see also Chogay, p. 55.

772 See TRP, p. 269, and the text by the Fifth Dalai Lama translated on pp. 539–72.

773 See Chogay, p. 36.

774 This claim is highly questionable; there were, in fact, upholders of the Sakya tradition throughout Tibet in Thuken's time.

775 The three Khecarī cycles relate to the ḍākinīs of Nāropa, Maitrī, and Indra; the great red ones are Kurukulla, Gānapati, and Kāmarāja; the lesser red ones are Garbhasuvarṇasūtraśrī, Hinudevī, and Vasudhara; cf. Chogay, p. 55.

776 Perhaps in reference to Mangthö *Lu*drup Gyatso.

777 Thuken may actually have in mind the collection known as the *One Hundred Sādhanas (Sgrub thabs brgya rtsa)* by Amoghavajra and Bari Lotsāwa; see TR, p. 298.

778 So named because it derives from Ārya Nāgārjuna.

779 See, e.g., Robinson, pp. 22–24; Dowman, *Masters of Mahāmudrā,* pp. 33–38; Templeman, *Seven Instruction Lineages,* pp. 8–11; Kvaerne, *Anthology of Buddhist Tantric Songs;* Cleary, *Ecstasy of Enlightenment.*

780 Yangdak Heruka is one of the Nyingma eight deities *(bka' brgyad)* of the mahāyoga system of both oral tradition and treasure lineages. He was retained, along with the Vajrajumāra form of Vajrakīla, as a special protector of the Khön family, and his practice referred to as an ancestral teaching *(yab chos).*

781 That is, *lam 'bras bu dang bcas pa,* or *lam 'bras,* pronounced Lamdré. On the translation of this term, see TRP, p. 1. Stearns' book contains by far the most detailed collection of Lamdré texts available in English and is indispensable for any serious student of the tradition.

782 See, e.g., Farrow and Menon; Snellgrove, *Hevajra Tantra;* Davidson, "Preliminary Studies on Hevajra's *Abhisamaya.*"

783 The Nāgārjuna of whom Śākyamitra was a disciple is the later, "tantric" Nāgārjuna.

784 This is a speculative reconstruction of the Tibetan *'bar ba'i gtso bo.*

785 See, e.g., TRP, pp. 137–52; Chogay, pp. 8–12; Robinson, pp. 27–32; Dowman, *Masters of Mahāmudrā,* pp. 43–52; Templeman, *Seven Instruction Lineages,* pp. 15–17; Davidson, *Indian Esoteric Buddhism,* pp. 258–62, 281–88, 304–7; TR, 49–58, 183–89 *et passim.* The Sakyapas claim that Virūpa was the same as Dharmapāla, the Yogācāra author at Nālandā, who taught Xuanzang's (602–64) preceptor, Rāhulabhadra. According to Ronald Davidson, however (personal communication, August 4, 2003), the places in Virūpa's hagiography only existed between 976 and 1027, so he probably was a late-tenth-century figure.

786 BA, p. 206, lists these as guru and disciple, not the same person; see also TR, *passim.*

787 See BA, pp. 205–10; TR, pp. 161–207 *et passim,* TRP, pp. 163–81. Drokmi's dates often are given as 993–1077, but, according to Davidson, these appear to be an invention of Mangthö Ludrup Gyatso (1523–96). The *Blue Annals* supplies no dates for him. Davidson suggests a birthdate sometime between 990 and 1000 and a death date of 1064 (TR, pp. 164, 182).

788 See TR, pp. 166–67, 195–96, 202–4.

789 See Stearns, *Luminous Lives,* pp. 47–55; TR, pp. 178–83 *et passim;* TRP, pp. 163–78.

790 See BA, p. 208; Stearns, *Luminous Lives,* p. 58, and TRP, p. 189; TR, *passim.*

791 See BA, p. 208; Stearns, *Luminous Lives,* pp. 58–59, and TRP, pp. 189–92; TR, pp. 264–66. He also is known as Dromdepa.

792 Also known as Sé Kharchungwa. See Stearns, *Luminous Lives,* p. 59, and TRP, pp. 192–98; TR, pp. 168–69, 264–66, 299–301 *et passim.*

793 Much of this paragraph is taken from BA, pp. 208–9; cf. TRP, p. 180.

794 See BA, pp. 210, 219, *et passim;* Stearns, *Luminous Lives,* p. 60, and TRP, pp. 208–12.

795 See BA, pp. 218–26; Tachikawa speculates that Thuken avoids much discussion of Machik because "he would have been forced to deal with sexual practices up to a degree which might have proved embarrassing" (p. 101n18).

796 On these events, see Stearns, *Luminous Lives,* pp. 61–63, and TRP, pp. 219–24.

797 Following K, we read *dbang gis* for *dbang gi.*

798 See Nebesky-Wojkowitz, p. 285.

799 The term *rtsa yig* refers to channels that are in the form of crooked syllables in various locations in the body, including the cakras.

800 Following K, we read *dbang gis* for *dbang gi.*

801 For a panegyric to Virūpa by Sachen Künga Nyingpo, see TR, pp. 50–52.

802 We have not been able to locate this text.

803 See Davidson, "Masquerading as Pramāṇa."

804 According to Tachikawa (p. 100n17), this entire section is taken verbatim by Thuken from Mangthö Ludrup Gyatso's *Guidelines on the Three Appearances as Privately Explained: A Fortunate Rosary of Nectar Moon-Drops Opening the New Night Lily;* in *Lam 'bras slob bshad,* vol. *ba,* 52b6–58a6.

805 Āryadeva, *Four Hundred Stanzas* 8:15; Toh 3846 Tengyur, dbu ma, *tsha,* 9b5; cf. Lang, *Āryadeva's Catuḥśataka,* p. 83.

806 Āryadeva, *Four Hundred Stanzas* 8:16cd; Toh 3846 Tengyur, dbu ma, *tsha,* 9b6; cf. Lang, *Āryadeva's Catuḥśataka,* p. 83.

807 The other options would round out the classical four-cornered negation: both existence and nonexistence, and neither existence nor nonexistence.

808 Drakpa Gyaltsen, *Parting from the Four Attachments;* in *Grags-pa-rgyal-mtshan gyi bka' 'bum = The complete works of Grags-pa-rgyal-mtshan,* in *Sa skya pa'i bka' 'bum,* vol. *ta,* 1b3. See above, note 695; cf. translation in Jinpa, *Mind Training,* pp. 519–24.

809 Literally, "at the time of the ground" *(gzhi dus).*

810 Literally, the apprehended *(gzung)* and the apprehender *('dzin).*

811 Heat, peak, and acceptance are the first three of the four stages of the path of preparation, the second of the five standard meditative paths of Indo-Tibetan Buddhism.

812 The fourth and final stage of the path of preparation.

813 The two purities are the result of the removal of the two types of obstacles: delusion obstacles and knowledge obstacles. In most accounts, from the path of seeing through the tenth bodhisattva stage is equivalent to the fourth path, of meditation, while the eleventh stage, i.e., buddhahood, is the equivalent to the fifth path, of no-more learning. Occasionally, the path of no-more learning is said to begin at the highest level of the tenth stage.

814 According to Tachikawa (p. 102n25), this section also is taken verbatim by Thuken from Mangthö Ludrup Gyatso's *Guidelines on the Three Appearances,* 21a4–33b4. For a detailed account of these processes by Jamyang Khyentsé Wangchuk, see TRP, pp. 416–49.

815 See above, pp. 143–45.

816 The mind is like a mirror, which can reflect colors if clean, but its nature is not the color it reflects; it is intrinsically clear and empty of reflection.

817 This is the third of the three qualities of mind mentioned earlier in the paragraph.

818 That is, it will entail positing the ultimate existence of the mind.

819 Nāgārjuna, *Fundamental Treatise on the Middle Way,* 7:33; Toh 3824 Tengyur, dbu ma, *tsa,* 5b6, cf. Garfield, p. 22

820 We have been unable to locate the source of this expression.

821 *Perfection of the Five Dependent Arisings;* in *Collected Works,* in *Sa skya pa'i bka' 'bum,* vol. *na,* 106a1. The text also is known as the *Letter on the Five Dependent Arisings: Special Instructions on the Vajrayāna.*

822 Drakpa Gyaltsen, *Root Text on the View of the Indivisibility of Samsara and Nirvana,* 96b6. For Jamyang Khyentsé Wangchuk's detailed explication of these metaphors, all of which refer to advanced tantric practices, see TRP, pp. 443–49.

823 This is analogous to the symbolic clear light achieved on the illusory-body phase of the highest yoga tantra generation stage, prior to the direct realization of emptiness in the clear-light phase.

824 For other presentations of this system, see, e.g., Ngorchen, pp. 156–200; Deshung, pp. 394–492.

825 A famous Mahākāla image in Sakya that has a mask of hide or skin.

826 Philippe Golden contributed to an earlier version of the translation of this chapter. For an excellent alternative translation of the chapter, see Ruegg, "The Jo naṅ pas"; on Jonang, see also BA, pp. 762 ff.; TPS, vol. 1, pp. 91–92; Hookham, chap. 8;

Stearns, *Buddha From Dolpo;* Hopkins, *Mountain Doctrine* and *Essence of Other-Emptiness;* Mathes, "Tāranātha's 'Twenty-one Differences with Regard to Profound Meaning.'"

827 Following K and Z, we read *dol bu pa* for *don bu pa*. Although Thuken consistently calls him Dölbupa *(dol bu pa)*, we have chosen to use throughout the name he is more commonly known by, Dölpopa *(dol po pa)*.

828 See Ruegg, "The Jo naṅ pas," p. 79.

829 See BA, p. 766 ff.; Stearns, *Buddha from Dolpo,* pp. 44–45, 199–200nn10–11.

830 Although this could refer to the Kālacakra commentarial tradition in general, it probably denotes Puṇḍarīka's great commentary, *Stainless Light.*

831 See BA, p. 775; Stearns, *Buddha from Dolpo,* pp. 17–20 *et passim.*

832 See, e.g., BA, pp. 775–77; Stearns, *Buddha From Dolpo;* Kapstein, *Tibetan Assimilation,* pp. 106–19; Hookham, chap. 8; Mathes, "Tāranātha's 'Twenty-one Differences'"; Hopkins, *Mountain Doctrine.*

833 See Stearns, *Buddha from Dolpo,* pp. 13–14.

834 Ruegg ("The Jo naṅ pas," p. 81n32) identifies him as the same Sönam Drakpa who served as Butön's preceptor.

835 Literally, "site of a hundred thousand images" *(sku 'bum).* This structure, erected 1330–33, resembles the great Sakya stupa at Gyantsé built a century later in having multiple levels with many small chapels dedicated to particular deities. See Ruegg, "The Jo naṅ pas," p. 81n24; Stearns, *Buddha from Dolpo,* pp. 21–22.

836 For a translation, see Hopkins, *Mountain Doctrine.* A separate translation will also appear as volume 7 of *The Library of Tibetan Classics.*

837 The word for "broke forth" *(rdol)* is pronounced the same as the first syllable of Dölpopa's name. For the original context of this saying, see Stearns, *Buddha from Dolpo,* p. 22.

838 On these two, see Ruegg, "The Jo naṅ pas," p. 81nn26–27; Stearns, *Buddha from Dolpo, passim.*

839 See BA, p. 777 ff.; Ruegg, "The Jo naṅ pas," p. 81n28.

840 In central Tsang; it is not to be confused with a monastery in Kham by the same name that is associated with Thangtong Gyalpo.

841 See BA, p. 777; Ruegg, "The Jo naṅ pas," p. 82n40.

842 See Stearns, *Buddha from Dolpo,* pp. 64–67.

843 See, e.g., TPS, vol. 1, pp. 128–131; Stearns, *Buddha from Dolpo,* pp. 68–74; Chimpa and Chattopadhyaya; Mathes, "Tāranātha's 'Twenty-one Differences'"; Baker; Templeman, *Seven Instruction Lineages* and *Tāranātha's Life of Kṛṣṇācārya/Kāṇha;* Hopkins, *Essence of Other-Emptiness.*

844 See above, p. 125.

845 On these developments, see, e.g., Stearns, *Buddha from Dolpo,* pp. 70–74.

846 *Mdo khams* signifies Amdo and Kham together, though Dzamthang is in Amdo.

847 See Ruegg, "The Jo naṅ pas," p. 82n46.

848 In fact, Jonang monasteries and practices survived in parts of Tibet in Thuken's time and continue to this day, especially in the east.

849 This is comparable to the illusory body in other highest yoga tantra systems; see, e.g., Khedrup Norsang Gyatso, p. 675; Cozort, *Highest Yoga Tantra,* part 4.

850 For a translation of this, see Stearns, *Buddha from Dolpo,* pp. 123–73.

851 These are, most likely, the three divisions of the dharmakāya: the gnostic dharmakāya *(ye shes chos sku, jñānadharnmakāya)* and the two subdivisions of the natural body

(ngo bo nyid sku, svabhāvikakāya), its natural emptiness and its natural lack of any obstacles. Alternatively, it may refer to the dharmakāya as found in the three basic existential events: birth, death, and bardo.

852 Ruegg ("The Jo naṅ pas," p. 83n52) notes that the text may in fact be the *Praise of the Dharmadhātu (Dharmadhātustava* or *Dharmadhātustotra);* Thuken mentions this text below, p. 204.

853 Some of these points (especially in the first paragraph) are made in Dölpopa Sherap Gyaltsen, *Mountain Dharma: The Ocean of Definitive Meaning,* p. 117 (cf. Hopkins, *Mountain Dharma,* p. 184), but much of Thuken's citation appears to be instead his own summary of the standpoint and sources of the extrinsic-emptiness view and not a direct quotation from Dölpopa's text.

854 The Tibetan *tshangs pa* equally refers to the Sanskrit *Brahmā* (the creator god) and *Brahma* (the neuter nominative singular of *Brahman,* the power behind and within the cosmos); since we know that the view reported here involves *Brahman* rather than *Brahmā,* we have translated accordingly.

855 See above, p. 41.

856 As Ruegg notes ("The Jo naṅ pas," p. 84n54), this is the opening verse of the *Words in a Sentence* of the great grammarian/philosopher Bhartṛhari (570–651?), the Sanskrit of which is: *anādinidhanaṃ brahma ṣabdatattvaṃ yad akṣaram/ vivartate 'rthabhāvena prakriyā jagato yataṃ.* It is quoted occasionally in Buddhist literature—e.g., Kamalaśīla, *Detailed Explication of the Compendium of Principles,* in the chapter on Brahmā word (Toh 4267 Tengyur, tshad ma, *ze,* 184b1)—though we do not know where Thuken found the passage.

857 See Kamalaśīla, *Detailed Explication of the Compendium of Principles;* Toh 4267 Tengyur, tshad ma, *ze,* 184b5. *Nang gi byed pa* (inner agent) may refer to the *antaḥkaraṇa,* the conventional principle of inner awareness postulated by numerous Hindu schools, including that of Bhartṛhari.

858 For further details, see above, pp. 39–40.

859 On the principal, see above, note 93. The transformation complex *(rnam 'gyur gyi tshogs)* is a term for the various material evolutes of the principal, such as mind, the gross and subtle elements, etc.

860 A reference to the classic Indian example of mistaken apprehension, where, in limited light, a coil of rope is seen to be a snake.

861 Literally, "[mental] complexes" *(tshogs).*

862 See above, p. 42.

863 See above, p. 41.

864 The Tibetan has *bde gshegs* (*sugata,* or "well gone") rather than *de gshegs* (*tathāgata,* or "thus gone"), but the sutra in question almost certainly is the *Tathāgata Essence Sutra,* the name under which Thuken cited it above (p. 201).

865 These are the three aspects of a provisional or interpretable statement that must be fulfilled in demonstrating its status as provisional. In the case of a concept like the mind-basis-of-all, the purported meaning, i.e., what the Buddha really had in mind, is emptiness, which is the ultimate referent of the term; the purpose was to provide the ignorant with a way to approach the truth of emptiness indirectly; and the conflict with actuality lies in the fact if interpreted literally, the mind-basis-of-all will lead to the extreme of eternalism.

866 *Laṅkāvatārasūtra;* Toh 107 Kangyur, mdo sde, *ca,* 216a5; cf. Suzuki, *Laṅkāvatāra Sūtra,* pp. 70–72.

867 The reality-limit *(yang dag pa'i mtha', bhūtakoṭi)* has multiple meanings, including the boundary between saṃsāra and nirvāṇa, emptiness, and perfect wisdom. To describe it as the intentional basis of the Buddha's teaching is to imply that his teaching is grounded in a realization of the nature of reality.

868 Verses 25:4–6; Toh 3824 Tengyur, dbu ma, *tsa,* 16a7; cf. Garfield, pp. 73–74.

869 Verse 25:3; Toh 3824 Tengyur, dbu ma, *tsa,* 16a7; cf. Garfield, p. 73.

870 Verses 25:19–20; Toh 3824 Tengyur, dbu ma, *tsa,* 17a1; cf. Garfield, p. 75.

871 There may be a play on words here: *mtshang* is a defect; *tshang* is a nest.

872 See above, p. 153; the reference is to Losang Chökyi Gyaltsen, *Root Text on Mahāmudrā: The Main Path of the Conquerors;* in *Collected Works,* vol. *nga,* 12a5; cf. Dalai Lama and Berzin, pp. 98, 261–71.

873 See Ruegg, "The Jo nań pas," p. 88n70.

874 The text is not included among Gyaltsap Jé's *Collected Works,* and we have not been able to locate it elsewhere.

875 See Nebesky-Wojkowitz, pp. 310–11.

876 With regard to Madhyamaka, these are Āryadeva, Buddhapālita, Bhāvaviveka, and Candrakīrti; cf. below, note 976.

877 See Ruegg, "The Jo nań pas," p. 91n78. *Great Madhyamaka* is a term that proponents of extrinsic emptiness use for their view to distinguish it from Prāsaṅgika and Svātantrika Madhyamaka.

878 See, e.g., Shākya Chokden, *Treatise Explaining the Distinction Between the Two Chariot-Paths of the Great Vehicle and Proving They Have a Single Definitive Meaning;* in *Collected Works,* vol. *kha,* 25a2.

879 We are unaware of any textual basis for this claim.

880 Verse 12:10; Toh 3846 Tengyur, dbu ma, *tsha,* 13b3; cf. Lang, p. 113.

881 The holy mountain in Ngari associated with Śiva by Hindus and Cakrasaṃvara by Buddhists. It is also sacred for the Jain and Bön traditions.

882 Following K and BA, we read *kor* for *kong.* See BA, pp. 846–47.

883 See especially BA, chap. XI.

884 That is, Kharakpa Drak Gyalwa.

885 See BA, pp. 726–28 *et passim.* Translations of his songs of realization appear in Stearns, *Hermit of Go Cliffs.*

886 Cf. Stearns, *Hermit of Go Cliffs,* p. 3, for additional commentary about Kodrakpa's background and influence.

887 See E. G. Smith, p. 179–208; Martin, *Tibetan Histories,* pp. 70–71.

888 This almost certainly refers to Yakdruk Sangyé Pal, not the Yakdé Panchen who died when Bodong was three years old! See Stearns, *Buddha from Dolpo,* p. 194n107.

889 See Martin, *Tibetan Histories,* p. 74.

890 See E. G. Smith, p. 319n665.

891 See, e.g., BA, *passim;* Ruegg, *Life of Bu-ston Rinpoche;* Martin, *Tibetan Histories,* pp. 50–52, 54, 57; Obermiller, *History of Buddhism* and *Jewellery of Scripture.*

892 Southeast of Shigatsé.

893 This is Drakpa Gyaltsen (thirteenth/fourteenth century); see Ruegg, *Life of Bu-ston Rinpoche,* pp. 89–90.

894 That is, Lotsāwa Rinchen Namgyal, mentioned above, p. 209.

895 See Martin, *Tibetan Histories,* pp. 63–64.

896 Lori Cayton contributed to an earlier version of the present translation of this and the following two chapters. Following K and Z, we consider the chapter on Geluk to be the eighth in a series on Tibetan traditions, not, as in S, a second major division within the section on Tibetan schools. On Geluk in general, see, e.g., TPS, vol. 1, pp. 39–80, 92–93, 116–24; Shakabpa; Snellgrove and Richardson, part 3; Powers, *Introduction to Tibetan Buddhism,* chap. 15; Samuel, *passim;* E. G. Smith, part IV; Ray, *Indestructible Truth,* chap. 8; Lopez, *Religions of Tibet in Practice,* chaps. 17, 20, 23, 28, 29.

897 Following K, we read *dga'* for *dge.*

898 The "Tsongkhapa" here is an insertion for clarity. In this chapter, as throughout Thuken's text, Tsongkhapa is referred to by a variety of honorific titles, the most common of which are Jé, Jé Rinpoche, Jé Lama, and Jetsün Lama; his given name is Losang Drakpa. Much has been written on Tsongkhapa; see, e.g., BA, pp. 1073–80; TPS, vol. 1, pp. 116–19, and vol. II, pp. 339–45, 417–36; Jinpa, *Self, Reality, and Reason;* Thurman, *Life and Teachings of Tsong Khapa,* pp. 3–55, 231–47, and *The Central Philosophy of Tibet,* pp. 1–173; Newland, *Introduction to Emptiness.* For works by Tsongkhapa, see, e.g., GT; Thurman, *Life and Teachings of Tsong Khapa,* pp. 56–230, and *The Central Philosophy of Tibet,* pp. 175–385; Mullin, *Tsongkhapa's Six Yogas of Naropa;* Kilty; Wangyal; Sparham, *Fulfillment of All Hopes, Tantric Ethics,* and *Ocean of Eloquence;* Hopkins, *Tantra of Tibet, Yoga of Tibet, Yoga Tantra, Emptiness in the Mind-Only School of Buddhism,* and *Tsong-kha-pa's Final Exposition of Wisdom;* Batchelor, pp. 171–206; Samten and Garfield, including the useful bibliographies of works in English in appendixes III–IV. See also Berzin, "A Short Biography of Lama Tsongkhapa."

899 Geluk *(dge lugs)* means "the virtuous tradition." Although the phrase has meaning and historical resonance of its own, Thuken insists that it came about initially through a mispronunciation that later was universalized and interpreted accordingly. By the same logic, another later name for the tradition, Gedenpa (*dge ldan pa,* meaning "virtuous"), would have come about through a mispronunciation of Gandenpa *(dga' ldan pa).*

900 *Book of Kadam,* p. 754. Cf. above, in the Kadam chapter (p. 104) for an earlier citation of the same verse, and note 356.

901 See E. G. Smith, pp. 149–50; BA, *passim.*

902 Desi Sangyé Gyatso, *Yellow Beryl,* p. 68.

903 S places this rubric title after the next paragraph, at 166:16.

904 *Rgyal sras snying stobs chen po.*

905 In Amdo; later the site of the Kumbum Monastery, it is located just southwest of Xining in present-day Qinghai province.

906 The *bar ma rab byung gi tshul khrims* involves shaving the head, wearing robes, observing celibacy, and becoming a follower of the Buddha—without, however, taking full monastic vows.

907 Thuken simply has *bod,* which means "Tibet," but implies Ü and Tsang, in contradistinction to lower Tibet, i.e., Amdo and Kham, and upper Tibet, i.e., Ngari.

908 In S, this rubric title is located at 167:17.

909 Dharmakīrti, *Thorough Exposition of Valid Cognition,* 2:132; Toh 4210 Tengyur, tshad ma, *ca,* 113b3; cf. R. Jackson, *Is Enlightenment Possible?,* p. 318.

910 Sadāprarudita ("ever-weeping") is an extremely empathetic bodhisattva who is the

subject of chapter 30 of the *Perfection of Wisdom in Eight Thousand Verses;* see Conze, *Perfection of Wisdom in Eight Thousand Lines*, pp. 277–90.

911 Tsongkhapa, *Song of Realization;* in *Collected Works*, vol. *kha*, 53a2; cf. Thurman, *Life and Teachings of Tsong Khapa*, p. 41.

912 This is the "reality" (Skt. *tattva*) chapter of Asanga's *Bodhisattva Stages;* see Willis, *On Knowing Reality*.

913 The text here actually says "twenty thousand," but that is a common shorthand for the *Perfection of Wisdom in Twenty-Five Thousand Verses*, which is usually taken to be the sutra that the *Ornament of Higher Realization* comments on.

914 This text is not listed in the Tōhoku catalogue.

915 A short commentary on the *Ornament of Higher Realization*.

916 A large commentary on *Ornament of Higher Realization*.

917 A summary of the eighth chapter of the *Ornament of Higher Realization;* this is not listed in the Tōhoku catalogue and may simply refer to the section on the eighth chapter from the *Commentary Clarifying the Meaning*.

918 See Lopez, *Elaborations of Emptiness*.

919 There is no commentary on the *Diamond-Cutter Sutra* by Vasubandu listed in the Tōhoku catalogue; Kamalaśīla's is the *Explication of the Diamond-Cutter Sutra*.

920 There is no commentary on the *Ornament of Mahayana Sutras* by Vasubandu listed in the Tōhoku catalogue; Thuken may be referring to Vasubandhu's *Explanation of the Summary of Mahayana*.

921 The two distinguishings are *Distinguishing the Middle from the Extremes* (see Stcherbatsky, *Madhyānta-vibhaṅga;* Dharmacakra Translation Committee) and *Distinguishing Dharmas from the Dharma Realm* (see Thrangu, *Distinguishing Dharma and Dharmata*), both attributed by Tibetan tradition to Maitreya.

922 A great Sakya master; see above, note 739.

923 This is one of the major divisions of vinaya literature in the Mūlasavāstivāda vinaya as found in the Kangyur.

924 In the Tōhoku catalogue, no author is credited with this text.

925 The only text with a title like this in the Tōhoku catalogue is attributed to Jinamitra, not Vimalamitra.

926 Neither the author nor a Vinaya commentary by this name is listed in the Tōhoku catalogue.

927 The only text in the Tengyur that comments on novice vows in three hundred stanzas (Toh 4126) is attributed not to Śākyaprabhā, but to Vinītadeva. Also, there is no text attributed to Vinītadeva that comments on those vows in fifty stanzas, though there is a poetic text on the topic by Śākyaprabhā (Toh 4124) that might match Thuken's description. It is possible, therefore, that Thuken simply reversed the authors of the two texts he had in mind.

928 Tsongkhapa, *Song of Realization;* in *Collected Works*, vol. *kha*, 53a3; cf. Thurman, *Life and Teachings of Tsong Khapa*, p. 41.

929 Dignāga's *Compendium of Valid Cognition* is regarded as a sutra not in the usual Buddhist sense of a text spoken by the Buddha, but in its broader Indic usage, as the fundamental text for a particular line of study and commentary. Dharmakīrti's *Thorough Exposition of Valid Cognition* is framed as a commentary on Dignāga's basic text, though in fact it strays from it considerably.

930 The one subcommentary to Dignāga's autocommentary listed in the Tōhoku

catalogue is the *Vast and Stainless: An Explication of the Autocommentary on the Compendium of Valid Cognition,* by Jinendrabuddhi (eighth century).

931 This pair almost certainly includes Ravigupta, author of the *Commentary on the Thorough Exposition of Valid Cognition,* and perhaps Mahābrahmaṇa (Great Brahman), who in some cases is listed as the author of the *Explication of the Thorough Exposition of Valid Cognition;* these are the only major commentators on the *Thorough Exposition* not otherwise named by Thuken.

932 These are the *Explication of the Ornament of the Thorough Exposition of Valid Cognition,* by Jina, and the *Very Pure: An Explication of the Ornament of the Thorough Exposition of Valid Cognition,* by Yamāri.

933 There is no autocommentary on the *Ascertainment of Valid Cognition* listed in the Tōhoku catalogue.

934 For a translation, see Stcherbatsky, *Buddhist Logic,* vol. II.

935 Dharmakīrti was not, however, a direct disciple of Dignāga, but of Dignāga's disciple, Īśvarakṛṣṇa.

936 *Song of Realization;* in *Collected Works,* vol. *kha,* 53a4; cf. Thurman, *Life and Teachings of Tsong Khapa,* p. 41.

937 *Collected Works,* vol. *kha,* 53a5; cf. Thurman, *Life and Teachings of Tsong Khapa,* pp. 41–42.

938 See Khedrup Jé, *Entryway to Faith;* in *Collected Works of Tsongkhapa,* vol. *ka,* 25a2.

939 A disciple of Butön.

940 Dönyö Dorjé *(don yod rdo rje)* in Sanskrit would be Amoghavajra; Karmavajra in Tibetan would be would be Trinlé Dorjé *('phrin las rdo rje).*

941 That is, with legs extended down to touch the floor.

942 See Khedrup Jé, *Entryway to Faith;* in *Collected Works of Tsongkhapa,* vol. *ka,* 26a1; cf. Thurman, *Life and Teachings of Tsong Khapa,* p. 15.

943 Also known as the *vajrācārya,* this is an initiation unique to the yoga and highest yoga tantras, which binds one to tantric vows and pledges. In either case, it comes at the culmination of the initiatory sequence, though in highest yoga tantra, there sometimes is a distinction between a lesser ācārya initiation at the conclusion of the first of the four initiatory sequences, the vase initiation, and a greater one at the end of the entire sequence of initiations.

944 Atiśa, *Lamp for the Path to Enlightenment,* 61c–63; Toh 3947 Tengyur, dbu ma, *khi,* 240b6; cf. Davidson, "Atiśa's Lamp on the Path," pp. 300–301; Sherburne, pp. 11–12; Rinchen and Sonam, *Atisha's Lamp for the Path,* p. 158.

945 For lists of action tantras, see, e.g., Lessing and Wayman, p. 145; Hopkins, *Yoga of Tibet,* p. 238ff.; for performance tantras, see, e.g., Lessing and Wayman, p. 205; Hopkins, *Yoga of Tibet,* p. 37.

946 For a translation, see Bhattacharyya.

947 On Vajrayoginī, see, e.g., English; K. Gyatso, *Guide to Dakini Land.*

948 This is presumably the same as the *Vajra Garland Tantra.*

949 The *Vajra Source* contains the Vajradhātu mandala.

950 On the *Compendium,* see, e.g., Snellgrove, *Indo-Tibetan Buddhism,* vol. I.

951 For a translation, see Skorupski.

952 A commentary on the *Compendium of Reality.*

953 See Lessing and Wayman, p. 221ff.

954 On these four "general action tantra" systems, see Lessing and Wayman, pp. 135–39.
955 See Lessing and Wayman, pp. 129–31.
956 See Lessing and Wayman, p 131.
957 See Lessing and Wayman, p. 227.
958 See Skorupski, pp. xxvii–xxviii.
959 Tokden Jampal Gyatso, *Short Biography of Jetsün Tsongkhapa;* in *Collected Works of Tsongkhapa,* vol. *ka,* 5b2.
960 Following K, we read *gcod* for *dpyod.*
961 *Collected Works,* vol. *ca,* 37b5.
962 All editions have *mar do,* but the reference most likely is to Marpa and Lochung (or Ngok Lotsāwa Loden Sherap), the two master translators referred to below, so we have read *lo* for *do.*
963 Tsongkhapa, *Clarifying the Whole Hidden Meaning;* in *Collected Works,* vol. *nya,* 5b2.
964 See Wayman, *Yoga of the Guhyasamājatantra,* pp. 56–57, 94.
965 See Wayman, *Yoga of the Guhyasamājatantra,* p. 114ff.
966 The only work by Praśāntajñāna listed in the Tōhoku catalogue is indeed a commentary on Guhyasamāja (Toh 1843), but under the title *Ascertaining the Special Instruction: A Commentary on the Glorious Guhyasamāja.*
967 See Wayman, *Yoga of the Guhyasamājatantra,* p. 100 *et passim.* Cilupa is listed in the Tōhoku catalogue as Celuka.
968 This is the *Explication of the King of Tantras, the Glorious Guhyasamāja;* see Wayman, *Yoga of the Guhyasamājatantra,* p. 107.
969 In the Tōhoku catalogue, the text is attributed to Ratnākaraśānti, who often is taken to be identical to Śāntipa.
970 On all these, see Wayman, *Yoga of the Guhyasamājatantra, passim.*
971 Although Śraddhākaravarman is credited with many translations and a number of original works in the Tōhoku catalogue, no commentary on the *Prophetic Intention* is mentioned.
972 Thuken (or his source) may have mistaken Ānandagarbha for Jñānagarbha. The former has no commentary on the *Questions of the Four Goddesses* listed in the Tōhoku catalogue, while the latter does: the *Explanation of the Questions of the Four Goddesses.* Śraddhākaravarman's commentary on the *Questions of the Four Goddesses* is not found in the Tōhoku catalogue.
973 Śākyamitra's is the *Extensive Explanation of The Lamp Summarizing Conduct;* Nāgabodhi is credited with two texts on the five stages of Guhyasamāja (Toh 1833, Toh 1840), but neither of them is explicitly a commentary on *The Lamp Summarizing Conduct.*
974 Nāgabodhi is credited with three texts on Guhyasamāja, but none bears the title cited by Thuken.
975 Nāgabodhi's would be the *Jewel Garland Explaining the Five Stages* and *Illumining the Meaning of the Five Stages.*
976 In a tantric context, the four sons are: Āryadeva, Candrakīrti, Nāgabodhi, and Śākyamitra. Cf. above, note 876.
977 See Davidson, "Preliminary Studies on Hevajra's *Abhisamaya,*" p. 112.

978 This refers to the *Commentary on a Short Teaching on Initiations,* a Kālacakra tradition text.

979 Or, as in Tōhoku, Indrabhūti.

980 Following K and the Tōhoku catalogue, we read *rnal 'byor ma'i* for *rnal 'byor mkha' 'gro ma'i.*

981 There are numerous texts in praise of Cakrasaṃvara in the Tōhoku catalogue, but none that has commentarial status, and none by Vajrapāṇi.

982 This Sanskrit name is conjectural for *skar rgyal zla ba;* no author by that name is found in the Tōhoku catalogue. The only other detailed exposition of Cakrasaṃvara found in the catalogue is that by Bāpabhati (Toh 1403), which may be what Thuken has in mind. The texts by Jayabhadra and Bhavyakīrti are, respectively, the *Detailed Exposition of the Root Tantra of Cakrasaṃvara* and the *Allure of the Hero: Detailed Exposition of the Root Tantra of Cakrasaṃvara.*

983 The text listed as *Commentary on Difficult Points in Cakrasaṃvara* (Toh 1415) is attributed not to Vīravajra but to Bhavabhadra. Vīravajra is credited with text called *Elucidating the Verbal Meaning: An Extensive Explanation of Cakrasaṃvara* (Toh 1412). It is unclear which of these Thuken intends.

984 Khedrup Jé, *Entryway to Faith;* in *Collected Works of Tsongkhapa,* vol. *ka,* 24a5.

985 In the Tōhoku catalogue, this text is attributed to Samādhibhadra.

986 This probably refers to the *Detailed Explication of the Distilled Essence of the Vajra Verses,* a commentary on the *Hevajra Tantra* that also draws on Kālacakra sources. Thanks to John Newman for this information..

987 This is the title given by Butön to the *Essential Kālacakra Tantra,* which, like the condensed tantra, is said to consist of extracts of the *Kālacakra Root Tantra.* Thanks to John Newman for clarifying this reference.

988 See Thoyön Yeshé Döndrup, *Advice from Grandmother Yoginī;* in *Storehouse of the Cherished Jewel Collection of the Kadam,* p. 135.

989 For Tsongkhapa's writings on this, see Mullin, *Tsongkhapa's Six Yogas of Naropa* and *Readings on the Six Yogas of Naropa,* pp. 93–136.

990 *Collected Works,* vol. *kha,* 62a1.

991 On these events, which began around 1390, see, e.g., Thurman, *Life and Teachings of Tsong Khapa,* p. 14ff., and *The Central Philosophy of Tibet,* p. 77ff.

992 This is a peaceful form, holding a sword and perfection of wisdom text, red-gold in color.

993 In vol. *da.*

994 This is the old name for the Jokhang; it invokes the legend of the white goat who brought building materials for the construction.

995 Thuken is suggesting that the notation found in the old manuscripts is more reliable than that which made its way into Tsongkhapa's collected works.

996 This is in relation to the so-called thirty-five confession buddhas.

997 In the elaborate form of the common practice of offering the mandala of Mount Meru to one's lama and/or to deities, one wipes an offering plate with one's forearm before placing various symbolic substances on it—usually grains of rice. It says elsewhere that during this retreat, Tsongkhapa performed 3.5 million full prostrations and 1.8 million mandala offerings; see, e.g., Thurman, *Life and Teaching of Tsong Khapa,* p. 17.

998 The lineage from Gönpawa is on the stages of the path. That stemming from Chengawa is on the special instructions. See Kadam chapter above, p. 111.

999 Following K, we read *gus pas* for *gus pa'i.*

1000 Jamyang Chöjé Tashi Palden, *Biography of Tsongkhapa the Great,* p. 141; or Khedrup Jé, *Entryway to Faith;* in *Collected Works of Tsongkhapa,* vol. *ka,* 17a4–17b6.

1001 Fully ordained monks stop eating food after noon. Liquids such as tea, juice, and water were permitted after noon, but monks who were not fully ordained had to sprinkle a little water on their drink beforehand.

1002 For fully ordained monks, there are five divisions of the 253 downfalls. The two heaviest are *pham pa sde,* involving expulsion, and *lhag ma sde,* involving suspension. The three lighter categories are *ltung byed sde,* minor transgressions, *sor gshags sde,* "confessable" sins, not mentioned here, and *nyes byes sde,* infractions. Between the heavy and light sections is an intermediate group of downfalls, requiring "return" of forbidden items, called *sbom po sde.* Tsongkhapa is saying he never committed any of the intermediate or heavy downfalls.

1003 Khedrup Jé, *Entryway to Faith;* in *Collected Works of Tsongkhapa,* vol. *ka,* 33b1–2.

1004 Probably the *Heart Sutra.*

1005 Jamyang Chöjé Tashi Palden, *Biography of Tsongkhapa the Great,* p. 290.

1006 Khedrup Jé, *The Jewel Cluster: Secret Biography of Tsongkhapa;* in *Collected Works of Tsongkhapa,* vol. *ka,* 2b5.

1007 This view, common to many earlier Tibetan scholars, denied the four extremes (existence, nonexistence, both, neither) in the manner of Nāgārjuna, but did not leave room for the affirmation of conventionalities, and therefore inclined toward nihilism.

1008 Literally, "close and distant" *(nye ring).* Emptiness should not be emphasized at the expense of appearance (e.g., cause and effect, dependent arising, etc.) and vice versa.

1009 Khedrup Jé, *The Jewel Cluster: Secret Biography of Tsongkhapa;* in *Collected Works of Tsongkhapa,* vol. *ka,* 2b5.

1010 That is, in common perception.

1011 A major debate among Mādhyamikas (and modern scholars of Madhyamaka) concerns whether there is a Madhyamaka position to establish, and whether it can be argued using standard inferential procedures. See, e.g., Thakchoe.

1012 Khedrup Jé, *The Jewel Cluster: Secret Biography of Tsongkhapa;* in *Collected Works of Tsongkhapa,* vol. *ka,* 3a2.

1013 Khedrup Jé, *The Jewel Cluster: Secret Biography of Tsongkhapa;* in *Collected Works of Tsongkhapa,* vol. *ka,* 3a6.

1014 Khedrup Jé, *The Jewel Cluster: Secret Biography of Tsongkhapa*; in *Collected Works of Tsongkhapa*, vol. *ka,* 3a6.

1015 Lechen Künga Gyaltsen, *Lamp Illuminating the Dharma History of the Kadam,* 346b4.

1016 Nāgabodhi is regarded as a disciple of Nāgārjuna who received important tantric teachings from him. He probably lived in the late first millennium. Like many Indian masters, however, he is given a very long lifespan by Tibetans, hence the possibility that he might still have been alive in Tsongkhapa's time.

1017 See above, note 144.

1018 In fact, both Odantapuri and Nālandā had been destroyed by Muslim armies some two centuries earlier.
1019 Author of a text on the meditations related to 108 deities; see TBRC W27761.
1020 That is, of the temple at Bodhgaya; the five sciences are probably the five major sciences.
1021 That is, Madhyamaka and secret mantra, respectively.
1022 See above, p. 238.
1023 Namely, Āryadeva, Buddhapālita, Bhavaviveka, and Candrakīrti; cf. the list above, note 976.
1024 Following K, we read *'jug* for *'dug*.
1025 Khedrup Jé, *The Jewel Cluster: Secret Biography of Tsongkhapa;* in *Collected Works of Tsongkhapa,* vol. *ka,* 9a1.
1026 This is *yid ches kyi dad pa,* the second of the three levels of faith; the first is *beginning faith (dang pa'i dad pa)* and the third is *irreversible faith (phyir mi ldog pa'i dad pa).*
1027 See translations at, e.g., Thurman, *Life and Teachings of Tsong Khapa,* pp. 99–107, and *The Central Philosophy of Tibet,* pp. 177–84; Kilty, pp. 216–45. The text begins: "Homage to Buddha whose vision and speech/Made him unexcelled as sage and teacher,/To the Conqueror, who saw dependent arising and then taught it!"
1028 Nāgārjuna, *Fundamental Treatise on the Middle Way,* 8:12; Toh 3824 Tengyur, dbu ma, *tsha,* 6a6. The version of the one line of Tibetan cited by Thuken—*brten nas 'byung ba med pa yi*—may also be read as an independent statement to the effect that because of dependence, there is [ultimately] no arising. Cf. Garfield, p. 25. Thurman (*The Central Philosophy of Tibet,* p. 85) cites, as the basis for Tsongkhapa's turning point, a different passage from Nāgārjuna's text, 18:1, which affirms that the self is neither the same as nor different from the aggregates.
1029 This story is found at, e.g., Khedrup Jé, *Entryway to Faith;* in *Collected Works of Tsongkhapa,* vol. *ka,* 37b3. We have not yet located the source in Changkya Rölpai Dorjé's writings cited by Thuken. Tsongkhapa's commentary on the *Fundamental Treatise* is the *Ocean of Reasoning;* see Samten and Garfield.
1030 Khedrup Jé, *Entryway to Faith;* in *Collected Works of Tsongkhapa,* vol. *ka,* 37b5.
1031 We have not yet located the source in Changkya Rölpai Dorjé's writings cited by Thuken.
1032 See above, p. 239.
1033 In fact, this long passage is drawn from the *Entryway to Faith*; see below, note 1037.
1034 The same passage is cited on p. 259. It is found in Khedrup Jé, *The Jewel Cluster: Secret Biography of Tsongkhapa;* in *Collected Works of Tsongkhapa,* vol. *ka,* 10a1.
1035 The king of Shambhala who, according to legend, requested the Kālacakra initiation and teachings from the Buddha; see below, p. 382.
1036 *Mixing and transference (bsre 'pho)* is another way of denoting the six Dharmas of Nāropa. In the explanatory tradition handed down from Rechungpa (who received it from Marpa via Milarepa), the nine aspects of the instruction are: (1) inner heat, which mixes desire with great bliss, (2) illusory body, which mixes anger with lack of true existence, (3) clear light, which mixes ignorance with nonconceptuality, (4) the daytime meditation that mixes inner heat with illusory body, (5) the nighttime meditation that mixes dream with clear light, (6) the death-time meditation that mixes bardo with the transference of consciousness, (7) inner-heat practice for en-

ergetic individuals, (8) dream practice for lazy individuals, and (9) mixing greater and lesser transference practices. See *Bod rgya tshig mdzod chen mo,* vol. 3, p. 3054. Thuken's text actually reads: *bsre ba skor dgu dang 'pho ba.*

1037 Khedrup Jé, *Entryway to Faith;* in *Collected Works of Tsongkhapa,* vol. *ka,* 42a5.

1038 Following K, we read *med de* for *med dam.*

1039 Khedrup Jé, *The Jewel Cluster: Secret Biography of Tsongkhapa;* in *Collected Works of Tsongkhapa,* vol. *ka,* 9a1.

1040 That is, an embodied sexual partner.

1041 The fifth of the five phases of highest yoga tantra completion-stage practice, equivalent to complete buddhahood.

1042 That is, an inwardly visualized female figure, sometimes referred to as a gnosis seal *(ye shes phyag rgya, jñānamudrā).*

1043 This is a very rough translation of *ting 'dzin pir* [or *bir*] *legs ma,* which may refer to an offering song related to Cakrasaṃvara practice called *Song of the Spring Queen,* that nowadays is chanted as part of the ritual feast *(tshogs)* portion of the *Offering to the Lama,* a central Geluk liturgy composed by the First Panchen Lama, Losang Chökyi Gyaltsen. The song in question begins with the two-line refrain: *ting 'dzin sngags dang phyag rgyas byin brlabs pa'i/ zag med bdud rtsi'i tshogs mchod rgya mtsho 'di/... 'bul* ("This ocean of feast offerings of uncontaminated nectar that is blessed by concentration, mantra, and mudra...I offer"). See, e.g., *Bla ma'i rnal 'byor,* pp. 71–72.

1044 Chenga Lodrö Gyaltsen, *Flowing River of Faith: Biography of Jetsün Jampal Gyatso;* in *Collected Works,* vol. *kha,* 10b1.

1045 We have been unable to locate the source of this claim.

1046 *The Hand-Offering Rite of the External Offering Rites of Cakrasaṃvara, and Song of the Spring Queen;* in *Collected Works,* vol. *na,* 13a3. For verses directed by Tsongkhapa to Sarasvatī, see Kilty, pp. 20–21, 166–77.

1047 *Prayer to Cakrasaṃvara;* in *Collected Works,* vol. *kha,* 231b3.

1048 Khedrup Jé, *Song to the Glorious Master of the Three Worlds;* in *Collected Works,* vol. *ta,* 5b6; cf. Thurman, *Life and Teachings of Tsong Khapa,* p. 236.

1049 Mañjughoṣa is the father of all the conquerors, or buddhas, because wisdom (which he represents) is the seed of enlightenment. Wisdom also, of course, is often personified as female in the goddess Prajñāpāramitā ("perfection of wisdom").

1050 Khedrup Jé, *Entryway to Faith;* in *Collected Works of Tsongkhapa,* vol. *ka,* 38a4.

1051 See Kilty, pp. 115–50.

1052 The previous two sentences are nearly identical to those found above, on p. 237.

1053 It is better known as Namtseng Deng, the name by which Thuken refers to it below, p. 254.

1054 In Sanskrit, *Mahāvārga.* Within the vinaya, it is the subsection of the Sections (Skt. *Skāndhaka*) that deals with rules for ordinations, special observance days, rainy-season retreats, clothing, food, medicine, and community procedures.

1055 In both Sanskrit and Pali, *Mahāvibhaṅga.* Within the vinaya, it is the subsection of the Division of Rules (Skt. *Sūtravibhaṅga*) that deals with the 253 vows observed by a fully ordained monk.

1056 There are a number of different types of downfalls that require confession, and the number of monks to whom these downfalls must be confessed varies according to the gravity of the downfall.

1057 An example of this would be the following. If, after blessing your robes, you are separated from them for more than one day, you would be required to stop using them for a certain period of time before confessing the downfall to the community of monks.

1058 Other requisites may include a belt, a razor, a staff, a needle and thread, water strainer, and the monk's three-part robe.

1059 Khedrup Jé, *Entryway to Faith;* in *Collected Works of Tsongkhapa,* vol. *ka,* 58a3.

1060 There are three motivations for taking the prātimokṣa vows: from fear, from admiration, and from renunciation. *Authentic individual liberation (so so'i thar pa)* is the Tibetan translation of the term *prātimokṣa;* it is fully enacted only when the last of the three motivations has taken root.

1061 Gö Lotsāwa Shönu Pal, *Blue Annals,* 75:6–76:2; cf. BA, p. 83.

1062 On the question of authorship, see Sparham, *Fulfillment of All Hopes,* p. 135n59.

1063 Translated in Sparham, *Fulfillment of All Hopes.*

1064 That is, for nineteen days.

1065 *Rgya gar skad du* refers to the titles at the beginning of the Kangyur and Tengyur texts translated into Tibetan. Tsongkhapa probably read aloud the first few pages of each text before starting the commentary.

1066 The monastery north of Lhasa with ancient connections to the Kadam tradition.

1067 See, e.g., Stcherbatsky, *Madhyānta-vibhanga;* Dharmacakra Translation Committee.

1068 Located close to what would become Ganden Monastery.

1069 The *Thorough Exposition of Valid Cognition*'s presentation of practice is most evident in the second chapter, which includes logical demonstrations of, e.g., the reality of past and future lives and the truth of the four noble truths. On this chapter, see, e.g., R. Jackson, *Is Enlightenment Possible?;* Franco.

1070 Van der Kuijp (in "An Early Tibetan View of the Soteriology of Buddhist Epistemology") has presented evidence of the use of the *Thorough Exposition* for practice purposes in the writings of Drigung Jikten Gönpo, who predates Tsongkhapa by over two centuries.

1071 This probably refers to Drakpa Gyaltsen (1374–1434/36), who is sometimes referred to as Dülzinpa. No text meeting Thuken's description is listed among Drakpa Gyaltsen's works, however.

1072 In the Geluk study system, the monks master five main subject areas and their five main texts: (1) abhidharma via Vasubandhu's *Treasury of Higher Knowledge,* (2) vinaya via Guṇaprabha's *Vinaya Sutra,* (3) Madhyamaka via Candrakīrti's *Entering the Middle Way,* (4) perfection of wisdom via Maitreya's *Ornament of Higher Realization,* and (5) valid cognition via Dharmakīrti's *Thorough Exposition of Valid Cognition.* On this system, see, above all, Dreyfus, *Sound of Two Hands Clapping.*

1073 The governor is Ngawang Drakpa, an important disciple who had requested the *Three Principal Aspects of the Path,* one of Tsongkhapa's most influential short texts (see, e.g., Sopa and Hopkins, part 1; Wangyal, chap. VI).

1074 It must be remembered that in Tsongkhapa's time the Potala had not yet attained the size or magnificence it would under the Fifth Dalai Lama.

1075 These three commentaries are available in translation in, respectively, Tatz, *Asanga's Chapter on Ethics;* Sparham, *The Fulfillment of All Hopes;* and Sparham, *Tantric Ethics.*

1076 Following K and TBRC, we read *gu shrī* for *shrī.*

1077 Tsongkhapa's retreat house on the shoulder of the mountain above Sera Monastery.

1078 This is the subtitle of the *Essence of Excellent Explanation.*

1079 Gö Lotsāwa Shönu Pal, *Blue Annals,* 699:1–2; cf. BA, p. 795.

1080 The *grwa skor* reflects a style of teaching in which a teacher would visit a series of monastic centers to teach on one main topic, which he then would debate with various students and visiting scholars.

1081 See above, note 745.

1082 Literally, *spu long,* "hair-raising, horripilating."

1083 *Collected Works of Tsongkhapa,* vol. *ka,* 7b5.

1084 Khedrup Jé, *Song to the Glorious Master of the Three Worlds;* in *Collected Works,* vol. *ta,* 4b3; cf. Thurman, *Life and Teachings of Tsong Khapa,* p. 233.

1085 In the Indian and Tibetan debate tradition, reasons only can be put forward to prove a thesis that has not yet been proven.

1086 *Dbu yon ma che.*

1087 This is the same as the *Great [Treatise on the] Stages of the Path to Enlightenment,* the *Byang chub lam rim chen mo*. For a translation, see GT.

1088 This is popularly known, however, as the *Middle-Length [Treatise on the] Stages of the Path,* the *Lam rim 'bring*. For partial translations, see, e.g. Thurman, *Life and Teachings of Tsong Khapa,* pp. 108–85.

1089 Khedrup Jé, *Teaching on the View, Clearing Away Darkness;* in *Collected Works,* vol. *ta,* 193a5.

1090 A wrathful god abiding in the mountains south of Namtso Lake in central Tibet.

1091 *Song of Experience Related to the Stages of the Path;* in *Great Treatise on the Stages of the Path,* in *Collected Works,* vol. *pa,* 519b5–520a3; cf. GT, vol. 3, pp. 368–69.

1092 This verse is known only through its citation by Geluk authors; Thuken may have drawn it from the *Excellent Wish-Fulfilling Tree* of his teacher, Sumpa Khenpo (p. 522). Taktsang Lotsāwa was a Sakya master who at one time tried to refute Tsongkhapa.

1093 These are detailed, among other places, in Candrakīrti's *Entering the Middle Way* (6:181–201, 215–23).

1094 See Samten and Garfield.

1095 See Thurman, *The Central Philosophy of Tibet.*

1096 Tsongkhapa; in *Collected Works,* vol. *pha,* 1a6; cf. Thurman, *The Central Philosophy of Tibet,* p. 188.

1097 There is no text by this name attributed to Nāgabodhi in the Tōhoku catalogue. He is, however, credited with three texts on the five stages of Guhyasamāja completion-stage practice (Toh 1810, 1833, 1840), and the title cited by Thuken may be a shorthand for one or all of these.

1098 Khedrup Jé, The *Jewel Cluster: Secret Biography of Tsongkhapa;* in *Collected Works of Tsongkhapa*, vol. *ka*, 6a6.

1099 Khedrup Jé, *The Jewel Cluster: Secret Biography of Tsongkhapa;* in *Collected Works of Tsongkhapa,* vol. *ka,* 10a1. This passage is quoted above, p. 243.

1100 That is, the *Great Treatise on the Stages of Mantra;* see Hopkins, *Tantra in Tibet, Yoga of Tibet,* and *Yoga Tantra.*

1101 Khedrup Jé, *The Jewel Cluster: Secret Biography of Tsongkhapa;* in *Collected Works of Tsongkhapa,* vol. *ka,* 10a2.

1102 A translation of this work will appear as volume 15 in this series, under the title *Lamp Thoroughly Illuminating the Five Stages of Completion.*

1103 We have not been able to locate an explanation of this image in the *Secret Biography*, and its meaning is not entirely clear—though the "moon" *(tsa ndra)* is almost certainly a reference to Candrakīrti, whose *Bright Lamp* is central to Tibetan traditions of Guhyasamāja interpretation.

1104 *Collected Works*, vol. *nga*, 311a4.

1105 *Collected Works*, vol. *nya*, 58a3.

1106 There are several texts that might be intended, including the *Exposition of the Completion Stage of Cakrasaṃvara According to the System of Lūipa*, the *Completion Stage of Cakrasaṃvara According to the System of Lūipa*, and the *Cluster of Yogic Achievements*.

1107 See Kilty, pp. 115–50.

1108 Another song in praise of Maitreya.

1109 See Kilty, pp. 83–96.

1110 *Collected Works*, vol. *nga*, 472b5. The metaphor involves the root tantra as the cream, the explanatory tantra the churning rod tied with the rope of wisdom and method, producing butter—the essential meaning of the root tantra. It refers back to the Hindu myth in which the nectar of immortality is churned up from the bottom of the sea by the gods and titans.

1111 *Cluster of Yogic Achievements: An Explanation of the Great Completion-Stage Yoga of Śrī Cakrasaṃvara;* in *Collected Works*, vol. *ta*, 1a3.

1112 Khedrup Jé, *Song to the Glorious Master of the Three Worlds;* in *Collected Works*, vol. *ta*, 5b1; cf. Thurman, *Life and Teachings of Tsong Khapa*, p. 235.

1113 Meditation with gnosis, through which one will see oneself as a deity, is the beginning point for generation-stage meditation, while dissolution of the deity's mandala is its endpoint.

1114 These are the first and fifth of the five Guhyasamāja-based stages of completion-stage meditation. The union of no more learning is equivalent to the fifth of the five standard Buddhist paths, which in a Mahayana context denotes full buddhahood.

1115 Literally, "dharmas in their immediacy" *(da gzod chos)*.

1116 This text is unavailable. On Jamyang Chöjé, see below, p. 276.

1117 *Collected Works*, in *Sa skya pa'i bka' 'bum*, vol. *cha*, 138a1.

1118 This verse is known to us only through its citation in Geluk sources, e.g., Sumpa Khenpo, *Excellent Wish-Fulfilling Tree*, p. 523.

1119 This was the founding of the present-day Great Prayer *(smon lam chen po)* festival.

1120 *Rgyal ba* usually refers to the Buddha, but the only prophecy concerning Tsongkhapa mentioned by Thuken is that of Atiśa; see above, p. 215.

1121 On these events, see Thurman, *Life and Teachings of Tsong Khapa*, pp. 26–27.

1122 See Tsongkhapa, *The Nectar Garland: Supreme Medicine of Answers to Questions;* in *Collected Works*, vol. *ka*, 12b; cf. BA, p. 1079.

1123 Tsongkhapa, *The Nectar Garland: Supreme Medicine of Answers to Questions;* in *Collected Works*, vol. *ka*, 10b; cf. BA, p. 1079. Matibhadra is the Sanskrit equivalent of Losang *(blo bzang)*, the first part of Tsongkhapa's name.

1124 Lechen Künga Gyaltsen, *Lamp Illuminating the Dharma History of the Kadam*, 363a1.

1125 We were not able to find the source of this quotation.

1126 *Song of Realization;* in *Collected Works*, vol. *kha*, 52b6; cf. Thurman, *Life and Teachings of Tsong Khapa*, p. 40.

1127 Changkya Rölpai Dorjé. *Great Treatise on the Establishment of Philosophical Systems;* in *Collected Works,* vol. *cha,* 26a3.

1128 *Song to the Glorious Master of the Three Worlds;* in *Collected Works,* vol. *ta,* 5b3; cf. Thurman, *Life and Teachings of Tsong Khapa,* p. 236.

1129 These are, strictly speaking, teachers rather than students of Tsongkhapa. As we have seen, however, many of his teachers came to respect him so much that they played both roles.

1130 See Tharchin and Roach, pp. 21–24.

1131 These also are the "eight pure ones" who accompanied Tsongkhapa to Ölkha Chölung for intensive practice.

1132 In most contexts, Khedrup Jé is considered the other principal spiritual son of Tsongkhapa, but as will be evident shortly, he receives a special designation in Thuken's list.

1133 These are, respectively, the founder of Drepung, the third abbot of Sera, the founder of Gyümé, and the founder of Tashi Lhünpo; the last would posthumously be designated as the First Dalai Lama.

1134 The founder of Sera Monastery.

1135 The languages are Sanskrit and Tibetan. The former is the author of the *Blue Annals;* the latter was initially a critic of Tsongkhapa but later wrote in praise of him.

1136 The connotation of *spyan snga,* which literally means "five eyes," refers to various sorts of conventional and ultimate vision possessed by ordinary and ārya beings. It is a title of particular importance to the Drigung Kagyü.

1137 The Tibetan *jo ldan* means "noble," as in the common title for Atiśa, Jowo *(jo bo).*

1138 A *rtogs ldan* is someone who has attained profound realization; the term often is added as an honorific.

1139 *Collected Works,* vol. *cha.*

1140 Those, that is, who did not have extensive interactions with Tsongkhapa.

1141 *Gser gyi lung.* It may refer metaphorically to writings of golden quality or perhaps more literally to writings highlighted in gold, in which case it would be synonymous with *gser yig.*

1142 Pawo Tsuklak Trengwa, *Scholars' Banquet: A Dharma History,* p. 964.

1143 This is a famous pilgrimage place, on which see Huber.

1144 Khedrup Jé, *The Jewel Cluster: Secret Biography of Tsongkhapa;* in *Collected Works of Tsongkhapa,* vol. *ka,* 7b5.

1145 Yisang Tsewa is another name for Gö Lotsāwa Shönu Pal. This statement does not appear to be drawn from the *Blue Annals;* it may be elsewhere in Gö's works.

1146 See TPS, vol. 1, pp. 119–20. For translations of Gyaltsap's work, see, e.g., R. Jackson, *Is Enlightenment Possible?;* Blumenthal; Rinchen and Sonam, *Yogic Deeds of Bodhisattvas.*

1147 See TPS, vol. 1, pp. 120–22. For translations of works by Khedrup, see e.g., Lessing and Wayman; Cabezón, *Dose of Emptiness.* The latter includes a short biography.

1148 Tib. *pho nya;* see Nebesky-Wojkowitz, pp. 303–4.

1149 Khedrup Jé, *Letter to Geshé Shersang;* in *Collected Works,* vol. *ta,* 85a4.

1150 Jamyang Chöjé, *Biography of Khedrup Jé;* in *Collected Works of Mkhas grub rje,* vol. *ka* 5a6. The passage there is not quoted verbatim by Thuken, who may, in fact, have drawn it from another biography of Khedrup Jé, e.g., that of Sera Jetsünpa.

1151 This is *Clearing Away Misconceptions about the Sadhana of Kālacakra.*

1152 According to legend, the white conch had been placed there by Śāriputra to show the place where a great monastery would later be established.

1153 That is, the Kangyur.

1154 The last text is the *Explanatory Treatise on Epistemology.*

1155 See, e.g., Boord and Tsonawa; Lati et al., part 2.

1156 He was the main teacher of the Fifth Dalai Lama and author of the well-known *Guru Puja* that is the staple of Geluk ritual calendar. See, e.g., TPS, vol. 1, pp. 131–33; E. G. Smith, chap. 10; Cabezón, "On the *sGra pa rin chen pa'i rtsod lan*"; Willis, *Enlightened Beings,* pp. 85–96; R. Jackson, "dGe ldan bka' brgyud Tradition of Mahāmudrā"; Dalai Lama and Berzin; Mullin, *Readings on the Six Yogas of Naropa,* pp. 137–53; Lopez, "Prayer to the Lama."

1157 For a translation of Jamyang Shepa's text on philosophical systems, see Hopkins, *Maps of the Profound.* The five root texts are Candrakīrti's *Entering the Middle Way* (see Huntington), Dharmakīrti's *Thorough Exposition of Valid Cognition* (see Mookerjee and Nagasaki; R. Jackson, *Is Enlightenment Possible?;* Franco; Tillemans), Maitreya's *Ornament of Higher Realization* (see Conze, *Abhisamayālaṃkāra*), *Vinaya Sutra,* and *Treasury of Higher Knowledge* (see La Vallée Poussin)

1158 If the Tibetan *zon* is equivalent to the Chinese *zong,* this might indicate one of Yunglo's successors as Ming emperor.

1159 See, especially, Sera Monastery website.

1160 This verse is quoted at, e.g., Panchen Sönam Drakpa, *Beautiful Ornament of Thought;* in *Collected Works,* vol. *ta,* 111a2.

1161 We have been unable to locate this text, but the passage in question is cited by Panchen Sönam Drakpa, *Beautiful Ornament of Thought;* in *Collected Works,* vol. *da,* 11a2

1162 He established Sera Jé.

1163 This is another name for the *Book of Kadam.*

1164 See, e.g., Mullin, *Bridging the Sutras and Tantras* and *Training the Mind in the Great Way.*

1165 Thuken presumably is taking 1408 as the founding date of Ganden; 1409 is the most commonly given date, but any one Tibetan year covers parts of two years in the Gregorian calendar.

1166 These are all Sakya masters.

1167 At Lhamo Lhatso, a mountain lake in eastern Ü that traditionally yields up prophecies involving the Dalai Lamas. On these events, see Mullin, *Fourteen Dalai Lamas,* pp. 105–9.

1168 Mangyül is north of the Annapurna Range of the Himalayas. The Śītā River, important in Kālacakra mythology, remains elusive, but most would place it considerably farther north, perhaps in the Tarim Basin in present-day Xinjiang; see Newman, *Outer Wheel of Time,* p. 309n12. Perhaps Thuken believes that its basin extends well to the south.

1169 The king who brought Atiśa to Tibet in 1042; see above, pp. 99–100.

1170 While giving these dates, the TBRC entry (P427) also suggests he may have been born around 1450 and died around 1500.

1171 Following K, we read *shod* for *bshong.*

1172 We have been unable to identify the members of these groups.

1173 Thuken's home monastery; see E. G. Smith, pp. 154–55.

1174 Thuken's immediate predecessor in his incarnation lineage; see E. G. Smith, pp. 152–53.

1175 Another name for Hor Ngawang Trinlé Lhundrup.

1176 This, the largest Geluk monastery in Amdo, is better known as Labrang; see Nietupski.

1177 That is, as a political and spiritual leader; literally, "through the two systems" *(lugs gnyis kyi sgo nas).*

1178 Pema Karpo, *Dharma History;* in *Collected Works,* vol. *kha,* 192a6–192b1.

1179 Pema Karpo, *Dharma History;* in *Collected Works,* vol. *kha,* 192a5–6. Thuken is paraphrasing; Pema Karpo's actual claim is that (a) Gendün Drup is rightly considered the emanation of Dromtönpa (hence standing in the same relation to Tsongkhapa as Dromtönpa to Atiśa) and (b) because Gendün Drupa founded Tashi Lhunpo, and his successive incarnations protected the Gelukpa teaching, he was the greatest of Tsongkhapa's disciples.

1180 Another name for Yama, an important protector deity.

1181 We were unable to find this passage, which presumably is from a biography of Tsongkhapa.

1182 We were unable to find this passage in the works of Khedrup Norsang Gyatso.

1183 *G.yag shi,* "where the yaks die."

1184 The *Gsang 'dus bzhi sbrags ma* is not found among the collected works of Tsongkhapa but here is attributed to him; it consists of the root text of the *Guhyasamāja Tantra* accompanied by four sets of annotations; see TBRC W23690.

1185 A *shok lhe* is a small carrying case for texts.

1186 For a text by Dülnakpa, see Thurman, *Life and Teachings of Tsong Khapa,* pp. 246–47.

1187 Probably the *Lamp Illuminating Guhyasamāja* and the *Precious Sprout that Severs Extremes.*

1188 Although all editions have *lo,* it probably should be *lū,* indicating Lūipa, the transmitter of one of the two great Cakrasaṃvara traditions.

1189 These yogas, roughly equivalent to the first four of the five stages of Guhyasamāja, are: mantra, commitment, form, and pure wisdom. A fifth yoga, great union, is equivalent to the fifth of the Guhyasamāja stages, namely, union. See, e.g., Mullin, *Selected Works of Dalai Lama II,* pp. 83–90.

1190 This may refer to the sixty-three torma offerings to Dharmarāja Riding a Buffalo.

1191 This may refer to practice of the six Dharmas of Nāropa, though the term *'khrul 'khor (yantra)* is widely applied both to yogic exercises and to the diagrams employed in them.

1192 A text by Sangpo Tashi (1410–78/79) related to the practice of Vajrabhairava.

1193 It is unclear what the four great reversals are, but Sitātapatrā *(gdugs dkar),* also known as Uṣṇīṣasitātapatrā, is often invoked to reverse worldly misfortune; she has a retinue of wrathful female deities to assist her.

1194 See Berzin, "A Brief History of Gyumay and Gyuto Tantric Colleges."

1195 Yisang Tsewa is another name for Gö Lotsāwa Shönu Pal. We have been unable to locate this statement in the *Blue Annals,* though Sherap Sengé is mentioned there; see, e.g., BA, p. 339. The statement is cited in Lechen Künga Gyaltsen, *Lamp Illuminating the Dharma History of the Kadam,* 379a1.

1196 See, e.g., Willis, *Enlightened Beings;* R. Jackson, "dGe ldan bka' brgyud Tradition of Mahāmudrā."

1197 See Willis, *Enlightened Beings,* pp. 33–42.

1198 See Willis, *Enlightened Beings,* pp. 43–48. As Thuken noted above, Baso was Khedrup Jé's younger brother (p. 275).

1199 Cited in Losang Chökyi Gyaltsen, *Biographies of the Lineage Holders of the Geden Oral Lineage*; in *Collected Works,* vol. *ka,* 8b5.

1200 See Willis, *Enlightened Beings,* p. 46.

1201 See Willis, *Enlightened Beings,* pp. 49–56.

1202 Ngawang Losang Gyatso, *Vajra Life-Tree of Long-life Initiations;* in *Collected Works,* vol. *tha,* 2a4.

1203 *Chariot of Oceanic Yogic Achievements: A Biography of the Omniscient Jetsün Sönam Gyatso;* in Ngawang Losang Gyatso, *Collected Works,* vol. *nya,* 60b1. Jan Willis argues (*Enlightened Beings,* p. 178, notes 197 and 199) that the Third Dalai Lama's biography is likely mistaken in this matter and cites a text stating that it was, in fact, the Second Dalai Lama with whom Palden Dorjé had a relationship. Palden Dorjé's exact dates are unknown, but if he were a student of Baso Chökyi Gyaltsen (1402–73), he would more likely have been an older contemporary of the Second Dalai Lama (1475–1542) than of the Third (1543–88)—though this chronology, of course, fails to take into account the extraordinarily long lives, or communication from the rainbow body, often attributed to great adepts like Palden Dorjé. The initiation from Padmasambhava was presumably received in a vision.

1204 We have been unable to locate these verses.

1205 See Willis, *Enlightened Beings,* pp. 57–72; Mullin, *Readings on the Six Yogas of Naropa,* pp. 71–92.

1206 On these, see Willis, *Enlightened Beings,* pp. 73–82, 85–96.

1207 The Panchen Lamas are said to be emanations of Amitābha, the Dalai Lamas of Avalokiteśvara. In most Tibetan pantheons of deities, Avalokiteśvara is said to emanate from Amitābha and, hence, is in some sense his "son."

1208 As has been noted by numerous scholars, the name found in Sanskrit texts is Sambhala. Its location (if there is one), remains a matter of dispute; Newman ("Itineraries to Sambhala," p. 487) argues on the basis of the Kālacakra literature that it is north of the Śītā (Tarim) River, which cuts through the middle of present-day Xinjiang.

1209 There are two systems for enumerating the Panchen Lamas. Under one system, Losang Chökyi Gyaltsen is considered the first, which would make the current incarnation the eighth. Under another system, Khedrup Jé is the first Panchen, Sönam Chökyi Langpo the second, Ensapa the third, and Losang Chökyi Gyaltsen the fourth; this would make the current incarnation the eleventh.

1210 For a text by the Fourth Panchen, see Sopa and Hopkins, part 1.

1211 On the Dalai Lamas in general, see, e.g., Brauen; Mullin, *Fourteen Dalai Lamas;* Snellgrove and Richardson, part 3; Shakabpa.

1212 Here and elsewhere, Thuken simply refers to the "conquerors" *(rgyal ba),* the most common Tibetan term for the Dalai Lamas, but because this is an epithet used for many exalted beings, we have substituted the more familiar "Dalai Lama."

1213 See, e.g., Mullin, *Fourteen Dalai Lamas,* pp. 51–86, and *Bridging the Sutras and Tantras.*

1214 Gendün Drupa, *Song of the Eastern Snow Mountain;* in *Collected Works,* vol. *cha,* 28a5. This poem was written while the First Dalai Lama, residing in Tsang, in the west, longed to see Tsongkhapa, who was in the east. See also Mullin, *Bridging the Sutras and Tantras,* pp. 109–14.

1215 See, e.g., Mullin, *Fourteen Dalai Lamas,* pp. 87–130; *Selected Works of the Dalai Lama II* and *Mystical Verses of a Mad Dalai Lama.*

1216 See, e.g., Mullin, *Fourteen Dalai Lamas,* pp. 131–64, and *Selected Works of Dalai Lama III.*

1217 That is, Mongolia, where he was born, and where he received, from Altan Khan, the title "Oceanic Guru" *(dalai lama).*

1218 See, e.g., Mullin, *Fourteen Dalai Lamas,* pp. 164–83.

1219 See, e.g., TPS, vol. 1, pp. 133–36, 145–48; Mullin, *Fourteen Dalai Lamas,* pp. 185–238; Snellgrove and Richardson, pp. 195–201; Shakabpa, chap. 7; Ahmad, *A History of Tibet by Ṅag-dBaṅ Blo-bZaṅ rGya-mTsho;* Karmay, *Secret Visions of the Fifth Dalai Lama.*

1220 See, e.g., Mullin, *Fourteen Dalai Lamas,* pp. 239–72; Aris; Fields; Williams, *Songs of Love, Poems of Sadness.*

1221 This refers to his being deposed by the Qosot Mongol governor Lhapsang Khan, then kidnapped and taken to eastern Tibet, where he died or was murdered at a relatively early age; on these events, see, e.g., Snellgrove and Richardson, pp. 204–17; Skakabpa, chap. 8.

1222 See, e.g., Mullin, *Fourteen Dalai Lamas,* pp. 273–322, and *Songs of Spiritual Change.*

1223 See Mullin, *Fourteen Dalai Lamas,* pp. 323–42.

1224 The eight are: Tsongkhapa's *Great Treatise on the Stages of the Path* (see GT), *Small Treatise on the Stages of the Path* (see, e.g., Thurman, *Life and Teaching of Tsong Khapa,* pp. 59–66), and *Song of Experience Related to the Stages of the Path* (see, e.g., Thurman, *Life and Teaching of Tsong Khapa,* pp. 40–46); the Third Dalai Lama's *Essence of Refined Gold* (a commentary on number 3; see Mullin, *Selected Teachings of the Dalai Lama III*), the Fifth Dalai Lama's *Sacred Words of Mañjuśrī* (which is a commentary on number 4), the First Panchen Lama Losang Chökyi Gyaltsen's *Path to Bliss* (see Dalai Lama, *Path to Bliss*), the Third Panchen Palden Yeshé's *Swift Path* (which is a commentary on number 6), and (8) Dakpo Ngawang Drakpa's verse text, the *Essence of Well-Spoken Advice.*

1225 Changkya Rölpai Dorjé, *Great Treatise on the Establishment of Philosophical Systems;* in *Collected Works,* vol. *cha,* 8a3.

1226 See above, p. 95; *thod rgal* and *khregs chod* are the highest levels of practice in Dzokchen, or ati yoga, the consummate yoga in the Nyingma tradition. Following K, we read *chod* for *chos.*

1227 This is a fuller title of Changkya's *Great Treatise on the Establishment of Philosophical Systems.*

1228 *Collected Works,* vol. *cha,* 7b5.

1229 Literally, "has the essence *(snying po can)* of compassion."

1230 Maitreya, *Ornament of Mahayana Sutras,* 2:10; Toh 4020 Tengyur, sems tsam, *phi,* 2b5; cf. Thurman et al., p. 13, where it is treated as verse 1:10.

1231 Literally, "lineages" or "types" *(rigs);* the reference is to the forty-two peaceful and fifty-eight wrathful deities found in early Tibetan tantric traditions and in meditations on the bardo.

1232 See above, pp. 38–39.

1233 This is the view of certain Yogācāras, who interpret the assertion of a thoroughly established nature *(yongs grub, pariniṣpanna)* for dependent phenomena *(gzhan dbang, paratantra)* as implying that emptiness exists absolutely.

1234 This is the Jonang view, on which see above, chapter 9.

1235 Nāgārjuna, *Fundamental Treatise on the Middle Way* 13:8; Toh 3824 Tengyur, dbu ma, *tsa,* 8a6; cf. Garfield, p. 36.

1236 See above, p. 49.

1237 See above, p. 72.

1238 Mutually exclusive direct opposition *(rnam bcad yongs gcod)* occurs when the affirmation of one entity automatically entails the rejection of the other, and vice versa.

1239 The latter two are, respectively, the *Ocean of Reasoning*—see Samten and Garfield—and *Clarifying the Meaning of Entering the Middle Way,* which will be translated in volume 19 of this series.

1240 For a translation, see Cabezón, *Dose of Emptiness.*

1241 Among the many works on the Geluk interpretation of Prāsaṅgika Madhyamaka, see, especially, Hopkins, *Meditation on Emptiness;* Napper; Thurman, *The Central Philosophy of Tibet;* Jinpa, *Self, Reality and Reason in Tibetan Philosophy;* Magee; Samten and Garfield; GT vol. 3.

1242 *Entryway for the Conqueror's Children: Exposition of the Way of the Bodhisattva;* in *Collected Works,* vol. *nga,* chap. 9, 159a1.

1243 This is another name for Yogācāra or Cittamātra. On Tsongkhapa's interpretation of Cittamātra, see, e.g., Thurman, *The Central Philosophy of Tibet;* Hopkins, *Absorption in No External World* and *Emptiness in the Mind-only School of Buddhism;* Sparham, *Ocean of Eloquence.*

1244 *A Dose of Emptiness;* in *Collected Works,* vol. *ka,* 22a3; cf. Cabezón, *Dose of Emptiness,* p. 68. Cabezón reads the verse as Khedrup describing his own opening of the treasury, while Thuken reads it as a reference to the work of Tsongkhapa.

1245 *Collected Works,* vol. *pha,* 1a6; cf. Thurman, *The Central Philosophy of Tibet,* p. 188.

1246 Tsongkhapa, *Prayer of the Virtuous Beginning, Middle, and End;* in *Collected Works,* vol. *kha,* 238a1; cf. Thurman, *Life and Teachings of Tsong Khapa,* p. 93.

1247 *Great Tantra of the Perfectly United;* Toh 381 Kangyur, rgyud, *ga,* chap. 10, 158a3.

1248 We have not traced these views to particular texts or persons, but roughly speaking, the first five represent approaches to meditation typical of Dzokchen and Mahāmudrā, the latter six to scholastic discussions of advanced tantric practices.

1249 There are four qualities of placement meditation *('jog sgom):* abiding on the object, raising the level of mind, tightening the mind, and nonconceptual placement.

1250 *Treasury of Dohas;* Toh 2224 Tengyur, rgyud 'grel, *wi,* 73a4; cf. R. Jackson, *Tantric Treasures,* p. 78.

1251 That is, the clarity side of placement meditation.

1252 That is, when they experience mere torpor *(rmugs pa),* they think it is the meditative fault known as sinking *(bying ba),* while when they experience excitation *('phro ba)* with respect to some object, they believe they are experiencing the meditative fault of distraction *(rgod pa).* Since sinking and distraction are subtler counterparts to the grosser faults and only occur when one has made some progress in concentration meditation, the implication is that these meditators have made no progress at all.

1253 Khedrup Jé, *Entryway to Faith;* in *Collected Works of Tsongkhapa,* vol. *ka,* 28b5.

1254 That is, there is no separation within the great texts of topics fit for study and topics fit for practice.

1255 *Collected Works,* vol. *pa,* 363b3; cf. GT vol. 3, pp. 102–3.

1256 Following K, we read *gso* for *'tsho.*

1257 Tsongkhapa, *Great Treatise on the Stages of the Path to Enlightenment;* in *Collected Works,* vol. *pa,* 363b3; cf. GT vol. 3, p. 103.

1258 *Vajra Garland of Excellent Explanation;* Toh 445 Kangyur, rgyud, *ca,* chap. 65, 271b2.

1259 This section may be interpreted to refer either to Tsongkhapa or to those who followed in his wake, i.e., the Geluk tradition as a whole.

1260 This verse is found in Jamyang Chöjé, *Biography of Tsongkhapa the Great,* p. 632.

1261 This verse is also found in Jamyang Chöjé, *Biography of Tsongkhapa the Great,* p. 632.

1262 See Taktsang Lotsāwa, *Dharma History: Root and Commentary on All Knowledge,* pp. 149–67.

1263 We have not been able to locate this passage in the works of the Fifth Dalai Lama. This may be read as referring either to Tsongkhapa or the Geluk system as a whole.

1264 *Collected Works,* vol. *pha,* 112a6; cf. Thurman, *The Central Philosophy of Tibet,* p. 382.

1265 The completion stage is introduced by the fourth, or *word,* initiation.

1266 On the completion stage, conventional truth is the illusory body, and ultimate truth is the clear-light awareness.

1267 *Hevajra Tantra,* II:12:5; Toh 417 Kangyur, rgyud 'bum, *nga,* 29b7; cf. Farrow and Menon, p. 294.

1268 In other words, what these deluded tantric practitioners take to be a profound understanding of the nature of reality is merely a replication of the fifth stage of meditative absorption, known as *infinite space.* Hence it is a common rather than a tantric attainment, and it involves concentration but not insight.

1269 This involves coordinating the chanting of *oṃ āḥ hūṃ* with the rhythms of the breath.

1270 The three empties are the empty, the very empty, and the greatly empty, which correspond to the experiences of white appearance, red increase, and black near attainment, respectively. These precede the experience of the clear light, which is equated to the all empty; cf. the glossary of enumerations, under *four empties.*

1271 Thuken is here giving Tsongkhapa's explanation of certain aspects of the five stages of the completion stage of the Guhyasamāja tantra tradition: isolated speech, isolated mind, illusory body, clear light, and union. In tantra, the mind is said to "ride" on various subtle physical winds that course through the body in a network of channels. The dissolution of the elements refers to a series of visions that occur at death as each of the body's four elements of earth, water, fire, and wind lose their potency and the mind becomes unhinged from the body, a process that is mimicked in certain tantric visualization practices. For overviews of these processes, see, e.g., Cozort, *Highest Yoga Tantra;* K. Gyatso, *Tantric Grounds and Paths.*

1272 *Guhyasamāja Tantra,* chap. 16; Toh 442 Kangyur, rgyud 'bum, *ca,* 135a3. See, e.g., Broido, "Killing, Lying, Stealing, and Adultery"; Davidson, *Indian Esoteric Buddhism,* chaps. 6–7.

1273 The "other" buddhas are buddhas other than oneself, since it is one's own innate wind and mind that serve as the basis for enlightenment through completion-stage practice.

1274 This association has roots in early Mahayana, where the perfection of wisdom, which is the realization of emptiness, was—much like *sophia* in the West—feminized and divinized as the goddess Prajñāpāramitā.

1275 Tsongkhapa, *Great Treatise on the Stages of Mantra;* in *Collected Works,* vol. *ga,* 306a1. The passage quoted by Tsongkhapa is: Nāgārjuna, *Five Stages,* chap. 64; Toh 1802 Tengyur, rgyud 'bum, *ngi,* 45b3; cf. Thurman, *Essential Tibetan Buddhism,* p. 251.

1276 When the vinaya was restored in Tibet during the second spread of Buddhism, one lineage came from Kashmir to the west (upper Tibet), another from China to the east (lower Tibet). See TR, chap. 3.

1277 See also above, page 232, where the lineage is said to derive from Ra, Kyo, and Nyö (Nyö Gyalwa Lhanangpa, 1164–1224).

1278 Literally, "carrying onto the path" *(lam khyer),* a series of practices which transforms ordinary events and attitudes into vehicles for meditation and realization.

1279 The Tibetan *bde legs* connotes both happiness and goodness, and so has an ethical component, as well.

1280 Thuken is advising his readers to regard all traditions as pure, just as in tantric practice one attempts to see all beings as phenomena in their pure rather than their samsaric aspects.

1281 This is third subdivision within "The History of Philosophical Systems in Tibet, the Land of Snows," the second of the book's five major sections outlined above on page 71.

1282 We might expect Thuken to list the five traditional sutra-level subjects, namely, vinaya, Madhyamaka, valid cognition, abdhidharma, and the perfection of wisdom, and not to list a specific text such as the *Thorough Exposition of Valid Cognition,* but all available editions read: *mdo phyogs la 'dul ba dang/ dbu tshad/ rnam 'grel.*

1283 José Cabezón contributed an early version of the present translation of the chapter. For alternative translations of the chapter, see Das, "Contribution on the Religion, History, etc., of Tibet," vol. L, part 1, (1881), pp. 187–205; Hoffman, *Quellen zur Geschichte der tibetischen Bon-Religion,* pp. 328–38. We have received valuable assistance on our analysis of this chapter from Dan Martin. There is a fine, concise discussion of Thuken's sources for the Bön chapter in his *Unearthing Bon Treasures,* pp. 133–36. Martin notes that, sometimes with and sometimes without attribution, Thuken draws approximately 80 percent of his chapter from other sources. See also E. G. Smith, p. 148.

1284 On Bön in general, see especially the introduction to Kvaerne, *Bön Religion of Tibet.* Also see Tucci, *Religions of Tibet,* chap. 7; Hoffmann, *Religions of Tibet,* chaps I, V; Snellgrove and Richardson, *passim;* Powers, *Introduction to Tibetan Buddhism,* chap. 16; Stein, *Tibetan Civilization,* pp. 229–47; Lopez, *Religions of Tibet in Practice,* chaps. 4, 25, 31; Karmay, *Treasury of Good Sayings;* Snellgrove, *Nine Ways of Bon;* Martin, *Unearthing Bon Treasures.*

1285 On Shenrap, see, e.g., Tandar.

1286 There is no universal agreement on the location of Shangshung, but most sources place it in Ngari, to the west of Mount Kailash.

1287 This is drawn from the *Ornament of Sunlight in the Breach in the Citadel of Secret Mantra,* pp. 5–10.

1288 That is, he prevented lower rebirths.

1289 Desi Sangyé Gyatso, *White Beryl,* vol. 1, p. 227; see Martin, *Unearthing Bon Treasures,* pp. 135–36. The *swastika path* refers to an actual path of painted paper swastikas used to symbolically guide the deceased down the path to enlightenment.

1290 This is one way of classifying Bön teachings and practices: (1) whitewater Bön, concerned with esoteric matters, (2) blackwater Bön, concerned with narratives, magic, funeral rites, and ransom rituals, (3) the Phenyül teaching, concerned with monastic rules and philosophical expositions, and (4) the divine-guide teaching, containing expositions of Dzokchen. The *treasury* contains essential elements of the other doors. See Namdak, p. 142; Snellgrove, *Nine Ways of Bon,* pp. 18–19, 43.

1291 From Shangshung; see Karmay, *Treasury of Good Sayings,* p. 16.

1292 From Sumpa; see Karmay, *Treasury of Good Sayings,* p. 16.

1293 In the ancient times in question, *mi nyag* refers to the Tangut kingdom of Xixia; later, after Tangut immigration to Tibet, it came to refer to a place in Kham.

1294 In Bönpo sources, this is generally spelled *sha ri;* K has *sha ra.*

1295 On these three, see, e.g., Stein, *Tibetan Civilization,* pp. 230–35, Martin, *Unearthing Bon Treasures,* p. 41.

1296 The first king of Tibet, who is dated by some traditional sources to the third century B.C.E. In fact, all dates for kings before Songtsen Gampo are conjectural, so any attempt to date either Nyatri or Tridé is suggestive at best.

1297 The term *gshen* refers to a Bönpo religious officiant, whose functions somewhat resemble those of a priest in Roman Catholicism or a shaman in Altaic societies.

1298 Also known as Ngamshö Bön *(ngam bshod bon);* see Martin, *Unearthing Bon Treasures,* p. 187.

1299 The entire paragraph up until this point is a direct citation of Wön Sherap Jungné's *Textbook on the Single Intention;* see Martin, *Unearthing Bon Treasures,* esp. chapters 13–14. Chapter 14 includes a complete translation of the text (pp. 183–99). This passage is translated on pp. 187–88.

1300 See Nebesky-Wojkowitz, pp. 300–303.

1301 See Das, "Contribution," vol. L, part 1, pp. 196–98n8. This threefold list is cited directly from the *Textbook on the Single Intention;* cf. the translation at Martin, *Unearthing Bon Treasures,* p. 189.

1302 Or Shenrap Miwo; cf. Martin, *Unearthing Bon Treasures,* p. 191.

1303 A knife funeral *(gri shid)* is a funeral rite for someone who has suffered an untimely and/or violent death; see Martin, *Unearthing Bon Treasures,* p. 191n24.

1304 According to Bön, he was the first king not to climb the spirit ladder back to heaven, having been tricked into cutting it. Therefore, he needed to be buried.

1305 See Martin, *Unearthing Bon Treasures,* p. 191n25.

1306 *Ju thig.* See Hoffmann, *Religions of Tibet,* p. 105: "The oracle is consulted by means of colored ribbons, and the answers come through exclamations uttered in a shamanistic trance and are regarded as being inspired by the gods and spirits." *Ju thig* are, however, more properly strings or cords.

1307 The entire paragraph up to this point is taken from the *Textbook on the Single Intention;* cf. Martin, *Unearthing Bon Treasures,* pp. 191–92.

1308 That is, Īśvaravādins or Śaivas.

1309 See Martin, *Unearthing Bon Treasures,* pp. 192–93.

1310 See the extensive discussion of this figure in Martin, *Unearthing Bon Treasures,* pp. 40–80.

1311 *Gtan la dbab pa,* a class of texts related to the codification of scripture after the death of the Buddha; see Martin, *Unearthing Bon Treasures,* pp. 43n7, 186n5.

1312 A treasure text; see Martin, *Unearthing Bon Treasures,* p. 43n8.

1313 The entire section up until this point is taken from the *Textbook on the Single Intention,* though mostly in the form of loose paraphrases, and with considerable abridgment; cf. the translation at Martin, *Unearthing Bon Treasures,* p. 192–97.

1314 See Martin, *Unearthing Bon Treasures,* p. 44n11.

1315 See, e.g., the discussion and references in Kvaerne, "Literature of Bon"; this sentence is taken straight from the Geluk author Chenga Lodrö Gyaltsen's *Treatise on Nyingma and Bön*. For a translation, see Martin, *Unearthing Bon Treasures*, pp. 131–33.

1316 The entire list that follows in the next six paragraphs (i.e., up through that on guardian deities) is taken—though sometimes with abbreviations or paraphrases—from the *Textbook on the Single Intention,* pp. 5–10.

1317 Though literally referring to a hundred thousand, the Tibetan *'bum* also stands in for an unspecified very large number.

1318 The last four listed here are the Bön equivalents of the four tantras *(rgyud bzhi)* of Tibetan medical tradition.

1319 Perhaps related to the four tantric activities: pacifying, increasing, empowering, and destroying; or, according to Hoffmann, *Religions of Tibet,* pp. 105–6, related to the practices of the first four of the Bön vehicles.

1320 Following K, we read *'dur thabs* for *shi thabs.*

1321 *Srog gi sag gdar.*

1322 The Red and Black Razor *(spu gri dmar nag)* are manifestations of the deity Takla Mebar. See Karmay, *Treasury of Good Sayings*, p. 46n.

1323 See Nebesky-Wojkowitz, pp. 267–73.

1324 See Nebesky-Wojkowitz, p. 277.

1325 See Nebesky-Wojkowitz, p. 281.

1326 See Snellgrove, *Nine Ways of Bon,* p. 297.

1327 This is our tentative translation for: *ro ku shag pa sbyang rgyug than gyi skor.*

1328 This sentence is taken from Chenga, with Thuken's own additions. The activities *(las)* may be those of pacifying, increasing, empowering, and destroying.

1329 According to Martin (*Unearthing Bon Treasures,* p. 195n40) the correct form of this is *sa trig er sangs.*

1330 Contra Z and S *(sad),* as well as K *(sang),* this should read *sangs*. See Martin, *Unearthing Bon Treasures*, p. 195n43, for a discussion of the term.

1331 All editions read *'a me nyid,* but the term is more commonly rendered *'a mo nyid.* Emptiness is *stong pa nyid.*

1332 The first seven examples in this list are drawn from the *Textbook on the Single Intention;* the remaining ones probably come from the *Ornament of Sunlight.*

1333 Cited in Drigung Jikten Sumgön, *Forty Statements on the Holy Dharma of the Single Intention;* in *Collected Works,* vol. 1, 20b2. On Jikten Sumgön's outlook on Bön, see Martin, *Unearthing Bon Treasures,* pp. 176–82.

1334 Drigung Jikten Sumgön, *Forty Statements on the Holy Dharma of the Single Intention;* in *Collected Works,* vol. 1, 20b2.

1335 Despite the reference to Drigung Jikten Gönpo, much of the preceding is taken directly from or based upon the *Textbook on the Single Intention,* whose authorship Thuken probably did not know; cf. Martin, *Unearthing Bon Treasures,* p. 190.

1336 According to Martin (*Unearthing Bon Treasures,* p. 131n20), "this text is most commonly referred to as the *Gzer-mig,* the two-volume version of the life of Teacher Shenrab."

1337 Following K, we read *zhen* for *zhan.*

1338 Following K, we read *gsal dangs* for *gsol drangs.*

1339 Chenga Lodrö Gyaltsen, *Presentation of Nyingma and Bön;* in *Collected Works,* vol. *ca,* 4b1. In Chenga's text, there is a considerable amount of other material between the beginning of the citation and the section quoted by Thuken; see Martin, *Unearthing Bon Treasures,* pp. 131, 132.

1340 See Martin, *Unearthing Bon Treasures,* p. 116.

1341 See, e.g., Taktsang Lotsāwa Sherap Rinchen, *Dharma History: Root and Commentary on All Knowledge,* p. 68; c.f. Martin, *Unearthing Bon Treasures,* pp. 144–47.

1342 *Ornament of Sunlight,* pp. 376–85.

1343 See, e.g., Snellgrove, *Nine Ways of Bon;* Tucci, *Religions of Tibet,* pp. 228–29. Sometimes the nine are referred to as *shen (gshen),* but more often they are considered *vehicles (theg pa).*

1344 In most lists, the white *a* and the sage are reversed; even Thuken reverses them later in the same section.

1345 This paragraph is drawn directly from the *Ornament of Sunlight,* p. 41.

1346 Or perhaps the four *doors* of chanting, if *sgo* be read in preference to *sgom.* Cf. Tucci, *Religions of Tibet,* p. 228.

1347 *Lta byang rdzu 'phrul.* This may relate to destroying the wrong views of enemies and purifying the circumstances of sentient beings and thereby establishing the doctrine and suppressing false views through ritual; see Snellgrove, *Nine Ways of Bon,* p. 99. Hoffmann (*Religions of Tibet,* p. 106) suggests it is related to four ways of arranging burial places.

1348 Snellgrove, *Nine Ways of Bon,* p. 18.

1349 Snellgrove (*Nine Ways of Bon,* p. 261) says this person corresponds to a Buddhist in the śrāvaka vehicle.

1350 See Snellgrove, *Nine Ways of Bon,* pp. 18 and 139.

1351 Snellgrove (*Nine Ways of Bon,* p. 261) says the last three vehicles constitute the tantric path; the ninth is Bönpo Dzokchen.

1352 The purity or impurity of both the subject and object.

1353 These are equivalent to the four stages of the path of preparation; they are on a conceptual level because they are not yet seen directly.

1354 The preceding two paragraphs are paraphrased from the *Ornament of Sunlight,* pp. 49–53.

1355 That is, in the *Textbook on the Single Intention.*

1356 Actually, Thuken seems to have drawn on this text for his material on view and meditation, but, as noted above, from the *Textbook on the Single Intention* for his account of the nine vehicles.

1357 Perhaps what is now Tajikistan, at the eastern reaches of the cultural sphere of Persia.

1358 This is not the Ganden Monastery founded near Lhasa by Tsongkhapa but a much later Geluk institution founded on the ruins of a Bönpo monastery.

1359 Das's translation ("Contribution," vol. L, part 1, p. 205) adds here: "The Gonparituo of Kham contains 500 priests. Formerly the Bönpo had no monastic system. Now after the example of the Buddhists they have monks and nuns, some of whom have pretensions to incarnate existence. But in general they are great drinkers of wine and eaters of meat. They are not careful to refrain from female company." This passage is not found in any of the editions consulted for this translation, and seems to be an editorial interpolation, though by whom is not clear. We surmise that "Gonparituo" is a phonetic spelling of *dgon pa ri khrod,* referring to Ritrö Monastery, an important Bön center in Kham.

1360 The following verses, made up quatrains of nine-syllable lines, have as their major conceit repetition of certain words. In each of the first two quatrains, the same word begins each line: in the first *chos* (dharma), and in the second *bon*. The third through fifth quatrains employ repetitions of certain words (either directly linked or separated by several syllables), e.g., *tshe* ("when" and "life"), *su* ("at" and "who"), etc. None of these patterns can be adequately captured in English.

1361 The original translation and annotation of this and the following chapter were prepared by Michael Sweet and Leonard Zwilling, who would like to extend their thanks to Martin Amster for his assistance. For a rough translation of this chapter, see Das, "Contribution on the Religion, History, etc. of Tibet," vol. LI, part 1, no. 2 (1882), pp. 99–114.

1362 The history of *chos,* or the Buddhadharma, is the subject of the next chapter. Daoism had long been associated with Bön by the Tibetans, who believed Laozi, the founder of Daoism, to be the founder of Bön as well, under the name of Miwo Shenrap. Using Bön to designate the Daoist tradition would have suggested to the Tibetan reader that Daoism played the same role when Buddhism was introduced to China as Bön had in Tibet, that is, as a hostile antagonist; this is exactly how Thuken portrays "the indigenous Bön" in the following chapter. The association of the Veda with China, as improbable as it might seem, was already of long standing before Thuken; see Döndam Mawai Sengé, p. 418ff. We surmise that the equation of Confucianism with the Veda lies in the fact that both of these traditions were regarded as the bases of their respective cultures. According to Mala ("A Mahayanist Rewriting of the History of China," pp. 151–54), the metaphor of the three luminaries *(sanguang)*—used not only by Thuken but by his predecessors Gönpo Kyap and Sumpa Khenpo—derives through intermediate sources from a Sui dynasty Buddhist layman, Li Shiqian (523–88).

1363 The distinction between "Cīna" and "Mahācīna" is an old one and was drawn both by Indian authors and Tibetans. On the basis of inscriptional and literary evidence, Cīna originally referred to the area of what is now western Tibet; see Tucci, *Preliminary Report on Two Scientific Expeditions in Nepal,* pp. 103–4. Some later Tibetan authors maintained the distinction—for example, Sumpa Khenpo, who introduces his chapter on the origin of Buddhism in China by saying that he will describe how Buddhism came "to China and Great China." Thuken, however, uses "China" and "Great China" interchangeably.

1364 Following K, we read *shen ṭe'u* for *she'u na ṭe.*

1365 Videha *(lus 'phags),* or Pūrvavideha, is the eastern continent, the second of the four principal continents according to the geography of the abhidharma; see *Treasury of Abhidharma,* 3:53b–55d.

1366 See Mala, "A Mahayanist Rewriting," pp. 151–54.

1367 *Ru,* literally "scholar," is the traditional Chinese term for the Confucian tradition or, as it came to be called by eighteenth-century Europeans, Confucianism.

1368 The use of *jing* to designate Chinese Buddhism here (and at the beginning of the next chapter) presents a problem: this is not one of the standard terms used by the Chinese themselves for Buddhism, such as Fojiao or Shijiao. It may be that Thuken is referring to the Chinese word *jing,* meaning pure or clear. This is used in many Buddhist Chinese compounds, including the name of the Pure Land school *(jingjia),* but not in reference to Buddhism as a whole. What Thuken may have done here is give the Chinese translation of the first half of the Tibetan word for Buddha (the *sangs* in *sangs rgyas*), which means "pure." This is analogous to the Chinese use of the first syllable of the Chinese transcription of Śākyamuni, *shi,* to refer to the religion (Shijiao or Shimen). In the Chinese translation of Thuken, Liu sometimes renders *jing* as *shi* (e.g., p. 206), although at other times he substitutes *fo,* the standard Chinese term for Buddha.

1369 Anu is another name for Thönmi Sambhota.

1370 Anu, *The Thirty;* Toh 4348 Tengyur, sna tshogs, *co,* 160b2.

1371 While it is the case that *ru* does mean "letter," "letters" would be more accurate, for what is meant by *ru* is "belle lettres, literature, letters." Thönmi uses *yi ge* when he means a written graph. Thuken, however, from his comment about "reading and writing letters," apparently understood *ru* in Thönmi's terms as an actual "letter." But he did know *ru* in the traditional Confucian sense of "literature," as is clear from his discussion of the four textbooks; see below, p. 334.

1372 That is, Veda *(rig byed).*

1373 Said traditionally to have lived from 2952 to 2836 B.C.E. or from 2852 to 2737 B.C.E.

1374 The terms for the six types of characters are, in order, *xiangxing* (Tib. *dbyibs gzugs*), *zhishi (dmigs gsal), huiyi (dngos bstan), xingsheng (zung 'jug), zhuanzhu ('phrul shes),* and *jiajie (sgra sbyor);* see Xie.

1375 For "regular style" and "running script" Thuken employs the words for Tibetan "head letters" *(gzab ma)* and "headless letters" *(gshar ma),* respectively.

1376 This whole discussion on the origin of writing closely covers the same ground, employing the same Tibetan name forms, as in Gönpo Kyap. On the six types of characters, Gönpo Kyap quotes a verse employing the same terminology and in the same order as Thuken; see Gönpo Kyap, pp. 417–19.

1377 It appears that Gönpo Kyap (p. 421) ascribes this possibly apocryphal work to the Yellow Emperor, but Thuken agrees with Sumpa Khenpo (p. 93).

1378 All editions have *ming 'dogs,* but we believe *mi 'dogs* better conveys the sense of the passage.

1379 Thuken transliterates the "correct" Chinese pronunciation of Confucius as *khung tse* and the "incorrect" Tibetan pronunciation as *kong tse.* In pinyin, the transcription of the contemporary Mandarin pronunciation of Confucius is Kongzi.

1380 Kongtse is an important figure for the Bönpos, who, however, hotly contest the Buddhist view that seeks to identify Kongtse with Kongzi; they regard this as an error made by Changkya Rölpai Dorjé, and by Thuken in particular.

1381 Zhu Xi was the great Song dynasty synthesizer of "neo-Confucianism," which incorporated Buddhist and Daoist philosophical and psychological conceptions into a reformed Confucian system. See Chan, pp. 588–653.

1382 Literally, "calculation" *(rtsis).*

1383 *Spor thang.* Thuken (or his source) may have confused *thang,* "scroll painting on cloth" (on which materials from the *Classic of Changes* would have been displayed) with *thang,* the conventional spelling for the Tang dynasty. From occurrences of *spor thang* elsewhere in Thuken's text, he is clearly using it to mean the *Classic of Changes,* though this leads him into an anachronism when he writes later on of the three early (pre-Tang) commentaries on *Thang Changes* rather than the *Classic of Changes.* He also writes that his teacher, Changkya, talked about commenting on the *Classic of Changes*, which title Thuken employs, and not *Thang Changes.*

1384 Tradition assigns the former to the fourth millennium B.C.E. and the latter to the third millennium B.C.E., but there is no real historical backing for these assignments.

1385 Thuken erroneously ascribes this work to Fu Xi; tradition ascribes it to the time of the Xia dynasty, traditionally 2205–1766 B.C.E.

1386 The ten roots, that is, *tian gan* or "heavenly stems," and twelve branches, or *di zhi,* "earthly branches."

1387 This entire section on Yi Xuan Shi is found nearly verbatim at Gönpo Kyap, p. 421, including the unglossed Chinese for armillary sphere, chiming clock, watch, and pitch pipe.

1388 Liu gives *duo* for *shi.*

1389 This is also Thuken's birth year. This passage is virtually identical to those at Gönpo Kyap, p. 423, and Sumpa Khenpo, p. 94.

1390 Although the hexagrams themselves of the early and later heavenly systems are the same, their orientation to the points of the compass and their numerological values differ in the two systems. Both the *Hetu* and the *Luoshu* are best described as numerological charts rather than books.

1391 Contrary to Thuken, Chinese tradition asserts that it is precisely the books on divination that Qin Shihuang exempted from burning, believing them to have practical utility, unlike the Confucian texts on social ethics, which were burned.

1392 Thuken's rationalist critique of traditional Tibetan accounts of the history of Chinese divination is an attack on the Nyingmapas, among whom such accounts originated, and upon Desi Sangyé Gyatso, who repeated them in his *White Beryl;* see Macdonald, pp. 74–75.

1393 The Bönpos believe that the Buddhists regard the four tantras as a translation from the Chinese; see Karmay, *Treasury of Good Sayings,* p. 24.

1394 *Shao* is not a treatise on music, but the style of music composed by Yi Xuan Shi, the "Yellow Emperor," which involved dancers, singers, and instrumentalists, and for that reason may have been regarded as the ancestor of the Chinese opera.

1395 The term we have translated as "model individual" is *tshad ma'i skyes bu,* which in other contexts is an epithet of the Buddha as the "authoritative person." This passage is a paraphrase of a well-known section from the *Liehzi,* a Daoist classic written ca. 300 C.E. The original passage refers only to a sage from the west, presumably referring to Laozi, although this was referred to by later Buddhist and Christian apologists as presaging their saviors; see Graham, pp. 78–79.

1396 Throughout this chapter, Thuken utilizes the Chinese term *heshang*, referring to a bhikṣu. It is the same term used to refer to the Chinese participant at the Samyé debate, Heshang Mahāyāna.

1397 The earliest great Chinese pilgrim to India; see Ch'en, pp. 89–92.

1398 The translation here is purely conjectural.

1399 Literally "had the features of a face and hands."

1400 For Zhu Xi's discussion of this subject, see Chan, pp. 644–46. Zhu Xi generally follows the argument given here, although *hun* and *po* are considered as single entities, and not divided into threefold and sixfold as here.

1401 The Jade Emperor was considered the head of the Daoist popular pantheon from the Song dynasty onward. See Little, pp. 170–71.

1402 Thuken gives a rather loose translation of the beginning of the *Great Learning.* Following Legge (pp. 308–10), the Chinese reads: "The way of great learning is in illuminating illustrious virtue, in renovating the people, and resting in the greatest good. Knowing when to rest, then one has certainty, having certainty then one is able to be calm, being quiet one is later able to have peace, having peace one is later able to have deliberation, having deliberation one is later able to attain. Things have their root and branch, affairs have their beginning and end. Knowing what is first and last, then one is close to the Way."

1403 These represent degrees of scholastic attainment within the Geluk tradition of monastic education.

1404 In fact, Zhufuxi, or Zhu Xi, while very indebted to Buddhist philosophy, was a powerful critic of Buddhism as an institution.

1405 This is probably a reference to Zhou Dunyi (1017–73), the great predecessor of Zhu Xi and the Neo-Confucian school. He was very much influenced by Daoism and the *Classic of Changes,* but is not particularly known as a critic of Buddhism; see Chan, pp. 460–80.

1406 This is similar to many Confucian critiques of Buddhism; see for example that of Cheng Hao, in *Sources of Chinese Tradition,* vol. 1, p. 697.

1407 Sakya Pandita, *Well-Spoken Advice from Sakya;* in *Collected Works,* in *Sa skya pa'i bka' 'bum,* vol. *na,* 106a4.

1408 During the latter Han dynasty, from the middle of the second century C.E., the deified Laozi was credited with a number of incarnations, later reaching the number eighty-one, including the Buddha. This is found in an apocryphal anti-Buddhist polemic, *Classic of Laozi's Conversion of the Barbarians (Laozi Huahu Jing);* see Kaltenmark, pp. 109–10; Little, pp. 91, 163, 174–76.

1409 We think Thuken (or the copyists or carvers) reversed the two syllables, as the text reads *shyan sheng*, which would be equivalent to *xian sheng.*

1410 Actually, Laojun was often held to be subordinate to Yuanshi Tianzun, the Celestial Venerable of the Primordial Beginning, as his emanation or disciple; see Kaltenmark, pp. 112–13; Little, pp. 228–29, 231.

1411 That is, the five sacred peaks *(wuyue):* Wutai Shan in the east, Hua Shan in the west, Nan Heng Shan in the south, Bei Heng Shan in the north, and Song Shan in the center; see Little, pp. 17, 147–48, 359.

1412 Following K, we read *lha'i* for *bla'i.*

1413 Although all editions have *sā dung,* the appropriate Tibetan equivalent of the Chinese is *ba dung.*

1414 This refers to Zhang Daoling, first Celestial Master *(tianshi),* a Taoist hermit who proclaimed himself a Celestial Master in 142 C.E. and founded the influential school called the Way of the Celestial Masters *(Tianshi Dao);* see Little, pp. 41–42.

1415 Following K, we read *ring lugs* for *rang lugs.*

1416 Liu (p. 332n1383) amends Thuken here to "in the time of Yao of Jin," considering "Han" to be a mistake, as the king mentioned following this, Yao Xiang, was the founder of the Latter Jin dynasty, taking power in 384 C.E. See Zürcher, pp. 111–12.

1417 *Tho dkar* may refer to the land of the Tokharians, the easternmost speakers of an Indo-European language, who settled in the Tarim Basin in what is now Xinjiang.

1418 For parallels see Sumpa Khenpo (who has additional information), p. 106, and Gönpo Kyap, p. 461.

1419 This probably refers to Genghis's conquest of the western border regions of China in 1219.

1420 Literally, "Western Ocean." This is a toponym that first referred to coastal Southeast Asia and was extended during the Ming and early Qing to include the Indian Ocean and Europe; see Wilkinson, p. 695. For Gönpo Kyap (p. 410), it is said to be in "the western region" *(nub phyogs).*

1421 Thuken's wording is nearly identical to that of Gönpo Kyap, p. 461. Gönpo Kyap, like Sumpa Khenpo (p. 102)—and unlike Thuken—includes this story of the teacher from Xiyang in his account of the precursors of Buddhism. On the basis of what follows it would appear that Islam is the religion referred to, yet *tianzhu* is the common Chinese designation for Christianity; note that Genghis Khan's mother was a Nestorian Christian, so perhaps there has been some confusion here. The conflation of Islam with the other Western monotheisms was not uncommon, at least as late as the early seventeenth century (from which Thuken's sources may date); see Spence, pp. 95–120.

1422 In the section on Shambhala; the reference here is to the destruction of Islam by the last kalkin of Shambhala, as predicted in the Kālacakra literature.

1423 For a rough translation of this chapter (up through the first paragraph of the section on Chan), see Das, "Contribution on the Religion, History, etc. of Tibet," vol. LI, part 1, no. 2, pp. 87–99.

1424 Thuken has modeled his treatment of Chinese Buddhism up to his discussion of the introduction of Tibetan Buddhism on part 2 of Gönpo Kyap's *History of Buddhism in China;* see especially the verse summary at the conclusion of part two, pp. 547–51. On Gönpo Kyap and his history, see Vostrikov, pp. 166–67, and the works of Mala.

1425 The doctrine of universal love *(jianai)* is a hallmark of Moism; however, the Buddhist doctrine of the intrinsic purity of mind attributed to him here is more characteristic of the thought of Mencius.

1426 Liehzi is a figure of doubtful historicity; the earliest parts of the book that bears his name may date to the third century B.C.E.; see Graham, p. 1.

1427 This is the same passage from Liehzi quoted in the previous section; see Graham, pp. 78–79. We have used Graham's translation of this passage, except for the last phrase, which is apocryphal. The Western sage presumably refers to Laozi, although it was later used by Buddhist (and Christian) apologists (Graham, p. 79).

1428 This is one of the most famous passages from the eponymous *Zhuangzi,* in chapter 2. See Watson, p. 45.

1429 For an overview of Geluk religious historians' knowledge of Christianity, see Sweet, "Jesus the World-Protector."

1430 Note the way in which Thuken suggests that a variety of non-Buddhist teachers who preceded Buddhism in China are somehow a product of the Buddha's miraculous activity. It is unclear whether Thuken believed Jesus to have visited China. According to historians, Christianity probably arrived in China no earlier than the seventh century, at least half a millennium after Buddhism, though it is possible that Jesus was known earlier through other sources.

1431 Zhao's date of accession to the throne traditionally is given as 1052 B.C.E., which would make this date 1026 B.C.E. The Zhou chronology is, however, uncertain.

1432 At present, the significance of this year to Thuken is unclear.

1433 Presumably the year in which Thuken was writing or dictating this section.

1434 Successor to King Zhao, whose date of accession traditionally is given as 1001 B.C.E.

1435 This date would correspond to 947 B.C.E, though the Chinese generally assign the final nirvana to 949 B.C.E. We have been unable to find the source of this passage.

1436 *Great Nirvana Sutra;* Toh 120 Kangyur, mdo sde, *tha,* chap. 11, 143a4.

1437 Tibetan: *mu dbang* (*dbang* = Ch. *wang,* "king").

1438 On this legend, see Zürcher, p. 22.

1439 The text simply has *grub mtha'* (philosophical system), but the reference clearly is to the whole of the Buddha's Dharma.

1440 Neither Sumpa Khenpo nor Gönpo Kyap identifies the meeting place. Lü and Liu (the latter perhaps following the former) identify it as Yue Zhi; in this, they are following some of the many differing accounts of the mission.

1441 Recall that in a Chinese context Thuken identifies Bönpos with Daoists.

1442 The original source of this poem appears to be the preface to the *Sutra in Forty-two Sections* (Taisho no. 784), where it is uttered by the two pandits, not the king; on this sutra, see Sharf, in Lopez, *Religions of China in Practice,* pp. 360–71.

1443 Following K, we read *a sho ka* for *a shwa ka.*

1444 According to Zürcher (pp. 29–30), it is unclear as to whether this was truly a work with a Sanskrit original or a Chinese compilation, although its original content clearly derives from a Hinayana source.

1445 This was An Shigao, the eminent early Parthian translator. See Liu, p. 333n1391; Zürcher, p. 23; Ch'en, pp. 43–44.

1446 An Indian teacher in the state of Wei; see Zürcher, p. 50.

1447 Or Kang Senghui, the son of a Sogdian merchant, who was born in southern China; see Zürcher, pp. 23, 36, 13ff.

1448 A scholar and translator of Scythian descent; see Zürcher, pp. 23–24ff.

1449 This was the famous Kumārajīva, whose name appears in Tibetan historiography as Kumāraśrī.

1450 This is likely *Huangshi,* one of the reign titles *(nianhao)* of the Latter Qin emperor Yao Xing (366–416), Kumārajīva's patron; see Ch'en, pp. 81–83.

1451 In Lü's text, but unaccountably not in Liu's translation, the Hva shang Ce'u of the Tibetan is identified as Seng Zhao, Kumārajīva's chief disciple and renowned master of Madhyamaka thought; see Ch'en, pp. 86–88, Feng, vol. 2, pp. 258–70.

1452 Thuken gives the Sanskrit in Tibetan transliteration, but he errs: it should be Buddhayaśas.

1453 Amoghavajra arrived during the reign of Emperor Xuanzong (713–55); see Ch'en pp. 335–36. *Minghuang,* "illustrious emperor," is an abbreviation of his posthumous title: *zhidao dasheng daming jiao huangdi* (Emperor Great Sage of the Supreme Path of the Great Illustrious Teaching).

1454 Although Dānarakṣita's dates are uncertain, most accounts place him in the eighth or ninth century, hence during the Tang rather than the Song.

1455 Following K, we read *thang pa* for *thang sang.*

1456 The "Tang monk" is how Xuanzang was known in the fictionalized account of his pilgrimages, Wu Chengen's *Journey to the West [Xiyou ji],* and this became his usual appellation. See Liu, p. 334n1402.

1457 *Dul ba bzang po.* Thuken's Tibetan does not allow any other reconstruction, but it is clearly a mistake, as Xuanzang's teacher is well known to have been Śīlabhadra (see Ch'en, p. 236), which in Tibetan would be *tshul khrims bzang po.* Inexplicably, Sumpa Khenpo, p. 120 also has *dul bzang,* as does Gönpo Kyap, p. 523. Gönpo Kyap should certainly have known the correct name, as he translated Xuanzang's account of his travels, the *Xiyou ji,* into Tibetan.

1458 According to Gönpo Kyap, p. 526, a Mādhyamika; the scholiast notes that he is the same as Seng bzang or Siṃhabhadra.

1459 Another name of Haravardhana.

1460 This Kumāra, the king of Kāmarūpa, commissioned a Sanskrit translation of the *Daodejing* through some Chinese envoys who had made it known to him; it was executed by Xuanzang. Unfortunately, it has not survived; see Pelliot, pp. 384–85.

1461 A *betweener* is one who has taken lay vows but has yet to take novice vows.

1462 According to Liu (p. 334n1406) this refers to Zhiyi (531–97), the founder of the Tiantai school, although he could not have been a pupil of Xuanzang.

1463 Liu states (p. 334n1407) that this school *(shenguan)*—also known as the Dharmatā *(faxing)* or Emptiness *(kong)* school—has two divisions in China, Tiantai and Huayan, and that the Madhyamaka or Sanlun (Three-Treatise) school is also reckoned as part of this division.

1464 Lü identifies Ye shes dpal as possibly the Sanlun master Jizang (549–623), whereas Liu (p. 334n1408) believes he is Huiwen, one of the predecessors of the Tiantai school (see Ch'en, p. 303). While Huiwen is closer to the Tibetan Ye shes dpal than is Jizang—which isn't close at all—Jizang better fits the context.

1465 According to Liu (p. 334n1409) this refers to Wendi (r. 560–67) and Houzhu (r. 583–87) of the Chen dynasty, one of the Five Dynasties of the Period of Division; it was located in southern China.

1466 The *Sutra of the Ornamented Tree* period corresponds to the Huayan school, and the Deer Park period to the Hinayana sutras or *āgamas.* The *Sutra of the Ornamented Tree* forms a portion of the *Flower Ornament Sutra,* though they also are reckoned separately at times.

1467 The eleventh lunar month.

1468 This was Zhiyi's successor, Zhangan Guanding; see Liu, p. 334n1411.

1469 Fahua was the name of a monastery. The venerable Wei is Zhiwei (d. 680), the third Tiantai patriarch (Liu, p. 334n1411).
1470 This refers to the fourth Tiantai patriarch, Huiwei; see Liu, p. 334n1412.
1471 Zuoqi (Eastern Spring) is a place name; Xuanlang was the fifth Tiantai patriarch (Liu, p. 334n1413).
1472 Jingqi (Thorny Spring) is a place name, the site of a monastery; Ven. Jingqi refers to Zhanran (711–82), a great Tiantai teacher of the period.
1473 Fashun or Dushun was the earliest exponent of the Huayan school (Liu, p. 335n1416); see Ch'en, p. 314.
1474 Yunhua was the temple in which Zhiyan preached the *Flower Ornament Sutra* (Ch'en, p. 314).
1475 He systematized the Huayan doctrines and is usually considered the real founder of this school; see Chen, pp. 314–15.
1476 He was the fourth patriarch of the Huayan; see Ch'en, p. 315; Liu, p. 335n1419.
1477 Zongmi was the fifth patriarch of the Huayan school; see Liu, p. 335n1420; Ch'en, p. 316; Gregory.
1478 Changkya Rölpai Dorjé, *Song in Praise of the Five-Peaked Mountain;* in *Collected Works,* vol. *nga,* 3a4.
1479 This is the *Huayan Gangyao.*
1480 Perhaps this is his *Shi Song (Collected Verses).*
1481 Perhaps his *Huayan Fajie Xuanjing.*
1482 Probably the *Xuanjing Denglun.*
1483 Probably the *Ru Putidao Cidi Wumen.*
1484 Gönpo Kyap calls it Tsung Men (p. 504). This may be an abbreviated reference to one of the synonyms for the Chan school, namely the mind or Buddha-mind school ([Fo]xin zong).
1485 Alternatively, Śanavāsika.
1486 Following K, we read *dhi ti ka* for *dhi dhi ka.*
1487 Alternatively, Madhyāntika.
1488 Following K, we read *dhi ta ka* for *dhi dhi ka.*
1489 Following K, we read *su na sha da* for *pu na sha da.*
1490 Following K, we read *a shwa bha ka* for *a sho bha ka.*
1491 More commonly known as Bodhidharma.
1492 This is just one of a number of possible enumerations of the twenty-eight patriarchs. For a variant list, see, e.g., D. T. Suzuki, *Zen Buddhism,* p. 60.
1493 Historically, at that time in the north, the Northern Wei was the ruling dynasty; while they were not Han, neither were they Huige (Uyghur).
1494 That is, the Yantgze.
1495 On the story of Bodhidharma, Thuken covers the same ground as Gönpo Kyap, pp. 504–7. Note that Gönpo Kyap does not remark on Bodhidharma's representation in art. The theme of the single sandal is common in saints' lives; see Dumoulin, *A History of Zen Buddhism,* pp. 68–69.
1496 In Japan, these are the Rinzai and Soto schools, respectively.
1497 Thuken follows Gönpo Kyap, p. 550, here, but a Gung Yöl of the Tang dynasty cannot be identified; according to Sumpa Khenpo, p. 132, the triple division of the Buddhadharma dates from the later Tang dynasty.
1498 It is interesting to note that nowhere in Thuken's account is the Pure Land school mentioned, despite its great antiquity, importance, and popularity in China.

1499 Following K and TBRC, we read *bkra shis dpal ldan* for *dpal ldan bkra shis.*

1500 Thuken routinely refers to the Manchu emperors by their Chinese dynastic titles. Until this point, he has called all the rulers of China *rgyal po,* or "king." With the Qing rulers, however, all are styled *gong ma,* or "emperor." It also should be noted that, throughout his treatment of Chinese religions, Thuken usually incorporates the titles of king *(wang)* or emperor *(huangdi)* along with the ruler's name, but additionally prefaces the Chinese name and title with Tibetan *rgyal po* or *gong ma,* e.g., "Emperor Shizu Huangdi," i.e., literally, "the emperor *(gong ma)* Emperor *(huangdi)* Shizu."

1501 Now called Liaoning.

1502 The embassy to Mukden took place in 1642. The rulership was actually in the hands of the regent Dorgön, the emperor being but a small child.

1503 Li Zicheng, who was born 1606, led a major revolt against the Ming and occupied Beijing in 1644; see Roberts, vol. 1, pp. 198, 200, 203–4. In calling Li the pejorative "bandit king," Thuken was following the official historiological line of the Qing, given in the Qing annals (see Ahmad, *Sino-Tibetan Relations in the Seventeenth Century,* p. 16), where they portray themselves as the saviors of China from banditry.

1504 The last of the Ming emperors.

1505 *Mun ten.* This form for Mukden also appears in the Tibetan version of the quadrilingual Imperial Edict of 1721 in Lhasa; see Richardson, *Ch'ing Dynasty Inscriptions at Lhasa,* pp. 11, 13.

1506 This "mountain," actually a hill, was renamed Jingshan (Prospect Mountain) during the Qing. As the place where the last Ming emperor had committed suicide, the site was considered dangerous, so it was geomantically stabilized by the erection of temples; see Naquin, pp. 309–10. As in the case of rulers where the Tibetan equivalent is also given along with the Chinese title, the same is true for topographic terms; here we have "on top of the mountain Mount Jing," as if one were to write "on top of the mountain Mont Blanc."

1507 *Lha khang ser po,* in Chinese, *huangsi.* This famous temple was founded in 1652 to accommodate the Fifth Dalai Lama.

1508 Whether this refers to the lama-adept or to the Panchen Lama, who sent him, is not clear. Most probably the Panchen is meant.

1509 *Tham ka bla ma.*

1510 These two men were instrumental in bringing the Mongols under Qing rule, Neichi Toyon, also known as Bogdo Gegen, in Inner Mongolia, and Losang Tenpai Gyaltsen, the First Jetsundampa, in Outer Mongolia.

1511 The Fifth Dalai Lama's visit to Beijing took place in 1653; Ahmad, *A History of Tibet by Ṅag-dBaṅ Blo-bZaṅ rGya-mTsho,* p. 39.

1512 The highest Tibetan Buddhist rank in China.

1513 Perhaps the Perfection and Secret Mantra vehicles of Mahayana.

1514 As with the other titles, this one too is found spelled variously, e.g., *no mon han.* This is actually *nom un qagan,* the Mongolian translation of Tibetan *chos kyi rgyal po* or Sanskrit *dharmarāja.*

1515 This is the famous Yong He Gong founded in 1743 by Qianlong. It had been his father's personal residence.

1516 This is a reference to the Nepalese incursions of 1788 and the war of 1792–93, in which Chinese armies defeated the invaders. That victory marked the zenith of Manchu military power.

1517 *Bogdo* is from the Mongolian *bogda,* "holy one, master." The core ethnic group of the people who later became known as Manchus were the Jurchid, who ruled northern China in the twelfth century under the name of Jin.

1518 The original translation and annotation of the section on Mongolia was prepared by Leonard Zwilling. For an earlier translation, see Das, "Contribution on the Religion, History, etc. of Tibet," vol. LI, part 1, no. 1 (1882), pp. 58–75.

1519 Hor and Sog in narrowly restricted senses refer respectively to the eastern Mongols of Manchuria and Inner Mongolia, and the western Mongols in the rest of the Mongol lands. Tibetan historians customarily use *Hor* almost exclusively when writing about the Yuan dynasty or referring to the dynasty itself. The two are otherwise used interchangeably.

1520 According to Das *(Tibetan-English Dictionary,* p. 998, under *tsam pa ka),* "one of the 96 provinces of Śambhala (prob. the Greco-Bactrian empire situated to the north-west of Kashmir)"; it should be noted, however, that Das assumes (p. 1231) that Shambhala corresponds to the Greco-Bactrian empire, an identification that is, like all assertions as to the location of Shambhala, highly problematic.

1521 *Spre'u,* literally, "monkey." Kiṣkindha: "the residence of the monkey-prince Vālin, who was slain by Rāma; the territory which is said to be in the northern part of Mysore" (Monier-Williams, p. 284); cf. also Das, *Tibetan-English Dictionary,* p. 812.

1522 Literally, "golden eye"; At the moment, this is unidentified.

1523 Following K, we read *rug ma* for *rgyug ma;* according to Das (*Tibetan-English Dictionary,* p. 1186), it is a "town in the country of Sindhu," presumably in what is now southern Pakistan.

1524 A district in Burma between Chittagong and Arakan; Liu, p. 337n1446.

1525 The four islands or lands (Skt. *dvīpa*) from Tāmra- to Yamuna- are associated with four of the sixteen arhats; Tāmradvīpa with Kālika, Siṅgaladvīpa with Vajraputra, Priyaṅkudvīpa with Rāhula, and Yamunadvīpa with Bhadra. There is probably no way to know whether any actual places were in mind behind those names. Tāmradvīpa (Copper Island) is also sometimes used for Jambudvīpa, but then again it could be Sri Lanka, or for that matter Tāmralipta, the area around the western mouth of the Ganges; see BA, p. 796. Siṅgaladvīpa (Lion Island) suggests Sri Lanka, but it is thought by some to be a district in northwest India, doubtless the area from which the ancestors of the Sinhalese emigrated. Priyaṅkudvīpa (Spice Island) remains unidentified; Yamunadvīpa certainly suggests an island in the Yamuna River.

1526 Possibly Indonesia, but perhaps Pegu (Lower Burma; see Das, *Tibetan-English Dictionary,* p. 1310).

1527 "A small island in the delta of the Ganges where Chandra Gomi was exiled by the order of a king of Varendra; it now forms a part of the district of Bakerganj in Bengal" (Das, *Tibetan-English Dictionary,* p. 1100, s.v *zla ba'i gling*).

1528 It is likely that *kha sha* should be *kha shya:* "name of a mountainous country in the north-east of India...the Khasya Hills in Assam" (Das, *Tibetan-English Dictionary,* p. 136).

1529 According to Liu, p. 337n1455, "a place in northern A Li," but we have not been able to identify it.

1530 *A sha:* the name of a warrior people living in Qinghai, i.e., Kokonor; see Liu, p. 337n1457.

1531 The name of an ancient tribe that once inhabited northern Tibet and parts of Central Asia and which was the family name of the scholar Sumpa Khenpo; see Yang, p. 3. According to Liu, p. 337n1458, who reads *bum pa* with K, a place in Bhutan.

1532 See above, note 255.

1533 Or "western Xia," site of the early-second-millennium Tangut Mongol empire, and now including parts of Gansu, Shanxi, and Ningxia provinces.

1534 *'Jang yul* is located between Tibet and Yunnan.

1535 Presumably in the south of India; see Das, *Tibetan-English Dictionary,* p. 300, s.v. *'gro lding;* Monier-Williams, p. 501, s.v. *draviḍa;* also Liu, p. 337n1464.

1536 *Lod pa'i yul;* If the *d* is an error for *nga,* then *Long po* would be the district of that name in Kongpo, southeastern Tibet; see Liu, p. 337n1465, and also Das, *Tibetan-English Dictionary,* p. 1224, s.v. *long po'i stod.*

1537 This section is based on the treatment by Sumpa Khenpo, incorporating parts of his text verbatim.

1538 *Mnga' ris skor gsum:* the three myriarchies of Ngari were Gugé, Purang, and Mangyul. See also Wylie, p. 119n53.

1539 *Ru* is "horn" or "wing." The four horns or wings were administrative and military units as early as the end of the seventh century, as is evident from Dunhuang texts. The four divisions of Ü-Tsang were, in the west, Rulak (Supplementary Ru) and Gyeru (Right Ru), and in the east, Üru (Center Ru) and Gyönru (Left Ru). Note that the perspective is from the north looking south. These are the names as known by Longdöl Lama; see Wylie, p. 128n122. For a masterful treatment of the whole subject, see Uray.

1540 The reason for the obvious incongruity between the dates of Genghis Khan and Sachen Künga Nyingpo is that the story is a fiction, as demonstrated by Petech (p. 6).

1541 We read *nga gsum* for *dang gsum.* The significance of 1760 has yet to be determined.

1542 Lanzhou, in the northwest inside the wall (in present-day Gansu), was the gateway to inner Asia, on the well-frequented northern trade route. It was the headquarters of the large appanage that the Tibetans call Jang Ngö, granted to Godan in 1239.

1543 All editions mention the fire dragon year, or 1257, which is mistaken, as both Sapan and Godan were dead by then. It is difficult to believe that Thuken himself was responsible for such an obvious error.

1544 The Lion's Roar, or Siṃhanāda, is a form of Avalokiteśvara who is depicted riding on a snow lion and carrying a spear from which hang snakes, or nāgas. *Nāgas* are associated with skin diseases.

1545 For *ha khe ki,* read: *ha he hi.* The letters bearing the vowels are supposed to be the same.

1546 For *a' e' i',* read: *sa se si.*

1547 The story of Sakya Pandita's devising a Mongol writing system and alphabet with its characteristic loops and notches ("the edge of a saw") is entirely unhistorical but is a staple of Tibetan historiography, where it is recounted in various forms.

1548 According to Sumpa Khenpo (p. 273), Trüldé lies to the east of the palace. The story of "Miraculous Monastery" is a commonplace in the later biographical accounts of Sapan, though there are a number of variations in the story regarding the circumstances in which the monastery *(sde)* came into being. All involve a magical temple, or even a city, created by one of the Khan's magicians, but when Sapan blesses it, often with a scattering of flowers, the magician is unable to undo his spell, so that what was illusory was made real. It is unclear from when this story dates, but it does not seem to be found in the earliest biographical accounts at our disposal, e.g., that of Ngorchen Künga Sangpo.

1549 Conceivably, in calling Karma Pakshi "bearded," the king may have thought him to be northern Chinese, since to Mongols the northern Chinese are considered relatively hairy.

1550 Following K, we read *thol* for *thal*.

1551 See, e.g., Jamgön Anyé Shap, *Wonderful Treasure-House of Sakya Genealogy*, p. 159.

1552 *'ja' sa bzang po*. The Tibetan *'ja' sa*, according to Petech, is a transcription of the Mongolian *jasag* (rule, administration) but always understood in the sense of *jarlig*, or imperial decree; see Petech, p. 12n21. However, according to the *Bod rgya tshig mdzod chen mo*, *'ja' sa*, "proclamation, edict," is so called because at some time in the past a rainbow design *('ja' ris)* was placed at the head of a royal proclamation—this being an obvious folk-etymology.

1553 Gö Lotsāwa Shönu Pal, *Blue Annals*, 424:2; cf. BA, p. 487.

1554 According to Gö Lotsāwa Shönu Pal, *Blue Annals*, pp. 423–24 (cf. BA, pp. 486–87), Karma Pakshi did in fact return to Tibet, where he died. In 1261, he was arrested by Kublai for having sided with a brother and rival in a civil war, was apparently sentenced to death, but was reprieved and sent into exile in southern China. After eight years, he was allowed to return to Tibet. Petech (p. 16) accepts this as historical; for other references, see Petech's note there.

1555 Tibetan *li shim*. In the *Erdeni-yin Tobči* (1662), the name of the city is given as Silimji; see Sagang Sechen, p. 77.

1556 The Mongols divided the whole of the Tibetan-speaking areas into three great divisions called *Čölge* in Mongolian, transcribed as *chol kha* in Tibetan. They were Ü-Tsang or central and west-central Tibet, Dotö or modern Kham, and Domé or modern Amdo and parts of northern Kham. See Petech, p. 39.

1557 *'Bangs*. This is part of the accepted Tibetan historical tradition but is misleading, as the Sakyapas did not exercise temporal authority in Tibet but administered it for the Mongols. See Petech, p. 17.

1558 The Mongols were perfectly happy with the Uyghur script (vertical notches and loops), but what Kublai wanted was a script that could be used for writing all the languages of the empire, and as such Phakpa's invention, a phonetic script, irritated the Chinese and was passively resisted by the Mongols. The "square script" never gained any real currency, though it was used as an official script by the Yuan dynasty until its demise in 1368 and was occasionally used in official documents down to the twentieth century.

1559 He was the author of the *Jirüken-ü Tolta*, which established rules for writing in Mongol-Uyghur script; according to Poppe (p. 11), "Only a few facts about Chos Kyi Od Zer's life are known."

1560 This is a famous story, and recounted at BA, p. 337. Jamyang put on a mask of a religious protector and appeared before his teacher in the moonlight, frightening him and chasing him around the monastery. As a result, Rikral refused him permission to stay, and Jamyang went to Sakya and then to Mongolia, where he became guru to Buyantu.

1561 Also known as Rinchenbal; he was the younger brother of Togon Temur. Though he "reigned" but a single year, dying at the age of six, Rinchenbal is reckoned the last ruler of the Mongolian empire. His elder brother and successor, Togon Temur, lost the empire to the Ming.

1562 The Ongghot were ancestral spirits worshipped in the form of statuettes or effigies that were believed to incarnate them, and slaves as well as animals were sacrificed to them; see Tucci and Heissig, especially pp. 360ff.

1563 Siregetü Guoshi Corji *(chos rje)* was one of the great translators of the early seventeenth century. He was a direct disciple of the Fourth Dalai Lama; among other works, he translated the biography of Milarepa and his *Hundred Thousand Songs* into Mongolian.

1564 Künga Öser headed the committee that translated the Kangyur. Ligden patronized the Karmapas and was an opponent of the Gelukpa.

1565 In the letter sent by the Fifth Dalai Lama and Panchen Losang Chökyi Gyaltsen to Shizu in 1640 (referred to by Thuken in the previous chapter), they addressed him as "Mañjuśrī Great Emperor." This was an allusion to a prophecy by the Third Dalai Lama that an incarnation of Mañjuśrī would join forces with the Dalai Lama to unite China, Mongolia, and Tibet under the Gelukpas. The Fifth Dalai Lama and the Panchen were thus giving their sanction to the Manchu claim to be the heirs of the Mongol Yuan dynasty, which in its last stages also identified the emperor with Mañjuśrī. See Berger, pp. 58–58. The emperors Kangxi and Qianlong made much of their identification with Mañjuśrī. In 1635 Abahai, on the eve of overthrowing the Ming dynasty, decreed a new name for his people, changing it from Jurchen to Manju, likely deriving from a word meaning "brave." The similarity to the first two syllables of Mañjuśrī furthered the identification.

1566 *Dag yig mkhas pa'i 'byung gnas*, in *Collected Works,* vol. *ja*.

1567 The Third Dalai Lama had been called back to Mongolia in 1585 by Altan Khan's son Sengé Dügerüng Khan to perform the funeral rites for his father. In 1586, the two met but Sengé died soon after. The Dalai Lama continued on his progress and met Abadai in Inner Mongolia, Abadai having come all the way from Outer Mongolia to meet him. Thus, the meeting was not in Khalkha itself, as Thuken seems to have it. The monastery of Erdeni Juu, the oldest in Mongolia, is built on the site of Qara Qoram. Its construction began in 1586, before the two men had even met.

1568 The Torgod form one of the four divisions of the Oirat or West Mongols along with the Jungars, Khoshot, and Derbet. The Torgod are sometimes referred to collectively as Kalmucks. Between 1616 and 1675 they progressively settled the "Kalmuck steppe" in Russia, but in 1771 a considerable number returned to what was then the Chinese empire and resettled in the territory of the Jungars, whose last revolt against China had been crushed and their land laid waste. It is to this that Thuken may be referring.

1569 The Choros comprised three tribes, the Jungar, the Derbet, and Khoit. For a biography of Galden see Arthur W. Hummel, *Eminent Chinese of the Ch'ing Period,* p. 265.

1570 The Fifth Dalai Lama had given Ocirtu the title of Sechen in 1668.

1571 For his biography, see Hummel, p. 757.

1572 Namtsé Ding Monastery is not far from Radreng and is associated with a style of monastic discipline that was transmitted from there.

1573 Most commonly, these are, respectively, statues, texts, and stupas.

1574 The history of the rebellion, which ended in 1757 with the depopulation of Jungaria and the reduction of the survivors to beggary, is too complicated to summarize; useful accounts are found in Bawden, pp. 110–34, and in the article on Amursana in Hummel's *Eminent Chinese.*

1575 What follows is based almost entirely on the writings of the Fifth Dalai Lama, especially his *Royal Annals,* much of it incorporated verbatim; see, e.g., Ahmad, *Sino-Tibetan Relations in the Seventeenth Century* and *A History of Tibet by Ṅag-dBaṅ Blo-bZaṅ rGya-mTsho,* p. 192ff.

1576 This was a name bestowed on him by the Fifth Dalai Lama in 1639.

1577 That is, a bodhisattva who has attained at least the first stage of the path of seeing, and hence has realized emptiness directly.

1578 That is, Turks.

1579 Klafkowski (p. 130) remarks that this man, also known as Tongkhor Dorjé, was a well-known incarnation from Kokonor, that Klafkowski's own teacher, an eastern Khampa, knew very well who he was, and that he was still remembered.

1580 Just before the new moon, and ordinarily pitch black.

1581 That is, Karma Tenkyong Wangpo. Orthodox Geluk historians like Thuken call him *sde srid*—as they do not wish to dignify him with the title of king, although he was entitled to it—and often refer to him as Thuken does here by the more unassuming *gtsang pa,* "the man from Tsang." Tenkyong Wangpo patronized the Jesuits Cacella and Cabral and became known in Europe through a laudatory account of him in a work published in the 1680s by the French Jesuit Gerbillon. See TPS, vol. 1, p. 51ff. and Shakabpa, p. 102ff.

1582 *Ra kho shing:* Most likely a petty king on the Indo-Tibetan border; see Ahmad, *A History of Tibet by Ṅag-dBaṅ Blo-bZaṅ rGya-mTsho,* p. 312n1658.

1583 *Dga' ldan pho brang* was the name of the Fifth Dalai Lama's palace at Drepung, where he lived from 1622 (brought there at the age of five due to the aggressive policies of Tsang) until 1642, when he entered Lhasa, declared it the capital of Tibet, and decreed that the government would be known as Ganden Phodrang.

1584 The destruction visited on the Amdo region is described in the biography of the second Thuken incarnation and in the third—our—Thuken's biography of Changkya; this includes the destruction of Gönlung Monastery—the "home monastery" of the Changkya and Thuken incarnations—and the execution of high lamas and incarnations. The second Thuken also reports earthquakes in Beijing as signs of Chinese excesses in Amdo. In 1729, the second Thuken obtained permission to rebuild Gönlung.

1585 On the northwest frontier and in northern Manchuria, respectively.

1586 On Khotan, which is located in what is now southwest Xinjiang, see, e.g., M. A. Stein, *Ancient Khotan;* Emmerick, *Tibetan Texts Concerning Khotan* and *Guide to the Literature of Khotan.*

1587 Toh 4202 Tengyur, spring yig, *nge,* 168b2–188a7. See Emmerick *Tibetan Texts Concerning Khotan,* esp. p. 16ff. This would appear to be Thuken's main source. Its designation as a sutra and inclusion in the Kangyur notwithstanding, it appears to be a Tibetan text.

1588 Toh 357 Kangyur, mdo sde, *a,* 232b–277b.

1589 Literally, "sucking the nipple from the earth" *(sa las nu ma nu)*. His name may be the source of the word Khotan.

1590 Following K, we read *a sho ka'i* for *a sho'i*.

1591 Following K, we read *bi dza ya birya'i* for *bi dza ya birma'i*.

1592 In the *Liyül Prophecy*, this boy is not identified as a prince; he is simply a small boy who, when wandering lost, comes upon the site of the Kāśyapa stupa.

1593 John Newman contributed significantly to the translation of this section. On Shambhala, see, e.g., Bernbaum; Newman, *Outer Wheel of Time;* Sopa et al. Much of Thuken's description is based on material about Kālacakra found in the works of Butön.

1594 Like Shambhala itself, none of these rulers can be located historically. Nevertheless, Kālacakra tradition assigns very specific dates to their reigns, keyed to the supposed revelation of the Kālacakra by the Buddha in 881 B.C.E. With the exception of that of Sucandra (four years), each reign lasted precisely a hundred years. The traditional regnal dates are supplied in the entries in the glossary of enumerations. There are some variations in the Sanskrit names assigned to the rulers in various sources; we have followed those given in Khedrup Norsang Gyatso, pp. 612–14.

1595 The earlier Sureśvara is said to be an emanation of Kṣitigarbha, the later one of Jambhaka; see Khedrup Norsang Gyatso, p. 612. Note that the Tibetan for each is different: *lha dbang* for the former, *dbang phyug che* for the latter.

1596 Puṇḍarīka, *Stainless Light,* chap. 1; Toh 845 Kangyur, rgyud, *shī,* 22a6.

1597 The Tibetan for the sixth Dharma king (Viśvamūrti) and the thirteenth kalkin (Viśvarūpa) is identical: *sna tshogs gzugs*.

1598 Khedrup Norsang Gyatso, p. 614, has Hari.

1599 This implies the reincarnation of the first kalkin, Yaśas *(grags pa),* as the twenty-fifth kalkin, Rudra, or Raudracakrin.

1600 Puṇḍarīka, *Stainless Light;* Toh 845 Kangyur, rgyud, *shī*, chap. 1, 22b1.

1601 Khedrup Norsang Gyatso, p. 612, identifies the year of the Buddha's enlightenment as 927 B.C.E.

1602 In Rājagṛha, the capital of Magadha.

1603 As manifestations of either Mañjuśrī or Avalokiteśvara.

1604 Following K, we read *ka lā pa'i* for *kā la pa'i*.

1605 Actually, this should be sixty thousand.

1606 An emanation of Mañjuśrī.

1607 The head of the extremists in Shambhala.

1608 An emanation of Avalokiteśvara.

1609 All editions have *chu sprel* ("water-monkey"), but Thuken must have intended *lcags sprel,* "iron-monkey."

1610 The *me mkha' rgya mtsho* refers to a period of 403 years, comprising the reigns in Shambhala of the tenth and eleventh kalkins, Samudravijaya (Gyatso Namgyal) and Aja (Gyalka). It runs from roughly the beginning of the Muslim era (traditionally dated at 622) until 1027, when the Kālacakra was brought to India from Shambhala; the latter year marks the inception of the Tibetan calendrical cycle. See, e.g., Khedrup Norsang Gyatso, pp. 41–42, 613.

1611 On this list, see Newman, *Outer Wheel of Time,* pp. 594–612.

1612 Or Noah *(a no gha);* see Newman, *Outer Wheel of Time,* pp. 601–2.

1613 Newman suggests (*Outer Wheel of Time,* pp. 603–9) that this mysterious figure is not—as first suggested by Helmut Hoffmann—Mani, the third-century founder of Manicheism, but rather the archangel Gabriel, who revealed the *Qur'an* to Muhammad.

1614 Both *mngar ldan* and *sbrang rtsi'i* translate the Sanskrit *madhu;* combined with *blo gros,* or *mati,* they yield Muhammad's Sanskrit name, Madhumati.

1615 Literally, the "age of strife" *(rtsod ldan gyi dus).*

1616 This refers to the Mahdi.

1617 Madhyadeśa (the Middle Land) refers to north-central India; "Tibet" here refers primarily to western and central Tibet.

1618 Puṇḍarīka, *Stainless Light;* Toh 845 Kangyur, rgyud, *shī,* chap. 1, 22b2.

1619 As we have seen, the Śītā is most commonly associated with the Tarim River in Xinjiang, and Thuken himself has just implied that its location is to the north of both Tibet and India. However, given his earlier suggestion (p. 282) that its basin extends as far as Mangyül, perhaps Thuken imagined the Śītā to comprise an immense system, to the point where it might be described as having an Indian section.

1620 This is an error; it should be the Mahdi *('joms byed).*

1621 This should be Aśvatthamān, best known in Indic lore as a Kaurava general in the great war described in the *Mahābhārata.*

1622 This is the *rdzogs ldan,* or *kṛtayuga,* the most glorious of the four ages recognized in Indian tradition.

1623 These probably refer to the Uyghur and Turks, respectively.

1624 We have been unable to find the source of this passage.

1625 Losang Palden Yeshé, *Source of Billions of Wonders;* in *Collected Works,* vol. *nya,* 47a2. The quote is not verbatim.

1626 We have been unable to locate this text or passage.

1627 Changkya Rölpai Dorjé, *Secret Biography of the [Seventh] Dalai Lama;* in *Collected Works,* vol. *ka,* 3b2. As noted, Hanuman is the name of Raudracakrin's general. The "twelve lords" apparently refers to the twelve Hindu gods that will assist Raudracakrin, but the epithet *mi rje* more properly applies to the satraps of Shambhala, which number ninety-six, not twelve. This information was supplied by John Newman.

1628 *Collected Works,* vol. *ka,* chap. 21, 314a5.

1629 Namely, Bodhgaya, sometimes regarded in Buddhist cosmology as the center of the world.

1630 The number of syllables in each line of the quatrain is indicated in parentheses at the end of the quatrain.

1631 That is, ordinary sentient beings.

1632 That is, outside the seventh and last circle of mountains at the center of the Meru mandala. Alternatively, lands beyond Tibet.

1633 The philosophical systems come from the inner oceans, which are pure, but outside the seven mountains the water is salty and undrinkable.

1634 A precious stone said to purify water.

1635 That is, Losang Drakpa, or Tsongkhapa.

1636 Following K, we read *'dun ma* for *mdun ma.*

1637 This verse and the previous refer to the three wisdoms arising from study, reflection, and meditation.

1638 Each of the lines of this quatrain begins with the Tibetan *grub,* signifying accomplishment or completion.

1639 There is a play on the word *mu la stegs,* which refers to non-Buddhist "extremists" but more literally means "keeping to the edge." Samsara is often imagined as a river, so the image here perhaps is of a ghat descending to water's edge, as opposed to the stairway leading up into the Buddha's house.

1640 Literally, not relying on others' kindness *(gzhan drin mi 'jog pa'i).*

1641 Perhaps indicating his mastery or memorization of a large number of texts.

1642 That is, the fifty-fifth year of a calendrical cycle. The date of the text's completion should be January 12 or 13, 1802.

1643 In all editions, there follows an editor's afterword praising Thuken's accomplishment (S 333:9–334:5, K 482:20–485:8, Z 518:2–519:4). Since it is not part of Thuken's text, we have not translated it here.

Glossary

N.B.: In the parentheses after each term, where both are listed, Tibetan equivalents are listed before their Sanskrit counterparts. Terms italicized in the course of a definition are cross-referenced in the glossary.

abhidharma *(mngon rtogs)*. Literally, "higher knowledge," the branch of Buddhist discourse and the section of the Buddhist canon concerned with categorizing and describing the basic constituents of existence, or *dharmas*. In Tibetan tradition, the two most influential abhidharma texts are Vasubandhu's *Treasury of Higher Knowledge* and Asaṅga's *Compendium of Higher Knowledge*.

action seal *(las kyi phyag rgya, karmamudrā)*. One of the three or four seals of practice in the higher tantras. In *highest yoga tantra,* it most often is used to refer to a sexual partner whose embrace assists one in manipulating energies in the subtle body so as to hasten enlightenment.

adept *(grub pa, siddha)*. A *bodhisattva* who has, through tantric practice, gained both worldly and transmundane *yogic achievements*. The great adepts of medieval India, whose lifestories are both colorful and inspirational, were instrumental in transmitting the tantras and are at the source of many Tibetan practice lineages.

aggregates *(phung po, skandha)*. For all Buddhists, the five constituent factors that comprise what we usually call a "person": form or matter, sensation or feeling, perception or recognition, mental formations or dispositions, and consciousness or awareness.

analytical meditation *(dpyad sgom)*. With *placement meditation,* one of the two basic types of meditation recognized in Buddhism. Analytical meditation may involve philosophical analysis, review of categories, or observation of mental and physical events. When sufficiently developed, it results in *superior insight* into the nature of things.

arhat *(gra bcom pa)*. From a *Hinayana* perspective, any being who has eliminated all defilements, completed the path, and attained *nirvana*. According to most Mahayanists, arhatship, while tranquil, is a goal inferior to the full *buddhahood* altruistically sought by the *bodhisattva,* and arhats eventually will have to move beyond the limitations of their quiescent state.

ārya *('phags pa).* In all Buddhist traditions, a practitioner whose *enlightenment* is certain, usually because of his or her direct insight into the nature of things with a mind that is deeply concentrated. In a five-path system, whether *Hinayana* or *Mahayana,* the point at which one becomes an ārya is one's entrance onto the path of seeing.

awakening mind *(byang chub sems, bodhicitta).* In *Mahayana,* a state of mind cultivated by a *bodhisattva.* The conventional awakening mind is the vow to attain *enlightenment* for the sake of all sentient beings; the ultimate awakening mind is the empty nature of all *dharmas,* including the enlightened mind.

bardo *(bar do, antarabhāva).* Broadly speaking, any interval, but used most commonly to refer to the period, no longer than forty-nine days, that occurs between death and a subsequent rebirth. During this period, mourning rituals are conducted, and the *liberation* of the mind still may be effected.

bhikṣu *(dge slong).* A fully-ordained Buddhist monk. In the Mūlasarvāstivāda tradition followed in Tibetan monasticism, a bhikṣu observes 253 vows, as opposed to the 227 of the Theravada tradition of Sri Lanka and Southeast Asia, and the 250 of the Dharmaguptaka tradition predominant in east Asia.

bodhisattva *(byang chub sems dpa').* In any Buddhist tradition, a buddha to be. In *Hinayana* schools, *buddhas* are rare (though arhats are not), so bodhisattvas are the exception rather than the rule. According to most *Mahayana* schools, all beings will eventually become buddhas, so each of us must become a bodhisattva, motivated by compassion and the *awakening mind* to attain *enlightenment* for the sake of all beings.

buddha/buddhahood *(sangs rgyas/sangs rgyas nyid, buddha/buddhatva).* A being who has achieved the highest goal of sentient striving: unsurpassed, perfect *enlightenment.* In *Hinayana,* a buddha is a special type of *arhat,* appearing only periodically to start a dispensation of the *Dharma.* For most proponents of *Mahayana, buddhahood* is the destiny of all beings, and a buddha is asserted to consist of three "bodies" or aspects *(kāya): dharmakāya, enjoyment body,* and *emanation body.*

buddha nature *(bde gshegs snying po/de gshegs snying po, tathāgatagarbha/sugatagarbha).* The capacity for *enlightenment* inherent in all beings according to *Mahayana* Buddhism. Debates about the negative or positive characterization of buddha nature form the basis of the debate in Tibet between proponents of *extrinsic emptiness* and *intrinsic emptiness.*

cakra *('khor lo).* In tantric theory, one of a number of "wheels" at the intersection of important channels in the *subtle body.* The cakras are important for understanding human physiology and meditative praxis, and are replete with symbolic significance. The most commonly mentioned are those at the sexual organ, navel, heart, throat, forehead, and crown.

Chö *(gcod).* Literally, "severance," or "cutting through," a meditative practice, probably stemming from India, introduced to Tibet within the Shijé school by Machik Lapdrön. Chö aims to sever attachment to self through a variety of contemplations, the most dramatic of which involves the visualized offering of one's cut-up body to various gods, titans, and animals. Chö practices are found to this day in most Tibetan traditions.

Cittamātra *(sems tsam).* Literally, the "mind-only" school of *Mahayana* philosophy. Roughly synonymous with Yogācāra and Vijñānavāda, Cittamātra defines the crucial concept of *emptiness* in terms of either an object's lack of difference from the subject perceiving it, or dependent phenomena's lack of the imaginary nature imputed to them. Tibetan tradition identifies two major types of Cittamātrins: those following scripture (e.g., Asaṅga) and those following reasoning (e.g., Dharmakīrti).

clear light *('od gsal, prabhāsvara).* On the *completion stage* of *highest yoga tantra,* the luminous, blissful realization of *emptiness* that is a prelude to the attainment of a buddha's *dharmakāya* at the moment of *enlightenment.* In the Guhyasamāja tradition, it is the fourth of the five stages of the *completion stage.* The term also may refer to the natural clarity of the mind in its subtlest state, which may be manifest at death and on various other occasions.

completion stage *(rdzogs rim, niṣpannakrama).* In *highest yoga tantra,* the second and final stage of practice, usually involving manipulation of energies in the *subtle body* and culminating in *buddhahood.* Completion-stage practices are divided in various ways, e.g., the five stages of the Ārya tradition of Guhyasamāja, the six yogas of the Kālacakra, the six Dharmas of Nāropa, etc.

concentration *(ting nge 'dzin, samādhi).* In virtually all Indic traditions, a state in which one is deeply focused in meditation on a particular object. In Buddhism, concentration presupposes *tranquil abiding,* and is roughly synonymous with *meditative equipoise.* Concentrations are as various as the objects of meditation and may involve states of inner absorption, the mastery of extraordinary powers, or insight into the nature of things.

concept/conceptual thought *(rnam rtog, vikalpa).* The constructive mental activity that dominates the inner life of sentient beings and obstructs them from seeing things as they really are. Like *elaboration,* it involves a process of *superimposition* on reality that must be eliminated before *enlightenment* can be attained.

conventional *(tha snyad pa/kun rdzob; vyāvahara/saṃvṛti).* In *Madhyamaka* thought, one of the two levels of discourse or truth. Unlike *ultimate* discourse, the conventional conceals the true nature of things, and is a mere nominal designation, acceptable by worldly standards but unable to withstand analysis, hence sublated in the attainment of an ultimate realization.

ḍākinī *(mkha' 'gro ma).* In advanced tantric traditions, a female figure who assists a practitioner in deepening meditative realization. As with their male counterparts, ḍākas, there are both worldly and transmundane ḍākinīs. Ḍākinīs may manifest as embodied human beings or in subtler forms, and they may appear alluring or wrathful. In consonance with Buddhist gender symbolism, they signify *gnosis,* or transcendental wisdom.

debate circuit *(grwa skor).* Literally, the "monk's circuit," a tour of monasteries in a given region undertaken by a monk so as to debate other monks on the classic topics of monastic education: *abhidharma, vinaya, Madhyamaka,* the *perfection of wisdom,* and *valid cognition.*

definition vehicle *(mtshan nyid theg pa, lakṣaṇayāna).* In Mahayana discourse, an alternative name for the *perfection vehicle* or sutra vehicle. It sometimes is translated as "dialectical vehicle" or "philosophical vehicle."

delusion(s) *(nyon mongs, kleśa).* Also translated as "affliction(s)" or "defilement(s)," these are the fundamental negative factors that, along with *karma,* serve to keep sentient beings in their samsaric condition and must be uprooted for *liberation* to occur. Lists of delusions are manifold, and range from the so-called three poisons (ignorance, desire, anger), to the twenty deluded mental factors specified in *abhidharma,* to symbolically potent but nonspecific references to 84,000 delusions.

delusion obstacles *(nyon mongs kyi sgrib, kleśāvaraṇa).* According to *Mahayana* soteriology, the obstacles to liberation removed by both *śrāvakas* and *bodhisattvas* en route to liberation. Śrāvakas remove only delusion obstacles, whereas bodhisattvas subsequently remove *knowledge obstacles,* which are the subtle traces of *delusion* that keep one from the full omniscience of a *buddha.*

dependent arising *(rten 'brel 'byung ba, pratītya samutpāda).* The general causal law in Buddhism that asserts that whatever arises does so in dependence upon causes and conditions. Sometimes taken to be the essential Buddhist teaching, it is given specific instantiation in the twelve links of dependent arising, which explain how it is we continually take birth in *samsara.* It is also explained by Nāgārjuna as equivalent to—and the major proof of—*emptiness.*

dharma/Dharma *(chos).* A multivalent term in Indic religions more generally and Buddhism in particular. In English orthography, Dharma (capitalized) refers to the entirety of the Buddha's teachings or to a particular teaching or set of teachings (e.g., the six Dharmas of Nāropa), while dharma (not capitalized) denotes the basic constituents of reality as described by the Buddha and categorized in the texts of the *abhidharma* tradition.

Dharma king *(chos rgyal, dharmarāja).* In general, an honorific term for an individual who has mastery of or is a great supporter of the Buddhist *Dharma;* it also is an epithet of the lord of death, Yama. In a Tibetan context the term usually refers to a set of three great kings who helped to establish Buddhism in the land: Songtsen Gampo (617–49/50), Trisong Detsen (r. 755/56–97), and Ralpachen (r. 815–38).

dharmadhātu *(chos dbyings).* The "field," "sphere," "realm," or "element" in which (metaphorically, at least) one who has attained the ultimate resides, as contrasted with the "element" connected to the sensory fields that comprise *samsara.* The term sometimes is synonymous with *emptiness* or *dharmakāya,* and also refers to a *gnosis* attained when one becomes a *buddha.*

dharmakāya *(chos sku).* In earlier traditions, the corpus of the Buddha's teaching; in *Mahayana,* the aspect of *buddhahood* that is equivalent to enlightened mind and is the basis of the *enjoyment body* and *emanation body.* It sometimes is singular and sometimes is divided into a natural dharmakāya, which is a buddha's *emptiness* or suchness, and a gnostic dharmakāya, which is a buddha's perfect knowledge, compassion, power, and other "positive" qualities.

Dzokchen *(rdzogs chen, mahāsandhi).* In the Nyingma as well as Bön traditions, the "great perfection" is an advanced tantric perspective and practice in which one opens oneself to the primordial perfection that is the intrinsic nature of oneself and all beings. It is regarded by Nyingmapas as the supreme attainment, functioning for them much like *Mahāmudrā* (to which it bears certain similarities) does for Kagyüpas.

ear-whispered lineage *(snyan brgyud).* A confidential transmission in which special instructions have been handed down orally from guru to disciple. Ear-whispered lineages often preserve tantric traditions that have been transmitted outside of major institutional structures. Though primarily oral/aural, they may eventually be written down.

early spread of the teaching *(snga dar).* In traditional Tibetan historiography, the period from approximately 650 to 850, during which Buddhism, under the sponsorship of numerous *Dharma kings,* first began to take hold in Tibet. Crucial events of the early spread included the foundation (ca. 775) of the first monastery, Samyé, and the beginning of the process of translating Indian Buddhist texts into Tibetan. The Nyingma tradition traces its roots back to the early spread.

elaboration *(spros pa, prapañca).* Mental activity that is prone to discursiveness, complication, and fantasy. Useful in everyday life, elaboration, like *conceptual thought,* is an impediment to the direct realization of *emptiness* and so must be overcome on the path to *liberation.*

emanation body *(sprul sku, nirmāṇakāya).* Within the compass of the *form body,* the aspect of a *buddha* that appears for the sake of ordinary sentient beings. A single buddha may manifest multiple emanation bodies, which may be in human, animal, or inanimate form. The "historical Buddha" Śākyamuni is generally regarded as an emanation body. The Tibetan term for emanation body, *trulku,* is used to designate a deliberately reincarnated lama.

emptiness *(stong pa nyid, śūnyatā).* The central term in *Mahayana* philosophy, especially the *Madhyamaka* school, and the truth that must be realized if *enlightenment* is to be attained. A radicalization and universalization of the early Buddhist idea of no-self, emptiness is the true nature of all entities and concepts in both *samsara* and *nirvana,* variously taken to be the absence of *inherent existence,* the enlightened mind's lack of samsaric *dharmas,* or external objects' nondifference from the mind that perceives them.

enjoyment body *(longs sku, sambhogakāya).* Within the compass of the *form body,* the glorified aspect of a *buddha* that appears only to selected disciples. The enjoyment body is said to be possessed of the major and minor marks of a buddha and to teach *Mahayana* Dharma in Akaniṣṭha heaven to high-level *bodhisattvas* for as long as *samsara* lasts.

enlightenment *(byang chub, bodhi).* More properly "awakening," this is the goal of the Buddhist path, achieved by Śākyamuni Buddha under the bodhi tree in Bodh Gaya, and attainable by all sentient beings. In *Hinayana,* it is the *nirvana* attained by an *arhat;* in *Mahayana,* it is *buddhahood,* entailing omniscience, infinite compassion, and the power to manifest in countless ways to assist sentient beings.

extrinsic emptiness *(gzhan stong, paraśūnyatā).* A controversial view of *emptiness,* implicit in some Indian Buddhist sutras and tantras, and explicit to various degrees in the Jonang, Nyingma, Kagyü, and Sakya traditions of Tibetan Buddhism, which asserts that all samsaric *dharmas* are empty of intrinsic existence, while a *buddha*'s *dharmakāya* is empty of everything extrinsic to it, namely all samsaric dharmas, but is itself eternally replete with all buddha qualities.

father tantra *(pha rgyud).* In the four-tantra scheme recognized by most Tibetan new translation schools, one of two major types of tantra in the *highest yoga tantra* class. Father tantras (also known as method tantras) are said particularly to stress development of the *illusory body,* which is a transformation of subtle physical energies. The primary father-tantra corpus is the Guhyasamāja; cycles related to Yamāntaka and Vajrabhairava are important, too.

form body *(gzugs sku, rūpakāya).* In the most general terms, a *buddha*'s physical body, in contrast to the "body of Dharma" *(dharmakāya).* In *Mahayana,* the form body is the aspect taken by dharmakāya for the sake of others. It is achieved through the accumulation of merit and is usually subdivided into the *enjoyment body* and *emanation body.*

generation stage *(bskyed rim, utpattikrama).* In advanced tantric systems (e.g., mahāyoga or *highest yoga tantra*), the phase of practice, preceding the climactic *completion stage,* in which one "overcomes ordinary appearances" by visualizing oneself as a *buddha*-deity at the center of a complex *mandala,* identifying one's body, speech, and mind with that of a buddha.

geshé *(dge bshes, kalyāṇamitra).* Generally speaking, a "virtuous friend" who assists one on the spiritual path. The Tibetan term is used most commonly to refer to great masters of the Kadam tradition and, since the seventeenth century, to Geluk monks with a high level of scholastic achievement.

gnosis *(ye shes, jñāna).* In contrast to wisdom *(prajñā, shes rab),* which may be either worldly or transmundane, gnosis usually connotes a realization of the nature of things that is profound and liberating. The "accumulation" of gnosis on the *bodhisattva* path eventuates in the attainment of a *buddha*'s *dharmakāya.*

gnosis being *(ye shes pa, jñānasattva).* In tantric meditation practices, the "actual" *buddha*-deity that is absorbed into the "pledge being" one has visualized in place of one's ordinary body. The absorption of the gnosis being seals one's identification with the buddha's body, speech, and mind.

gradualist *(rim gyis pa).* In any Buddhist tradition, a practitioner who advances toward the goal in a step-by-step sequence, moving on to advanced stages only when more basic procedures have been thoroughly mastered. Despite much literature celebrating the *simultaneist,* or sudden, approach, it is presumed that most people must practice the path gradually.

guidelines *('khrid).* A set of instructions for practice conveyed by a guru to a disciple or group of disciples, either orally or in writing. Among Buddhist pedagogical styles, guidelines are less broad than teachings *(bstan)* or explanations/expositions *(bshad),* and more like *instructions, praxis,* or *special instructions,* which tend to be quite specifically focused.

heshang *(hvā shang,* Chinese *heshang).* A monk from the Chinese Buddhist tradition.

highest yoga tantra *(bla med rnal 'byor rgyud, niruttarayogatantra).* The last of the Buddhist tantric systems to develop in India, regarded by *new translation schools* as the most advanced of Buddhist practices. It often is divided into *father tantras* (e.g., Guhyasamāja), which stress methods for generating the *illusory body,* and *mother tantras* (e.g., Cakrasaṃvara), which emphasize attainment of the *clear-light* mind. Its practices are twofold: *generation stage* and *completion stage.*

Hinayana *(theg dman, hīnayāna).* From the perspective of *Mahayana,* the "lesser vehicle" teachings and practices expounded by the Buddha in his initial turning of the Dharma wheel. It sets as its ideal the *nirvana* of an *arhat.* Philosophically, it is prone to realism, as expressed in two major schools,

Vaibhāṣika and *Sautrāntika*. From the Tibetan point of view, Hinayana is foundational but is superseded by the Buddha's later Mahayana and *secret-mantra vehicle* teachings.

illusory body *(sgyu lus, māyādeha)*. In *completion-stage* practice in *highest yoga tantra,* the simulacrum of the *buddha's form body* that one will attain at the moment of *enlightenment*. In the Guhyasamāja tradition, it is the third of the five stages of the *completion stage*. It is based on the extremely subtle energy that is the basis of our physical being.

inherent existence/establishment *(rang yod/rang grub, svabhāva/svasiddha)*. A quality of *dharmas* that, if they possessed it, would define them as permanent, partless, and independent. The notion of inherent existence (generally synonymous with true existence) is the primary object of refutation in *Madhyamaka* philosophy, and realization of dharmas' *emptiness* of inherent existence is the necessary condition for the elimination of *delusions* and the attainment of *liberation*.

initiation *(dbang bskur, abhiṣeka)*. A tantric ritual anointment, coronation, or empowerment, in which a guru confers upon disciples the blessings of the practice lineage of a particular deity and allows them to undertake practices related to that deity. There are different types and categorizations of initiations, but all of them require that the disciple visualize the lama as the deity, make offerings, and undertake vows.

innate gnosis *(lhan skyes ye shes, sahajajñāna)*. In tantric contexts, the fundamental, luminous awareness that is intrinsic to all beings. Tantric practice aims at the actualization of this gnosis, which is roughly synonymous with *buddha nature* and *clear light*.

instruction *(gdams/gdams ngag, avavāda)*. Like *guidelines, praxis,* and *special instructions,* a specifically focused set of teachings imparted by a guru to a disciple or disciples.

intrinsic emptiness *(rang stong, svaśūnyatā)*. The view of *emptiness* most prominent in the Geluk tradition (but found in other traditions as well), which insists that all *dharmas* of both *samsara* and *nirvana* are empty in the same fashion, namely as intrinsically devoid of inherent existence. It is stated in contradistinction to the *extrinsic emptiness* view, in which nirvanic dharmas are seen to be empty in a different way than are samsaric dharmas.

isolated mind *(sems dben, cittaviveka)*. The second of the five stages of *completion-stage* practice in the Guhyasamāja tantra tradition. Following upon isolated speech, in which energies are brought into the central channel of the *subtle body,* this stage involves mimicry of the death process, in which energies are brought to the heart center, then the indestructible drop within it; there, conceptuality is stilled, or "isolated." On the basis of isolated mind, one creates an impure *illusory body,* attains *clear-light* realization of the nature of reality, and attains the final union of *buddhahood*.

karma *(las)*. Actions of body, speech, and mind, as well as their effects. Karma is, with *delusion,* one of the two basic forces that drive sentient beings from rebirth to unsatisfactory rebirth.

knowledge obstacles *(shes sgrib, jñeyāvaraṇa)*. In *Mahayana* soteriology, the obstacles to complete *buddhahood* that are removed by *bodhisattvas* on the final three stages of the ten-stage sequence. Knowledge obstacles are not *delusions* per se, but the subtle propensity to them that remains even when delusions have been removed. When the last knowledge obstacle is removed on the tenth bodhisattva stage, one is enlightened in the next instant.

Lamdré *(lam 'bras, mārgaphala)*. The "path-and-result" tradition of the Sakyapas, which is the definitive tantric transmission in that order. It is rooted in the Hevajra corpus and was introduced in Tibet in the eleventh century by Drokmi Lotsāwa on the basis of *instructions* from the Indian master Gayādhara and a root text composed by the great adept Virūpa.

later spread of the teaching *(phyi dar)*. In traditional Tibetan historiography, the period from approximately 950 to 1300, during which Buddhist institutions and practices were revived in Tibet after the chaos ensuing from the collapse of the empire around 850. Many new Indian Buddhists texts were introduced and new translations undertaken. Traditions traced to the later spread include the Kadam, Kagyü, Sakya, Shijé, and Geluk.

liberation *(thar pa, mokṣa)*. The state of release, or emancipation, from *samsara* achieved by every *arhat,* hence the same as *nirvana*. In *Hinayana,* it is the highest achievement. In *Mahayana,* it either is synonymous with the highest achievement, buddhahood, or is regarded as an attainment preliminary to following the *bodhisattva* path to full enlightenment.

Madhyamaka *(dbu ma)*. With *Cittamātra,* one of the two major *Mahayana* philosophical schools. Founded by Nāgārjuna, it focuses on the doctrine of *emptiness* expounded in the *perfection of wisdom* literature. Madhyamaka was the most influential single philosophical tradition in Tibet and spread in other parts of the Mahayana world as well.

Mahāmudrā *(phyag rgya chen po)*. Originally part of a system of three or four tantric seals, the "great seal" is synonymous with *inter alia, buddhahood, buddha nature,* and the *emptiness* that "seals" all *dharmas*. Among the Kagyüpa (and Gelukpa) in Tibet, it also refers to a system of meditation, with both *sutra* and *tantra* versions, in which one meditates on the true nature of the mind.

Mahayana *(theg chen, mahāyāna)*. With *Hinayana,* one of the two great divisions of Buddhism. Based on *sutras* (and *tantras*) allegedly taught by the Buddha later in his career (and regarded by Hinayanists as spurious), it became the dominant style of Buddhism in east and central Asia, including Tibet.

mandala *(dkyil 'khor, maṇḍala)*. In any tantric system, the abode of a *buddha-*deity, which represents an enlightened transformation of our ordinary environment. Upon initiation into a particular tantric practice, the disciple is introduced to the mandala and its inhabitants, and in *sādhana* practice, he or she will visualize him or herself at the center of the mandala.

mantra *(sngags).* In virtually all Indic traditions, a potent syllable or phrase, most often in Sanskrit, which may or may not have denotative meaning. In Buddhist *tantra,* a mantra evokes the *buddha*-deity with whom one identifies, and is uttered as the speech of that deity, with the power to affect and effect events in the mind and in the world.

master *(slob dpon, ācārya).* At the time of monastic ordination, the officiating monk who will serve as one's primary teacher. More generally, it denotes an especially learned and accomplished member of the community.

meditational deity *(yi dam, iṣṭadevatā).* In Buddhist *tantra,* the "chosen deity" who becomes the principal focus of one's meditation practice. The meditational deity may be chosen by the practitioner or the practitioner chosen by the deity; in most cases, one must receive confirmation from one's guru that the deity is the one with which one has a true affinity.

meditative equipoise *(mnyam gzhag, samāpatti).* A highly concentrated state of mind in which one is focused effortlessly on a particular object of meditation. Like *concentration,* meditative equipoise presupposes *tranquil abiding* and has a range of possible objects that are its focal point, including *emptiness* itself.

mental absorption *(bsam gtan, dhyāna).* One of a series of increasingly concentrated states attained in *placement meditation.* On the basis of the attainment of *tranquil abiding,* one may pass through four form-world absorptions and four formless absorptions, with the *meditative equipoise* of cessation sometimes added as a ninth. Mental absorptions may result in various *yogic achievements,* but they do not assure *liberation* unless combined with *superior insight* into the nature of reality.

mind-basis-of-all *(kun gzhi rnam shes, ālayavijñāna).* Among *Cittamātrins* following scripture, a foundational or "storehouse" consciousness that is the source of the other seven consciousnesses (six sense consciousnesses and a deluded consciousness) as well as their objects. It is the carrier of various cognitive and affective tendencies as well as of the seeds of *karma,* and it will be transformed at *enlightenment* into the *gnosis* of a *buddha.*

monastic seat *(gdan sa).* In Tibetan traditions, the main monastery of a particular lineage, which usually will have associated with it various subsidiary monasteries, retreat houses, and other religious institutions.

mother tantra *(ma rgyud).* In the four-*tantra* scheme recognized by most Tibetan *new translation schools,* one of two major types of tantra in the *highest yoga tantra* class. Mother tantras (also known as wisdom or yoginī tantras) are said particularly to stress development of the *clear-light* wisdom that is inseparable from great bliss. The primary mother-tantra practices are the Hevajra, Cakrasaṃvara, and Kālacakra, with Vajrayoginī and Vajravārāhī having great importance, too.

muni *(thub pa).* A term that can refer to an anchorite, ascetic, visionary, or silent sage in a range of Indian religious traditions. For Buddhists, the Buddha is *the* Muni, the ascetic par excellence.

new translation schools *(gsar ma).* Those traditions of Tibetan Buddhism—Kadam, Kagyü, Sakya, Shijé, and Geluk—that arose during the *later spread of the teaching* (post-950) and relied upon the translations of Indian Buddhist texts made during that period rather than the "old translations" made during the *early spread of the teaching.*

nirvana *(mya ngan las 'das pa, nirvāṇa).* The most common term for the *summum bonum* of Buddhism. Nirvana is a state of transcendent peace in which all *delusions* have been uprooted, *karma* is no longer created, and rebirth need no longer be taken. In *Mahayana,* nirvana sometimes is regarded as a mere way-station en route to full *buddhahood,* but it may also be considered synonymous with a *buddha*'s complete *enlightenment.*

old translation school *(rnying ma).* The tradition of Tibetan Buddhism, the Nyingma, that arose during the *early spread of the teaching* (650–850) and relies upon the translations of Indian Buddhist texts made during that period, rather than the "new translations" made during the *later spread of the teaching.*

oral tradition *(bka' ma).* In Nyingma, one of the three major lineages, with the *treasure* and *pure vision* lineages. It consists of the triad of sutra, magical net, and mind class: the *Sutra that Gathers Intentions,* the *Net of Illusion,* and the mind-side teachings.

perfection of wisdom *(shes rab kyi pha rol tu phyin pa, prajñāpāramitā).* One of the six or ten perfections that must be mastered by a *bodhisattva;* also, a corpus of literature related to wisdom. The main subject matter of the corpus is the career of the *bodhisattva,* with a special emphasis on the compassionate methods he or she must develop, and the wisdom realizing *emptiness* that he or she must attain.

perfection vehicle *(phar phyin theg pa, pāramitāyāna).* In later Indian and in Tibetan categorizations, one of two traditions within Mahayana, along with the *secret-mantra vehicle.* The perfection vehicle (also called the *sutra* vehicle or the *definition vehicle*) draws primarily from *Mahayana* sutras and their commentaries and focuses on the development of the six or ten perfections by a *bodhisattva* exclusive of tantric methods.

philosophical system *(grub mtha', siddhānta).* The term used most often by Tibetan Buddhists to designate both a school of thought and a system of religious practice. It is broader than the Sanskrit notion of a philosophical viewpoint *(darśana)* but somewhat narrower than the modern notion of a "religion."

placement meditation *('jog sgom).* With *analytical meditation,* one of the two basic types of meditation recognized in Buddhism. Placement meditation usually involves focus on a single object; when seriously practiced, it leads to states of *tranquil abiding, meditative absorption, meditative equipoise,* and *concentration.* Though a necessary condition for attaining *enlightenment,* it is not sufficient on its own and must be combined with analytical meditation.

Prāsaṅgika Madhyamaka *(dbu ma thal 'gyur).* According to Tibetan scholarly tradition, the school of *Madhyamaka* philosophy that (a) stresses the use of *reductio ad absurdum (prasaṅga)* rather than syllogistic reasoning in establishing *emptiness* as the nature of *dharmas* and (b) denies that dharmas possess inherent defining characteristics *(svalakṣaṇa)* even conventionally. The greatest Indian representative of the Prāsaṅgika is generally regarded to be Candrakīrti.

pratyekabuddha *(rang sangs rgyas).* A being who has attained enlightenment without recourse to a teacher or who, having attained enlightenment, chooses not to teach but to remain solitary. Along with the *śrāvaka* vehicle, the vehicle of the pratyekabuddha is often treated as a *Hinayana* approach to *liberation,* requiring a thorough realization of *dependent arising.*

praxis *(lag len).* Literally "taking in hand." These are instructions for practice conveyed by a guru to disciples, somewhat akin to *guidelines,* and often included within *instructions* or *special instructions.*

preceptor *(mkhan po, upadhyāya).* At the time of monastic ordination, the officiating monk who actually confers the vows. In Tibetan tradition, it is the most common term for the abbot of a monastic community.

pure vision *(dag snang).* In general, the mode in which a *buddha* or *meditational deity* is properly encountered in tantric practice, whether deliberately evoked or unbidden. It also refers to a way of seeing beings and the world, as essentially pure. In Nyingma *Dzokchen* tradition, it is the name given to one of three major lineages.

sādhana *(sgrub thabs).* Literally a "means of accomplishment," it refers to the meditative procedures applied in tantric practice whereby one visualizes oneself as a deity at the center of a *mandala.* It also may refer to a text that describes those procedures.

samsara *('khor ba, saṃsāra).* The general term for the worlds inhabited by sentient beings. It is marked by suffering, impermanence, and absence of self, and entails for those beings repeated rebirth in one or another unsatisfactory realm due to the force of *delusions* and *karma.*

Sautrāntika *(mdo sde pa).* According to Tibetan traditions, one of the two major *Hinayana* philosophical schools. Ontologically, Sautrāntikas subscribe to a doctrine of radical momentariness and accept some *dharmas* as real and others as conceptual; epistemologically, they assert a representational realism. Vasubandhu's *Autocommentary on the Treasury of Higher Knowledge* reflects Sautrāntika views, as do some of the writings of Dignāga and Dharmakīrti.

scholar-adept *(mkhas grub)*. In Tibetan Buddhism, an honorific term applied to a master who is widely and deeply learned as well as spiritually developed, displaying the best qualities of a pandit and a yogin.

secret-mantra vehicle *(gsang sngags theg pa, guhyamantrayāna)*. In later Indian and in Tibetan categorizations, one of two traditions within *Mahayana,* along with the *perfection vehicle.* The secret-mantra vehicle (also called the *tantra* vehicle or the vajra vehicle) draws primarily from Mahayana tantras and their commentaries, and focuses on the identification of the practitioner with a *buddha*-deity through a range of ritual and contemplative methods.

shen *(gshen)*. In Bön, a sacrificial officiant or "priest." Applied more abstractly, the term also has connotations of ultimacy.

simultaneist *(cig car ba)*. In any Buddhist tradition, a practitioner who attains the final goal either very rapidly or instantaneously. The simultaneist approach is generally reserved for advanced meditators and is particularly celebrated in Chan Buddhism and, among Tibetans, by those in *Dzokchen* and *Mahāmudrā* lineages.

single intention *(dgongs gcig)*. A set of vajra sayings in the Drigung Kagyü traditions that explicates basic features of the Drigung understanding of Buddhist tradition.

single taste *(ro gcig, ekarasa)*. In tantric traditions, the single savor—of emptiness—that all dharmas possess. Also referred to as the taste of sameness *(ro snyoms, samarasa),* it is a practice tradition in Kagyü and the third of the four yogas in the sequence of Mahāmudrā meditations.

special instruction *(man ngag, upadeśa)*. Like *guidelines, praxis,* and *instructions,* a pithy, esoteric, and highly important set of teachings imparted by a master to a disciple or disciples. In most Tibetan traditions, special instructions are regarded as the most vital teachings of all.

special oral tradition *(bka' 'babs)*. Literally, a "descent of the word," a lineage of transmission related to highly specialized and esoteric practices, most often related to the *tantras,* as for instance, the four special oral traditions received by Tilopa.

śrāvaka *(nyan thos)*. A "hearer" or "disciple," most often of *Hinayana* teachings. The term may refer either to one who follows a Hinayana path or to an *arhat* who has reached the end of that path. As distinguished from the Hinayana *pratyekabuddha* vehicle, the śrāvaka vehicle refers to an approach to the path in which one receives teachings from others rather than proceeding independently.

stages of the path *(lam rim)*. A gradual approach to the attainment of *enlightenment* (especially prominent among the Geluk) in which one develops progressively stronger motivation and understanding, moving from a narrowly focused desire for self-improvement to an altruistic aspiration to *enlightenment* for the sake of all beings, and from the acceptance of common Buddhist truths to the cultivation of the *Mahayana* perfections and, ultimately, the path of the *secret-mantra vehicle.*

subtle body *(phra mo'i lus, sukṣmaśarīra).* In tantric theory, the network of channels that interpenetrates, and is more basic than, the gross physical body. Manipulation of the consciousnesses, breath-related energies, and hormonal drops that move through these channels is basic to advanced meditative practice on the *completion stage* of *highest yoga tantra.*

superimposition *(sgro 'dogs).* The attribution to a phenomenon of characteristics that it does not possess, most notably the imputation of *inherent existence* to entities through *conceptual thought* or *elaboration.*

superior insight *(lhag mthong, vipaśyanā).* One of two crucial attainments in Buddhist meditation, the other being *tranquil abiding.* Superior insight involves a penetrating realization of the nature of reality, whether articulated in terms of the four noble truths, no-self, or *emptiness.* Though based on intellectual analysis, superior insight is only effective in uprooting *delusions* if conjoined with tranquil abiding.

supernormal powers *(mngon shes, abhijñā).* Powers attained by advanced meditators: retrocognition, clairvoyance, clairaudience, telepathy, yogic achievements, and knowledge of the destruction of the corruptions, i.e., delusions. The first five can be gained through deep *concentration,* and are not specific to Buddhism; the last is unique to Buddhists and is attained only on the basis of *superior insight* into the nature of reality.

sutra *(mdo, sūtra).* A discourse of the Buddha, contained in the canonical collection of either a *Hinayana* or *Mahayana* school. There is significant disagreement between Hinayana and Mahayana schools over which sutras were actually taught by the Buddha, with the former having a narrower, and the latter a more expansive, understanding of "what the Buddha taught."

Svātantrika Madhyamaka *(dbu ma rang rgyud).* According to Tibetan scholarly tradition, the school of *Madhyamaka* philosophy that (a) stresses syllogistic reasoning rather than the use of *reductio ad absurdum (prasaṅga)* in establishing the nature of *dharmas* as *emptiness* and (b) asserts that dharmas possess inherent defining characteristics *(svalakṣaṇa),* at least conventionally. The school is subdivided into Sautrāntika Svātantrika Madhyamaka (represented by Bhāvaviveka and Jñānagarbha) and Yogācāra Svātantrika Madhyamaka (represented by Śāntarakṣita and Kamalaśīla).

tantra *(rgyud).* A type of text taught by the Buddha to expound the doctrines and practices of the *secret-mantra vehicle,* in contradistinction to the *sutras* through which he expounded the *śrāvaka* and *perfection vehicles*. In English, the term also has come to connote the doctrines, practices, and outlook described in the tantras.

tantric master *(rig 'dzin, vidyādhara)*. Literally, a "knowledge holder" or "spell possessor." In India, the term has connotations of "wizard" or "sorcerer," while in Tibet it generally refers to a *secret-mantra vehicle* practitioner of great proficiency, somewhat akin to an *adept*.

Tathāgata *(de bzhin gshegs pa)*. One of the most common epithets of the Buddha, literally meaning one who is "thus gone" *(tathā agata)* beyond *samsara* to the far shore of *nirvana*, or who is "thus come" *(tathā āgata)* to the world to show the way to nirvana.

torma *(gtor ma, bali)*. In tantric Buddhist ritual practice, one of a variety of sculpted dough images that are offered to a range of deities, from worldly gods and demons to *buddha*-deities, in order to secure their noninterference in or blessings for the advancement of one's aims.

tranquil abiding *(gzhi gnas, śamatha)*. One of two crucial attainments in Buddhist meditation, the other being *superior insight*. Tranquil abiding is a state of effortless *concentration* upon an object of meditation accompanied by mental and physical ease, and is the doorway to the *mental absorptions*. In most Buddhist path-systems, a practitioner must join tranquil abiding with superior insight to become an *ārya* being and assure the attainment of *liberation* or *buddhahood*.

treasure *(gter ma)*. In the Nyingma tradition (and occasionally in others), a special teaching that was "buried" in an earlier era then discovered centuries later by a treasurer revealer *(gter ston)*. Treasures may be found in the earth, through pure visions, or in the mind of the revealer. Their status as "word of the Buddha" has been controversial at times, with some Gelukpas, in particular, questioning their validity.

Tripiṭaka *(sde snod gsum)*. The basic threefold collection of Buddhist canonical scriptures, divided into *vinaya, sutra,* and *abhidharma*. This organization of scriptures is most applicable in the cases of the Pali and other *Hinayana* canons; the Tibetan and Chinese Tripiṭakas are organized along rather different lines.

Tripiṭaka master *(sde snod 'dzin pa, tripiṭakadhara)*. An expert in the *Tripiṭaka*, the three canonical collections of Buddhism; the term implies extraordinary scholarly achievement.

true existence/establishment *(bden par yod pa/grub pa)*. A quality of *dharmas* that, if they possessed it, would define them as "true" in the sense of being permanent, partless, and independent. True existence (generally synonymous with *inherent existence*) is an important object of refutation in *Madhyamaka* philosophy, and realization of *dharmas' emptiness* of true existence is the necessary condition for the elimination of *delusions* and the attainment of *liberation*.

trulku *(sprul sku)*. Literally the *"emanation body"* of a *buddha*. In a Tibetan context, a trulku (often given the epithet rinpoché, "precious one") denotes the chosen reincarnation of a lama of high spiritual stature. A trulku usually inherits his (or her) predecessor's prestige, wealth, and institutional seat. Important trulku lineages include the Dalai and Panchen Lamas and the Karmapas, who originated the tradition in the thirteenth century.

ultimate *(don dam pa/mthar thug pa; paramārtha/niṣṭa)*. In *Madhyamaka* thought, one of the two levels of discourse or truth. Unlike *conventional* discourse, the ultimate is the true and final nature of things, revealed through an analysis (and/or direct realization) of the ontological status of all entities and concepts. That search reveals them to be empty, and *emptiness* is the term most often used to indicate the ultimate, though its meanings have been interpreted in many ways.

uniting and freeing *(sbyor grol)*. Euphemism for exploitative sex and murder as practiced by self-styled tantric teachers in Tibet, especially in the period between the *early* and *later spreads of the teaching*.

Vaibhāṣika *(bye brag smra ba)*. According to Tibetan traditions, one of the two major *Hinayana* philosophical schools. Sometimes divided into eighteen subschools, the Vaibhāṣika is most often identified with the Sarvāstivāda tradition typified by Vasubandhu's *Treasury of Higher Knowledge*. Vaibhāṣikas espouse ontological and epistemological realism, asserting that all *dharmas* exist and that sense cognitions directly encounter the objects that they cognize.

vajra *(rdo rje)*. A fundamental term in Buddhist *tantra*, indicating the indestructibility of the state of *enlightenment*. In Hindu mythology, the vajra is the thunderbolt wielded by Indra; in a Buddhist context, it sometimes is translated as "diamond" or "adamantine." It also refers to a scepter-like ritual object utilized by tantric practioners.

valid cognition *(tshad ma, pramāṇa)*. In Indian and Tibetan philosophical systems, an authoritative source of knowledge. Buddhist schools generally accept only two types of valid cognition—perception and inference. The analysis of valid cognition promulgated by Dharmakīrti is a major topic of study in the Tibetan system of monastic education.

vinaya *('dul ba)*. The branch of Buddhist discourse and the section of the Buddhist canon concerned with monastic discipline. In Tibetan tradition, the most influential vinaya text is the *Vinaya Sutra* of Vasumitra.

white simple *(dkar po gcig thub)*. In Kagyü traditions of *Mahāmudrā* practice, the "single powerful" medicine, realization of the nature of mind or reality, that is all that is required to attain *enlightenment*. The concept was utilized by Gampopa and Shang Tsalpa and criticized by Sakya Pandita.

wind-mind *(lung sems, prāṇacitta).* In tantric theory, the related physical and mental energies that course through the *subtle body* and are the true basis for what sentient beings are and become. In its subtlest form, the wind-mind is found in the indestructible drop at the heart *cakra;* it is through transformation of the subtlest wind-mind through the practices of the *completion stage* that *buddhahood* is achieved.

yogic achievements *(dngos grub, siddhi).* Generally speaking, any powerful attainment that results from spiritual practice. Yogic achievements are generally divided into the transmundane—i.e., complete *buddhahood*—and the mundane, which includes such powers as invisibility, flying, walking through solids, curing disease, and prolonging life.

Glossary of Enumerations

THIS GLOSSARY does not contain every numerical list in Thuken's text. There are some too large or too nonspecific for inclusion, some that cannot easily be identified, and some that are clearly identified in the text itself. We have, however, tried to include the most significant and oft-repeated listings, most of which are explicit in the text, a few of which are mentioned in notes.

two collections *(tshogs gnyis)*. The collections of merit and gnosis, which produce the form and dharma bodies of a buddha, respectively.

two compendiums *(sdom rnam gnyis)*. Asaṅga's *Compendium of Mahayana Sutras* and *Compendium of Abhidharma*.

two distinguishings *('byed gnyis)*. *Distinguishing the Middle from the Extremes* and *Distinguishing Dharmas from the Dharma Realm,* both attributed by Tibetan tradition to Maitreya.

two divisions of dharmakāya *(chos sku'i dbye ba gnyis)*. Gnostic dharmakāya and natural dharmakāya.

two divisions of Kagyü *(bka' brgyud kyi dbye ba gnyis)*. Shangpa and Dakpo.

two divisions of Mahāmudrā *(phyag chen dbye ba gnyis)*. The perfection-vehicle system and the mantra-vehicle system.

two extremes *(mtha' gnyis)*. Eternalism and nihilism.

two great chariot-paths *(shing rta'i srol chen po gnyis)*. Madhyamaka and Cittamātra.

two great charioteers *(shing rta chen po gnyis)*. Nāgārjuna and Asaṅga.

two great mandalas of yoga tantra *(rnal 'byor rgyud kyi dkyil 'khor chen po gnyis)*. Vajradhātu and Garbhadhātu.

two higher vows *(sdom pa gong ma gnyis)*. The eighteen root and forty-six auxiliary bodhisattva and the fourteen root and eight auxiliary tantric vows.

two knowledges *(mkhyen gnyis)*. Ultimate knowledge of the nature of reality and conventional knowledge of particulars.

two lamas who were expert in the systems of the two charioteers *(shing rta chen po gnyis kyi lugs la mkhas pa'i bla ma gnyis)*. In Kadam: Serlingpa and Vidyākokila.

two Madhyamaka schools *(dbu ma'i lugs gnyis)*. Svātantrika and Prāsaṅgika.
two obstacles *(sgrib gnyis)*. Delusion obstacles and obstacles to omniscience.
two purities *(dag pa gnyis)*. The purity resulting from the elimination of delusion obstacles and knowledge obstacles, respectively.
two spiritual sons of Tsongkhapa *(tsong kha pa'i sras po gnyis)*. Gyaltsap Jé and Khedrup Jé.
two śrāvaka schools *(snyan thos lugs gnyis)*. Vaibhāṣika and Sautrāntika.
two stages of highest yoga tantra *(bla na med pa'i rgyud kyi rim gnyis)*. Generation stage and completion stage.
two supremes of Jambudvīpa *('dzam gling mchog gnyis)*. Guṇaprabha and Śākyaprabhā (or Nāgārjuna and Asaṅga).
two truths *(bden pa gnyis)*. Ultimate and conventional.
two types of apprehension of self *(bdag 'dzin gnyis)*. Imputed and innate.
two types of Cittamātrins *(sems tsam pa gnyis)*. Cittamātrins following scripture and Cittamātrins following reasoning.
two types of Svātantrika Mādhyamikas *(dbu ma rang rgyud kyi lugs gnyis)*. Sautrāntika Svātantrikas and Yogācāra Svātantrikas.
two vehicles of Mahayana *(theg chen gyi theg pa gnyis)*. Sutra/perfection/definition and tantra/secret mantra/vajra.

three activities of scholars *(mkhas pa'i bya ba gsum)*. Teaching, debating, and writing or, more properly, composing.
three appearances *(snang gsum)*. In Sakya tradition: the appearance of phenomena as impure falsities, through which one develops renunciation; the appearance of experience in meditation, through which one develops the awakening mind of a bodhisattva; and pure appearance, through which, practicing secret mantra, one perfects one's body, speech, and mind.
three aspects of a perfect logical reason *(rtags yang dag gsum)*. The reason's presence in the logical subject, pervasion by the predicate, and absence from all instances of the nonpredicate.
three bases *(gzhi gsum)*. Fortnightly confession, the summer rains retreat, and the end-of-retreat ceremony.
three bodies *(sku gsum)*. The dharmakāya, enjoyment body, and emanation body.
three brothers *(sku mched gsum)*. In Kadam tradition: Geshé Potowa, Geshé Chengawa, and Geshé Puchungwa.
three characteristics *(mtshan nyid gsum)*. In Cittamātra ontology, the three types of phenomena: imaginary, dependent, and thoroughly established.
three classes of Dzokchen *(rdzogs chen gyi sde gsum)*. The mind class, expanse class, and special-instruction class.
three Dharma kings *(chos rgyal gsum)*. Songtsen Gampo, Trisong Detsen, and Ralpachen.

three Dharma robes *(chos gos gsum)*. The skirt, tunic, and robe.
three districts of Ngari *(mnga' ris skor gsum)*. Gugé, Purang, and Mangyul.
three divisions of the dharmakāya *(chos sku'i dbye ba gsum)*. Gnostic dharmakāya and the two subdivisions of the natural body: natural emptiness and natural lack of any obstacles.
three doors *(sgo gsum)*. Body, speech, and mind.
three doors of liberation *(thar pa'i sgo gsum)*. Signlessness, wishlessness, and emptiness.
three empties *(stong pa gsum)*. The empty, very empty, and greatly empty. Cf. *four empties*.
three essential works of Saraha *(sa ra ha'i snying skor gsum)*. *People Treasury of Dohas, Queen Treasury of Dohas,* and *King Treasury of Dohas.*
three fallacies of a logical reason *(ltar snang gsum)*. When a reason is uncertain (where the presence of the predicate in subject is debatable), inconclusive (where the reason's positive or negative pervasion of the predicate is not determined), or contradictory (where the reason and the predicate are opposites).
three families of the action tantras *(bya rgyud kyi rigs gsum)*. The vajra, lotus, and tathāgata.
three inner tantric yogas *(nang ba'i rnal 'byor gsum)*. In Nyingma: mahāyoga, anuyoga, and atiyoga.
Three Jewels *(dkon mchog gsum)*. The triple refuge: Buddha, Dharma, and Saṅgha.
three levels of faith *('dad pa gsum)*. Beginning faith, faith through understanding, irreversible faith.
three lineages of Nyingma *(rnying ma'i rgyud gsum)*. The long lineage of oral tradition, the short lineage of treasure, and the profound lineage of pure vision.
three lineages of Shijé *(zhi byed kyi rgyud gsum)*. Early, middle, and later Shijé.
three lower tantra classes *(rgyud sde 'og ma gsum)*. In the four-tantra scheme accepted by new translation schools, the action, performance, and yoga tantras.
three mothers *(ma gsum)*. See *three perfection of wisdom sutras*
three perfection of wisdom sutras *(shes rab kyi pha rol tu phyin pa'i mdo gsum)*. The extensive *Perfection of Wisdom in a Hundred Thousand Verses;* the middle-length *Perfection of Wisdom in Twenty-five Thousand Verses;* and the condensed *Perfection of Wisdom in Eight Thousand Verses.*
three persons *(skyes bu gsum)*. In Kadam and Geluk traditions, persons of: small scope (seeking higher rebirths), intermediate scope (seeking individual liberation), and great scope (seeking enlightenment for the sake of all beings).
three *piṭakas* *(sde snod gsum)*. The Buddhist canon, or Tripiṭaka, consisting of the Sūtra, Vinaya, and Abhidharma *piṭakas*.

three pledges *(sdom gsum)*. See *three vows*

three poisons *(sdug gsum)*. Greed, hatred, and ignorance.

three principal aspects of the path *(lam gyi gtso bo'i gsum)*. In the Geluk tradition: renunciation, the awakening mind, and right view.

three provinces of Tibet *(bod kyi chol kha gsum)*. Ü-Tsang, Amdo, and Kham.

three pure stages *(sa dag pa gsum)*. The eighth through tenth bodhisattva stages, on which one has fully abandoned all delusion obstacles but is separated from buddhahood by knowledge obstacles.

three requisites *(rgyu tshogs gsum)*. Praying to and doing intensive retreat on the inseparable guru/meditational deity; striving well in both accumulation of merit and purification of negativities; and analyzing the meaning of textual systems carefully through reason, and thinking about them in detail.

three Saṃmatīya sects *(mang bkur ba'i gyes pa gsum)*. Kurukullaka, Āvantika, and Vātsīputrīya.

three secret treasuries *(gsang mdzod gsum)*. In Shijé: the guru secret treasury, meditational-deity secret treasury, and ḍākinī secret treasury.

three Sthavira sects *(gnas brtan pa'i gyes pa gsum)*. Jaitavanīya, Abhayagirivāsīya, Mahāvihāravāsīya.

three supports *(rten gsum)*. Stupas, texts, and images, which symbolize the Buddha's body, speech, and mind, respectively.

three systems *(lugs gsum)*. In Chinese religion: Confucian, Daoist, and Buddhist traditions.

three times *(dus gsum)*. Past, present, and future.

three trainings *(bslab gsum)*. The trainings in morality, meditation, and wisdom.

three turnings of the Dharma wheel *(chos kyi 'khor lo'i 'khor ba gsum)*. The Buddha's teaching of: dharma realism through Hinayana sutras at Sarnath; emptiness through the perfection of wisdom sutras on the Vulture Peak at Rājagṛha; and mind-only and/or buddha nature through various sutras at Mount Malaya and/or Vaiśālī.

three types of inference *(rjes dpag gsum)*. Inference based on: causation, identity, and nonapprehension.

three types of persons *(skyes bu gsum)*. See *three persons*

three types of practitioners *(sgrub pa gsum)*. In Dzokchen: gradualist, simultaneist, and transcender.

three types of worldly gods *('jig rten pa'i lha gsum)*. Deities of the desire, form, and formless worlds.

three vehicles *(theg pa gsum)*. The Hinayana, Mahayana, and Vajrayana.

three vows *(sdom gsum)*. The 253 prātimokṣa vows, the eighteen root and forty-six auxiliary bodhisattva vows, and the fourteen root and eight auxiliary tantric vows.

three worlds *(khams gsum)*. The worlds, or realms, of desire, form, and formlessness, which together constitute the Buddhist samsaric cosmos.

four activities *(las bzhi)*. In tantric traditions: peaceful, increasing, empowering, and wrathful.

four ages *(dus bzhi)*. In Indic mythology: the *kṛta, treta, dvapara,* and *kali* yugas. These are roughly equivalent to the gold, silver, bronze, and iron ages of Western mythology.

four aspects of the path of conduct *(spyod lam rnam bzhi)*. Walking, standing, sitting, lying down.

four attachments *(zhen pa bzhi)*. This life, samsaric existence, one's own aims, and the self.

four authenticating seals of the Buddhist view *(lta ba bkar btags kyi phyag rgya bzhi)*. All compounded phenomena are impermanent; all contaminated phenomena are suffering; all dharmas are without self; nirvana is peace. Cf. *four seals.*

four basic schools of Vaibhāṣika *(bye brag pa'i rtsa ba sde bzhi)*. Mahāsāṃghika, Sarvāstivāda, Sthavira, and Saṃmatīya.

four basic transgressions *(ltung byed rtsa bzhi)*. Violations of monastic conduct that result in immediate expulsion: killing a human being, stealing from the Three Jewels, lying about one's attainments, and engaging in sexual intercourse.

four bodies *(sku bzhi)*. A buddha's natural and gnostic dharmakāyas and the enjoyment and emanation bodies.

four causes *(rgyu bzhi)*. Objective cause, immediate cause, cooperative cause, dominant cause.

four classes of tantra *(rgyud kyi sde bzhi)*. Action tantra, performance tantra, yoga tantra, and highest yoga tantra.

four continents *(gling bzhi)*. In traditional Indian cosmo-geography: the eastern continent of Pūrvavideha, the southern continent of Jambudvīpa, the western continent of Aparagodanīya, and the northern continent of Uttarakuru.

four deities *(lha bzhi)*. In Kadam: Śākyamuni Buddha, Avalokiteśvara, Tārā, Acala.

four difficult subjects *(dka' bzhi)*. In Tibetan monastic education, the subject matters of: Madhyamaka (or valid cognition), the perfection of wisdom, vinaya, and abhidharma, as well as the basic texts for each course of study: Candrakīrti's *Entering the Middle Way* (or Dharmakīrti's *Thorough Exposition of Valid Cognition*), Maitreya's *Ornament of Higher Realization,* Guṇaprabha's *Vinaya Sutra,* and Vasubandhu's *Treasury of Higher Knowledge.*

four empties *(stong pa bzhi).* On the completion stage of highest yoga tantra, four experiences induced by the absorption of consciousness into the heart cakra: the empty, the very empty, the greatly empty, and the all empty.

four fearlessnesses *(mi 'jigs pa bzhi).* A buddha's fearlessness regarding: knowledge of all things, knowledge of the cessation of all affliction, the declaration that path obstructions do not recur, and the fact that the path of renunciation has been realized.

four great elements *('byung ba chen po bzhi).* Earth, water, fire, and air.

four great men *(skyes mchog bzhi).* In Chinese traditions: Fu Xi, Wen Wang, Zhou Gong, and Kongzi (Confucius).

four great monasteries of Ü-Tsang *(dbus gtsang gi chos sde chen po bzhi).* In Geluk tradition: Ganden, Sera, Drepung, and Tashi Lhünpo.

four great rivers *(chu klang chen po bzhi).* In China: Yangtze (in the south), Huanghe (in the north), Huai (in the center), and Ji (in the east).

four immeasurables *(tshad med pa bzhi).* Love, compassion, sympathetic joy, and equanimity.

four initiations *(dbang bskur bzhi).* In highest yoga tantra: vase, secret, wisdom-gnosis, and fourth (or word).

four joys *(dga' bzhi).* On the completion stage of highest yoga tantra (especially the mother tantras), four experiences induced by the movement of energies within the central channel: joy, ultimate joy, joy of cessation, and innate joy.

four kinds of birth *(skyes gnas bzhi).* From a womb, egg, moisture, or miracle.

four māras *(bdud bzhi).* The aggregates, delusions, death, and the divine youth.

four medical tantras *(rgyud bzhi).* These are the *Root Tantra (Rtsa ba'i rgyud), Explanatory Tantra (Bshad rgyud), Tantra of Special Instruction (Man ngag gi rgyud),* and the *Supplementary Tantra (Phyi ma'i rgyud).*

four mental absorptions *(bsam gtan bzhi).* The first, which involves investigation, analysis, joy, happiness, and one-pointedness; the second, which involves joy, happiness, and one-pointedness; the third, which involves happiness and one-pointedness; and the fourth, which involves one-pointedness.

four negative tendencies *('gro ba bzhi).* The major impediments to receiving secret teachings: desire, fear, anger, and confusion. Alternatively, it may refer to the sorts of beings who are controlled by these tendencies.

four noble truths *('phags pa'i bden bzhi).* There is suffering, there is an origin of suffering, there is a cessation of suffering, and there is a path to the cessation of suffering.

four opponent powers *(stobs bzhi).* In confession practice: recognition of one's transgression, regret at its commission, a promise not to repeat, and purification, e.g., through visualization and mantra recitation or meditation on emptiness.

four philosophical systems *(grub mtha' bzhi).* Vaibhāṣika, Sautrāntika, Cittamātra, and Madhyamaka.

four preparations *(sngon 'gro sbyor ba bzhi).* The preliminary practices for tantra: prostration, Vajrasattva purification meditation, guru yoga, and mandala offerings.

four profound Dharmas not allowed outside the fence *(lcags ri mi 'da' ba'i zab chos bzhi).* In Sakya: the path-time Hevajra sādhana, the Vajrayoginī sādhana, the Virūpa protection meditation, and the profound-path guru-yoga meditation.

four seals *(phyag rgya bzhi).* In advanced tantric systems: action seal, dharma seal, pledge seal, and great seal *(mahāmudrā).* Cf. *four authenticating seals.*

four special oral traditions *(bka' babs bzhi).* Four transmissions received by Tilopa, regarding, respectively, Guhyasamāja, the *Four Seats Tantra,* the illusory body, and transference of consciousness; Mahāmāyā and dreams; Cakrasaṃvara and clear light; and Hevajra and inner heat.

four stages of the path of preparation *(sbyor lam gyi sa bzhi).* Heat, peak, patience, and supreme mundane achievement.

four syllables *(yi ge bzhi).* In Mahāmudrā meditation: *a, ma, na, si.*

four tantras *(rgyud bzhi).* See *four medical tantras*

four textbooks (*yig cha bzhi,* Ch. *sishu*). In Confucian tradition: the *Daxue (Great Learning),* the *Zhongyong (Doctrine of the Mean),* the *Lunyu (Analects),* and the *Mengzi (Book of Mencius).*

four texts *(lung sde bzhi).* In vinaya: *Elements of Vinaya, Divisions of Vinaya, Elements of Lesser Vinaya,* and *Higher Text of Vinaya.*

four times *(dus bzhi).* Past, present, future, and indefinite time.

four trainings of a recluse *(dge sbyong gi chos bzhi).* Not to hate others despite being the object of their hatred, not to retaliate in anger even when angry, not to injure others even when injured, and not to beat others even when one is beaten by them.

four yogas of Mahāmudrā *(phyag rgya chen po'i rnal 'byor bzhi).* One-pointedness, nonelaboration, single taste, nonmeditation.

four yogas of Vajrabhairava *(rdo rje 'jigs byed kyi rnal 'byor bzhi).* Mantra, commitment, form, and pure wisdom.

five aggregates *(phung po lnga).* That which comprises the "person": form, sensations, perceptions, mental formations, and consciousness.

five classics (*gzhung lnga,* Ch. *wujing*). In Chinese, especially Confucian, tradition: the *Yijing (Classic of Changes),* the *Shijing (Classic of Odes),* the *Shujing (Classic of Records),* the *Lijing (The Classic of Rites),* and the *Chun Qiu (Spring and Autumn Annals).*

five conquerors *(rgyal ba lnga).* In tantric Buddhism: Akṣobhya, Vairocana, Ratnasambhava, Amitābha, and Amoghasiddhi.

five deities of Cakrasaṃvara *(bde mchog lha lnga).* Buddha Heruka, Vajra Heruka, Ratna Heruka, Padma Heruka, and Karma Heruka.

five dhāraṇī texts *(gzungs grwa lnga).* Sādhanas related to Mahāsahasrapramarsanī, Mahāmayurī, Mahāmantrānudhāriṇī, Mahāśītavatī, and Mahāpratisara.

five divisions of the 253 downfalls *(ltung ba sde lnga).* Downfalls entailing expulsion, downfalls entailing suspension, minor transgressions, "confessable" transgressions, and small infractions.

five early Sakya manifestations *(sa skya gong ma lnga).* Sachen Künga Nyingpo, Sönam Tsemo, Drakpa Gyaltsen, Sakya Pandita, Phakpa.

five elemental essences *(dwangs ma lnga).* The distilled forms of earth, water, fire, air, and space.

five elements *('byung ba lnga).* In Indo-Tibetan tradition: earth, water, fire, air, and space. In Chinese tradition: wood, fire, earth, metal, and water.

five families *(rigs lnga).* The families of tantric tradition: tathāgata or buddha, vajra, jewel, lotus, and action.

five gnoses *(ye shes lnga).* The mirror-like gnosis, the gnosis of equality, the discriminating gnosis, the all-accomplishing gnosis, and the gnosis of the dharmadhātu.

five impurities *(snyigs ma lnga).* Short lifespan, false view, domination by the delusions, and the impurities of beings, and the age they live in. Alternatively, killing brahmans, taking intoxicants, theft, adultery with wives of one's elders, and association with those who commit any of the first four (see Mittal, p. 35, note).

five lineages of Chinese Buddhism *(rgya nag gi nang pa'i brgyud lnga).* According Tibetan analyses: vinaya (Lu), secret mantra (Chenyen), extensive practice (school of Xuanzang), profound view (Tiantai and Huayan), and essential meaning (Chan).

five Mahāsāṃghika sects *(phal chen pa las gyes pa lnga sde).* Pūrvaśaila, Aparaśaila, Haimavata, Lokottaravāda, and Prajñaptivāda.

five major sciences *(rig gnas che ba lnga).* Linguistics, logic, medicine, arts and technology, and "inner meaning" (i.e., Buddhism).

five minor sciences *(rig gnas chung ba lnga).* Grammar, poetic theory, prosody, drama, and lexicography.

five paths *(lam lnga).* In both Hinayana and Mahayana traditions: the paths of accumulation, preparation, seeing, meditation, and no-more-learning.

five recollections *(rjes dran lnga).* A Kadam special instruction involving recollection of: your lama as an object of refuge, your body as a deity, your speech as mantra, all beings as your parents, and your mind as empty.

five root texts *(po ti lnga)*. The five basic texts of the Geluk monastic educational system: Candrakīrti's *Entering the Middle Way* (for Madhyamaka), Dharmakīrti's *Thorough Exposition of Valid Cognition* (for valid cognition), Maitreya's *Ornament of Higher Realization* (for perfection of wisdom), Guṇaprabha's *Vinaya Sutra* (for vinaya), and Vasubandhu's *Treasury of Higher Knowledge* (for Abhidharma).

five sacred peaks *(ri lnga)*. In China: Wu Tai Shan in the east, Hua Shan in the west, Nan Heng Shan in the south, Bei Heng Shan in the north; and Song Shan in the center.

five sense objects *(de tsam lnga)*. In Sāṃkhya: forms, sounds, smells, tastes, tangibles.

five stages *(rim lnga)*. The completion-stage phases described by the Guhyasamāja tantric tradition: isolated speech, isolated mind, illusory body, clear light, and union.

five supernormal powers *(mngon shes lnga)*. Five mundane attainments: retrocognition, clairvoyance, clairaudience, telepathy, and various physical powers.

five transworldly classes *('jig rten las 'das pa'i sde lnga)*. Deities in the Nyingma tradition of eight transmitted precepts: Manjuśrī/Yamāntaka, Hayagrīva, Heruka, Vajrāmṛta, and Vajrakīla.

five treatises of Maitreya *(byams chos sde lnga)*. *Ornament of Higher Realization, Ornament of Mahayana Sutras, Sublime Continuum, Distinguishing the Middle from the Extremes,* and *Distinguishing Dharmas from the Dharma Realm.*

five treatises on the stages *(sa sde lnga)*. Asaṅga's *Stages of Yogic Practice, Compendium of Bases, Compendium of Ascertainments, Compendium of Enumerations,* and *Compendium of Explanations.*

five virtues *(ring lugs lnga,* Chinese *wuchang)*. In Confucian tradition: *ren* (humaneness), *yi* (righteousness), *li* (propriety), *zhi* (wisdom), and *xin* (trustworthiness).

five winds *(lung lnga)*. The breath-related energies of the subtle body: the vitalizing, pervasive, upward-moving, downward-moving, and equalizing winds.

fivefold *(lnga ldan)*. In Drigung Kagyü: the awakening mind, deity yoga, guru yoga, Mahāmudrā, and dedication of merit.

six about the taste of sameness *(ro snyom skor druk)*. In Kagyü: using conceptual thoughts as the path, using delusions as the path, using illness as the path, using gods and *dré* demons as the path, using suffering as the path, and using death as the path.

six bardos *(bar do drug)*. This life, the stages of dying, the dharmadhātu, "becoming" one's next rebirth, dreaming, and meditative absorption.

six categories *(tshig don drug).* In the Vaiśeṣika system of Hindu philosophy: substance, quality, generality, particularity, activity, and inherence.

six classes of beings *('gro ba rigs drug).* Hell beings, hungry ghosts, animals, humans, titans, and gods.

six collections of reasoning *(rigs pa'i tshogs drug).* Nāgārjuna's six major texts: *Fundamental Treatise on the Middle Way, Sixty Stanzas on Reasoning, Seventy Stanzas on Emptiness, Finely Woven Scripture, Refutation of Objections,* and *Precious Garland.*

six Dharmas of Nāropa *(nā ro'i chos drug).* Inner heat, illusory body, dream, clear light, transference of consciousness, and the bardo.

six Dharmas of Niguma *(ni gu ma'i chos drug).* Inner heat, illusory body, dream, clear light, transference of consciousness, and the bardo.

six Kadam texts *(bka' gdams gzhung drug).* Asaṅga's *Bodhisattva Stages,* Maitreya's *Ornament of Mahayana Sutras,* Śāntideva's *Compendium of Training* and *Way of the Bodhisattva,* Āryaśūra's *Garland of Birth Stories,* and the *Collection of Uplifting Verses.*

six lineages of Nyingma *(rnying ma'i brgyud drug).* The meaning lineage of the conquerors, the symbol lineage of mantra adepts, the ear-whispered lineage of ordinary persons, the lineage of prophecies of the special oral tradition, the lineage of the karmically projected treasure, and the lineage of the mind-seal prayer.

six ornaments of Jambudvīpa *('dzam gling rgyan drug).* Āryadeva, Vasubandhu, Nāgārjuna, Asaṅga, Dignāga, and Dharmakīrti.

six perfections *(pha rol tu phyin pa drug).* In Mahayana: generosity, morality, patience, diligence, mental absorption, and wisdom.

six sources of valid cognition *(tshad ma drug).* In Mīmāṃsā: perception, inference, testimony, comparison, implication, and cognition of nonexistence.

six types of object *(yul drug).* Sight, sound, smell, taste, touch, dharma.

six types of sensory equipment *(tshogs drug).* Eye, ear, nose, tongue, body, and mind.

six yogas *(rnal 'byor drug).* In the Kālacakra tantric corpus, the completion-stage yogas of: withdrawal, mental absorption, breath control, retention, recollection, and concentration.

seven Dharma kings *(chos rgyal bdun).* In Kālacakra traditions: Sucandra (d. 877 B.C.E.), Sureśvara (r. 877–777 B.C.E.), Tejin (r. 777–677 B.C.E.), Somadatta (r. 677–577 B.C.E.), Sureśvara (r. 577–477 B.C.E.), Viśvamūrti (r. 477–377 B.C.E.), and Sureśāna (r. 377–277 B.C.E.).

seven integrated factors *(kha sbyor yan lag bdun).* Qualities of the enjoyment body: complete enjoyment, union, great bliss, essencelessness, perfect compassion, noninterruption, and noncessation.

seven limbs *(yan lag bdun)*. Seven aspects of ritual offering that are crucial to meditation in Mahayana Buddhism: prostration, offering, confession, rejoicing in the virtue of others, requesting the buddhas to turn the Dharma wheel, entreating them not to enter final nirvana, and dedication of merit.

seven Mañjughoṣas *('jam dbyangs bdun)*. In Sakya: Khöntön Künga Bar, Sönam Tsemo, Drakpa Gyaltsen, Chungpal Ö, Sakya Pandita, Sangtsa Sönam Gyaltsen, and Phakpa.

seven-point mind training *(blo sbyong don bdun)*. In Kadam: thinking through the basic Dharma, the preparatory practices; training in the awakening mind, which is the actual practice; changing adverse conditions into the path to enlightenment; the teaching condensed into practice for a single life; the criteria of mind training; the pledges involved in mind training; and how one studies mind training.

seven Sarvāstivādin sects *(gzhi thams cad yod par smra ba las gyes pa bdun)*. Sarvāstivāda, Kāśyapīya, Mahīśāsaka, Dharmaguptaka, Bahuśrutīya, Tāmraśāṭīya, and Vibhajyavāda.

seven treatises on valid cognition *(tshad ma sde bdun)*. Dharmakīrti's *Thorough Exposition of Valid Cognition, Ascertainment of Valid Cognition, Drop of Reasoning, Proof of Other Minds, Analysis of Relations, Principles of Debate,* and *Drop of Reasons.*

seven yogic attainment texts *(sgrub pa sde bdun)*. Padmavajra's *Secret Yogic Attainment,* Anaṅgavajra's *Yogic Attainment Ascertaining Wisdom and Means,* Indrabhūti's *Yogic Attainment of Gnosis,* Lakṣmīṅkarā's *Yogic Attainment of Nonduality,* Dārikapa's *Special Instruction on the Reality of the Greatest Secret,* Yoginī Cintā's *Yogic Attainment of Reality Following the Clarification of Entities,* and Ḍombi Heruka's *Yogic Attainment of the Innate.*

sevenfold analysis *(rnam bdun gyi dpyad pa)*. In Madhyamaka, the investigation whether an entity exists: as separate from its components, as identical to its components, possessing its components, inherently dependent upon its components, as the basis upon which the components depend, as the collection of components, or the shape of its components.

sevenfold deities and Dharmas *(lha chos bdun ldan)*. In Kadam tradition: four deities—the Buddha, Avalokiteśvara, Tārā, and Acala—and the triple Dharma of the three sections of the Tripiṭaka.

eight *bagua* *(pā bkwa brgyad)*. The trigrams of the *Classic of Changes: qian* (heaven), *kun* (earth), *zhen* (thunder), *xun* (wind), *kan* (water), *li* (fire), *gen* (mountain), and *dui* (valley).

eight consciousnesses *(tshogs* [or *rnam shes*] *brgyad)*. In Yogācāra: consciousness related to eye, ear, nose, tongue, body, mind, the afflicted mind, and the mind-basis-of-all.

eight dissertations *(pra ka ra ṇa sde brgyad).* Vasubandhu's *Twenty Stanzas, Thirty Stanzas, Dissertation on the Five Aggregates, Rational System of Exposition, Dissertation on the Proof of Deeds, Explanation of the Ornament of Mahayana Sutras, Explication of Distinguishing the Middle from the Extremes,* and as the last either the *Treasury of Higher Knowledge* or *Commentary on Distinguishing Dharmas from the Dharma Realm.*

eight emanations *(sprul pa brgyad).* In Sakya: Khöntön Künga Bar, Sönam Tsemo, Drakpa Gyaltsen, Chungpal Ö, Sakya Pandita, Sangtsa Sönam Gyaltsen, Phakpa (all emanations of Mañjughoṣa), and Chakna (an emanation of Vajrapāṇi).

eight entrances *('jug sgo rnam pa brgyad).* In the Tiantai system: the sudden entrance, gradual entrance, secret or special entrance, indefinite entrance, entrance to the *piṭakas,* entrance to awareness, entrance to discrimination, and entrance to perfection.

eight factors for abandoning obstacles *(spong ba'i 'du byed brgyad).* In tranquil-abiding meditation: faith, determination, perseverance, confidence (all of which counter laziness), mindfulness (which counters lack of mindfulness), introspection (which counters sinking and distraction), investigation (which counters further association with sinking and scattering), and equanimity (which counters unnecessary prolongation of countermeasures).

eight great guidelines *(khrid chen brgyad).* In Geluk, in the Mé tantra system: the direct instructions on the five stages of Guhyasamāja; the two guidelines on Cakrasaṃvara, by Lūipa and Ghaṇṭapa; the stages of the four yogas of Vajrabhairava; the six yogas of Kālacakra; the fourfold blessing of the Great Wheel Vajrapāṇi; the six Dharmas of Nāropa; and the opening of the golden door to the guidelines on transference of consciousness.

eight great guidelines *(khrid chen brgyad).* In Kagyü: the guidelines on the lama as the three buddha bodies, the guidelines on love and compassion, the guidelines on cause and effect and dependent arising, the guidelines on the fivefold nectar drip, the guidelines on the yoga of the coemergent, the guidelines on the six Dharmas of Nāropa, the guidelines on equalizing the eight worldly dharmas, and the guidelines meditation to reverse ill fortune through secret conduct.

eight great men *(skyes mchod brgyad).* The eight immortals of Daoist tradition: Zhong Liquan, Zhang Guolao, Lu Dongbin, Li Tieguai, He Xiangu, Nan Caihe, Han Xiangzi, and Chao Guojiu.

eight higher realizations *(mngon rtogs brgyad).* As taught in the *Ornament of Higher Realization,* by Maitreya: realization of all aspects, realization of the path, realization of everything, perfectly manifest realization of all aspects, reaching the summit of existence, final realization, instantaneous realization, and dharmakāya.

eight-limbed rule *(yan lag brgyad pa'i khrims)*. Abstention for twenty-four hours from killing, stealing, lying, sexual activity, intoxicants, eating after noon, sitting on high beds or thrones, and singing, dancing, or enjoying theatrical shows.

eight manuals *(be'u bum brgyad)*. In Shijé: the *Manual of the Profound Initiation, Manual of the Root Identification, Manual of the Guidelines of the Ear-Whispered Lineage, Manual of the Vital Points of the Four Doors, Manual of the Various Magical Powers, Manual of the Profound Mantra, Manual of the Dākiṇī Doctrine-Protector,* and *Manual of the Three-Part Royal Special Instruction.*

eight proponents of eternalism *(rtag par smra ba brgyad)*. Sāṃkhyas, Brahmavādins, Vaiṣṇavas, Mīmāṃsakas, Śaivas, Vaiśeṣikas, Naiyāyikas, and Nirgranthas.

eight pure ones *(dag pa rnam brgyad)*. Disciples of Tsongkhapa: Jampal Chösang, also known as Lama Jamkarwa; the venerable Sangkyongwa; the venerable Rinchen Gyaltsen; the venerable Jangsengwa; Tokden Jampal Gyatso; Geshé Sherap Drak; Geshé Jampal Tashi; and Geshé Palkyongwa.

eight sessions on mind training *(blo sbyong thun brgyad)*. In Kadam, special instructions on: mind training based on food, mind training based on the breath, emanating as many bodies as there are sands in the Ganges, mind training based on flesh and blood, mind training based on tormas, mind training based on the elements, training the mind to emanate the body as a wish-granting jewel, and the time just before death.

eight transmitted precepts *(sgrub pa bka' brgyad)*. In the triad lineage of Nyingma: the five transworldly classes—of Manjuśrī/Yamāntaka; lotus/Hayagrīva; purity/Heruka; nectar/Vajrāmṛta; and dagger/Vajrakīla—and the three worldly classes—sending invitations to the mother goddesses, reciting the destructive wrathful mantra, and praising and making offerings to worldly deities.

eight worldly dharmas *(['jig rten pa'i] chos brgyad)*. Preoccupation with: pleasure and pain, praise and blame, fame and shame, loss and gain.

eight yogic achievements *(dngos grub brgyad)*. Eye medicine, speed walking, magic pills, penetration of matter, suppression of diseases, the magic sword, flying, invisibility.

eightfold special instruction *(brgyad ldan gyi man ngag)*. In Geluk: Tsongkhapa's *Great Treatise on the Stages of the Path, Small Treatise on the Stages of the Path,* and *Song of Experience Related to the Stages of the Path;* the Third Dalai Lama's *Essence of Refined Gold* (a commentary on the preceding), the Fifth Dalai Lama's *Sacred Words of Mañjuśrī* (a commentary on the preceding), the First Panchen Lama Losang Chökyi Gyaltsen's *Path to Bliss,* the Third Panchen Palden Yeshé's *Swift Path* (a commentary on the preceding), and Dakpo Ngawang Drakpa's *Essence of Well-Spoken Advice.*

nine categories of knowledge objects *(shes bya tshig don dgu).* In Jainism: These are souls *(jīva),* the non-living *(ajīva),* evil *(pāpa),* afflictions *(āsrava),* bondage *(bandha),* merit *(puṇya),* stopping affliction *(saṃvara),* destruction of bondage *(nirjarā),* and liberation *(mokṣa).* See also Hopkins, *Maps of the Profound,* pp. 179–80.

nine expanses *(klong dgu).* In Nyingma, the expanses or spaces in which: the view is unchanging, meditation is neither present nor absent, there is neither hope nor doubt for the result, the essence is neither accomplished nor clarified, natural expression is unimpeded, appearance and mind are liberated with respect to characteristics, the expanse is unchanging, display unimpededly and naturally arises, and there is the total presence of spontaneous sameness and primordial liberation. See NS, vol. II, p. 45n591; cf. BA, p. 172.

nine lamps of pacification *(zhi byed sgron ma dgu).* In Shijé: the *Lamp of the Body Instruction, Lamp of the Speech Vehicle, Lamp of Secret Mind, Lamp of Pure View, Lamp of Precious Meditation, Lamp of Enlightened Conduct, Lamp of Basic Equanimity, Lamp of the Yoga Path,* and *Lamp of the Ultimate Result.*

nine methods for stabilizing the mind *(sems gnas pa'i thabs dgu).* The nine stages of tranquil abiding: mental placement, continuous placement, patched placement, close placement, taming the mind, pacification of the mind, complete pacification, one-pointed attention, and balanced placement.

nine obstacles *(sgrib dgu).* To be abandoned on the path of meditation: coarse-coarse, medium-coarse, subtle-course, coarse-medium, medium-medium, subtle-medium, coarse-subtle, medium-subtle, and subtle-subtle.

nine uncorrupted stages *(zag med sa dgu).* The preparatory mind of the first mental absorption, and then the actual experiences of the four form-realm and four formless-realm mental absorptions.

nine vehicles *(theg pa dgu).* In Bön: the shen of prediction, the shen of appearance, the shen of magic, the shen of existence, the vehicle of the layperson, the vehicle of the white *a,* the vehicle of the seer, the vehicle of the primordial shen, and the especially great vehicle.

nine vehicles *(theg pa dgu).* In Nyingma: śrāvaka, pratyekabuddha, bodhisattva, kriyā tantra, upa tantra, yoga tantra, mahāyoga, anuyoga, and atiyoga.

ninefold cycle on mixing and transference *(bsre 'pho dgu skor).* In Kagyü Mahāmudrā: inner heat, which mixes desire with great bliss; illusory body, which mixes anger with lack of true existence; clear light, which mixes ignorance with nonconceptuality; the daytime meditation that mixes inner heat with illusory body; the nighttime meditation that mixes dream with clear light; the death-time meditation that mixes bardo with the transference of consciousness; inner-heat practice for energetic individuals; dream practice for lazy individuals; and mixing greater and lesser transference practices.

ten avatars of Viṣṇu *(khyab 'jug gi 'jug pa bcu).* Fish, Tortoise, Boar, Man-Lion, Dwarf, Rāma, Rāma with the Ax, Kṛṣṇa, Buddha, Kalkin.

ten difficult texts *(dka' bcu).* Dharmakīrti's *Thorough Exposition of Valid Cognition,* Maitreya's *Ornament of Higher Realization,* Guṇaprabha's *Vinaya Sutra,* Asaṅga's *Compendium of Abhidharma,* Nāgārjuna's *Fundamental Treatise on the Middle Way,* Candrakīrti's *Entering the Middle Way,* Āryadeva's *Four Hundred Stanzas,* Maitreya's *Sublime Continuum,* Vasubandhu's *Treasury of Higher Knowledge,* and the *Guhyasamāja Tantra.*

ten directions *(phyogs bcu).* East, southeast, south, southwest, west, northwest, north, northeast, up, and down.

ten powers of a buddha *([sangs rgyas kyi] stobs bcu).* Knowing what abides and does not; knowing the maturation of acts; knowing the various inclinations of beings; knowing various sensory realms; knowing whose faculties are superior and whose are not; knowing all paths leading everywhere; knowing meditative absorption, liberation, concentration, meditative equipoise, delusions, and purification; remembering past lives; knowing death and birth; and knowing the cessation of affliction.

ten sciences *(rig gnas bcu).* Linguistics, logic, medicine, arts and technology, "inner meaning" (i.e., Buddhism), grammar, poetic theory, prosody, drama, and lexicography.

ten stages *(sa bcu).* The levels traversed by a bodhisattva: the joyous, the stainless, the illuminating, the radiant, the hard-to-conquer, the manifest, the far-reaching, the unmoving, the good-minded, the Dharma cloud.

ten virtues *(dge ba bcu).* Refraining from killing, stealing, sexual misconduct, lying, abusive speech, slander, gossip, covetousness, malice, and wrong views.

eleven sense faculties *(dbang po bcu gcig).* In Sāṃkhya thought: Eye, ear, nose, tongue, body, mind, speech, hand, foot, generative organ, and excretory organs.

eleven sources of valid cognition *(tshad ma bcu gcig).* Among Cārakīya Jaiminīyas: perception, inference, testimony, comparison, implication, cognition of nonexistence, reasoning, nonapprehension, renown, occurrence, and thinking.

twelve deeds of Bön *(bon gyi mdzad pa bcu gnyis).* Miwo Sherap's birth, dissemination of teachings, pacification of beings, guidance of beings, marriage, emanation, conquest of demons, victory, knowledge, isolation, and liberation.

twelve links of dependent arising *(rten cing 'brel bar 'byung ba'i yan lag bcu gnyis).* Ignorance, karmic formations, consciousness, name-and-form, six sense faculties, contact, feeling, craving, grasping, becoming, rebirth, and aging and death.

thirteen districts of Tibet *([bod kyi] khri skor bcu gsum).* Lho, Jang, Chu, Ja, Lha, Shang, Ya, Phak, Gyal, Tsal, Dri, Tak, and Yardrok.

thirteen golden Dharmas not allowed outside the fence *(lcags ri'i phyir mi 'da' ba'i gser chos bcu gsum).* See *thirteen golden Dharmas of the Tsar-system Lamdré*

thirteen golden Dharmas of the Tsar-system Lamdré *(tshar lugs kyi lam 'bras gser chos bcu gsum).* The three *khecarīs:* Nāro Khecarī, Indra Khecarī, Maitrī Khecarī; the three great red ones: Kurukulla, Gaṇapati, Ṭakkirāja; the three lesser red ones: Kurukulla with a Golden Heartdrop, Red Norgyünma, Tinuma; and Amāravajradevī, Red Jambala, Siṃhamukhā, and Black Mañjughoṣa.

thirteen great provinces of China *(rgya nag gi zhing sa chen po bcu gsum).* Shandong, Shanxi, Henan, Zhili, Zhejiang, Fujian, Jiangxi, Guandong, Guangxi, Yunnan, Guizhou, Sichuan, Huguang.

fourteen golden Dharmas of Lupa *(klu pa'i gser chos bcu bzhi).* In Sakya: The three *kecarīs:* Nāro Khecarī, Indra Khecarī, Maitrī Khecarī; the three great red ones: Kurukulla, Gaṇapati, Ṭakkirāja; the three lesser red ones: Kurukulla with a Golden Heartdrop, Red Norgyunma, Tinuma; and Amāravajradevī, Red Jambala, Siṃhamukhā, Black Mañjughoṣa, and Siṃhanāda Avalokiteśvara.

fourteen root downfalls *(rtsa ltung bcu bzhi).* In tantric practice: scorning or deriding the guru, transgressing the words of a buddha, criticizing vajra brothers or sisters because of anger, giving up love for sentient beings, giving up the awakening mind, criticizing our own or others' philosophical systems, revealing teachings to those who are unready, reviling or abusing our aggregates, denying emptiness, abetting malevolent people, not meditating on emptiness continually, discouraging the faithful, not properly utilizing the substances for tantric practice, deriding women.

sixteen arhats *(gnas brtan bcu drug).* Piṇḍola Bharadvaja, Ajita, Subinda, Kalika, Vajraputra, Bhadra, Kanakavatsa, Kanakabhadra, Nakula (Vakula), Rāhula, Chuḍapaṇṭhaka, Aṅgaja, Paṇṭhaka, Nāgasena, Jīvaka, Vanavasin.

sixteen aspects of the four noble truths *(bden bzhi'i rnam pa bcu drug).* Suffering is: suffering, impermanence, emptiness, no-self; origin is: origination, production, cause, condition; cessation is: cessation, peace, excellence, renunciation; path is: path, reasoning, attainment, and disillusionment.

sixteen drops *(thig le bcu drug).* The Kadam lineage's central tantric practice, wherein the meditation's focus gets progressively smaller, moving from: the entire universe, to your world in particular, to the realm of Tibet, to your own dwelling. Within your heart, there lie in sequence—one inside the heart of the other—the deity Prajñāpāramitā, the Buddha, Avalokiteśvara, Wisdom Tārā, Wrathful Tārā, the protector Acala, Atiśa, and Dromtönpa, inside of whose heart are the drops of the three lineages—extensive conduct, profound view, and inspirational practice—finally culminating in the drop of great awakening.

eighteen sects of the Vaibhāṣika *(bye brag smra ba'i gyes pa bco brgyad).* Pūrvaśaila, Aparaśaila, Haimavata, Lokottaravāda, Prajñāptivāda (all Mahāsāṃghika), Sarvāstivāda, Kāśyapīya, Mahīśāsaka, Dharmaguptaka, Bahuśrutīya, Tāmraśāṭīya, Vibhajyavāda (all Sarvāstivāda), Jaitavanīya, Abhayagirīvāsīya, Mahāvihāravāsīya (all Sthavira), Kurukullaka, Āvantika, Vātsīputrīya (all Saṃmatīya).

eighteen sense fields *(khams bco brgyad).* Eye, form, eye consciousness; ear, sound, ear consciousness; nose, smell, nose consciousness; tongue, taste, tongue consciousness; body, sensation, body consciousness; mind, dharmas, mind consciousness.

twenty Dharma treatises related to Maitreya *(byams pa dang 'brel ba'i chos nyi shu).* The five treatises of Maitreya, the five treatises on the stages, the two compendiums, and the eight dissertations.

twenty emptinesses *(stong nyid nyi shu).* The emptiness of the inner, the emptiness of the outer, the emptiness of the inner and the outer, the emptiness of emptiness, the emptiness of the great (i.e., the ten directions), the emptiness of the ultimate (i.e., nirvana), the emptiness of the composite, the emptiness of the noncomposite, the emptiness of that which is beyond extremes, the emptiness of that which is without beginning or end, the emptiness of that which should not be discarded (i.e., the path), the emptiness of true nature, the emptiness of all dharmas, the emptiness of defining characteristics, the emptiness of the imperceptible (i.e., the three times), the emptiness that is the absence of entities, the emptiness of entities, the emptiness of nonentities, the emptiness of intrinsic nature, the emptiness of an entity that is other. The last four are sometimes considered to be a summary of the first sixteen.

twenty-four power places of Jambudvīpa *('dzam gling gnas mchog nyi shu rtsa bzhi).* In the Yoginī tantras: Jālandhara, Uḍḍiyāna, Paurṅagiri, Kāmarūpa, Mālava, Sindhu, Nagara, Munmuni, Kāruṇyapāṭaka, Devīkoṭa, Karmārapāṭaka, Kulatā, Arbuda, Godāvarī, Himādri, Harikela, Lampāka, Kañci, Saurāṣṭra, Kaliṅga, Kokaṇa, Caritra, Kośala, Vindhyākumārapaurikā.

twenty-five categories of Sāṃkhya *(grangs can pa'i shes bya nyer lnga)*. The principal (or fundamental nature), the great, the I-principle, form, sound, smell, taste, tangibles, earth, water, fire, air, space, eye, ear, nose, tongue, body, voice, hands, feet, excretory organs, generative organs, mind, and the person.

twenty-five kalkins *(rigs ldan nyer lnga)*. In Kālacakra tradition: [Mañjughoṣa] Yaśas (r. 277–177 B.C.E.), Puṇḍarīka (r. 177–77 B.C.E.), Bhadra (r. 77 B.C.E.–24 C.E.), Vijaya (r. 24–124), Sumitrabhadra (r. 124–224), Ratnapāṇi (r. 224–324), Viṣṇugupta (r. 324–424), Sūryakīrti (r. 424–524), Subhadra (r. 524–624), Samudravijaya (r. 624–806), Aja (r. 806–1027), Sūrya (r. 1027–1127), Viśvarūpa (r. 1127–1227), Śaṣiprabha (r. 1227–1327), Ananta (r. 1327–1427), Mahīpala (r. 1427–1527), Śrīpala (r. 1527–1627), Siṃha (r. 1627–1727), Vikrama (r. 1727–1827), Mahābala (r. 1827–1927), Aniruddha (r. 1927–2027), Narasiṃha (r. 2027–2127), Maheśvara (r. 2127–2227), Ananatavijaya (r. 2227–2327), Yaśas or Raudracakrin (r. 2327–2427).

twenty-eight powerful goddesses *(dbang mo nyer brgyad)*. Yak-headed Rākṣasī, serpent-headed Brahmaṇī (Brahmī), leopard-headed Mahādevī, mongoose-headed Vaiṣṇavī (Lobhā), snow-bear-headed Kumārī, bear-headed Indraṇī, cuckoo-headed Vajrā, sow-headed Vajrī, water-dragon-headed Śānti, scorpion-headed Amṛtā, hawk-headed Candrā, fox-headed Daṇḍā, tiger-headed Rākṣasī, antelope-headed Vajrā, vulture-headed Bhakṣiṇī, horse-headed Ratī, garuda-headed Mahābalī, dog-headed Rākṣasī, crane-headed Abhilāsī, stag-headed Vasurakṣā, lion-headed Vajrā, wolf-headed Vajudevī, buffalo-headed Nārī, sow-headed Vārāhī, crow-headed Vajrī, elephant-headed Mahāhastini, serpent-headed Varuṇī, serpent-headed Vajrā.

thirty-two marks *(mtshan sum bcu rtsa gnyis)*. As found in, e.g., *Ornament of Higher Realization,* 8:13–17: palms and soles marked with wheels, feet firm like a tortoise's, webbed finger and toes, soft and supple hands and feet, well-proportioned limbs, long toes and fingers, broad arches, a tall and straight body, hidden ankles, upward-curling body-hair, calves like an antelope's, long and beautiful arms, contracted sex organ, golden complexion and delicate skin, body hairs curling to the right, hair-ring between the eyebrows, leonine chest, rounded shoulders, broad back, superior sense of taste, body symmetrical like a banyan, protuberance at the crown, long tongue, voice like Brahmā's, leonine jaws, white teeth, equal teeth, closely spaced teeth, forty teeth, sapphire blue eyes, bovine eyelashes.

thirty-five confession buddhas *(ltung bshags kyi sangs rgyas so lnga).* Amoghadārśin, Anantaujas, Aśokaśrī, Bhadrarṣi, Brahman, Brahmadatta, Brahmajyotis, Candanaśrī, Dhānaśrī, Indraketudhvaja, Kusumaśrī, Nageśvaraja, Nārāyaṇa, Padmajyotis, Parikīrtitanāmaśrī, Prabhāsari, Ratnacandra, Ratnacandraprabhā, Ratnāgni, Ratnārcis, Ratnapadma, Śailendrarāja, Samantavabhāsa, Śākyamuni, Smṛtiśrī, Suradatta, Suvikranta, Vajragarbha, Varuṇa, Varuṇadeva, Vikranta, Vimala, Virānanda, Virasena, Yuddhajaya.

forty-two peaceful deities *(zhi lha zhe gnyis).* Samantabhadra (buddha), Samatabhadrī, Vairocana, Akṣobhya, Ratnasambhava, Amitābha, Amoghasiddhi, Ākāśadhātvīśvarī, Buddhalocanā, Māmakī, Paṇḍaravāsinī, Samayatārā, Kṣitigarbha, Vajrapāṇi, Ākāśagarbha, Avalokiteśvara, Lāsyā, Mālyā, Gītā, Nartī, Maitreya, Nivaraṇaviśkambhin, Samantabhadra (bodhisattva), Mañjuśrī, Dhūpā, Puṣpā, Ālokā, Gandhā, Amṛtakuṇḍalin, Hayagrīva, Mahābala, Yamāntaka, Aṅkuśā, Pāśā, Sphoṭā, Ghaṇṭā, Munīndra, Vemacitra, Śākyamuni, Siṃha, Jvālamukha, Yamarāja.

fifty-eight wrathful deities *('khro bo lnga bcu lnga brgyad).* Buddha Krodheśvarī, Buddha Heruka, Vajra Krodheśvarī, Vajra Heruka, Ratna Krodheśvarī, Ratna Heruka, Padma Krodheśvarī, Padma Heruka, Karma Krodheśvarī, Karma Heruka, Kerima (or Gaurī), Pukkaśī, Caurimā (Chaurā), Ghasmarī, Pramohā, Caṇḍalī, Vetalī (Vaitalī, Petalī), Śmaśalī (Śmaśaṇī), Siṃhamukhī, Gṛdhramukhī, Vyāghramukhī, Kaṅkamukhī, Sṛgalamukhī, Kākamukhī, Śvamukhī, Úlumukhī, Ankuśā, Paśadhārī, Vajraśṛṅkhalā, Ghaṇṭā, yak-headed Rākṣasī, Brahmaṇī (Brahmī), Mahādevī, Vaiṣṇavī (Lobhā), Kumārī, Indraṇī, cuckoo-headed Vajrā, sow-headed Vajrī, Śānti, Amṛtā, Candrā, Daṇḍā, tiger-headed Rākṣasī, antelope-headed Vajrā, Bhakṣiṇī, Ratī, Mahābalī, dog-headed Rākṣasī, Abhilāsī, Vasurakṣā, lion-headed Vajrā, Vajudevī, Nārī, sow-headed Vārāhī, crow-headed Vajrī, Mahāhastini, Varunī, serpent-headed Vajrā.

sixty-two debased views *(lta ngan drug bcu re gnyis).* In, e.g., the *Brahmajala Sutta* of the *Dīgha Nikāya:* four grounds for asserting the eternity of the self and world; four grounds for asserting the partial eternity and partial noneternity of the self and world; four grounds for asserting the finitude and infinitude of the self and world; four grounds for avoiding assertion altogether; two grounds for asserting origination through chance; sixteen assertions regarding the self after death, to the effect that it is healthy and conscious and either material, immaterial, both material and immaterial, neither material nor immaterial, finite, infinite, both, neither, of uniform perception, of varied perception, of limited perception, of unlimited perception, wholly happy, wholly miserable, both, or neither; eight assertions regarding the self after death, to the effect that it is healthy and unconscious and either material, immaterial, both, neither, finite, infinite, both, or neither; eight assertions regarding the self after death, to the effect that it is healthy and unconscious and either material, immaterial, both, neither, finite, infinite, both, or neither; seven grounds for asserting the annihilation of the self after death; and five grounds for wrongly asserting the attainment of nirvana here and now.

eighty-four great adepts *(grub thob brgyad bcu rtsa bzhi)*. Aciṅta, Ajogi, Anaṅga, Āryadeva, Babhaha, Bhadrapa, Bhandepa, Bhikṣanapa, Bhusuku (Śāntideva), Cāmāripa, Campaka, Carbaripa, Catrapa, Cauraṅgipa, Celukapa, Dārikapa, Ḍeṅgipa, Dhahulipa, Dharmapa, Dhilipa, Dhobīpa, Dhokaripa, Ḍombipa, Dukhaṅdhi, Ghaṇṭāpa, Gharbari, Godhuripa, Gorakhnāth, Indrabhūti, Jālandhara, Jayānanda, Jogipa, Kālapa, Kambala, Kamparipa, Kanakhalā, Kāṇhapa, Kaṅkaṇa, Kaṅkarīpa, Kantalipa, Kapālapa (Āryadeva), Khaḍgapa, Kilakilapa, Kirapālapa, Kokilipa, Koṭalipa, Kucipa, Kukkuripa, Kumbharipa, Lakṣmīṅkarā, Līlapa, Lucikapa, Lūipa, Mahipa, Maṇibhadrā, Medhini, Mekhalā, Mekopa, Mīnapa, Nāgabodhi, Nāgārjuna, Nalinapa, Nāropa, Nirguṇapa, Pacaripa, Paṅkajapa, Putalipa, Rāhula, Ratnākaraśānti (Śāntipa), Samudra, Saraha, Saroruha, Sarvabhakṣa, Śavaripa, Śyalipa, Taṅtepa, Tantipa, Thaganapa, Tilopa, Udhilipa, Upanaha, Viṇāpa, Virūpa, Vyālipa.

Bibliography

Key:

NA = text not available
NGB = Nying ma rgyud 'bum number
P = Peking Tibetan Tripitaka catalogue number
Toh = Tōhoku Dergé Tibtan Tripitaka catalogue number

Works Cited by the Author

Kangyur and Bönpo Canon *(Canonical Scriptures)*

Descent to Laṅka Sutra. Āryalaṅkāvatāramahāyānasūtra. 'Phags pa lang kar gshegs pa'i theg pa chen po'i mdo. Toh 107, mdo sde *ca.* P775, *ngu.* English translation: D. T. Suzuki. The *Laṅkāvatāra Sūtra: A Mahayana Text.* London/New York: Kegan Paul International, 1998 (1932).

Great Drum Sutra. Āryamahābherīhārakaparivartanāmamahāyānasūtra. 'Phags pa rnga bo che chen po'i le'u zhes bya ba theg pa chen po'i mdo. Toh 222, mdo sde *dza.* P888, *tshu.*

Great Nirvana Sutra. Āryamahāparinirvāṇanāmamahāyānasūtra. 'Phags pa yongs su mya ngan las 'das pa chen po'i mdo. Toh 120, mdo sde *tha.* P788, *tu.*

Great Tantra of the Perfectly United. Saṃpūṭanāmamahātantra. Yang dag par sbyor ba zhes bya ba'i rgyud chen po. Toh 381, rgyud *ga.* P26, *ga.*

Guhyasamāja Tantra. Sarvatathāgatakāyavākcittarahasyaguhyasamājanāmamahākalpatantrarāja. De bzhin gshegs pa thams cad kyi sku gsung thugs kyi gsang chen gsang ba 'dus pa zhes bya ba brtag pa'i rgyal po chen po. Toh 442, rgyud *ca.* P81, *ca.*

Heart Sutra. Bhagavatīprajñāpāramitāhṛdaya. Bcom ldan 'das ma shes rab kyi pha rol tu phyin pa'i snying po. Toh 21, sher phyin *ka.* P160, *na.* English translation: Edward Conze, *Buddhist Wisdom Books: Containing* The Diamond Sutra *and* The Heart Sutra. New York: Harper & Row, 1958.

Hevajra Tantra. Hevajramahātantrarāja. Kye rdo rje shes bya ba rgyud kyi rgyal po. Toh 417, rgyud *nga.* P10, *ka.* English translations: G. W. Farrow and I. Menon. *The*

Concealed Essence of the Hevajra Tantra, with the Commentary Yogaratnamālā. Delhi: Motilal Banarsidass, 1992; David L. Snellgrove. *The Hevajra Tantra: A Critical Study.* London/New York: Oxford University Press, 1959.

Kālacakra Root Tantra. Paramādibuddhoddhṛtaśrīkālacakranāmatantrarāja. Mchog gi dang po'i sangs rgyas las phyung ba rgyud kyi rgyal po dpal dus kyi 'khor lo. Toh 363, rgyud *ka.* P4, *ka.*

King of Concentration Sutra. Āryasarvadharmasvabhāvasamatāvipañcitasamādhirājanāmamahāyānasūtra. 'Phags pa chos thams cad kyi rang bzhin mnyam pa nyid rnam par spros pa ting nge 'dzin gyi rgyal po zhes bya ba theg pa chen po'i mdo. Toh 127, mdo sde *da.* P795, *thu.*

Langru Prophecy. Āryagośiṅgavyākaraṇanāmamahāyānasūtra. 'Phags pa glang ru lung bstan pa zhes bya ba theg pa chen po'i mdo. Toh 357, mdo sde *a.* P1026, *ke.*

Mañjuśrī Root Tantra. Āryamañjuśrīmūlatantra. 'Phags pa 'jam dpal rtsa rgyud. Toh 543, rgyud *na.* P162, *na.*

Precious Collection Tantra. 'Dus pa rin po che'i rgyud. (Bön text; NA)

Puṇḍarīka. *Stainless Light. Vimalaprabhānāmamūlatantrānusāriṇīdvādaśasāhasrikālaghukālacakratantrarājaṭīkā. Bsdus pa'i rgyud kyi rgyal po dus kyi 'khor lo'i 'grel bshad rtsa ba'i rgyud kyi rjes su 'jug pa stong phrag bcu pa bcu gnyis pa dri ma med pa'i 'od.* Toh 845, rgyud *shī.* P2064, *ka.*

Vajra Garland of Excellent Explanation. Vajramālābhidhānamahāyogatantrasarvatantrahṛdayarahasyavibhaṅga. Rnal 'byor chen po'i rgyud dpal rdo rje phreng ba mngon par brjod pa rgyud thams cad kyi snying po gsang ba rnam par phye ba. Toh 445, rgyud *ca.* P82, *ca.*

Verse Summary of the Perfection of Wisdom. Prajñāpāramitāsañcayagāthā. Shes rab gyi pha rol tu phyin pa sdud pa tshigs su bcad pa. Toh 13, sher phyin *ka.* P735, *tsi.* English translation: Edward Conze, *The Perfection of Wisdom in Eight Thousand Lines and Its Verse Summary.* Bolinas: Four Seasons Foundation, 1973.

White Lotus of Compassion Sutra. Āryamahākaruṇāpuṇḍarīkanāmamahāyānasūtra. 'Phags pa snying rje chen po'i pad ma dkar po zhes bya ba theg pa chen po'i mdo. Toh 111, mdo sde *cha.* P779, *chu.*

Tengyur *(Canonical Treatises)* and Non-Canonical Treatises

Anu (Thönmi Sambhota). *The Thirty. Vyākaraṇamūlatriṃśaka. Lung du ston pa rtsa ba sum cu pa.* Toh 4348, sna tshogs *co.* P5834, *ngo.*

Āryadeva. *Four Hundred Stanzas. Catuḥśatakaśāstrakārikā. Bstan bcos bzhi rgya pa.* Toh 3846, dbu ma *tsha.* P5246, *tsha.* English translation: Karen Lang. *Āryadeva's Catuḥśataka.* Copenhagen: Akademisk Forlag, 1986.

Asvabhāva. *Explication of the Ornament of Higher Realization. Mahāyānasūtrālaṃkāraṭīkā. Theg pa chen po'i mdo sde'i rgyan gyi rgya cher bshad pa.* Toh 4029, sems tsam *bi.* P5530, *bi.*

Atiśa. *Lamp for the Path to Enlightenment. Bodhipathapradīpa. Byang chub lam gyi sgron ma.* Toh 3947, dbu ma *khi*. P5343, *ki*. English translations: Richard Sherburne. *A Lamp for the Path and Commentary of Atīśa*. London/Boston: Allen and Unwin, 1983; Ronald M. Davidson. "Atiśa's Lamp on the Path." In Donald S. Lopez, Jr., ed. *Buddhism in Practice*. Princeton: Princeton University Press, 1995, pp. 290–301.

Bhāvaviveka. *Blaze of Logic. Madhyamakahṛdayavṛttitarkajvālā. Dbu ma'i snying po'i 'grel pa rtog ge 'bar ba.* Toh 3856, dbu ma *dza*. P5256, *dza*.

———. *Precious Lamp of Madhyamaka. Madhyamakaratnapradīpa. Dbu ma rin po che'i sgron ma.* Toh 3854, mdo 'grel *tsha*. P5254, *tsha*.

Candrakīrti. *Bright Lamp. Pradīpoddyotananāmaṭīkā. Sgron ma gsal bar byed pa zhes bya ba'i rgya cher bshad.* Toh 1785, rgyud 'grel *ha*. P2650, *sa*.

Dharmakīrti. *Ascertainment of Valid Cognition. Pramāṇaviniścaya. Tshad ma rnam nges.* Toh 4211, tshad ma *ce*. P5710, *ce*.

———. *Thorough Exposition of Valid Cognition. Pramāṇavārttika. Tshad ma rnam 'grel.* Toh 4210, tshad ma *ce*. P5709, *ce*.

Dharmamitra. *Clear Words. Abhisamayālaṃkārakārikāprajñāpāramitopadeśaśāstraṭīkāprasphuṭapadā. Shes rab kyi pha rol tu phyin pa'i man ngag gi bstan bcos mngon par rtogs pa'i rgyan gyi tshig le'ur byas pa'i 'grel bshad tshig rab tu gsal ba.* Toh 3796, mdo 'grel *nya*. P5194, *nya*.

Exposition of Praises of the Stages. Yogācārabhūmivyākhyā. Rnal 'byor spyod pa'i sa rnam par bshad pa. Toh 4043, sems tsam *'i*. P5544, *yi*.

Jñānakīrti. *Distinguishing Clearly the Entire Sum of the Buddha's Words. Tattvāvatārākhyasakalasugatavacastātparyavyākhyāprakaraṇa. De kho na nyid la 'jugs pa zhes bya ba bde bar gshegs pa'i bka' ma lus pa mdor bsdus te bshad pa'i rab tu byed pa.* Toh 3709, rgyud 'grel *tsu*. P4532, *nu*.

Kamalaśīla. *Detailed Explication of the Compendium of Principles. Tattvasaṃgrahapañjikā. De kho na nyid bsdus pa'i dka' 'grel.* Toh 4267, tshad ma *ze*. P5765 *'e*. English translation: Ganganatha Jha. *The Tattvasaṃgraha of Śāntarakṣita with the Commentary of Kamalaśīla*. 2 vols. Baroda: The Oriental Institute, 1937–39.

Liyül Prophecy. Kaṃsadeśavyākaraṇa. Li'i yul lung bstan pa. Toh 4202, spring yig *nge*. P5699, *nge*.

Maitreya. *Ornament of Mahayana Sutras. Mahāyānasūtrālaṃkāra. Theg pa chen po'i mdo sde rgyan.* Toh 4020, sems tsam *phi*. P5521, *phi*. English translation: Robert A. F. Thurman et al. *The Universal Vehicle Discourse Literature (Mahāyānasūtrālaṃkāra)*. New York: American Institute of Buddhist Studies, 2004.

Maitrīpa. *Commentary on the Ten Principles. Tattvadaśakaṭīkā. De kho na nyid bcu pa'i rgya cher 'grel pa.* Toh. 2254, rgyud 'grel *wi*. P3099, *mi*.

———. *Ten Principles. Tattvadaśaka. De kho na nyid bcu pa.* Toh 2236, rgyud 'grel *wi.* P3080, *mi.* English translation: Karl Brunnhölzl. *Straight from the Heart: Buddhist Pith Instructions.* Ithaca, NY: Snow Lion, 2007, pp. 140–41.

Nāgārjuna. *The Five Stages. Pañcakrama. Rim lnga.* Toh 1802, rgyud 'grel *ngi.* P2667, *gi.*

______. *Fundamental Treatise on the Middle Way. Prajñāmūlamadhyamakakārikā. Dbu ma rta ba'i tshig le'ur shes rab ces bya ba.* Toh 3824, dbu ma *tsa.* P5224, *tsa.* English translation: Jay L. Garfield. *The Fundamental Wisdom of the Middle Way: Nāgārjuna's Mūlamadhyamakakārikā.* New York: Oxford University Press, 1995.

Nāropa. *Explication of the Lamp of All Secrets. Sarvaguhyapradīpaṭīkā. Gsang ba thams cad kyi sgron ma'i rgya cher 'grel pa.* Toh 1787, rgyud 'grel *ha.* P2652, *sa.*

______. *The Epitome. Ājñāsaṃyakpramāṇanāmaḍākiṇyupadeśa. Bka' yang dag pa'i tshad ma shes bya ba mkha' 'gro ma'i man ngag [Kā dpe].* Toh 2331, rgyud 'grel *zhi.* [No P.]

Sahajavajra. *Explication of the Ten Principles. Tattvadaśakaṭīkā. De kho na nyid bcu pa'i rgya cher 'grel pa.* Toh 2254, rgyud 'grel *wi.* P3099, *mi.* English translation: Karl Brunnhölzl. *Straight from the Heart: Buddhist Pith Instructions.* Ithaca, NY: Snow Lion, 2007, pp. 141–90.

Saraha. *Treasury of Dohas. Dohākoṣagīti. Do ha mdzod gyi glu.* Toh 2224, rgyud 'grel, *wi.* P3068, *mi.* English translation: Roger R. Jackson. *Tantric Treasures: Three Collections of Mystical Verse from Buddhist India.* New York: Oxford University Press, 2004, pp. 53–115.

Śavaripa [attributed to Saraha]. *Doha Treasure Mahāmudrā Instruction. Dohākoṣanāmamahāmudropadeśa. Do ha mdzod ces bya ba phyag rgya chen po'i man ngag.* Toh 2273, rgyud 'grel *zhi.* P3119, *tsi.* English translation: Jampa Thaye. *A Garland of Gold: The Early Kagyu Masters of India and Tibet.* Bristol: Ganesha Press, 1990, pp. 80–86.

Tilopa. *Ganges Mahāmudrā Instruction. [Gaṅgā]mahāmudropadeśa. Phyag rgya chen po'i man ngag [gangā ma].* Toh 2303, rgyud 'grel *shi.* P3132, *tsi.* English translation: Samuel Bercholz and Sherab Kohn, eds. *Entering the Stream.* Boston: Shambhala, 1993, pp. 266–72.

Udbhaṭasiddhasvāmin. *Special Praise of the Holy. Viśeṣastava. Khyad par 'phags stod.* Toh 1109, bstod tshogs *ka.* P5476, *gi.*

Vasubandhu. *Treasury of Higher Knowledge. Abhidharmakośa. Chos mngon pa mdzod kyi tshig le'ur byas pa.* Toh 4089, mngon pa *ku.* P5590, *gu.* English translation from La Vallée Poussin's French translation found in Leo M. Pruden. *Abhidharmakośabhāṣyam.* Fremont, CA: Asian Humanities Press, 1991.

Vinītadeva. *A Summary of the Teachings of the Various Sects by Way of a Progressive Reading of Various Critiques. Samayabhedoparacanacakrenikāyabhedopadeśasaṃgraha. Gzhung tha dad pa rim par bklag pa'i 'khor lo las sde pa tha dad pa bstan pa bsdus pa.* Toh 4140, 'dul ba *su.* P5641, *su.*

Tibetan Works

Biography of Tsültrim Rinchen of Shalu. Zha lu ba tshul khrims rin chen gyi rnam thar. NA.

Book of Kadam, The. Bka' gdams glegs bam. 2 vols. Kansu: Mi rigs dpe khrun khang, 1993. English translation: Thupten Jinpa. *The Book of Kadam: The Core Texts.* Boston: Wisdom Publications, 2008.

Butön Rinchen Drup. *Bu ston chos 'byung [Chos 'byung gsung rab rin po che'i mdzod]*. [Sining]: Krun go Bod kyi shes rig dpe skrun khang, 1991. Partial English translation: E. Obermiller, trans. *History of Buddhism (Chos-ḥbyung)*. Delhi: Sri Satguru Publications, 1986 (Heidelberg, 1931–32); E. Obermiller, trans. [Bu-ston.] *Jewellery of Scripture*. Delhi: Paljor, 2000 (Heidelberg, 1931–32).

Changkya Rölpai Dorjé. *Great Treatise on the Establishment of Philosophical Systems. Grub mtha'i rnam gzhag chen mo*. In *[Collected Works] Lcaṅ-skya Rol-pa'i-rdo-rje'i gsuṅ 'bum*, vol. *cha*. Dharamsala: Library of Tibetan Works and Archives, 2002– . Translation forthcoming as volume 24 of the *Library of Tibetan Classics*.

———. *Secret Biography of the [Seventh] Dalai Lama, Kalsang Gyatso. Rgyal ba bskal bzang rgya mtsho'i zhal snga nas gsang ba'i rnam thar pa'i sgo nas stod pa thugs rje'i nyin byed 'dren pa'i skya rengs*. In *[Collected Works] Lcaṅ-skya Rol-pa'i-rdo-rje'i gsuṅ 'bum*, vol. *ka*. Dharamsala: Library of Tibetan Works and Archives, 2002– .

———. *Song in Praise of the Five-Peaked Mountain. Ri bo rtse lnga'i gnas bstod dang 'brel ba'i mgur.* In *[Collected Works] Lcaṅ-skya Rol-pa'i-rdo-rje'i gsuṅ 'bum*, vol. *nga*. Dharamsala: Library of Tibetan Works and Archives, 2002– .

———. *Songs on Correct View. Lta mgur a ma ngos 'dzin nam lta ba'i gsung mgur zab mo*. In *[Collected Works] Lcaṅ-skya Rol-pa'i-rdo-rje'i gsuṅ 'bum*, vol. *nga*. Dharmaṣala: Library of Tibetan Works and Archives, 2002– .

Chenga Lodrö Gyaltsen. *Flowing River of Faith: Biography of Jetsün Jampel Gyatso. Rje btsun 'jam dpal rgya mtsho'i rnam thar dad pa'i chu rgyun*. In *The Collected Works (gsuṅ 'bum) of Spyan-sṅa blo-gros-rgyal-mtshan of rgya-ma rin-chen-sgaṅ*, vol. *kha*. New Delhi: Ṅagwang Gelek Demo, 1983.

———. *A Presentation of Nyingma and Bon. Rnying ma dang bon gyi rnam gzhag*. In *The Collected Works (gsuṅ 'bum) of Spyan-sṅa blo-gros-rgyal-mtshan of rgya-ma rin-chen-sgaṅ*, vol. *ca*. New Delhi: Ṅagwang Gelek Demo, 1983.

———. *Seven-Point Mind Training. Blo sbyong don bdun ma*. In *The Collected Works (gsuṅ 'bum) of Spyan-sṅa blo-gros-rgyal-mtshan of rgya-ma rin-chen-sgaṅ*, vol. *nga*. New Delhi: Ṅagwang Gelek Demo, 1983.

Desi Sangyé Gyatso. *White Beryl. Phug lugs rtsis kyi legs bshad ba'i dūra dkar po*. 2 vols. Beijing: Khrung go'i bod kyi shes rig dpe khrun khang, 1996.

———. *Yellow Beryl. Bai ḍūr ser po.* New Delhi: Ṅagwang Gelek Demo, 1980.

Dölpopa Sherap Gyaltsen. *Mountain Dharma: The Ocean of Definitive Meaning: An Uncommon Special Instruction on the Ultimate. Ri chos nges don rgya mtsho zhes bya ba mthar thug thun mong ma yin pa'i man ngag.* Beijing: Mi rigs dpe skrun khang, 1998. English translation: Jeffrey Hopkins. *Mountain Doctrine: Tibet's Fundamental Treatise on Other-Emptiness and the Buddha Matrix.* Ithaca, NY: Snow Lion, 2006.

Drakpa Gyaltsen. *Parting from the Four Attachments. Zhen pa bzhi bral.* In *Grags-pa-rgyal-mtshan gyi bka' 'bum = The Complete Works of Grags-pa-rgyal-mtshan.* Compiled by Bsod nams rgya mtsho. In *Sa skya pa'i bka' 'bum,* vol. *ta.* Tokyo: Toyo Bunkyo, 1968.

———. *Root Text on the View of the Indivisibility of Samsara and Nirvana. 'Khor 'das dbyer med kyi lta ba'i rtsa ba.* In *Lam 'bras slob bśad: The Sa-skya-pa Teachings of the Path and the Fruit, according to the Tshar-pa Transmission, as Arranged by 'Jam-dbyaṅs-blo-gter-dbaṅ-po and Supplemented by Texts Continuing the Lineage through Khaṅ-gsar Dam-pa and Sga-ston Ṅag-dbaṅ-legs pa.* Sa-skya Lam-'bras Literature Series, vol. II *da.* Dehra Dun: Sakya Centre, 1983.

———. *Wishing Tree of Higher Realization. Mngon rtogs ljon shing.* In *Grags-pa-rgyal-mtshan gyi bka' 'bum = The Complete Works of Grags-pa-rgyal-mtshan.* Compiled by Bsod nams rgya mtsho. In *Sa skya pa'i bka' 'bum,* vol. *cha.* Tokyo: Toyo Bunkyo, 1968.

Drigung Jikten Sumgön. *Forty Statements on the Holy Dharma of the Single Intention. Dam chos dgongs gcig nang tshan gsung bzhi bcu pa.* In *Collected Works (gsuṅ 'bum) of 'Bri-guṅ Skyob-pa 'Jig-rten-mgon-po Rin-chen-dpal,* vol. *ka.* Bir, H.P.: D. Tsondu Senghe, 1976.

———. *Root Song. Phyag rgya chen po lnga ldan rtogs pa'i mgur [Rtsa ba'i mgur].* In *Collected Works (gsuṅ 'bum) of 'Bri-guṅ Skyob-pa 'Jig-rten-mgon-po Rin-chen-dpal,* vol. *tha.* Bir, H.P.: D. Tsondu Senghe, 1976.

Dromtön Gyalwai Jungné. *Short Work on the Sevenfold Divinity and Teaching. Lha chos bdun ldan chung ba.* NA. Cited by Jamgön Anyé in his *Collected Works.*

Gampopa. *Collected Works (gsung 'bum) of Sgam-po-pa Bsod-nams-rin-chen.* 3 vols. Darjeeling: Kargyud Sungrab Nyamso Khang, [1982].

Gendün Drupa (Dalai Lama I). *Song of the Eastern Snow Mountain. Shar kang ri ma.* In *The Collected Works of the First Dalai Lama Dge-'dun-grub-pa,* vol. *cha.* Gangtok: Dodrup Lama Sangye, 1978–81. English translation: Glenn H. Mullin. *Bridging the Sutras and Tantras.* Valois, NY: Gabriel/Snow Lion, 1982, pp. 109–114.

Gendün Gyatso (Dalai Lama II). *A Ship to Sail the Ocean of Philosophical Systems. Grub mtha 'rgya mtshor 'jug pa'i gru rdzings.* Varanasi: Dge ldan spyi las khang, 1993. English translation: Glenn Mullin. *Selected Works of the Dalai Lama II: The Tantric Yogas of Sister Niguma.* Ithaca, NY: Snow Lion, 1985, pp. 153–82.

Geshé Potowa. *Blue Udder. Be'u bum sngon po.* In *Gangs can rigs brgya'i sgo 'byed lde mig,* vol. 10. Beijing: Mi rigs dpe khrun khang, 1991. Translation forthcoming in volume 10 of the Library of Tibetan Classics.

Gö Lotsāwa Shönu Pal. *The Blue Annals. Deb ther sngon po.* New Delhi: International Academy of Indian Culture, 1974. English translation: G. Roerich, *The Blue Annals.* Delhi: Motilal Banarsidass, 1979 (1949).

Gomchen Ngawangpa. *Garland of Yogic Achievements. Lan dngos grub gyi phreng ba mkhas rgyan.* In *Collected Works of Dwags po sgom chen ṅag dbaṅ grags pa,* vol. *kha.* New Delhi: Ngawang Sopa, 1980–82.

———. *Reply to Questions About the View and Meditation of the Inquiry into the Pure Noble Intention. Dri ba lhag bsam rab dkar lta sgom gyi dris lan.* In *Collected Works of Dwags po sgom chen ṅag dbaṅ grags pa,* vol. *kha.* New Delhi: Ngawang Sopa, 1980–82.

Gönpo Kyap. *History of Buddhism in China. Rgya nag chos 'byung.* Khreng-tu'u: Si-khron mi rigs dpe skrun khang, 1998 (1983).

Gyaltsap Jé Darma Rinchen, *Entryway for the Conqueror's Children: Exposition of the Way of the Bodhisattva. Byang chub sems dpa'i spyod pa la 'jug pa'i rnam bshad rgyal sras 'jug ngogs.* In *The Collected Works (gsuṅ 'bum) of the Lord Rgyal-tshab Rje Dar-ma-rin-chen,* vol. *nga.* New Delhi: Mongolian Lama Gurudeva, 1982.

Jamgön Anyé Shap Ngawang Künga Sönam. *Collected Works.* [Kathmandu:] Sa skya rgyal yongs gsung rab slob gnyer khang, 2000.

———. *Wonderful Treasure-House of Sakya Genealogy. Sa skya'i ngo mtshar gdung rabs bang mdzod.* [Kathmandu:] Sa skya rgyal yongs gsung rab slob gnyer khang, 2000.

Jamyang Chöjé Tashi Palden. *Biography of Khedrup Jé. Mkhas grub rje'i rnam thar.* In *The Collected Works (gsuṅ bum) of the Lord Mkhas-grub Rje Dge-legs-dpal-bzaṅ-po,* vol. *ka.* New Delhi: Mongolian Lama Gurudeva, 1980–82.

———. *Biography of Tsongkhapa the Great. 'Jam mgon chos kyi rgyal po tsong kha pa chen po'i rnam thar.* Xining: Mtsho sngon mi rigs dpe skrun khang, 1992.

Joden Sönam Lhundrup. *Biography of Tsongkhapa. Tsong kha pa'i rnam thar.* NA; see TBRC W18630.

Khedrup Jé Gelek Pal Sangpo. *A Dose of Emptiness. Stong thun chen mo.* In *The Collected Works (gsuṅ bum) of the Lord Mkhas-grub Rje Dge-legs-dpal-bzaṅ po.* vol. *ka* New Delhi: Mongolian Lama Gurudeva, 1980–82. English translation: José Ignacio Cabezón. *A Dose of Emptiness: An Annotated Translation of the Stong Thun Chen Mo of Mkhas Grub Dge Legs Dpal Bzang.* Albany: State University of New York Press, 1992.

———. *Entryway to Faith: A Biography of the Marvelous and Amazing Jetsün Tsongkhapa the Great. Rje btsun bla ma tsong kha pa chen po'i ngo mtshar rmad du byung ba'i rnam par thar pa dad pa'i 'jug ngogs.* In *Collected Works of Rje Tsoṅ Kha Pa Blo bzaṅ Grags pa (gSuṅ 'Bum),* vol. *ka.* New Delhi: Ngawang Gelek Demo, 1975.

———. *The Jewel Cluster: Secret Biography of Tsongkhapa. Tsong kha pa'i gsang ba'i rnam thar rin po che'i snye ma.* In *Collected Works of Rje Tsoṅ Kha Pa Blo bzaṅ Grags pa (gSuṅ 'Bum),* vol. *ka.* New Delhi: Ngawang Gelek Demo, 1975.

———. *Letter Sent to Geshé Shersang. Dge bshes sher bzang la gnang ba'i chab shog.* In *The Collected Works (gsuṅ bum) of the Lord Mkhas-grub Rje Dge-legs-dpal-bzaṅ-po,* vol. *ta.* New Delhi: Mongolian Lama Gurudeva, 1980–82.

———. *Song to the Glorious Master of the Three Worlds. Dpal ldan sa gsum ma.* In *The Collected Works (gsuṅ bum) of the Lord Mkhas-grub Rje Dge-legs-dpal-bzaṅ-po,* vol. *ta.* New Delhi: Mongolian Lama Gurudeva, 1980–82. English translation: Robert Thurman, ed. *Life and Teachings of Tsong Khapa.* Trans. Sherpa Tulku et al. Dharamsala: Library of Tibetan Works and Archives, 1982, pp. 232–37.

———. *Teaching on the View, Clearing Away Darkness. Lta khrid mun sel.* In *The Collected Works (gsuṅ bum) of the Lord Mkhas-grub Rje Dge-legs-dpal-bzaṅ-po,* vol. *ta.* New Delhi: Mongolian Lama Gurudeva, 1980–82.

Khedrup Norsang Gyatso. *Lamp Illuminating Mahāmudrā. Phyag chen gsal ba'i sgron me.* Ms. in Library of Tibetan Works and Archives, accession 20379.

Lechen Künga Gyaltsen. *Lamp Illuminating the Dharma History of the Kadam. Bka' gdams chos 'byung gsal ba'i sgron me.* 2 vols. New Delhi: B. Jamyang Norbu, 1972.

Lingrepa Pema Dorjé. *The Collected Works (bka' 'bum) of Gliṅ-chen Ras-pa Padma-rdo-rje.* 2 vols. Tashijong, Palampur, Distt. Kangra, H.P. : Khampa Gar Sungrab Nyamso Gyunphel Parkhang, Tibetan Craft Community, 1985.

Losang Chökyi Gyaltsen (Panchen Lama I). *Biographies of the Lineage Holders of the Geden Oral Lineage. Dge ldan bka' brgyud brgyud pa'i rnam thar.* In *Collected Works (gSuṅ 'bum) of Blo bzaṅ chos kyi rgyal mtshan, the First Paṇchen bLa ma of bKra śis lhun po,* vol. *ka.* New Delhi: Mongolian Lama Gurudeva, 1973.

———. *Lamp Re-Illuminating Mahāmudrā. Phyag chen rtsa ba yang gsal sgron me.* In *Collected Works (gSuṅ 'bum) of Blo bzaṅ chos kyi rgyal mtshan, the First Paṇchen bLa ma of bKra śis lhun po,* vol. *nga.* New Delhi: Mongolian Lama Gurudeva, 1973.

———. *Reply to Questions: Sweet Words of Explanation for Those with Good Minds. Dri ba lhag bsam gyi rab dkar gyi dris lan blo bzang bshad sgra dbyangs.* In *Collected Works (gSuṅ 'bum) of Blo bzaṅ chos kyi rgyal mtshan, the First Paṇchen bLa ma of bKra śis lhun po,* vol. *nga.* New Delhi: Mongolian Lama Gurudeva, 1973.

———. *Root Text on Mahāmudrā: The Main Path of the Conquerors. Dge ldan bka' brgyud rin po che'i phyag chen rtsa ba rgyal ba'i gzhung lam.* In *Collected Works (gSuṅ 'bum) of Blo bzaṅ chos kyi rgyal mtshan, the First Paṇchen bLa ma of bKra śis lhun po,* vol. *nga.* New Delhi: Mongolian Lama Gurudeva, 1973. English translation: H. H. the Fourteenth Dalai Lama and Alexander Berzin. *The Gelug/Kagyü Tradition of Mahamudra.* Ithaca, NY: Snow Lion, 1997, pp. 97–102.

Losang Palden Yeshé (Panchen Lama III). *Secret Teaching. Gsang ba'i gsung.* NA.

———. *Source of Billions of Wonders: An Exposition of Shambhala, Great Abode of Attainment, and an Expression of the Realizations of the Holy Land. Grub pa'i gnas chen po sham bha la'i rnam bshad 'phags yul gyi rtogs brjod bcas pa ngo mtshar bye ba'i 'byung gnas.* In *The Collected Works (gsuṅ 'bum) of the Third Panchen Lama of Tashilhunpo Blo-bzaṅ-dpal-ldan-ye-śes,* vol. *nya.* New Delhi: Mongolian Lama Gurudeva, 1975–78.

Losang Rinchen. *Harmonizing the Stages of the Path [Traditions]. Lam rim gyi 'bril bsgrigs.* NA.

Ma ṇi bka' 'bum: A Collection of Rediscovered Teachings Focussing upon the Tutelary Deity Avalokiteśvara (Mahākaruṇika). Delhi: Trayang and Jamyang Samten, 1975.

Mangthö Ludrup Gyatso. *Almanac of the Teaching. Bstan rtsis gsal ba'i nyin byed.* [Lhasa:] Bod ljongs mi dmangs dpe skrun khang, 1987.

———. *Guidelines on the Three Appearances as Privately Explained: A Fortunate Rosary of Nectar Moon Drops Opening the New Night Lily. Gsung ngag slob bshad snang gsum gyi khrid yig zla ba bdud rtsi'i thigs phreng skal bzang ku mud gsar ma'i kha 'byed.* In *Lam 'bras slob bśad: the Sa-skya-pa teachings of the path and the fruit, according to the Tshar-pa transmission, as arranged by 'Jam-dbyaṅs-blo-gter-dbaṅ-po and supplemented by texts continuing the lineage through Khaṅ-gsar Dam-pa and Sga-ston Ṅag-dbaṅ-legs-pa Rin-po-ches,* vol. *ba.* Dehra Dun, U.P.: Sakya Centre, 1983[–1985].

Ngawang Losang Gyatso [Dalai Lama V]. *Chariot of Oceanic Yogic Achievements: A Biography of the Omniscient Jetsün Sönam Gyatso. Rje btsun thams cad mkhyen pa bsod nams rgya mtsho'i rnam thar dngos grub rgya mtsho'i shing rta.* In *The Collected Works (gsung 'bum) of Vth Dalai Lama Ngag-dbang-blo-bzang-rgya-mtsho,* vol. *nya.* Gangtok, Sikkim: Sikkim Research Institute of Tibetology, 1991–95.

———. *Vajra Life-Tree of Long-Life Initiations. Tshe dbang rdo rje'i srog shing.* In *The Collected Works (gsung 'bum) of Vth Dalai Lama Ngag-dbang-blo-bzang-rgya-mtsho,* vol. *tha.* Gangtok, Sikkim: Sikkim Research Institute of Tibetology, 1991–95.

Ngok Lawachen. *Thorny Plant. Gze ma ra mgo.* NA.

The Ocean of Kagyü Songs. Bka' brgyud mgur mtsho. Dehradun, U.P.: Drikung Kagyu Institute, 1991. English translation: Nālandā Translation Committee. *The Rain of Wisdom: The Essence of the Ocean of True Meaning, the Vajra Songs of the Kagyü Gurus.* Boston: Shambhala, 1980.

Orgyen Lingpa, *Five-Part Edict. Bka' thang sde lnga.* Beijing: Mi rigs dpe skrun khang, 1990.

Ornament of Sunlight in the Breach in the Citadel of Secret Mantra. Gsang sngags rdzong 'phrang nyi 'od rgyan. In *Man-ngag Gnad-kyi Rdzong-'phrang-gi Skor: Two Texts of the Bonpo Tradition Parallel to the Rnying-ma-pa Rdzong-'phrang Bka'-ma Transmissions.* Dolanji, H.P.: Lopon Tenzin Namdak, 1981.

Panchen Sönam Drakpa. *Beautiful Ornament of Thought. Bka' gdams gsar rnying gi chos 'byung yid kyi mdzas rgyan.* In *[Collected Works:] Mdo sngags rab 'byams pa paṇ chen bsod nams grags pa'i gsung 'bum,* vol. *da.* Mundgod, Karnataka: Drepung Loseling Library Society, 1982–90.

Pawo Tsuklak Trengwa. *Scholars' Banquet: A Dharma History. Chos 'byung mkhas pa'i dga' ston.* Delhi: Delhi Karmapae Chodey Gyalwae Sungrab Partun Khang, 1980.

Pema Karpo. *Dharma History. Chos 'byung bstan pa'i padma rgyas pa'i nyin byed.* In *Collected Works (gsuṅ-'bum) of Kun-mkhyen Padma-dkar-po,* vol. *kha.* Darjeeling: Kargyud Sungrab Nyamso Khang, 1973–74.

———. *Storehouse of Mahāmudrā. Phyag chen gan mdzod.* In *Collected Works (gsuṅ-'bum) of Kun-mkhyen Padma-dkar-po,* vol. *zha.* Darjeeling: Kargyud Sungrab Nyamso Khang, 1973–74.

Pha Dampa Sangyé. *Hundred Root [Verses] for the People of Dingri. Źal gdams diṅ ri brgya rtsa ma.* In *Bka' rnying gi skyes chen du ma'i phyag rdzogs kyi gdams ngag gnad bsdus nyer kho rin po che'i gter mdzod,* vol. *sha.* Delhi: Bka' brgyud gsung rab nyams so khang, 1985.

Phakmo Drupa Dorjé Gyalpo. *The Jeweled Stairway. Rin chen them skas.* In *The Collected Works (gsung 'bum) of Phag-mo-gru-pa Rdo-rje-rgyal-po,* vol. *ga.* Delhi: Mkhan po shes sgrub bstan 'dzin and Bla ma 'phrin las rnam rgyal, 2003.

———. *Joining the Coemergent. Phyag rgya chen poi' skor lhan cig skyes sbyor sogs chos mtshan nyer drug.* In *Collected Works of Phag mo gru pa Rdo rje rgyal po,* vol. *nga.* Delhi: Mkhan po shes sgrub bstan 'dzin and Bla ma 'phrin las rnam rgyal, 2003.

———. *Verses on the Four Yogas. Rnal 'byor bzhi'i tshigs bcad ma chung ba.* In *Collected Works of Phag mo gru pa Rdo rje rgyal po,* vol. *nga.* Delhi: Mkhan po shes sgrub bstan 'dzin and Bla ma 'phrin las rnam rgyal, 2003.

Sakya Pandita Künga Gyaltsen. *Distinguishing the Three Vows. Sdom gsum rab dbye.* In *Paṇḍi-ta Kun-dga'-rgyal-mtshan gyi bka' 'bum = The Complete Works of Paṇḍita Kun-dga'-rgyal-mtshan.* Compiled by Bsod nams rgya mtsho. In

Sa skya pa'i bka' 'bum, vol. *na*. Tokyo: Toyo Bunkyo, 1968. English translation: Jared Rhoton. *A Clear Differentiation of the Three Codes: Essential Distinctions Among the Individual Liberation, Great Vehicle, and Tantric Systems*. Albany: State University of New York Press, 2002.

______. *Perfection of the Five Dependent Arisings. Rten 'brel lnga rdzogs [= Letter on the Five Dependent Arisings: Special Instructions on the Vajrayāna (Theg chen man ngag rten 'brel lnga'i yi ge)]*. In *Paṇḍi-ta Kun-dga'-rgyal-mtshan gyi bka' 'bum = The Complete Works of Paṇḍita Kun-dga'-rgyal-mtshan*. Compiled by Bsod nams rgya mtsho. In *Sa skya pa'i bka' 'bum,* vol. *na*. Tokyo: Toyo Bunkyo, 1968.

______. *Well-Spoken Advice from Sakya. Sa skya legs bshad*. In *Paṇḍi-ta Kun-dga'-rgyal-mtshan gyi bka' 'bum = The Complete Works of Paṇḍita Kun-dga'-rgyal-mtshan*. Compiled by Bsod nams rgya mtsho. In *Sa skya pa'i bka' 'bum,* vol. *na*. Tokyo: Toyo Bunkyo, 1968. English translation: John Davenport. *Ordinary Wisdom: Sakya Pandita's Treasury of Good Advice*. Boston: Wisdom, 2000.

Shākya Chokden. *Reply to the Inquiry into the Pure Noble Intention. Dri ba lhag bsam rab dkar gyi dris lan man ngag gi dgongs rgyan*. In *The Complete Works (gsuṅ 'bum) of Gser-mdog Paṇ-chen Śākya-mchog-ldan,* vol. *'a*. Thimphu: Kunzang Tobgey, 1975–.

______. *Treatise Explaining the Distinction Between the Two Chariot-Paths of the Great Vehicle and Proving They Have a Single Definitive Meaning. Shing rta chen po'i srol gnyis kyi rnam par dbye ba bshad nas nges don gcig tu bsgrub pa'i bstan bcos*. In *The Complete Works (gsuṅ 'bum) of Gser-mdog Paṇ-chen Śākya-mchog-ldan,* vol. *kha*. Thimphu: Kunzang Tobgey, 1975– .

Shang Yudrakpa Tsöndrü Drakpa. *Shang's Special Instruction on the Ultimate Profound Path of Mahāmudrā. Phyag rgya chen po lam zab mthar thug zhang gi man ngag*. In *Dpal Tshal-pa Bka'-brgyud kyi bstan pa'i mṅa' bdag Zhaṅ Gyu-brag-pa-brtson-'grus-grags-pa'i gsuṅ 'bum rin po che glegs bam = The Collected Works of Zhaṅ Brtson-'grus-grags-pa, 1123–1193,* vol. *nga*. Kathmandu: Khenpo Shedup Tenzin and Lama Thinley Namgyal, 2004. English translation (and alternative edition): Dan Martin. "A Twelfth-Century Tibetan Classic of Mahāmudrā: *The Path of Ultimate Profundity: The Great Seal Instructions of Zhang*." *The Journal of the International Association of Buddhist Studies* 15, 2 (1992), pp. 243–319.

Situ Panchen Chökyi Jungné, *Spotless Crystal Mirror. Tā'i si tur rang rnam rang tshul drangs por brjod pa dri bral shel gyi me long*. In *Collected Works,* vol. *a,* Delhi: Dpal sprungs dpar ma Shes rab rgyal mtshan, 1990

Soksokpa Lodrö Gyaltsen. *Dragon's Roar of Definitive Meaning. Nges pa don gyi 'brug sgra: Refutations of the Charges Leveled Against the Tantric Works of the Nyingmapa at Various Periods in Tibetan History*. Delhi: s.n. 1968.

Sumpa Khenpo Yeshé Paljor. *Excellent Wish-Fulfilling Tree. 'Phags yul rgya nag chen po bod dang sog yul du dam pa'i chos 'byung tshul dpag bsam ljon bzang.* New Delhi: International Academy of Indian Culture, 1975.

Taklung Ngawang Namgyal. *Wonderful Ocean Dharma History. Chos 'byung ngo mtshar rgya mtsho.* In *Chos 'byung Ngo mtshar rgya mtsho: A Detailed Account of the Development of Buddhism in Tibet with Special Emphasis on the Stag-lung Bka'-brgyud-pa,* by Stag-lung-pa Ngag-dbang-rnam-rgyal and supplemented by Khams-sprul Don-brgyud-nyi-ma. Palampur: Sungrab Nyamso Gyunpel Parkhang, 1972.

Taktsang Lotsāwa Sherap Rinchen. *Dharma History: Root and Commentary on All Knowledge. Grub mtha' kun shes kyi rtsa 'grel.* Beijing: Mi rigs dpe skrun khang, 2000.

Thoyön Yeshé Döndrup, *Advice from Grandmother Yoginī. Rnal 'byor ma myes kyi gsung bgros.* In *Storehouse of the Cherished Jewel Collection of the Kadam. Bka' gdams gces btus nor bu'i bang mdzod.* Ed. Don grub ye shes bstan pa'i rgyal mtshan. Bir, Distt. Kangra, H.P., India: D. Tsondu Senghe, 1985.

Thuken Losang Chökyi Nyima. *Biographical Ornament Beautifying the Geden Doctrine. Rnam thar dge ldan bstan pa'i mdzes rgyan.* In *Collected Works of Thu'-bkwan Blo-bzang-chos-kyi-nyi-ma,* vol. *ka.* Edited and Reproduced by Ṅawang Gelek Demo. Delhi: Ngawang Gelek Demo, 1969–71. Introduction by E. Gene Smith republished in E. G. Smith, pp. 147–70.

Tokden Jampal Gyatso. *Short Biography of Jetsün Tsongkhapa. Rje btsun tsoṅ kha pa'i rnam thar chen mo'i zur 'debs rnam thar legs bśad kun 'dus.* In *Collected Works of Rje Tsoṅ Kha Pa Blo bzaṅ Grags pa (gSuṅ 'Bum),* vol. *ka.* New Delhi: Ngawang Gelek Demo, 1975.

Tsangnyön Heruka. *The Hundred Thousand Songs of Milarepa. Rnal 'byor gyi dbang phyug chen po mi la ras pa'i rnam mgur.* Xining Shi: Mtsho sngon mi rigs dpe skrun khang, 1981. English translation: Garma C. C. Chang. *The Hundred Thousand Songs of Milarepa.* 2 vols. Boston and Shaftesbury: Shambhala, 1989 (1962).

———. *Life of Marpa. Mar pa'i rnam thar.* In *Biographies of the Kagyüpa. Bka' brgyud pa'i rnam thar,* vol. 1. Bkra shis ljong, Palampur: Gsung rab nyams gso rgyun sel par khang, 1972. English translation: Nālandā Translation Committee. *The Life of Marpa.* Boston: Shambhala, 1986.

Tsongkhapa Losang Drakpa. *Annotations Clarifying the Meaning of the Five Stages. Rim lnga gsal sgron gyi mchan gyi yang 'grel.* In *Collected Works of Rje Tsoṅ Kha Pa Blo bzaṅ Grags pa (gSuṅ 'Bum),* vol. *nga.* New Delhi: Ngawang Gelek Demo, 1975.

———. *Clarifying the Whole Hidden Meaning: An Extensive Commentary on the Shorter Saṃvara Tantra. Bde mchog bsdus pa'i rgyud kyi rgya cher bshad pa sbas pa'i don kun gsal ba.* In *Collected Works of Rje Tsoṅ Kha Pa Blo bzaṅ Grags pa (gSuṅ 'Bum),* vol. *nya.* New Delhi: Ngawang Gelek Demo, 1975.

_____. *Cluster of Yogic Achievements: An Explanation of the Great Completion Stage Yoga of Śrī Cakrasaṃvara. Dpal 'khor lo bde mchog kyi rdzogs rim rnal 'byor chen po'i rnam bshad dngos grub snye ma.* In *Collected Works of Rje Tsoṅ Kha Pa Blo bzaṅ Grags pa (gSuṅ 'Bum),* vol. *ta.* New Delhi: Ngawang Gelek Demo, 1975.

_____. *Direct Explanation of the Five Stages. Rgyud kyi rgyal po dpal gsang ba'i 'dus pa'i rdzogs rim rim lnga gdan rdzogs kyi dmar khrid.* In *Collected Works of Rje Tsoṅ Kha Pa Blo bzaṅ Grags pa (gSuṅ 'Bum),* vol. *nya.* New Delhi: Ngawang Gelek Demo, 1975.

_____. *Essence of Excellent Explanation: Distinguishing Provisional and Definitive. Drang nges rnam 'byed legs bshad snying po.* In *Collected Works of Rje Tsoṅ Kha Pa Blo bzaṅ Grags pa (gSuṅ 'Bum),* vol. *pha.* New Delhi: Ngawang Gelek Demo, 1975. English translation: Robert A. F. Thurman. *The Central Philosophy of Tibet: A Study and Translation of Jey Tsong Khapa's "Essence of True Eloquence."* Princeton: Princeton University Press, 1991.

_____. *Great Treatise on the Stages of Mantra. Rgyal ba khyab rdo rje chang chen po'i lam gyi rim pa gsang ba kun gyi gnad rnam par phye ba, Sngags rim chen mo.* In *Collected Works of Rje Tsoṅ Kha Pa Blo bzaṅ Grags pa (gSuṅ 'Bum),* vol. *ga.* New Delhi: Ngawang Gelek Demo, 1975. Partial English translation: Jeffrey Hopkins. *The Tantra of Tibet.* London: George Allen and Unwin, 1977; *The Yoga of Tibet.* London: George Allen and Uwin, 1981; *Yoga Tantra.* Ithaca, NY: Snow Lion, 2005.

_____. *Great Treatise on the Stages of the Path to Enlightenment. Byang chub lam rim gyi chen mo.* In *Collected Works of Rje Tsoṅ Kha Pa Blo bzaṅ Grags pa (gSuṅ 'Bum),* vol. *pa.* New Delhi: Ngawang Gelek Demo, 1975. English translation: Lamrim Chenmo Translation Committee. [Tsong-kha-pa.] *The Great Treatise on the Stages of the Path to Enlightenment.* Ed. Joshua W. C. Cutler and Guy Newland. 3 vols. Ithaca, NY: Snow Lion, 2000–2004.

_____. *The Hand-Offering Rite of the External Offering of Cakrasaṃvara, and Song of the Spring Queen. Dpal 'khor lo sdom pa'i phyi rol mchod pa'i cho ga lag mchod dang spyid kyi rgyal mo'i glu dang bcas pa.* In *Collected Works of Rje Tsoṅ Kha Pa Blo bzaṅ Grags pa (gSuṅ 'Bum),* vol. *na.* New Delhi: Ngawang Gelek Demo, 1975.

_____ [sic]. *Inquiry into the Pure Noble Intention. Dri ba lhag bsam rab dkar.* In *Collected Works of Rje Tsoṅ Kha Pa Blo bzaṅ Grags pa (gSuṅ 'Bum),* vol. *ka.* New Delhi: Ngawang Gelek Demo, 1975.

_____. *Lamp Illuminating the Five Stages: A Special Instruction on the King of Tantras, Śrī Guhyasamāja. Rgyud kyi rgyal po'i dpal gsang ba 'dus pa'i man ngag rim lnga rab tu gsal ba'i sgron me.* In *Collected Works of Rje Tsoṅ Kha

Pa Blo bzaṅ Grags pa (gSuṅ 'Bum), vol. *nga.* New Delhi: Ngawang Gelek Demo, 1975. Translation forthcoming as volume 15 of the Library of Tibetan Classics.

———. *Letter of Questions Offered to Lamas Rendawa and Umapa. Bla ma red dbu ma pa la phul ba'i zhu yig.* In *Collected Works of Rje Tsoṅ Kha Pa Blo bzaṅ Grags pa (gSuṅ 'Bum),* vol. *kha.* New Delhi: Ngawang Gelek Demo, 1975.

———. *The Nectar Garland: Supreme Medicine of Answers to Questions. Zhu lan sman mchog bdud rtsi 'phreng ba.* In *Collected Works of Rje Tsoṅ Kha Pa Blo bzaṅ Grags pa (gSuṅ 'Bum),* vol. *ka.* New Delhi: Ngawang Gelek Demo, 1975.

———. *Prayer of the Virtuous Beginning, Middle, and End. Thog ma dang bar dang tha mar dge ba'i smon lam.* In *Collected Works of Rje Tsoṅ Kha Pa Blo bzaṅ Grags pa (gSuṅ 'Bum),* vol. *kha.* New Delhi: Ngawang Gelek Demo, 1975. English translation: Tsongkhapa. *Splendor of an Autumn Moon.* Trans. Gavin Kilty. Boston: Wisdom, 2001, pp. 193–208.

———. *Prayer to Cakrasaṃvara. Bde mchog smon lam.* In *Collected Works of Rje Tsoṅ Kha Pa Blo bzaṅ Grags pa (gSuṅ 'Bum),* vol. *kha.* New Delhi: Ngawang Gelek Demo, 1975.

———. *Precious Sprout that Severs Extremes with Regard to the Difficult Points in the Illuminating Lamp, the Great Commentary on the Guhyasamāja, the King of Tantras. Rgyud kyi rgyal po dpal gsang ba'i 'dus ba'i rgya cher bshad pa sgron ma gsal ba'i dka' ba'i gnad kyi mtha' gcod rin po che'i myu gu.* In *Collected Works of Rje Tsoṅ Kha Pa Blo bzaṅ Grags pa (gSuṅ 'Bum),* vol. *ca.* New Delhi: Ngawang Gelek Demo, 1975.

———. *Song of Experience Related to the Stages of the Path. Lam rim nyams mgur.* In *Great Treatise on the Stages of the Path to Enlightenment. Byang chub lam rim gyi chen mo.* In *Collected Works of Rje Tsoṅ Kha Pa Blo bzaṅ Grags pa (gSuṅ 'Bum),* vol. *pa.* New Delhi: Ngawang Gelek Demo, 1975. English translation: Lamrim Chenmo Translation Committee. [Tsong-kha-pa.] *The Great Treatise on the Stages of the Path to Enlightenment.* Ed. Joshua W. C. Cutler and Guy Newland, vol 3. Ithaca, NY: Snow Lion, 2002, pp. 367–69.

———. *Song of Realization. Rtogs brjod mdun legs ma. Collected Works of Rje Tsoṅ Kha Pa Blo bzaṅ Grags pa (gSuṅ 'Bum),* vol. *kha.* New Delhi: Ngawang Gelek Demo, 1975. English translation: R. Thurman, ed. *Life and Teachings of Tsong Khapa.* Trans. Sherpa Tulku et al. Dharamsala: Library of Tibetan Works and Archives, 1982, pp. 40–46.

Wön Sherap Jungné. *Textbook on the Single Intention. Dgongs chig yig cha.* Bir, H.P., India: D. Tsondu Senghe, 1975.

Yongzin Yeshé Gyaltsen, *Biographies of the Masters of the Stages of the Path Lineage. Lam rim bla ma brgyud pa'i rnam thar.* Beijing: Bod ljongs mi dmangs dpe skrun khang, 1990.

Works Consulted by the Translators

Ahmad, Zahiruddin, trans. *A History of Tibet by Ṅag-dBaṅ Blo-bZaṅ rGya-mTsho, Fifth Dalai Lama of Tibet*. Bloomington: Indiana University Research Institute for Inner Asian Studies, 1995.

———. *Sino-Tibetan Relations in the Seventeenth Century*. Roma, Istituto Italiano per il Medio ed Estremo Oriente, 1970.

Anacker, Stefan. *Seven Works of Vasubandhu, the Buddhist Psychological Doctor*. Delhi: Motilal Banarsidass, 1984.

Apte, Vaman Shivaram. *The Practical Sanskrit-English Dictionary*. Rev. ed. Delhi: Motilal Banarsidass, 1998.

Aris, Michael. *Hidden Treasures and Secret Lives: A Study of Pemalingpa (1450–1521) and the Sixth Dalai Lama (1683–1706)*. London/New York: Kegan Paul International, 1989.

———, and Aung Saan Suu Kyi, eds. *Tibetan Studies in Honour of Hugh Richardson: Proceedings of the International Seminar on Tibetan Studies, Oxford, 1979*. Warminster, England: Aris and Phillips, 1980.

Āryaśūra. *The Marvelous Companion: Life Stories of the Buddha*. Berkeley: Dharma Publishing, 1983.

Aung, Shwe Zan, and Mrs. Rhys Davids. *Points of Controversy, or, Subjects of Discourse: Being a Translation of the Kathā-vatthu from the Abhidhammapiṭaka*. London: Luzac and Co., 1969 (1915).

Aziz, Barbara Nimri. "The Work of Pha-dam-pa Sangs-rgyas as Revealed in Ding-ri Folklore." In Aris and Aung Saan Suu Kyi, pp. 21–29.

———, and Matthew T. Kapstein, eds. *Soundings in Tibetan Civilization*. New Delhi: Manohar, 1985.

[BA]. See Roerich.

Baker, Willa, trans. *Essence of Ambrosia: A Guide to Buddhist Contemplations*. Dharamsala: Library of Tibetan Works and Archives, 2005.

Bareau, André. *Les sectes bouddhiques du petit véhicule*. Paris: École Française d'Extrême-Orient, 1955.

Barron, Richard, trans. *The Precious Treasury of the Basic Space of Phenomena, by Longchen Rabjam*. Ed. Padma Translation Committee. Junction City, CA: Padma Publishing, 2001.

Batchelor, Stephen. *The Jewel in the Lotus: A Guide to the Buddhist Traditions of Tibet*. London: Wisdom, 1987.

Bawden, C. R. *The Modern History of Mongolia*. London: Kegan, Paul, 1989.

Bendall, Cecil, and W. H. D. Rouse, trans. [Śāntideva.] *Śikṣā samuccaya: A Compendium of Buddhist Doctrine*. Delhi: Motilal Banarsidass, 1971.

Bentor, Yael. "The Tibetan Practice of the Mantra Path According to Lce-sgom-pa." In White, pp. 326–46.

Bercholz, Samuel, and Sherab Kohn, eds. *Entering the Stream*. Boston: Shambhala, 1993.

Berger, Patricia. *Empire of Emptiness: Buddhist Art and Political Authority in Qing China*. Honolulu: University of Hawaii Press, 2003.

Bernbaum, Edwin. *The Way to Shambhala: A Search for the Mythical Kingdom Beyond the Himalayas*. Boston: Shambhala, 2001.

Berzin, Alexander, trans. [Thuken.] "Abbreviated Single-Deity Kalachakra Sadhana." *Berzin Archives:* http://www.berzinarchives.com/kalachakra/abbreviated_single_kc_sadhana.html.

______. "A Brief History of Gyumay and Gyuto Tantric Colleges." *Berzin Archives:* http://www.berzinarchives.com/web/en/archives/study/history_buddhism/buddhism_tibet/gelug/brief_history_gyumay_gyuto_tantric_college.html.

______. "A Short Biography of Lama Tsongkhapa." *Berzin Archives:* http://www.berzinarchives.com/web/en/archives/approaching_buddhism/teachers/lineage_masters/short_biography_lama_tsongkhapa.html.

______ et al. Long-ch'en Rb[sic]-jam-pa Dr'i-me wö-zer. *The Four-Themed Precious Garland (Chos-bzhi rin-chen phreng-ba): An Introduction to Dzogch'en, the Great Completeness*. Explanation and oral commentary by Dudjom Rinpoche and Beru Khyentze Rinpoche. Translated, edited, and prepared by Alexander Berzin, in conjunction with Sherpa Tulku and Matthew Kapstein. Dharamsala: Library of Tibetan Works and Archives, 1979.

Beyer, Stephan. *The Buddhist Experience: Sources and Interpretations*. Encino, CA: Dickenson Publishing, 1974.

Bhattacharyya, Benoytosh, ed. *Niṣpannayogāvalī of Mahāpaṇḍita Abhayākaragupta*. Baroda: Oriental Institute, 1972.

Biography of Atisa and His Disciple hBrom-ston. New Delhi: International Academy of Indian Culture, 1982.

Bjerken, Zeff. "Cracking the Mirror: A Critical Genealogy of Scholarship on Tibetan Bon and the 'Canonical' Status of *The Crystal Mirror of Doctrinal Systems*." *Tibet Journal* 23: 4 (Winter 1998), pp. 92–107.

Bka'-brg[y]ud Rinpoche'i mgur mtsho ye shes byin 'bebs: The collected songs of esoteric spiritual realisation (Mgur) of the Bka'-brgyud-pa school in general and the Bri-guṅ Bka'-brgyud-pa school in particular. Arranged and edited by the 7th Bri-guṅ Skyabs-mgon Che-tshan Dkon-mchog-bstan-'dzin-'phrin-las-lhun-'grub. Dehradun, India: Drikung Kagyu Institute, 1991.

Bla ma'i rnal 'byor dang/yi dam khag gi bdag bskyed sogs zhal 'don gces btus bzhugs so. Dharamsala: Tibetan Cultural Printing Press, 1974.

Blumenthal, James. *The Ornament of the Middle Way: A Study of the Madhyamaka Thought of Śāntarakṣita: Including Translations of Śāntarakṣita's Mādhyamakālaṃkāra (The Ornament of the Middle Way) and Gyel-tsab's dbU ma rgyan gyi brjed byang (Remembering "The Ornament of the Middle Way")*. Ithaca, NY: Snow Lion, 2004.

Bod rgya tshig mdzod chen mo. 3 vols. Beijing: Mi rigs dpe skrun khang, 1984.

Bodhi, Bhikku. *The Discourse on the All-Embracing Net of Views: The Brahmajāla Sutta and Its Commentarial Exegesis*. Kandy: Buddhist Publication Society, 1978.

Boord, Martin J. *The Cult of the Deity Vajrakīla: According to the Texts of the Northern Treasures Tradition of Tibet (Byang-gter phur-ba)*. Tring, U.K.: The Institute of Buddhist Studies, 1993.

______, and Losang Norbu Tsonawa, trans. [Panchen Sonam Dragpa.] *Overview of Buddhist Tantra: General Presentation of the Classes of Tantra, Captivating the Minds of the Fortunate Ones*. Dharamsala: Library of Tibetan Works and Archives, 1996.

Broido, Michael M. "Killing, Lying, Stealing and Adultery: A Problem of Interpretation in the Tantras." In Lopez, *Buddhist Hermeneutics*, pp. 71–118.

______. "Padma dKar-po on Integration as Ground, Path and Goal." *Journal of the Tibet Society* 5 (1985), pp. 5–54.

______. "Sa-skya paṇḍita, the White Panacea and the Hva-shang Doctrine." *The Journal of the International Association of Buddhist Studies* 10: 2 (1987), pp. 27–68.

______. "Padma dKar-po on Tantra as Ground, Path and Goal." *Journal of the Tibet Society* 4 (1984), pp. 59-66.

______. "Padma dKar-po on the Two *Satyas*." *The Journal of the International Association of Buddhist Studies* 8: 2 (1985), pp. 7–60.

Brunnhölzl, Karl. *The Center of the Sunlit Sky: Madhyamaka in the Kagyü Tradition*. Ithaca, NY: Snow Lion, 2004.

______. *Straight from the Heart: Buddhist Pith Instructions*. Ithaca NY: Snow Lion, 2007.

Cabezón, José Ignacio. "The Canonization of Philosophy and the Rhetoric of *Siddhānta* in Indo-Tibetan Buddhism." In Griffiths and Keenan, pp. 7–26.

______. *A Dose of Emptiness: An Annotated Translation of The sTong thun chen mo of mKhas-grub dGe-legs-dpal-bzang*. Albany: State University of New York Press, 1992.

______. "On the *sGra pa rin chen pa'i rtsod lan* of Paṇ chen bLo bzang chos rgyan." *Asiatische Studien/Études Asiatiques* XLIX: 4 (1995), pp. 643–69.

______. "Rong ston Shākya rgyal mtshan on Madhyamaka Thesislessness." In Krasser et al., pp. 97–105.

______. "Two Views of the Svātantrika-Prāsaṅgika Distinction in Fourteenth-Century Tibet." In Dreyfus and McClintock, pp. 289–316.

Cabezón, José Ignacio, and Geshé Lobsang Dargyay. *Freedom from Extremes: Gorampa's "Distinguishing the Views" and the Polemics of Emptiness*. Boston: Wisdom, 2007.

Cabezón, José Ignacio, and Roger R. Jackson, eds. *Tibetan Literature: Studies in Genre*. Ithaca, NY: Snow Lion, 1996.

Campany, Robert Ford. "On the Very Idea of Religions (in the Modern West and in Medieval China)." *History of Religions* 42: 4 (2003), pp. 287–319.

Carelli, M. E., ed. *Śekoddeśaṭīkā by Nāḍapāda*. Gaekwad's Oriental Series, vol. XC. Baroda, India: Oriental Institute, 1941.

Chan, Wing-tsit. *A Sourcebook in Chinese Philosophy*. Princeton: Princeton University Press, 1963.

Chandra, Lokesh, ed. *Materials for a History of Tibetan Literature*. 3 vols. New Delhi: International Academy of Indian Culture, 1963.

———. *Tibetan-Sanskrit Dictionary*. 2 vols. Kyoto: Rinsen Book Company, 1976.

Chang, Garma C. C., trans. *The Hundred Thousand Songs of Milarepa*. 2 vols. Boston and Shaftesbury: Shambhala, 1989 (1962).

———, trans. *Six Yogas of Naropa and Teachings on Mahamudra*. Ithaca, NY: Snow Lion, 1986.

Chattopadhyaya, Alaka, with Lama Chimpa. *Atiśa and Tibet*. Delhi: Motilal Banarsidass, 1981 (1967).

Chattopadhyaya, Debiprasad. *Lokāyata*. Delhi: People's Publishing House, 1978 (1959).

Ch'en, Kenneth K. S. *Buddhism in China: A Historical Survey*. Princeton: Princeton University Press, 1964.

Chimpa, Lama, and Alaka Chattopadhyaya, trans. *Tāranātha's History of Buddhism in India*. Simla: Indian Institute of Advanced Study, 1970.

Chogay Trichen Rinpoche. *The History of the Sakya Tradition: A Feast for the Minds of the Fortunate*. Trans. Ven. Phende Rinpoche, Jamyang Khandro, Jennifer Stott. Bristol, U.K.: Ganesha, 1983.

Cleary, Thomas, trans. *The Ecstasy of Enlightenment: Teachings of Natural Tantra*. York Beach, ME: Samuel Weiser, 1988.

———, trans. *The Flower Ornament Scripture: A Translation of the Avatamsaka Sutra*. 3 vols. Boulder: Shambhala, 1984–87.

Coleman, Graham. *A Handbook of Tibetan Culture*. Boston: Shambhala, 1993.

Cologne Digital Sanskrit Lexicon. http://webapps.uni-koeln.de/tamil/.

Conze, Edward, trans. *Abhsamayālaṃkāra*. Roma: Istituto Italiano per il Medio ed Estremo Oriente, 1954.

———, ed. *Buddhist Texts Through the Ages*. New York: Harper and Row, 1954.

———. *Buddhist Wisdom Books: Containing* The Diamond Sutra *and* The Heart Sutra. New York: Harper and Row, 1958.

———, trans. *The Large Sutra on Perfect Wisdom, with the Divisions of the Abhisamayālaṃkāra*. Berkeley: University of California Press, 1975.

———, trans. *The Perfection of Wisdom in Eight Thousand Lines and Its Verse Summary*. Bolinas: Four Seasons Foundation, 1973.

Coward, Harold G., and K. Kunjunni Raja, eds. *The Philosophy of the Grammarians*. Encyclopedia of Indian Philosophy, vol. V. Princeton, NJ: Princeton University Press, 1990.

Cozort, Daniel. *Highest Yoga Tantra*. Ithaca, NY: Snow Lion, 1986.

Cozort, Daniel, and Craig Preston. *Buddhist Philosophy: Losang Könchok's Short Commentary to Jamyang Shayba's* Basic Text on Tenets. Ithaca, NY: Snow Lion, 2003.

Crosby, Kate, and Andrew Skilton, trans. [Śāntideva.] *The Bodhicaryāvatāra*. Oxford/New York: Oxford University Press, 1996.

Crossley, Pamela Kyle. *The Manchus*. Oxford: Blackwell Publishing, 1997.

Cuevas, Bryan J., and Kurtis R. Schaeffer, eds. *Power, Politics, and the Reinvention of Tradition: Tibet in the Seventeenth and Eighteenth Centuries*. (Proceedings of the Tenth Seminar of the IATS, 2003.) Leiden: Brill, 2006.

Cüppers, Christoph. *The IXth Chapter of the Samādhirājasūtra: A Text-Critical Contribution to the Study of Mahāyāna Sūtras*. Stuttgart: F. Steiner, 1990.

Dagyab, L. S. *Tibetan Dictionary*. Dharmsala: Lama L. S. Dagyab, 1966.

Dalai Lama, H. H. the Fourteenth. *The Path to Bliss*. 2nd ed. Ithaca, NY: Snow Lion, 2003.

———. [Kamalashila.] *Stages of Meditation*. Trans. Geshé Lobsang Jordhen, Losang Choephel Ganchenpa, and Jeremy Russell. Ithaca, NY: Snow Lion, 2001.

———. *The World of Tibetan Buddhism*. Trans. Thupten Jinpa. Boston: Wisdom, 1995.

Dalai Lama, H. H. the Fourteenth, and Alexander Berzin. *The Gelug/Kagyü Tradition of Mahamudra*. Ithaca, NY: Snow Lion, 1997.

Das, Sarat Chandra. *Tibetan-English Dictionary*. Kyoto: Rinsen Book Company, 1979 (1902).

———. "Contribution on the Religion, History, etc., of Tibet." *Journal of the Royal Asiatic Society of Bengal*, vol. L, part 1, no. 3 (1881), pp. 187–205; vol. LI, part 1, no. 1 (1882), pp. 1–14, 58–75; vol. LI, part 1, no. 2 (1882), pp. 87–114.

Dasgupta, Surendra Nath. *History of Indian Philosophy*. Vol. 1. Cambridge: Cambridge University Press, 1924.

Davenport, John, et al., trans. *Ordinary Wisdom: Sakya Pandita's Treasury of Good Advice, by Sakya Pandita Kunga Gyaltsen; With Commentary Entitled: A Hive Where Gather Bees of Clear Understanding, by Sakya Khenpo Sangye Tenzin*. Boston: Wisdom, 2000.

Davidson, Ronald M., trans. "Atiśa's Lamp on the Path." In Lopez, *Buddhism in Practice*, pp. 290–301.

———. *Indian Esoteric Buddhism: A Social History of the Tantric Movement.* New York: Columbia University Press, 2002.

———. "The Litany of Names of Mañjuśrī: Text and Translation of the *Mañjuśrī-nāmasaṃgīti*." In Strickmann, pp. 1–69.

———. "Masquerading as Pramāṇa: Esoteric Buddhism and Epistemological Nomenclature." In Katsura, pp. 25–35.

———. "The Ṅgor-pa Tradition." *Wind Horse* 1 (1981), pp. 79–97.

———. "Preliminary Studies on Hevajra's *Abhisamaya* and the *Lam-'bras Tshogs-bshad*. In Goodman and Davidson, pp. 107–32.

———. *Tibetan Renaissance: Tantric Buddhism in the Rebirth of Tibetan Culture and the Rise of Sakya*. New York: Columbia University Press, 2004. [TR]

Davidson, Ronald M., and Christian K. Wedermeyer, eds. *Tibetan Buddhist Literature and Praxis: Studies in Its Formative Period, 900–1400*. [PIATS 2003.] Leiden/Boston: Brill, 2006.

de Bary, William Theodore, and Irene Bloom, eds. *Sources of Chinese Tradition,* vol. 1, 2nd ed. New York: Columbia University Press, 1999.

Decleer, Hubert, trans. "Atiśa's Journey to Tibet." In Lopez, *Religions of Tibet in Practice,* pp. 157–77.

Demiéville, Paul. *Le Concile de Lhasa*. Paris: Imprimerie Nationale de France, 1952.

Deshung Rinpoche, Kunga Tenpai Nyima. *The Three Levels of Spiritual Perception: An Oral Commentary on the Three Visions (Snang gsum) of Ngorchen Konchog Lhundrub*. Trans. Jared Rhoton. 2nd ed. Boston: Wisdom, 2003.

Deutsch, Eliot. *Advaita Vedanta: A Philosophical Reconstruction*. Honolulu: East-West Center Press, 1969.

Dewar, Tyler, trans. The Ninth Karmapa, Wangchuk Dorje. *The Ninth Karmapa's Middle Way.* Ithaca, NY: Snow Lion, 2008.

Dharamacakra Translation Committee. *Middle Beyond Extremes: Maitreya's Madhyāntavibhāga with Commentaries by Khenpo Shenga and Ju Mipham.* Ithaca, NY: Snow Lion, 2006.

Dilgo Khyentse Rinpoche. *Zurchungpa's Testament*. Trans. Padmakara Translation Group. Ithaca, NY: Snow Lion, 2007.

Ding Fubao, ed. *Foxue Dacidian*. Taipei: Taibeishi Huayan Lianshe, 1969.

Doctor, Andreas. *Tibetan Treasure Literature: Revelation, Tradition, and Accomplishment in Visionary Buddhism.* Ithaca, NY: Snow Lion, 2005.

[Döndam Mawai Sengé.] Don Dam sMra Ba'i Senge. *A 15th Century Compendium of Knowledge, the bŚad mDzod Yid bZhin Nor Bu*. Ed. Lokesh Chandra. New Delhi: Sharada Rani, 1969.

Douglas, Nik, and Meryl White. *Karmapa: The Black Hat Lama of Tibet*. London: Luzac, 1976.

Dowman, Keith, trans. *The Divine Madman: The Sublime Life and Songs of Drukpa Kunley*. 2nd ed. Middletown, CA: Dawn Horse Press, 1998.

______, trans. *The Flight of the Garuda. Teachings of the Dzokchen Tradition of Tibetan Buddhism*. Boston: Wisdom, 1994.

______. *Masters of Mahāmudrā: Songs and Histories of the Eighty-Four Buddhist Siddhas*. Albany: State University of New York Press, 1985.

Dreyfus, Georges B. J. *Recognizing Reality: Dharmakīrti's Philosophy and Its Tibetan Interpretations*. Albany: State University of New York Press, 1997.

______. *The Sound of Two Hands Clapping: The Education of a Tibetan Buddhist Monk*. Berkeley/Los Angeles/London: University of California Press, 2003.

Dreyfus, Georges B. J., and Sara L. McClintock, eds. *The Svātantrika-Prāsaṅgika Distinction: What Difference Does a Difference Make?* Boston: Wisdom, 2003.

Dudjom Rinpoche Jikdrel Yeshe Dorje. *The Nyingma School of Tibetan Buddhism: Its Fundamentals and History*. Trans. and ed. Gyurme Dorje and Matthew Kapstein. Boston: Wisdom, 1991. [NS]

Dumoulin, Heinrich. *A History of Zen Buddhism*. Trans. Paul Peachey. New York: Pantheon, 1963.

______. *Zen Buddhism: A History*. Trans. James W. Heisig and Paul Knitter. New York: Macmillan; London: Collier Macmillan, 1988–90.

Dutt, Nalinaksha. *Buddhist Sects in India*. Calcutta: Firma K. L. Mukhopadhyay, 1970.

Eckel, Malcolm David. *Jñānagarbha's Commentary on the Distinction Between the Two Truths: An Eighth-Century Handbook of Madhyamaka Philosophy*. Albany: State University of New York Press, 1987.

Edgerton, Franklin. *Buddhist Hybrid Sanskrit Grammar and Dictionary*. 2 vols. New Haven, CT: Yale University Press, 1953.

Edou, Jerome. *Machig Labdron and the Foundations of Chöd*. Ithaca, NY: Snow Lion, 1996.

The Eighth Situpa. *Mahāmudrā Teachings of the Supreme Siddhas: The Eighth Situpa Tenpa'i Nyinchay on the Third Gyalwa Karmapa Rangjung Dorje's "Aspiration Prayer of Mahāmudrā of Definitive Meaning."* Trans. Sherab Dorje. Ithaca, NY: Snow Lion, 1995.

Emmerick, Ronald E. *A Guide to the Literature of Khotan*. 2nd ed. Tokyo: International Institute of Buddhist Studies, 1992.

______. *Tibetan Texts Concerning Khotan*. London, New York [etc.]: Oxford University Press, 1967.

English, Elizabeth. *Vajrayoginī: Her Visualizations, Rituals, and Forms*. Boston: Wisdom, 2002.

Epstein, Lawrence, and Richard F. Sherburne, eds. *Reflections on Tibetan Culture: Essays in Memory of Turrell V. Wylie*. Lewiston/Queenston/Lampeter: Edwin Mellen Press, 1990.

Evans-Wentz, W. Y., ed. *The Tibetan Book of the Great Liberation*. London: Oxford University Press, 1954.

———, ed. *Tibetan Yoga and Secret Doctrines*. New York: Oxford University Press, 1958.

Fairbank, John King, and Merle Goldman. *China: A New History*. Enlarged ed. Cambridge, MA: Belknap Press of Harvard University Press, 1998.

Farrow, G. W., and I. Menon, ed. and trans. *The Concealed Essence of the Hevajra Tantra, with the Commentary Yogaratnamālā*. Delhi: Motilal Banarsidass, 1992.

Fields, Rick, et al., trans. *The Turquoise Bee: The Tantric Lovesongs of The Sixth Dalai Lama*. San Francisco: HarperSanFrancisco, 1998.

Fitzgerald, Timothy. *The Ideology of Religious Studies*. New York: Oxford University Press, 2000.

Franco, Eli. *Dharmakīrti on Compassion and Rebirth*. Wiener Studien zur Tibetologie und Buddhismuskunde, heft 38; Vienna: Arbeitskreis für Tibetische und Buddhistische Studien Universität Vienna, 1997.

Garfield, Jay L. *The Fundamental Wisdom of the Middle Way: Nāgārjuna's Mūlamadhyamakakārikā*. New York: Oxford University Press, 1995.

Garrett, Frances. "Critical Methods in Tibetan Medical Histories." *Journal of Asian Studies* 66: 2 (2007), pp. 363–87.

Germano, David. "Architecture and Absence in the Secret Tantric History of the Great Perfection *(rdzogs chen)*." *The Journal of the International Association of Buddhist Studies* 17: 2 (1994), pp. 203–335.

———. "The Elements, Insanity, and Lettered Subjectivity." In Lopez, *Religions of Tibet in Practice*, pp. 313–34.

Gnoli, Raniero, and Giacomella Orofino. *Iniziazione Kālacakra*. Milano: Adelphi, 1994.

Goodman, Steven, and Ronald Davidson, eds. *Tibetan Buddhism: Reason and Revelation*. Albany: State University of New York Press, 1992.

Graham, A. C. *The Book of Lieh-tzu*. London: John Murray, 1960.

Gray, David B. *The Cakrasaṃvara Tantra: A Study and Annotated Translation*. New York, Columbia University Press, 2007.

Griffiths, Paul J., and John Keenan, eds. *Buddha Nature: A Festschrift in Honor of Minoru Kiyota*. Las Vegas: Buddhist Books International, 1990.

Grousset, René. *The Empire of the Steppes: A History of Central Asia*. Trans. Naomi Walford. New Brunswick, NJ: Rutgers University Press. 1970.

[GT]. See Lamrim Chenmo Translation Committee.

Guenther, Herbert V. *Buddhist Philosophy in Theory and Practice*. Baltimore: Penguin, 1972.

———, trans. *Ecstatic Spontaneity: Saraha's Three Cycles of Dohā*. Nanzan Studies in Asian Religions, 4. Berkeley: Asian Humanities Press, 1993.

———, trans. Sgam.po.pa. *The Jewel Ornament of Liberation*. Berkeley, Shambhala, 1971.

———. *The Life and Teaching of Nāropa*. London/Oxford/New York: Oxford University Press, 1963.

———. *The Royal Song of Saraha: A Study in the History of Buddhist Thought*. Seattle and London: University of Washington Press, 1969.

Gungthang Könchok Tenpai Drönmé [Gung thang Dkon mchog bstan pa'i sgron me.] *White Lotus Expressing Realization of the Marvelous Triple Secret of Jetsün Losang Chökyi Nyima, Lord of an Ocean of Realizations and Mandalas. Rigs dang dkyil 'khor rgya mtsho mnga bdag rje btsun blo bzang chos kyi nyi ma'i gsang gsum rmad du byung ba'i rtogs brjod padma dkar po*. In *Collected Works of Thu'u-bkwan Blo-bzang-chos-kyi-nyi-ma*. Edited and reproduced by Ṅawang Gelek Demo, with an introduction by E. Gene Smith. Gedan Sungrab Minyam Gyunphel Series, vol. 9, pp. 479–949; vol. 10, pp. 5–815. Delhi: Ngawang Gelek Demo, 1971.

Gyaltsen, Khenpo Könchog, trans. *The Garland of Mahamudra Practices: A Translation of Kunga Rinchen's Clarifying the Jewel Rosary of the Profound Fivefold Path*. Ithaca, NY: Snow Lion, 1986.

———, trans. *The Great Kagyu Masters: The Golden Lineage Treasury*. Ed. Victoria Huckenpahler. Ithaca, NY: Snow Lion, 1990.

———, trans. Gampopa. *The Jewel Ornament of Liberation. The Wish-fulfilling Gem of the Noble Teachings*. Ed. Ani K. Trinlay Chödron. Ithaca, NY: Snow Lion, 1998.

———, trans. *Prayer Flags: The Life and Spiritual Teachings of Jigten Sumgön*. Ithaca, NY: Snow Lion, 1986.

Gyaltsen, Sakyapa Sonam. *The Clear Mirror: A Traditional Account of Tibet's Golden Age*. Trans. McComas Taylor and Lama Choedak Yuthok. Ithaca, NY: Snow Lion, 1996.

Gyatso, Geshe Kelsang. *Clear Light of Bliss: Mahamudra in Vajrayana Buddhism*. Trans. Tenzin Norbu. London: Wisdom, 1982.

———. *Guide to Dakini Land: A Commentary to the Highest Yoga Tantra Practice of Vajrayogini*. London: Tharpa, 1991.

———. *Tantric Grounds and Paths*. London: Tharpa, 1994.

Gyatso, Janet. *Apparitions of the Self: The Secret Autobiographies of a Tibetan Visionary: A Translation and Study of Jigme Lingpa's Dancing Moon in the Water and Ḍākki's Grand Secret-Talk*. Princeton, NJ: Princeton University Press, 1998.

———. "The Development of the *Gcod* Tradition." In Aziz and Kapstein, pp. 320–41.

———. "Drawn from the Tibetan Treasury: The *gTer ma* Literature." In Cabezón and Jackson, pp. 147–69.

———. "Genre, Authorship, and Transmission in Visionary Buddhism: The Literary Traditions of Thang-stong rGyal-po." In Goodman and Davidson, pp. 95–106.

Halbfass, Wilhelm. *On Being and What There Is: Classical Vaiśeṣika and the History of Indian Ontology*. Albany: State University of New York Press, 1992.

Harding, Sarah, trans. *Machik's Complete Explanation Clarifying the Meaning of Chöd*. Ithaca, NY: Snow Lion, 2003.

Harrison, Paul M., trans. *Pratyutpanna Samadhi Sutra*. Berkeley, CA: Numata Center, 1998.

Heissig, Walther. *The Religions of Mongolia*. Trans. Geoffrey Samuel. Berkeley: University of California Press, 1980.

Hirakawa Akira. *A History of Indian Buddhism: From Śākyamuni to Early Mahāyāna*. Trans. and ed. Paul Groner. Honolulu: University of Hawaii Press, 1990.

Hoffman, Frank J. *Rationality and Mind in Early Buddhism*. Delhi: Motilal Banarsidass, 1987.

Hoffman, Helmut. *Quellen zur Geschichte der tibetischen Bon-Religion*. Wiesbaden: Akademie der Wissenschaften und der Litteratur, 1950.

———. *The Religions of Tibet*. New York, MacMillan, 1961.

Hookham, S. K. *The Buddha Within: Tathagatagarbha Doctrine According to the Shentong Interpretation of the Ratnagotravibhaga*. SUNY Series in Buddhist Studies. Albany: State University of New York Press, 1991.

Hopkins, Jeffrey. *Absorption in No External World: 170 Issues in Mind-Only Buddhism*. Ed. Kevin Vose. Ithaca, NY: Snow Lion, 2005.

———, trans. *Buddhist Advice for Living and Liberation: Nāgārjuna's Precious Garland*. Ithaca, NY: Snow Lion, 1998.

———. *Emptiness in the Mind-Only School of Buddhism*. Berkeley: University of California Press, 1999.

———, trans. *The Essence of Other-Emptiness by Tāranātha*. Ithaca, NY: Snow Lion, 2007.

———, trans. *Maps of the Profound: Jam-yang-shay-ba's Great Exposition of Buddhist and Non-Buddhist Views on the Nature of Reality*. Ithaca, NY: Snow Lion, 2003.

———. *Meditation on Emptiness*. Asst. ed., Elizabeth Napper. Rev. ed. Boston: Wisdom, 1996.

———, trans. *Mountain Doctrine: Tibet's Fundamental Treatise on Other-Emptiness and the Buddha Matrix*. Ed. Kevin Vose. Ithaca, NY: Snow Lion, 2006.

———, trans. Tsong-ka-pa. *The Tantra of Tibet: The Great Treatise on the Stages of Mantra*. The Wisdom of Tibet Series, 3. London: George Allen and Unwin, 1977.

______. "The Tibetan Genre of Doxography." In Cabezón and Jackson, pp. 170–86.

______, trans. *Tsong-kha-pa's Final Exposition of Wisdom.* Ithaca, NY: Snow Lion, 2008.

______, trans. Tsong-ka-pa. *The Yoga of Tibet: The Great Treatise on the Stages of Mantra—2 and 3.* The Wisdom of Tibet Series, 4. London: George Allen and Unwin, 1981.

______, trans. and ed. Tsong-ka-pa. *Yoga Tantra: Paths to Magical Feats.* Ithaca, NY: Snow Lion, 2005.

Huber, Toni. *The Cult of Pure Crystal Mountain: Popular Pilgrimage and Visionary Landscape in Southeast Tibet.* New York: Oxford University Press, 1999.

Hummel, Arthur W., ed. *Eminent Chinese of the Ch'ing period (1644–1912).* 2 vols. Washington, DC: U.S. Government Printing Office, 1943–44.

Huntington, Jr., C. W., with Geshé Namgyal Wangchen. *The Emptiness of Emptiness: An Introduction to Early Indian Mādhyamika.* Honolulu: University of Hawaii Press, 1989.

Huntington, John, and Dina Bangdel. *The Circle of Bliss: Buddhist Meditational Art.* Columbus: Columbus Museum of Art; Chicago: Serindia, 2003.

Jackson, David P., *Enlightenment by a Single Means. Tibetan Controversies on the "Self-Sufficient White Remedy."* Beiträge zur Kultur- und Geistesgeschichte Asiens nr. 12. Vienna: Verlag der Österreichischen Akademie der Wissenschaften, 1994.

______. *The Entrance-Gate for the Wise (Section III): Sa-skya Paṇḍita on Indian and Tibetan Traditions of Pramāṇa and Philosophical Debate.* 2 parts. Wiener Studien zur Tibetologie und Buddhismuskunde, heft 17. Vienna: Arbeitskreis für Tibetische und Buddhistische Studien Universität Wien, 1987.

______. "The *bsTan rim* ('Stages of the Doctrine') and Similar Graded Expositions of the Bodhisattva's Path." In Cabezón and Jackson, pp. 229–43.

Jackson, Roger R. "Buddhism in India." In Mahalingam and Carr, pp. 318–48.

______. "The dGe ldan bka' brgyud Tradition of Mahāmudrā: How Much dGe ldan? How Much bKa' brgyud?" In Newland, *Changing Minds,* pp. 155–92.

______, trans. and annot. *Is Enlightenment Possible? Dharmakīrti and rGyal tshab rje on Knowledge, Rebirth, No-self and Liberation.* Ithaca, NY: Snow Lion, 1993.

______. "Mahāmudrā." In *Encyclopedia of Religion.* 2nd ed. Ed. Lindsay Jones. Vol. 8, pp. 5596–6501. Detroit: Wadsworth Gale, 2005.

______. *Tantric Treasures: Three Collections of Mystical Verse from Buddhist India.* New York: Oxford University Press, 2004.

______, trans. "A Tibetan Fasting Ritual," in Lopez, *Religions of Tibet in Practice,* pp. 271–92.

———. "Triumphalism and Ecumenism in Thu'u bkwan's *Crystal Mirror*." *Journal of the International Association of Tibetan Studies* 2 (2006), THDL #T2720, 23 pp. [online: www.thdl.org/collections/journal/JIATS.html].

Jäeschke, H. A. *A Tibetan-English Dictionary to Which Is Added an English-Tibetan Vocabulary*. London: Routledge and Kegan Paul, 1972 (1881).

Jaini, Padmanabh S. *The Jaina Path of Purification*. Berkeley: University of California Press, 1979.

Jayatilleke, K. N. *Early Buddhist Theory of Knowledge*. Delhi: Motilal Banarsidass, 1998.

Jinpa, Thupten, ed. and trans. *The Book of Kadam: The Core Texts*. Boston: Wisdom, 2008.

———, ed. and trans. *Mind Training: The Great Collection*. Compiled by Shönu Gyalchok and Könchok Gyaltsen. Boston: Wisdom, 2006.

———. *Self, Reality and Reason in Tibetan Philosophy: Tsongkhapa's Quest for the Middle Way*. London/New York: RoutledgeCurzon, 2002.

———, and Jaś Elsner, trans. *Songs of Spiritual Experience: Tibetan Buddhist Poems of Insight and Awakening*. Boston: Shambhala, 2000.

Jorden, Ngawang. *Buddha-Nature Through the Eyes of Go rams pa Bsod nams seng ge in Fifteenth-Century Tibet*. Ph.D. dissertation, Harvard University, 2003.

[K]. Thu'u bkwan Blo bzang chos kyi nyi ma. *Thu'u bkwan grub mtha'*. Lanzhou: Kan su'u mi rigs dpe skrun khang, 1984.

Kaltenmark, Max. *Lao Tzu and Taoism*. Palo Alto, CA: Stanford University Press, 1969.

Kalupahana, David J. *Buddhist Philosophy: A Historical Analysis*. Honolulu: University of Hawaii Press, 1976.

Kämpfe, Hans-Reiner, ed. *Die Biographie des 2. Pekinger lCaṅ skya-Qutuqtu*. St. Augustin, Germany: VGH Wissenschaftsverlag, 1976.

Kapstein, Matthew T. "Chronological Conundrums in the Life of 'Khyung po rnal 'byor." *Journal of the International Association of Tibetan Studies* 1 (2005) THDL #T1221, 14, pp. [on-line: www.thdl.org/collections/journal/JIATS.html].

———. "*gDams ngag:* Tibetan Technologies of the Self." In Cabezón and Jackson, pp. 275–89.

———, trans. "The Journey to the Golden Mountain." In Lopez, *Religions of Tibet in Practice*, pp. 177–87.

———. *Reason's Traces: Identity and Interpretation in Indian and Tibetan Buddhist Thought*. Boston: Wisdom, 2001.

———. "The Shangs-pa Bka' brgyud; An Unknown Tradition of Tibetan Buddhism." In Aris and Aung Saan Suu Kyi, pp. 138–44.

———. *The Tibetan Assimilation of Buddhism: Conversion, Contestation, and Memory*. Oxford: Oxford University Press, 2000.

———. *The Tibetans*. Malden, MA: Blackwell, 2006.

Karmay, Samten G. *The Great Perfection: A Philosophical and Meditative Teaching of Tibetan Buddhism*. Leiden: Brill, 1988.

———, ed and trans. [Grub dbang Bkra shis rgyal mtshan dri med snying po.] *The Treasury of Good Sayings: A Tibetan History of Bon*. London: Oxford University Press, 1972.

———, ed. *Secret Visions of the Fifth Dalai Lama: The Gold Manuscript in the Fournier Collection*. London: Serindia, 1988.

Karthar Rinpoche, Khenpo. *The Instructions of Gampopa: A Precious Garland of the Supreme Path*. Trans. Lama Yeshe Gyamtso. Ithaca, NY: Snow Lion, 1996.

Katsura Shoryu, ed. *Dharmakīrti's Thought and Its Impact on Indian and Tibetan Philosophy—Proceedings of the Third International Conference on Dharmakīrti and Pramāṇa*. Vienna: Österreichischen Akademie der Wissenschaften, 1999.

Khedrup Norsang Gyatso. *Ornament of Stainless Light: An Exposition of the Kālacakra Tantra*. Trans. Gavin Kilty. Boston: Wisdom, 2004.

Kilty, Gavin, trans. Tsongkhapa. *The Splendor of an Autumn Moon: The Devotional Verse of Tsongkhapa*. Boston: Wisdom, 2001.

Klafkowski, Piotr, trans. and ed. [Damchø Gyatsho Dharmatāla.] *Rosary of White Lotuses: Being the Clear Account of How the Precious Teaching of Buddha Appeared and Spread in the Great Hor Country*. Wiesbaden: O. Harrassowitz, 1987.

Kochumuttom, Thomas A. *The Buddhist Doctrine of Experience: A New Translation and Interpretation of the Works of Vasubandhu, the Yogācārin*. Delhi: Motilal Banarsidass, 1982.

Koller, John M., and Patricia Koller, eds. *A Sourcebook in Asian Philosophy*. New York: Macmillan, 1991.

Komarovski, Iaroslav, trans. [Shākya Chokden.] *Three Texts on Madhyamaka*. Dharamsala: Library of Tibetan Works and Archives, 2000.

Komito, David Ross, et al. *Nagarjuna's Seventy Stanzas: A Buddhist Psychology of Emptiness*. Ithaca, NY: Snow Lion, 1987.

Kongtrul, Jamgön. *Systems of Buddhist Tantra*. The Treasury of Knowledge, book 6, part 4. Trans. Elio Guarisco and Ingrid McLeod. Ithaca, NY: Snow Lion, 2005.

———. *Esoteric Instructions*. The Treasury of Knowledge, book 8, part 4. Trans. S. Harding. Ithaca, NY: Snow Lion, 2007.

Kragh, Ulrich. *Culture and Subculture: A Study of the Mahāmudrā Teachings of Sgam po pa*. M.A. Research Paper (speciale), University of Copenhagen, 1998.

Krasser, Helmut, et al., eds. *Tibetan Studies: Proceedings of on the International Conference on Tibetan Studies [Graz, Austria]*. Vienna: Verlag der Österreichischen Akademie der Wissenschaften, 1997.

Kuijp, Leonard W. J. van der. *Contributions to the Development of Tibetan Buddhist Epistemology: From the Eleventh to the Thirteenth Century*. Wiesbaden: F. Steiner, 1983.

———. "An Early Tibetan View of the Soteriology of Buddhist Epistemology: The Case of 'Bri-gung 'Jig-rten mGon-po." *Journal of Indian Philosophy* 15 (1987), pp. 57–70.

Küng, Hans, et al. *Christianity and the World Religions: Paths to Dialogue with Islam, Hinduism, and Buddhism*. Trans. Peter Heinegg. Garden City, NY: Doubleday, 1986.

Kunga Rinpoche, Lama, and Brian Cutillo, trans. *Miraculous Journey: New Stories and Songs by Milarepa*. Novato, CA: Lotsawa, 1986.

———, trans. *Drinking the Mountain Stream: Songs of Tibet's Beloved Saint, Milarepa*. Boston: Wisdom, 1995.

Kvaerne, Per. *An Anthology of Buddhist Tantric Songs: A Study of the Caryāgīti*. Oslo/Bergen/Tromso: Universitetsforlaget, 1977.

———. *The Bön Religion of Tibet: The Iconography of a Living Tradition*. Boston/London: Shambhala, 1995.

———. "The Literature of Bon." In Cabezón and Jackson, pp. 138–46.

La Vallée Poussin, Louis de, trans. *Abhidharmakośabhāṣyam*. English translation by Leo M. Pruden. Berkeley: Asian Humanities Press, 1988–90.

Lamotte, Étienne, trans. *L'Explication des Mystères [Saṃdhinirmocanasūtra]*. Paris: A. Maisonneuve, 1935.

———. *History of Indian Buddhism: From the Origins to the Śāka Era*. Trans. Sara Webb-Boin. Louvain-la-Neuve: Université Catholique de Louvain, Institut Orientaliste, 1988.

———. *La Somme du Grand Véhicule d'Asaṅga (Mahāyānasaṃgraha)*. 2 vols. Louvain: Bureaux du Muséon, 1938–39.

Lamrim Chenmo Translation Committee, trans. Tsong-kha-pa. *The Great Treatise on the Stages of the Path to Enlightenment*. Ed. Joshua W.C. Cutler and Guy Newland. 3 vols. Ithaca, NY: Snow Lion, 2000–2004. [GT]

Lang, Karen. *Āryadeva's Catuḥśataka*. Copenhagen: Akademisk Forlag, 1986.

———. "Spa-tshabs Nyi-ma-grags and the Introduction of Prāsaṅgika Madhyamaka in Tibet." In Epstein and Sherburne, pp. 127–42.

Larson, Gerald J., and Ram Shankar Bhattacharya. *Sāṃkhya: A Dualist Tradition in Indian Philosophy*. Encyclopedia of Indian Philosophies, vol. IV. Princeton: Princeton University Press, 1987.

Lati Rinbochay et al. *Meditative States in Tibetan Buddhism: The Concentrations and Formless Absorptions*. Trans. Jeffrey Hopkins, ed. Leah Zahler. London: Wisdom, 1983.

Legge, James, ed. and trans. *The Four Books*. New York: Paragon Book Gallery, 1966 (1923).

Lessing, F. D. *Mongolian-English Dictionary*. Bloomington: The Mongolia Society, 1995.

Lessing, F. D., and Alex Wayman. *Introduction to the Buddhist Tantric Systems, Translated from Mkhas grub rje's* Rgyud sde spyi'i rnam par gzhag pa rgyas par brjod, *With Original Text and Annotation*. Delhi: Motilal Banarsidass, 1978 (1968).

Lhalungpa, Lobsang, trans. *The Life of Milarepa*. Boston and London: Shambhala. 1998.

______, trans. *Mahāmudrā—The Moonlight: The Quintessence of Mind and Meditation*. Boston: Wisdom, 2006 (1986).

Li An-che, "The Bkaḥ-brgyud Sect of Lamaism." *Journal of the Royal Asiatic Society* 69 (1949), pp. 51–59.

______. "Rñiṅmapa, the Early Form of Lamaism." *Journal of the Royal Asiatic Society* 68 (1948) pp. 142–63.

______. "The Sakya Sect of Lamaism." *Journal of the West China Border Research Society* XVI: A (1945) pp. 72–86.

Lindtner, Christian. *Nagarjuniana: Studies in the Writings and Philosophy of Nāgārjuna*. Copenhagen: Akademisk Forlag, 1982.

Linrothe, Rob, ed. *Holy Madness: Portraits of Tantric Siddhas*. New York: Rubin Museum of Art/Chicago: Serindia, 2006

Little, Stephen, ed. *Taoism and the Arts of China*. Chicago: Art Institute of Chicago, 2000.

Liu Liqian. *Tuguan Zongpai Yuanliu*. Chengdu: Xizang Renmin Chubanshe, 1985.

Loizzo, Joseph. *Nagarjuna's Reason Sixty (Yuktiṣaṣtikā) with Candrakīrti's Commentary (Yuktiṣaṣtikāvṛtti)*. New York: American Institute of Buddhist Studies, 2007.

Lopez, Jr. Donald S., ed. *Buddhism in Practice*. Princeton Readings in Religions. Princeton: Princeton University Press, 1995.

______, ed. *Buddhist Hermeneutics*. Honolulu: University of Hawaii Press, 1992.

______. *Elaborations on Emptiness: Uses of the Heart Sūtra*. Princeton, NJ: Princeton University Press, 1996.

______. "A Prayer to the Lama." In Lopez, *Religions of Tibet in Practice*, pp. 276–386.

______, ed. *Religions of China in Practice*. Princeton Readings in Religions. Princeton, NJ: Princeton University Press, 1998.

. *A Study of Svātantrika*. Ithaca, NY: Snow Lion, 1987.

Lü Cheng. *A Short History of Chinese Buddhism by Thuhu-bkwan. Studia Serica Monographs*, Series B, No. 1. Chengdu: The Chinese Cultural Studies Research Institute, 1942.

Macdonald, Ariane. "Préambule à la lecture d'un rGya-Bod Yig-Cha." *Journal Asiatique* 251: 1 (1963) pp. 53–159.

Magee, William. *The Nature of Things: Emptiness and Essence in the Geluk World.* Ithaca, NY: Snow Lion, 1999.

Mahalingam, I., and B. Carr, eds. *Companion Encyclopedia of Asian Philosophy.* London: Routledge, 1997.

Makransky, John J. *Buddhahood Embodied: Sources of Controversy in India and Tibet.* Albany: State University of New York Press, 1997.

Mala, Guilaine. "A Mahayanist Rewriting of the History of China by Mgon po skyabs in the Rgya nag chos 'byung." In Cuevas and Schaeffer, pp. 145–69.

———. *Perception of Chinese Religions in Eighteenth-Century Tibet: A Study of Thu'u-bkwan's Grub-mtha' shel-gyi me-long and Related Tibetan Works written by Mongol Authors.* Ph.D. dissertation, Oxford University, 2006.

Martin, Dan. "The Early Education of Milarepa." *The Journal of the Tibet Society* 2 (1982), pp. 53–76.

———. "Meditation Is Action Taken: On Zhang Rinpoche, A Meditation-Based Activist in Twelfth-Century Tibet." *Lungta* 14 (2001), pp. 45–56.

———. *Tibetan Histories: A Bibliography of Tibetan-Language Historical Works.* London: Serindia, 1997.

———. "Padampa Sangye: A History of Representation of a South Indian Siddha in Tibet." In Linrothe, pp. 108–23.

———. "A Twelfth-Century Tibetan Classic of Mahāmudrā: *The Path of Ultimate Profundity: The Great Seal Instructions of Zhang.*" *The Journal of the International Association of Buddhist Studies* 15: 2 (1992), pp. 243–319.

———. *Unearthing Bon Treasures: Life and Contested Legacy of a Tibetan Scripture Revealer, with a General Bibliography of Bon.* Leiden: Brill, 2001.

Mathes, Klaus-Dieter. "Blending the Sūtras with the Tantras: The Influence of Maitrīpa and His Circle on the Formation of Sūtra Mahāmudrā in the Kagyu Schools." In Davidson and Wedermeyer, *Tibetan Buddhist Literature and Praxis: Studies in Its Formative Period, 900–1400,* pp. 201–227.

———. "Tāranātha's 'Twenty-One Differences with Regard to the Profound Meaning' Comparing the Views of the Two *gzhan stoṅ* Masters Śākya mchog ldan and Dol po pa." *The Journal of the International Association of Buddhist Studies* 27: 2 (2004), pp. 285–328.

Matilal, B. K. *Perception: An Essay on Classical Indian Theories of Knowledge.* Oxford: Clarendon Press / New York: Oxford University Press, 1986.

Matsunaga Yukei. *The Guhyasamāja Tantra: A New Critical Edition.* Osaka: Toho Shuppan, 1978.

Matthews, R. H. *Chinese-English Dictionary.* Revised American edition with revised English index. Cambridge, MA: Harvard University Press, 1975 (1931).

Miller, Amy. *Jeweled Dialogues: The Role of 'The Book' in the Formation of the*

Kadam Tradition within Tibet. Ph.D. dissertation, University of Virginia, 2004.

Mimaki Katsumi, ed. and trans. *Blo gsal grub mtha': chapitres IX (Vaibhāṣika) et XI (Yogācāra) et chapitre XII (Mādhyamika)*. Kyoto: Zinbun Kagaku Kenkyusyo, Université de Kyoto, 1982.

Mishra, Ramprasad. *Advayasiddhi: The Tāntric View of Lakṣmīṅkarā*. Delhi: Kant Publications, 1995.

Mittal, Kewal Krishan, with Lama Jamspal. *A Tibetan Eye-View of Indian Philosophy*. New Delhi: Munshiram Manoharlal, 1984.

Molk, David, with Lama Tsering Wangdu Rinpoche. *Lion of Siddhas: The Life and Teachings of Phadampa Sangye*. Ithaca, NY: Snow Lion, 2008.

Monier-Williams, Sir Monier. *A Sanskrit-English Dictionary*. New edition. Oxford: Oxford University Press, 1899.

Mookerjee, S., and Nagasaki Hojun. *The Pramāṇavārttikam. An English Translation of the First Chapter with the Autocommentary and with Elaborate Comments (kārikās I–LI)*. Nalanda, Patna: Nava Nālandā Mahāvihāra, 1964.

Mote, F. W. *Imperial China, 900–1800*. Cambridge, MA: Harvard University Press, 1999.

Mullin, Glenn H., trans. Gyalwa Gendun Druppa. *Bridging the Sutras and Tantras*. Ithaca, NY: Gabriel/Snow Lion, 1982.

———. *The Fourteen Dalai Lamas: A Sacred Legacy of Reincarnation*. Santa Fe, NM: Clear Light Publishers, 2001.

———, trans. Gyalwa Gendun Gyatso. *Mystical Verses of a Mad Dalai Lama*. Wheaton, IL: Theosophical Publishing House, 1994.

———. *The Practice of Kalachakra*. Ithaca, NY: Snow Lion, 1991.

———, trans. *Readings on the Six Yogas of Naropa*. Ithaca, NY: Snow Lion, 1997.

———, trans. Gyalwa Kalzang Gyatso. *Songs of Spiritual Change*. Ithaca, NY: Gabriel/Snow Lion, 1982.

———, trans. *Selected Works of the Dalai Lama II: The Tantric Yogas of Sister Niguma*. Ithaca, NY: Snow Lion, 1985.

———, trans. Gyalwa Sönam Gyatso. *Selected Works of the Dalai Lama III: Essence of Refined Gold*. Ithaca, NY: Gabriel/Snow Lion, 1982.

———, trans. Gyalwa Gendün Druppa. *Training the Mind in the Great Way*. Ithaca, NY: Snow Lion, 1993.

———, trans. *Tsongkhapa's Six Yogas of Naropa*. Ithaca, NY: Snow Lion, 1996.

Nakamura Hajime. *Indian Buddhism: A Survey with Bibliographical Notes*. Hirakata, Japan: KUFS Publication, 1980.

Nālandā Translation Committee, trans. *The Life of Marpa*. Boston: Shambhala, 1986.

———, trans. "The Life of Tilopa." In Lopez, *Religions of Tibet in Practice*, pp. 137–56.

———, trans. *The Rain of Wisdom: The Essence of The Ocean of True Meaning, the Vajra Songs of the Kagyü Gurus*. Boston: Shambhala, 1980.

———, trans. "The Yogin Lorepa's Retreat at Lake Namtso." In Lopez, *Religions of Tibet in Practice*, pp. 200–211.

Namdak, Tenzin, trans. Shardza Tashi Gyaltsen. *Heart Drops of Dharmakaya: Dzogchen Practice of the Bon Tradition*. Ithaca, NY: Snow Lion, 1993.

Napper, Elizabeth. *Dependent Arising and Emptiness: A Tibetan Buddhist Interpretation of Mādhyamika Philosophy Emphasizing the Compatibility of Emptiness and Conventional Phenomena*. Boston: Wisdom, 2003.

Naquin, Susan. *Peking Temples and City Life, 1400–1900*. Berkeley: University of California Press, 2000.

Nebesky-Wojkowitz, Réne de. *Oracles and Demons of Tibet: The Cult and Iconography of the Tibetan Protective Deities*. Kathmandu: Tiwari's Pilgrims Book House, 1992 (1956).

Newland, Guy, ed. *Changing Minds: Contributions to the Study of Buddhism and Tibet in Honor of Jeffrey Hopkins*. Ithaca, NY: Snow Lion, 2001.

———. *Introduction to Emptiness: As Taught in Tsong-kha-pa's Great Treatise on the Stages of the Path*. Ithaca, NY: Snow Lion, 2008.

Newman, John R. *The Outer Wheel of Time: Vajrayāna Buddhist Cosmology in the Kālacakra Tantra*. Ph.D. dissertation, University of Wisconsin–Madison, 1987.

———. "Vajrayoga in the Kālacakra Tantra." In White, pp. 587–94.

Ngorchen Konchog Lhundrub. *Three Visions: Fundamental Teachings of the Sakya Lineage of Tibetan Buddhism*. Trans. Lobsang Dakpa and Jay Goldberg. Ithaca, NY: Snow Lion, 2002.

Nietupski, Paul. *Labrang: A Tibetan Buddhist Monastery at the Crossroads of Four Civilizations*. Ithaca, NY: Snow Lion, 1998.

Norbu, Chögyal Namkhai, and Adriano Clemente, trans. *The Supreme Source: The* Kunjed Gyalpo, *The Fundamental Tantra of the Dzokchen Semde*. Trans. Andrew Lukianowicz. Ithaca, NY: Snow Lion, 1999.

[NS]. See Dudjom.

Nydahl, Ole. *Mahamudra: Boundless Joy and Freedom: A Commentary on The Wishing Prayer for the Attainment of the Ultimate Mahamudra Given by His Holiness Rangjung Dorje (The Third Karmapa, 1284–1339)*. Nevada City, CA: Blue Dolphin, 1991.

Obermiller, E., trans. *History of Buddhism (Chos-ḥbyung)*. Delhi: Sri Satguru Publications, 1986 (1931–32).

———, trans. Bu-ston. *Jewellery of Scripture*. Delhi: Paljor, 2000 (1931–32).

———, trans. "Sublime Science of the Great Vehicle to Salvation." *Acta Orientalia* 9 (1931), pp. 81–306.

Orofino, Giacomella. *Contributo allo Studio dell'Insegnamento di Ma gcig Lab sgron.* Napoli: Istituto Universitario Orientale, 1987.

———. "The Great Wisdom Mother and the Gcod Tradition." In White, pp. 396–416.

Padmakara Translation Group, trans. Shantideva. *The Way of the Bodhisattva: A Translation of the Bodhicharyāvatāra.* Boston: Shambhala, 2006.

Peking Tripitaka Online Search. Website: http://web.otani.ac.jp/cri/twrp/tibdate/Peking_online_search.html.

Pelliot, Paul. "Autour d'une traduction sanscrite du Tao Tö King." *T'oung Pao* 33 (1912).

Perdue, Peter C. *China Marches West: The Qing Conquest of Central Eurasia.* Cambridge, MA: Belknap Press of Harvard University Press, 2005.

Petech, Luciano. *Central Tibet and the Mongols.* Rome: Istituto Italiano per il Medio ed Estremo Oriente, 1990.

Phyag chen Rgya gzhuṅ: The collected texts of the Mahamudra practice translated from Sanskrit, representing the tradition which has passed in the Mar-pa Bka'-brg[y]ud-pa. Bir, Distt. Kangra, H.P.: D. Tsondu Senghe, 1985.

Poppe, Nicholas. *The Twelve Deeds of Buddha.* Seattle: University of Washington Press, 1967.

Potter, Karl R., ed. *Bibliography of Indian Philosophies.* 3rd ed. Encyclopedia of Indian Philosophies, vol. I. Princeton, NJ: Princeton University Press, 1995.

———, ed. *Buddhist Philosophy from 100 to 350 A.D.* Encyclopedia of Indian Philosophies, vol. VIII. Delhi: Motilal Banarsidass, 1999.

———, ed. *Buddhist Philosophy from 350 to 600 A.D.* Encyclopedia of Indian Philosophies, vol. IX. Delhi: Motilal Banarsidass, 2003.

———, ed. *Indian Metaphysics and Epistemology: The Tradition of Nyāya-Vaiśeṣika to Gaṅgeśa.* Encyclopedia of Indian Philosophies, vol. II. Princeton, NJ: Princeton University Press, 1977.

———. *Presuppositions of India's Philosophies.* Seattle: University of Washington Press, 1968.

———, et al., eds. *Abhidharma Buddhism to 150 A.D.* Encyclopedia of Indian Philosophies, vol. VII. Delhi: Motilal Banarsidass, 1996.

Powers, John. *Introduction to Tibetan Buddhism.* Ithaca, NY: Snow Lion, 1995.

———, trans. *Wisdom of Buddha: The Saṃdhinirmocana Sūtra.* Berkeley: Dharma, 1995.

Quintman, Andrew. *Mi la ras pa's Many Lives: Anatomy of a Tibetan Biographical Corpus.* Ph.D. dissertation, University of Michigan, 2006.

Radhakrishnan, Sarvepalli. *Indian Philosophy.* London: G. Allen and Unwin, 1941.

———, and Charles A. Moore, eds. *A Sourcebook in Indian Philosophy.* Princeton, NJ: Princeton University Press, 1957.

Rahula, Walpola, trans. Asaṅga. *Abhidharmasamuccaya. The Compendium of the Higher Teaching (Philosophy).* English version from the French by Sara Boin-Webb. Fremont, CA: Asian Humanities Press, 2001.

Rambachan, Anantanand. *The Advaita Worldview: God, World, and Humanity.* Albany: State University of New York Press, 2006.

Rangjung Yeshe Tibetan-English Dictionary. http://www.nitartha.org/dictionary.html.

RangjungYesheWiki. http://rywiki.tsadra.org/index.php/Main_Page.

Ray, Reginald A. *Indestructible Truth. The Living Spirituality of Tibetan Buddhism.* Boston: Shambhala, 2002.

———. *Secret of the Vajra World: The Tantric Buddhism of Tibet.* Boston: Shambhala, 2001.

Régamy, C., trans. *Philosophy in the Samādhirājasūtra: Three Chapters from the Samādhirājasūtra.* Delhi: Motilal Banarsidass, 1990 (1938).

Rhoton, Jared, trans. Sakya Pandita. *A Clear Differentiation of the Three Codes: Essential Distinctions Among the Individual Liberation, Great Vehicle, and Tantric Systems.* Albany: State University of New York Press, 2002.

Rhys Davids, T. W., trans. *The Questions of King Milinda.* 2 vols. Delhi: Motilal Banarsidass, 1965 (1890).

Ricard, Matthieu. *Geographical Glossary from Matthieu Ricard.* http://rywiki.tsadra.org/index.php/Geographical_Glossary_from_Matthieu_Ricard.

Richardson, Hugh E. *Ch'ing Dynasty Inscriptions at Lhasa.* Roma: Istituto Italiano per il Medio ed Estremo Oriente, 1974.

———. "The Karma-pa School: A Historical Note." *Journal of the Royal Asiatic Society* 1 (1973), pp. 12–20.

———. *Tibet and Its History.* London: Oxford University Press, 1962.

Riggs, Nicole. *Like an Illusion: Lives of the Shangpa Kagyu Masters.* Eugene, OR: Dharma Cloud, 2000.

Rigzin, Tsepak. *Tibetan-English Dictionary of Buddhist Terminology.* Dharamsala: Library of Tibetan Works and Archives, 1986.

Rinchen, Geshe Sonam, with Ruth Sonam. *Atisha's Lamp for the Path: An Oral Teaching by Geshe Sonam Rinchen.* Ithaca, NY: Snow Lion, 1997.

———. *The Yogic Deeds of Bodhisattvas: Gyeltsap on Aryadeva's Four Hundred.* Ithaca, NY: Snow Lion, 1994.

Ringu Tulku. *The Ri-Me Philosophy of Jamgön Kongtrul the Great: A Study of the Buddhist Lineages of Tibet.* Boston: Shambhala, 2006.

Roberts, J. A. G. *A History of China,* vol. 1. Phoenix Mill, UK: Alan Sutton, 1996.

Robinson, James B., trans. Abhayadatta. *Buddha's Lions: The Lives of the Eighty-Four Siddhas.* Berkeley, CA: Dharma Publishing, 1979.

Rockhill, W. Woodville, trans. *Udânavarga: A Collection of Verses from the Buddhist Canon.* London: Trübner and Co., 1883.

Roerich, George N., trans. [Gö Lotsāwa Shönu Pal.] *The Blue Annals*. Delhi: Motilal Banarsidass, 1976 (1949). [BA]

Rona-Tas, A. *Tibeto-Mongolica: The Tibetan Loanwords of Monguor and the Development of the Archaic Tibetan Dialects*. The Hague: Mouton, 1966.

Ruegg, David Seyfort. *Buddha-Nature, Mind and the Problem of Gradualism in a Comparative Perspective: On the Transmission and Reception of Buddhism in India and Tibet*. London: School of Oriental and African Studies, University of London, 1989.

______. "The Jo naṅ pas: A School of Buddhist Ontologists According to the *Grub mtha' Śel gyi me loṅ*. *Journal of the American Oriental Society* 83: 1 (1963), pp. 73–91.

______. "A Kar ma bKa' brgyud Work on the Lineages and Traditions of the Indo-Tibetan dBu ma (Madhyamaka)." In G. Gnoli and L. Lanciotti, eds. *Orientalia Iosephi Tucci Memoriae Dicata*. Serie Orientale Roma: LVI, 3. Roma: Istituto Italiano per il Medio ed Estremo Oriente, 1988.

______. *The Life of Bu-ston Rinpoche, with the Tibetan Text of the Bu ston rNam thar*. Serie Orientale Roma, XXXIV. Roma: Istituto Italiano per il Medio ed Estremo Oriente, 1966.

______. *The Literature of the Madhyamaka School of Buddhism in India*. Wiesbaden: Harrassowitz, 1981.

[S]. Thu'u bkvan blo bzang chos kyi nyi ma. *Grub mtha' thams cad kyi khungs dang 'dod tshul ston pa legs bshad shel gyi me long zhes bya ba zhugs so*. Ed. Thupten Jinpa et al. Bod kyi gtsug lag gces btus pod phreng, 25. Delhi: Institute of Tibetan Classics, 2007.

Sagang Sechen. *The Bejewelled Summary of the Origin of Khans*. Trans. John R. Kruger. In *The Mongolia Society Occasional Papers Number Two*. Bloomington, IN: Mongolia Society, 1967.

Samdhong Rinpoche and Vrajallabh Dwivedi, eds. *Guhyādi-Aṣṭasiddhi-Saṅgraha (gSang ba grub pa la sogs pa'i grub pa sde brgyad)*. Rare Buddhist Text Series, 1. Sārnāth: Central Institute of Higher Tibetan Studies, 1987.

Samten, Geshe Ngawang, and Jay L. Garfield, trans. *Ocean of Reasoning: A Great Commentary on Nāgārjuna's Mūlamadhyamakakārikā*. Oxford/New York: Oxford University Press, 2006.

Samuel, Geoffrey. *Civilized Shamans: Buddhism in Tibetan Societies*. Washington, DC: Smithsonian Institution Press, 1993.

Samye.org. http://www.samye.org.

Schaeffer, Kurtis. *Dreaming the Great Brahmin: Tibetan Traditions of the Buddhist Poet-Saint Saraha*. New York: Oxford University Press, 2005.

______. *The Enlightened Heart of Buddhahood: A Study and Translation of the Third Karma pa Rang byung rdo rje's Work on Tathāgatagarbha, the* De bzhin gshegs pa'i snying po gtan la dbab pa. M.A. thesis. Seattle: University of Washington, 1995.

———. "Future Directions for Modern Tibetan Studies: Religion/History." *Bulletin of the CSSR* 35: 1 (February 2006), pp. 17–19.

Schram, Louis. *The Monguors of the Kansu-Tibetan Frontier*. 2 vols. Philadelphia: American Philosophical Society, 1954–57.

Sera Monastery. http://www.thdl.org/collections/cultgeo/mons/sera/.

Shahidullah, M. *Chants Mystiques de Kāṇha et de Saraha: Les Dohā-koṣa et les Caryā*. Paris: Adrien-Maisonneuve, 1928.

Shakabpa, Tsepon W. D. *Tibet: A Political History*. New Haven, CT: Yale University Press, 1967.

Sharf, Robert. "The Scripture in Forty-Two Sections." In Lopez, ed. *Religions of China in Practice*, pp. 360–71.

Sharma, Chandradhar. *A Critical Survey of Indian Philosophy*. London: Rider, 1960.

Shastri, Haraprasad, ed. *Advayavajrasaṃgraha*. Gaekwad's Oriental Series, XL. Baroda: Oriental Institute, 1927.

Shendge, Malati. "*Śrīsahajasiddhi*." *Indo-Iranian Journal* 10: 2/3 (1967), pp. 126–49.

Sherburne, Richard. *A Lamp for the Path and Commentary of Atīśa*. London/Boston: Allen and Unwin, 1983.

Skorupski, Tadeusz, trans. *The Sarvadurgatipariśodhana Tantra: Elimination of All Evil Destinies*. Delhi: Motilal Banarsidass, 1983.

Smart, Ninian. *Doctrine and Argument in Indian Philosophy*. 2nd ed. Leiden/New York: E.J. Brill, 1992.

Smith, E. Gene. *Among Tibetan Texts: History and Literature of the Himalayan Plateau*. Boston: Wisdom, 2001.

Smith, Jonathan Z. "Religion, Religions, Religious." In Taylor, pp. 269–84.

Snellgrove, David L., trans. "The Attainment of the Realization of Wisdom and Means." In Conze, *Buddhist Texts Through the Ages*, pp. 240–46.

———. *The Hevajra Tantra: A Critical Study*. 2 vols. London/New York: Oxford University Press, 1959.

———. *Indo-Tibetan Buddhism*. 2 vols. Boston: Shambhala, 1987.

———, ed and trans. *The Nine Ways of Bon: Excerpts from gZi-brjid*. Boulder, CO: Prajñā Press, 1980.

———, trans. "Saraha's Treasury of Songs." In Conze, *Buddhist Texts Through the Ages*, pp. 224–39.

Snellgrove, David L., and Hugh Richardson. *A Cultural History of Tibet*. New York: Praeger, 1967.

Sopa, Geshe, trans. *Peacock in the Poison Grove: Two Buddhist Texts on Training the Mind*. With Michael Sweet and Leonard Zwilling. Boston: Wisdom, 2001.

Sopa, Geshe, and Jeffrey Hopkins, trans. *Cutting Through Appearances: The Practice and Theory of Tibetan Buddhism*. Ithaca, NY: Snow Lion, 1990.

Sopa, Geshe, Roger Jackson, and John Newman. *The Wheel of Time: Kalachakra in Context*. Ed. Beth Simon. Ithaca, NY: Snow Lion, 1991.

Sørensen, Per K., and Guntram Hazod, in cooperation with Tsering Gyalbo. *Rulers on the Celestial Plain: Ecclesiastic and Secular Hegemony in Medieval Tibet; A Study of Tshal Gung-thang*. Vienna: Verlag der Österreichischen Akademie der Wissenschaften, 2007.

Sparham, Gareth, trans. Tsongkhapa. *The Fulfillment of All Hopes: Guru Devotion in Tibetan Buddhism; A commentary on Aśvaghoṣa's* Gurupañcaśīkā *entitled* Bla ma lnga bcu pa'i rnam bshad slob ma'i re ba kun skong shes bya ba. Boston: Wisdom, 1999.

______, trans. *Ocean of Eloquence: Tsong Kha Pa's Commentary on the Yogācāra Doctrine of Mind*. In collaboration with Shotaro Iida. Albany: State University of New York Press, 1993.

______, trans. Tsongkhapa. *Tantric Ethics: An Explanation of the Precepts for Tantric Buddhist Practice*. Boston: Wisdom, 2005.

______, trans. *The Tibetan Dhammapada*. Compiled by Dharmatrata. Ed. Beth Lee Simon. New Delhi: Mahayana, 1983.

Spence, Jonathan D. *The Memory Palace of Matteo Ricci*. New York: Viking Penguin, 1984.

Sprung, Mervyn, et al., trans. *Lucid Exposition of the Middle Way: The Essential Chapters from the Prasannapadā of Candrakīrti*. London: Routledge and Kegan Paul, 1979.

Stcherbatsky, F. Th. *Buddhist Logic*. 2 vols. Osnabrück: Biblio Verlag, 1970 (1930–32).

______. *The Central Conception of Buddhism and the Meaning of the Word "Dharma."* London: Royal Asiatic Society, 1923.

______, trans. *Madhyānta-vibhanga: Discourse on Discrimination Between Middle and Extremes, Ascribed to Bodhisattva Maitreya and Commented by Vasubandhu and Sthiramati*. Osnabrück, West Germany: Biblio, 1970 (1936).

Stearns, Cyrus, trans. *The Buddha from Dolpo: A Study of the Life and Thought of the Tibetan Master Dolpopa Sherab Gyaltsen*. Albany: State University of New York Press, 1999.

______, trans. *Hermit of Go Cliffs: Timeless Instructions from a Tibetan Mystic*. Boston: Wisdom, 2000.

. *King of the Empty Plain: The Tibetan Iron-Bridge Builder Tangtong Gyalpo*. Ithaca, NY: Snow Lion, 2006.

______, trans. *Luminous Lives: The Story of the Early Masters of the Lam 'bras Tradition in Tibet*. Boston: Wisdom, 2001.

———. "Sachen Kunga Nyingpo's Quest for *The Path and Result*." In Lopez, *Religions of Tibet in Practice*, pp. 188–99.

———, trans. *Taking the Result as the Path: Core Teachings of the Sakya Lamdré Tradition*. Boston: Wisdom, 2006. [TRP]

Stein, M. Aurel. *Ancient Khotan: Detailed Report of Archaeological Explorations in Chinese Turkestan*. New York: Hacker Art Books, 1975.

Stein, R. A. *Tibetan Civilization*. Trans. John E. Stapleton Driver. Palo Alto: Stanford University Press, 1972.

———, trans. *Vie et chants de 'Brug-pa kun-legs le yogin*. Paris: G.-P. Maisonneuve et Larose, 1972.

Steinkellner, Ernst. *Dharmakīrti's Pramāṇaviniścaya, Kapitel 2: Svārthānumnam.* Vienna: Österreichische Akademie der Wissenschaften, 1973.

Stewart, Jampa Mackenzie. *The Life of Gampopa: The Incomparable Dharma Lord of Tibet*. Ithaca, NY: Snow Lion, 1995.

Streng, Frederick J. *Emptiness: A Study in Religious Meaning*. Nashville: Abingdon Press, 1970.

Strickmann, Michel, ed. *Tantric and Taoist Studies in Honor of R. A. Stein. Mélanges chinois et bouddhiques* 20 (1981).

Studholme, Alexander. *The Origins of* Oṃ Maṇipadme Hūṃ*: A Study of the* Karaṇḍavyūha Sūtra. Albany: State University of New York Press, 2002.

Suzuki, D. T., trans. *The Laṅkāvatāra Sūtra: A Mahayana Text.* London/New York: Kegan Paul International, 1998.

———. *Zen Buddhism: Selected Writings*. Ed. William Barrett. Garden City, NY: Doubleday, 1956.

Sweet, Michael J. "Jesus the World Protector: Eighteenth-Century Gelukpa Historians View Christianity." *Buddhist-Christian Studies* 26 (2006), pp. 173–78.

———. "Mental Purification *(Blo sbyong)*: A Native Tibetan Genre of Religious Literature." In Cabezón and Jackson, pp. 244–60.

Tachikawa Musashi. "The Tantric Doctrine of the Sa skya pa according to the *Śel gyi me loṅ*." *Acta Asiatica* 29 (1975), pp. 95–106.

Taipei Tibetan Tripitaka. Ed. A.W. Hanson-Barber. Taipei: SMC Publishing, 1991.

Tandar, Sangye, trans. [Menri Lopon Sangye Tenzin.] *The Twelve Deeds: A Brief Life Story of Tonpa Shenrab, The Founder of the Bon Religion*. Ed. Richard Guard. Dharamsala: Library of Tibetan Works and Archives, 1995.

Tatz, Mark. *Asanga's Chapter on Ethics, With the Commentary of Tsong-Kha-pa, the Basic Path to Awakening, the Complete Bodhisattva.* Lewiston NY/ Queenston U.K.: The Edwin Mellen Press, 1986.

———. "The Life of the Siddha-Philosopher Maitrīgupta." *Journal of the American Oriental Society* 107: 4 (1987), pp. 695–711.

Tauscher, Helmut. "Phya pa chos kyi seng ge as a Svātantrika." In Dreyfus and McClintock, pp. 207–56.

Taylor, Mark C., ed. *Critical Terms for Religious Studies*. Chicago: University of Chicago Press, 1998.

[TBRC]. *Tibetan Buddhist Resource Center*. www.tbrc.org

Templeman, David, ed. and trans. [Tāranātha.] *The Seven Instruction Lineages [Bka 'babs bdun ldan]*. Dharamsala: Library of Tibetan Works and Archives, 1983.

———, trans. *Tāranātha's Life of Kṛṣṇācārya/Kāṇha*. Dharmasala: Library of Tibetan Works and Archives, 1989.

Thakchoe, Sonam. *The Two Truths Debate: Tsongkhapa and Gorampa on the Middle Way*. Boston: Wisdom, 2007.

Tharchin, Geshe Lobsang, and Michael Roach, trans. Tsongkapa, with commentary by Pabongkha Rinpoche. *The Principal Teachings of Buddhism*. Howell, NJ: Mahayana Sutra and Tantra Press, 1988.

Thaye, Jampa. *A Garland of Gold: The Early Kagyu Masters of India and Tibet*. Bristol, U.K.: Ganesha Press, 1990.

Thrangu Rinpoche, Khenchen. Asaṅga and Maitreya. *Distinguishing Dharma and Dharmata*. Trans. Jules Levinson. Delhi: Sri Satguru, 2001.

———. *The Eighth Situpa on the Third Karmapa's Mahāmudrā Prayer*. Trans. Sherab Dorje. 2nd ed. Ithaca, NY: Snow Lion, 2004.

———. *King of Samadhi: Commentaries on the Samadhi Raja Sutra and The Song of Lodrö Thaye*. Trans. Erik Pema Kunsang. Hong Kong / Boudhanath / Århus: Rangjung Yeshe, 1994.

———. *The Life of Tilopa and the Ganges Mahamudra*. Crestone, CO: Namo Buddha, 2002.

———. *The Ninth Karmapa's Ocean of Definitive Meaning*. Trans. Lama Tashi Namgyal. Ithaca, NY: Snow Lion, 2003.

———. *A Song for a King: Saraha on Mahamudra Meditation*. Ed. Michele Martin. Boston: Wisdom, 2006.

———. *Songs of Naropa: Commentaries on Songs of Realization*. Trans. Erik Pema Kunsang. Boudhanath/Hong Kong/Esby: Rangjung Dorje, 1997.

———. *Teachings from the 100,000 Songs of Milarepa*. Boulder, CO: Namo Buddha, 1994.

———. *Transcending Ego: Distinguishing Consciousness from Wisdom of Rangjung Dorje, the Third Karmapa*. Trans. Peter Roberts. Boulder, CO: Namo Buddha, 2001.

———. *The Uttara Tantra, a Treatise on Buddha Nature: A Commentary on the Uttara Tantra Śāstra of Asaṅga*. Trans. Ken and Katia Holmes. Delhi: Sri Satguru, 1994.

Thurman, Robert A. F., trans. *The Central Philosophy of Tibet: A Study and Translation of Jey Tsong Khapa's "Essence of True Eloquence."* Princeton, NJ: Princeton University Press, 1991 (1984).

———. *Essential Tibetan Buddhism.* San Francisco: HarperSanFrancisco, 1995.

———, trans. *The Holy Teaching of Vimalakīrti.* University Park, PA: Pennsylvania State University Press, 1975.

———, ed. *Life and Teachings of Tsong Khapa.* Trans. Sherpa Tulku et al. Dharamsala: Library of Tibetan Works and Archives, 1982.

———, et al. *The Universal Vehicle Discourse Literature (Mahāyānasūtrālaṃkāra).* New York: American Institute of Buddhist Studies, 2004.

Tibetan and Himalayan Digital Library. www.THDL.org

Tillemans, Tom J. F. *Dharmakīrti's Pramāṇavārttika: An Annotated Translation of the Fourth Chapter (Parārthānumāna).* Vienna: Österreichische Akademie der Wissenschaften, 2000.

[Toh]. See Uji.

Tola, Fernando, and Carmen Dragonetti, trans. *Nāgārjuna's Refutation of Logic (Nyāya) Vaidalyaprakaraṇa.* Delhi: Motilal Banarsidass, 1995.

[TPS]. See Tucci, *Tibetan Painted Scrolls.*

[TR]. See Davidson, *Tibetan Renaissance.*

[TRP]. See Stearns, *Taking the Result as the Path.*

Trungram Gyaltrul Rinpoche Sherpa. *Gampopa: The Monk and the Yogi: His Life and Teachings.* Ph.D. dissertation, Harvard University, 2004.

Tsuda Shiníchi, ed. and trans. *The Saṃvarodaya Tantra: Selected Chapters.* Tokyo: The Hokuseido Press, 1974.

Tsultrim Gyamtso Rimpoche, Khenpo. *Progressive Stages of the Meditation on Emptiness.* Oxford: Longchen Foundation, 1986.

Tucci, Giuseppe, ed. *Minor Buddhist Texts, Part II.* Roma: Istituto Italiano per il Medio ed Estremo Oriente, 1958.

———. *Preliminary Report on Two Scientific Expeditions in Nepal.* Rome: Istituto Italiano per il Medio ed Estremo Oriente, 1956.

———. *The Religions of Tibet.* Trans. Geoffrey Samuel. London/New York: Kegan Paul International, 2000 [1980].

———. *Tibetan Painted Scrolls.* 3 vols. Roma: Libreria dello Stato, 1949. [TPS]

———, and H. Heissig. *Les religions du Tibet et de la Mongolie.* Paris: Payot, 1973.

Tulku Thondup Rinpoche. *Buddha Mind: An Anthology of Longchen Rabjam's Writings on Dzogpa Chenpo.* Ed. Harold Talbott. Ithaca, NY: Snow Lion, 1989.

———. *Hidden Teachings of Tibet: An Explanation of the Terma Tradition of Tibetan Buddhism.* Boston: Wisdom, 1997 (1986).

Uji Hakuju et al., eds. *A Complete Catalogue of the Tibetan Buddhist Canons (Bkaḥ-ḥgyur and Bstan-ḥgyur)*. Sendai, Japan: Tōhoku Imperial University, 1934. [Toh]

Uray, G. "The Four Horns of Tibet According to the Royal Annals." *Acta Orientalia Hungaricae* X (1960), pp. 33–57.

Vaidya, P. L., ed. *Samādhirājasūtra*. Buddhist Sanskrit Texts, no. 2. Darbhanga: Mithila Institute, 1961.

van Schaik, Sam. *Approaching the Great Perfection: Simultaneous and Gradual Methods of Dzogchen Practice in the Longchen Nyingtig*. Boston: Wisdom, 2004.

Verpoorten, Jean-Marie. *Mīmāṃsā Literature*. Wiesbaden: O. Harrassowitz, 1987.

Vostrikov, A. I. *Tibetan Historical Literature*. Trans. Harish Chandra Gupta. Calcutta: Indian Studies Past and Present, 1970.

Wallace, Vesna A. *The Inner Kālacakratantra: A Buddhist Tantric View of the Individual.* New York: Oxford University Press, 2001.

———, trans. *The Kālacakratantra: The Chapter on the Individual Together with the* Vimalaprabhā. New York: American Institute of Buddhist Studies, 2004.

Walser, Joseph. *Nāgārjuna in Context: Mahāyāna Buddhism and Early Indian Culture*. New York: Columbia University Press, 2005.

Wang Xiangyun. *Tibetan Buddhism at the Court of the Qing: The Life and Work of lCang-skya Rol-pa'i-rdo-rje (1717–86)*. Ph.D. dissertation, Harvard University, 1995.

Wang-chug Dor-je, the Ninth Karmapa. *The Mahamudra Eliminating the Darkness of Ignorance*. Trans. Alexander Berzin et al. Dharamsala: Library of Tibetan Works and Archives, 1978.

Wangyal, Geshe, trans. *The Door of Liberation: Essential Teachings of the Tibetan Buddhist Tradition*. 3rd ed. Boston: Wisdom, 1995.

———, and Brian Cutillo, trans. Sakya Pandita. *Illuminations: A Guide to Essential Buddhist Practices*. Novato, CA: Lotsawa, 1988.

Warder, A. K. *Indian Buddhism*. 2nd ed. Delhi: Motilal Banarsidass, 1980.

Watson, Burton. *Chuang Tzu*. New York: Columbia University Press, 1964.

Wayman, Alex. *The Buddhist Tantras: Light on Indo-Tibetan Esotericism*. New York: Samuel Weiser, 1973.

———. *Yoga of the Guhyasamājatantra: The Arcane Lore of the Forty Verses*. New York: Samuel Weiser, 1980.

White, David Gordon, ed. *Tantra in Practice*. Princeton Readings in Religions. Princeton, NJ: Princeton University Press, 2000.

Wilkinson, Endymion. *Chinese History: A Manual*. Cambridge, MA: Harvard University Asia Center, 1998.

Williams, Paul. *Mahāyāna Buddhism: The Doctrinal Foundations*. London/New York: Routledge, 1989.

———. "A Note on Some Aspects of Mi-bskyod rDo-rje's Critique of dGe lugs pa Madhyamaka." *Journal of Indian Philosophy* 2 (1983), pp. 125–46.

———. *Songs of Love, Poems of Sadness: The Erotic Verse of the Sixth Dalai Lama*. London/New York: I.B. Tauris, 2004.

Williams, Paul, and Anthony Tribe. *Buddhist Thought: A Complete Introduction to the Indian Tradition*. London/New York: Routledge, 2000.

Willis, Janice D. *Enlightened Beings: Life Stories From the Ganden Oral Tradition*. Boston: Wisdom, 1994.

———, trans. *On Knowing Reality: The Tattvārtha Chapter of Asaṅga's Bodhisattvabhūmi*. New York: Columbia University Press, 1979.

Wylie, Turrell V. *The Geography of Tibet According to the 'Dzam-gling-rgyas-bshad*. Rome: Istituto Italiano per il Medio ed Estremo Oriente, 1962.

Xie Guanghui, "Introduction to the Chinese Script." http://faculty.virginia.edu/cll/chinese/introduction.html

Yang, Ho-chin. *The Annals of Kokonor*. Bloomington: Indiana University Press, 1969.

Yangchen Gawai Lodoe. *Paths and Grounds of Guhyasamaja According to Arya Nagarjuna*. Trans. Tenzin Dorjee. Dharmasala: Library of Tibetan Works and Archives, 1995.

[Z]. *Grub mtha' thams cad kyi khung dang 'dod tshul ston pa legs bshad shel gyi me long*. In *Collected Works of Thu'u-bkwan Blo-bzang-chos-kyi-nyi-ma*. Edited and reproduced by Ṅawang Gelek Demo, with introduction by E. Gene Smith. Gedan Sungrab Minyam Gyunphel Series, vol. II. (kha), pp. 5–519. Delhi: Ngawang Gelek Demo, 1969.

Zangpo, Ngawang, trans. *Guru Rinpoché: His Life and Times*. Ithaca, NY: Snow Lion, 2002.

———, trans. *Timeless Rapture: Inspired Verses of the Shangpa Masters*. Compiled by Jamgon Kongtrul. Ithaca, NY: Snow Lion, 2003.

Zürcher, E. *The Buddhist Conquest of China*. Leiden: E. J. Brill, 1959.

Index

THIS INDEX has been enhanced in several ways to make it a more valuable tool for researchers. Dates have been provided for historical figures, where known. For certain figures, page references are given to selected works, such as the *Blue Annals,* where additional information on them can be found. (In general, references for major figures are found in the notes.) Tibetan names and places—which are spelled phonetically throughout the book—have been supplied with their proper transliterated Wylie spellings, and the Tibetan has been provided for most translated technical terms. Entries on Tibetan texts—which we have rendered in English throughout the book—include their transliterated Tibetan title and the name of the author, where known. Entries on Indic-language texts—also in English throughout—include transliterated Tibetan and Sanskrit titles, Tōhoku catalog numbers, and the name of the author, where known. Most place names include a general indication as to their location.

Key

AU	author unknown
BA	Gö Lotsāwa, *Blue Annals*
DU	date unknown
NGB	Nying ma rgyud 'bum number
NS1	Dudjom, *Nyingma School of Tibetan Buddhism,* vol. 1
r.	regnal dates
Toh	Tōhoku catalogue number
TR	Davidson, *Tibetan Renaissance*
TRP	Stearns, *Taking the Result as the Path*
TU	Tōhoku catalog number unknown
*	title as cited by Thuken; correct title not found

About the Contributors

Born in central Tibet in 1923, Geshe Lhundub Sopa is one of the few remaining Tibetan masters to have been trained in his homeland prior to the Chinese occupation. He gained a reputation early on as a dedicated and brilliant scholar and was chosen as one of the Dalai Lama's debate examiners during the annual Prayer Festival of 1959. Shortly thereafter, he joined the exodus of Tibetans to India, and in 1962 moved to New Jersey. In 1967 he was invited to teach in the recently formed Buddhist Studies Program at the University of Wisconsin–Madison, where he is now Professor Emeritus. He is the founder of Deer Park Buddhist Center in Oregon, Wisconsin, where he lives.

Roger R. Jackson teaches the religions of South Asia at Carleton College in Northfield, Minnesota. He has authored numerous articles and books, the latter including *Is Enlightenment Possible?*, *Tibetan Literature* (coedited), *Buddhist Theology* (coedited), and *Tantric Treasures: Three Collections of Mystical Verse from Buddhist India*.

Geshe Thupten Jinpa was trained as a monk at the Shartse College of Ganden Monastic University, South India, where he received the Geshe Lharam degree. Jinpa also holds a B.A. honors in philosophy and a Ph.D. in religious studies, both from Cambridge University, England.

Jinpa has been the principal English-language translator for His Holiness the Dalai Lama for nearly two decades and has translated and edited numerous books by the Dalai Lama. His own works include *Songs of Spiritual Experience* (coauthored) and *Self, Reality and Reason in Tibetan Philosophy*. He is currently the president of the Institute of Tibetan Classics and lives in Montreal with his wife and two daughters.

The Institute of Tibetan Classics

The Institute of Tibetan Classics is a nonprofit, charitable educational organization based in Montreal, Canada. It is dedicated to two primary objectives: (1) to preserve and promote the study and deep appreciation of Tibet's rich intellectual, spiritual, and artistic heritage, especially among the Tibetan-speaking communities worldwide; and (2) to make the classical Tibetan knowledge and literature a truly global heritage, its spiritual and intellectual resources open to all.

To learn more about the Institute of Tibetan Classics and its various projects, please visit www.tibetanclassics.org or write to this address:

Institute of Tibetan Classics
304 Aberdare Road
Montreal (Quebec) H3P 3K3
Canada

The Library of Tibetan Classics

"This new series edited by Thupten Jinpa and published by Wisdom Publications is a landmark in the study of Tibetan culture in general and Tibetan Buddhism in particular. Each volume contains a lucid introduction and outstanding translations that, while aimed at the general public, will benefit those in the field of Tibetan Studies immensely as well."

—Leonard van der Kuijp, Harvard University

"This is an invaluable set of translations by highly competent scholar-practitioners. The series spans the breadth of the history of Tibetan religion, providing entry to a vast culture of spiritual cultivation."

—Jeffrey Hopkins, University of Virginia

"Erudite in all respects, this series is at the same time accessible and engagingly translated. As such, it belongs in all college and university libraries as well as in good public libraries. *The Library of Tibetan Classics* is on its way to becoming a truly extraordinary spiritual and literary accomplishment."

—Janice D. Willis, Wesleyan University

Following is a list of the thirty-two proposed volumes in *The Library of Tibetan Classics*. Some volumes are translations of single texts, while others are compilations of multiple texts, and each volume will be roughly the same length. Except for those volumes already published, the renderings of titles below are only tentative and are liable to change. The Institute of Tibetan Classics has contracted numerous established translators in its efforts, and work is progressing on all the volumes concurrently.

1. *Mind Training: The Great Collection*, compiled by Shönu Gyalchok and Könchok Gyaltsen (fifteenth century). NOW AVAILABLE.
2. *The Book of Kadam: The Core Texts*, attributed to Atiśa and Dromtönpa (eleventh century). NOW AVAILABLE
3. *The Great Chariot: A Treatise on the Great Perfection*, Longchen Rapjampa (1308–63)
4. *Taking the Result As the Path: Core Teachings of the Sakya Lamdré Tradition*, Jamyang Khyentsé Wangchuk (1524–68) et al. NOW AVAILABLE
5. *Mahāmudrā and Related Instructions: Core Teachings of the Kagyü School*
6. *Stages of the Path and the Ear-Whispered Instructions: Core Teachings of the Geluk School*
7. *Ocean of Definitive Meaning: A Teaching for the Mountain Hermit*, Dölpopa Sherap Gyaltsen (1292–1361)
8. *Miscellaneous Tibetan Buddhist Lineages: The Core Teachings*, Jamgön Kongtrül (1813–90)
9. *Sutra, Tantra, and the Mind Cycle: Core Teachings of the Bön School*
10. *The Stages of the Doctrine: Selected Key Texts*
11. *The Bodhisattva's Altruistic Ideal: Selected Key Texts*
12. *The Ethics of the Three Codes*
13. *Sādhanas: Vajrayana Buddhist Meditation Manuals*
14. *Ornament of Stainless Light: An Exposition of the Kālacakra Tantra*, Khedrup Norsang Gyatso (1423–1513). NOW AVAILABLE
15. *Lamp Thoroughly Illuminating the Five Stages of Completion*, Tsongkhapa (1357–1419)
16. *Studies in the Perfection of Wisdom*
17. *Treatises on Buddha Nature*
18. *Differentiations of the Profound View: Interpretations of Emptiness in Tibet*
19. *Elucidation of the Intent: A Thorough Exposition of "Entering the Middle Way,"* Tsongkhapa (1357–1419)
20. *Tibetan Buddhist Epistemology I: The Sakya School*

21. *Tibetan Buddhist Epistemology II: The Geluk School*

22. *Tibetan Buddhist Psychology and Phenomenology: Selected Texts*

23. *Ornament of Higher Knowledge: A Exposition of Vasubandhu's "Treasury of Higher Knowledge,"* Chim Jampalyang (thirteenth century)

24. *A Beautiful Adornment of Mount Meru: Presentation of Classical Indian Philosophies*, Changkya Rölpai Dorjé (1717–86)

25. *The Crystal Mirror of Philosophical Systems: A Tibetan Study of Asian Religious Thought*, Thuken Losang Chökyi Nyima (1737–1802). NOW AVAILABLE

26. *Gateway for Being Learned and Realized: Selected Texts*

27. *The Well-Uttered Insights: Advice on Everyday Wisdom, Civility, and Basic Human Values*

28. *A Mirror of Beryl: A Historical Introduction to Tibetan Medical Science*, Desi Sangyé Gyatso (1653–1705)

29. *Selected Texts on Tibetan Astronomy and Astrology*

30. *Art and Literature: An Anthology*

31. *Tales from the Tibetan Operas*

32. *Selected Historical Works*

To receive a brochure describing all the volumes or to stay informed about *The Library of Tibetan Classics*, please write:

Wisdom Publications
Attn: Library of Tibetan Classics
199 Elm Street
Somerville, MA 02144 USA
or send a request by email to info@wisdompubs.org.

The complete catalog containing descriptions of each volume can also be found online at www.wisdompubs.org, where you can sign up for an email newsletter dedicated to *Library of Tibetan Classics* news.

Become a Benefactor of the Library of Tibetan Classics

The Library of Tibetan Classics' scope, importance, and commitment to quality make it a tremendous financial undertaking. Please consider becoming a benefactor. Contributors of us$2,000 or more will receive a copy of each volume as it becomes available and will have their names listed in all subsequent volumes. Simply send a check made out to Wisdom Publications or credit card information to the address below.

Library of Tibetan Classics Fund
Wisdom Publications
199 Elm Street
Somerville MA 02144
USA

Please note that contributions of lesser amounts are also welcome and are invaluable to the development of the series. Wisdom is a 501(c)3 nonprofit corporation, and all contributions are tax-deductible to the extent allowed by law.

To keep up to date on the status of the *Library of Tibetan Classics*, visit the series page on the Wisdom website, wisdompubs.org. Sign up for the email news list for the *Library of Tibetan Classics* while you are there.

About Wisdom Publications

Wisdom Publications is dedicated to making available authentic Buddhist works for the benefit of all. We publish translations of the sutras and tantras, commentaries and teachings of past and contemporary Buddhist masters, and original works by the world's leading Buddhist scholars. We publish our titles with the appreciation of Buddhism as a living philosophy and with the special commitment to preserve and transmit important works from all the major Buddhist traditions.

Wisdom Publications
199 Elm Street
Somerville, Massachusetts 02144 USA
Telephone: 617-776-7416
Fax: 617-776-7841
Email: info@wisdompubs.org
www.wisdompubs.org

Wisdom is a nonprofit, charitable 501(c)(3) organization affiliated with the Foundation for the Preservation of the Mahayana Tradition (FPMT)

Mind Training

The Great Collection

Translated and edited by Thupten Jinpa

720 pages, cloth, ISBN 0-86171-440-7, $49.95

"The practice of mind training *(lojong)* is based on the essential Mahayana teachings of impermanence, compassion, and the exchange of self and other that the eleventh-century master Atisha brought to Tibet from India. The *lojong* teachings are a source of inspiration and guidance shared by masters of all Tibetan traditions. This makes Thupten Jinpa's translation of *Mind Training: The Great Collection* a natural choice for publication as part of the *Library of Tibetan Classics* series. For the first time, this early collection of the instructions of the great Kadampa masters has been translated in its entirety. The clarity and raw power of these thousand-year-old teachings are astonishingly fresh, whether studied as a complete anthology or opened at random for inspiring verses on the heart of Buddhist practice."

—*Buddhadharma: The Practitioner's Quarterly*

"Thupten Jinpa has done us all a great service by editing and translating this marvelous volume. In an era when Buddhist meditation is largely equated with simply calming the mind and developing mindfulness, this compendium of methods for training the mind gives a glimpse of the tremendous richness and depth of the Buddhist tradition for enhancing mental health and balance and realizing the full potential of consciousness in terms of wisdom and compassion. With the current rise of positive psychology, in which researchers are seeking a fresh vision of genuine happiness and well-being, this volume can break new ground in bridging the ancient wisdom of Buddhism with cutting-edge psychology. Such collaborative inquiry between spirituality and science is especially timely in today's troubled and divisive world."

—B. Alan Wallace, author of *The Attention Revolution*

Taking the Result as the Path

Core Teachings of the Sakya Lamdré Tradition

Translated and edited by Cyrus Stearns

His Holiness Sakya Trizin, Foreword

784 pages, cloth, ISBN 0-86171-443-1, $59.95

"The Sakya school of Tibetan Buddhism has been the most conservative in maintaining the secrecy of its lineage's special practices. *Taking the Result as the Path* represents a major breakthrough by bringing these teachings to light with the full blessings of the Sakya masters. In nearly seven hundred pages of translation, the indefatigable Cyrus Stearns presents an anthology of essential texts on Lamdré. This collection will be an invaluable resource for practitioners of the Lamdré system."

—*Buddhadharma: The Practitioner's Quarterly*

"No one is better suited than Cyrus Stearns to offer the first major translation of Lamdré teachings to the world. He has studied intimately with the most revered leaders of the Sakya tradition for decades. Beyond this, Stearns possesses a quality that sets him apart from most translators today—he is a poet. Few have transmuted the verse or the prose, the earthy imagery or the celestial style of Tibetan Buddhist teachings, with comparable eloquence and inspiration; few are endowed with the capacity to inspire students of Tibetan Buddhism through force of the sheer beauty of the translated word. The Sakya tradition will henceforth be known to English audiences in all its splendor thanks to this new translation."

—Kurtis R. Schaeffer, University of Virginia

"In this volume, Stearns makes available for the first time a selection of key texts from the highly prized esoteric transmission of the great Tsarpa masters, translated with enormous effort and care. Students of the Lamdré will rejoice to see these often enigmatic Tibetan yoga manuals transformed into such lucid English."

—David P. Jackson, University of Hamburg

Ornament of Stainless Light

An Exposition of the Kālacakra Tantra

Khedrup Norsang Gyatso

736 pages, cloth, ISBN 0-86171-452-0, $49.95

"A radiant gem drawn from the vast ocean of Tibetan literature on the Kālacakra tantra. It provides a clear, comprehensive summary of the basic structure and essential features of this important system of mysticism. Also, Khedrup Norsang Gyatso's interpretations of controversial issues in the Kālacakra contribute to our understanding of the evolution of Tibetan theories of mysticism. Gavin Kilty's faithful translation makes this work easily accessible—it is a fitting inaugural volume for the *Library of Tibetan Classics.*"

—John Newman, MacArthur Professor of
Asian Religions, New College of Florida

"When the Dalai Lama performed the Kālacakra initiation for a crowd of 20,000 at Madison Square Garden in 1991, a page was turned in the history of tantra. It was perhaps because of the popularity of this event and the success of others like it that when he was asked to select a text for the inaugural volume of the important new *Library of Tibetan Classics* series, the Dalai Lama chose a commentary on the Kālacakra tantra. The inaugural volume, *Ornament of Stainless Light,* is an important resource for anyone who has attended or will attend one of the many public performances of the Kālacakra initiation around the world."

—Buddhadharma: The Practitioner's Quarterly

The Book of Kadam

The Core Texts

Atisa Dīpaṃkara (982–1054) and Dromtönpa (1005–64)

Translated by Thupten Jinpa

752 pages, cloth, ISBN 0-86171-441-5, $59.95

The Kadam School, which emerged from the teachings of the Indian master Atisa and his principal student, Dromtönpa, is revered for its unique practical application of the bodhisattva's altruistic ideal in day-to-day life. One of the most well-known sets of spiritual teachings stemming from Atisa and Dromtönpa is a special collection of oral transmissions enshrined in the two-volume *Book of Kadam (Bka' gdams glegs bam)*. The texts in this volume include the core texts of *The Book of Kadam*, notably the twenty-three-chapter dialogue between Atisa and Dromtönpa that is woven around Atisa's *Bodhisattva's Jewel Garland*. Sometimes referred to as the "Kadam emanation scripture," *The Book of Kadam* is undisputedly one of the greatest works of Tibetan Buddhism. This volume contains (1) Atisa's *Bodhisattva's Jewel Garland*, (2) the twenty-three chapters of the *Jewel Garland of Dialogues*, (3) Dromtönpa's *Self-Exhortation*, (4) *Elucidation of the Heart-Drop Practice* by Khenchen Nyima Gyaltsen (1223–1305), (5) four selected chapters from Dromtönpa's birth stories, (6) two brief verse summaries of the *Book of Kadam*, one by the second Dalai Lama (1476–1542) and the other by Yongzin Yeshé Gyaltsen (1713–93), and (7) *Sayings of the Kadam Masters*, compiled by Chegom Sherap Dorjé (ca. twelfth century). Although the Kadam school no longer exists as an autonomous lineage within Tibetan Buddhism, its teachings have become fully incorporated into the teachings of all four major schools of Tibetan Buddhism, especially the Geluk School.

A Note About Dust Jackets

In response to readers' requests, Wisdom has elected to change the dust jackets on the *Library of Tibetan Classics* series from the vellum covers initially produced to conventional paper jackets. If you have purchased either of the first two releases in the series, *Ornament of Stainless Light* or *Mind Training*, and would like to receive a replacement jacket free of charge, please email us at info@wisdompubs.org with your mailing address. You can also send your request to Wisdom Publications, 199 Elm Street, Somerville MA 02144.